A History of Europe in the Twentieth Century

A History of Europe in the Twentieth Century

Eric Dorn Brose

New York   Oxford
OXFORD UNIVERSITY PRESS
2005

Oxford University Press

Oxford   New York
Auckland   Bangkok   Buenos Aires   Cape Town   Chennai
Dar es Salaam   Delhi   Hong Kong   Istanbul   Karachi   Kolkata
Kuala Lumpur   Madrid   Melbourne   Mexico City   Mumbai
Nairobi   São Paulo   Shanghai   Taipei   Tokyo   Toronto

Published by Oxford University Press, Inc.
198 Madison Avenue, New York, New York, 10016
http://www.oup.com

Oxford is a registered trademark of Oxford University Press

Library of Congress Cataloging-in-Publication Data
Brose, Eric Dorn, 1948–
   A history of Europe in the twentieth century / by Eric Dorn Brose.
      p. cm.
   Includes index.
   ISBN 0-19-513571-7 (alk. paper)—ISBN 0-19-513570-9 (pbk. : alk. paper)
   1. Europe—History—20th century. I. Title.
D424.B76 2004
940.5—dc22   2004041473

Printing number: 9 8 7 6 5 4 3 2 1

Printed in the United States of America
on acid-free paper

CONTENTS

▼

MAPS

ACKNOWLEDGMENTS

I would like most to thank my wife, Christine, for having the deep reservoir of patience that writers of projects like this one require in a spouse, but surely do not always find. She appreciated the necessity of so many hours of work behind a closed study door and never questioned my need to buy books, make long-distance calls, and take trains and planes—she has been through this before. My wife also has a real gift for politely and artfully shifting the subject away from history when the "enough is enough" point has been reached. This book is dedicated to Christine with good reason.

Others in my immediate family as well as many colleagues in my professional family at Drexel University have also performed yeoman service. My father, Robert Brose, made many interesting observations about the Proctor & Gamble and American business experience in Europe in the 1960s. My son, Christian Brose, steered me to numerous important articles on contemporary Europe. Thanks also to Dean Cecilie Goodrich and Provost Richard Astro at Drexel for tolerating a department head with a scholarly agenda, and, later, after I stepped down from this post, to my present department head, Don Stevens, for supporting the project in many ways; to Nunzio Pernicone for lending so many volumes on Italian history and giving me many tips and insights; to Christian Hunold, Andrei Muntean, and Olga Kucherenko for commenting on various chapters; to Peter Groesbeck in Graphics for reproducing some of the book's illustrations and crafting the collage on World War Two technology; and to Deidre Harper in Interlibrary Loan for tracking down everything I asked her to find.

Outside my university many others deserve an energetic nod of appreciation: Volker Berghahn of Columbia University for his insightful comments on parts of the manuscript; Philip Cannistraro of City University of New York and freelance acquisitions editor Bruce Borland for initial contacts with Oxford University Press as well as help during the proposal stage; John Williams of Bradley University for organizing two informative seminars in Berlin and Prague in 2001 and 2003; the circulation staffs of the libraries at the University of Pennsylvania and Swarthmore College for not charging for every overdue book; the staff of Swarthmore's Peace Collection for help with photographing an important Käthe Kollwitz print; Michael Slade of Art Resource and Anthony Sullivan of Getty Images for quick, professional, personal service; and Northild Eger of the Otto Dix Stiftung in Liechtenstein for making sure I got the correct transparency.

I would also like to extend thanks to my editor at Oxford University Press, Peter Coveney. He let me write when it was time to write, nudged me a bit when it was time to be finished writing, and then guided me through the intricacies of acquiring and producing so many maps, illustrations, and copyright permissions—the leap from the level of previous, relatively easy monographs to an intricate upper-level textbook would have fallen short without him. Peter's hard-working assistant, June Kim, also provided invaluable services in acquiring illustrations and saving me time as the final deadline neared. Finally, the six outside readers at Oxford University Press in the proposal stage, and the final six who read the first draft of the manuscript, deserve special thanks. Each one spent weeks with recommendations, the overwhelming majority of which made their way into the revised manuscript. There is no doubt that these suggestions have greatly improved a final product that remains, of course, "my thing." Everyone makes these kinds of standard disclaimers, but with very good reason. Authors benefit from comments, but scholarly books, after all, are not written by committee. I have made the final excruciating choices as to what to include and exclude, and any and all weak points that remain are my responsibility alone.

Philadelphia
April 2004

A History of Europe in the Twentieth Century

INTRODUCTION

From the vantage point of early 2004, Europe's history of the last century appears to straddle the end of one era that stretches back centuries into a violent and authoritarian past and the beginning of another era, more democratic and peaceful, that may represent the future. The turning points came in 1945 with the end of World War Two and in 1989–1991 with the end of the Cold War. The spores of the new era germinated well before the end of the old, while the seeds of the old era, although much less potent now, continue to sprout. Contemporary Europe is no utopia, but European leaders are making conscious efforts to root out a catastrophic recent past.

THEMES

This history of twentieth-century Europe has five main thematic emphases. Readers should think of the themes presented here as separate, shifting lenses through which to focus on specific aspects of the history of this troubled century. The chapters that follow combine these thematic perspectives into a composite image.

1. War and the Quest for Alternatives to War

Europe in 1900 was torn between the well-entrenched notion that war was an acceptable means of settling differences between states and another idea, also possessing ancient provenance, that nonviolent alternatives to war were superior and feasible. The peace movement of the late nineteenth century believed that it had found these workable alternatives in the form of arbitration and disarmament. Unfortunately, internal divisions and a deficient power base doomed the anti-war movement to failure when World War One broke out in 1914.

After millions died in that conflagration, champions of peace redoubled their efforts. The so-called Interwar Period (1919–1939) witnessed the world's first intergovernmental peace-keeping organization, the League of Nations, and even more promising policing agreements between the sovereign nations of Europe. During the more hostile environment brought on by the Great Depression of the 1930s, however, the pacifist cause foundered. Although international law had changed and aggression was no longer legally acceptable, older aggressive attitudes, never far from the surface, welled up again. The resulting World War Two, which killed nearly sixty million people, led to a successor intergovernmental body, the United Nations (UN), and progress to-

1

ward economic and political union among European states, but these developments were overshadowed for decades by the threat of nuclear destruction during the "Cold War" between the communist and democratic blocs. The fall of communism; the evolving importance of the UN; the transformation of the West's military alliance, the North Atlantic Treaty Organization (NATO), to a peace-keeping role; and the emergence of the European Union (EU) seem to have created a war-free zone on a once conflict-ridden continent. Ongoing ethnic strife and terrorism serve as a reminder, however, that much work remains to be done.

2. Ethnic/Racial Belligerency and Efforts to Create Ethnic/Racial Harmony

By 1900 a tense and unstable hierarchy of dominant, middling, and subjugated peoples existed in Europe. Millennia of warfare had pushed certain powerful "ethnic- or nation-state" groupings to the top: the English, the French, the German-speaking Austrians, the Germans per se, and the Russians. The Italians were also on the rise. These imperial peoples dominated much of the world, too, either through their economic and financial connections or outright through military conquest and colonization. Below the dominant nation-states, weaker European peoples had exited the power struggle in the hope that diplomacy or neutrality would preserve their independence. These waning states included Turkey, Spain, Portugal, Switzerland, Belgium, Holland, Denmark, and Sweden. On the bottom, subjugated ethnic groups like the Finns, the Poles, the Czechs, the Slovaks, the South Slavs, the Basques, and the Irish longed for freedom. Europe's ethnic and racial tensions sparked war in 1914, contributed to democratic instability in the Interwar Period, led to the horrible genocide of World War Two, and opened up lines of fissure in the Communist Bloc after 1945. Perhaps the greatest accomplishment of today's EU, in fact, has been to find a cooperative modus operandi and vivendi between different peoples with troubled pasts. So far it is working.

3. Authoritarianism and the Struggle for Democracy

The peoples of Europe in 1900 were organized politically into two basic types of systems. Authoritarian monarchies, where hereditary heads of state wielded awesome decision-making powers, prevailed over much of the land mass, most prominently in the Russian, Austro-Hungarian, and German empires. Popular forces pushing for democracy in these states created instability and turmoil. Europe possessed only three well-established democracies at this time: Switzerland, France, and Britain, although all three states were rocked by class and gender disorders. Europe's remaining states were politically somewhere in between, which usually meant monarchies or republics where elected representatives ruled but were chosen undemocratically by upper-class elites—where most of the people, in other words, could not vote.

Although World War One swept away the German, Austro-Hungarian, and Russian monarchies and seemed to open a new era of democracy as the

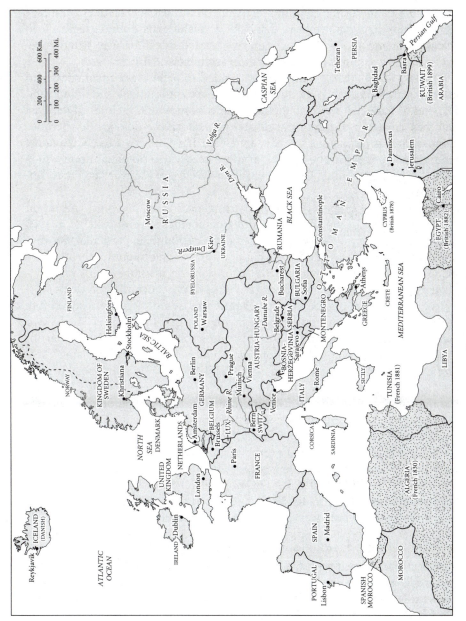

Europe in 1900

people nearly everywhere came into power, many of the unstable young democracies of East-Central Europe succumbed to a complex of problems in the 1920s, while others did not survive the hardships of the Great Depression. By the late 1930s seemingly more resilient communist and fascist or military dictatorships had undermined democracy, pushing its boundaries back to Scandinavia and Western Europe. Europe carried this three-way struggle between fascism, communism, and democracy into World War Two.

After 1945 the triple competition yielded to a two-way ideological and military standoff between the surviving systems, communism and democracy. The end of the Cold War and the toppling of communist regimes in the East Bloc has created a Europe that is almost exclusively democratic. Because democracies, as far as most scholars are aware, have never waged war against other democracies, Europe is thus far more peaceful, a potential upon which the EU is trying to build. Those who say "never again" to war keep their fingers crossed.

The story of Europe's democratic struggle contains three very important sub-themes. First, if the continent's three democracies were unstable in 1900 this is largely because they were not democratic enough, in particular, because the lower classes demanded a "social democracy" that would improve their living standards and provide social security in an insecure era of rapid industrialization. Much of the history of European democratization deals with a struggle for social democracy that experienced some success already before World War One, but did not register its biggest gains until after World War Two. A second factor limiting European democracy in 1900 was gender inequality, for women could not vote in national elections and remained second-class citizens in a legal sense as well. Like the struggle for social justice, the quest for women's rights began well before 1914, achieved some key breakthroughs in the 1910s and 1920s, but did not gain significant momentum until gender relations stabilized somewhat after the world wars. Third, that Europe's great democracies in 1900 were also its great imperial powers, namely Britain and France, represented a double standard. How genuinely democratic were they if voters at home were responsible for suppressing and exploiting other people in Africa and Asia? This double standard did not fall away until European empires fell after 1945.

4. Technological Revolutions and Technological Systems

Inextricably entwined with many of the other themes introduced here is that of technological change. In 1900 a "second industrial revolution" featuring a new system of tightly integrated technologies was underway. Steel, new electrical and chemical industries, ingenious machine tools, automobiles, airplanes, and new sources of power and energy like oil and the internal combustion engine were altering beyond easy recognition the means of production of the late eighteenth-century industrial revolution. Like that first revolutionary transformation, progress was not spread evenly among the Great Powers of Europe, for Germany was overtaking Britain and France, which had led during the first industrial revolution, and leaving Russia, which had yet to industrialize fully, far behind. These developments exacerbated the pre-1914 arms race, generating anxiety among peoples as the likelihood of war increased. Once war erupted, the second industrial revolution's dark potential to decimate armies became shockingly evident. Germany and its allies were defeated in World War One because of the weight of British, French, and Russian numbers; British blockading; the intervention of Italy and eventually the United States; and Berlin's counterproductive authoritarian policies at home.

The modern technological system matured and spread during the Interwar Period. The most noteworthy change, the industrial acceleration of Russia under the communists, factored in important ways in their victory on the Eastern Front after 1941 and the ultimate defeat of Nazi Germany in 1945. By the end of World War Two, however, a new technological system had begun to emerge directly out of the old as the previous set of techniques reached its limit in the race against time to develop new weapons to win the war. Significantly, World War Two spawned jet airplanes, missiles, nuclear power, miniaturization of product parts, and computers. This technological system—our contemporary system—matured during the 1970s and 1980s, but, like circumstances in the early 1900s, did not spread evenly among power rivals. Indeed, the inability of the Soviet Union to keep pace with the United States and Western Europe, especially with computers and consumer technologies, exacerbated popular discontent over the Soviet Union's rigid authoritarianism and contributed to the fall of communism.

5. Elite and Popular Culture

This history's final thematic emphasis is the world of culture, both highbrow and lowbrow. Sometimes organized in separate subchapters, sometimes as part of the overall social and political narrative, the discussion of cultural developments like art, music, literature, philosophy, film, sport, and other leisure time activities is an integral part of the history of twentieth-century Europe—its inclusion cements the final pieces of the mosaic into place. Important in their own right, high cultural and mass cultural phenomena can also be used as important "primary" evidence to buttress and expand upon the book's other themes.

SOURCES

For the most part, however, the history that follows is a work of synthesis—one that builds, in other words, on the primary investigations of other scholars. These "secondary" sources are cited in endnotes linked to the relevant part of the text. This is not done to intimidate readers by showing them the voluminous extent of the literature on twentieth-century Europe—most readers will already know the extensive nature of this research—but rather to facilitate the independent research of the reader by connecting the bibliographic information to the text site of the discussion. The opening of every chapter and most every subchapter have endnotes with suggested readings for those who wish to probe deeper. Direct quotes are also cited in the traditional way, and such quotes, taken from the classic, the standard, or the most recent studies, are employed as yet another way of putting readers on the correct path for their own research projects.

It is time to raise the curtain now on Europe at the turn of the twentieth century. Was it the best of times or the worst of times? To the elites, even to alarmed upper-class leaders of the peace movement, the answer was clear: the best of times. As we have learned in our own times, however, things are not always as they seem, especially on the placid eve of shocking events.

Chapter 1

▼

"A SPECTER IS HAUNTING EUROPE"

It was May 1899, the last springtime of the old century. The Hague radiated with resplendent, spirit-lifting color. Coaches carrying representatives from twenty European and six non-European states streamed in grand succession past the fountains, flower gardens, and marble nymphs surrounding wooded Huis ten Bosch, site of the world's first peace conference. A military honor guard took position in front of this exquisite "House in the Woods," whose black enameled gate, red bricks, and white window frames reflected the sunlight of early afternoon as if beaming its confidence in mankind to the heavens. The beautiful scene seemed to presage the opening of a pacific new era.[1]

The guard received each coach of dignitaries, announced the parties with great pomp, and ushered them inside. Green-baize desks for scores of delegates were set up in a great ballroom, the Oranje Zaal. On walls rising three stories to the ceiling hung golden damask and frescoes by the Great Masters, most depicting—fittingly or unfittingly—martial triumphs of past Dutch princes on horseback. Accompanying Cupid and Venus on high, leering eerily and insidiously at the throng below, hovered Death in the form of a skeleton. Optimists shuddered, but soon found a more appropriate omen in a mural allegorically representing the Treaty of Westphalia that had ended a vicious, thirty-year round of fighting in 1648. Peace enters the Oranje Zaal to close the doors of the Temple of Janus, whence issue, according to an old Roman legend, the "dogs of war." A brief opening address by Dutch Foreign Minister Maurice de Beaufort reinforced the spirits of all champions of a new, nonviolent world order. He pointed out that they, like allegorical Peace, had the same higher purpose "of preventing calamities which threaten the whole world."[2]

One lone woman listened with the others, Bertha von Suttner, the Austria anti-war activist. Ten years earlier she had written her highly controversial novel, *Lay Down Your Arms*, and for a decade champions of "the ancient ideal of war," as a diary entry described them, had ridiculed her followers as "utopians," or less charitably as "wrong-headed idiots." She knew that her enemies had stacked their delegations with militarists: Germany sent Baron von Stengel, an advocate for war, and America included Alfred Mahan, a well-known proponent of sea power. A seasoned crusader, Suttner knew a move-

7

Champion of peace: Bertha von Suttner. (Library of Congress)

ment was afoot to "civilize" warfare with more rules about treatment of prisoners, and thereby scuttle the most ambitious goals of the peace movement—arbitration and disarmament. Still, she could not help but feel the power of the moment. For the first time in history pacifists had convened a conference to root out the still potent "remnants of the old barbarism" and secure a just and lasting peace. Since time immemorial the Dutch had built their dykes to control the fury of the sea. Was it really so utopian to construct institutions to dam up "the rage of one people against another"? After the twentieth century had passed, would peace advocates make pilgrimages to The Hague as the site of the first permanent court of international justice? Bertha von Suttner was determined to make it happen.[3]

ETHNIC DIVERSITY AND THE RISE OF THE GREAT NATION STATES

More than anyone else, Bertha von Suttner appreciated the need to reverse the long violent history of Europe. For millennia, indeed since well before the dawn of written history, Europe's many tribes had warred against one another. On the historical record the shedding of blood worsened as successive waves of migrating groups subjugated indigenous European peoples, warred against others, and then defended themselves against subsequent invaders. Flooding into Europe were fierce Celts, aggressive Germanic Teutons, hard-charging Bulgars, land-hungry Slavs, rapacious Hungarians, and, the most vicious of all, the Mongols. After the Mongolian wave ebbed, Ottoman Turks marched far into Europe, unsuccessfully besieging Vienna in 1683.[4]

Amidst so much slaughtering, notions of war as a natural, albeit reprehensible, occurrence became deeply embedded in European culture. The commingling of a plethora of polities and diverse cultures in a geographically restricted area helped to perpetuate armed conflict, for rival economic bases, power centers, and contrasting political systems increased friction, especially with relations often strained by different languages, religions, customs, and physical appearances, all of which could breed suspicion and dislike. Of course, none of this made war inevitable. Diplomacy, dynastic marriages, and the instinct for self-preservation sometimes kept fear, vanity, and lust for conquest in check. Christian teachings also represented a force for peace. From the ancient writings of Saint Augustine to the medieval elaborations of Saint Thomas Aquinas and beyond, churchmen taught that the only just war was one fought in defense or retaliation against the injustice of evildoers. "But greater is that glory that slays war with speech rather than men with the sword, and acquires or maintains peace through peace rather than through war."[5] Unfortunately the opponents of war rarely prevailed. A later scholar identified only 230 years of peace in the western world over three strife-torn millennia stretching back to antiquity.[6]

It is not surprising, therefore, that Christian moral teachings had little influence on a growing body of secular international law that began to sanction bellicose behavior in the sixteenth, seventeenth, and eighteenth centuries, legitimating the concept of *ex factis jus oritur*. By possessing or taking land, in other words, one has a right to it. As one grasping German king observed, "the jurisprudence of sovereigns is commonly the right of the stronger."[7] By the early 1800s a long list of peoples subdued over the centuries could testify to the accuracy of his statement: in the west, Catalans, Basques, Bretons, Walloons, Welsh, Scots, and Irish; in the north and east, Norwegians, Finns, Latvians, Lithuanians, Estonians, White Russians, and Ukrainians. Like Greek (Byzantine), Serbian, Bulgarian, and Hungarian states that fell earlier to the Turks, Poland had also disappeared, devoured by stronger neighbors. Others like Spain, Portugal, Switzerland, Holland, Sweden, and Denmark had withdrawn into the ranks of the secondary or tertiary powers, while once-dreaded Turkey had also conceded greatness to others and retreated into the Balkans. Out of Europe's multilateral power struggle, the states of certain peoples had grappled their way over others to the top of the ethnic heap. Five great "nation-states" towered over Europe by 1815—Britain, France, Prussia, Austria, and Russia.

Although the national competition was less convoluted, war could still break out among five wary, jealous contenders. Because the recent conflagrations of the French Revolution and Napoleon Bonaparte (1792–1815) had been so deadly—a shocking five million had died—the possibility of more large-scale bloodshed elicited the first serious challenges to traditional warring ways.[8] Victimized repeatedly by conquerors, Switzerland sought and acquired European recognition for the novel notion of neutrality—under international law, essentially, she could not attack or be attacked. For the first time nations subordinated rights of conquest in advance to a people's right of "self-determination," lending some small weight to the notion of *ex injuria jus non oritur*—rights cannot arise from an illegal act.[9] Belgium and Luxembourg joined Switzerland as neutral nations in 1839 and 1867, respectively.

Could laws and treaties replace violence as the final arbiter among nations? Some thought so. Between 1815 and 1830 pacifists founded the London Peace Society, the American Peace Society, the Parisian Society of Moral Christians, and the Peace Society of Geneva. Religiously inspired, these organizations saw Christ, the Prince of Peace, as a pacific model for modern times. Simultaneously, innovative economic thinkers like Henri de Saint-Simon and Augustin Thierry argued that war had grown far too costly for Europe's burgeoning commerce and industry. They presented a peace plan to the rulers who gathered at Vienna in 1815 to reestablish order after the final defeat of Napoleon.

The greatest prospect for peace came from monarchs in Russia, Austria, and Prussia who had survived a series of French aggressions aimed not only against their countries, but also against the institution of monarchy itself. They managed to stay the hand of war for forty years. After the generation of sovereigns who remembered Napoleonic times passed, however, wars returned to European soil in the 1850s and 1860s. One result was the first united Italian state since ancient times. After Prussia won wars against Austria and France, moreover, it joined other German states north of Austria in a mighty German Empire in 1871. Afterward Germany gave the annexed people of Alsace and Lorraine time to freely emigrate to France. Under "new moral pressures" to respect a people's wishes, rights of conquest were yielding—cynically, disingenuously, and only slightly, but yielding all the same—to rights of self-determination.[10]

By the 1890s a showdown loomed between Germany and Austria, on the one side, and France and Russia, on the other. The former states had buried their old differences and allied in 1879. To counter this, France and Russia agreed to an alliance in 1894. Soon Britain would be forced to choose sides. It was just such a European-wide cataclysm that the peace advocates who gathered at The Hague in May 1899 hoped fervently to prevent.

The ancient legacy of Europe's diversity, however, made matters worse. Ethnic differences lay at the root of Europe's early struggles, triggering strife in former times and setting in place the continent's unique polycentric pattern of rival states. Eventually the sovereigns of the dominant states ceased to fight for "tribal" causes, trying to divorce the people's vulgar impulses from politics and substituting dynastic agendas and the cold reason of state. In one of the most remarkable developments of the nineteenth century, however, a revived, or, better, a new ethnic/national consciousness surfaced among the many subjugated nationalities of Europe—among peoples, that is, without states of their own. To some extent this resulted from a growing desire to be free from oppression—*ex injuria jus non oritur*. Thus the Irish rose up in 1798; the Greeks in 1822; the Belgians, Italians, and Poles in 1830; the Irish, Italians, and Hungarians in 1848; the Poles again in 1863; and the Irish for a third time in 1867. In 1882 a secret Irish society brutally murdered the British chief and undersecretary for Ireland. The Greeks, Belgians, and Italians succeeded in their revolts, while the Hungarians managed to wrest full autonomy from Austria in 1867. With Russian assistance in 1878, moreover, Serbia, Rumania, and Montenegro broke free of Turkish control and Bulgaria received autonomy. German nationalism of the early 1800s can be viewed similarly, for many Germans had resented Napoleon's domination of their ancestral lands. German nationalists believed their troubles had begun centuries earlier when the medieval German Empire declined. Only the restoration of a powerful empire would end this troubled condition.

Adding an extra anxious dimension to nationalism, however, was its ideological charge. As historians of this phenomenon have argued, it takes a powerful act of imagination to bridge the local or provincial outlook typical in most communities and perceive oneself as part of a larger transregional nation.[11] The rise of printing, the spread of literacy, and the acceleration of transportation and communications facilitated the growth of imagined communities all over Europe as national leaders rediscovered and reshaped their conquered peoples' histories, folklore, and ancient languages; consolidated and manipulated local dialects into standardized written form; and then used all of this to fire revolutionary passions. The artificially stimulated "memory" of past great German (i.e., Holy Roman), Italian (i.e., Roman), Bulgarian, Serbian, and Polish empires and kingdoms became explosive forces in European politics, for much of its population lived under alien ethnic rule.

These developments generated anxieties among the established powers. There were clever reactionary responses, to be sure, from states like Prussia, which rode the tiger of nationalism to promote and control the kind of imperial German union that many national revolutionaries desired. The tsars also knew how to exploit Russian nationalism as an integrating force within their far-flung and rapidly expanding empire, but there was nothing subtle about it: "Russification" meant terminating experiments in ethnic autonomy and brutally suppressing any protests, as occurred in Finland in 1898–1899—another cloud hanging over deliberations at The Hague. In more precarious multiethnic states like Austria-Hungary, patriots' dreams of Greater Serbia or Greater Rumania induced nightmare scenarios. Would subject Serbs and Rumanians chafing under Austro-Hungarian rule secede in order to join the adjacent nation-states of Serbia and Rumania? Would it not serve the cold interests of state to crush these upstart neighboring nations and remove the source of secessionist temptation? Three thousand years after it began, therefore, ethnic diversity remained a thorny problem.

Revolutionary new developments sweeping across Europe further complicated issues for champions of peace as well as champions of violence, for the awesome technologies of a "second industrial revolution" threatened to kill many more combatants than had perished in the bloody Napoleonic Wars. Pacifists shuddered at the thought that the generalissimos would suppress soldierly anxieties about unsustainably high casualties and unleash the dogs of industrialized, mechanized war. Indeed, a specter was haunting Europe.

INDUSTRIALIZATION AND IMPERIALISM

Industrialization did not occur anywhere in the world until the late eighteenth century. The substitution of coal for wood to fuel iron manufacture; the coming of coal-fired, steam-driven factories; and the application of scientific principles to chemical production occurred first in Great Britain. During the nineteenth century much of this system of production spread to the United States and parts of Europe. The driving forces behind this migration of early industrial technologies were the competitive needs of foreign businessmen to emulate Britain's low-cost production methods as well as the desire of rival states to derive military benefits from industry in Europe's anxious power struggle. Translating these needs and desires into reality, however, required not only a lengthy lead time for planning and investment but also a basic level of scientific and engineering know-how commensurate with Britain's.[12]

The military imperative to further modern industry grew as the ongoing process began to generate technological by-products beneficial to the armies of Europe. Prussia, for example, recognized the great potential for its army of railroads—not one technology, but rather a cluster of technologies encompassing mining, metallurgy, machine tools, the steam engine, and construction engineering. As one officer put it, railroads were "an indispensable tool of war"[13] against France. The resulting expansion of strategic railroad networks benefited Prussia's growing economy, but it also returned handsome dividends in 1866 and 1870 when Berlin's armies stole marches on Austrian and French forces, which were unable to mobilize their battalions as rapidly. Not to be outdone, France paid more attention to its own railroad grid, constructing numerous strategic rail lines between Paris and the eastern frontier in the 1870s and 1880s.

By this time, however, the technological system of the first industrial revolution had begun to break down. The mutually reinforcing, converging, and interdependent functions of three basic technologies, or clusters of technologies, lent the industrial sector of early nineteenth-century Britain its systemic character. The first, wrought iron, was a material used in machines, rails, and building construction. The second, the reciprocating steam engine, powered the factories, locomotives, boats, and tractors. The third, sulfuric acid made in large lead vats or chambers, processed dyes and bleaches for textiles; soda for soap, glass, and gunpowder; and phosphates for fertilizer. As material demands on "the system" grew rapidly in the late 1800s, these basic component "parts" failed. Wrought iron was too soft and weak for the weight of bigger locomotives and the stress of heavier, faster-moving machines. The reciprocating motion of the steam engine was too inefficient, its power impossible to

Technological bottleneck: locomotives of the late 1800s too heavy for iron rails. (Corbis, Inc./Bethmann Archive)

transport over long distances, and its size-to-power ratio prohibitively high. Lead chamber acid, moreover, proved increasingly difficult to mass-produce.

While finding solutions to technological bottlenecks is never automatic or given, the technicians of Europe and the United States managed to solve this set of problems. Cheap, strong, flexible steel replaced wrought iron; powerful steam turbines supplanted reciprocating engines; and chemical researchers found ways to make large quantities of more highly concentrated sulfuric acid. But the scientists, engineers, and inventors went further, solving other problems as—or sometimes *before*—they arose. By the beginning of the twentieth century a new technological system had spawned a "second industrial revolution." Many of its parts are recognizable today: electrical power and equipment, wireless telegraphs, telephones, a host of synthetic chemicals for manufacturing and medicinal uses, nitrogen-based high explosives, and precision machine tools to shape bicycles, automobiles, airships, and airplanes.

These radical scientific and technological breakthroughs also revolutionized the art of warfare, producing killing machines like magazine-fed repeating rifles shooting thirty fo forty bullets a minute; machine guns shooting hundreds of bullets a minute; rapid-firing, semi-recoilless, steel alloy artillery pieces firing a few shells a minute, and hundreds per hour; and high-caliber shells packed with nitroglycerin and trinitrotoluene (TNT). Soldiers found it difficult, in fact, to cope with the rapid pace of change. The tightly packed ranks of infantry and cavalry that had charged in Napoleon's day would be killed so fast and in such horrendous quantities, complained one German general, that there would not be enough troops left to bury the dead.

Some argued that modern military technology favored defenders and ruled out attacks, especially by cavalry, while others insisted that charges would succeed if artillery crews prepared assaults by pummeling defensive positions, and if infantry spread out on the battlefield and occasionally dived for cover to avoid casualties. Still others refuted the necessity of such novel reforms, stubbornly maintaining the worth of older, allegedly more masculine "shock tactics."[14]

But soldiers of all countries closed ranks to condemn the arguments of Ivan Bloch, whose multivolume tract, *The Future of War*, appeared in 1892. The insightful Russian businessman predicted that the next European-wide conflagration would devastate the old order. Industrialized warfare would kill millions of soldiers over many years, ruin Europe's interdependent economy, draw civilians into the same vortex of death, and eventually trigger violent social upheavals. His conclusion that no nation could afford such a fate, and that all nations should therefore find alternatives to war, led him into the peace movement. Here was added reason for the generals to be furious about Bloch's critique of their ancient craft. In the end, military establishments felt they had to accept the wares of war offered up by Europe's rapidly evolving technological system. Fear that neighboring enemy countries might adopt these weapons and win a crushing victory overwhelmed whatever doubts and anxieties remained.

Killer technology: the German 420-mm howitzer. (Karl Justrow, *Die Dicke Berta und der Krieg* [Berlin, 1935])

As noted earlier, however, adopting modern weapons presupposed the necessary industrial plant, engineering savvy, and lead time to acquire these, for importation was rarely possible—and unreliable during the disruptions of wartime. A country had to reach and pass the threshold of its industrial revolution, in other words, before it could wield power against potential enemies in modern times. And only four Great Powers in Europe had reached this point: Britain, France, Germany, and Austria. Britain, the first nation to industrialize—and the only nation to have really perfected the interlocking clusters of technologies that comprised the first industrial revolution—possessed a tremendous lead in 1850, and still led in 1900. However, industrial latecomer Germany had made rapid strides to close this gap. The industries of this mighty nation wedged between its rivals were growing at twice the rate of Britain's, which meant a doubling of industrial output every fifteen years. Germany had also forged ahead *qualitatively* by pioneering or widely adopting many of the newest technologies of the second industrial revolution. Germany's steel, machine tool, chemical, and electrical industries had no equal in Europe by the early twentieth century.

On the other hand, Southern and Eastern Europe, including the Russian colossus, had just begun to industrialize. Thus Russian steam engine capacity—a reliable barometer of industrial strength—lagged nine years behind that of Germany in 1870, and twenty years in 1888 despite three decades of serious state efforts to accelerate industrial growth. As Minister of Finance Sergei Witte observed in the early 1890s, Russian backwardness represented a very definite economic and military peril.[15] Russia's immediate response to this predicament took the form of a defensive alliance with more highly developed France in 1894. Clearly the spiraling, mutating process of industrialization had exacerbated relations between nations with little history of resolving disputes peacefully. Fixing his eye on the long run, however, Witte managed to convince Tsar Alexander III (1881–1894) to take a quantum leap into the advancing second industrial revolution. Saint Petersburg provided subsidies to struggling entrepreneurs, raised protective tariffs, and facilitated foreign loans and investments, all of which targeted the acquisition of foreign expertise and technology. So that urban factories had laborers, he issued special internal passports to peasants still restricted to village communes (see later in this chapter). These measures accelerated production during the late 1890s. Railroad expansion provided the major stimulus to industrial growth as the length of track soon doubled. Mining and metallurgy grew proportionally—quicker, in fact, than in Germany. By the time Russia began the catch-up process, however, she stood twenty-four years behind Germany in steam engine capacity. Ominously, moreover, key components of the second industrial revolution like chemicals and machine tools, both of military importance, lagged even further behind (see Chapter 3).

Russia desperately needed modern industry to avoid slipping from the ranks of Europe's Great Powers. She did not require steam turbines or state-of-the-art steel mills, however, to become the greatest imperial state in Asia.[16] In-

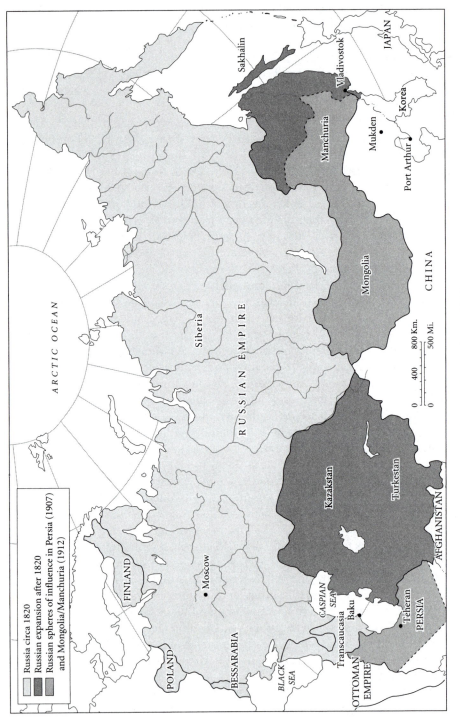

Russian Expansion to 1914

South Asia 1914

Map labels:

PACIFIC OCEAN

HONG KONG (British 1841)

PHILIPPINES ISLANDS U.S., from Spain 1898

TAIWAN Japanese, from China 1895

FRENCH INDOCHINA

BRITISH MALAYA

Singapore

DUTCH EAST INDIES

AUSTRALIA

Shanghai

CHINA

SIAM

BURMA

TIBET

Calcutta

INDIA

Bombay

INDIAN OCEAN

AFGHANISTAN
Kabul

Russian Sphere

British Sphere

PERSIA

Teheran

OMAN

KUWAIT
BAHRAIN
QATAR

ADEN

BRITISH SOMALILAND

OTTOMAN EMPIRE

EGYPT

Red Sea

British
Dutch
French
Russian

0   800 Km.
0   500 Mi.

17

deed, by the 1820s tsarist power extended from European Russia, into the Caucasus, and far beyond the Urals into Siberia. Utilizing this massive territorial base and an impressive pre-industrial manufacturing establishment, moved by a desire for new markets and the lust for fame typical of captains in the field, and propelled by belligerency acquired over a millennium of intense warfare, Russian armies went on the march. Between 1830 and 1885 they rolled around the Caspian Sea and over the khanates of Central Asia, and eastward as far as the Amur River and the Pacific Ocean. The city they founded on the coast, Vladivostok, means "Rule over the East." It was a fitting name.

The imperial age in Western Europe also began prior to industrialization. Spain captured its vast American holdings in the fifteenth and sixteenth centuries, but by 1820 had lost nearly all of them to independence movements as well as British and French encroachment. Holland seized much of present-day Indonesia, the so-called Dutch East Indies. The best example of early modern imperialism, of course, is British expansion into North America, the Caribbean, South Africa, India, portions of the East Indies, and Australia—the colonial demand for British goods contributed significantly, in fact, to Britain's eighteenth-century quest for new industrial technologies to break production bottlenecks.

With European industrialization in the nineteenth century, however, imperialism greatly accelerated. Europeans had never lacked aggressiveness before, but now they possessed vastly superior weaponry as well as the means of transporting armies quickly around the globe. Lethal repeating rifles, machine guns, field artillery, and intimidating steam-powered battleships and gunboats expedited the subjugation of the entire African hinterland by British, French, and German forces, for instance, in the relatively short span of the 1880s and 1890s. Only the Abyssinians resisted successfully, overwhelming an Italian invasion force at Adowa in 1896 with the aid of modern French artillery. Zulus, Matabeles, the Congo tribes, the Sudanese, and scores of other African peoples were not as fortunate.

Industrialization provided Europeans not only with the weaponry to subdue the world, but also with a greater incentive to do so. For they went in search of oil, rubber, copper, nitrates, and other scarce natural resources vital to Europe's burgeoning industries. They sought colonies as markets to amortize domestic investments more quickly; as farm sites for the coffee, tea, fruit, and sugar products craved by continental consumers of all classes with increasingly more purchasing power; and as a welcome high-risk, high-return investment outlet for capital accumulating rapidly back home. By 1900 the English had invested ten billion dollars abroad, France five billion, and Germany nearly four billion—a total amount roughly equivalent to the combined annual domestic product of these three mighty nations. Europe was indeed the world's banker. When revolt or expropriation threatened oil wells in Mexico, banana plantations in Guatemala, nitrate mines in Chile, or the Suez Canal and territories straddling the sea route to India, and when debt cancellation terminated lucrative loans to the Tunisian Bey, the Egyptian Khedive, the Turkish Sultan, the Persian Shah, or the Chinese Empress, Europe responded with

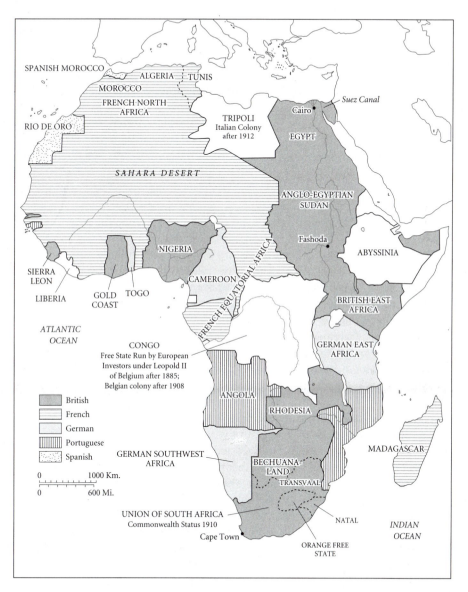

political pressure, intimidation, or the establishment of military protectorates. Thus European flags followed trade and investment—and European empires grew.

Historians have debated additional motivations beyond those related to industrialization that drove the complex phenomenon of imperialism inexorably forward.[17] The French push into Indo-China received major impetus from the appeals of French missionaries, for instance, while similar calls from Christian proselytizers accelerated the simultaneous "scramble for Africa." A settlement drive something akin to the British migration to their eighteenth-century American colonies also moved Dutch pioneers north from British Capetown as well as French emigrants into Algeria. Moreover, a unique European imperialism of sorts combining religious, settler, and *nationalistic* motives—Zionism—brought European Jews to Ottoman Palestine circa 1900 with the aim of escaping persecution and reestablishing the Hebrews' ancient homeland. Perceived as encroachment by local Muslims, Jewish immigration created tensions and sparked disagreements that have sadly intensified, seemingly without solution, throughout the twentieth century to the present day.[18] Researchers make subtle distinctions, furthermore, between the market motives driving Britain's eighteenth-century expansion into India and financial- and investment-related aims behind the establishment of an Egyptian protectorate, on the one hand, and the *strategic* need to protect the Suez Canal and control territories along the connecting route to India, on the other. It is important to remember in this respect that oil did not become important until Persian (e.g., Iranian) resources were tapped after 1900—Iraqi and Arabian fields did not factor into imperial formulas until the 1920s and 1930s. Closely related to strategic considerations, finally, were the nationalistic rivalries between European Great Powers that magnified the significance of territories throughout the world with little or no economic value. If the British had coaling stations for their ships on Pacific islands, Germany and America needed them too. And could any European power stand idly by while Britain established a chain of possessions from Capetown to Cairo?

As empires expanded, the number of flashpoints between jealous imperial rivals multiplied. At Adowa in 1896, for instance, the French armed the Abyssinians to bludgeon the Italians and indirectly thwart Italy's patron, Britain. Two years later at Fashoda, on the Nile south of Sudan, French and British expeditions butted heads and nearly triggered war. As the Russians conquered more of Central Asia and their agents pushed farther into Persia and Afghanistan, moreover, the British watched anxiously from their huge colony in India. The so-called Great Game of matching an opponent move for move on the chessboard of Central Asia brought Great Britain and Russia to the brink of war more than once during the 1800s. With relations still simmering as the century drew to a close, Britain opened secret talks in Berlin, for a deal with Germany seemed a logical way to gird for a possible war against imperial nemeses Russia and France. Thus industrialization, imperialism, and other factors fueled one another and increased the likelihood of worldwide war.

EUROPEAN SOCIETY

Karl Marx, the famous philosopher and revolutionary, observed Europe's militant industrial-technological transformation from his native Germany in the 1840s, and later from exile in London, where he died in 1883. His political creed would become one of the twentieth century's most influential. Although scholars have long discounted the self-styled "scientific" nature of his analysis, many academic investigators have benefited from his model of thinking, for it was perhaps the first to incorporate economic, social, political, and intellectual/artistic factors into a dynamic, interactive whole.[19]

The Upper Classes

One of Marx's political predictions involved the "bourgeoisie," the owners of the technological "means of production" driving the industrial revolution—and the new age—forward. Just as wealthy industrialists and bankers rose to the top of the business world, so too, he believed, they would sweep into political power, ousting or marginalizing the blue-blooded kings and landed aristocrats who had ruled for many centuries. The new governors would quickly introduce laws to protect private property and investments, bolster themselves against the lower classes, and generally establish cultural norms in keeping with bourgeois conventions.

In Marx's lifetime this seemed to be happening in Western Europe, first in Belgium, where revolution opened government to industrialists in 1830, and in Britain, where reforms brought the middle class into parliament in 1832. Reformers subsequently established rule of law and plutocratic or otherwise limited representative institutions in Holland (1848), Denmark (1849), Italy (1860), Sweden (1866), Austria/Hungary (1861–1867), and Germany (1867–1871). Eighty years of turmoil in France culminated with the founding of more democratic institutions in 1871. Although only France and Switzerland, Europe's first democracy, elected presidents, others retaining their monarchs as heads of state, momentum appeared to be with the bourgeoisie. "We are the times," boasted a German publicist. In France confident men bragged that "wicked" kings and emperors had been driven out and "everything was happening for the best," while a British middle-class historian asserted that "a new and brighter spiritual era is slowly evolving itself for all men."[20]

This kind of optimism and dogmatic certainty characterized the "liberal" ideology undergirding the advance of the bourgeoisie. Liberals tended to believe that all phenomena in the universe were knowable, that science and rational investigation represented the keys to understanding, and that these tools, hard work, and virtue cleared a path for the ineluctable progress of mankind. The rapidly unfolding industrial and sci-tech marvels of the time, especially the conquest of the skies by balloon, airship, and airplane, epitomized man's upward trajectory. Even the worried pacifists of fin de siécle Europe bore the same infectious optimism in their heady determination to establish peace on earth. Liberalism had its caveats and contradictions, of course, for progress seemed reserved for the propertied, not the propertyless; for men, not women; for Christians, not Jews, Muslims, or Hindus; and for white Europeans, not the colored peoples of Africa and Asia.

Marx's notion of a historically inevitable bourgeois or "liberal" revolution begins to break down, however, in Central and Eastern Europe.[21] Thus the autocratic Russian monarchy, which had sponsored industrialism since the 1850s, backed away from representative institutions at the local level in the 1880s and condemned more radical proposals for a nationwide elected body as contrary to the tradition of authoritarian rule "by the grace of God." This so-called divine right of kings had a corollary of sorts among arrogant noblemen in Russia who maintained immense landholdings, enjoyed privileged appointments in the bureaucracy and army, and expected peasants to be submissive and deferential despite the fact that they were no longer legally expropriated serfs. Nor had the bourgeoisie cracked the social and political monopoly of the aristocracy in Russia by century's end. In Austria-Hungary and Germany, furthermore, the king-kaisers sacrificed only a small portion of their powers, retaining exclusive control over their armies and foreign policies, including declarations of war. Politics here is more accurately characterized as an upper-class/middle-class political compromise featuring limited parliamentary rights. Socially in German Europe, moreover, the worlds of aristocracy and bourgeoisie rarely met—upwardly mobile bourgeois families ennobled by the king usually suffered through a generation of ostracizing before their children were accepted by blue bloods. Even in Scandinavia and Britain titled aristocrats and lords continued to hold high office and lead exclusive lives. Lavish eight-course dinner parties, "posh" outings along the French coast, and weekend shooting parties were the rage, such as the one in Buckinghamshire during which seven men shot 3,937 pheasants, all beaten out of the bush by lower-class locals sometimes unlucky enough to be accidentally shot themselves.

Since Marx's day historians also pay more attention to subclass distinctions among the many groupings and factions located socially in the "middle" between the aristocracy and the masses, but possessing little else in common.[22] Vast differences of income, for instance, separated barons of industry from other more modestly situated bourgeois. A good example is German armaments maker Alfred Krupp, whose palatial Villa Hugel near Essen boasted its own train stop for special visits by Kaiser William II. Scholars make another distinction between the "propertied" middle class of wealthy, largely self-made businessmen like Krupp and the "cultivated" middle class of highly educated clergymen, bureaucrats, professors, lawyers, scientists, and engineers. The numbers of the cultivated grew rapidly as the first industrial revolution yielded to the second. High school and university enrollment in the prominent German state of Prussia, for instance, rose from sixteen thousand in 1820 to over one hundred thousand in the 1880s. Despite such growth, those with university degrees still represented an elite one thousandth of Europe's population. The "new" men of property and professionalism must be distinguished in their turn from an "old" or preindustrial middle class of artisans, handicraftsmen, and small shopowners, and both the old and new middle classes from a rapidly growing subclass of moderately paid government clerks and business functionaries. Joining these "white-collar" office workers in what has been called the lower middle class were those skilled "blue-collar" mechanics whose high wages elevated them above the masses.

In recent decades historians have delved deeper into another aspect of middle-class existence that interested Marx and many of his early associates: the world of women, in particular the cult of domesticity surrounding wives of prominent businessmen and professionals.[23] As the bourgeoisie grew in wealth and influence, men built fortunes and careers and struggled for status and political rights in the outside world. Meanwhile, their women were relegated to the private sphere of the home, where they were expected to bear children, preside over the servants, and manage the household in isolation from the public domain of men. Thus women, who for centuries had toiled at different tasks on the farms of the preindustrial era, lived even more separate lives in the bourgeois age. This hierarchy of gender became fixed in law with the Civil Code of Napoleon Bonaparte in 1800—statutes that remained on the books well into the twentieth century not only in France, but also in Belgium, Holland, Luxembourg, and Italy. It would be difficult to exaggerate the persistent influence in these parts of Europe of the Civil Code, which had an aura of perfection among male jurists who practically enshrined its principles. The great conqueror's legal reforms empowered male "heads" of the household to decide on the upbringing and education of children, determine whether wives could work or engage in any sort of activity outside the home, and control all property and resources, even income from a wife's dowry or work. The writings of Karl Marx and his longtime colleague in London, Friedrich Engels, as well as German follower August Bebel, one of the founders of the Marxist Social Democratic Party, emphasized this propertied aspect of marriage, focusing on the importance for family heads of producing sons to inherit male wealth.

While many women in Western Europe made the most of the public opportunities available to them, becoming active in church, leading the community's charitable causes, and generally parlaying the husband's status into a female respectability far above that of ordinary women, others chafed at their "dollhouse"[24] existence and sometimes thought about—or even acted on—the need to enter politics and overturn woman's legal inferiority. In France, for instance, voting-rights pioneers Maria Deraismes and Hubertine Auclert braved male opposition and organized campaigns for women's suffrage in the late 1800s, but Napoleon's legacy, buttressed by a conservative Catholic Church that saw feminism as a threat to the family, preserved gender order. The first signs of change came, not coincidentally, in Germany, Scandinavia, and British or formerly British lands where Germanic or common law made fewer claims on private life than the patriarchal Civil Code. Because under these traditions law was used more for settling disputes, not for regulating civil and private matters for public-political purposes, women tended to be somewhat less subordinate to men. It is significant, moreover, that these countries were Protestant (or largely so), for a religion begun to correct perceived abuses seems to have generated greater concern for individual rights and thus found itself slightly more accommodating to the feminist spirit.[25] Pressured by reformers in the 1860s and 1870s, for instance, the Universities of Zurich and London became the first to admit women for degrees. Simultaneously, Britain, Sweden, and Russian Finland introduced municipal voting rights for single women of property. The single women of many states in the American West could vote in statewide elections by the 1890s, sometimes with property qualifications, sometimes not, and Australia inaugurated full-fledged women's voting in national elections in 1902. Finally, married women in Britain and Swedish Norway earned legal competency and the right to control earnings and property in the 1880s; Germany passed an attenuated version of these laws in 1900. Women's organizations across Europe and the English-speaking world ushered in the new century by pushing governments to grant women a wider range of political rights and educational and economic opportunities.

Women's groups also backed the cause of peace. One of the earliest signs of a gender-specific pacifism came in Germany with the emergence of "spiritual motherhood." Bourgeois female activists in this citadel of militarism believed that the nurturing qualities of mothers could transform society once women exited the private sphere of home and family. German feminists wanted women to acquire formal education, pedagogical training, and jobs as teachers at all levels from kindergarten to the university. The combined effect of childrearing and teaching would enable women to transform culture and affect a gentler, more peaceful way of doing things. Eventually their valuable contribution to a public world dominated by men would earn females voting rights, and the suffrage, in turn, would carry this peaceful maternal revolution into national and international politics. "We women are created not to hate, but to love,"[26] said Henriette Goldschmidt in 1866 after one of Europe's many wars.

Female pacifism had become more pronounced by the 1890s. An influx of "spiritual mothers" to elementary school classrooms reinforced the trend. Women made up 20 percent of teaching staffs in German grade schools in 1899, but the figure came to nearly 50 percent in France, where activists like Mme. St. Croix wanted to utilize the "mother heart of the world" to achieve moral betterment. Women occupied 60 percent of elementary school positions in Sweden, and almost 70 percent in Britain. Speaking for many of them, the International Council of Women (ICW), an American-based, pro-suffrage organization packed with teachers and women professionals from eighteen nations, condemned war-mongering teachers and textbooks. Led by Mary Wright Sewall, a feminist school administrator, the ICW strove to purge the curriculum of reading material that "eulogizes vanity and arrogance in the name of patriotism." Rather, history, civics, and literature should include "training in citizenship and encouragement to a life of peace." Consistent with this goal, the ICW established a standing committee on peace and arbitration in 1899 to add momentum to the intensifying quest for alternatives to war. One year earlier, moreover, Margarethe Selenka of the Federation of German

Women's Organizations overcame the doubts of comrades who worried that peace activism would turn governments against the movement's efforts to improve the status of women. The Federation decided to support the upcoming Hague conference with public agitation against "race hatred" as the best way to demonstrate "true love of country." They circulated a petition among women in twelve countries that gathered a million signatures by the following spring. An international demonstration of pacifist women at the Hague Conference declared "the woman question" inseparable from "the peace question," for both were essentially "struggles for the power of law against the law of power."[27]

The signatures of a million women impressed contemporaries. As Bertha von Suttner had repeatedly reminded readers, however, female solidarity against the "military spirit" did not yet exist. Women could make no claim to superiority on the issue of peace versus war, she wrote in 1894, for there were also "women's groups that start collections for torpedo boats and within a short time bring 800,000 [Austrian] crowns together for this cause." Nor did motherhood seem to improve the situation. "Mothers are the best customers of factories that make tin soldiers—great numbers of them are either indifferent or proud that their boys are cadets."[28] Suttner saw most women as captives of Europe's age-old tradition of war and hatred—a legacy propagated by both sexes. All solutions relying exclusively on gender or class, therefore, would fail to exorcize Europe's martial demons. For that, men and women of all classes had to unite.

The Social Question

"A specter is haunting Europe" opens *The Communist Manifesto* (1848) by Karl Marx and Friedrich Engels. As many readers will already know, the two revolutionaries were not thinking mainly about *international* war in this first line, but rather an inevitable *class* war between the bourgeoisie and blue-collar "proletarians." They believed that factory owners had begun an inevitable revolutionary process by paying laborers who toiled in dangerous conditions subsistence wages far below the value of output. These dire conditions would not improve, for competition and profit imperatives dictated harshness, and states allegedly controlled by the bourgeoisie would not introduce ameliorating social legislation. Although such exploitation gradually shaped a coherent class of workers highly conscious of their collective plight, an "intelligentsia" of disgruntled educated members of the upper classes was necessary to guide the proletariat toward fulfillment of its historical destiny—a bloody uprising to wrest control of state and society from the expropriators.

Marx and Engels believed that the first proletarian revolution would occur in Britain, whose bourgeois stage of history had evolved the furthest, followed by somewhat less advanced countries like France and Germany, and eventually more backward industrializing nations like Russia, whose bourgeois revolution had not yet occurred. For an indefinite period after the first revolutions proletarian dictatorships would be required to defend the revolution from bourgeois counterrevolutionaries at home and abroad—thus class war would eventually spill over into international war. The dictatorship's ultimate task was to lay the socialist groundwork for communism. Once workers had power they would own and operate their plants collectively and produce according to an economic plan—Marx did not trust market forces and saw privately owned means of production as the root cause of exploitation. Through planning and worker solidarity socialism would not only facilitate industrial productivity unmatched in the previous bourgeois era but also terminate class struggle, exploitation, poverty, crime, and war—workers' societies would never fight one another. Socialism, in short, would eliminate the need for state structures and take history into its final stage: a "communist"[29] utopia.

Throughout much of the nineteenth century the verdict of unfolding historical developments appeared to be on Marx's side. Europe's year of revolutions, 1848, witnessed shocking lower-class violence and revolts in France, Central Europe, and Italy. Although revolutionaries did not prevail, another eruption of class bloodshed shook Paris in 1870. The city's leftist "Commune" also succumbed to brutal upper-class counterrevolution, but contemporaries agonized over the possibility that the next volcanic surge of proletarian ire would topple existing society. These worries stayed alive in the 1880s and 1890s as governments in Spain, Italy, Belgium, Sweden, and Russia resorted to military suppression of striking workers. That Switzerland called out troops twelve times against strikers between 1860 and 1894 conformed exactly to Marxist prescriptions and conveyed more anxiety than hope for what the next century held in store.

Modern social and demographic studies highlight this image of late nineteenth-century Europe undergoing a turbulent and wrenching transition to modern times.[30] Population from the Bay of Biscayne to the Urals burgeoned from 300 to 450 million in forty years (1870–1910) as falling mortality rates overcompensated for the tendency of families to have fewer children in crowded urban environments, particularly in West-Central Europe. Metropolises like London, Paris, Rome, Berlin, Vienna, and Saint Petersburg doubled in numbers, the British capital with 6.6 million in 1900 far exceeding the next largest, Paris, with 2.7 million, and the third largest, Berlin, with 1.9 million. Cities and towns claimed a growing share of the populace, climbing from 60 to 80 percent in Britain, 33 to 45 percent in France, and 29 to 55 percent in Germany. Many of the rural newcomers or those born in cities entered the industrial labor force, whose numbers roughly doubled in the last third of the century, reaching 10 million in Britain, 5 million in Germany, 3.5 million in France and Austria-Hungary, and 2 million in Italy and Russia. Trade union membership also soared above very humble mid-century beginnings to levels that alarmed employers: 2 million in Britain, nearly a million in Germany, and half a million in France. Although unions were illegal in Draconian Russia, 170,000 proletarians downed tools there in 1897. Like the fast-charging second industrial revolution, life itself seemed to be accelerating, surging forth in different directions, and placing myriad excessive demands on strained abilities to comprehend the changes—a form of future shock that affected the

Europe's largest city: London circa 1890.   (Hulton/Archive by Getty Images)

anxious haves more than the dissatisfied have-nots. "Time was moving faster than a cavalry camel," remembered Austrian writer Robert Musil. "No one knew what it was moving towards [nor] could anyone quite distinguish between what was above and what was below, between what was moving forward and what backward."[31]

Times were not changing fast enough, however, for the lower classes. While historians have hotly disputed whether the workers' standard of living rose or fell during early industrialization, a consensus has emerged that proletarian lives improved marginally in the late 1800s.[32] Thus average "real wages" rose a percentage point or so every year, enough to bring a welcome variety of food to the table.[33] Mixed occasionally now with bread, butter, and a pail of beer was some meat, cheese, vegetables, fruit, or sweets. In some big cities at least, workers sometimes splurged with an evening of singing and slapstick comedy in a music hall. But these improvements affected only some of the working class. Studies conducted in Britain, Europe's most prosperous society, showed that about 30 percent of the people lived in chronic poverty in the 1890s, while around 35 percent did not possess the minimum physical requirements for military service—the proportion of army rejects rose to 90 percent in heavily industrialized cities like Manchester and London. Even the more fortunate faction of the working class had to cope, moreover, with harsh, unameliorated sides of proletarian life such as poor, packed, unsanitary housing; long working hours in unsafe conditions; and, worst of all perhaps, social insecurity. Thus unemployment during recessions or the off-season of the

The people have needs: poor family in Britain circa 1900. (Getty Images)

building trades created months of crisis for poor families, not to mention a disabling injury or accidental death to the breadwinner, which plummeted surviving wives and children into society's underclass. These cruel realities mixed cynically with the marginal advances of lower-class Europeans to spawn an angry, insistent mood among the masses—a kind of proletarian, atonal variation on the era's dominant theme of optimism. In November 1899, for example, workers marched into the center of Paris singing a menacingly sinister melody: "To the lamp-post with the bourgeois/The bourgeois, let's string 'em up/And if we don't get to hang 'em/ We'll flatten the bastards out." For hours the crude procession went by, its banners confidently proclaiming the need for justice, equality, liberty, and emancipation. "It would be good to know," said one alarmed observer, "just what these words mean to these men."[34]

Recent gender research deepens our understanding of proletarian misery, for working women clearly led even more precarious lives than their men.[35] At century's end they worked either at home sewing and button-holing for nearby factories, in upper-class homes as domestic servants, or in garment shops, textile plants, and tobacco and food-processing factories. Women worked in great numbers, constituting 20 percent of the industrial labor force in Russia, 20 percent in Germany, 26 percent in Britain, and 34 percent in France. They had to work as teenagers or wives to support the meager incomes of fathers and husbands. On the job, females experienced the same problems of low pay, long hours, and unsafe surroundings, but sexual harassment from male bosses and coworkers often added an ugly dimension. Abuse of this sort became so extreme in one Russian factory that women weavers revolted and almost destroyed the entire plant. At home, cooking and cleaning lengthened the workday to the point of total exhaustion. Here, too, dangers frequently lurked in the form of male drunkenness, wife beating, or marital rape.

The Great Powers could not afford to ignore the great social problems of the day and risk revolution, as Marx had predicted they would. Britain, Europe's pioneering industrial nation and thus also the first to face the squalor, pollution, and harsh working conditions of early industrialization, reacted in pragmatic ways that especially defied Marxist analysis.[36] Always compromise-prone, the nation's moderate, parliamentary monarchy yielded to the demands of the nation's rapidly growing working class. Reform acts enfranchised most men in 1867 and 1884. Balloting became secret in 1872, thereby assuring that laborers could vote without the scrutiny of employers. Britain's young democracy responded immediately to the wider, freer electorate. In 1875 trade unions won a fifty-year struggle for the right to organize, strike, and bargain collectively. An early form of workman's compensation followed in the 1880s. British trade unions also committed the bulk of their considerable funds to insure members against sickness, accidents, unemployment, old age, and death. Despite impressive progress, however, much social work remained to be done.

Late nineteenth-century France did not negotiate the narrows of working-class protest as adequately as did Britain.[37] This was because workers had revolted in 1830, 1848, and 1870–1871 with many thousands dying when soldiers intervened—and neither side forgot. Frightened by the seething discontent below them, for example, bourgeois leaders of the republic denied workers full rights of trade union organization until 1884. French proletarians had the right to vote, organize unions, and strike, but received nothing more in the way of social legislation before 1900. Memories of violence prejudiced many legislators against bills guaranteeing shorter working days, higher wages, and social insurance programs, while deep suspicions of urban workers among rural voters comprising over half of the population further reduced the likelihood of social reforms. The paucity of reform and earlier history of repression helps to explain the "to the lamp post with the bourgeois" attitude of French workers. Their clenched-fisted approach kept class relations very tense as trade union militants argued that only strikes, sabotage, and boycotts would advance the workers' cause.

The escalating scandal known as the Dreyfus Affair created further tension.[38] The army framed a Jewish officer, Alfred Dreyfus, on espionage charges in 1894, sentencing the innocent man to life in prison and hauling him away to the bleak, cruel Caribbean confines of Devil's Island. Relatives and political sympathizers refused to accept the verdict. Their struggle to reopen the case triggered a huge crisis that nearly tore France apart from 1897 to 1899. Military top brass, civilian super patriots, the conservative church establish-

ment, and most of the press rallied to the army's defense, accusing the "Drey-
fusards" of besmirching the soldier's caste, the nation's only weapon against
Germany. Anti-Semitism flared up as petit bourgeois Frenchmen, who were
extremely anxious in an era of rapid socioeconomic change and transition,
sought scapegoats for their troubles. "Death," they shouted, "death to the
Jew." On the other side champions of Dreyfus believed that the case threatened cherished traditions of justice and liberty stretching back to the great
revolution of 1789. Anyone who subverted these virtuous institutions—even
if they wore the red and blue uniform of France's glorious army—had to be
stopped. Anti-clericalism also motivated radical leftist deputies like Georges
Clemenceau, who felt that the army was "in the hands of the Jesuits." Supporters of Dreyfus were prepared to match the intensity of the enemies of justice blow for blow. "God give me struggle, enemies, howling crowds," said
one of them, "all the combat of which I am capable."[39]

Socialist factions in the chamber initially scoffed at pro-Dreyfus pleas.
"Strikers are unjustly condemned every day without having committed treason and deserve our sympathies more than Dreyfus."[40] As the scandal unfolded,
however, advocates of the laborers' cause also entered the fray. Foremost among
them stood the brilliant socialist orator, Jean Jaures, who believed that republican institutions, however flawed, were far superior to the reactionary decrees
that would follow a rightist coup d'etat. The impassioned speeches of Jaures
in defense of Dreyfus appealed to rank-and-file unionists and blue-collar workers whose leftist republicanism was aroused by the affair. The Parisian laborers who chanted death to the bourgeoisie typified the complexity of this proletarian spirit, for they marched to the Place de la Nation to view the unveiling
of a great bronze statue celebrating the triumph of the republic.

The Central European powers experienced somewhat greater social stability, mainly because they responded more cleverly to challenges from the
lower classes.[41] Thus Germany introduced universal manhood suffrage and
legalized trade unions and strikes in 1869–1870. Pioneering old age pensions
along with accident and long-term disability insurance programs followed in
the 1880s. For twelve years Germany combined the carrot of reform with the
stick of discriminatory anti-socialist laws (1878–1890), but early in his reign
Kaiser William II (1888–1918) abolished this legislation. Austria also permitted trade union activity and patterned social insurance policies after its northern neighbor and ally. But Vienna denied workers the suffrage as a means of
preserving law and order: "You should not believe that we would be inclined
to introduce mob rule into Austria," officials told one labor leader. It would
be foolish to allow "proletarians with caps on their heads and pikes in their
hands to run into the council hall."[42] Prolonged labor protests and the violence of anarchism (see later in this chapter) finally elicited a more prudent
response in 1897 when the state enfranchised industrial workers.

This pattern of reform as insurance against revolution certainly contributed to the moderation of trade unionists and Social Democrats, whose numbers were growing quickly, especially in more rapidly industrializing Germany. Serious crisis was banished from neither realm, however, for the unions

kept pushing for more far-reaching reforms like collective bargaining rights, while their socialist parliamentary friends demanded democratization of political institutions that were still transparently authoritarian. Parliamentarization (i.e., the sharing of decision making between monarch and parliament) did not mean democratization, in other words, and by century's end soldiers stood ready to march on factory districts if proletarians pressed their unacceptable demands too forcefully.

The Vatican also responded to labor issues with a mix of social theology and political pragmatism. In a dramatic encyclical, *Rerum Novarum* (1891), Pope Leo XIII (1878–1903) urged European Catholics and the states that governed them to intensify efforts to solve the social question and thereby prevent further disruptions of families and society. Both governmental efforts like those begun in Germany, and private action like the founding of Christian labor organizations, also initiated in Germany, could make an immeasurable difference. Leo reminded Catholics what Saint Thomas Aquinas had written centuries earlier about the rights of the poor to share the proceeds of the land, and the obligation of owners to ensure that their property served the community. Although *Rerum Novarum* stimulated great social activity among Catholic workers and some of their "red" priests, employers, even Catholic employers, tended to look askance at the Pope's "Christian Socialism."[43]

The expansion of cities, the growth of the industrial working classes, the proliferation of urban social problems, and the turbulent air of rising expectations were not the only perils to the establishment. In order to gain a fuller appreciation of societal tremors it is important to shift focus to a segment of society that Marx and Engels believed history would relegate to insignificance— rural workers.[44] A significant portion of Europe's labor force still lived and worked on the land in 1900: 10 percent in Britain, 40 percent in France and Germany, 51 percent in Italy, 61 percent in Austria-Hungary, and 70 percent in Russia. They no longer toiled under the degrading and dehumanizing institution of serfdom, which the ruling classes had eliminated in the decades between the French Revolution of 1789 and the Russian Emancipation of 1861. Farming remained a hard life that still retained an exploitative side, however, especially for small farmers and rural laborers in Spain, Southern Italy, and Russia.

Rural conditions in Russia were particularly harsh.[45] In order to assuage noblemen who opposed the abolition of serfdom, "Tsar Liberator" Alexander II (1856–1881) insisted that peasants pay noblemen for the farm plots they received with emancipation. Coming on top of taxes, these indemnification payments made life acutely trying for the small man. It is doubtful that the tsar achieved his goal of completely defusing what had been a revolutionary threat to the regime. Rural life deteriorated further under Alexander III (1881–1894) and his ill-prepared son, Nicolas II (1894–1917). Convinced that liberation had been a mistake, Alexander III began to turn back the clock to former times. "Land captains" appointed from the nobility received police powers that reminded many of the sordid side of serfdom. Further decrees largely disenfranchised peasants from the "Zemstvos," rural councils that Alexander II had introduced as a first step toward self-government. Meanwhile, population in the countryside rose 57 percent from 1860 to 1897 while household plot size simultaneously decreased 22 percent. The onus of taxes and indemnities added to the burden of extra mouths to feed on smaller plots. These conditions triggered famine and cholera in 1891–1892 that killed many hundreds of thousands. Soon another type of hunger—for more land—mobilized agitated petty farmers to rise up against local noblemen who, it was said, had too much land. Rural violence in the 1890s was as bad as it had been on the eve of Tsar Alexander's "liberating" decrees.

The riotous phenomenon of "land hunger" fueled the rise of the "Socialist Revolutionaries" (SRs). Inspired by the revolutionary potential of the countryside, these disaffected intellectuals and frustrated Zemstvo functionaries hoped to incite a violent upsurge and establish a communistic society based on the institution of the village commune. At first scattered throughout Russia without contact or viable national organization, the SRs began to coalesce in 1897–1898. Two years later they succeeded in founding a national party.

With 70 percent of the labor force still working on the land, the SRs represented a serious threat. A backlog of problems unsolved during the preindustrial era obviously plagued Russia, but by accelerating industrialization in the 1890s its rulers had added a second revolutionary challenge: the proletariat. At the head of Russia's striking workers in the late 1890s, for instance, stood the so-called Fighting Union for the Liberation of the Working Class, a radical Marxist group led by a ruthlessly determined man, Vladimir Ilyich Lenin, the later founder of the Soviet Union.

Russia's absolute monarchy was singularly ill equipped to cope successfully with these diverse challenges. No national parliament or elected body existed to diffuse conflict and conciliate protesting groups with the kind of political deals and compromises that eventually result when the lower classes have representatives in government. Absolute monarchy had possessed a definite rationale during the seventeenth century, filled as it was with martial threats demanding immediate warlike responses that allowed no time for deliberation. Indeed, stronger monarchies arose throughout Europe in response to the political imperatives of this terrible period. The French and industrial revolutions, however, ushered in a new era of mass political pressures. If insightful advisers had gotten the ear of the monarch, warning him to ward off revolution with timely social and political reforms, pressures would probably have decreased. But Nicolas II, naively trusting the autocratic ideas and policies of Alexander III, stubbornly opted to rule with many of his father's deeply conservative appointees. Removed physically, emotionally, and socially from the problems of lower-class Russia, the tsar and his bureaucrats stayed the reactionary course. Middle-class Zemstvo liberals who greeted Nicholas's ascension in 1894 as a portent of parliamentarization were disappointed when he dismissed their ideals as "senseless" dreams. "Let everyone know that I shall safeguard the principles of autocracy as firmly and unwaveringly as did my father."[46] This was a revolutionary disaster waiting to happen in the land where Marx expected it least.

Italy, one of the most unstable monarchies in Europe, also faced acute social and political pressures.[47] Somewhat like Russia, industrial and pre-industrial circumstances combined to create a very explosive situation. Poverty gripped Italy's southern provinces mainly because of an unequal distribution of land that forced most farmers into a scandalously low paid rural proletariat. Roughly 57 percent of Italy's agrarian laborers possessed no land, earning a pittance of one lira or less per day. Those who owned a plot typically worked marginal, unproductive land; utilized antiquated agricultural techniques; and struggled to afford crushing tax and mortgage payments.

Not surprisingly, therefore, Italy became a fertile breeding ground for the dangerous anarchist creed. Its earliest formulator, Frenchman Pierre-Joseph Proudhon, castigated private property as "theft" and state institutions upholding such injustice as evil. Europe's most famous anarchist, Russian Michael Bakunin, focused on the social inequity of Russia and Austria-Hungary, predicting that peasant anger, combined with ethnic tensions, would blow the lids off both. This would be a fitting punishment across the continent, he thought, for "the [European] state was born historically of the marriage of violence, rape, and pillage—it has been since its origin the divine sanction of brutal force and triumphant inequality." Crossing the frontier into Italy in 1864, Bakunin quickly realized the peasantry's potential to trigger an uprising that would spread throughout Eastern Europe to Russia. Thus the man who all his life had "blindly stumbled after the unknown god of destruction" found an intellectual home in Italy. He soon attracted a circle of devoted followers for "the holy mission of the militant church of democracy."[48] After Bakunin's death in 1876 Errico Malatesta emerged as the most determined disciple of the "propaganda of the violent deed." Killings and assassinations, in short, would enlighten the masses to their plight and spark further action. The uprisings that shook the Italian countryside in the 1890s owed much of their intensity to him.

The late nineteenth century also witnessed Italy's industrial revolution, which created social unrest as laborers crowded into ill-prepared urban districts. Labor leaders reacted to these harsh conditions with fiery determination by establishing a militant Marxist party, the Social Democratic Party of Italy, in 1891–1892. Thus Rome, like Moscow, felt the squeeze of mounting pressures from both town and country. Italy's elitist political system, however, had little chance of coping with these rapid changes. Suffrage rights extended to only 2 percent of the population in 1861—a mere 7 percent voted after reforms in 1882. Anarchists, radical democrats, and Marxists pointed to the unfairness of a system that disenfranchised the entire lower class. They also condemned the nation's plutocracy for ignoring social problems and banning rights of association—trade unions and strikes remained illegal. Colonial expeditions fueled more anti-governmental propaganda as tribunes of the people charged that monies should be spent curing the ills of a neglected "Africa at home." Accusations of this sort mounted after the nation's humiliation at Adowa in 1896.

Workers and peasants took matters into their own hands during the 1890s. Great numbers made the tough choice for emigration: Every year of that feverish decade 110,000 departed rural districts, joined by 112,000 from industrial areas, most heading for the United States. The pressure release valve of emigration did not suffice, however, to prevent serious unrest at home. Riots and strikes disrupted the countryside, the worst occurring in Sicily when irate peasants and sulfur miners attacked banks, customs houses, police stations, and city halls in 1893. Underpaid and underfed workers rose up in Milan in 1898, erecting barricades and issuing calls for a general strike. The army intervened and killed four hundred street fighters. Frightened and angry, the government imposed nationwide martial law in July 1899.

The Second International

In Russia, peasant-oriented Socialist Revolutionaries and a belligerent, worker-oriented Marxist Fighting Union stirring up the workers; in Italy, a Marxist Social Democratic Party recruiting and striking while Bakunin-oriented anarchists shook the countryside—obviously the threat to European establishments was more variegated, complex, and frightening, somehow, than the apocalyptic images projected in *The Communist Manifesto*. Indeed, for a time before the turn of the century anarchist violence seemed to be the greatest threat to the established order. Thus Spanish followers of this creed organized downtrodden rural laborers in the 1880s, unleashing violent strikes that were brutally squashed by Madrid. Other adherents of the propaganda of the deed assassinated President Carnot of France in 1894, Premier Canovas of Spain in 1897, Empress Elizabeth of Austria-Hungary in 1898, King Umberto I of Italy in 1900, and U.S. President McKinley in 1901.

Severe and persistent police surveillance, infiltration, and repression would eventually take a heavy toll, however, on the anarchists. Simultaneously Marx's followers assured their movement a significant place in the political history of twentieth-century Europe by building up impressive grassroots organizations.[49] Guided from London by Marx and Engels, most socialists preached the inevitable and violent collapse of capitalism. Mixed with this revolutionary credo, however, was a pragmatic determination to cooperate with trade unions and enter parliaments to improve the lot of men and women workers under the existing system of private property.[50] Political activists founded socialist or social democratic political parties to further these somewhat contradictory goals in Germany (1875), France (1879), Spain (1882), Britain (1883), Russia (1883), Belgium (1885), Austria (1888), Scotland (1888), Switzerland (1888), and Sweden (1889). By the latter year proposals circulated in the socialist world to secure the kind of international cooperation among toilers that Marx had called for. "Workers of the world unite," he proclaimed, "you have nothing to lose but your chains." Marx's own attempt to unite socialists succeeded only briefly in the 1860s before this "First Socialist International" fell apart amidst doctrinal wrangling and ideological discord with Bakunin and the anarchists. The great enemy of all states never trusted that Marx's "dictatorship of the proletariat" would avoid the suppression typical of Europe's police regimes.

Representatives from the ten established socialist parties gathered in Paris in July 1889 to establish a "Second International." They were joined by aspiring party organizers from Portugal, Italy, Holland, Denmark, Swedish Norway, Russian Finland, Russian Poland, Austrian Bohemia, Hungary, and Rumania. In the centennial year of the great French Revolution, organizers hoped to set something equally historic in motion. The congress passed resolutions favoring an eight-hour workday and improved conditions of labor, not just for men but also for women. What were the means to these ends? A second resolution urged parties to strive for universal suffrage in countries where workers could not yet vote. Within more democratic countries socialists should amass followers and capture parliamentary power, eschewing cooperation with upperclass enemies. In a third resolution, delegates chose May 1 as the day to demonstrate working-class solidarity in pursuit of these ambitious goals.

The Paris Congress passed its fourth and final resolution against war. Socialists believed fervently that workers should never fight fellow workers. One means to guard against the institutionalized killing of warfare, therefore, was to abolish conscripted standing armies and replace them with popular militias like the citizens' army of neutral Switzerland that would never support unjust wars. Over the long run, however, the abolition of capitalism offered the best defense against the scourge of war. Indeed, from the socialist perspective, social, economic, and political institutions dominated by greedy, profit-seeking private property owners represented the root cause of military conflagration. The class struggle to overthrow the bourgeoisie was in a very real sense, therefore, "war against war."

The anti-militarism of socialism found some common ground in the 1890s with Europe's growing pacifist movement. While the social democrats formulated their resolutions in Paris, Bertha von Suttner's novel *Lay Down Your Arms* raced through its first edition. With good reason the Austrian noblewoman regarded socialism as a great force for peace and thus an attractive ally. "The social democrats and the fear of them will bring the world forward after all," she wrote. "They take a resolute position on the peace issue." In 1892 the Swiss Social Democratic Party joined the International Peace Bureau, an organization established in Geneva to coordinate worldwide peace efforts. The Bureau's president, Henri Lafontaine, led the Belgian workers' movement. That same year Karl Liebknecht, son of a founder of the German Social Democratic Party, printed Suttner's novel in the party newspaper. Forging an alliance with socialism would prove highly frustrating for pacifists, however, for Marx's maxim of class struggle prejudiced the movement against extensive cooperation with bourgeois pacifists. As the London Congress of the Second International made very clear in 1896, "only the working class can seriously have the will to take power and create world peace."[51]

This resolution greatly disappointed Suttner and compatriots who refused to acknowledge an "only" way to peace. German pacifist Friedrich Förster spoke for many in the movement when he lambasted the London resolution as "a repetition of the ancient talk of a chosen people." As long as the working class resorted to "warring instincts" it had no right "to eulogize itself as the protector of world peace."[52] Pacifists hoped that reason and logic would eventually prevail over class chauvinism.

THE HAGUE

The immediate stimulus for the Hague Peace Conference came from Russia. This once-mighty eastern colossus strained to industrialize in order to avoid slipping into the ranks of Europe's second-class powers. The notion of achieving disarmament or finding alternatives to war like arbitration treaties struck a responsive, albeit cynical and opportunistic chord in the Russian ministries of War and Finance. Adoption by Austria of rapid-firing, semi-recoilless artillery pieces already adopted by the armies of Britain, France, and Germany threatened to undermine the effectiveness of Russia's Army. The crushing burden of military expenditure detracted, moreover, from Sergei Witte's program of heavily state-subsidized industrial development. It seems that more altruistic concerns motivated Tsar Nicholas II and Foreign Minister Mikhail Muraviev. Both had read Ivan Bloch's searing condemnation of modern military conflict, *The Future of War*, and were especially shocked by his predictions of societal collapse and revolution after a European-wide conflagration. In August 1898 the tsar approved the proposal of his three ministers for an international peace conference to help "put an end to these incessant armaments and to seek the means of warding off the calamities which are threatening the whole world."[53]

The announcement polarized Europe. "The thing is simply impossible," scoffed Prince Edward, the English heir apparent. "France could never consent to it—nor we." Kaiser William II reacted with incredulity. "Imagine a monarch [who holds] personal command of his army dissolving his regiments sacred with hundreds of years of history and handing over his towns to Anarchists and Democracy." Francis Joseph of Austria-Hungary found the tsar's invitation to discuss disarmament "unacceptable." Diplomatic imperatives made participation at The Hague difficult to refuse, however, for Nicholas ruled one of Europe's greatest states. On the other extreme, a host of anti-war and women's organizations greeted the surprising good news from Russia. "This good word, coming from so on high, will move the entire world— people are starting to think,"[54] said Bertha von Suttner.

Pacifist ranks, unfortunately, were badly broken. Many men in the peace movement recoiled from the anti-war feelers of women's voting rights organizations for fear that pacifism would be branded as effete and unmanly because of its association with "emotional" females. Similarly, suffragettes sometimes voiced tactical arguments for withholding public support for a controversial cause that might alienate male politicians otherwise sympathetic to female voting. Consequently, not one woman took a delegate's seat at The Hague—Suttner sat with the invited guests. European socialists refused to support the conference, moreover, arguing that nothing worthwhile could result from upper classes whose material interests so clearly contradicted the goals of maverick peaceniks. As Suttner saw it, by mocking the conference as a farce socialists seemed to be serving the cause of militarists who hoped that nothing positive or concrete would exit the House in the Woods. "How the Social Democrats have fallen into the trap laid by the chauvinists!"[55] Suttner lamented to no avail. For their part, however, most bourgeois pacifists were as glad to be rid of the socialists as they were of the suffragettes, for association with these lower-class subversives would surely contaminate the cause of peace within the chancelleries of power.

After the splendor of opening ceremonies and the first plenary session, delegates broke up into working committees on disarmament, rules of war, and arbitration. They registered no progress in the first committee because the military figures present immediately squelched the noble ideal of "laying down your arms." The German delegate, Colonel Gross von Schwarzkopf, refused to discuss the matter, while Admiral Sir John Fischer dismissed the whole notion with his bombastic assertion that "the supremacy of the British Navy is the best security for the peace of the world." The second committee proceeded to build on the Geneva Red Cross Convention of 1868, which had formulated rules for the humane treatment of prisoners, by outlawing "dum-dum" expanding bullets, poison gas, and the dropping of bombs from balloons. These accords angered and frustrated pacifists like Suttner who crusaded for "the codification of peace" not the "humanization of war." Militarists were unhappy too, but for different reasons. It was "silly ass," scoffed Fischer. "You might just as well talk of humanizing hell!"[56]

Pressure built, nevertheless, to prevent a total failure. Margarethe Selenka's petition had demonstrated how quickly the new morality was spreading. In an increasingly democratic age, the ruling classes had to respond in some way. No one wanted to embarrass Tsar Nicholas completely, moreover, or prove the socialists right. And for their part, the pacifists redoubled efforts to keep their cause alive. But something else was happening. After a few weeks of serious work by the first truly international peace congress, the notion of substituting cooperation for conflict seemed more realistic to a growing number of delegates. "That is the dream that begins to rise here," observed one of them. "Europe must choose to pursue the dream—or anarchy."[57]

The dream arose at The Hague—albeit just barely. It took the form of arbitration. Widely lauded for decades, the concept nevertheless remained vague until 1894, when two jurists' conferences formulated specific models for peaceful conflict. The Hague Conference took a moderate approach, creating a Permanent Court of Arbitration that was not "permanent," however, for it would be convened on an ad hoc basis when wars threatened—and only if both parties to a dispute agreed to arbitration. Twenty-six states signed the convention.

It was a start—but no more than that. In August 1899, when war threatened to break out between Britain and the Dutch "Boers" in South Africa, the latter wanted to arbitrate but the British, confident of victory, did not. Pacifists courageously demonstrated against impending war in Trafalgar Square. "A war of aggression and annexation will excite in South Africa such fierce racial hatred," they warned, and "will create a second Ireland."[58] But war, not peace, prevailed. "Our time civilized? Ridiculous!" lamented Suttner. "There are a few thousand civilized people, no more than that."[59] She had exaggerated, but the statement reflected well her depressed mood. In four months it would be the twentieth century.

Chapter 2

▼

EUROPE BEFORE THE GREAT WAR

Frankfurt's Municipal Museum pulsated with energy for the premier performance of *A Hero's Life* by Richard Strauss. The concert hall overflowed with distinguished VIPs who had used their influence to acquire a ticket. Fifteen minutes after the orchestra began, however, most in the audience sat with arms folded in doubt and faces furrowed in incredulity as they struggled to understand the odd "tone poem." Conducting was Strauss himself, a tall, slim, elegant-looking man whose odd style matched the polyphony of the strange piece. His gestures and beat were simple and decided with no wild or exaggerated motions, but his fists were clenched and contorted and he occasionally signaled the players with an awkward knock-kneed crouch. Simultaneously his foot tapped the dais in a stiff military manner. Suddenly Strauss stood upright and pointed ominously to the wings as if ordering soldiers to charge. Hidden brass trumpeted the opening of battle.[1]

A vibrant thirty-four in March 1899, Richard Strauss was still on his way up in the music world. As a younger man he had patterned his creations after Franz Liszt and Richard Wagner, composing giants whose scores had variously shocked and entranced German audiences in the 1850s and 1860s. Their "music of the future" featured glaring polyphonic combinations of contrasting melodies, frequent modulations of key, odd time signatures, and uneven rhythms that reflected the turbulence and confusion of accelerating industrialization and the drama of German unification. Like Liszt and Wagner, Strauss seemed in tune with the Zeitgeist. "While reading Schopenhauer or Nietzsche or some history book, I will get an uncontrollable urge to go to the piano," he wrote in 1895. "Before long a quite distinct melody appears."[2]

Friedrich Nietzsche was clearly the greatest influence on Strauss in the years immediately before *A Hero's Life*. The eccentric philosopher from the University of Basel struggled to understand the nature of modernity before failing health forced him to retire in 1879. A life of painful asceticism, harsh nihilism, frightening portents, and final descent to insanity followed in the 1880s. The shallow materialism of industrialism, the ugliness of cities, and the depressing mediocrity of a leveling democracy revolted Nietzsche. As an atheist, he turned his back on the regenerative potential of Christianity. Rather, a breed of courageous fighters and superior intellects possessing a higher morality would seize the day. The new superior man, a "Roman Caesar with the soul of Christ," needed to "wage wars for the sake of thoughts and their consequences." In *Thus Spake Zarathustra*, Nietzsche asked, "O my brothers, am I cruel?" The answer—that only destruction was creative—made readers familiar with traditional philosophy's idealism tremble. "For creators are hard. . . . This new commandment, O my brothers, I give unto you: *become hard!*"[3] Strauss put *Zarathustra* to music in 1896 before beginning to sketch what would be his paean to the triumph of "heroic strength" in the wider world. Kaiser William II of Germany liked the notion of heroic progress, but modern music repulsed him. *A Hero's Life* premiered in Frankfurt, far away from William's disapproving ears.

Trumpets heralded the beginning of battle between heroic strength and its enemies. The following minutes of noisy cacophony were difficult to appreciate at the time, even for those accustomed to the overpowering effects of Wagner. Strings, brass, and percussion feuded in a welter of conflicting chords, beats, and melodies. Deeply moved, French writer Romain Rolland, himself eager to do battle with right-wing intellectual and political enemies in the Dreyfus Affair, praised his friend's tone poem. In the "tremendous din and uproar" he could hear "the storming of towns, the terrible charge of cavalry which makes the earth tremble and our hearts beat." As a Frenchman, however, Rolland was greatly disturbed by a tendency he perceived in Strauss— and other German artists—to reflect "that heroic pride which is on the verge of becoming delirious, that contemptuous Nietzscheism, that egotistical and practical idealism which makes a cult of power and disdains weakness." Across the Rhine, "Neroism"[4] drifted ominously in the wind.

ESCALATING INTERNATIONAL TENSIONS

The premonitions of violence felt by sensitive artists like Strauss and Rolland came into general focus in October 1899 when hostilities erupted between Great Britain and two Dutch South African republics. War broke out again in 1904, this time between Russia and Japan in the Far East. Over the next decade Great Power crises over Morocco (1905–1906), Bosnia (1908–1909), and Morocco again (1911) nearly triggered European conflagrations, as did two localized wars between Balkan countries in 1912 and 1913.[5] None of these troubles sufficed to undermine Europe's characteristic optimism or fully shake its trademark confidence in unlimited progress as 1914 approached. Anxieties mounted among pacifists, however, while a mood of nervous anticipation of something ominous about to happen overtook others, particularly the artists. Thus one German poet, Kasimir Edschmid, described life on the eve of Europe's Great War as "uncertainty, hanging in the air, so to speak—frantic, raging life—the sensation of being in an express train which roars through a small station."[6]

Wars and Crises, 1899–1907

The so-called Boer War began for many of the same ethnic and diversity-related reasons that had set Europeans against Europeans for centuries. The colony of Cape Town, belonging to Holland since 1713, fell into British hands in 1815. Dutch subjects soon amassed ethnic, religious, and legal grievances against their English overlords. Fleeing this perceived persecution in the 1830s, tens of thousands of Boer "trekkers" migrated to the northeast, where they seized rich farmland from native tribes, resulting in two new nations: the Orange Free State and the Transvaal. Britain only reluctantly recognized their independence in the 1850s. Discovery of gold in the Transvaal in 1886 brought matters to a head as thousands of English settlers flooded into Boer territory. More numerous than their Dutch rulers by the late 1890s, British subjects paid taxes but could not vote or use English in schools or law courts. Rights of citizenship were denied. The British High Commissioner in Cape Town castigated Boer rule as "a medieval race oligarchy." The ethnic minority establishment refused to introduce reforms, however, fearing a return of the anti-Dutch discrimination they had fled decades earlier. As the imperialist "scramble" for African lands accelerated, Boer leaders warily eyed encroaching English expansion, especially after a botched cavalry raid from neighboring British territory failed in 1896. "It is our country you want,"[7] said Transvaal President Paul Kruger accusatorily. When Dutch police killed an Englishman in 1899— and a judge acquitted the officer, praising his behavior—emotions ratcheted up for war. There were calmer heads on both sides, but they did not prevail.

The Boer War loomed as a frightening portent of warfare in the twentieth century, for it debuted magazine rifles and semi-recoilless cannon firing smokeless powder that enabled soldiers to kill quickly from long range without being seen. Both sides also used deadly machine guns. The Boers cut down hapless British troops deploying in old "shock" formations in December 1899—seven thousand fell during one "Black Week." Reeling after a series of humiliating defeats, the British gained the upper hand in 1900 by emulating the enemy's far more pragmatic loose-order tactics and by building up a vastly superior force of nearly half a million soldiers. The Boers refused to relinquish the sacred ground of "the Volk" to a hated ethnic foe, however, disputing the seemingly inevitable outcome for two more years with guerrilla tactics. British generals responded by cordoning off provinces with barbed-wire fences and concrete blockhouses, and then "bagging" fighters and their family members as well as other innocent Boers and Africans caught in these regional traps. The British confined over 150,000 people to "concentration camps,"[8] where food shortages and disease took 42,000 lives—many more deaths than the combat itself. Final defeat in 1902 brought the Transvaal and Orange Free State into the burgeoning British Empire.

Considerable self-doubt accompanied victory as the army that smaller Boer forces stymied for years reexamined itself, adopted new technologies, and discarded outmoded practices. The mighty British Empire also ended a half-century of self-proclaimed "splendid isolation." Official pro-Boer sentiments and vitriolic press attacks in France and Russia, Britain's bitter imperial rivals, heightened a sense of national vulnerability with large forces committed in South Africa. So Britain turned to Germany, the continental foe of France and Russia, with an offer of alliance. Germany remained aloof, however, confident that growing industrial and military strength would exact better concessions later. This proved to be a serious blunder, for Britain, surprised by the rebuff—and now doubly anxious about the Kaiser's rapidly expanding fleet—concluded that sinister dictatorial motives lay behind Germany's refusal to negotiate. The British quickly changed course, finalizing a defensive alliance with modernizing Japan in 1902. The deal offered Britain a counterbalance to the growing Russian threat in Asia, while Japan had insurance against a combination of hostile European nations. With the ink barely dry on this treaty, Britain and France settled outstanding imperial differences. The so-called cordial understanding of 1904 greatly reduced the possibility of another Fashoda showdown (see Chapter 1) by dividing North Africa into spheres of mutual influence—the British in Egypt and the Sudan, France in Morocco, Algeria, and Tunisia. The *Entente Cordiale* left both sides freer to oppose Germany.

As Franco-British talks neared an end in February 1904, the first war of the twentieth century between two Great Powers broke out. Russia had continued its push into the Far East, stationing troops that threatened Japan in Manchuria in 1900. Emboldened by its alliance with Britain, and frustrated after years of failed diplomatic efforts, Tokyo opted for war. The daring island nation launched a surprise attack against Russia's Far East Fleet at Port Arthur, destroying or incapacitating half of the tsar's naval forces with one bold stroke. Eventually Port Arthur succumbed to a lengthy siege and battered Russian armies were forced out of Korea and southern Manchuria. A desperate bid to reverse Russian fortunes by steaming a second fleet around the world ended disastrously at the Tsushima Straits in May 1905. Disaster erupted at home, too, as angry Russian peasants, industrial workers, and subject ethnic minorities, frustrated by the deaf ear and armored fist of tsarist autocracy, demonstrated, rioted, and revolted. Beaten, humiliated, and fearful of the revolution's mounting force, Nicholas sued for peace and reluctantly announced the convening of a national Duma with limited parliamentary rights (see later in the chapter).

At the treaty table Russian "Rule over the East" receded as the victor compelled Moscow to recognize Japan's sphere of influence in Korea and Manchuria. The "demonstration effect" of successful resistance to European superiority in the world soon became evident as China introduced Japanese-style westernizing reforms, Indian patriots increased independence efforts, and anti-imperialist movements actually seized power in Persia (1906) and Turkey (1908). The Russo-Japanese War was significant in other respects, for like the Boer War it foreshadowed warfare in the twentieth century. Infantry units were forced to master dispersed-order tactics and dig trenches and foxholes to protect soldiers from the awesome firepower of modern weaponry. Field artillery began to fire from hidden "defiladed" positions, unleashing a steel rain on defenders surprised in the open field. The Japanese also experimented with heavier artillery calibers to overcome the defensive advantages of field fortifications. And the Russian Army became the first to rely heavily on machine guns. One French observer testified to the "uncontestable value" of these "soulless devices without nerves" that "literally mow down the attackers."[9] The two-week battle of Mukden in 1905 illustrated the potential of modern killing machines, claiming 160,000 men on both sides. Nearly half a million soldiers fell before the war ended. Military experts concluded with an optimism characteristic of the era, nevertheless, that technology had not made the soldier's task impossible. In particular, the Japanese had shown that infantry attacks could overrun defenders if officers demonstrated patience. That these assaults succeeded against the inefficient and poorly led Russian Army—and might fail against better-prepared European forces—had been widely overlooked.

The Far Eastern explosion almost ignited war in Europe. Russia watched angrily as its nemesis in Central Asia, Great Britain, lent huge sums of money to Japan. While steaming to its terrible fate in October 1904, moreover, Russia's Baltic Fleet strained relations nearly to the breaking point when it mistakenly fired on English fishing boats in the North Sea. Now Germany sought to exploit the crisis by offering Russia an alliance that contradicted tsarist obligations to France. While Russia pondered the terms, Germany attempted to bully its way into French Morocco. Kaiser William II landed at Tangier in March 1905 and proclaimed the North African state open to the interests of all powers. Masterminded by Friedrich von Holstein, a top official in the Foreign Office, the move was designed to humiliate France and break apart its entente with Britain, for surely France would crumble under German pressure, knowing that the Russian Army, tied down in Manchuria, could offer no assistance. Afterward the British would abandon demonstratively weak France and ally with mighty Germany.

Holstein's ploy backfired miserably. Wavering at first, France found encouragement from British diplomats convinced after Tangier that the German Army and Navy represented a menace to British interests. Paris received further encouragement when the unstable and contradictory William II undercut Holstein by telling French officials that Germany had no intention, after all, of making war over Morocco. Events now ran a humiliating course for Berlin. An international conference at Algerciras in 1906 essentially supported the French position in Morocco. While the treaty guaranteed German commercial interests and preserved some face-saving appearances, it was clear that bluff and bluster had only solidified Franco-British relations. Moreover, Russia turned down Germany's alliance offer. The bleak and meager outcome shocked a German public that saw enemies all around and questioned, for the first time, whether the nation's leaders, especially the kaiser and his most intimate entourage, could deal competently with foreign challenges.

Britain, meanwhile, began to maneuver itself into a more favorable position should war break out. The British General Staff held war games designed to test the feasibility of sending an expeditionary force to France and Belgium. The results were shared with the French General Staff. Simultaneously, construction began on the *Dreadnought*, an awesome new battleship armed with twelve-inch guns. Superior to anything afloat, the ship became Britain's answer to Germany's naval challenge. London also gave tacit approval to President Theodore Roosevelt's policy of policing all foreign investments in Latin America—the so-called Roosevelt corollary to the Monroe Doctrine—by withdrawing its Caribbean Fleet and concentrating these ships in home waters opposite Germany. In August 1907, furthermore, Great Britain negotiated spheres of influence and buffer zones with Russia in Persia, Afghanistan, and Tibet. Like the entente with France in 1904, this agreement reduced the likelihood of imperial brushfires to distract London from a more worrisome Germany. The so-called Triple Entente of France, Russia, and Great Britain took definite shape.

Peace Efforts

During the Russo-Japanese War of 1904–1905 Bertha von Suttner received the fifth Nobel Peace Prize. In accepting the award she claimed "that two philosophies, two eras of civilization are wrestling with one another," and that "a vigorous new spirit is supplanting and threatening the old." On a deeper level the "instinct for self-preservation in human society" was beginning to rise in rebellion, she asserted, "against the constantly refined methods of annihilation." The dedicated idealists of the peace movement complemented this "subconscious striving toward an era free of war."[10] Suttner had fewer illusions since 1899, however, for the escalating violence of the young century had shown that the same human instincts for survival could be used to subvert peace when governments, having convinced peoples of threats to national security, swamped the new spirit with the old. Because the recent war in Asia and subsequent crisis over Morocco had twice postponed a second peace conference, Suttner urged pacifists to intensify their efforts.

Since 1899 arbitration seemed to be the most promising method judging from the increasing tendency among nations to sign bilateral treaties of this sort.[11] Neutral Switzerland set the example with nineteen separate agreements, while Great Britain and France led the way among the larger powers, respectively, with ten and seven each. Most of these dealt with disagreements arising over routine matters like navigation or copyrights, but a few, namely those negotiated by Denmark with Holland and Italy, called for mandatory arbitration of all disputes. The ad hoc mediation procedures of the World Court established in 1899 gained a first small measure of prestige in 1905, moreover, by arbitrating the dispute triggered by Russia's destruction of English fishing boats. Indeed, a "vigorous new spirit" seemed to be operating on the outskirts of the world order, challenging the ancient preference for war as the final arbiter of relations among nations.

The most ardent champions of arbitration appreciated the need to widen the World Court's competence. This they attempted at the second Hague Peace Conference, which brought together forty-four nations in June 1907. As months passed without any substantive results, governmental delegates returned to the agenda of "civilizing" warfare by insisting on declarations or ultimatums before military action, by formulating rules of naval engagement, and by renewing the ban on hurling projectiles from balloons. "St. George rode out to slay the dragon," lamented Suttner, "not to clip its claws."[12] Finally the U.S. delegation introduced a motion identifying numerous types of minor disputes that would fall automatically under the jurisdiction of the existing Hague machinery—cases the ad hoc tribunal would decide without national governmental review. Advocates assumed that states, once accustomed to the sacrifice of sovereignty on less threatening issues like trade, commerce, communications, debts and finance, fishing and navigation, and health and labor, would gradually learn to accept mediation in times of serious international crisis. Britain and France supported the motion; Germany and Austria-Hungary opposed it. Russia, militarily humbled two years earlier, gave lukewarm backing to America's position.

The outcome of the conference hinged on the ability of the western democracies to sway world opinion against the arguments of the Central European authoritarian regimes. Joseph Choate, former U.S. ambassador in London, presented the American case, imploring listeners to prevent the "incalculable amount of human suffering and misery" witnessed recently in "two terrible wars" by providing nations with "a loophole of escape from all those evils and mischiefs." Passage of a general treaty, however limited in scope, would greatly strengthen arbitration's legitimacy by lending it the emphatic sanction of the "whole civilized world."[13] The champions of Saint Augustine's "slaying war with speech" met their match, unfortunately, in Alfred Marschall von Bieberstein. Germany's urbane and eloquent ambassador to Turkey took the moral high ground by heaping praise on the principle of arbitration, and then charging that America's proposal was unworthy of this great ideal. He pointed with cynical effectiveness to the contradictions of an "obligatory arbitration" agreement that allowed so many exceptions to the application of arbitration that the mandatory principle disappeared in practice. The American Senate, he added, would never allow disputes, even minor ones, to go automatically before a world court. There were so many loopholes as to call seriously into question the support of the movers for their own motion.

Marschall von Bieberstein's sophistry undermined the consensus by convincing neutral states like Belgium, Luxembourg, and Switzerland that their desire to avoid war would not be served by the American proposal. Joining them were Rumania, Bulgaria, Greece, and Turkey—states so caught up in ethnic Balkan imbroglios that they rejected any limitation whatsoever to national sovereignty. Reflecting the same concerns, Montenegro abstained. Authoritarian Russia undercut the motion's fading chances by reminding delegates that a world minority outnumbered more than three to one (33–11) could never accept a majority vote.[14] With consensus shattered, progress on arbitration proved impossible.

Authoritarian Germany, Austria-Hungary, and Russia had strong convictions behind the stances they took. Privately, for instance, Marschall von Bieberstein vented his real feelings on—and deep opposition to—arbitration. As a "kind of leveling scheme" based on the "principle of absolute equality of states," arbitration, if allowed to put down roots, would eventually substitute binding legal ties for the power relationships that had ruled the world for millennia. "A kind of spider web would be created in which even the smallest states would feel like spiders—and perhaps here and there the great powers will become the flies in the web." Why should Germany sacrifice its position of strength and power for a seat on the parliamentary backbench of international politics? Worse still, the democratic spider principle could easily carry over to domestic politics. Already in 1906 Austrian officials reacted vehemently to the "strongly socialistic"[15] practice of parliamentary deputies, largely without influence at home, attending a pacifist conference in London to formulate arbitration models for their government. An international victory for arbitration would strengthen the hand of leftists at home, in other words, by allowing them to meddle successfully in foreign affairs during times of crisis. Russia deserted the arbitration cause, moreover, as soon as the majority of nations began to consider voting for a general arbitration treaty. Struggling against leftists at home, the monarchy could not tolerate leftist tendencies abroad.

Britain, France, and the United States, the democratic Great Powers, had emerged as champions of sorts for peace by arbitration. This may have been an early sign of a trend more entrenched by the 1930s, namely, the inclination of democratic states to seek conciliation and compromise abroad just as they did at home. The arbitrational concept on which the pacifists' main hopes rested, however, needed better friends. Indeed, Marschall's critique of Washington had cut to the quick. Despite a democratic tradition stretching back to the 1820s, a strong peace movement, and the backing of both the Roosevelt and Taft administrations, the Senate had refused to ratify a long list of bilateral treaties with European countries calling for arbitration of all disputes lest arbitration fetter the nation's ability to enforce its blatantly self-interested Monroe Doctrine in Latin America. This kind of hypocrisy shone through the pro-arbitration postures of Britain and France too, for they might sign arbitration understandings with one another and criticize the scheming of authoritarian governments at The Hague, but they could also conquer colonial peoples and refuse to arbitrate, as the British with the Boer republics, when it suited their interests. Not until much later in the twentieth century would soul-searching democracies in Europe discard their double standards.

By 1907 threats to the peace also troubled the Socialist International. For nearly two decades since its founding, this worldwide organization of working-class parties maintained the facile belief that capitalism caused war. Peace would come with the victory of the proletariat. Successive tri-annual congresses, including the 1904 Congress in Amsterdam, did not seriously discuss the notion of unleashing a general strike to ward off capitalist war. A war in Asia, a revolution in Russia, and a near European war over Morocco, however, transformed proletarian anti-war action into a real agenda item. Accordingly, the Stuttgart Congress of August 1907 faced pressing demands from French and Russian radicals who were convinced that labor solidarity would both stop war and topple regimes.

The huge host delegation did not agree. Having to contend with the best army in the world, German Social Democrats feared that direct action would trigger confiscation of the movement's assets and imprisonment of its leaders. A compromise resolution saved international working-class face. Delegates renounced war as unacceptable and obligated every member organization to employ the anti-militarist means it deemed most effective. The resolution had tactfully omitted all mention of general strikes.

Advent of the Dragon, 1908–1914

Europe neared the brink of war in October 1908 when Austria-Hungary annexed Bosnia and Herzegovina. Although Vienna had long administered these Turkish provinces, it thought formal acquisition would stop Serbia from demanding—or perhaps just seizing—a territory inhabited by Slavic brethren. The "Young Turk" revolution in Constantinople that summer (see later) precipitated the annexation, for Austria-Hungary worried that disgruntled Balkan states would use Turkish weakness to grab land. The bold move reflected Vienna's waning desire to coexist amicably with expansion-minded Serbia. Ruling over substantial South Slav elements itself, the Danube Monarchy feared that a Greater Serbia would "tear the empire to pieces," as one official put it, by encouraging Austria-Hungary's Serbs to secede. The annexation would forestall a final "appeal to the sword" if it intimidated the Serbs, but if they retaliated, Konrad von Hötzendorff, the Austrian chief of staff, stood ready. The firebrand commander had counseled war for years as the only sure means to eradicate "the dangerous nest of vipers"[16] in Belgrade. The ensuing crisis worsened when Russia backed Slavic, Orthodox Serbia and the Germans supported their Austrian cousins. In no position to make war again after its Far Eastern debacle, Russia backed down in March 1909, then Serbia a few days later. Pan-Slav zealots in the chancelleries of Saint Petersburg and Belgrade swore revenge, however, against the Germanic powers.

A series of North African incidents soon pushed national anxieties in Europe to even higher levels. In April 1911 France sent troops to Morocco to suppress rioting. Germany perceived this action as a violation of the Algeciras Treaty of 1906 that had stopped short of sanctioning a French protectorate. Germany dispatched a gunboat to Morocco as a blunt signal that there must be some form of compensation. Officials also hoped to assuage nationalist politicians and agitators who insisted on erasing the humiliation of the First Moroccan Crisis. France bristled, and Britain expressed alarm at Germany's bullying tactics. "It is a trial of strength," concluded Sir Eyre Crowe of the Foreign Office. "National honor"[17] was at stake, barked David Lloyd George of the Exchequer. Germany eventually backed down after receiving part of the French Congo. In the aftermath, Britain finalized plans for a British Expeditionary Force to block an anticipated German invasion through Belgium. Britain and France also initiated naval talks to divide fleet assignments: The British Mediterranean Fleet was withdrawn to home waters, leaving French ships in charge. Much more than the First Moroccan Crisis, therefore, the Second served to transform a cordial diplomatic understanding into a military alliance.

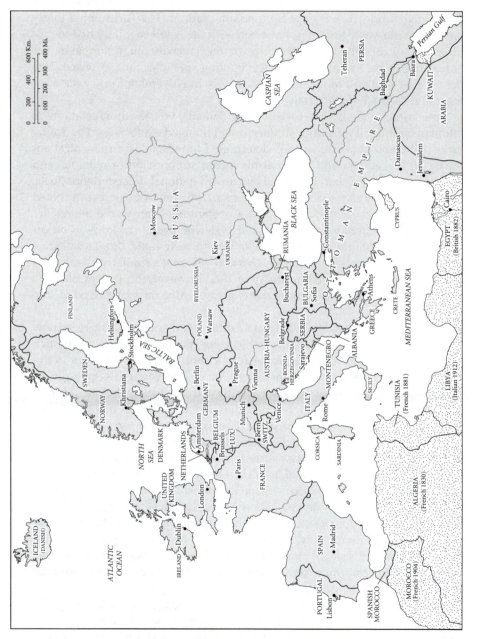

Europe in 1914

One crisis sparked another. Sensing that France wanted to extend its position in North Africa, Italy declared a protectorate in Turkish Tripoli. Rome wanted to seize the province to preempt France as well as to prevent a quickly revitalizing Young Turk regime from holding onto it. The Turks opted to defend their vulnerable holdings, however, with the result that Italy had to mobilize one hundred thousand troops for an unexpectedly tough campaign. For a brief time in the autumn of 1911, the fighting spread as far as Constantinople: the first war on European soil since 1878. In November Turkey sued for peace and ceded Tripoli to Italy.

International crisis now revisited the Balkans, where ethnic relations in Ottoman-controlled territories simmered and bubbled explosively. The Young Turks had come to power in 1908 determined to reestablish firm central authority. In Macedonia and Albania this meant suppression of religious and community rights, disbanding of all clubs with national independence goals, and, worse still in Macedonia, settlement of Muslims on the expropriated lands of Bulgarians, Serbs, and Greeks. Constantinople answered the retaliation of ethnic terrorist bands in 1910 and 1911 with brutal crackdowns on entire villages. Many thousands of people were arrested and dozens killed. A rising of Albanian nationalists in Kosovo that year met a similarly grizzly fate. When a second revolt made headway in 1912, however, the Turks yielded to Albanian demands for an autonomous greater Albania that extended into Macedonia.

The surrounding states of Bulgaria, Serbia, Montenegro, and Greece now formed a "Balkan League." Fearing the "extermination" of fellow Christian nationals by Muslim Albanians, eager for a chunk of Turkish territory in Europe, and determined to preempt Great Power intervention—especially by Vienna—they were ready to seize territory from Turkey before Austria-Hungary did the same. In October 1912 the four small nations mobilized over half a million soldiers who soon pushed Turkey's smaller force back toward Constantinople. Casualties quickly exceeded a shocking one hundred thousand on all sides, but there was worse to come. As the Turkish rulers pulled out, Christian soldiers and civilians lashed back at Muslims, murdering, raping, and burning in village after village as a harsh payback for Ottoman oppression. The "liberation" of the Balkans "unleashed the accumulated hatreds, the inherited revenges of centuries."[18] Although peace came in May 1913, war broke out again immediately when Bulgaria—which had already taken the lion's share of the spoils—attacked Serbia. Greek, Serbian, and Rumanian forces easily defeated Bulgaria that summer, once again perpetrating terrible atrocities.

Twice in one year European diplomats had managed to contain the escalating killing in the Balkans before it triggered a wider war. Increasingly, however, many in Europe considered the peacemakers' task impossible. As this belief spread, spokesmen for solving international problems in traditional ways stepped to the fore. German Army leader Helmuth von Moltke urged the kaiser to strike sooner rather than later, despite gloomy premonitions that the war would not be as short as some of his colleagues believed. Cavalry

General Friedrich von Bernhardi's paean to the inevitability of combat, *Germany and the Next War*, also called for preemptive war. His message resonated in the aggressive imperialist circles of the Pan German League and the German Defense League. The French, too, had found a tribune of "vitalistic" action in Henri Bergson, a philosophy lecturer at the Collège de France. His immensely influential *Creative Evolution* attacked the dominant rationalism of science and shifted emphasis to man's nonrational drives and "real self" that lay deeply buried in the subconscious. At this level one tapped into *élan vital*, the vital urge that made man—and nations of men—great, enabling them to achieve destinies against seemingly overwhelming forces of resistance. Bergson "set the cat among the piedgons,"[19] observes Eugen Weber. Thus one attendee of the philosopher's lectures, Georges Sorel, became a firebrand of class warfare and international armageddon with his *Reflections on Violence*. "Sorel's unrelenting prediction of war and anarchy, his characterization of Europe as the soil of armed cataclysms, his theory that the nations of this continent have always been able to unite around only one idea, that of engaging in war—all that entitled this to be called the book of the age,"[20] recalled German novelist Thomas Mann. French military men also drank deeply of Bergson, translating his ideas into a new spirit of offensive action that revolutionized French operational doctrine in 1913 by discarding decades of prudent defensive thinking for the idea of an energetic rush to recapture Alsace and Lorraine.

The foundering of the peace movements added to an ominous sense of despair. To be sure, the Socialist International sent representatives from twenty-six nations to a special congress in Basle as casualties and atrocities mounted during the First Balkan War. The ringing of church bells and noble anti-war rhetoric of French Socialist Jean Jaures could not hide the fact, however, that the international labor movement did not agree on a strategy to stop war. Two years earlier at Copenhagen German moderates had again thwarted a decision to declare a general strike if war neared. The 1910 Congress had postponed further discussion to August 1914—a special gathering scheduled to coincide with the twenty-fifth anniversary of the International. Victor Adler of the Austrian movement saw through the emotions expressed so eloquently in Switzerland to the hard, unpleasant reality: "It unfortunately does not depend on us Social Democrats whether there is a war or not."[21]

Bourgeois pacifists fared no better. Plans for a third peace conference to meet at The Hague in 1913 faded as crisis descended on the Balkans. The champions of arbitration were not ready in any event, for five years of lobbying and negotiation in various nations had produced no breakthrough agreement on mandatory procedures. "We thought there was a far more widespread sense of justice," lamented Suttner in one of her last statements. "The peace movement is not yet powerful enough," she admitted, "to overthrow the deep-seated forces of ancient despotism."[22]

There was good reason to worry, for either Balkan war could have touched off a greater European explosion by pulling Austria-Hungary into the conflict. Indeed, many in this multinational empire advocated using war to solve the empire's internal problems. Vienna watched with mounting alarm, for example, as Serbia—the Danube monarchy's main antagonist in the Balkans, and the greatest threat to its dismemberment—expanded southward over Kosovo and parts of Macedonia during the first war, and then sent troops across Albania to the Adriatic during the second. Belgrade's insistence on an outlet to the sea triggered an Austro-Hungarian ultimatum in 1913 that forced Serbia to withdraw its soldiers from Albania. Even more disconcerting to Vienna was Russia's meddlesome role in the Balkans. The Russian minister in Belgrade referred openly to Austria-Hungary as "the next sick man of Europe," a derisive reference to Turkish weakness. In early 1914 the Russian military press inflamed Balkan relations even more by tauntingly writing about "the partition of Austria-Hungary."[23] In a hostile, tit-for-tat reply, Vienna reminded Saint Petersburg of its own precarious multinational empire. Successive nerve-fraying crises militarized Habsburg diplomacy after 1912, leaving its leaders committed to a subsequent policy of force.

They would not have long to wait. On June 28, 1914, Serbian terrorists assassinated Archduke Francis Ferdinand, the heir to the Austro-Hungarian throne, in Sarajevo. The killing triggered a chain reaction of events that touched off a European war six weeks later.

Long-Term Origins of the War

Before discussing at the end of this chapter the specific personal, diplomatic, and operational factors that contributed to the outbreak of war, it will be instructive to summarize the deeper, underlying causes of the conflict that have been identified by historians.[24] Europe's ethnic diversity and long history of struggle between peoples spawned a system of dominant states that eyed one another warily by the late nineteenth century. Many Europeans considered war a natural and unavoidable occurrence—the final arbiter, in fact, of national disputes that were resolved when one state took another's territory and held it by legal right of conquest. The legitimacy of such claims was attenuated only marginally in the case of neutral states like Switzerland, Belgium, and Luxembourg.[25] Existing tensions between Britain, France, Italy, Germany, Austria-Hungary, and Russia worsened as industrialization and technological change generated novel weapons; strengthened certain nations like Britain, and later Germany; but heightened the fears and anxieties of the others. Simultaneously, imperialism offered up new colonies, potential markets, and arenas of struggle in the wider world.[26] As the Great Powers, including industrial leaders Britain and Germany, realized that they could not afford to stand alone, they formed alliances that divided Europe into two armed camps—Germany and Austria-Hungary on the one side; Russia, France, and Britain on the other; and Italy officially tied to Berlin and Vienna but unofficially leaning away as patriots eyed Austro-Hungarian territory across the Adriatic Sea. These entangling alliances endangered the wider peace by threatening to drag allied countries into a local war that one ally or patron had entered or provoked. The likelihood of such a scenario increased with the resurgence of ethnic nationalism, particularly in the Balkans, Europe's powder keg.[27]

Arrayed against the forces pushing events toward belligerence were the opponents of war. The pacifist/anti-militarist causes attracted millions of people to their banners, certainly enough to justify Bertha von Suttner's 1905 claim that "a vigorous new spirit" had arisen to challenge the old attitudes. Although far from a tiny minority, however, the anti-war activists had little or no influence where it counted. Thus Suttner was feted in small countries like Switzerland or across the ocean in America but reviled at home in Central Europe, while the socialists, for all their influence among workers and ability, right into July 1914, to mobilize greater numbers in the streets than their pro-war opponents, could do little in schools and universities, the opinion-making bourgeois press, or the chancelleries of power. The pacifists and anti-militarists were also sorely divided against and among themselves. Men, women, bourgeois, and socialists all professed reasons why no solid front was possible or desirable— even workers disagreed about the feasibility of the general strike. When war finally came, furthermore, it became hard to distinguish the "vigorous new spirit" from the old, for no one denied the need to defend the nation, and peoples of all nations believed that enemies had provoked the conflict.[28]

POLITICAL TURMOIL INSIDE EUROPE

The music of Richard Strauss pulsated with more than the sound of impending battle between nations: Its atonal chords and odd rhythms also shook from the blaring, vibrating sounds of social transformation that worried his philosophical mentor, Friedrich Nietzsche. Edvard Munch's painting *The Scream* (1893) captured the same revulsion with the distortions and fevers of modern times. Europe's rising temperature resulted, in part, from rapid industrialization and technological change occurring within authoritarian or conservative political structures poorly designed to withstand such challenges, but even the democracies of Western Europe could not make labor concessions quickly enough to calm things down. The simultaneous deterioration of gender relations and exacerbation of long-standing ethnic grievances caused more disruption.[29]

Internal societal tensions are another factor among the many that scholars have considered in explaining the coming of war in 1914. To a radical nationalist minority among the upper classes, and in certain artistic circles, it seemed that only a great war could purge society of its divisiveness. That national leaders actually adopted this stance, fomenting war mainly to rally divided home fronts, seems unlikely. Russia abhorred this prospect after such an attempt completely backfired in 1904–1905. The major exception was Austria-Hungary, which definitely sounded the tocsin of war to eliminate Serbia as a haven for the Dual Monarchy's potentially secessionist South Slavs. In discussing the so-called July Crisis set off by Vienna's punitive action against Belgrade we shall see that other powers may have welcomed the prospect of war uniting their quarreling classes, sexes, and ethnic minorities, but this functioned as a secondary factor reinforcing primarily power- and honor-related motives.[30]

Edvard Munch, **The Scream.** (Photo credit: Erich Lessing/Art Resource, NY/©2004; The Munch Museum/The Munch-Ellingsen Group/Artists Rights Society (ARS), NY)

Class Relations

The classic study of pre-war England by R. C. K. Ensor aptly describes "the seething and teeming" of this period, "its immense ferment and restless fertility."[31] Nearly two decades of rule by the Conservative Party ended with the 1906 elections. Over the next years the triumphant Liberal Party and its Labour Party allies passed an impressive series of reforms, including old age pensions, improved workman's compensation, more secure strike rights, labor exchanges, unemployment insurance in the building trades, an eight-hour day for miners, and national health insurance. This coalition also introduced progressive income taxes to pay for these programs (as well as the ongoing naval race with Germany), and then clipped the powers of a recalcitrant House of Lords when it threatened to block passage of these levies. The Parliament Act of 1911, coming after so many pathmark social reforms, strengthened British democracy. But organized labor did not respond gratefully. Affecting over four million workers, 4,725 strikes broke out from early 1910 to mid-1914. "One felt as though some magical allurement had seized upon the people,"[32] wrote Labour Party leader Ramsay MacDonald. The government called out troops on numerous occasions and killed strikers in a few instances. The escalation of labor disputes in 1914—there were 937 strikes in the first seven months— seemed a buildup to a planned general strike of the shipyard, transport, and mining unions in October. Would England, which had always managed to avoid violent, French-style solutions to social problems, lose its characteristic restraint and ability to compromise?

The workers' strike activity is all the more intriguing to historians today given what they know about blue-collar life before 1914.[33] Indeed, trends stretching back to the late 1800s had deepened and widened over the two pre-war decades, bringing steady improvements for the upper echelons of the la-boring classes. Diets and housing were better, jobs plentiful, unemployment low, and hours of work shorter—the ten-hour day and fifty-four hour week, freeing up Saturday afternoon and all day Sunday, became more common. Free time coupled with the spread of inexpensive tram lines made an outing to the racetrack, boxing arena, or football match a regular weekend occurrence—over 120,000 predominantly working-class and lower middle-class fans saw Aston Villa and Sunderland play, for example, in 1913. The same factors facilitated an hour at the cinema or a raucous Saturday evening in one of London's sixty-three big vaudevillian music halls, where seating prices divided people by class but comedy routines poking fun at society's high and low served a nationally integrative function. These benefits and comforts did not extend downward to the underclass of the underpaid and the overworked who continued in great numbers to suffer from poverty, however, nor did leisure activities for those

Mass culture: British soccer crowd in 1913.   (Getty Images)

enjoying them outweigh negative impressions acquired during the workweek. And so, angered by the anti-unionism of employers and judges, anxious about rising living costs, resentful of still long hours, and spurred by rumors of workers' gains in other branches, British unionists began to strike, unleashing "an enormous energy—an unparalleled, inarticulate, irrational energy . . . which leavened the whole lump of society from top to bottom."[34]

Political life also surged with heat in France.[35] After the Dreyfus Affair the Radical Party rose to the fore, an amorphous grouping of factions determined to shield the republic from democracy's enemies on the Right and the Left. Educational and military reforms after 1900 reduced the perceived threat from reactionaries in the church and army, but novel challengers surfaced like the angry young writer, Charles Maurras, founder of the proto-fascistic *Action Française*. While favoring a return to monarchical institutions, other traits of his politics looked forward to fascism in the 1930s: appeals to the masses to attack bourgeois liberalism; organized brutality by the ruffians of the *Camelots du Roi*, especially their violence against Jews, socialists, leftist intellectuals, and other alleged subversives; a willingness to sacrifice legality and justice for the greater goal of discipline, strength, and order; and a tendency to accept struggle as an eternal part of life. When war came in August 1914, Maurras barely reacted: "I saw it and predicted it,"[36] he said with steely calm.

The Radical Party faced greater dangers on the Left. To ward them off the Chamber of Deputies passed numerous labor reforms, including old age pensions, accident insurance, minimal medical coverage, the ten-hour day for women and children, and the eight-hour day for miners. But these measures did not purchase domestic peace, despite the fact that proletarian living standards and lifestyles kept close to those of blue-collar compatriots across the Channel. Indeed, incremental gains and occasional amenities did nothing to attenuate the ideology of "revolutionary syndicalism" espoused by France's dominant trade union organization, the General Confederation of Labor (CGT). Formulated mainly by Fernand Pelloutier but also influenced by Georges Sorel, this doctrine advocated strikes, boycotts, and sabotage, culminating, it was hoped, in a general strike—the ultimate act of working-class emancipation from bourgeois exploitation. The CGT initiated its strategy on May Day 1906, triggering over four thousand strikes in four years.

The state responded forcefully, arresting CGT leaders and shooting down workers on many occasions. The worst incident occurred in 1908 at Villeneuve-Saint George, where troops killed four workers and injured fifty. CGT resolutions protested bitterly against a "government of assassins" which "murdered"[37] its poor, but repression continued in 1909–1910 as the Interior Ministry fired striking postal employees, railway workers, and seamen and drafted them into the army. Although the crackdown sapped some of the spirit of revolutionary syndicalism, allowing anti-strike moderates to elect their candidate for CGT Secretary in 1909 by a majority of one, the moderating trend did not carry over into parliamentary politics. Moderate Socialists eager to form a "Bloc of the Left" with governmental Radicals got nowhere, for the memory of democracy's most recent crushing of the workers was too bitterly fresh for any such reconciliation.

In Germany too, workers generated friction despite social and political gains.[38] A rich proletarian subculture flourished by 1914, featuring singing, drama, cycling, hiking, swimming, and other activities organized mainly by the Social Democrats and various Catholic lay and church groups. A prevailing ten-hour day and Sunday off combined with urban transit and rising real wages to make a rudimentary social life possible. Like Britain, Germany had numerous music halls and cabarets, but cinema was more the rage: Twenty-five hundred movie theaters had sprouted up across the empire, visited by 1.5 million people a day. We should recall, furthermore, that since the 1870s and 1880s workers possessed the vote, the right to unionize and strike, and basic social insurance benefits (see Chapter 1). As in France and Britain, however, improvements did not eliminate poverty for about a third of the urban population, nor did simple pleasures for better-off workers eliminate the general glaring inequality between upper- and lower-class people. Thus one Berlin mechanic, a "labor aristocrat" and lover of the countryside, pined that "I'd like to go walking all day the way the rich people do."[39] So the Social Democratic Party (SPD) pressed for more reforms, including unemployment insurance, collective bargaining, eight-hour workdays, and the democratization of a state controlled by conservative aristocrats, reactionary soldiers, haughty industrialists, and the unbalanced William II. Socially conscious Catholic reformers and Christian trade unionists repeated many of these demands. Meanwhile, workers generated the largest strike wave west of Russia—over eight thousand outages from 1910 to 1913. Employers hostile to trade union activity created more disruption by barring laborers from factories in hundreds of "lockouts" every year.

Despite increasing pressure from below, however, legislative victories for the workers grew rarer after 1900 as the authorities sought mainly to protect upper-class interests. Agricultural tariffs raised in 1902 shielded large landowners from foreign competition at the cost of higher bread for the poor, while consumer taxes rose in 1909 to fund Germany's arms race. After leftist street demonstrations in 1910 failed to alter plutocratic voting procedures in Prussia, Germany's most powerful state, working-class voters protested all of these setbacks at the polls. The "red" elections of 1912 threw 34.8 percent of votes to the SPD—a million more than in 1907—as previously non-socialist Catholic and Protestant workers defected from the Center Party, the Progressives, and other parties.

The reaction from the Right came immediately. Heinrich Class, a lawyer with a small practice who chaired the rabidly nationalistic Pan German League, published *If I Were the Kaiser*, an angry venting of extremist sentiments. The irreverent tract advocated disenfranchisement of workers, a rollback of labor legislation, discriminatory laws against Jews, and a militant foreign policy to expand Germany abroad—and purge unhealthy elements at home. When the state seemed to ignore this warning in 1913 by making the wealthy pay for army increases, Class took political action, convening a reactionary "Cartel of the Producing Social Estates" to stiffen the backbone of allegedly weak rulers and reverse what they perceived as a dangerous leftist drift in German politics. In reality, leftist majorities demanding unemployment insurance and the eight-hour day had never moved imperial ministers. The entire Left—socialist and non-socialist trade unionists, SPD and Catholic Center deputies, and an assortment of bourgeois social reformers—assembled in Berlin in May 1914 to protest Germany's inadequate social legislation in an unprecedented show of solidarity. As war clouds gathered in Europe that summer, the kaiser's generals drew up lists of subversives to arrest when bugles sounded.

Political strife also plagued Sweden, where King Gustav V shared power with a parliament chosen plutocratically by the wealthiest twelfth of the population. The dominant landowners and industrialists answered the rapidly growing labor movement with anti-socialist "muzzle" laws, lockouts, and legislation protecting strikebreakers. A workman's compensation act (1901) proved unable to ameliorate labor relations. Denied the right to register protests with votes, workers responded with industrial sabotage, ugly bombing attacks on scab laborers, and a general strike involving over three hundred thousand employees in 1909. Stockholm finally yielded to this pressure by granting universal male suffrage. Following leftist gains during the first elections under the expanded suffrage in 1911, Karl Staaff's Liberal Party implemented factory safety laws and old age pensions. When Staaff and his Social Democratic allies prepared to reduce military expenditure to fund more social insurance, however, rightists lashed back, alleging that naïve pacifism and anti-militarism would reduce Sweden to Finland's fate as a Russian protectorate. Amidst angry demonstrations and counterdemonstrations, new elections in 1914 split the Liberals and polarized the nation between Conservatives with 34.8 percent of seats in parliament and Social Democrats with 32.2 percent.

The Kingdom of Italy exhibited equally turbulent political trends.[40] The century dawned amidst widespread poverty, escalating societal violence, and Draconian state repression (see Chapter 1), but insightful progressive politicians like Giovanni Giolitti realized the need for immediate reform. "The ascending movement of the lower classes becomes faster by the day," he declared in 1901. No one should think that the "invincible" masses could be denied their "rightful share of economic and political influence."[41] Serving many terms as prime minister over the next thirteen years, Giolitti put the principles of his speech into practice, introducing workman's compensation and old age pensions, a weekly day of rest, and limits to child and female labor. Italy initiated prison reforms, support for homeless children, some low-income housing, and public works projects in impoverished southern Italy and Sicily. By 1913 illiteracy had dropped, medical care had improved, and infant mortality rates were lower. Living standards remained poor, however, as workers continued to pack into industrial centers like Milan—as it doubled in size, dwellers per room also shot up to three or four. Laborers struck less frequently than in France, whose industrial work force was roughly equivalent in size, but relations were not good— nearly a thousand strikes brought

385,000 workers into the streets in 1913. Riotous leftist disturbances in June 1914, moreover, forced Rome to place the army on alert once again. A year earlier upper-class reactionaries disgusted by these tensions had formed the Italian Nationalist Association, favoring domestic repression and foreign expansion as an antidote for popular unrest. Harsh lower-class living conditions coupled with the continued disenfranchisement of the masses, however, dampened the ameliorative effects of Giolitti's reforms. When the government finally granted universal male suffrage in 1913, the "invincible" people expressed past decades of dissatisfaction by casting nearly 40 percent of their votes for militant socialists and other extreme leftist parties.

As disturbing as sociopolitical problems remained in Italy and among the underclasses of Northwestern Europe, their troubles paled in comparison with those of Russia.[42] Proletarians in heavy industry worked a sixty-six hour week by law, but frequently more in practice, as did those in light industry. Housing was so crowded that five or six workers had to share a room or, worse, sleep on plank beds in factory barracks with other men, women, children, bugs, fleas, and stench. Even cities like the capital of Saint Petersburg had few toilets and limited running water, turning into smelly breeding grounds for typhus and cholera, which reached epidemic proportions about every three years in the early twentieth century. At the bottom of urban society were the working women, whose proportion of industry's work force rose from 20 to 33 percent in prewar decades as employers learned to exploit their cheap labor. "One cannot help but note the premature decrepitude of the factory women," observed one doctor in 1913. They saw and heard poorly; their shoulders hunched over and heads trembled; one aged fifty "looks about seventy."[43]

Such atrocious conditions help to explain the ferocity of revolution in 1905, but tsarist autocratic habits, exacerbated by postwar political chaos, blocked much-needed progress. Tsar Nicholas II responded grudgingly to the disturbances, for example, by holding elections for a national parliament (Duma) in March 1906. The balloting spawned a welter of forty-two political parties or national caucuses—the typical kind of political fragmentation that happens when dissent and opposition, suppressed for decades, surface during the first small burst of freedom: small conspiratorial factions, local or regional groupings of kindred spirits, and extended friendship circles competing with one another, all made worse by extreme polarization between leftist peasant, proletarian, and ethnic parties demanding far-reaching land, labor, and ethnic autonomy reforms, on the one side, and rightist delegations supporting the tsar's determination to resist such demands, on the other. After a second Duma election in 1907 produced even greater gains for radicals—82.8 percent of deputies opposed the government—Nicholas disenfranchised the masses to ensure moderate upper-class majorities.

The bloody campaign of the Socialist Revolutionaries greatly exacerbated parliamentary vitriol. In 1906 and 1907 the assassins of this terrorist peasant party murdered thirty-one hundred state officials. The government answered in kind with courts-martial executions for several thousand revolutionaries and hard labor sentences or deportation for additional tens of thousands. The crackdown extended to the radical Bolsheviks around Vladimir Lenin, the most extreme Marxist party in Europe. By 1908 most Bolsheviks, like most SRs, had been jailed or exiled. Lenin himself waited in Switzerland for more opportune times. Two right-wing extremist groups assisted with these Draconian policies: the Union of the Russian People, an organization with close ties to the tsar, and the so-called Black Hundreds, vigilante gangs that wreaked terror on Jews scapegoated for the ills of Russian society.

Peter Stolypin, the tsar's chief minister from 1907 to 1911, added the carrot of reform to the stick of reactionary violence. The state legalized trade unions with limited rights—not including strikes. Workers also received minimal sickness, accident, and disability benefits. A more ambitious reform sought to transform at least a portion of the peasantry into politically loyal landed proprietors. A complex series of laws and decrees gave peasants an opportunity to convert communal village lands into private property. The reforms also facilitated the consolidation of strip holdings, still scattered about village communes in medieval fashion, into enclosed farms that could accommodate tractors and other modern agricultural techniques. By 1913 about a third of peasant households had converted communal into private properties, while only a quarter of these—a twelfth of all families—had acquired consolidated farms.

Stolypin's legislation helped to lessen rural violence. Government colonization programs supporting migration to Siberia released further societal steam, for well over two million people left European Russia during these years. It seems likely, however, that social pressures continued to mount toward some sort of violent eruption. Thus many colonists streamed back—257,000 in 1908–1909—disillusioned with Siberia's harsh climate, immense distances, shortage of water, and lack of roads. The returnees joined crowded former neighbors, many of whom complained that government officials who allegedly favored richer peasants had forced through an unwanted conversion to private property in the face of strong opposition from village assemblies. The poorer farmers also alleged that strip holdings had been redistributed unfairly and, worse, that their burgeoning families still did not possess enough land. A huge problem before the Revolution of 1905, the Stolypin reforms did not appreciably diminish "land hunger."

Then in 1912 shocking news arrived in the villages from cousins who had migrated to factories and mines in search of a better life: Tsarist troops had gunned down five hundred striking workers in the Lena gold fields. The bloody action touched off protests and demonstrations throughout the empire. Urged on by Bolsheviks and SRs, strikers grew bolder throughout 1912 and 1913. In the first half of 1914 alone their agitation triggered thirty-five hundred strikes—twenty-four hundred of them overtly political—involving 1,340,000 workers, the worst strike wave since the earlier revolution. If tsarist ministers had hoped for "a little victorious war to stem the revolution"[44] in 1904, the uprising of 1905 amidst national humiliation in a foreign war soured them on such risk-taking adventurism in subsequent years. Russia went to war for other reasons in 1914, not to solve problems of lower-class unrest (see later in this chapter).

Women

Compounding Britain's labor problems in the years before 1914 was the fact that women also demanded radical change. The turn from moderation came in 1903 when Emmeline Pankhurst founded the Women's Social and Political Union (WSPU). Together with her daughters Christabel and Sylvia, Pankhurst rejected the patient approach to gaining suffrage rights favored by older women's groups. The WSPU heckled male speakers, organized street demonstrations, and held mass rallies—250,000 women gathered at Hyde Park in 1908, for instance, to demand the vote. Two years later, after the Liberal government of Herbert Asquith refused to be forced, the Pankhursts tromped in great numbers to the House of Commons. They never got there on this "Black Friday" in November 1910, as police ringing Parliament Square vented male anger on women who allegedly showed no respect for authority. "They were pummeled and they were pinched, their thumbs were forced back, their arms twisted, their breasts gripped, their faces rubbed against the palings: and this went on for nearly six hours."[45] Britain's sex war had begun. Over the next three years WSPU members disrupted debates in the House, put jam in parliamentary mailboxes, chained themselves to fences around government buildings, broke windows, went on debilitating hunger strikes when arrested, and continued to march—all to no avail.

This pressure release of women's energy poses explanatory problems for historians.[46] That the WSPU recruited many working-class women who had

Women on the march: British suffragettes in 1908.   (Getty Images)

benefited only marginally from rising living standards and leisure time possibilities in Britain (see earlier in this chapter) explains some of this suffrage anger, but the movement also appealed to educated daughters from skilled working-class and somewhat better-off middle-class families. By 1901 a quarter of a million women from these backgrounds had jobs as teachers, nurses, typists, telephonists, department store clerks, and office workers, many of whom may have regarded the vote as a means to attain equal pay with better-paid men in the same jobs. Many wealthier bourgeois women also marched, however, displaying obvious dissatisfaction with the status quo despite markedly improving circumstances for females of their class. Indeed, falling infant mortality rates and the trends toward fewer children and children born earlier in marriage meant not only better mother-child relationships but also more time for middle-age mothers to engage in other activities. About half a million women did philanthropic work in 1900, for instance, many dedicated to these pursuits as unpaid professional careers. The secondary and higher educational opportunities becoming available in the late nineteenth century reinforced the tendency to seek fulfillment outside the home, as did gradually expanding political rights. Female ratepayers had voted in local elections since 1869, for instance, and by 1900 a million British women exercised this right. Others not content merely to vote locally also served as Poor Law Guardians, members of school boards and local educational committees, and after 1907 as elected members of town and county councils. For some women of the British upper classes, however, the glass was half empty, not half full. Ongoing improvements accentuated the possibility of positive change, in other words, while also highlighting the illogic in women's eyes of the remaining social, economic, legal, and political inferiorities—and chief among the latter was the denial of the national suffrage.

Elsewhere in Europe many of the same factors worked to spread the women's movement.[47] In 1894 German women founded the Federation of German Women's Organizations, which pushed mainly for better educational opportunities, legal rights, child welfare, and public health, but also for world peace, and after 1902, for the vote. French women similarly campaigned for a variety of female causes, including the suffrage, but a concerted voting drive waited until the founding of the French Union for Women's Suffrage in 1909. Furthermore, the American-based International Council of Women (ICW), founded in 1888, had spawned affiliated or allied councils in sixteen European countries by 1914. The ICW formed a separate organization in 1904, the International Alliance of Women (IAW), designed specifically to gather and disseminate information about methods of obtaining the vote for women. Within a few years the IAW had founded national affiliates or fellow-traveling organizations in nine European countries.

An egalitarian, progressive spirit reigned in the IAW. "The Great Powers and the small nations, those who can boast of bayonets and dreadnoughts, and those who have none, are on the same footing," said a proud Annie Furuhjelm of Finland. "Some people will probably shrug their shoulders, saying, 'A woman's dream'—yes, a woman's dream, and a vision of justice and peaceful evolution."[48] Adopting assertive but nonviolent tactics, Finnish women acquired the right to vote in elections to the Provincial Diet in 1906. Showing similar tact, Norwegian women gained the national suffrage in 1913. No other European women had the national franchise. Joining Sweden and Britain with their longstanding female voting rights in local elections, however, were the women of Denmark (1908) and Iceland (1909).

The proliferation of women's organizations, particularly their growing insistence on getting the vote, elicited a wide range of negative responses. Mrs. Humphrey Ward, a respected English author, argued that women's expanding public experience in the local community did not prepare them for national and international service better performed by men, nor were such positions commensurate with women's true dignity and special mission. Ellen Key, a Swedish feminist, favored extension of the vote but was also troubled by exaggerated demands for equality that allegedly ignored the unique aspects of motherhood. Similarly, Swedish writer August Strindberg supported women's emancipation while worrying about the possibility of women ruling over men in a repressive matriarchy.

Frequently, however, male critics chose harsher words. Thus Russian nationalists lashed out at suffragist "whores," while French militarists envisioned alarming scenarios of women's emancipation, declining birthrates, and national enervation. Italian advocates of violence worried similarly about the "castration"[49] of the race threatened by feminism. These more extreme sentiments clearly reflected Europe's worsening international tensions and the exaggerated fear that women would somehow weaken the nation in its hour of peril.

German Europe displayed the most extreme forms of anti-feminism. Viennese author Otto Weininger published a scathingly misogynous tract in 1903 entitled *Sex and Character* that castigated women for being "in constant close relation with the lower life." He saw a woman's demand for emancipation "in direct proportion to the amount of maleness in her." Weininger advised men to save their sexual energy for nobler military endeavors. These twisted seeds bore political fruit in Germany after the "red" elections of 1912, for the Social Democrats advocated women's Reichstag suffrage, while some middle-class parties were willing to grant municipal voting rights—which anti-feminists viewed as national voting rights "through the back door." To create a dike against these unacceptable possibilities, rightist men founded The German League for the Prevention of Women's Emancipation in June 1912. Supported mainly by Pan Germans and anti-Semites, the new anti-feminist organization grouped politicized women in the same category as other alleged "internal enemies" like Catholics, Socialists, and Jews. These reactionaries believed female suffrage meant a "womanization" of the state and a deterioration of its "manly militant character." They pointed to Scandinavia, where feminism and pacifism allegedly produced mothers who could raise only "sissies." When German feminists adopted WSPU heckling tactics in 1913 they were shouted down as "perverse, degenerate men-women."[50]

The masculine backlash against women prompted Carrie Chapman Catt, American chairwoman of the IAW, to speak up for the WSPU's controversial methods at the Alliance's Budapest Congress in June 1913. The international suffrage movement owed Emmeline Pankhurst an immense debt for provoking a worldwide debate about women's voting demands, Catt argued. Like the crazed American abolitionist John Brown, Pankhurst was a martyr for a worthy cause. Catt added, however, that Pankhurst and her followers did not deserve to be treated like "military prisoners."[51]

By this time, in fact, a martyr had fallen for the cause in Britain. On Derby Day in May 1913 Emily Davison stepped onto the track in front of the king's hard-charging racehorse, which trampled her to death. When the Liberals still refused to take political action, the WSPU increased pressure by setting fire to buildings—107 feminist acts of arson occurred between January and July 1914, including the total destruction of churches at Whitekirk, Wargrave, and Breadsall. Meanwhile, the marches, arrests, and hunger strikes continued.

Ethnic Tensions

Another source of unrest in Britain, perhaps the most threatening of all, emanated from subjugated Ireland. After the abortive rising of 1867 Irish politics revolved mainly around the question of "home rule," but backers of Irish autonomy could not muster majority support in the House of Commons until 1910. The Liberal majority disappeared in that year's elections, forcing the government to rely on Irish Nationalists for a majority. Irish members of parliament (MPs) consequently used their leverage to procure a Home Rule Bill in 1912 that called for an autonomous Irish parliament deferring to London in matters of trade, foreign policy, and defense. Irish Protestants in the northern province of Ulster condemned the bill, preferring union with England to submersion in a mainly Catholic and—it was feared—vindictive Irish state. Almost immediately "unionists" recruited an Ulster Volunteer Force to prevent separation from the Motherland should home rule become law. In 1913 southern patriots formed the Irish Nationalist Volunteer Army to push for autonomy.

A violent showdown seemed inevitable by 1914. Filled with unionist sympathizers, however, the British Army balked at imposing parliament's will by force. A compromise effort whereby each of the nine Ulster counties could vote to join Ireland or postpone this step, perhaps indefinitely, broke down in late July when unionists refused to contemplate loss of the large Protestant minorities in the Catholic counties of Tyrone and Fermanagh. Europe's Great War intervened before the worst scenario—the first civil war in Britain in over two and half centuries—could happen. Like most English, most Irish set aside their quarrel and concentrated their considerable energies against Germany.

All over Europe subject nationalities—other "Irelands"—expressed their massive discontents. In Spain a strong Catalan movement pressed for its own version of home rule, while Basque nationalists preached a violent and racist separatism that aimed to reverse Castille's centuries-old conquest of Navarre. In German Alsace, pro-French demonstrations plagued haughty army officers in this annexed province. The manhandling and arrest of protestors at Zabern in 1913 brought Alsatian anti-German sentiments to a fever pitch. The Norwegians seceded from Sweden a few years earlier, weathering a crisis that saw both sides mobilize military forces. In Saint Petersburg, rulers kept a wary eye on nationalist movements all over European Russia. The Finns and Poles were by far the biggest troublemakers. Thus Finnish dissidents resorted to assassination and a general strike in 1906 before sinking back into a sullen defiance of tsarist rule, while an alliance of exiled Polish revolutionaries in Vienna plotted to overthrow the Russians and regain Polish independence.

Centrifugal forces in Austria-Hungary also grew stronger on the eve of Europe's Great War. Czech deputies in Vienna and Prague demanded home rule rights so intransigently that Francis Joseph suspended the Bohemian constitution and prorogued the Austrian Diet in 1913, ruling thereafter by decree. The suffocating Hungarian rule over Rumanians in Transylvania triggered bomb attacks against Catholic clergy and fueled both autonomist and secessionist movements. The latter were cheered at officially sponsored demonstrations across the border in independent Rumania, whose leaders hoped Hungary's loss would be their gain. Serbs and Croats in Hungarian Croatia-Slovenia made provincial Diet speeches protesting Magyar racial arrogance, some demanding an independent state for all South Slavs (i.e., Yugoslavia). Like Rumania's fanning of ethnic flames in Transylvania, expansionists in neighboring Serbia agitated and intrigued for Serbo-Croatian secession from Austria-Hungary. Serbian nationalists welcomed dissent in adjacent Bosnia-Herzegovina for the same reasons, perpetrating six assassination attempts against Austro-Hungarian officials in the four years before Archduke Francis Ferdinand's fateful trip to Sarajevo. In 1909, moreover, Italian irredentists blew up a railroad tunnel near Trieste, narrowly missing the Habsburg heir apparent.

Firsthand experience with the empire's "volcanic social forces"[52] helped convert the normally reactionary Francis Ferdinand to the notion of a "United States of Greater Austria." The plan, first proposed by a Rumanian autonomist in 1906, advocated federal home rule for Czechs, Slovaks, Poles, Ruthenes (Ukrainians), Rumanians, South Slavs, and Italians. The Hungarians could be expected to resist tooth and nail, for control and security meant everything to a people harboring a deep sense of insecurity and ethnic paranoia born over centuries of violence.[53] But Francis Ferdinand viewed the restructuring of Austria-Hungary as a way to reduce centrifugal secessionist dangers and appease subject nationalities. The bold scheme got him killed, for the archduke's intentions were public knowledge, also to the Order of the Black Hand, a Serbian terrorist sect that feared that the plan's implementation after the old emperor's passing would defuse secessionist sentiments within the Dual Monarchy and block Serbian expansion.

VARIATIONS OF MODERNIST CULTURE

The first decade of the twentieth century was a time of accelerating industrial growth and technological change in Europe. Industrial sectors expanded at annual rates of 5 to 6 percent, pushing output in most industrial nations by 1913 to twice 1900 levels. This was also the decade of the automobile, the airplane, the airship, and the first luxury liners—among them, the allegedly unsinkable *Titanic*. The dynamic subcontinent that ruled most of the world had become a tremendous mega-machine, funneling prodigious quantities of capital, raw material, and labor into its mines, factories, and shipyards. Reflecting Europe's industrial upsurge, world energy consumption experienced a six-and-a-half-fold increase from 1870 to 1913. Some historians point to this accumulating economic and technological dynamism as one of the major contributing factors to war's outbreak in 1914.[54]

Contemporaries reacted with mixed feelings as the second industrial revolution gained momentum. Always sensitive to the possibility that "frantic, raging life"[55] might erupt in revolution, the ruling establishments of Europe questioned anxiously whether governmental structures could withstand the seismic pressures of social change that accompanied industrial expansion. Matching the awesome generation of natural energy, in fact, was an earth-shaking rumbling of societal energy measured not in tons of coal or electric wattage, but rather in industrial strikes, leftist electoral gains, angry women's suffrage demonstrations, ethnically inspired political violence, and assassinations. Leader of the Italian "Futurist" avant-garde, F. T. Marinetti, felt these tremors. "Reality vibrates around us, assaulting us with squalls of fragments of inter-connected events, wedged into each other, confused, tangled, chaotic."[56] When war finally erupted in 1914, Austrian novelist Stefan Zweig believed it had "nothing to do with ideas and hardly even with frontiers—I cannot explain it otherwise than by this surplus force, a tragic consequence of the internal dynamism that had accumulated in forty years of peace and now sought violent release."[57]

There existed a tragic interlocking unity, in other words, to the technological, the social, the political, and the military in Europe. As demonstrated in this section, all of these developments were also inextricably bound up with "modernist" artistic and cultural movements that reflected "raging life."[58] Of course, modernist culture before the war is important in its own right—what the great artists created from their scaffolds, music rooms, ateliers, and writing desks need not be viewed politically to appreciate it. Readers gain a better understanding of that day by investigating the avant-garde, however, for its creators were in tune with the tragic side of the spirit of the times. As Thomas Messer notes, "one of the most interesting aspects of the artists is to have antennae that sense somehow the end of an order before it occurs externally."[59] Modernist culture, in short, provides some of the most convincing historical evidence that Europe was generating too much dynamism and energy for those in high places to control.

Like the music of Richard Strauss, avant-garde culture revolted against the underlying assumptions and external structures of dominant art forms. Traditional culture circa 1900 tended to reflect society's rationalism and optimism. The sonatas, concertos, and symphonies of composers like Johannes Brahms, for instance, were tonal, harmonious, lyrical, and well-ordered. Portraits of the confident servant-keeping classes, beautiful landscapes, and com-missioned scenes of victorious battles for public buildings occupied most painters. Popular novels and plays also stressed stability, the triumph of good over evil, and other nondisturbing messages. Modernist art broke from these traditions by dwelling on the fragmented, the fractured, and the discordant as opposed to the finished and harmonious whole. It rejected philosophical idealism, gravitating more to the frightening moral relativism of Friedrich Nietzsche. Modernist culture penetrated beneath external consciousness to the realm of the unconscious, both drawing from and contributing to the emerg-ing abnormal psychology of its pioneering Viennese practitioner, Sigmund Freud (see Chapter 4). There was a scandalous new openness with regard to sexuality, and in some members of the avant-garde, an uncomfortable sus-picion or even hatred of women. The new art also believed itself to be far above the ugly crowds, its complex meaning far beyond the grasp of the masses. Related to this elitism was a preoccupation with the consequences of rapid technological modernization, with most (but not all) modernists anx-ious about the "express train" momentum of the brave new world. Under-pinning much avant-garde art, in fact, was a cultural pessimism and despair that produced visions of apocalyptic martial ends. Some welcomed ap-proaching war as a great societal purge, others suffered nightmares and feared bloodshed, but most—again, not all—saw these things coming. The self-appointed prophets of modernity's dark side conflated art and life, finally, believing that their works genuinely expressed the human experience—indeed, that their creations *were* the soul of humanity. Given the dominant culture's contrasting assumptions, such messianism generated tremendous controversy.

Richard Strauss's *Salome* premiered in Dresden in December 1905. The opera told the story of John the Baptist's gruesome beheading at the erotic urging of King Herod's voluptuous daughter, Salome. Drawn from Oscar Wilde's play, the drama portrays decadent authority, depravity, and gore. "Volcani-cally violent," the music resonated with emotions that lured audiences in-creasingly anxious over the likelihood of domestic eruptions and European conflagrations. "Using more instruments than ever, he composed a score of tremendous difficulty and exaggerated dissonance with the orchestra at times divided against itself, playing in two violently antagonistic keys as if to ex-press the horror of the subject by horrifying the ear." Strauss made unheard-of demands on musicians, asking cellos to reach the realm of violins and trom-bones that of flutes. The opera's "barbaric noise" culminated misogynously in "thudding, screeching discords when Herod's soldiers crush Salome be-neath their shields."[60] The work made Strauss a fortune as it moved through other German cities, Graz, Milan, London, and New York.

Salome would be the height of Strauss's experimentation with modernist "music of the future." In *Elektra*, which premiered in Dresden in January 1909, the composer used Hugo von Hoffmansthal's extremely popular psy-chodrama as a study in contrasting and conflicting musical styles. It relates the tale of the daughter of murdered King Agamemnon, Elektra, whose vengeful monomania eventually triumphs over her father's slayers. Life is tragically drained out of her, however, all of this despite the virtuous, maternal, life-affirming efforts of her sister, Chrysothemis. In the opera's central scene Strauss used clashing major and minor keys and the chromatic twelve-tone scale—a hallmark of modernist music—to capture the twisted anger of Elektra.[61] This dissonance is controlled in other scenes, however, by the dominance of major keys and the traditional diatonic eight-tone scale. After the killing of Clytemnestra and Aegisthus, and Elektra's enervating death dance, gloomy motifs and atonality yield to a major chord finale that signals the restoration of harmony and the continuity of life.

Nevertheless, the message that order cannot prevail without bloodshed left Viennese writer Hermann Bahr unable to shake the queasy feeling that sinister events were luring the world "back toward chaos."[62] The composer may have reacted similarly, for afterward he turned to cheerier pieces with lighter styles. Had Strauss become frightened after his experiments had led him unwittingly into a brutal and disturbing world?[63]

German "expressionist" poetry provides further examples of modernism's revolt. Circa 1911 the poets of this school began to break the mold of inherited romantic verse. They sought to delve beneath the allegedly rational, realistic, descriptive *surface* of language to find and release its expressive energy. As Kasimir Edschmid declared, the new poet "doesn't depict, he experiences, he doesn't reproduce, he fashions, he doesn't take, he searches." Another spoke of the need "to defeat [reality] and dominate it through . . . the intense, explosive power of feeling."[64] They accomplished this with a duel of structural elements locked in precarious equilibrium, somewhat like the musical struggles of key and scale in *Elektra*, and by revolutionary uses of the parts of speech. These poetic devices amplified thematic concerns with industrial society's dynamism, lower-class misery, and impending cataclysms.

The poems of Ernst Stadler, one of the best-known and today most highly regarded German expressionists, illustrate these points well. In "Noontide" he describes a sunlit garden at midday with all its seeming beauty and calm, yet under the surface tranquility heat is rising dangerously. Gods' statues "radiate," trellises "heat-glisten," meadows are "rust-red," and even the shadows are "warm." The sense of explosiveness is heightened by tension between the order of a strict rhyming pattern and the countervailing disorder arising from lines that are jammed together, verbs that control nouns, and adjectives that have anthropomorphic meaning. And then an invisible presence enters the garden: "softly the gravel crunches." Readers familiar with Nietzsche's *Zarathustra* might recognize the coming of "superior man" after humankind has passed the "great noontide" of evolution. In "Train Stations" the poet switches to an urban scene as huge steam locomotives pull in and out of cavernous, electric-lit grand centrals. Stadler employs run-on, almost gasping syncopation, mixed with violent, animalistic, sensual, and erotic metaphors— which all feud with a rhyming pattern that gradually weakens—to evoke a tense excitement. Indeed, he seems to transcend the bounds of language to place readers on the throbbing pulse beat of the modern technological world, thereby achieving the modernistic goal of conflating art and life.[65]

The so-called New Club of Berlin brought a different variation of expressionist poetry to the podium; witness Jakob van Hoddis's "End of the World," recited shortly before his death in 1912, which describes a storm that makes landfall and wreaks havoc, knocking hats off heads, roofers off houses, and dykes off their foundations. "Most people have caught a cold/Railway trains tumble off the bridges."[66] There is glaring dissonance in this poem between the tight symmetry of lines rhyming in the original German and the lines' subject matter, which leaps illogically, almost mockingly from one scene to another. Such poems "resemble unsecured scaffoldings," writes Richard Sheppard, "within which an explosion seems about to occur."[67] Indeed, at the thematic level the poet leaves no doubt about society's fate. Hoddis truly wanted the old bourgeois world to die, for its poverty, harsh inequities, and decadence disgusted him. Another star of the New Club, Georg Heym, expressed similar sentiments: "If only someone would start a war, it needn't be a just one," reads a diary entry. "This peace is so stagnant, oily and greasy, like a patina on old furniture."[68]

The pessimism and despair epitomizing modernist culture also surface in Thomas Mann's brilliant novella, *Death in Venice* (1913).[69] Its author had joined the modernist revolt after moving to Munich in 1893. There he imbibed Nietzsche, whose philosophy of decadence, decline, and violent regeneration swept him past the city's dominant visual arts with their vogue realistic depiction of things, beyond the naturalist literary style of late nineteenth-century writers Émile Zola and Henrik Ibsen, which dwelt on the ugly surface of society, to a new mode of writing that plunged readers into the psychological and pathological depths of human suffering. His third major work, *Death in Venice* follows writer Gustav von Aschenbach to the famous city on the water. Unable to sustain his workday with the usual energy and unselfish discipline, Aschenbach is lured to Venice for relaxation and literary rejuvenation. Instead he becomes enraptured and infatuated with a beautiful teenage boy, Tadzio, prolonging his stay and resisting the inclination to return home. Delayed departure means death, however, for a cholera epidemic claims the great artist as victim.

There are contrasting, seemingly clashing modes of writing in the novella, each carrying a different meaning. Mann uses the detailed, labored realistic mode of earlier fiction from beginning to end. This was the style of writers like Aschenbach, and it propels the storyline. Omens point the way below the surface, however, to darker meanings embedded in myth, for beneath the writer's suppressed inner cravings that appear to be his undoing demons are at work, in particular Dionysus, dark God of springtime regeneration and intoxication, the nemesis of Apollo, bright God of clarity and order. As the tragedy nears its end the myths rise to the surface when Aschenbach dreams of partaking in a wild and bloody Dionysian orgy. Upon awakening he can no longer resist Tadzio, cares nothing about his work, and sinks into willing self-abandon. In a fortnight Dionysus has shattered the ordered existence of a lifetime. Death soon follows.

Death in Venice certainly expressed Mann's personal anxiety over reception, frustration with creative blocks, and self-doubts about his own homoeroticism—hidden demons that could undo careers. The novella went far beyond autobiography, however, to make a statement about the times. In the first line, for instance, he alludes to an international crisis "glowering so ominously at our continent."[70] It is the last such allusion, but the book can be read as Mann's sense of collective urges and passions rising dangerously to the surface in Germany and Europe. "There is no doubt a political will was alive in me," he wrote during the war. Older brother Heinrich Mann, whose novels always lambasted unthinking patriotism, also sensed the perils as man's ability to reason grew weak and "surrender[ed] the field to the orgies of a complicated naiveté [and] the outbreaks of a deep and ancient anti-reason."[71]

The expressionist school of painting emerging in Germany after 1905 perhaps best illustrates modernism's desire to expose society's passionate substrata. The two main loci were Dresden, where Ernst Kirchner founded the "Bridge," and Munich, whose "Blue Rider" group formed around Vassily Kandinsky and Franz Marc. Both camps rejected the attempts of earlier artists to reproduce near photographic depictions of people, objects, and landscapes. Crying out to these avant-garde types was the alternative of inventing a new painterly language capable of expressing, according to Kirchner, "the great mystery which lies behind all circumstances and things in our environment," or showing, as Marc put it, "the mighty laws that surge behind the beautiful appearance of things." Only the gifted, possessed artist could lead the way. "A demon allows us to peep through the cracks in the world's surface," said Marc, "and, in our dreams, leads us behind the world's bright backdrop."[72] The Bridge's structural break with the past took shape in distorted forms, angular strokes, and a kind of primitivism. Representation was stripped of all nonessentials. Blue Rider also valued pictorial reduction, but blazed its own trail with otherworldly, dreamlike color schemes and a drift toward the abstract.

The "mighty laws" that expressionists discovered beneath Europe's surface grew more and more frightening after 1912. Many of their apocalyptic paintings depicted burning cities, exploding landscapes, battling Amazons, and the sinking *Titanic*. Marc's poignant *Fate of the Animals* (1913) represents this trend. Destructive bolts from the sky wreak havoc on a forest of terrified horses, boars, and deer. The shots descend into the woods, and reverberate through it, diagonally. "These lines serve to provide an atmosphere of unremitting tension," writes Frederick Levine, "a tension further emphasized by both the nearly total absence of horizontals and verticals, and the utilization of a color scheme (green on red, red on blue) designed to produce the maximum intensity of tonal contrasts." But "despite all the frenzy, all the apparent confusion," argues Levine, "the composition nevertheless remains one of strict order, even balance, and overall unity."[73] The evocation of harmony and stability emerging from ongoing killing is reinforced by the image of four deer in the lower right that find haven beneath protective limbs. It is the great world-ash tree from Norse mythology, the Yggdrasil, whose roots draw sustenance from heaven, hell, and earth, rendering the tree eternally immune to catastrophic purges of evil recurring since time immemorial. Like these deer, mankind will survive the apocalypse and try again.

Clearly a strong case can be made for the centrality of German culture in the avant-garde movement.[74] The modernists' scoffing at older artistic standards, their anxious, trembling introspection, as well as their self-styled projection of "spirit at war" found best expression in the nation whose collective express train roared most rapidly through a small station. The roots of this strand of modernism extended, however, into other parts of Europe undergoing rapid socioeconomic transformations. Feeding the German revolt in painting, for example, were Frenchman Henri Matisse and his so-called Fauves (wild beasts), Belgian expressionists like Eugene Laermans and James Ensor, and the young Spanish cubist Pablo Picasso. Edvard Munch also made great contributions to German modernist art. Many regard *The Scream* as prototypically expressionist, but the painter who spent years in Munich and Berlin drew early formative influences from his Norwegian upbringing. Kandinsky grew to adulthood in Russia, similarly, while playwright August Strindberg found German commercial success for avant-garde pieces whose inspiration came in part from his native Sweden. Robert Musil lived in Germany and wrote in German, moreover, but tales of military school sadism like *Young Törless* (1906) originated in the Austria-Hungary he remembered from adolescence. In modernistic fashion this novel called for a new spirit to infuse a society racing toward disaster.[75]

In venturing to the southeast, in fact, one finds a veritable hotbed of modernist culture. Thus Vienna was home to psychoanalyst Sigmund Freud, whose interpretation of dreams foresaw widespread discontent in European societies that repressed sexuality. The Dual Monarchy also housed Arnold Schoenberg, a composer of dissonant and atonal scores that seemed to predict catastrophe, and Béla Bartók, the transformer of Hungarian folk music into gloomy tones and dissonances that conveyed a sense of social malaise. Also working inside the Habsburg realms was Franz Kafka, a writer of stories about alienation and the absurdity of irrational and impersonal power. And finally there were Gustav Klimt, an artist whose images often mixed eroticism and death, and Oscar Kokoschka, painter of the shockingly misogynous *Hope, Murderer of Women*. It was said that after seeing a Kokoschka exhibit Archduke Francis Ferdinand wanted to break every bone in the artist's body.[76]

The avant-garde also thrived in Russia. One hears the loud, violently cacophonous sound of the modern, for example, in the music of Igor Stravinsky. A French critic lambasted Stravinsky's score for *Rites of Spring* (1913) as "the most discordant composition ever written—never has the cult of the wrong note been applied with such industry, zeal, and ferocity." Poets Vladimir Maiakovsky and Victor Khlebnykov, like Western European expressionists, broke with old structural conventions that no longer seemed to convey meaning. "We alone are the face of our era," they declared in a manifesto of 1910. "Through us sounds the bugle call of the era in the artistry of words." The paintings of Natalia Goncharova and Mikhail Larionov represented the same break with tradition. Although heavily influenced by the radically primitive works of the Blue Rider, the two nevertheless developed a distinctive neo-primitive style of their own. Thus Goncharova drew inspiration from her peasant background to imbue canvasses with the impersonal rough force of rural working folk. *Washerwomen* (1911), one of her best-known paintings, represents village launderers in the stylized poses of fierce Scythian stone sculptures. Life partner Larionov turned to Assyria and Persia, arguing that the future would be informed by antiquity, in particular the fertility cult of the goddess Astarte and the annealing fire of Zarathustra. Both painters evoked frightening ancient images that they hurled with Slavophile derision at allegedly inferior western cultures. "The West," declared Goncharova, "has shown me one thing: everything it has is from the East."[77]

The Russian avant-garde, in fact, had already taken the West by storm. In 1909 Serge Diaghilev's Ballets Russes opened in Paris, demonstrating convincingly that the East, for all its political anachronisms, had become a source of cultural modernity. Diaghilev introduced the sensational dance talent of Vaslav Nijinsky, complementing his fresh new technique with modernist musical scores and stage backdrops. With the debut of *Rites of Spring*, however, the Ballets Russes went too far for many Parisians. Stravinsky's "cult of the wrong note" was definitely hard on the ear, but Nijinsky compounded the disjointed effect created by the music with his flaunting of known dance steps. In place of pirouettes and arabesques came stomping and heavy jumping. His basic position "consisted of the feet turned inward with great exaggeration, knees bent, arms tucked in, head turned in profile as the body faced forward," a kind of "knock-kneed contortion." The dance troupe split into groups moving to different rhythms, struggling to follow musical beats that changed from bar to bar. The sense of being subjected to "spring from the inside, with its violence, its spasms, its fissions" was reinforced at the thematic level, for the ballet's plot flows from pagan springtime revelry to its interruption by village elders who prepare their trembling people for the tragic consecration of a virgin. "She sacrifices herself in the presence of the old men in the great holy dance, the great sacrifice." Only through death can the rejuvenation of spring occur. All of this was set against the backdrop of Nikolai Roerich's primitive stage designs, reminding Diaghilev of the camps of the Polovtsian Tartars who had brought devastation from the East. As Europe neared the brink of war a year later, one critic reflected on *Rites of Spring*'s nihilistic message, calling the ballet a "Dionysian orgy dreamed of by Nietzsche and called forth by his prophetic wish to be the beacon of a world hurtling toward death."[78]

In 1909 F. T. Marinetti, the Italian avant-garde poet, issued his "Futurist Manifesto" from Paris. Dubbed by Parisians "the caffeine of Europe" because of his seemingly boundless energy, this self-styled high priest of modernity envisioned a futuristic wonderland that pulsated and vibrated with electricity. "The energy of distant winds and the rebellions of the sea, transformed by man's genius into many millions of kilowatts, will spread everywhere with-out wires, through the muscles, arteries and nerves of the peninsula, with a fertilizing abundance regulated by keyboards that throb beneath the fingers of the engineers."[79] His close associate, painter Umberto Boccioni, projected the same worshipful confidence onto canvas in *The City Rises* (1910–1911). Drawn with every bright color on the palette, images of the city going to work blur into one another as if caught up in a whirlwind of movement and force. With one glance a viewer feels the raw dynamism of the second industrial revolution. There was a dark side to Futurism, however, for Marinetti and his friends were determined to throw out the old—baby with bathwater—to bring on the new.

This comes into clearer focus when examining the Futurists' aggressive, warlike conflation of art and life. Their artistic point of departure derived angry inspiration from the blunt fact that present-day Italy nauseated them. Political corruption, parliamentary deadlock, labor radicalism, the emerging women's movement, pacifism, and established culture—all these forces sapped technology's potential, war's potential, and man's potential. All were seen, in fact, as emasculating and feminizing bleedings of the male life force:

> Yes, our nerves demand war and despise woman, because we fear that the supplicating arms will wrap around our knees on the morning of our departure! What do women, the sedentary, the invalid, the sick and all the prudent counselors expect? To their vacillating lives, broken with dismal agonies, by fearful sleep and heavy nightmares, we prefer violent death and we glory it as the only worthy of man, beast of prey.

The Bergsonian mission of art was to blast away at all impediments to masculine virility and energy. "Poetry must be conceived of as a violent assault against unknown forces, so that they will be reduced to prostrating themselves before man." There could be no real beauty or true culture, however, in peacetime. Ultimately, the only genuine art was combat itself. After war broke out between Italy and Turkey in 1911, Marinetti became a newspaper correspondent in order to experience killing up close. "We can admire nothing else today but the formidable symphonies of bursting shells and the crazy sculptures modeled by our inspired artillery amongst the enemy hordes."[80] Inspired by the Balkan violence of 1912, he wrote an entirely asyntactical, un-punctuated, and ostensibly nonsensical poem entitled "Zang Tumb Tumb" (1914). The idea, however, was to simulate the intense, rushed speech mode soldiers might use when locked in a life-and-death struggle. Like other modernists, Marinetti had to break with established cultural structures to hammer home his point.

In England, J. M. Barrie anticipated some of Futurism's violent rush forward with *Peter Pan*, appearing as a play in 1904 and a novel in 1911. Better to escape the emasculating clutches of mother and the boring, life-sapping professionalism of father—better to have an adventure than experience mundane adulthood and grow old. "To die will be an awfully big adventure,"[81] says Peter Pan. Futurist painting came to the socially troubled British Isles,

too, advanced especially by C. R. W. Nevinson after 1912, but Marinetti's influence quickly dissipated as artists in Roger Fry's "Bloomsbury" group and
the Rebel Art Center around Wyndham Lewis took different modernist tacts,
the latter's coterie shouting down the Italian at one of his readings in London. Lewis and contributors to his journal *Blast* adhered more to the painting
of Pablo Picasso, now in Paris, whose unorthodox cubist reshaping of human
form catered to their elitist, conservative worldview. While the Spaniard's style
broke with traditional realist representations, thereby penetrating to a deeper,
truer world of human feeling, cubism also appealed to those around Lewis
because it seemed to achieve all this in a precise and orderly way. Futurism,
in other words, was too much in love with the speed and confusion of the
present. Superior art would anchor a turbulent society by linking it to allegedly better, more stable, and more hierarchical historical epochs.

This conservative strand of British modernism was even more pronounced
in a remarkable circle of writers that discarded literary structures perceived
as outmoded and embraced the avant-garde after 1909. Personally close to
Lewis, this clique boasted greats like poet-playwright William Butler Yeats,
novelist Ford Maddox Ford, and poet Ezra Pound. Like continental modernists, they scoffed at bourgeois notions of progress, human perfectibility,
and a better life for all. On the contrary, the Liberal Party's social programs,
culminating with the enervating reform of the House of Lords in 1911, had
dismantled authority and opened the floodgates to a raging, uncontrollable
current of democracy. "If the Deity were really beneficent," wondered Ford,
"would [he] not send us a slaughter, famine, or a pestilence that would sweep
away . . . all the purely parasitic classes?"[82] For the most part, however, these
talented men did not envision or welcome any kind of cleansing apocalypse
or great purgative war; rather, they advocated a peaceful return to medieval-
like conditions of lorded authority and believed, furthermore, that modern art
presaged the merciful turn of history's wheel.

The variegated culture of prewar Europe produced other less violently vi-
sionary images for posterity. In H. G. Wells's *The History of Mr. Polly*, for example, the protagonist, a petit-bourgeois nobody, goes from one humiliation
to another, souring from the "grinding smallness of his life"[83] until finally contemplating suicide. Rather than end life, however, he gathers himself together
and manages to find happiness and honor in normal, peaceful, civilian pursuits. Thus Wells tried to convince contemporaries that, in fact, nonviolent alternatives existed to Peter Pan's "awfully big adventure." In France, Marcel
Proust also sent more pacific messages. Written between 1907 and 1919, his
classic *Remembrance of Things Past* takes readers into a kind of time warp. The
main characters move ineluctably forward in time, eventually reaching, like
confident Europe itself, the era of the Great War. But the protagonist, Marcel,
travels along another time plane into the past of his own self. In one chapter
the aroma of pastry induces a euphoric reliving of happy childhood moments
in the security of his grandmother's home. Proust's novel did not issue a call
to arms and the mad dash forward. But the only paradise, it seemed, was paradise lost.

Nonmartial sentiments of a somewhat different sort surfaced among the smaller nations of Europe. Having seen the folly of war centuries earlier, for instance, Switzerland managed to extricate itself from Europe's struggles by eliciting international recognition of its neutrality. The Swiss did not trust Great Power promises, however, for they prepared to defend themselves if others ignored international law. Ferdinand Hodler paid artistic tribute to these widespread Swiss emotions with his tripartite fresco *The Retreat from Marignano*, completed for the Hall of Arms of the Swiss Museum of History in Zurich. High on the windowless west wall appears the battered troop of warriors that slipped back over the mountains from Italy after losing thousands of comrades at Marignano in 1515. Hodler discarded the detailed style of academic realism, rendering his ancestors in stylized, symbolic poses and exaggerated color. With a fatigued yet fierce determination in their eyes, two veterans at the rear turn to face imaginary pursuers. Like the painter's Switzerland, the troop withdraws from fighting—but will fight again if it must. "The men of that time exist today," said Hodler proudly. "They are the same today, and they would still fight in the same way."[84]

Closely related emotions emerged architecturally and sculpturally where one would perhaps expect them least—in the Germany of 1913. The cyclopean monument to the Battle of Nations, commemorated on the centennial of the previous century's greatest bloodletting, rises three hundred feet above the old battlefield near Leipzig. Outside, a gargantuan head of the legendary

Ferdinand Hodler, **The Retreat from Marignano.** (Swiss National Museum, Zurich)

Barbarossa guards steps leading into the massive interior. It is not the mood of Germany awakening to the glory of imperial expansion, however, that one feels inside. For here arrogance mixes with the anxiety, uncertainty, and insecurity that cropped up in public structures throughout the Reich in the decade before 1914.[85] Above, in the Hall of Glory, a manly adult generation cradles youth protectively in its lap. Below, in the Crypt, death masks peer from the shadows as if to say, ambivalently: "Never again—but woe to him who awakens us!"

THE JULY CRISIS

By late June 1914 many long-term developments increased the likelihood of a martial explosion in Europe: (1) a long history of violence among different peoples culminating in a small set of victor states ruling over defeated ethnic groups that nevertheless retained an unquenchable desire for freedom or independence; (2) recent industrial and technological revolutions that exacerbated national and colonial rivalries between the increasingly anxious Great Powers, which maneuvered for security into two opposing alliance systems

Anxious nationalism: interior of monument to the Battle of Nations, Leipzig. (Stadtgeschichtliches Museum Leipzig)

or armed camps; (3) escalating political difficulties within the dominant states, prompting some Europeans to wish or actually call for war as a way to purge divisiveness or channel these pressures abroad; and (4) an overall international and societal dynamism accelerating the pace of events and further heightening anxieties, all of which complicated top-level decision making by leaders with human flaws. While no single factor—or even all of them interacting together—made war inevitable, the absence of the kind of institutional checks to war desired by pacifists heightened its chances.

As events turned out, the first fiery force at work—ethnic grievances—lit fuses that set off a terrible four-year conflagration.[86] Six Serbian terrorists united in a convoluted and still shadowy conspiracy to assassinate Archduke Francis Ferdinand on June 28, 1914. They had completed paramilitary training in Belgrade with the aid of sympathetic army officers and then crossed frontier checkpoints into Austrian Bosnia with the help of compatriot border guards. Although superiors in the so-called Order of the Black Hand initially tried to call off the mission, the six young men, eager to destabilize the Austro-Hungarian Empire and make way for a South Slav state, persevered and prevailed with their plot. Serbian political leaders knew the team had crossed the border, and that nothing good would come of it, but apparently saw no reason to issue anything more than vague warnings to the hated Habsburgs. After the violent deed Bosnian Muslims and Croats, eager to demonstrate their dissociation from the act to angry imperial authorities, and seeming to know who had armed and assisted the assassins, destroyed the shops and businesses of resident Serbs.

Jumping to the same correct conclusions, Vienna began to draft a stiff ultimatum to Serbia and to make other preparations for a war long advocated by anti-Serb zealots in the army like Hötzendorff. Before going forward, however, Austria-Hungary sought a blank check of military assistance from Berlin, for any action against Serbia might trigger Russian intervention. Kaiser William II and his advisers agreed to this carte blanche, gambling that Serbia could be quickly crushed and the declining power of Germany's only true ally shored up. Russia seemed too beset by internal unrest to risk war and another revolution, but if she did not stay her sword hand, German soldiers gave themselves a good chance of defeating both Russia and its ally France. Indeed, daring operational plans, perfected over many years of maneuvers and war games, called for a bold strike into Belgium and eastern France designed to weaken allied forces sufficiently to transfer unneeded army corps to the East. So Vienna got what it wanted in Berlin. Confident of German backing, Austria bombarded Belgrade early on July 29.

How would Russia react? Carefully weighing the internal and external risks, Tsar Nicholas II and his advisers decided that the prestige and honor of the nation demanded that it mobilize forces to stand by fellow Slavic/Orthodox ally Serbia. Emboldening Russia somewhat was the knowledge that she would not stand alone: With a probability bordering on certainty, France had made promises of support to Russia as Germany had made assurances to Austria-Hungary. Because mobilization schedules and timetables for millions of troops and tons of supplies were so complicated, however, the Russian Army had only one set—and these fateful orders would send troops to bivouacs not just in the southeast sector but all along a western frontier stretching from Rumania to the Baltic. Once Russia's grandiose call up began on July 30, Germany, possessing only one operational plan, grew nervous, for the limited time available for a western campaign started to tick away. Early on August 1, therefore, Berlin warned Russia to stand down within twelve hours or face war. Although little military action was anticipated in the East during the first month or so, German political leaders considered an actual declaration of war against Saint Petersburg necessary to rally the notoriously anti-war Social Democrats to a seemingly just cause against the most reactionary regime in Europe.

As upper-class pacifists looked helplessly and with increasing horror at what was unfolding on the continent, Britain, Europe's best hope for the kind of arbitration trumpeted at The Hague, made repeated attempts to mediate the rapidly escalating Balkan dispute. Last-minute wavering and willingness to consider such proposals in Vienna and Saint Petersburg amounted to nothing in the end, however, for Berlin, having received no favorable reply to its ultimatum, declared war on Russia as well as France late on August 1, 1914.

Now, as pacifists continued to pray, anxious eyes focused on London. But to specialists in the Foreign Office the decision seemed fairly clear cut: The British Empire could not afford German hegemony in Europe. Furthermore, as Prime Minister Herbert Asquith watched with frustration while his fourth mediation attempt floundered he found some solace in the knowledge that a European war "may incidentally have the effect of throwing into the background the lurid picture of civil war in Ireland."[87] The violation of Belgian neutrality by German cavalry units on August 4 precipitated the final decision for war in London later that same day.

And what of the anti-militarists of the Socialist International? Nationalist impulses undermined it. A general strike debate at Copenhagen in 1910, for instance, had quickly deteriorated into bickering and finger-pointing between German, French, and English delegates. Four years later European socialists were no closer to agreement on direct action to stop war. Now, as alarms sounded repeatedly in newspapers, parliaments, and the streets, widespread beliefs about the legitimacy of defending one's country assumed greater prominence. With crowds in Vienna clamoring for punishment of the Serbs, German workers peering anxiously eastward for the coming of the dreaded Cossacks, and French laborers listening to reports of enemy troops crossing the frontier, the "ancient despotism" of war easily prevailed.

Chapter 3

▼

THE GREAT WAR AND BEYOND

An American field hospital near Belgium bustled with activity as the hours drew on toward noon. Outside the hastily constructed structures of corrugated iron the day had remained cold and gray. Mist and drizzle exacerbated the dreariness of late autumn 1918 as if to accentuate, fittingly or unfittingly, the inevitability of more fighting in 1919. Inside, the inescapable stench of wounds clung to the young women of the Red Cross nursing corps. The sickly sweet odor filled up their nostrils when they walked into the countryside for fresh air, harassed them during rare opportunities to bathe, almost knocked them over when ambulance doors opened, attached itself to blankets, and sneaked into beds at day's end.

Since America joined the war in 1917 her female volunteers had witnessed all of the behind-the-lines horrors seen earlier by nurses of the European powers.[1] Were these the same men who had marched through the streets in 1914 so full of life and youthful vigor? No, machine guns and heavy artillery, the ghastly maiming machines of modern war, had changed all that. The wounds they inflicted defy ungratuitous description, but the worst casualties for the nurses to cope with, somehow, were the defaced ones, their lips and jaws blown away, feeding tubes inserted where mouths had been, wads of gauze stuffed in nose holes bigger than silver dollars.

The survivors among these half-men would somehow have to adjust to civilian life. As for the nurses, they learned to cope by growing immune and thick-skinned during the working day—even to the point of taking tea amidst piles of amputated body parts—then releasing the horrors with nightmares about the poor suffering men. Soon the caretakers would have to make the same transition to civilian life. The postwar world would bear little resemblance, however, to that imperfect peacetime world of 1914, now remembered wistfully as the end of a golden era.

At eleven o'clock on this eleventh day of November 1918, the guns fell strangely silent. Usually a dull thunder of artillery fire sounded at a distance. It had become as normal to the nurses and patients as the fetid odor and the maddening, emasculating pain. Now there was just an unnerving stillness: no explosive booms, no birds chirping, not even a cow mooing. Word spread that silence meant the long-awaited cease-fire—an end, perhaps, to four and a half years of war. But nobody in the hospital rejoiced. If the Great War were really over, there was time to celebrate after tending to today's horrible casualties.

WAR OF ATTRITION

Europe's armies mobilized quickly in August 1914 and marched to the front.[2] Along the German-French-Belgian frontier seven German armies collided catastrophically with five French armies reinforced by smaller Belgian and British forces. The worst losses occurred when artillery and machine gun fire caught whole brigades and divisions and corps—sometimes tens of thousands of men—packed in dense formations forming up in the rear, marching along roads, or attacking. The mutilating effects, which left battlefields from Belgium to the Swiss border strewn with corpses and body parts, contradicted not only the unshakeable confidence generals had expressed in offensive warfare, but also an era's confidence in itself. Casualty figures confirmed the impression made by such gory visages: of the three million soldiers who battled in the west that first month, eight hundred thousand were dead or badly wounded, nearly twice as many as fell during the eighteen-month Russo-Japanese War. Magnifying the horror, the Germans executed nearly a thousand Belgian civilians in brutal retaliation for persistent sniper attacks.

During the fighting, German divisions overran Belgium and northern France, pushing the exhausted British and French divisions back to Paris. As new research demonstrates, German planners did not intend to fight the critical battles near the capital, as historians have long held—even the legendary Alfred von Schlieffen, chief of the General Staff (1890–1905), had seen this as a worst-case scenario. Rather, they strove for victories along the frontier that would decimate the French, force an abandonment of their fortresses, and permit immediate redeployment of eight or ten German corps to meet the Russians while the rest of the army gradually finished off surviving allied defenders. But the French and their allies avoided this trap, and the Germans gave chase, extending lines of supply, exhausting troops, and eventually exposing an open flank near the Marne River.[3] In early September a surprise Franco-British counterattack halted the German advance. Fierce fighting later that autumn killed many thousands more, but produced only stalemate and the lone option of burrowing deep into the blood-soaked earth. A frightful new phenomenon—trench warfare—awaited combatants in 1915.

The eastern campaigns proved even costlier. Russia sent five armies into Austrian Galicia and two armies into East Prussia, but the latter forces, divided, outmaneuvered, and ineptly led, fell to Germany's eastern army group, whose commanders, Paul von Hindenburg and Erich Ludendorff, achieved instant legendary status by stopping the dreaded "Cossacks." As the snow fell their reinforced divisions ran into stiffer Russian resistance during an unsuccessful drive on Warsaw. Russian armies fared much better in Galicia, overrunning the entire province and crushing incompetently led Austro-Hungarian forces. Serbia also registered victories against the Danube Monarchy, remarkably freeing the homeland of invaders by Christmas. Losses in all of these campaigns

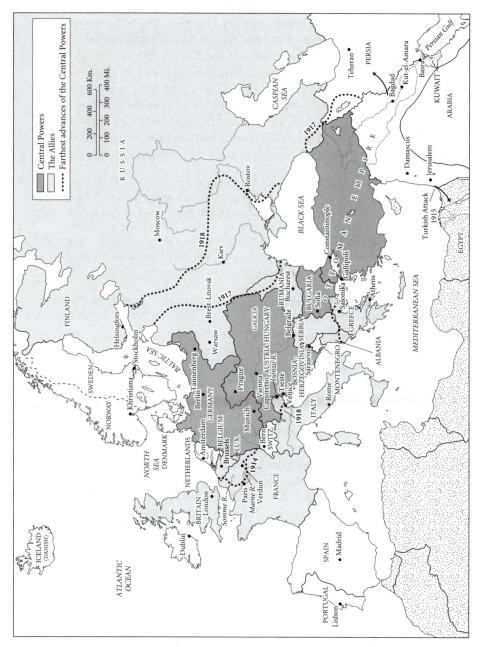

The Great War

rose to levels unprecedented in the history of warfare—from the Baltic to Belgrade over two and a half million men lay dead or wounded.

Both armed camps believed that 1914's elusive victory would occur in 1915, but incredibly enough the overall bloodbath just got worse. On the eastern front Hindenburg and Ludendorff attacked out of East Prussia while Austro-Hungarian armies sought to recapture Galicia. Both winter offensives failed, the latter turning into a Russian romp that included capturing the massive fortress at Przemysl. Greatly reinforced with new armies and heavy artillery in May, however, the Central Powers broke through Russian lines in Poland and Galicia, nearly pushing the tsar's forces out of these provinces by autumn 1915. A British nurse trying to help one Russian infantryman who had temporarily survived Germany's metallic onslaught fought off feelings of guilt:

> I pushed the clothes back and saw a pulp, a mere mass of smashed body from the ribs downwards. The stomach and abdomen were completely crushed and his left leg was hanging to the pulped body by only a few shreds of flesh. The soldier's dull eyes were still looking at me and his lips moved, but no words came. What it cost me to turn away without aiding him, I cannot describe, but we could not waste time and material on hopeless cases, and there were so many others waiting.[4]

Indeed, the numbers waiting on all sides were staggering. Austria-Hungary and Russia suffered four and a half million casualties in 1915, twenty times more than the better-equipped and better-led Germans.

Technological deficiencies headed a long list of problems dragging down the Russian war effort. Industrialization had been late relative to the West, and then quick and impressive after the 1890s. Russia had not adequately negotiated the steep gradient of the second industrial revolution, however, for her chemical and machine tool industries—key components of the modern technological system and integral parts in the subsystem of armaments manufacture—remained badly underdeveloped. The country, in fact, remained dangerously dependent on Germany for chemical and machine tool imports, which of course Berlin cut off in August 1914. When Hindenburg and Ludendorff overran what little the Russian Empire possessed of nitric and sulfuric acid plants in 1915 ammunition deficiencies vis-à-vis Germany worsened. Machine tool production had also lagged far behind Western Europe, triggering wartime difficulties in weapons output as well as replacement of locomotives and rolling stock. As the latter wore out and could not be replaced, supplies of armaments, inadequate to begin with, became literally sidetracked in a nationwide transportation crisis. To the poor soldier at the front, technological deficiencies usually meant having to fight the German Army without many rifle cartridges or much artillery support.

Early in the war Austria-Hungary experienced an even more complex set of problems. Although the industry of the Dual Monarchy's Austrian and Czech regions had expanded since the mid-1800s, armaments manufacture never factored highly in the empire's priorities. Outgunned, even by the Russians, and even more incompetent than the tsar's poorly led forces, Austro-

Hungarian armies squandered huge numbers of soldiers—two and a half million in 1915 alone. The casualties included dead and wounded as well as hundreds of thousands of soldiers from subject ethnic groups who preferred to surrender or desert rather than fight for a state that ignored their political demands. Over 28 percent of troops mobilized by Austria-Hungary in the Great War became prisoners or went missing, far above Russia's 21 percent, Germany's 10 percent, or France's 6 percent.

On other fronts in 1915 the Germans and Austrians stayed largely on the defensive. In France allied armies assaulted the Germans' impregnable trench networks, suffering terrible losses without breaking through. The nightmare of charging infantrymen, these killing zones typically featured two zigzagging trench lines about two hundred yards apart, both protected by tangles of barbed wire. Seven hundred yards or so behind these lines the Germans placed a deadly belt of machine-gun nests to mow down soldiers who made it past the front trenches. Then came support trenches with reinforcements for counterattacks, and still farther back the heavy artillery. In one of their own limited attacks in April 1915, German units unleashed an even greater horror on the enemy: a thick yellowish-green, ground-hugging cloud of poison gas that caught gagging, choking, dying allied soldiers completely by surprise—gas masks were not yet available. As much suffering as hapless French and British men went through that year, entrenched men on the other side also sacrificed life or limb, hoping desperately that the unbearable suffering had a deeper meaning. "Have you ever seen a butcher's shop where slaughtered people are laid out for sale, with machines making a terrific racket as they slaughter more and more people with their ingenious mechanism?" wrote one horrified German. "Yesterday one of those butchers smashed the person next to me into pieces with one blow and mockingly covered me with blood and flesh and guts." Artist Otto Dix added his own thoughts on life in the trenches. "Lice, rats, barbed wire, fleas, shells, bombs, underground caves, corpses, blood, liquor, mice, cats, artillery, filth, bullets, mortars, fire, steel: that is what war is—it is the work of the devil."[5] Well over two million men fell on the western front in 1915.

Bulgaria also entered the fray in 1915, helping Austrian and German forces outflank hated Balkan rival Serbia, which was overrun in four months. Both victors and vanquished suffered heavy losses. The accession of Italy to the bloodied Triple Entente of England, France, and Russia in May lifted allied spirits. Rome launched four offensives along the Isonzo River designed to penetrate to Vienna, but there were no breakthroughs—only high Italian and Austrian casualties. One survivor remembered the intense artillery exchanges as "unparalleled butchery . . . Blood is running everywhere, and all about, the dead and pieces of corpses lie in a circle."[6]

Elsewhere that year Turkey, which had joined Berlin and Vienna in 1914, mounted an unsuccessful assault on the Suez Canal. Another Turkish force had more success on the Dardenelles, pinning down assaulting British divisions at Gallipoli and forcing them to withdraw after months of bloody carnage. The Turks also stymied a British drive on Baghdad, defeating a largely

Otto Dix, War. (Photo credit: Erich Lessing/Art Resource, NY/© 2004 Artists Rights Society (ARS), New York/VG Bild-Kunst, Bonn)

Indian force at Kut-el-Amara south of Baghdad. One journalist described the "dreadful stream of broken men"[7] shipped daily back to Bombay.

Turkish victories did not ease the anxiety felt in Istanbul, however, as it considered the many powerful enemies that encircled the nation. Arch foe Russia, a Christian land, threatened Turkey's northern flank, which was further weakened, assumed Turkish Muslims, by the presence of Armenian Christians. When the Armenians refused to support the war against Russia, therefore, the Turks forced the recalcitrant ethnic minority to relocate, which turned into a death march as over a million Armenians perished from disease, hunger, and systematic executions.

The German commander-in-chief, Erich von Falkenhayn, had good reason to be optimistic at the end of 1915. Eighteen months of warfare had produced no great breakthroughs for either alliance, but the enemy seemed to be bleeding himself white, and Serbia had been knocked out of the war. The depletion of Austro-Hungarian armies alarmed Falkenhayn, to be sure, but Germany had suffered far less. Thus he gambled on the Central Powers holding in the east while a powerful German army group punched through the line around the Fortress of Verdun. Victory on one front would surely lead to quick triumphs on others. Throughout the winter of 1915–1916, therefore, he amassed the largest artillery force ever assembled for one battle. On February 21, 1916, shock troops went over the top after more than a million shells had been fired. The assault made encouraging progress for a few days because the artillery had performed its morbid mission well. Thousands of

French infantrymen lay buried in forward trenches or their bodies decapitated and dismembered in the most grisly fashion imaginable. Those who survived were too "shell shocked" to resist effectively. The French quickly brought up massive reinforcements of men and materiel, however, and by March the German attack bogged down. Now Verdun turned into industrialized, high-tech killing on a horrendous scale. Month after month thousands of French and German cannons dueled each other. By the early summer of 1916 the kaiser's gunners had shot up twenty-two million shells. Both sides sent scores of fresh divisions into this veritable killing mill. When the guns finally fell silent around the ruined fortress complex that autumn, over a million soldiers had fallen and the front lines had barely changed.

The stalemate and escalating sacrifices of the Great War continued on other fronts in 1916. Britain launched a massive attack on the Somme River in June to relieve pressure on Verdun. It ground unsuccessfully to a halt months later. The Austrians and Italians again traded blows along the Isonzo, but neither side broke through. Sensing an opportunity for expansion, Rumania entered the war against the Central Powers in August, but was crushed before the end of the year. The horrible sacrifices continued on the main east-

The living, the wounded, the dead: French trench. (Getty Images)

ern front, too, without greatly changing the strategic situation by Christmas. Collectively these campaigns claimed over five million dead, maimed, or missing—almost half of the total were Russians.

What cruel calculus of killing allowed this war to grind on after eighteen million casualties by late 1916? Utilizing a formula based on standing army strength, population, and overall industrial capacity, one historian points to the rough balance of power between opposing alliances. His numbers indicate that Germany and Austria-Hungary wielded only slightly less strength in 1914 than Britain, France, and Russia.[8] Of the neutral powers recruited by each side, however, only Italy reinforced the Triple Entente while Turkey and Bulgaria now stood with Austria-Hungary and Germany. The "Central Powers" had matched their enemies' capacity. Fairly evenly balanced with huge populations to draw on, the warring alliances could not gain a decisive edge.

HOME FRONTS

A balance of hate also existed between opposing camps as nations held ancient enemies—or perceived ancient enemies—responsible for deaths and wounds affecting almost every family. Wartime propaganda that demonized enemy peoples fueled the fires of this feud, especially among western democracies outraged by German atrocities in Belgium, but also by Germany against arch foe France and its "perfidious" ally Britain. Remarkably enough, Russians also vented hatred against German-speaking enemies despite the awkward fact that Empress Alexandra was herself German—indeed, the people increasingly loathed her as the war dragged on. As this example demonstrates, such high levels of suffering could unleash passions and emotions in the opposite direction, namely, against the very political establishments that sent armies of men to their slaughter. The likelihood of revolution in terrible times hinged on the degree of distrust or, inversely, faith people had in their governments. Authoritarian systems in Germany, Austria-Hungary, and Russia that had denied equal rights to the lower classes in peacetime, and continued to treat workers as second- or third-class citizens during the war, suffered more serious home front disruptions than did maturing democracies in Britain and France, which responded to pressure with concessions. Aloof ruling elites in Central and Eastern Europe also proved more vulnerable to charges of mismanaging a war that dragged on with no victorious end in sight. Low prewar living standards factored explosively into the mix, furthermore, for states drafted or recruited heavily among—and asked greater wartime sacrifices of—the larger numbers of dissatisfied lower-paid unskilled workers, while the skilled "labor aristocrats" either stayed in armaments factories or were returned from the front. In Russia's case, reliance on larger numbers of poorer peasants who had benefited little from Stolypin's reforms compounded the blue-collar dilemma. While the conservative monarchies could still count on popular revulsion against enemies in 1914, the emotional tide began to shift in 1916, turning inward and upward against the top. The same phenomenon occurred in Italy, an outwardly democratic nation that had no democratic traditions.[9]

Britain and France

In July 1914 three movements pushed Britain to the brink of revolution: the suffragettes, the trade unions, and the Irish. As the crisis escalated tragically toward the first shots of August, however, attention shifted from domestic to foreign concerns. For one Liberal leader, future Prime Minister Winston Churchill, the distraction occurred when hearing about Austria's ultimatum to Serbia. "The parishes of Tyrone and Fermanagh faded back into the mists and squalls of Ireland," he recalled, "and a strange light began immediately, but by perceptible gradations, to fall and grow upon the map of Europe."[10] Like Churchill, all Britain soon rallied to the colors.

John Redmond, leader of the Irish MPs, revealed his patriotic side too. He announced in August 1914 that Irish militiamen would defend the island's shores, thereby freeing up regular forces for continental fighting. In September Redmond went further, encouraging Irish nationalists to enlist in the British Army. They responded in great numbers. Political motives were also at play, for that month he convinced Prime Minister Herbert Asquith to implement the long-delayed Home Rule Bill as soon as the war ended. "We have won at last a free constitution,"[11] Redmond declared. He aimed to exchange Irish wartime cooperation for a place alongside Canada and Australia in the British Commonwealth. Support for the war effort might even mollify die-hard Ulster Unionists. Redmond's popular stance provoked panicky Irish nationalists around Patrick Pearse and James Connolly to accelerate plans for an armed coup to win outright independence from London. The so-called Dublin Castle uprising of March 1916 failed badly.

One observes the same pattern of cooperation, restraint, and minority dissent among the British working classes. The threatened general strike of miners, railway men, and dockyard workers evaporated in 1914 as masses of common people—two million by 1916—volunteered to fight Germany. Already during the first winter, however, problems of unemployment in nonessential industries, overtime in armaments works, the influx of non-union, mainly female laborers, and soaring prices and rents threatened the industrial truce. During the spring of 1915 the government negotiated deals with the trade union leadership for a renunciation of strikes and tolerance of non-union labor in return for compulsory arbitration of disputes and state safeguarding of wage standards. Rank-and-file militants simply ignored the pact, especially in the mines, where two hundred thousand struck that summer. The government responded with wage concessions, and when similar pressures mounted in December 1915 over rents, controls were introduced. These timely concessions preserved solidarity on the domestic front.

Like Irish nationalists and trade unionists, militant women also exchanged domestic for foreign targets of wrath. Thus Britain's radical suffragette, Christabel Pankhurst, initially described the war as "God's revenge upon [those] who held women in subjection," but by 1915 she stood squarely behind men "who at the risk of death are resisting the leader of the Anti-Suffragettes—William II." Turnabouts like this created some discord in the ranks, however, among pacifist zealots like Helena Swanwick, who refused to change course. "The sanction of brute force by which a strong nation 'hacks its way' through a weak one is precisely the same as that by which the stronger male dictates to the weaker female," she asserted. "Not till the idea of public right has been accepted by the great nations will there be freedom and security for small nations; not till the idea of moral law has been accepted by the majority of men will there be freedom and security for women." Swanwick led a determined anti-war faction, reduced by now to a small minority, which insisted on participating in a third Hague Peace Conference in 1915 that went on to pass resolutions favoring arbitration, disarmament, and a "league of nations" to monitor international relations. Most women in Britain's National Union of Women's Suffrage Societies, however, mocked the peace activists as "wild women of theory" and "poisonous pacifists."[12] Arguing that anti-war agitation would prejudice even pro-suffrage males against votes for women, this majority of pragmatic tacticians registered some progress in early 1917 when a parliamentary committee recommended extending the suffrage to women of property or wives of householders over thirty. That the proposal excluded from the franchise five million out of twelve million adult females, especially younger, single, working women, generated more dissension.

France also entered the war amidst serious class tension. These problems faded but did not completely disappear as the nation's armies went on the offensive in 1915 and defended Verdun in 1916. Armaments workers grumbled about not having the "English" eight-hour day, women complained about male rudeness on the job, and men griped about women supplanting them in the labor force. The "sacred union" of August 1914 remained alive in subsequent years, however, reminding Frenchmen of the need for sacrifice. Impressive material assistance to the masses reinforced this spirit of solidarity. From the first days of the war women with husbands in uniform received allowances generous enough in most cases to replace lost wages. Legislators also moved quickly to shield lower-class incomes by freezing rents. Such egalitarian measures prevented grumbling from escalating to riot or revolt.

French women's leaders needed far less to keep the domestic peace, for somehow the nation's emergency made campaigning for the female franchise seem untimely and inappropriate. "We will claim our rights when the triumph of Right is assured," said one of them. Wartime conditions also pushed feminist pacifism far offstage into the backroom of politics. Although all organizations that campaigned vigorously for the female vote before 1914 also advocated peace, the German invasion and the deaths of so many French men defending their own soil brought an abrupt reversal. "United with those who battle and die," wrote one feminist, "French women do not know how to talk of peace." Not surprisingly, none went to The Hague, for how would it be possible "to meet with the women of enemy countries [like Germany] . . . [until] they disavowed the political crimes of their government?"[13]

Italy, Austria-Hungary, and Germany

The situation in Italy contrasted greatly with that in Britain and France. Prime Minister Giovanni Giolitti inaugurated the democratic era with universal manhood suffrage in 1913, but the ruling elite possessed little patience for democracy. The absence of a true democratic culture was reflected in the problematic agenda of Giolitti's successor, Antonio Salandra. Shocked by leftist gains in the 1913 elections and the riotous "Red Week" of June 1914, he viewed Giolitti's experiment as a failure that should be replaced by governmental authoritarianism buttressed by rightist patriotic societies like the Nationalist Association. King Victor Emmanuel III supported his minister, seemingly tempted by the prospect of restoring royal prerogatives eroded by decades of parliamentary interference. Such considerations led in spring 1915 to Italy's entry to the war by government fiat against the wishes of the parliamentary majority, the Vatican, and the overwhelming majority of the Italian people. The disasters along the Isonzo River, coupled with Salandra's semi-dictatorial regime, inflamed home front politics until parliament finally mustered the courage to oust him in June 1916. Trouble lay ahead, however, for the nationalist Right and its dandy, Army Chief Raffaele Cadorna, now began to lash out rhetorically at the alleged "defeatists" running the country.

Austria-Hungary enjoyed better conditions than did Italy when entering the war, but martial enthusiasm had all but receded as 1915 yielded to 1916. Rigid censorship and the refusal of Austrian Prime Minister Karl Sturgkh to convene parliament exacerbated the stress and misery of escalating casualties and worsening food shortages. Official pro-war propaganda depicting a high degree of popular enthusiasm "has become a travesty of the innermost feelings of the people," declared the socialist *Worker Times*, "and stands in sharpest opposition to secret general opinion." Bread riots in 1916 led by angry women who lashed out at an uncaring establishment clearly expressed the real sentiments. Worse still, the murder of Sturgkh that November by a disgruntled socialist, and the high desertion rate among soldiers of the subject nationalities, particularly Czechs, presaged the breakup of the empire desired by intriguing Czechoslovak, Yugoslav, and Hungarian patriots. Hungarian Prime Minister István Tisza's refusal to grant universal manhood suffrage further complicated matters. "The Hungarian soldier in the trenches does not care about [voting]," mocked Tisza callously, "he is only longing for a leave of two weeks to till his lot."[14]

Octogenarian Kaiser Francis Joseph seemed to sense the bleak reality of things better than his top ministers. "The starving people can't stand much more," he admitted in July 1916. The emperor doubted whether his armies and subjects could last through another winter. "I mean to end the war next spring, whatever happens, for I can't let my realm go to hopeless ruin."[15] Still widely respected and revered after sixty-two years on the throne, the fragile ruler represented the only stabilizing force. His passing in November 1916 triggered an inevitable legitimacy crisis as a torrent of protests gushed forth about incompetent military leadership, the army's dictatorial rule, and the people's increasingly unbearable hardships. These outcries peaked in March 1917 after Russian Tsar Nicholas II succumbed to revolutionary disturbances and abdicated his throne (see later in this chapter). Wanting to avoid the same fate, Kaiser Charles, great nephew of the assassinated Francis Ferdinand, wisely decided to convene parliament in Vienna.

Similar disturbances would occur in Germany, but like other peoples going to war in 1914, most Germans responded patriotically. Christian trade unionists, bourgeois social reformers, and left-wing parties immediately swung into line behind the government, and when the Social Democrats voted for war credits, William II declared exuberantly that beneath the "red varnish" lay "good German wood." For its part the women's movement had moved into patriotic waters already before the war, discarding pacifism as "outmoded" according to Gertrud Bäumer, leader of the Federation of German Women's Associations. The peace movement's "cosmopolitan aims and internationalist policies" seemed even less acceptable to her in 1915 when a recalcitrant minority wanted to denounce war in The Hague. Bäumer lambasted these efforts as "incompatible with the patriotic character and the national duty of the German women's movement."[16]

Already during the first winter, however, tensions and unresolved problems from peacetime began to resurface. Trade unionists, Social Democrats, and other reform-oriented politicians urged Chancellor Theobald von Bethmann Hollweg to implement democratic electoral procedures in Prussia and strengthen labor's hand in the workplace by introducing collective bargaining and permitting youths to join unions. He made the latter concession in May 1916 as a sign of the government's "new orientation" toward the masses. With the number of striking workers rising tenfold to 130,000 that year, worried trade union leaders had warned that wildcat stoppages would worsen unless the chancellor initiated reforms.

Now reactionary groups protested that leftists had exploited wartime conditions to squeeze the upper classes. That Bethmann succumbed to such "extortionist" tactics, charged rightists, was an unforgivable sign of weakness. They reacted angrily when he refused to expand submarine warfare to include the targeting of ships from neutral nations supplying Britain and France. What seemed to the chancellor a prudent policy to avoid provoking nonbelligerents like the United States struck members of the Pan-German League and other extremists as treasonous softness. First expressed by the "Cartel of the Producing Classes" in 1913, rightist doubts about the stiffness of governmental backbone grew.

The Great War undermined the empire's political stability in still more fundamental ways. The Social Democratic Party (SPD) always favored republican over monarchical institutions in theory while tolerating monarchy in practice, but as 1916, the year of Verdun, unfolded, common people who usually voted SPD began condemning the kaiser's opulent lifestyle of three-course meals and lavish day-trips while loved ones died for the Fatherland. The Battle of Verdun inflicted further damage on monarchical legitimacy, for commanding Germany's bloodied army was none other than Crown Prince William, a dissolute womanizer whose frivolous sexual exploits became known to the men. In letters home they contrasted his carnal joys with their "hell" and blamed the monarchy for "the evil events" around them. Adding greatly to anti-monarchical sentiment in 1916, rightists also began to make ugly accusations against William II. The war had broken him down, they charged, into a crazed defeatist who prayed for deliverance and believed he spoke with Jesus in the royal bedchamber. The "half-English" monarch refused to unleash the submarines and zeppelins, it was said, because of his pro-English sympathies. Instead, artillery blew away hundreds of thousands. Government officials confiscated the pamphlets and arrested the ringleaders, but admitted that Pan-German venom had "undermined state authority, above all crown authority, in a highly dangerous fashion."[17] The replacement of Falkenhayn by the popular Hindenburg and Ludendorff in August 1916 soothed Pan-German feelings somewhat—but the monarchy's prestige dipped still more as increasing numbers of Germans placed their hopes in the heroes of 1914, not William II.

In Germany and other belligerent states of both alliances cracks appeared along many other societal fault lines. One important fissure opened up between the hapless men in the trenches who endured mud, stench, rats, and psychological breakdown triggered by constant exposure to death and disfiguring wounds, and safely homebound civilians whom soldiers loved and missed at first, but later came to resent. Because this was a young man's war, youthful fingers of blame pointed at the generation of fathers who started the conflict, pounded patriotic chests, and then ordered others to fight it. One British warrior-poet, Wilfred Owen, has biblical Abraham ignore an angel di-

Maintaining appearances: the kaiser with Hindenburg and Ludendorff.   (Getty Images)

recting him to slay the lamb of pride. "But the old man would not, and slew his son/And half the seed of Europe, one by one."[18] Many soldiers harbored similar resentments against patriotic mothers as well as sisters, girlfriends, and wives who had encouraged men to volunteer or cheered as they marched off to hell on earth. On top of this came issues of suspected infidelity, job market anxieties as women filled factory slots vacated by mobilized soldiers, and a general male perception of gender disorder as women played greater public roles and demanded more in return, including the vote (see later). Exacerbating these generational and gender frictions were a whole series of intraclass and interclass animosities generated by wartime conditions: Unskilled workers drafted into the ranks resented skilled factory operatives who stayed behind; lower middle-class clerks, white-collar functionaries, and pensioners on fixed incomes resented striking trade unionists who won wage increases and were thus better able to stay abreast of inflation; and urban dwellers resented farmers for alleged price gouging or hoarding of foodstuffs.[19] Like other problems mentioned here, city-country fissures created political difficulties in all warring nations, but especially in the beleaguered authoritarian monarchies. Thus food complaints added an ugly dimension to politics in Germany, nearly ripping apart parties like the Catholic Center, which joined people from all walks of life. Grocery-related issues also magnified centrifugal forces in the Dual Monarchy as hungry Austrians accused Hungarians of keeping harvests to themselves. And in Russia grain production problems exacerbated by a transportation breakdown drove bread-rioting city folk into the streets—and the history books, too, as their anger helped bring down the monarchy.

Russia and the West in 1917

Momentous events occurred in Russia during the Great War's fourth year. In early 1917 the monarchy collapsed, ending three centuries of hereditary rule by the Romanov Dynasty. The demonstration effect reverberated among would-be revolutionaries, not only in Germany and Austria-Hungary, but also within the relatively more stable western democracies. Later that autumn, however, before the import of these events could be assessed amidst wartime's disruptions, Vladimir Lenin's hard-line Marxist Bolsheviks overthrew the democratic successors of the tsars, initiating almost eighty years of communist rule. Two significant turning points had occurred within the short span of eight months. How do historians explain these events?

The demise of the Romanovs resulted from seismic wartime pressures. The macabre jubilation of 1914 quickly faded as families in every corner of the empire donned the black colors of mourning. Over the next two years a series of interlocking crises deepened, widened, and intensified Russia's modern time of troubles. First, the inadequate system of industrial technology failed as chemical, machine tool, and railroad sectors broke down (see earlier). Second, Russia's inefficient agricultural sector languished as the army siphoned off peasant labor and dwindling supplies of food rotted on side tracks due to the transportation crisis. Bread riots in the cities soon escalated, as did strikes by underfed workers whose wages could not keep pace with war-induced inflation. Finally, the odd beliefs of royal favorite Gregory Rasputin, who thought he could purge the sins of unhappily married women by having sexual intercourse with them, added scandal to the mix. The behavior of this obscure Siberian monk belied his claims to holiness—boasts that the German-born Empress Alexandra, desperate for someone to cure the hemophilia of Crown Prince Alexis, unfortunately believed.[20] As the country fell apart, outraged people blamed dissolute behavior and seeming treason on high.

In the midst of this crisis Nicholas and Duma leaders drifted farther apart. Urged on by Alexandra, the tsar treated them with contempt, preferring to rule through the ministries without parliament. Matters came to a head in November 1916 when Paul Miliukov, leader of the Constitutional Democrat Party (Kadets), lambasted the empress and her clique, ending each peroration with the refrain: "Is this stupidity or is this treason?"[21] His speech added another political dimension to mounting, rapidly overheating protests. The number of workers on strike in 1916 nearly doubled from the previous year—950,000 versus 540,000. After a group of highly placed conspirators brutally assassinated Rasputin in December 1916, the French ambassador wired home that another revolution could occur at any moment. In January and February 1917 another 676,000 workers struck—the highest level of labor unrest since 1905–1906.

Local leaders from many different organizations fomented most of the unrest in Saint Petersburg, working tirelessly at tremendous risk to themselves. Radical Socialist Revolutionaries (SRs) agitated in the factories and garrisons of the capital, appealing mainly to angry peasants. The "Trudovik" Labor Group, a non-Marxist worker and peasant faction of the Duma forced further and further left by wartime arrests, reinforced the work of the SRs. Both quarreling Marxist parties, the Mensheviks and Bolsheviks, were active too, joined by a bridge party advocating an end to this feud, the so-called Interdistrict Group. None of these organizations seems to have recruited a significantly greater number of followers than the others. Thus the notion later popularized by communist historians that the Bolsheviks spearheaded the monarchy's fall is exaggerated. Recent research not only spreads credit among a handful of groups, but also emphasizes how greatly wartime deprivations and miseries had politicized common workers, peasants, and soldiers, many of whom needed no prompting from party agitators.[22]

The first Russian revolution of 1917 demonstrates this point. On February 22 workers of the massive Putilov armaments factory outside Saint Petersburg struck. On February 23 working-class women protested in the city against bread shortages, appealing for support to men in factories who soon joined the irate females. In subsequent days chaos prevailed as the spontaneous revolt spread and soldiers fired on crowds, killing hundreds before finally joining the rioters. The revolutionary organizations initially held back, worried that army suppression would be swift. "There is no revolution," said one of the Bolsheviks, "we have to prepare for a long period of reaction."[23] But the garrison's defection emboldened these "reluctant revolutionaries" to move against the hated monarchy. By early March 1917 seven or eight thousand people had been killed or wounded. At this point army commanders concluded that Duma power was preferable to continued, seemingly futile street fighting on behalf of the tsar. They convinced Nicholas to pass the throne to his brother, Grand Duke Michael. When the latter prudently abdicated in his turn, the Romanov Dynasty came to an abrupt end.

Already on February 27, 1917, vivid memories of the 1905 Revolution spawned the formation of another "Soviet" in Saint Petersburg. This assembly of workers' and soldiers' deputies elected an executive committee headed by two Mensheviks and a fiery leader of the Trudoviks, Alexander Kerensky. Other socialist organizations, including the SRs, Bolsheviks, and the Interdistrict Group, were also represented. Two days later the political picture clouded with the creation of a Provisional Government dominated by Kadets in the Duma like Miliukov, but also including Kerensky. Fearing an army backlash if simple workers and soldiers tried to rule, the Saint Petersburg Soviet quickly expressed its support for the new government.

The two bodies settled into an uneasy truce. Meanwhile, the soviet movement spread across Russia like wildfire. About six thousand local councils had been founded by summer, organized hierarchically from the grass roots up to the "All-Russian" national level. Socialist leaders in the capital espoused peace talks, democratization of the army through soldiers' committees, national defense against the dreaded Germans—or even an offensive if necessary—and a host of radical reforms like the eight-hour day and redistribution of noble land to peasants. Upper-class members of the Provisional Government looked askance at much of this program. While they yielded pragmatically to the Soviet on soldiers' committees that elected officers and voted on orders, they hoped to avert a crisis over land reform by delaying a decision until the election of a constitutional assembly. Still fearing an army coup, the Saint Petersburg Soviet nevertheless reconfirmed its support for the Provisional Government in May 1917. Two prominent Mensheviks and an SR joined Kerensky as ministers.

On July 1, 1917, the Provisional Government unleashed a great offensive in Galicia, the site of so much suffering and dying. Forty-five divisions—almost a million soldiers—crashed into Austrian lines. Alexander Kerensky, the new minister of war and since March the rising star of the revolution, conceived the massive attack. The armies of democratic Russia overran enemy positions, even at points where Austrian units had the support of German divisions. The Habsburg army began to melt away, in fact, as whole regiments of Czechs bolted. Only the timely transfer of six German divisions from the western front prevented the crisis from escalating to mutinous French proportions. The Russians would certainly have routed their foes had the troops persevered, but their hearts were not in it. Some units ritually paraded through abandoned Austrian lines and retreated deliberately to their own lines. Whole waves of reserve divisions refused to join the fray. And when Austro-German forces counterattacked on July 19, the Russians fled east, shooting some officers who tried to rally defenses, evacuating captured ground so rapidly that the attackers took only a few thousand prisoners.

The military collapse in Galicia reflected a wider breakdown in Russian politics and society. Put simply, the moderate Provisional Government had progressively less control of extremist elements in a rapidly polarizing situation. The basic source of this instability was a deep-seated, thoroughgoing anger among the rural and urban masses. Although most socialist leaders who supported the new government wanted to hold elections for a constitutional assembly before discussing land reforms, most peasants did not. Seizures of noble estates by land-hungry common folk began to rise already in spring 1917. Most knowledgeable army officers also knew that the spontaneous revolution in March had been a product of hatred not just for the monarchy, but also for the war. It was doubtful, they predicted, how long the average soldier would stand his ground at home, let alone attack on foreign soil. Politicians and officers out of touch with mass sentiments got a harsh dose of reality in July as soldiers mutinied and peasant expropriations accelerated. Unable to keep pace with a runaway inflation or procure ample food, furthermore, factory workers struck in numbers that soon approached the level of early 1917. Moderate socialists, in particular, now paid a high price for losing touch with grassroots feeling. "They looked to the All-Russian Congress rather than to the local soviets, to the [Saint Petersburg] Soviet rather than to the district soviets in the capital, to the trade unions rather than the factory committees, to the provincial land committees rather than village assemblies, to conferences of soldiers' committees rather than to those closest to the rank and file." In each case, recent historians conclude, "the higher-level bodies tended to be less sensitive to popular opinion than lower ones."[24]

Although a socialist himself, Kerensky began to flirt with the idea of dictatorship. When his commander in Galicia counseled against a coup, warning that it would be like "building a dam when the river is in flood,"[25] Kerensky replaced him with Lavr Kornilov, a general surrounded by right-wing business, noble, and military men who insisted that he seize power, crush the Soviets, and save Russia. Miliukov and the bulk of the Kadets had also drifted rightward. Perhaps recalling the wise "dam and flood" analogy, Kerensky, who advanced to prime minister after the July debacle, seems to have suppressed dreams of becoming a latter-day Napoleon. Rather, he tried to rally centrist forces in August by convening a "State Conference" of all parties. But this body, torn by widely polarized factions of the propertied and the propertyless, accomplished nothing. Even Kerensky's best weapon, his passionate oratory, failed him as the conference disintegrated into chaos.

Reactionaries now urged Kornilov to strike quickly. What followed in late August 1917 has divided historians ever since.[26] Did Kornilov betray Kerensky, or just the opposite? Assured by numerous well-placed informants—some reputable, some not—that Kerensky wanted to impose order from above, it seems the general moved forces toward Saint Petersburg to rescue the "weak and womanly"[27] prime minister from the soviets' clutches. But whatever Kerensky's day-to-day vacillations may have led him to say to Kornilov, on August 27 he dismissed the surprised general and mobilized workers against "counterrevolution." Socialists of various party allegiances had no difficulty convincing Kornilov's soldiers to turn on their officers. Russia's raging river of revolution had swept away his reactionary dam before it could be lodged firmly in place.

The defeat of the Far Right meant victory for the Far Left. Vladimir Ilyich Lenin, leader of the Bolsheviks, seized this opportunity.[28] Since adolescence when his older brother had been executed for attempting to assassinate Tsar Alexander III, the resolute, hardened communist harbored a searing desire for justice against the establishment. Although he turned to Marxism in the 1890s, Lenin never abandoned the conspiratorial populism of his brother's associates. This insistence on action drove a wedge between the Bolsheviks and the Mensheviks, a more orthodox Marxist faction that believed in the historical inevitability of proletarian revolution—a spontaneous upheaval that would occur, in other words, without the machinations of hard-core, professional revolutionaries. But history seemed to favor Lenin's approach. The spontaneous revolution had been crushed after 1905, and now, in the midst of war and revolution's great opportunity, the survival of soviet power was far from guaranteed.

Returning to Russia from exile in April 1917, Lenin urged compatriots to take power from the Provisional Government, end the war, and attend to people's problems. By summer, the Bolshevik motto of "bread, land, and peace" appealed to increasing numbers of angry common folk impatient with a government that postponed, hesitated, and prevaricated on everything except the need to keep fighting. Lenin turned heads with his mocking parody of Kerensky: "Wait until the Constituent Assembly for the land, wait until the end of the war for the Constituent Assembly, wait until total victory for the end of the war."[29] After the Kornilov affair, army desertions, land seizures, and strikes spiraled rapidly upward—and so did Bolshevik popularity, especially in the soviets of Saint Petersburg, Moscow, and other large cities. Urban majorities once favoring Mensheviks or SRs changed hands as workers and soldiers abandoned politicians who, despite the glaring storm warning signals since July, remained strangely ignorant of street sentiments. On October 25, 1917, Bolshevik-led workers of the Military Revolutionary Committee of the Saint Petersburg Soviet—the same fighters Kerensky armed to stop Kornilov—seized power. Incensed with the Provisional Government since the general's arrest, army leaders did not lift a finger to help the prime minister. Instead, they plotted the next round of counterrevolution.

The momentous Russian events of 1917 reverberated throughout Europe. In Britain, radical shop stewards and rank-and-file workers ignored trade union pleas for order as strikes spiraled out of control. Alarmed government investigators reported that skilled and unskilled workers alike "expressed distrust in, and total indifference to, any promise the Government may make, while some referred to 'Russia,' and openly declared the one course open for Labor was a general 'down tools' policy to secure reforms that constitutional policy was failing to effect." As one laborite recalled, "the [Russian] Revolution was hailed enthusiastically by all sections of the working class movement."[30] The government of Prime Minister David Lloyd George responded cleverly by abolishing the "leaving certificate" system that restricted the mobility of workers, and consequently their ability to move to the highest paying jobs. Gradually an uneasy calm returned to factories and mines.

Meanwhile, a fourth season of killing brought warring nations close to their breaking points. The French and British attacked German trench lines at numerous points (Arras, Cambrai, the Aisne River, and Passchendaele), suffering two-thirds of a million casualties and inflicting the same on the Germans. Italy failed for a tenth and eleventh time along the Isonzo, adding another half million losses to the body count of the Great War. A worse sign for the Italians, however, was the torrent of deserters, shirkers, and draft evaders, amounting to many hundreds of thousands—some claimed half a million. French soldiers also lost faith in the operational wisdom of their generals. During the Aisne offensive of spring 1917 mutinies broke out in half of the army's divisions. While the high command managed to restore order by executing scores of "strikers," the fact remained that France's army was incapable of resuming offensive operations. Its new commander, Philippe Pétain, wisely introduced pay and furlough reforms and promised no more senseless attacks. Even the vaunted German Army started to crack. For the first time, large numbers of soldiers surrendered. Thousands of shirkers and hiders contrasted alarmingly, moreover, with the near universal willingness to sacrifice of earlier campaigns.[31]

It seemed that the French army mutineers breathed the same rebellious air that had felled the Romanovs. So apparently did the strikers who disrupted the Paris garment industry, the clothing trades, and the armaments factories that spring of 1917. Spearheaded by women who protested the soaring cost of living as well as the crude chauvinism of male foremen, the strikes featured the chanting of anti-war slogans—a clear indication that women sympathized with their suffering men in the trenches. Pacifism also affected left-wing parties in parliament. Both Socialist and Radical leaders became more insistent on peace talks with Germany as 1917 yielded to 1918. That last spring, moreover, revolutionary syndicalists determined to emulate Bolshevik successes of the previous autumn struck the metal trades. That they failed was a tribute to the resiliency of democracy and the leadership of the new premier, Georges Clemenceau. The "Tiger of France" offered workers the carrot and the stick: an eight-hour day, mandatory arbitration of strikes, and government pressure on employers for wage hikes, on the one hand; and swift repression of labor excesses, on the other. Pétain's commonsense army reforms also helped to maintain France's fighting spirit for a fifth campaign season.

The escalating body count along the Isonzo River in 1917 combined with the electrifying news from Russia to undermine Italy's war effort. Bread riots erupted in Turin and Lombardy, and in Milan the Socialists threatened a general strike. Pope Benedict XV joined a growing chorus of war-weary voices on August 1 by calling for an end to the "useless carnage." General Cadorna trumpeted angry retorts from the front against "the assaults of all forms of cowardice and hesitation from the interior."[32] The dam cracked on

October 24, however, when thirty-three Austro-German divisions attacked at Caporetto, killing ten thousand defenders and wounding many more. These losses panicked the others as hundreds of thousands surrendered or deserted. The fleeing soldiers left behind thousands of artillery pieces. After three disastrous weeks of retreat those who stuck to their guns finally rallied on the Piave River, their resolve stiffened by reinforcements London and Paris had rushed to Italy from other theaters. With front and home front crumbling, however, Rome could not last much longer.

But neither could Austria-Hungary. Although the news of victory at Caporetto improved spirits at military headquarters, at home people began to starve. "The physical strength of the great part of the population is so undermined with insufficient nourishment," declared Vienna's chief health officer, "that they are unable to withstand sickness." Indeed, deaths from tuberculosis tripled that year—and the rate, according to the same official, would be "much higher" in 1918. London papers published a cartoon that aptly described the bleak situation. The two kaisers, William II and Charles, press hard against the door of Austria in a desperate effort to stop a bony apparition from breaking out. "Remember Nicky!" shouts William, "We musn't let our skeleton get out of the closet as Russia did."[33]

Popular anger spilled into the streets in January 1918. Inspired by the Bolshevik example, two hundred thousand workers walked off the job in Vienna and Budapest amidst shouts for "peace," cries against "this life of slavery," and cheers for revolutionary Russia. It took troops to restore order. The empire's ethnic minorities also protested against an unrepentant German-Hungarian establishment. On May Day thousands of Czechs marched in Prague chanting "death to the kaiser" and carrying placards demanding peace, bread, and independence. To the Czechs' side rallied Poles, Slovenes, Croats, Serbs, and Italians. "We have not one Ireland," wrote Vienna's leading socialist paper, "but six Irelands."[34] In the Hungarian half of the monarchy centrifugal pressures from Serbs, Rumanians, Ukrainians, and Slovaks mounted to even greater levels. The empire was splitting apart along class and ethnic fault lines.

Germany and War's End 1917–1918

While Russian developments shook Europe, another event of great significance to the war's outcome occurred: On February 1, 1917, Germany initiated "unrestricted" submarine warfare. Now ships of all nations trading with the Reich's enemies, including neutrals like the United States, would be sunk. The decision reflected frustration with a seemingly unwinnable war and the desperate desire to starve Britain into submission and break up the Entente. The risky military move also reflected Germany's closely related, escalating domestic crisis. Both traditional and radical rightist cliques worried that Chancellor Bethmann Hollweg's concessions to Social Democrats and trade unionists would grow more generous the longer the war continued. These circles pressed for immediate victory to stave off democracy. The consequences of torpedoing American ships soon became apparent, however, when Washington broke diplomatic relations in February and armed its merchant marine in March. The newspaper publication of German Foreign Minister Arthur Zimmermann's ridiculous ploy to entice Mexico and Japan into a war against the United States further aggravated relations. The U.S. declared war on Germany in early April 1917. Under intensifying front and home front pressures, Germany's leaders had made an irrational decision that squandered all chances, good until now, of winning the war, for they had greatly overestimated the capabilities of an overstretched submarine force and sorely underestimated the allies' ability to expand production of ships and food. German submarines neither starved Britain nor sunk any of the troop transports that carried more than a million American soldiers to France over the next eighteen months.[35]

On the German home front politicians opposed to the SPD and other leftists had high stakes riding on a smashing, total victory. Anything short of such a triumph, rightists feared, would mire the nation in a democratic swamp. Indeed, domestic politics had become badly polarized in 1917. Against the backdrop of twin revolutions in Russia and the failed promise of unrestricted submarine warfare, two-thirds of a million German workers went on strike against economic hardships, the absence of democratic reforms—and, increasingly, the war itself. The Reichstag intensified matters by passing a "Peace Resolution" in July. A sizeable majority extending from the SPD and Progressives into the moderate Center and National Liberal parties voted for an immediate initiation of peace talks with the aim of returning to the status quo of 1914. The Reichstag wanted no territorial annexations or monetary indemnities.

The Right pulled in the opposite direction. Shortly before the Reichstag vote army commanders Paul von Hindenburg and Erich Ludendorff coerced William II into sacking the reform-minded Bethmann Hollweg. They ordered his lackluster replacement to accept the Peace Resolution as interpreted by the army. The meaning of this statement became evident almost immediately: Hindenburg and Ludendorff intended to ignore parliament and press for victory in the field. Reactionary political circles bolstered the powerful army duo in September 1917 by founding the "Fatherland Party." The new grouping strove to rally all classes for total victory, mobilizing over a million patriots by March 1918 to counteract the "defeatist" Reichstag. The most extreme elements based in the Pan-German League actually preferred a military coup, but neither the conservative Hindenburg nor the more radically minded Ludendorff wanted to unseat the kaiser. Their "silent dictatorship"[36] fully sufficed to control politics from behind the scenes.

The Left formed its counterweight to the Fatherland Party in October 1917. An umbrella organization of all leftist and moderate parties, trade unions, and reform societies, the "Peoples' League for Freedom and Fatherland" campaigned for reform and backed the Peace Resolution, but shrank from the intimidating, treasonous alternative of fomenting revolution against the army in wartime. Rank-and-file workers were obviously less timid, for in January 1918 over a half million struck against their employers and the war—the SPD claimed that two million downed tools. The army brutally suppressed the strikes, however, and then packed all ringleaders off to the trench-pocked fields of France.

One final victory there, it was hoped, would guarantee political victory at home. How many proletarians would dare to protest authoritarianism as the troops paraded through the Reich, fresh from their glorious conquests in the South, East, and West? This scenario did not appear illogical in the winter of 1917–1918. The near collapse of Italy was not the only sign, in fact, of apparent victory for the Central Powers. In the Middle East, Turkey fought doggedly against superior British might, yielding Baghdad in March and Jerusalem in December 1917. These were expensive victories, however, for they took a million British troops away from the fighting in Europe. Another three hundred thousand allied soldiers wasted away in Thrace. Malaria ravaged this motley force, ruling out any threat of offensive action against Germany and Austria-Hungary. In neighboring regions, moreover, prospects appeared bright for Vienna and Berlin. Serbia had been occupied in 1915, Rumania in 1916. The lone Rumanian army that escaped into Russian Moldavia surrendered to pursuing German armies in early December 1917. Six days later, once-mighty Russia signed a cease-fire agreement. As Germany and Austria-Hungary prepared to impose terms on Rumania and Bolshevik Russia in treaty talks opening that month, the German high command turned its attention to the western front. One big push, aided by scores of divisions from the East, could perhaps end the war before large numbers of Americans arrived. Shortly after Russia exited the war with the onerous Treaty of Brest-Litovsk in early March 1918, Germany rolled the iron dice in the West.

Hindenburg and Ludendorff chose the ruined terrain near the Somme River, site of such horrendous combat in 1916 and 1917, for their assault. Six thousand artillery pieces—five times more than the opening barrage at Verdun—supported the first wave. Sixty-seven divisions—twice the number that invaded Belgium in 1914—smashed into the weakest spot of the British line. Outnumbered and outgunned, battered and nearly broken, the British fell back, in some areas as far as the casualty clearing stations. "By day a thudding crescendo, by night sharp flashes in the sky," recalled one British nurse. "I don't suppose I was the only member of the staff whose teeth chattered with sheer terror."[37]

The Germans advanced for a week, but gradually lost momentum as the infantry outran artillery support, British reinforcements arrived, and the French, bolstered by increasing numbers of American divisions elsewhere on the front, rushed to the aid of their British comrades. The Germans shifted their attack to Flanders in April, and the Aisne River in May and June. Each time initial advances bogged down when the allies proved too strong. Massive transfers of troops from the eastern front enabled Hindenburg and Ludendorff to sustain their offensive, but nearly a million men fell from March to July 1918. The Germans were outnumbered and outgunned.

The allies swung over to the offensive in mid-summer near the historic Marne River. As summer gave way to fall, another half million Germans had been killed, wounded, or captured. Some regiments refused to fight, and as many as one million soldiers shirked or actually deserted. The German rank and file seemed determined to avoid death. Retreating soldiers greeted troop trains carrying reinforcements from Russia with howls of "strike breakers." A large portion of the German Army was, in a very real sense, on strike in the fall of 1918.

News from other fronts further dampened spirits. With the British driving toward Damascus, Turkey sued for peace. Shortly after the allies unleashed their long-delayed offensive from Thrace with frightening results, the Bulgarians, too, asked for an armistice. And in Vienna, Emperor Charles tried to extricate Austria-Hungary from the war before radical ethnic minorities seceded into separate states. Realizing that the end was also near for Germany, Hindenburg and Ludendorff advised Kaiser William in early October to arrange a cease-fire.

Germany's monarchy did not survive the rapidly approaching end of the war. Sailors of the High Seas Fleet mutinied on October 28, 1918, when ordered to fight a last-ditch battle with the overwhelmingly superior combined allied fleet. Workers' and soldiers' councils, formed in emulation of revolutionary Russia the previous year, spread quickly from the North Sea coast to other parts of Germany, including Berlin. On November 9 leaders of the SPD proclaimed a republic in hopes that the end of the monarchy would calm the masses and avert a more radical, Bolshevik-style takeover. Elections enfranchising all adult men and women would select members of a constitutional assembly for the new democratic Germany. Kaiser William wanted to break the revolution and republic at the head of his army, but went into exile instead after learning that his troops would not follow.

These developments typified revolutionary events that shook other parts of Central and Eastern Europe. After two revolutions in 1917, Russia fell apart in civil war in 1918. Austria-Hungary also disintegrated as the empire's major ethnic groups formed independent states and Austrian workers, like their German counterparts, proclaimed a republic in Vienna. When an armistice took effect on November 11, 1918, the Romanov, Hohenzollern, and Habsburg dynasties that had been so responsible for the outbreak of war over four years earlier had fallen. So had thirty-seven million men: the dead, the wounded, and the missing of the Great War.

THE TURBULENT ERA OF THE PEACE TREATIES

In January 1919 delegates from the victorious allied states assembled in Paris to negotiate the peace.[38] Over the next twenty months they tried to put a broken continent and troubled world back together again. All sides demanded justice after such a horrendous bloodletting, but nothing near consensus reigned, unfortunately, about what shape a just settlement would take. From across the ocean American President Woodrow Wilson brought a "fourteen-point" program, announced to Congress a year earlier, which included the worthy goal of self-determination for Europe's subject peoples. These independent democratic nations would sit in a League of Nations to safeguard the peace with moral, anti-war solidarity, and economic or military sanctions if necessary. The small states of Europe, in particular, rallied to Wilson's ideas. To French Premier Georges Clemenceau, however, justice meant punishment of guilty enemies and effective policing arrangements to guarantee that aggression did not occur again. Many of the new states emerging in Eastern Europe would benefit from and make common cause with Clemenceau. While these sets of goals were not mutually exclusive, they were different enough to spark quarrels between Washington and Paris. Britain, led by Prime Minister David Lloyd George, adopted a middle position, while Italy, somewhat like France, concerned itself more with power than matters of self-determination for other peoples. Rome's idea of a fair settlement meant fulfillment of wartime treaties that promised non-Italian Trans-Adriatic lands from Austria-Hungary as well as a healthy slice of the Ottoman Empire. Germany harbored other ideas of justice. Running the spectrum from national revenge to the *status quo ante* of the Reichstag Peace Resolution of 1917, such chimeras were obviously unacceptable to France and other allied states. Finally, the Marxist-Leninist notion of revolutionary international class justice emanating from Moscow caused nightmares in other countries. The fact that disorders swept Central and Eastern Europe and the Middle East in 1919 and 1920 further complicated the peacemakers' search for justice.

The Setting: Violence Continues

The collapse of the Romanov Dynasty and the revolutionary upheavals of 1917 triggered four of the worst years in Russian history—worse, after deaths from civil war, disease, and famine are counted, than the Great War itself. An early Bolshevik decree granting rights of self-determination to non-Russian nationalities of the former empire precipitated the new time of troubles. The Finns exploited this opportunity to declare independence on December 6, 1917, and within eleven months Estonia, Latvia, Lithuania, Poland, Ukraine, and the Transcaucasian republics of Georgia, Armenia, and Azerbaijan followed suit. The Cossacks of the Don Basin and Caucasus as well as the Tatars and Bashkirs of the Volga-Ural region wanted to do the same. All of these peoples were soon embroiled in Bolshevik efforts to avoid being overthrown, however, as the new "Red Army" moved against "white" counterrevolutionary bands in Kiev, Rostov, and Samara. Lenin also sent revolutionary expeditions into the Baltic republics, backed Finnish socialists in their civil war, and would eventually fight a war with Poland. From the beginning, therefore, ethnic strife intertwined inextricably with class struggle. As Western Europe celebrated the armistice in November 1918, and German and Austrian armies retreated from the Ukraine, Russia sank rapidly into a brutal, ethnically tinged civil war. What would allied leaders do about this deteriorating situation?

The Four Horsemen of the Apocalypse also galloped through much of "postwar" Central Europe.[39] Four years of allied blockade had reduced nourishment levels to alarmingly low levels by the cease-fire. Death from starvation by war's end was far more frequent in Austria-Hungary than Germany, but the weak and hungry populations of both empires were already succumbing in great numbers to tuberculosis, pneumonia, typhus, and a deadly new mutated strain of influenza that began invading human bodies that autumn. Showing no mercy to enemies of the worst war in history, however, the allies continued their debilitating blockade until July 1919. Five years after it started, the Great War had killed almost three million civilians in Germany and Austria-Hungary—most of these victims dying in the previous eighteen months, probably two-thirds of them from influenza.

While hunger and disease ravaged town and country from the North Sea to the Black Sea and Adriatic, revolution, civil war, and ethnic violence ripped into what remained of civil society. Germany first experienced these terrible disruptions. Taking the name of "Spartacus," the ancient gladiator who led a slave rebellion against Rome, left-wing extremists rejected the call of the Social Democrats and the majority of Workers' and Soldiers' Councils for democratic elections to a constitutional assembly in January 1919. Two weeks before the polling they unleashed their Bolshevik-style revolt in Berlin. The provisional government turned to the so-called free corps, the only armed forces it could rely on given the disintegrating state of the old imperial army. These militia units began to coalesce in December and January, recruiting from the small minority of soldiers that returns from all wars twisted by the bloodletting, caught up psychopathically in the camaraderie of combat, and determined to keep fighting. The Spartacists proved no match for these ruthless killers. A hundred revolutionaries lay dead in January after the revolt was crushed. A more serious uprising rocked the capital in March 1919, but afterward the free corps had twelve hundred new notches in their guns. Counterrevolutionary expeditions stamped out other revolts that spring, shooting hundreds of Reds in the port cities, the Ruhr, north-central Germany, and Saxony. The violence culminated in May with a shocking "cleansing action" against revolutionaries in Munich. Over six hundred executions marked the restoration of order.

By summer 1919 hundreds of thousands of free corps vigilantes wandered the country in scores of bands with little to do. Some of them set off for the Northeast, helping Baltic Germans battle against Latvians, Estonians, and Red Army units until finally forced to withdraw that autumn. Others attempted to seize power in Germany in March 1920, forcing the government to flee Berlin until a general strike of millions of trade unionists brought the ill-planned coup to an end. But when leftist militants rose up in the Ruhr, forming a "Red Army" some fifty thousand strong that brutally crushed local free corps units, the government allowed eastern free corps to accompany the regular army on a punitive expedition. About three thousand revolutionaries died in a week of rampage. Although Berlin now disbanded all free corps, the insatiate fighters turned their bloodlust on local and national democratic leaders, eventually assassinating hundreds of them. What would be done about all of this from Paris?

The Dual Monarchy of Austria-Hungary unraveled at the ethnic seams, meanwhile, as independent Austrian, Polish, Czechoslovakian, and Yugoslavian[40] states emerged days before the armistice took effect. These events soon presented the peacemakers with new dilemmas, for during the first months of 1919 Poland seized Galicia from what had been the Austrian half of the empire while Czechoslovakian, Rumanian, and Yugoslavian armies overran two-thirds of prewar Hungary, leaving only a rump territory around Budapest. Consequently, the bid of Hungarian democrats to establish themselves was made next to impossible.

In the closing weeks of the war, after soldiers mutinied and workers struck, Count Mihály Károli, leader of the parliamentary opposition, became prime minister. The new democratic government called for elections based on universal suffrage. It also prepared to implement radical land redistribution and equal rights for ethnic minorities—Hungary would become the "Switzerland of the East." Károli's administration failed to win widespread support, however, as the sick and weary masses demanded immediate relief that the prostrate nation could not deliver. Foreign policy victories would have strengthened his hand, but after Czech, Rumanian, and Yugoslav armies overran much of the country, the victorious Great Powers sanctioned these seizures. In protest, Károli resigned. His demise smoothed the way for a leftist takeover by Béla Kun, a Bolshevist sympathizer. During the spring and summer of 1919 squads of the "Red Terror" executed over five hundred conservative politicians and a refitted Hungarian army repulsed both the Czechs and the Rumanians in very bloody fighting. Aid from Russia failed to materialize that summer, however, as counterrevolutionary (i.e., anti-Bolshevik) forces temporarily won the upper hand in neighboring Ukraine. In August 1919 triumphant Rumanian units occupied Budapest and overthrew Kun. Now a "White Terror" began, perpetrated by the prewar elite of Hungary and its leader, Admiral Miklós Horthy. Two thousand heads rolled. Subsequent decrees eliminated voting for the young and the uneducated and forced peasants to cast ballots publicly, disenfranchising them for all intents and purposes.

In the Middle East, simultaneously, crises followed one another in rapid succession. The first signs of trouble came in March 1919 when widespread rioting occurred in Egypt after British authorities deported Saad Zaghlul, a popular nationalist. That same spring Amanullah Khan successfully challenged British rule in Afghanistan, and then proclaimed a jihad and invaded India. In December, furthermore, Mustafa Kemal, the hero of Gallipoli, held elections to a new Turkish Chamber of Deputies that promptly declared independence in defiance of secret wartime treaties, published by the Bolsheviks, which planned to split the Ottoman Empire into British, French, Italian, and Greek administrative areas and zones of influence. In early 1920 Kemal moved against French troops in southern Anatolia, one of France's promised spheres. Now the contagious unruliness ignited adjacent Syria, where Pan-Arab enthusiasts demanded creation of an Arab state encompassing present-day Syria, Lebanon, Israel, Jordan, and western Iraq, claiming, correctly, that British authorities had promised as much in 1915 in the hopes of undermining Ottoman rule. When moderate Arab leaders warned in January 1920 that the radical agenda meant war with France, the extremists replied curtly that "we are ready to declare war on both England and France."[41]

The Paris Settlement

The treaties ending the Great War received their names from the suburban Parisian palaces where the signing ceremonies took place. The first and most important, Versailles, imposed stiff terms on Germany in June 1919. The victors stripped the house that Bismarck built of its colonies, its high seas fleet, and much of its merchant marine. They reduced the army to a mere police force of one hundred thousand soldiers without airplanes, heavy artillery, or offensive weapons of any kind. The Rhineland would be occupied by the allies indefinitely with no German troops permitted on the west or east bank of the river. France regained Alsace and Lorraine, Belgium received Eupen and Malmédy, and Denmark took over part of Schleswig. Thanks mainly to support from France, the new republic in Warsaw got vast portions of former eastern Germany to establish a "Polish Corridor" to the sea. The petition of Germans living in border regions of Austria and Czechoslovakia that Wilson's principle of national self-determination be interpreted to allow their merger with Germany was denied on French insistence—Paris wanted a smaller, not a larger, Germany. France also insisted that Germany remain outside the League of Nations, whose charter was appended to the treaty. Furthermore, the allies held Berlin primarily responsible for the outbreak of war and imposed on the liable party reparations of an as yet undetermined amount.

Like most compromises, the treaty pleased no side. The minimum that leftist democrats in Germany could have accepted was a return to the *status quo ante* on the basis of Wilson's Fourteen Points, while even the most lenient settlement inflamed nationalist extremists because this still meant acceptance of German defeat. Great Britain disliked Versailles because its harsher provisions threatened European economic recovery and seemed to guarantee a war of revenge, perhaps in league with Moscow if the treaty drove suffering Germans into the arms of communism. In contrast, France viewed the defeated people as warlike by nature and argued, accordingly, that only a much more punitive treaty could enervate them sufficiently to prevent future aggression. Only after Britain and America made pledges of military assistance, in fact, did France drop its demand for separation of the Rhineland from Germany. The U.S. president clearly found much of Versailles hard to accept, but compromised in the knowledge that his League of Nations would surely correct the treaty's imperfections.

The allies dealt with the defunct Austro-Hungarian Empire in separate deals imposed on the successor states: the treaties of Saint Germain with the Republic of Austria in September 1919, and Trianon with the Republic of Hungary in June 1920. Like Germany, both had to accept disarmament, responsibility for the war, and reparations. These treaties also sanctioned post-armistice land-grabbing by Poland, Czechoslovakia, Rumania, and Yugoslavia that had come at the expense of Vienna and Budapest. With Britain looking the other way and America swallowing hard, France condoned this kind of claim-jumping in order to establish a cordon of states in Eastern Europe able to block future German aggression—with help from Paris, of course, which eventually negotiated military alliances with all four newcomers. While it is true that Eastern Europe's criss-crossing, patchwork jumble of different peoples made ethnic minorities inevitable wherever boundary lines were drawn—even Wilson admitted that implementation of national self-determination was much more complicated than he had initially realized—Saint Germain and Trianon nevertheless blatantly exacerbated Europe's age-old problems by isolating three million German-speaking Austrians in Czechoslovakia and three and a half million Hungarians in surrounding states. From the Baltic to the Adriatic and Aegean, in fact, ethnic minorities subjected to alien rule continued to be a problem (see Chapter 4). Wilson brought the Paris settlement more into line with his principles by insisting on interallied treaties committing the new states to constitutional guarantees of minority rights. He also pledged League of Nations protection for ethnic minorities, thereby augmenting the great hope that many Europeans already placed in the proposed new institution.

The remaining Central Powers received their treaties to sign in due course: Neuilly with Bulgaria in November 1919, and Sèvres with Turkey in August 1920. The former saddled Sofia with reparations, disarmament, and cession of territories with Bulgarian and Macedonian minorities to Yugoslavia and Greece. A worse fate awaited Turkey, which had to accept international control of Constantinople and the Straits; Greek administration of western Anatolia; independence for the Armenians; autonomy for the Kurds; French control of Syria and Lebanon; British control of Palestine, Jordan, and Iraq; and independence for Arabia. The treaty was made more palatable for Wilson by calling for a plebiscite in Greek Anatolia after five years, and "mandating" Britain and France, under League of Nations auspices, to prepare their Arab subjects for eventual independence.

By signing the liquidating Treaty of Sèvres, Ottoman rulers signed their own political death warrant, for the ambitious and charismatic Mustafa Kemal already questioned Ottoman legitimacy and favored a republic to resurrect the Turkish nation. By shackling that proud people the treaty virtually guaranteed further troubles. The same held true for the Arabs. Disturbances seemed inevitable, in fact, after British Foreign Minister Arthur Balfour promised Zionist leaders in 1917 that his government would favor a postwar Jewish homeland in Palestine, and then, in stark contrast to other ignored pledges, actually kept the commitment. "My personal hope is that the Jews will make good in Palestine and eventually found a Jewish state," he told Jewish dignitaries in early 1918, adding a year later that "Zionism . . . is rooted in age-old traditions, in present needs, in future hopes, of far profounder import than the desires and prejudices of the seven hundred thousand Arabs who now inhabit that ancient land." The arrangement satisfied the needs of both Britain, which would rule its Palestinian mandate indefinitely and thus provide extra security to the Suez Canal, and the Jews, whose leaders appreciated the interim need for British protection. To calls from diplomats in the Indian Office that Britain "[should] not for heaven's sake tell the [Muslim] what he ought to think," Balfour answered indifferently: "I am quite unable to see why heaven or any other power should object to our telling the [Muslim] what he ought to think."[42]

Finally, allied victors faced the dilemma of what to do about Russia. As the civil war intensified, pressures mounted from conservatives to strike a blow against Bolshevism and from labor unions and socialists to resist intervention. Among the Great Powers, France favored anti-communist action as punishment for deserting the allied cause in 1918 and later repudiating debts owed from foreign loans to tsarist Russia. Although Italy backed this position, Britain and America did not, preferring an end to the fratricidal violence and some kind of Russian representation in Paris. With no agreement on Russia, meanwhile, nearly two hundred thousand French, British, American, Canadian, and Japanese troops initially sent to Russia to aid against Germany turned against the Soviet regime by distributing money, weapons, ammunition, and supplies to anti-Bolshevik forces while allied navies blockaded coastlines held by the Red Army. In late January 1919 Wilson finally convinced his colleagues to invite all sides in the civil war to peace talks near the Black Sea, but leaders of the white armies refused and the Bolsheviks would only agree to negotiate if the West terminated its de facto intervention. In the course of 1919 domestic political pressure to "bring the boys home" and return to some kind of normalcy ended all talk of intervention. Thus almost by default the allies fell back on Wilson's initial preference for "letting [the Russians] work out their own salvation."[43]

The Fighting Runs Its Course

The Red Army quadrupled to three million men in 1919, expanding to five million in 1920. Against them fought three White armies led by disgruntled officers of the old imperial army aiming to restore "Great Russian" power and the rule of the propertied classes. General Nikolai Yudenich commanded a small contingent of fighters in the Baltic. A much greater army of one hundred thousand soldiers under Admiral Alexander Kolchak operated out of the Urals. The biggest threat to communist rule came from General Anton Denikin's somewhat larger army based in the lower Volga and Don River basins. Much better equipped and disciplined than the often rag-tag Red Army, the White armies almost won the war in 1919 as Yudenich advanced on Saint Petersburg, Kolchak approached the Volga, and Denikin overran the lower Volga, most of the Ukraine, and parts of central Russia. The Bolsheviks eventually prevailed, however, because of greater numbers, the failure of White generals to coordinate their offensives, and the reluctant support of many peasants whose dread of rumored White reestablishment of serfdom enabled them to tolerate, however grudgingly, the hated grain requisitioning practices of the Reds.

Ethnic animosities also played a major role. Bolshevik armies sweeping into the Ukraine in early 1919, for instance, treated peasants of Ukrainian descent like colonial vassals. The Reds also subjected Cossacks of the Don Basin to what has been described as "a war of genocide" aimed at "exterminating the rich Cossacks to the last man."[44] As Lenin's minions moved into the Urals, furthermore, they trampled upon the Tatars' and Bashkirs' Muslim traditions. Generals Denikin and Kolchak benefited from this blatant cultural arrogance when these peoples revolted against Moscow.

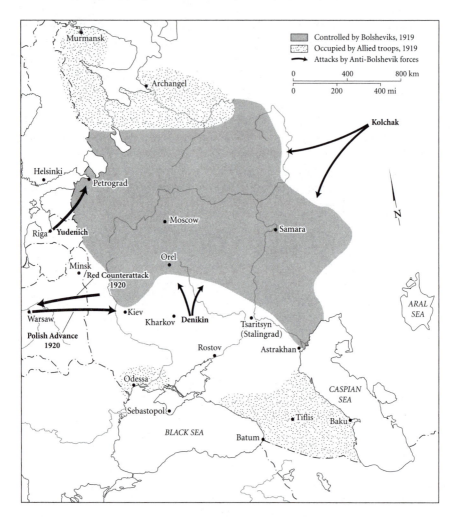

Fighting in Russia 1919–1920

White forces were even more chauvinistic than the Red Army, however, and therefore could not exploit their advantage. The aim of restoring Russian Great Power status blinded them to the tactical necessity of supporting the aspirations to statehood of ethnic groups that consequently either deserted the White cause or, in the case of the Cossacks, gave it only lukewarm support. Yudenich proved just as pigheaded, refusing to recognize the independence of Finland in 1919, an extremely shortsighted move, for Finnish leaders wanted to commit their divisions notwithstanding the Bolshevik threat of "merciless extermination"[45] of Finns if Helsinki intervened. Without diplomatic recognition, however, their hands were tied.

By early 1920 the main White armies had been defeated. Lenin and his henchmen had no time to celebrate, however, for Marshal Joseph Pilsudski's Polish army attacked that spring, advancing as far as Kiev in a bold campaign to restore "historic Poland." The Red Army counterattacked in June, and by August had driven all the way to Warsaw. Now the Poles struck back in their turn, pushing Soviet army groups into Byelorussia by September. Desperate and exhausted, the Reds sued for peace in October 1920, bringing to an end the civil war between the parts of the former Russian Empire.

The guns of the civil war and Polish conflagration probably killed as many people as the nearly two million tsarist soldiers shot dead in the Great War. Many hundreds of thousands died in combat or against the wall as prisoners, but "political" victims were far more numerous. Lenin's "Red Terror" and its sadistic security agency, the Cheka, took a comparable toll to the military casualties, and this sum was matched by psychopathic White executioners who murdered hostages and reputed Bolsheviks wherever their armies went. All sides singled out Jewish settlements for punishment, moreover, especially in the Ukraine. Fierce political warriors killed or severely wounded around three hundred thousand Jews in the worst pogroms on historical record. Incredibly, Russia's apocalypse was even worse than these figures indicate, for other mythic horsemen rode roughshod through the land. Typhus, influenza, smallpox, cholera, typhoid, and venereal diseases ravaged cities, villages, and armies without discrimination. And when war, political savagery, ethnic cleansing, and plague ran their course, famine struck in 1921. The death toll of the civil war years (1918–1921) may have topped a staggering ten million.[46]

American President Woodrow Wilson had preached in 1917 that his European crusade would be a "war to end all wars." Small wonder that many Americans came to agree with future president Herbert Hoover that they had been duped, for the bloodletting was apparently without end in a continent and surrounding regions where, at least to outsiders, it seemed "the genes of a thousand years of inbred hate and fear were in the blood."[47] Wilson had also claimed that the Great War would "make the world safe for democracy." But democracy had already flickered out in Hungary, and before that in Russia. Nor did Bolshevism appear to be weakening, despite the loss to Poland. On the contrary, the Red Army not only won the civil war, but also spread communist rule to Byelorussia in late 1918; the Ukraine, Armenia, and Azerbaijan in 1920; and Georgia in early 1921.

In Italy, too, government by the people did not appear that it would survive for long.[48] Combat veterans returned from the front in 1918–1919 to a series of disillusionments: unemployment after army demobilization, jeers from those who had opposed the war, and a seeming lack of respect from former allies abroad. Therefore, when Wilson insisted in the Treaty of Saint Germain that Austria cede Dalmatia to Yugoslavia, even though it had been promised to Italy in a secret wartime treaty, numerous veterans and other adventurers helped the flamboyant warrior-poet, Gabriele D' Annunzio, seize the port city of Fiume. They held it for a year until Italian naval vessels chased them out.

The parliamentary system had also gridlocked. Italy's second democratic elections in December 1919 threw together Social Democrats, Catholic populists, moderate liberals, radical nationalists, and other parties that agreed on nothing and, consequently, could find no governing formula. With legislators stymied, angry workers and peasants took law into their own hands, seizing factories and farms in an elemental outburst of revolutionary enthusiasm.

Unwilling to tolerate lawlessness and expropriation, property owners and local magnates turned to the *squadristi* for protection. Soon numbering in the hundreds, the fascist squads were typically led by tough ex-soldiers like those who wore the black shirts of the elite *arditti* shock troops. Many of them resented Italy's empty plate after the peace settlement and, like D'Annunzio, wanted to do something about this perceived national disgrace. In contrast to some veterans who merely longed for a semblance of the old normalcy, moreover, the fascist leaders and their tens of thousands of recruits had drunk deeply of the brutal way of life at the front. Now it spewed out at home. As 1920 turned to 1921, fascist squads won back the streets and country lanes from socialists, pro-Soviet communists, trade unionists, and peasant radicals. Over three thousand leftists and hundreds of *squadristi* fell in Italy's riotous civil war.

The political leader of the fascist movement, Benito Mussolini, sensed victory. A savvy politician and gifted orator who had begun his career on the extreme Left, Mussolini still harbored egalitarian ideas of rising up against established society. Because outspoken support for the war effort led to a break with the anti-war Socialists, however, he was forced to find a new political home. This Mussolini found among *squadristi* who knew much about breaking heads but little about the art of politics. Having risen to the top of the fascist movement by October 1922, the self-styled "Leader" (*Duce*) ordered twenty-five thousand of his black-shirted followers to encamp outside the capital. The legendary "March on Rome" succeeded where the free corps of Germany had failed, for an intimidated king appointed Mussolini prime minister even before the march began. The new premier would soon turn to the bloody business of eliminating political enemies and consolidating power (see Chapter 4).

With the Italian situation deteriorating and the Russian Civil War reaching its climax in 1920, Europe's position in the Middle East nearly fell apart. Pan-Arab rioting tinged with growing anti-Jewish sentiment swept British Palestine and Jordan, while the French faced a military threat in Syria that forced them to send a small army to Damascus to restore order. The British also faced a full-fledged uprising in Iraq led by former Ottoman officers who wanted at least a greater Arab state if they could no longer have the empire. Not until February 1921 was the revolt suppressed at a cost of two thousand British soldiers and perhaps five times as many Iraqis. The knowledge that London faced domestic political and fiscal pressures to bring soldiers home—indeed, troop strength had dropped from a million throughout the region to a third as much by 1921—emboldened pro-Arab, anti-colonial activists. Iranians under Reza Pahlavi took the cue too. Like Amanullah Khan in Afghanistan two years earlier, the military strongman seized power in February 1921 and forced the British out of oil-rich, strategically important Persia.

But worse was about to happen, for one month later Greece attacked Turkey, overrunning four hundred miles of Anatolia by the end of the summer. As the army advanced it perpetrated, according to a western observer, "a systematic plan of destruction of Turkish villages and extinction of the Muslim population."[49] In August 1922 the Turkish Republic, newly proclaimed by war hero Mustafa Kemal, counterattacked. The self-proclaimed "Father of the Turks" inflicted a terrible revenge on Greeks as he pushed their army back to Smyrna and into the sea. When the fighting and killing finally stopped, over a quarter of a million soldiers and civilians on both sides lay dead. Now Kemal faced down the British troops that Lloyd George had sent in 1920 to guard the Straits. Although the prime minister preferred to take a stand, the British people did not, and the boys came home.

These events forced a modification of the Middle Eastern postwar settlement in 1922–1923. At a conference in Lausanne, Switzerland, the allies made substantial concessions to Turkey, which regained eastern Thrace, won back partial control of the Straits, and was freed from about half of its foreign debt. Most importantly, Lausanne tacitly buried the wartime deals that had carved up Turkey among the victors. Elsewhere in the region the British recognized both their economic and strategic interests as well as the limits of their power by granting autonomy to Egypt, Jordan, and Iraq. Only Palestinian Arabs, chafing under a British administration that favored Jews for much of the Internar Period, continued to protest—with rioting in 1920–1921 and 1929, and then unleashing a more serious Intifada from 1936 to early 1939.

WAR'S EFFECTS ON MEN AND WOMEN

Europe's fighting continued until the Central Powers collapsed and postwar violence ran its course. Women did not stop this horrendous attrition. A few attempted to be peacemakers, and failed, but most women made no attempt to stay man's killing hands. Patriotism and ethnically charged emotions consumed both men and women in the Great War and its bloody aftermath.

Tactical issues were also involved. Most women supporting the war postponed suffrage reform efforts assuming that men would reward patriotism and service with female voting rights—and serve they did. In Britain, hundreds of thousands filled positions in local and national government and volunteered as auxiliaries in the army, navy, air force, and police corps and as doctors, nurses, and hospital orderlies. Others performed charitable work in private organizations. A million German women volunteered for nursing positions—at least ten times the number the army could actually fill. Additional tens of thousands inundated offices of the National Women's Service, a volunteer organization that fed the sick, housed refugees, helped war widows and their fatherless children, recruited women for the armaments industry, and supplemented city and town governments with volunteers. Many others donned army uniforms as auxiliaries behind the front. Large numbers of French women also served, entering the army as cooks, accountants, secretaries, and draftswomen or volunteering as nurses and nurses' aides. French feminists organized artistic and recreational programs in army hospitals, financed cantinas for soldiers on leave, and sent packages to POWs and soldiers at the front. Well-to-do women in Italy adopted similar auxiliary and voluntary roles. The one "certainty of the war," observed an Italian feminist in 1917, was that "women had undertaken a great integrative task."[50]

Working-class women also supported their countries' war efforts by filling workplaces vacated by men. Thus the female percentage of the labor force (including agriculture) increased from 24 to 38 in Britain, 32 to 40 in France, and 34 to 51 in Germany. Hidden in these figures, however, was a tremendous shift from domestic work and textiles to transport and other war-related sectors. In France, for instance, women employed by the state railways leaped tenfold, while numbers in the armaments industry skyrocketed more than forty-five-fold. The level of sacrifice can also be measured by the danger of manufacturing munitions. When a fire broke out in a German grenade factory in July 1918, for example, hundreds of women were killed or severely injured. All countries experienced these terrible industrial accidents.

And what did women earn for their service and sacrifice? In both contemporary accounts and recollections in interviews many decades later women stressed the liberating effects of the war: greater access to secondary and higher education, the freedom to work at a man's job, and the opportunity to enjoy leisure time less fettered by prudish prewar notions of domesticity—in short, women came "out of the cage."[51] The first wave of women's historians built on recollections of this sort to chart the beginnings of women's emancipation, including in some countries the right to vote. More recent scholarship, however, while recognizing that progressive forces had been set in motion by the war, stresses man's largely successful efforts to slam the cage shut again.[52] Such a "reconstruction" of gender order clearly took place, for example, in Italy, where returning soldiers chanting "down with women" and "women's jobs cause men's joblessness"[53] demanded that employers fire female employees. And the bosses listened, for most positions gained by Italian women during the war had been filled with men again by 1921. Meanwhile, legislation of 1919 blocked women from high-ranking public jobs and a 1920 ministerial decree invalidated all laws favoring women's employment. The consolation that women's suffrage would somehow reverse these setbacks faded as male leaders of political parties able to agree on little else refused to grant Italian females national voting rights, conceding only "nonpolitical" voting in local administrative elections. The story in France differed only slightly. The French Chamber of Deputies voted overwhelmingly for women's suffrage in 1919, but a slight majority of the Senate refused to consider the bill. Some senators feared the consequences of female majority rule after the deaths of nearly two million French men, while others assumed that matriarchy would undermine the republic when conservative Catholic women obeyed the Vatican.[54] Britain was no paragon of progress, of course, having introduced only half measures, and in both France and Britain returning soldiers took back their jobs, wiping out all employment gains of women by the early 1920s.

Clearly the Great War had generated a great deal of male hostility toward women—animosities that are not entirely or adequately explained by men's job anxieties and anti-suffrage emotions. Deeper underlying reasons must have caused Europe's gender crisis. Men had entered the war anticipating a great adventure, a quick and brutal reckoning followed by a triumphal return. After the grisly failure of the first offensives and the living nightmare of trench warfare made a cruel mockery of such notions, however, soldiers found themselves in a hellish world. The survivors of one decimated British unit, horrified by the sight of hundreds of fallen comrades, their "battered, mutilated bodies and blackened faces and hands" lying about "in distorted attitudes" felt "completely cut off from the world we had left behind us."[55] Thrust into a situation no one had imagined possible, many soldiers expressed resentment against younger brothers, fathers, and grandfathers who harbored naïve views of combat, but they also turned against the opposite sex—the women who had urged men to volunteer, it was said, for what now seemed certain death. A gap of understanding and empathy soon opened between females back home and male combatants, who complained that while they dug deeper into the earth to avoid a gruesome artillery death, women remained safe, dry, warm, and entirely free to enjoy civilian life. Thus one French infantryman received a letter from his mistress reporting that she had sprained an ankle while dancing. Imagine the clenched-fist misogyny welling up as he wondered within earshot of shell explosions: "With whom?" It was a layering of resentments, therefore, that exacerbated gender relations to the point of crisis. Men feared losing their power and their jobs as well as their women—of returning home from hell, writes Francoise Thébaud, "only to find themselves penniless cuckolds."[56] The fact that belligerent nations had mobilized sixty-eight million men underscores the Great War's potential to drive wedges between the sexes. France, for instance, mobilized over eight million, more than 70 percent of the nation's male population aged 18 to 40. Germany's eleven million represented well over 90 percent of the same cohort.

About 31 percent of European men who joined armies received wounds—more than 21 million males. This terrible combat and convalescence experience created a very special hospital relationship with the opposite sex. Sometimes seen as angels or heroines by male soldiers, the Great War's approximately half a million nurses represented a special category of women who were close enough to combat to know what men had endured. But even here, in the tender care of sacrificing and sensitive women knowledgeable about the reality of war, man's anger could fester, for now he was helpless and so obviously unable to conquer anything. A 1918 Red Cross poster, "The Greatest Mother in the World," featuring an oversized nurse cradling a doll-like, infantilized, emasculated casualty of war, illustrated well this relationship of inferiority. Because none of this humiliation and embarrassment could be hidden from the all-seeing nurses, some men directed their anger at the ones who saw. Poet D. H. Lawrence captured this sentiment in one verse of

Red Cross
Christmas
Roll Call
Dec. 16-23ʳᵈ

The
GREATEST MOTHER
in the WORLD

Man's helplessness: Red Cross poster, "The Greatest Mother in the World." (Imperial War Museum, London)

1915: "Why do the women follow us, satisfied/Feed on our wounds like bread, receive our blood/Like glittering seed upon them for fulfillment?"[57] There was a certain twisted logic to hating one's caretaker, in fact, for this woman sometimes nursed a man right back to the front, another horrendous wound, and the likelihood of death.

Indeed, men's anger at women found its most revealing expression in works of literature and art. Lawrence's wartime poem, "Tickets Please," is another good example. Fears of female employment and the boundless liberation it seemed to presage take extreme form as a group of the war's ubiquitous girl tram conductors performs a ritualistic bacchanalian rape of a hapless male inspector. The greater sexual freedom unleashed by the war did not mean, however, that women would perform their patriotic "duty" of repopulating the nation. Guillaume Apollinaire's 1917 play, *The Breasts of Tirésias,* spoofed this widespread fear on the French home front. Proclaiming "I am a feminist and do not recognize the authority of men," Thérèse refuses to have babies, transforms herself into a man, Tirésias, and goes to war. Her husband rises to the challenge by producing 40,049 offspring himself in one day. If woman "suddenly renounces prolific love," he asserts, "too bad, let men make [the babies]." Although rare, these war-induced, misogynous dreams of re-placing women did in fact occur. In Italy, for instance, Futurist F. T. Marinetti issued a manifesto advocating "multiplied man and the reign of the ma-chine,"[58] a world without women, while in Germany Ludendorff's chief ad-viser, Gustav Bauer, declared in 1917 that the war could be won if only there were "four million less women today" and a "million more men."[59]

German artist Otto Dix imagined a completely different threat from the reproductive patterns of women. In *Shellhole with Corpses* (1917) men who have sought refuge in Mother Earth are hurled violently out of her womb. Not only are mothers powerless to protect their sons from the horror of war, but also, as the soldier-producing side of humanity, they are responsible for it. One is reminded here of the "little mother" in Robert Graves's *Goodbye to All That* (1929), who declared that mothers should gladly "pass on the human am-munition" for the cause. "We will emerge [from the war] stronger women to carry on the glorious work [their] memories have handed down to us."[60] An-

Otto Dix, **Sexual Murder.**   (Otto Dix Stiftung, Vaduz/© 2004 Artists Rights Society (ARS), New York/VG Bild-Kunst Bonn)

other veteran of the fighting, German artist George Grosz, seemed to agree that women sacrificed men on the altar of war:

> Where have the nights gone? . . . Where are the women? [Where are the] adventures?—And our friends have been mutilated, dispersed, duped, bewitched and turned into gray uniformed butcher's boys!! . . . What a finale to this hell, to this brutal murdering on all sides—to this witch's Sabbath, to this horrifying castration.[61]

Grosz took a revenge of sorts with a shocking painting entitled *When It Was All Over, They Played Cards* (1917). Having mutilated a woman and stuffed her body parts into a crate, three men nonchalantly drink and deal. The same anesthetized indifference to death imposed on men in the trenches has been turned on women. Countryman Dix put his vengeful solution on canvas after the war in *Sexual Murder* (1922). A woman has been eviscerated by an intruder, but through the window one sees architectural order and symmetry symbolizing the reconstruction—through violence if necessary—of gender relations. Clearly Europe's Great War turned some men against the women in their lives, triggering a sort of postwar crackdown.

But how did women react to the experience of 1914–1918—and beyond? As memoir (and early historical) literature stressed, they certainly began to enjoy a wider range of social, economic, and educational freedoms together with the confident assurance that wartime work and service would procure voting rights. "It is the first hour in history for the women of the world," declared a women's trade union leader. "It is the woman's age."[62] The war "makes the blood course through the veins," wrote another women's advocate, because it "[compels] women to work," sending them "over the top . . . up the scaling ladder, and out into 'All Man's Land.' "[63] Initially some women could not get close enough to the firing, in fact, taking positions as motorcycle messengers, ambulance drivers, and nurses. "There is something about the sound of the first near gun of your first battle that, so far from being hateful or dreadful, will make you smile in spite of yourself with a kind of quiet exultation," wrote a British feminist. Another nurse admitted to being "obsessed by what may have been a kind of morbid curiosity."[64]

As the war dragged on, however, women's reactions began to change. Like many of her countrywomen, English suffragette Vera Brittain imbibed the martial mood of 1914, adopting army lingo in letters to her soldier fiancée, volunteering as a nurse's aide, and expressing eagerness to go to France. But by 1915 she had become embarrassed and angry that public opinion "made it a high and lofty virtue for us women to countenance the departure of [men like] you to regions where they will probably be slaughtered in a brutally degrading fashion." That this barbarity happened to one sex and not the other created a "barrier of indescribable experience between men and the women whom they loved" as well as "the possibility of a permanent impediment to understanding [between the sexes]."[65] As soldiers returned from the front, in fact, British women began to pay a price for their newfound social freedoms

The blurring of gender roles: nurse in gas mask.   (Getty Images)

and the gaping divide "of indescribable experience" between genders. "Murder, and brutal assault of women are of incessant occurrence," complained British suffragette Nina Boyle in 1916. "Men who have not gone to the trenches, and men who come back from them, vie with each other in this pleasing pastime." In 1919 an ugly wave of street violence swept the isles—much of it directed against women. And the ugliness did not soon dissipate. "The attitude of the public towards women," reported the *Daily News* in 1921, "is more full of contempt and bitterness than has been the case since the suffragette outbreaks [of 1913–1914]."[66]

It seems likely that male backlash of this sort contributed to the modification or abandonment of feminist goals in Britain during and after the war.[67] Before 1914 the WSPU and its allies had engaged in a sex war to force themselves into the arena of power. As the patriotic truce of 1914 gradually yielded to parliamentary discussions of women's suffrage in 1916, however, many suffragettes drew back from their goals. Thus Millicent Garrett Fawcett, president of the National Union of Women's Suffrage Societies, rationalized the sacrifice of voting rights for all women by arguing that "it might be fatal for us" not to compromise. "Such a course might very well bring the whole delicately balanced structure about our ears." Indeed, as Nina Boyles warned, male violence was already rising, and women shrank before it. We were "pursuing power," wrote another suffragette in 1917, but "saw how war spoke with a more powerful voice, and the women who had been snatching at power felt the quickening of a quite new spirit of humbleness." The brutality of the

Great War brought women "back to the primitive conception of the relative position of the two sexes. . . . Again man was the fighter."[68]

According to this argument, the experience of the war split the British women's movement of the postwar period between an "old" and a "new" feminism. The latter abandoned the cause of universal female suffrage and equality with men. It also placed greater emphasis on the complementary nature of male and female roles in society as well as the overriding national importance of women's reproductive function—the need for mothers to replace Britain's three-quarters of a million dead men. "New" feminists gave up the sex war, furthermore, in favor of efforts to calm men's anger, ameliorate gender relations, and reestablish social peace.

The war contributed to the transformation of the British women's movement in another significant way. For tens of thousands of single women who served as doctors, nurses, and hospital orderlies, relations with the opposite sex changed. The strictures of Victorian and Edwardian society had kept most of them ignorant of sexual relations or even male anatomy. Now the latter was exposed, but often in a hideous, or at the very least, damaged form. Nursing a man's body back to health, restoring it to its natural shape as much as possible, became a sort of innocent sexual act. Vera Brittain made explicit reference to this in her memoirs:

> From the constant handling of their lean, muscular bodies, I came to understand the essential cleanliness, the innate nobility, of sexual love on its physical side. Although there was much to shock in Army hospital service, much to terrify, much, even, to disgust, this day-by-day contact with the male anatomy was never part of the shame. . . . Short of actually going to bed with them, there was hardly an intimate service that I did not perform for one or another in the course of four years, and I still have reason to be thankful for the knowledge of masculine functioning which care of them gave me.[69]

Such hospital experiences, multiplied by the hundreds of thousands to include women who welcomed home and cared for their wounded spouses, created a reservoir of female sympathy for the tragic circumstances that had befallen men. Women felt the brunt of male anger after the war and knew they had to reduce men's provocation to anger, but now they also believed in woman's ability, indeed her charge, to maintain the fellowship gained with men during wartime in order to heal and replenish society in peacetime.

The combination of male anger at women and female fear and sympathy for men also helps to explain certain aspects of gender relations on the continent. According to German novelist Arnold Zweig, for example, the war "has brought us an upsurge of public and private male-manliness." Indeed, the country's "bloodied and enraged knighthood of men"[70] perpetrated a capital crime wave including sexual murders like those depicted by Otto Dix. On the other hand one finds the testimony of Marie-Elisabeth Lüders, a German civil administrator in occupied Belgium who also nursed behind the lines, which bears witness to the depth of feeling, the near guilt, in fact, that German women felt for their men:

Even though we pondered our loss and suffering, work and pain, deprivation and worry, even though we had to read the long death lists that brutally ripped apart ties of love and friendship, even though we did without the most necessary staples of life, were afraid for our children, and concerned about material things, we always felt the immeasurable essential difference between two realities: our everyday life here, and the fate-bedecked, blood-soaked field there. This other reality, whose traces lay on the faces of so many wounded, whose features we tried in vain to decipher, this reality that appeared so suddenly and strangely in our midst as if transformed from a new and completely unknown experience, impressed itself upon us at all times as that which it was: evidence of an alien existence, of a death and dying hidden from our eyes, evidence of a daily giving one's all, also for us. . . . As much as we pondered, worked, and worried, what was that compared to what was demanded of the millions of witnesses to that other cruel reality?! This world was silent on their lips because the soul dared not put it into words, and we did not ask, for in our short time together with them, death was not to have the last word.

Lüders states clearly, however, that the "silence" of Germany's convalescing and dying men could not be equated with guilt or, worse, male failure. For who would dare to accuse the nation's brave soldiers of this, especially given the naked fact that the greatest courage and will to victory will always fall victim to a brutal preponderance of men and materiel? Although Germany's men were defeated, "their courage loses nothing of its greatness; their suffering nothing of its hardship; their death nothing of its bitterness."[71]

In France and Italy after the armistice, male anger and female sympathy functioned similarly. Novelist Victor Margueritte's bestseller, *La Garconne* (1924), epitomized men's dislike of the wild new independent type of woman allegedly created by the war and the fervent desire to reconstruct gender order in traditional ways.[72] In both countries, however, men went a long way toward actually implementing the gender reconstruction agenda, removing women from their jobs, denying them voting rights, and accusing wives, sisters, and daughters of placing selfish female goals ahead of national rebuilding and repopulation. Those suffrage organizations that managed to survive the super-patriotic and hyperbolic masculine atmosphere of the war reacted defensively and cautiously to these charges. While they continued to advocate the franchise, and expected to receive it, Italian and French women's leaders admitted that their nations faced problems and challenges that had to be given higher priorities—especially the need to have babies. Their reaction blended prudence and sympathy, for any other response would have been provocative and, it was felt, unwomanly, after men had suffered and sacrificed so much in the Great War, that Calvary of men.

There were important differences from Britain, however, for France and Italy retained male voting monopolies, circumstances that reinforced the raison d'être of ongoing suffrage activism. In both countries, moreover, strong Catholic women's organizations began to campaign openly for votes after the Vatican amended its negative position on women's suffrage in 1919. By entering political arenas, it was said, women could protect the family and uphold morality, but a strong undercurrent of anti-Bolshevism mixed with these motives, for women were expected to vote more conservatively than men did.

Across the Rhine, too, the situation differed from Britain—in fact, it was far more complicated. Although angry men certainly committed atrocities against women, the pathetically weakened, emasculated, indeed *failed* man was far more common in Germany, where twice as many had been wounded—certainly more typical than guilt-ridden former nurses like Lüders could admit to themselves. "Had we returned home in 1916, out of the suffering and the strength of our experiences we might have unleashed a storm," lamented Erich Maria Remarque's most famous protagonist, Paul:

> Now if we go back we will be weary, broken, burnt out, rootless, and without hope. We will not be able to find our way any more. . . . We will be superfluous even to ourselves, we will grow older, a few will adapt themselves, some others will merely submit, and most will be bewildered—the years will pass by and in the end we shall fall into ruin.[73]

Other artists noticed the same "chronic inertia" and "widespread inner paralysis"[74] of German men after the war. This image appeared on screen in a string of postwar productions like *The Street* (1923) and *Sylvester* (1923) featuring male characters who tried life, were beaten by it, and returned anxious,

Man's defeat: still from film **The Street.** (Siegfried Kracauer, *From Caligari to Hitler: A Psychological History of the German Film* [Princeton, New Jersey, 1947])

insecure, and dejected to bury their heads in mother's bosom. German women also observed the sad postwar reality mirrored by this artistic imagery—a reality that contrasted sharply with their own anxious exhilaration as they prepared to exploit newly received voting rights. "When the iron wagon of history rolls over a people and the people stagger," wrote Else Hasse of the pro-republic Center Party, "then the bowed-down men look to women—the teachers of the coming generations."[75] Gertrud Bäumer, who moved from wartime service to a seat in the pro-republic German Democratic Party, advised female followers to learn about exercising power from the ancient sagas, for they recalled societies where "motherly authority" determined whether life should be sacrificed in war, but also had "to restore to order what men had disrupted and destroyed."[76] Her words reflected the man-made catastrophe of the Great War, but also her frustration with the fact that German men lay prostrate and helpless before the victors. Bäumer's former mentor and fellow Democrat, Helene Lange, similarly bemoaned "the terrible mess that men have made of the world." Lange's preferred solutions vacillated between some sort of Jean d' Arc matriarchy or, barring this ideal world, the rise of "strong men"[77] like Napoleon and Mussolini to set things straight.

The farther right into the German political spectrum one moved, in fact, the more women favored not a female takeover, but rather a revival of manhood. Thus Guida Diehl, a fervent nationalist and anti-Semite, encouraged women to appreciate "the historical transformation of your sex" created in wartime, but believed that only a resuscitation of masculinity would save Germany. In 1925 Diehl thought she had found the nation's savior: "And so the Leader stands before us: upright, honest, thorough-going, God-fearing, and heroic—the sort of Germanic man we women long for and demand in this our Fatherland's hour of direst need."[78] The young "Führer" was Adolf Hitler, "Leader" of Nazi Germany after 1933.

Chapter 4

▼

THE ILLUSION OF PEACE
AND DEMOCRACY

A squadron of bright red biplanes marked with the white cross of Switzerland buzzed over Lake Geneva. Almost summerlike warm weather and sunshine mocked the typical gray chill of late Genevese autumn. As the planes neared Mont Blanc Bridge their shadows raced over blue lake-top waters whose colors yielded quickly to the bright emerald hues of the Rhone River. The airman zoomed above the bridge and saluted the stately procession directly below them, then split into two formations, veering left and right over the dense, cheering crowds that lined the streets on either side. The marchers, walking to the sound of church bells ringing throughout the city, passed under multi-colored bunting and flags draped from windows and rooftops. Representing the city of Geneva, all the cantons of Switzerland, and delegations from forty-two nations of the world, they headed for the Salle de la Réformation.

Like the centuries-old, hurriedly renovated meeting hall, it was questionable whether the world was ready for the first session of the Assembly of the League of Nations. It was November 15, 1920. By this time, to be sure, the butchery of the Great War had widened and deepened antiwar sentiments that had existed for decades before the outbreak of hostilities. "We were journeying to Paris, not merely to liquidate the war, but to found a new order in Europe," recalled one of the League's British founders. "There was about us the halo of some divine mission."[1] The U.S. Senate, however, had twice rejected membership during the autumn and winter of 1919–1920. The blow fell hardest on the small nations of Europe that distrusted French and British commitment to League principles and had counted on Washington to check the old game of power politics. "It is not possible to speak of the League of Nations," wrote the *Zurich Post* as the delegations prepared to march in Geneva, "unless great and powerful America becomes a member."[2] Meanwhile, Europe festered as horrible wars, civil wars, and ethnic-cleansing campaigns dominated newspaper headlines.

Across the lake from the Salle de la Réformation another grand old building, the Hotel National, had been rapidly prepared for the world's gathering. The League purchased the two-hundred-room structure for 5.5 million francs that autumn. Scores of work crews were contracted to transform the hotel into the offices of the League of Nations Secretariat. Its head, Englishman Sir Eric Drummond, occupied his workspace on November 1, 1920. The League Council, the organization's steering committee, would meet around a large circular table in the hotel's glass-encased dining room. Drummond kept on the hotel director as League concierge as well as the hotel dog, a huge Saint Bernard, as League mascot. The latter decision seemed especially appropriate for a body crusading to save a world in dire need of a rescue.

The League of Nations 1919–1929

The term "League of Nations," unknown before 1914, had become current by 1915 when opponents of war founded a society of this name in Great Britain.[3] Simultaneously, a League to Enforce the Peace surfaced in the United States. Two years later Pope Benedict XV called for an international system of compulsory arbitration with punishment of violators, while France and Great Britain established parliamentary commissions to consider the exact form that such a league would take. President Woodrow Wilson joined the antiwar chorus in January 1918 with his seminal Fourteen Point address to Congress. He now became the spiritus rector of the League cause.

When the victor nations gathered in Paris in 1919, however, signs of trouble began to appear. France preferred to enforce the new world order with a league that wielded a standing army—or at least a general staff with strong national contingents at its disposal during crises. Initially leaning toward similar notions of automatic war against aggressors, Wilson eventually sided with the juridical preferences of Lord Robert Cecil, leader of the League movement in Britain, for mandatory arbitration of disputes—nonmartial options also favored by many American pacifists. Moreover, the United States and Great Britain, traditionally wary of standing armies at home, wanted to guard their sovereignty against an international army likely to be commanded by a Frenchman, Marshall Ferdinand Foch, allied supreme commander at war's end. Thus French wishes were sacrificed during the writing of the League Covenant for the legalistic approach favored by Wilson and the British. As opposed to the ad hoc, trouble-shooting favored by Cecil, however, the American president insisted on a permanent organization and staff capable of responding instantly to any crisis. He prevailed on this point.

In a prudent attempt to line up Senate support back home, Woodrow Wilson appended the document to the Treaty of Versailles imposed on defeated Germany. Voting against the League, he reckoned, would be less likely if it meant rejecting the treaty too. But the old congressional tactic failed to overcome a diehard Republican opposition that equated League membership with a loss of sovereignty. Wary of unwanted foreign obligations or, worse, League opposition to the Monroe Doctrine, the Senate rejected the treaty and the League. When Versailles went into effect in January 1920, the Covenant took effect too—but without the membership of the country whose president had pushed hardest for the League. America's empty chair on the League Coun-

A war to end all wars? Woodrow Wilson in Paris 1919.   (Library of Congress)

cil, which took up its work immediately, was flanked by those of permanent members Great Britain, France, Italy, and Japan, and the first set of rotating members: Belgium, Spain, Greece, and Brazil.

The absent American leader had nevertheless put his stamp on the organization. Arbitration, so much a part of prewar pacifism, remained the central solution. Members were pledged to bring international disputes before the League Council or the World Court for adjudication and not to resort to war while their cases were being heard—a maximum period of six months. A further three months after the rendering of arbitral decisions had to elapse before plaintiff nations could legally take up arms. The Council possessed the right to coax or coerce nonmember nations to accept the same obligations. Wilson believed fervently—he just knew, in fact—that the cooling off period guaranteed by the Covenant would eliminate the scourge of war. "Just a little exposure will settle most questions," he asserted confidently. "If the Central Powers had dared to discuss the whole purposes of this war for a single fortnight it never would have happened, and if, as should be, they were forced to discuss it for a year, war would never have been conceivable."[4] The champions of peace would depend primarily upon "the moral force of the public opinion of the world—the cleansing and clarifying and compelling influences of publicity—so that intrigues can no longer have their coverts, so that designs that are sinister can be drawn into the open, so that those things may be properly destroyed by the overwhelming light of the condemnation of the world." Wilson scoffed at the suggestion that rogue nations could successfully defy a world awakened by Europe's recent tragedy to the unacceptability of territorial aggression. Those that tried would "go down in disgrace."[5] That violence raked Europe from the Rhine to the Volga in early 1919 prompted no second thoughts in the mind of America's chief executive—in his thinking, these terrible events would have been prevented if a peacekeeping organization like the League had been in place.

Refusal to arbitrate or wait for a Council or World Court decision constituted an act of war against the League. Defiance of this sort triggered an immediate trade embargo, severance of financial ties, and an abrupt end to all personal contact. If necessary, the Council could also recommend military sanctions against an outlaw nation, suggesting which forces would be required from member armies. Decisions for war against aggressors had to be unanimous, however, exclusive of the parties to the dispute. Thus the League of Nations gave considerable protection to the sovereignty of member nations and did not, in the last instance, deny nations the right to wage war. However, the League shattered the centuries-old legal system that defended such violence as a natural and necessary occurrence. Indeed, the legal right of conquest—*ex factis jus oritur*—was abolished, for members pledged to respect the independence and territorial integrity of other member states. Even a punitive expedition by the League would not result in territory taken from the aggressor, thereby preventing the seeds of future wars from germinating.[6] The striking fact that forty-eight nations had signed the League Covenant by December 1920 accentuated the legal caesura marked by the birth of this novel organization.

Impressed in 1919 with his organization's potential for making a new departure in world history, League Secretary-General Sir Eric Drummond had his doubts by 1920 that the turning point could be reached and turned. His main fear was that the Covenant would be a mere scrap of paper after the disappointing votes in Washington. To an American colleague he expressed doubts that a League without the United States "would ever be an international instrument of really first class importance." The Englishman warned ex-President Wilson himself in 1921: "So long as great and powerful states remain outside, the League cannot, of course, be altogether what you and your collaborators at Paris intended to create." Later Drummond concluded that Washington's defection "left the League maimed at its inception."[7]

America's negative decision seemed to embolden cynics who assumed there would be an immediate return to the old rules. During the League's first year in existence (1920) Finland took the Aaland Islands from Sweden, League member Poland assaulted the Soviet Union and seized Vilnius from Lithuania, and League Council member Greece embarked on its land-grabbing expedition in Asia Minor. Council member Britain held its hand over Greece, eager for Athens to weaken Turkey's position in the region. Council member

France backed Poland, desperate for Warsaw to reproduce some of the security of the defunct Russian alliance. Not wanting to expend scarce League capital in a hopeless struggle with the Great Powers, Drummond largely ignored the Polish-Soviet and Greco-Turkish conflicts. Overextension and failure might lead to the embarrassment and bankruptcy of his organization. The mood in the Hotel National got darker as League staffers helplessly watched the Red Army march into Azerbaijan (April 1920), Ukraine (June 1920), Armenia (November 1920), and Georgia (February 1921). By this time it had become obvious that Wilson's "great wind of moral force moving through the world"[8] had become a breeze without America—and further, that the crosswinds and downdrafts of power politics and aggression, though now of dubious legality at best, still threatened.

The Great Powers and the League

The Franco-German problem caused the League additional worries, mainly because France did not feel that the Treaty of Versailles provided adequate guarantees of security. French apprehensiveness rose after the Anglo-American conception of the League of Nations prevailed over Paris's scheme for a collective security strike force. Pessimism deepened when Washington rejected the League and the treaty and began its retreat into isolationism, for America simultaneously withdrew the promise of military assistance Wilson and British Prime Minister David Lloyd George had given to France—the so-called Rhineland Pledge—which prompted Britain to renege as well. Only French vigilance and military might, it appeared, would guarantee the nation's security. German weakness served the same purpose, which explains French pressure to bleed the defeated nation through reparations. After two years of deliberations in London, an inter-allied reparations commission set the bill at 132 billion marks—a crushing amount over two and a half times Germany's prewar annual national income.

Thus League officials braced themselves for trouble. It came in March 1921 when France and Britain crossed the Rhine to occupy Düsseldorf and other Ruhr towns as a sanction against German attempts to lower reparations payments. Berlin protested formally in Geneva that the invasion threatened European peace, but Drummond dropped the matter when no member of the League Council would discuss Germany's petition. Once again League prudence won out over valor. "Was the League, in spite of the Assembly, no more than a tool of the Allied Powers, unable to do anything to save the world from the fatal effects of French intransigence and British opportunism?" asked League historian F. P. Walters.[9]

Prospects for improved Franco-German relations brightened in early 1922. That April a special conference convened in Genoa with the goal of greater political and economic cooperation among the Great Powers. The gathering owed a great deal to Lloyd George. The fiery Welshman believed that America, Germany, and Soviet Russia had to be economically reintegrated with Europe, and that such arrangements would smooth the way for their entry into the League, thus greatly strengthening it and enhancing the possibilities for world peace. The Great War, however, had erected huge barriers to economic recovery. During the hostilities Great Britain, France, and Italy borrowed 9.5 billion dollars from U.S. creditors who now asked for repayment. France and Italy owed British lenders 8.7 billion, and France expected nearly 2 billion from Moscow—even though the Soviets had renounced all responsibility for "capitalist" IOUs. Inter-allied indebtedness increased demands for prompt reparations payments from Germany, for Paris was supposed to receive about 16 billion dollars and London 9 billion. It seemed unlikely, however, that Germany could afford these sums—and certainly Berlin could not simultaneously pay reparations and rebuild a prosperous economy. Lloyd George hoped to reverse this vicious cycle by canceling all war debts and lightening Germany's burden of indemnities. These agreements would pave the way for the freer flow of credit and investments Europe needed to reconstruct its tattered economies.

As April 1922 approached, however, prospects dimmed. For one thing, the Americans refused to consider cancellation of war debts or even to participate in such a conference. France snuffed out most of the remaining hopes. Raymond Poincaré, the new premier and former hawkish president, adamantly refused to place reparations reductions or cancellation of Russian debts on the agenda. The Genoa conference had failed before it began. Matters deteriorated further when the offended Germans and Soviets met secretly at nearby Rapallo to sign a treaty guaranteeing "most favored nation" trading rights. The two pariahs also roundly denounced reparations. The specter of Russia's masses joining hands with German technology and science in an apparent alliance—indeed, secret military cooperation soon began—left the western powers, especially France, nervous and edgy.

The French riposte came soon after Rapallo. Since 1921 the new German republic had dragged its feet on reparations: protesting the bill when first presented, then requesting a moratorium, finally trumpeting its intent to "fulfill" allied terms but in reality denouncing them altogether, as at Rapallo. With the Germans failing to make prompt payments in January 1923, the French, Belgian, and Italian members of the Reparations Commission voted against the lone dissenter, Great Britain, to punish Germany by occupying the entire Ruhr industrial region. Two French divisions, accompanied by Belgian and Italian technical units, occupied the area and began exacting reparations in kind from production. Berlin retaliated by ordering passive resistance, that is, refusal to work for enemy occupiers. As winter turned to spring, France had to increase troop levels to run industries. With tempers flaring on both sides, Drummond could do nothing, for all three occupying powers were Council members which refused, under any conditions, to discuss the matter.

League fortunes soon reached low ebb. Italian naval forces bombarded the Greek island of Corfu in August 1923, killing many civilians before landing troops. The action came ostensibly in retaliation for the assassination by unknown gunmen of Italian General Enrico Tellini near the Greek-Albanian border. Benito Mussolini had coveted the island, however, since coming to power in 1922. By taking it, the Italian dictator gave an early sign of the utter contempt he felt for notions like peaceful coexistence and collective security. Greece protested the seizure in Geneva, claiming its innocence in the Tellini matter and warning, correctly, that Italy's violation was a "rude test" of League trustworthiness. Sweden demanded "energetic steps"[10] to counteract the clear breach of the Covenant. But France, aware of the shaky legal basis of its own incursion into Germany, sided with Italy, while Britain, now ruled by the Conservative government of Stanley Baldwin, also acquiesced to Rome in order to maintain unity among Great War victors. So the powers arranged a "compromise" whereby Greece paid a sizeable indemnity to Italy for the death of Tellini in return for Italian withdrawal from Corfu.

Once again a horribly frustrated Drummond felt he could no nothing. But this time irreparable damage had occurred. The crisis had "done much to weaken both the moral authority of the Council and the general confidence that the precise obligations of the Covenant will be universally accepted and carried out," he wrote in September 1923. A powerful member had "refused to carry out its treaty obligations . . . and has succeeded in doing so with impunity, some might even say with an increase in prestige."[11] To Mussolini, in fact, the legal foundations of the new world order were meaningless. The Corfu and Ruhr crises, as well as other unfortunate events of the early 1920s, had demonstrated clearly and irrefutably the unenforceability of the Covenant without British and French—and American—backing.

Determined to reverse these adverse trends, champions of collective security presented an ambitious plan to the League General Assembly in September 1923. The so-called Draft Treaty of Mutual Assistance was the inspiration of Britain's Lord Cecil. He wanted to promote general disarmament by tightening the League's collective security apparatus. The Draft Treaty expanded the Council's authority by permitting it to determine if aggression had occurred, to name the guilty party and invoke sanctions, and to decide—not merely recommend—which member nations in the region afflicted by aggression should march behind Geneva's banner. To qualify for League protection, however, nations had to participate in disarmament plans.

France and an overwhelming majority of League members enthusiastically endorsed the Draft Treaty, but not Britain, Canada, and the Commonwealth. Baldwin's Labour Party successor, Ramsay MacDonald, worried that the treaty would embroil League members in conflicts with nonmembers like the Soviet Union and the United States. With an imperial presence on every continent, moreover, Britain might have to march in every League action. For these reasons London and the dominions rejected the treaty in July 1924. A similar initiative, the so-called Geneva Protocol for the Pacific Settlement of International Disputes, failed when MacDonald's government yielded to Austen Chamberlain and his cabinet of League-wary Conservatives in October 1924. With MacDonald's fall and the failure of the Protocol, Wilson's dream of an intergovernmental authority above individual nations seemed to have gone up in smoke.

Solutions to European and world peace would have to originate outside Geneva as sovereign national proposals. This began to happen in late 1923, in fact, as a worried American business community and a sympathetic Republican administration surveyed the shambles of Europe's economy. Reparations, war debt, and an upward-spiraling inflation, almost out of control, threatened ruin throughout the interdependent transatlantic financial world. Therefore a commission of American, British, and Belgian experts chaired by Chicago banker Charles Dawes began deliberations in January that produced a workable solution by spring. The so-called Dawes Plan won European-wide approval in August 1924.

The new arrangements considerably lightened the burden on Germany. The plan stipulated a two-year reparations moratorium with reduced payments for another two years, but made in German marks rather than hard-to-obtain gold and foreign currencies. A private American bank loan of two hundred million dollars facilitated German rebuilding and repaying. Equally significant, the Dawes Plan included peacekeeping provisions. An American agent-general now headed the Reparations Commission instead of the rapacious French, Belgians, and Italians. France also agreed to evacuate the Ruhr and submit future reparations disputes to binding arbitration. Furthermore, Paris would receive a sizeable—and greatly needed—American loan as soon as it regularized political relations with Berlin. Thus Germany received the help it needed to pay Europe's victors, the latter received the reparations they required to repay American bankers, and all sides enjoyed a marked easing of tensions.

The acceptance of the Dawes Plan would have been impossible without political changes in Paris. Raymond Poincaré lost the premiership in May 1924 to Edward Herriot, leader of a center-left electoral coalition that swept into office by lambasting the vindictiveness of the Ruhr invasion. This prolonged occupation had hurt France financially by weakening its economy and diplomatically by souring its relationship with Britain. Indeed, both the Baldwin and MacDonald governments regarded Poincaré's course as reckless and irresponsible. What good was a policy designed to enhance French security, asked moderates in Paris, if it drove away Britain, the last remaining ally of the Triple Entente? Herriot's foreign minister, Aristide Briand, was especially pragmatic about the need to restore Britain's goodwill, even if this meant better relations with Germany. A one-time colleague of the combative Poincaré, Briand soon blossomed into a major champion of internationalism—a decisive personality, in fact, in the unfolding Great Power reconciliation of the mid-1920s.

Other key players included British Prime Minister Austen Chamberlain, German Foreign Minister Gustav Stresemann, British Ambassador in Berlin Edgar D' Abernon, and the hardworking man behind the scenes, Eric Drummond. Chamberlain's cabinet colleagues remained skeptical about the League of Nations, but he appreciated its principles and agreed to limited experiments with collective security. Although the Geneva Protocol went too far in the direction of supranationalism for his tastes, he felt it should be possible to further the spirit of the Covenant by making special arrangements. Stresemann originally opposed the League, seeing it as an oppressive tool of the victors. The patriotic minister also knew the extent of nationalist disdain for the

League in Germany, especially among members of his own German People's Party. Somewhat like Briand, however, he felt the time had come in history to serve one's nation in nonviolent ways. Lobbied strongly by D' Abernon, who mainly wanted to split Germany from the Soviets, Stresemann adopted the "special arrangements" approach dear to the British. In February 1925 he proposed that France and Germany mutually guarantee their common border. It fell to the indefatigable Drummond to work Geneva back into the mix by persuading Berlin to join the League—and by coaxing Paris to drop its fervent opposition to German entry.

This personal diplomacy produced an important series of agreements signed in October 1925 at the Swiss resort town of Locarno. A so-called Rhineland Security Pact permanently recognized the Franco-German-Belgian border with further provisos for arbitration of all disputes between the three nations. The League Council would arrange arbitration procedures. Moreover, the three neighbors renounced use of force in all area disputes. Thus the Pact went a big step further than the Covenant, which still allowed for war after a cooling-off period. Geneva would decide in most cases when to engage arbitration mechanisms, but if "flagrant military violations"[12] occurred (i.e., involving movement of troops across frontiers) the Pact provided for automatic punitive action by the armies of Britain and Italy. France, skeptical about leaving decisions of such magnitude to the League Council, had insisted that sovereign nations make police commitments.

However, the fact that Germany received membership along with a permanent Council seat considerably strengthened the League. Thus Germany became the League's fifty-fifth member. Twenty-seven nations of Europe now belonged—the whole continent, in fact, including defeated Central Powers Germany, Austria, Hungary, and Bulgaria. The only exception in Europe proper was tiny Lichtenstein. To the East, the Soviet Union remained a suspicious outsider, as did Mustafa Kemal's Turkey.

Briand had hoped to secure guarantees from Stresemann on Germany's eastern borders. But the wily foreign minister refused to budge past the kinds of pledges and commitments contained in the weaker League Covenant. He could not recognize the permanency of the German-Czechoslovakian and German-Polish borders without incurring the wrath of nationalists who would never accept the loss of prewar territory to upstart Poland or abandon Germans living under Prague's rule. Stresemann signed arbitration treaties with his two eastern neighbors, but would not put in writing an oral renunciation of force he made at Locarno—thus staying within the bounds of a Covenant that permitted the use of force after a cooling-off period. Briand suffered further disappointment when Chamberlain refused to agree to police the eastern arbitration treaties. The prime minister made a clear distinction between France and Belgium, "on which, as our history shows, our national existence depends," and Eastern Europe, "for which no British government ever will or ever can risk the bones of a British grenadier."[13]

The Bismarckian turn of phrase with its eerie evocation of nineteenth-century national interest politics and its self-serving restriction of "collective" security to Western Europe did not augur well. France, in particular, realized that aggression in Eastern Europe remained a distinct possibility, and worse, that it might go unpunished. Indeed, how much security derived from Stresemann's word at a time when the angry demagoguery of German nationalists threatened to drown him out? France renewed its military alliances with Poland and Czechoslovakia in an attempt to compensate in some small way for the absence of a reliable law enforcement team. Causes for worry abounded, in fact, as the statesmen departed Locarno. How secure was the West, let alone the East, with a British Army in the midst of disarming to its traditional expeditionary force level? Furthermore, would the United States, the savior of Britain and France in the Great War, make a binding peacekeeping commitment in Europe? Finally, what did it mean to be "protected" by a fascist like Benito Mussolini?

The answer to this final question was not immediately obvious to contemporaries. After his appointment as premier in 1922 the populist demagogue served up a confusing mix of authoritarianism and traditional parliamentary practice, inviting fascists, liberals, social democrats, Catholic populists, and royalist officers into his cabinet but undemocratically threatening parliament that he would "make an armed camp of this house."[14] So great was the desire throughout the upper classes for law and order, however, that most non-Marxist factions saw Mussolini as the savior, not the corrupter, of democracy. Clearer signs of trouble began to appear in 1923. The Fascists replaced police and state administrators with their own supporters and forcefully disarmed the Royal Guard and the Blue Shirts, a rival paramilitary group, and then later that year passed the so-called Acerbo Law. This dubious piece of legislation granted two-thirds of parliamentary seats to the party or coalition winning the most votes (as long as their electoral total reached 25 percent). The bill hardly proved necessary, in fact, for Mussolini's fairly broad-based coalition slate captured 65 percent in April 1924 with the remainder split among seven bickering opposition parties. The ominous meaning of fascism had become more discernible, however, as Blackshirts unleashed violence against non-Fascists at polling places and, worse, appeared to be behind the post-election murder of Giacomo Matteotti, a moderate Socialist deputy. Mussolini responded to newspaper criticism and persistent opposition party jabs by abolishing freedom of the press and banning all parties except his own. "Italy wants peace and quiet and to get on with its work," said the Duce in January 1925. "I shall give it all these, if possible in love, but if necessary by force."[15] Could Europeans after Locarno afford to ignore the old wisdom that strongmen like Mussolini tended to give foreign nations the same treatment as the domestic opposition?

Publicly, however, no one questioned the achievement of Locarno. Indeed, Europe had taken great strides toward more peaceful relations. With the Great War finally over, a euphoric mood began to sweep through the continent, starting in one little Swiss town. "Old women knelt in the dust to cross themselves; church bells rang out over the lake; fireworks erupted in the evening sky; and the normally staid citizens of Locarno celebrated the advent of peace until daybreak."[16]

The Era of Locarno

Europe's leading statesmen returned home skeptical because too many loopholes existed in the League Covenant and the Locarno agreements to feel confident about the future of peace. Nor was it prudent to overlook the dangers of German nationalists, Italian fascists, or Russian communists, all of whom worshipped some form of violence. The resumption of disarmament efforts in Geneva offered little cause to rejoice. To be sure, the League launched its unprecedented Preparatory Commission for the World Disarmament Conference in May 1926. Most champions of peaceful alternatives to war assumed that the technological revolution of the late nineteenth century, and the great arms race it spawned, had been primarily responsible for the Great War. The Treaty of Versailles had drastically reduced German armaments as a first step, therefore, toward the general arms reduction that would supposedly guarantee the end of war. The Preparatory Commission urgently sought to facilitate this giant second step of universal disarmament—a task "now seriously undertaken for the first time in human history."[17] Non-League representatives from the United States—and later from the Soviet Union—joined the effort.

Talks in Geneva soon bogged down, however, over a series of irresolvable questions. Should the convention limit trained reserves as well as regular armies? Should it limit navies by classes of ships (e.g., battleships, cruisers, etc.) or total fleet tonnage? Should there be budget restrictions or merely full disclosure of expenditures? And how could the world guarantee actual disarmament with a reliable system of inspection? The Preparatory Commission adjourned for six months in April 1927 in order that the great military powers could negotiate an end to the impasse.

The extreme caution and suspicion that characterized the Geneva deliberations reflected the insecure nature of the peace. Although the fact that talks of this sort were being held underscored the tremendous degree of progress over prewar days, nations still doubted whether the League and Locarno offered a form of international collective security superior to the ancient means of national security—and in the absence of the former, said the French repeatedly, no nation could dispense with the latter. For all the emotion invested in disarmament at Geneva, in fact, champions of peace had not overlooked the need for a workable system of collective security as a prerequisite for disarmament.

This awareness explains the feverish work in Geneva to improve collective security. The League session that opened in October 1927 passed a resolution introduced by Poland condemning war and calling for peaceful settlement of all disputes. That year the Assembly also instructed the Preparatory Commission to establish a parallel Arbitration and Security Committee. This body produced a set of nine "Model Treaties" approved during the 1928 session. One subset of treaty drafts was designed for small groups of nations wanting to emulate Locarno by signing arbitration and mutual assistance pacts. The other drafts were universal calls for pacific settlement of all conflicts, whether by compulsory arbitration, judicial action, or conciliation. The latter model treaties, like the Polish resolution, went beyond the Covenant to renounce war as a means of national policy. The 1928 Assembly marked the culmination of efforts to fill Covenant loopholes in order to ensure "first, that all disputes without exception should be submitted to peaceful processes of settlement; secondly, that any state which rejected such peaceful processes and resorted to war should be declared an aggressor; and thirdly, that any victim of aggression should be assured of automatic, swift, and effective assistance from the rest of the world."[18]

The famous—and later much-maligned—Kellogg-Briand Pact of August 1928 reinforced these efforts—and enhanced the chance of converting them into international legal reality. French Foreign Minister Aristide Briand remained dissatisfied with the accomplishments of Locarno. His general unease grew in April 1927 when Mussolini, one of the guarantors of Locarno, signed a friendship pact with Hungary, and then proceeded to violate the Treaty of Trianon by shipping arms to Budapest. So Briand attempted to lure Washington into France's security orbit with a bilateral non-aggression pact that he hoped would appeal to the American peace movement. Wanting to shield the Republican administration from isolationist backlash, Secretary of State Frank Kellogg delivered a clever riposte by floating the notion of a multilateral treaty renouncing war. Signed by fifty-five nations, the resultant Kellogg-Briand Pact was modeled closely on the 1927 Polish resolution. Although hedged about by declarations that nations still possessed the right to defend themselves— indeed, to decide unilaterally when recourse to defensive warfare was necessary, even if it meant defending one's colonial or overseas interests—the pact greatly reinforced the pacifist spirit which the League's own simultaneous efforts gave more concrete substance.

The election of Herbert Hoover in November 1928 lent further momentum to the cause of peace, for the new American president announced that he supported disarmament. Specifically, the United States would support compromise positions on army and navy reductions reached secretly by France and Britain the previous summer. Hoover's statement paved the way for Great Power negotiations in London over naval strengths during the fall of 1929. Although members of the Preparatory Commission criticized sidetracking the League in this way, realists knew that no progress on disarmament was possible without Great Power willingness to proceed.

As the 1920s drew to a close another happening reinforced the contemporary impression of the dawning of a more pacific era. On the occasion of the Tenth Assembly of the League of Nations in September 1929 Aristide Briand stated that it was time for the nations of Europe to form a closer federal union. At a private gathering of all continental delegations a few days later Europe's most tenaciously realistic champion of peace asked that each country give serious consideration to his idea, and that he be charged with the task of drawing up a plan before the next Assembly in 1930. The delegations agreed, but respectfully and prudently made no commitments—with one notable exception. German Foreign Minister Gustav Stresemann said that Germany welcomed further discussion of a promising idea, alluding to the nineteenth-century customs union that had preceded the political unification of Germany.

A world peacekeeping organization, binding international arbitration agreements, Great Power guarantees to punish aggressors, multilateral pacts renouncing wars of aggression, unprecedented Great Power willingness to discuss arms reductions, and a United States of Europe: Were these not the outlines of a new pacific world order? To optimists it seemed that only time was required for these seeds to bear fruit.

CULTURAL BELLWETHERS

Thomas Messer, former director of the Guggenheim museum in New York City, observed that "one of the most interesting aspects of the artists is to have antennae that sense somehow the end of an order before it occurs externally."[19] If that were true for the prewar period, what about the postwar years? Can culture, both of the elite and mass variety, tell us anything meaningful about Europe's course in the 1920s?[20] From what follows it seems clear that culture emanated pessimism in the turbulent aftermath of war, especially when the bloodshed did not end for years after the armistice. "Doubt and disorder are in us and with us," said French poet and critic Paul Valéry in 1922. "There is no thinking man, however shrewd or learned he may be, who can hope to dominate this anxiety." The "cruelly wounded mind" of Europe helps to explain the frenzied nature of much postwar culture, but its self-righteous exhilaration and excitement also stemmed from a realization that prewar modernists had been correct to criticize mainstream culture, an awareness that now led them further down the path of experimentation and innovation. This underlying mood of apprehension may have affected popular culture too, for its hedonistic preoccupation with entertainment probably contained an element of escapism. Culture began to emit a more tempered pessimism only as the settled times of mid-decade drew on, eventually yielding to a guarded optimism at the end of the 1920s. This found affirmation in literature, philosophy, psychology, music, and architecture—even in flying, the "extreme sport" of the time. Thus Charles Lindbergh's wildly celebrated solo flight across the Atlantic in 1927 reminded a Europe which still sought recovery from the deaths of the Great War that man, although alone in the modern world, could still manage to get by. "You are one of these men," said the cautiously sanguine president of the Paris Municipal Council, "whose examples will preserve humanity if it is ever tempted to doubt its greatness and despair of its future."[21]

The Cultural Aftermath

When the League of Nations opened its doors in 1920 few in the world of art and culture gave its rescue mission much of a chance. Indeed, the slaughter of the Great War and its immediate aftermath produced profound pessimism and deep despair. In the most extreme case, "Dada," this bleak mood festered and metamorphosed into a nihilistic backlash. The movement's odd name seems to have been chosen for its similarity to a baby's babbling, and to leading proponents like Rumanian Tristan Tzara and Frenchman Marcel Duchamp the world, too, made no sense. The means adopted to expose this truth were bizarre poems, abstruse paintings, meaningless collages of newspaper scraps and rubbish, or "ready-made" art like Duchamp's outrageous exhibit of a porcelain urinal. In one performance Tzara walked on stage, shaved himself, then exited—the show was over. "As far as Dada goes," he wrote, it is odorless, it means nothing, absolutely nothing."

> Dada is your hopes [Tzara continued]: it is nothing. It is your paradise: it is nothing. It is your idol: it is nothing. It is your political leader: it is nothing. It is like your heroes: it is nothing. It is like your artists: it is nothing. It is like your religion: it is nothing.[22]

Dada's systematized nonsense was briefly chic in the immediate postwar period because it held a mirror to the irrationality and absurdity of Europe's self-destruction.

Dada soon yielded to a related cultural phenomenon. As described by its founder, French poet André Breton, "surrealism" consisted in "going out into the street with a revolver in each hand, and firing as much as possible at random into the crowd." This was his slightly tongue-in-cheek way of stating the movement's Freudian aim of expressing subconscious urges without allowing superego's reason to disrupt their essence. They wanted, in other words, to unleash psychological forces thus far dammed up by civilization. Surrealism would influence many of the great artists of the 1920s like poet T. S. Eliot, painter Salvador Dali, and novelists James Joyce and Virginia Woolf. Its manifesto praised "the dream; the subconscious; love, freed from all moral or social fetters; revolutionary fervor; flamboyant atheism."[23]

The music of Alban Berg contained similarly defiant themes as well as a revolutionary sound that echoed Europe's troubles. Berg's mentor, Viennese composer Arnold Schoenberg, had followed Lizst, Wagner, and Strauss into the world of atonality before 1914, but his full "emancipation of dissonance"[24] was not completed until after the war when he developed a chromatic scale that reshuffled all twelve notes into different sequences and patterns. Schoenberg's disciple employed this novel twelve-tone technique in *Wozzeck* (1922), the haunting story of a soldier who, like Berg, himself a veteran of the Great War, feels "chained, sick, captive, resigned, in fact humiliated." His wife's betrayal eventually drives Wozzeck to murder and suicide, but not before vowing that if he and his fellow victims in uniform ever get to heaven they would set to work making thunder. "After Wozzeck's death," observes Peter Conrad, "his verbal motto is trumpeted forth in a symphonic interlude which, if played with proper force and intensity, should shake the earth's foundations . . . anticipating the day of wrath when society's outcasts will be vindicated."[25]

In T. S. Eliot's poem *The Waste Land* (1922), readers confront a different, far darker mood. The work moves surrealistically between two worlds: the contemporary London of bored office workers, lower-class bars, meaningless sexual encounters, rape, and trash floating in the Thames; and numerous other haunted wastelands drawn from medieval European legends and mystic eastern literature. Indeed, *The Waste Land* is nearly overloaded with literary allusions depicting the latter world—one critic, Edmund Wilson, counted more than thirty in the twenty-page work. Pervading the entire poem is a deep and dreary sense of all that was lost in the great conflagration:

> Unreal City,
> Under the brown fog of a winter dawn,
> A crowd flowed over London Bridge, so many,
> I had not thought death had undone so many.
> Sighs, short and infrequent, were exhaled,
> And each man fixed his eyes before his feet.
> Flowed up the hill and down King William Street,
> To where Saint Mary Woolnoth kept the hours
> With a dead sound on the final stroke of nine.
> There I saw one I knew, and stopped him, crying, "Stetson!"

The allusion to "Stetson," thought by some interpreters to symbolize a close friend who died off Galipoli in 1915, and the endless stream of the walking dead crossing to the inferno, anchor us squarely in the world of war's gruesome aftermath. Another bewildered, unpunctuated passage makes more direct allusions to martial destruction.

> What is that sound high in the air
> Murmur of maternal lamentation
> Who are those hooded hordes swarming
> Over endless plains, stumbling in cracked earth
> Ringed by the flat horizon only
> What is the city over the mountains
> Cracks and reforms and bursts in the violet air
> Falling towers
> Jerusalem Athens Alexandria
> Vienna London
> Unreal[26]

The Waste Land continues to find new and daring interpretations. Its meaning to contemporaries, however, was clear. "Sometimes we feel that he is speaking not only for a personal distress, but for the starvation of a whole civilization," wrote Wilson. Eliot's wasteland was "a place not merely of desolation, but of anarchy and doubt. In our postwar world of shattered illusions, strained nerves and bankrupt institutions, life no longer seems serious or coherent."[27]

On the continent many writers also looked despairingly into the future, seeing little earthly hope of escaping man's threatened existence. Thus German painter Paul Klee produced in *Angelus Novus* (1920) a machine-like winged angel who stares, mouth agape, at the recent past's human wreckage rapidly accumulating at his feet as he is blown backwards into the future.

"The angel would like to stay, awaken the dead, and make whole what has been smashed," observed the owner of the painting, "but a storm is blowing from paradise; it has caught in his wings with such violence that the angel can no longer close them." At the same time Frenchman Paul Valéry was still "restless [and] uneasy, as if the storm were about to break. . . . We think of what has disappeared, and we are almost destroyed by what has been destroyed; we do not know what will be born, and we fear the future, not without reason." On stage in Luigi Pirandello's *Six Characters in Search of an Author*, similarly, audiences saw two sets of actors, the first a family devastated by domestic tragedy, the second a troupe whom the mourning clan beseeches to act out their drama. The two groups talk past one another, projecting two different versions of reality. "We think we understand one another," laments one frustrated family member, "but we never really do." Austrian author Franz Kafka also wrote about individuals who were hopelessly trapped in an alien world. *The Trial* describes a doomed defendant who has forgotten his crime and never confronts prosecutor or judge, while *The Castle*'s protagonist is hired as a surveyor but fails to gain access to the castle that houses his employer. Both heroes are helpless and confused, the victims of unknown and inexplicable societal imperatives. Marcel Proust's magnum opus, *Remembrance of Things Past*, conveyed the same melancholy, futile pathos. Although the first volume had gone largely unnoticed in 1913, the second caused a sensation and won France's most prestigious literary award in 1919. "We are always feeling with Proust as if we were reading about the end of something," commented Edmund Wilson. "Not only do his hero and most of his other characters pass into mortal declines, but their world itself seems to be coming to an end."[28]

The turbulent, chaotic half-decade after the armistice and the peace treaties also witnessed the appearance of two of the century's most influential and widely studied novels. The first, *Ulysses*, by Irish surrealist James Joyce, was banned as obscene in England, only showing up on Parisian book shelves in 1922. Joyce had been at work on this unusual book since the beginning of the war. The second, Thomas Mann's *The Magic Mountain*, came out in 1924. The German author had first put pen to paper before the war, but then set the project aside. After 1919, however, it consumed him. With these two monumental works the most perceptive readers could begin to find some hope that the world would somehow return to stability.

Ulysses tells the story of one day in the life of an average man in Dublin. Bloom, Joyce's atypical hero, seems to epitomize the sheer banality of human existence as he wanders aimlessly through the city's maze of streets and pubs in 1904—apparently a cruel parody of Homer's hero returning circuitously from Troy. But more is at work here, for the gifted author's unorthodox grammatical presentation also serves as a mirror to the fragmented, disjointed world around him. Employing an unconventional style that disturbed and provoked many readers, Joyce wove complex wordplay, fragments of foreign languages, obscure historical allusions, bits of recollection, and surrealistic fantasy into over seven hundred pages of sometimes incomprehensible and bewildering stream of consciousness. At one point in the odyssey, for example, readers stumble upon the lair of Aeolus, Greek god of the winds, but find it in a newspaper office whose press, in stamping type on paper, seems "almost human" as if "doing its level best to speak." *Ulysses*, said Wilson, was the "prose equivalent of *The Waste Land.*"[29] Eliot himself, however, was more taken with Joyce's anchoring of modern Dublin in historical myth and allusion, for this "continuous parallel between contemporaneity and antiquity . . . is simply a way of controlling, or ordering, of giving shape and a significance to the immense panorama of futility and anarchy which is contemporary history."[30] Eliot drew an explicit connection between this literary method and prewar modernists like William Butler Yeats who sought comfort in the knowledge that history moves in cycles, and that man will once again enjoy a golden age. Thus Eliot the pessimist may have found a profound message of hope in *Ulysses*.

Most experts consider *The Magic Mountain* Mann's best work; some go further, asserting that it "is one of the very few great novels this century has produced."[31] The story begins innocently with an aspiring engineer from Hamburg, Hans Castorp, traveling to a sanatorium in Davos, high in the Swiss Alps, to visit an ailing cousin, Joachim Ziemssen. This aspiring artillery officer picks up his relative at the train station, and the narrative begins to unwind. It does so slowly at first as Mann describes each hour at this strange place of healing in minute detail, but more quickly as the tale accelerates, skipping over days, weeks, months, seasons—and eventually even longer unspecified periods of time to its terminus in 1914, seven years and one thousand pages later. The length and manipulation of the narrative affect a sense of time passing. Readers feel nostalgia for a fictional past that was once their reading present, and sympathy for a hero who once lived, learned, and dreamed between these pages, for Castorp enlists in the German army and perishes in the novel's brief final passage.

It is important to remember that Mann wrote *The Magic Mountain* during Europe's postwar years of mourning and intended it to serve—as all art serves—as a cultural bridge of understanding over life's perplexities. The grisly but psychologically necessary process of burying the dead had not been completed in the early 1920s; those not fortunate enough to find bodies turned by the hundreds of thousands to séances and mediums for some "contact" with loved ones and a semblance of closure. This background helps to explain the novel's fixation with death and dying. It is no coincidence that the story is set in a sanatorium where patients must cope with the death of others as well as the prospect of their own passing. "Guests" consider it taboo to discuss the topic, a form of denial that the house management respects by removing the deceased as discreetly as possible. Castorp rejects the callousness of ignoring the topic of death, which he sees as a lack of respect for the dying, by sending flowers to "moribund" cases, and eventually visiting them. There is a tendency at the sanatorium, moreover, to engage in modish flights of fancy: stamp collecting, amateur photography, gambling, and wild partying—a phenomenon one of the novel's main characters, the Italian humanist Lodovico Settembrini,

Unknown soldiers, unburied soldiers: German war remains in France circa 1920.   (Library of Congress)

recognizes as a form of "self-narcosis" that nature provides to paralyze and banish fear at the time of death.

Mann's greatest work is a Bildungsroman, a novel that tracks the protagonist's personal growth. Castorp's intellectual maturation occurs in a magical mountaintop airiness that enhances and magnifies his otherwise limited potential to learn. The most important part of his learning process—and the novel's climactic development—is the pedagogical struggle between Settembrini and the sinister Leo Naphta for Castorp's allegiance. Whereas the good Italian believes in rationality, research, peace, and the inevitability of human progress and perfectibility, Naphta scoffs at all of this. A Jew who converts to Catholicism, the maverick Jesuit preaches a frightening brand of revolutionary Christian Bolshevism. His ideology points longingly to a new dark age of bloodshed and obedience to absolute rulers. Castorp vacillates between the two teachings before achieving nobler insights during a dream while lost, and near death, high up the freezing mountain. The full panorama of human nature opens before him: its absolute best and worst, all its virtues and vices. He sees a courteous, respectful, reasonable, loving community of men and women on a classical Mediterranean seashore, but behind it, in a Doric Spartan temple, witches devour a baby. Death is ever present to the wary seaside humanists, but they carry on with unbending, stoic resolve. "For the sake of goodness and love," Castorp says in his frigid, dreamy state, "man shall grant death no dominion over his thoughts."[32] He vows never to forget these lofty insights to man's plight and salvation, but, within hours after he descends, forgets a dream that apparently even the mountain's magic cannot cement in his consciousness.

The Magic Mountain is also an allegorical novel. At this higher level Mann condemns the ideas and institutions of prewar Europe and rejects them as prescriptions for the future. The central characters, like most of the sanatorium's patients, are decaying on the inside—they are something that is dying on Europe's mountain. As the allegory ends, poor Hans Castorp, who stands for the average person, is swept up in the artillery barrage of Europe's sickness. He has forgotten his dream, but goes into battle singing a morbid song of love welling up from somewhere in his subconscious:

> Farewell Hans! [says the narrator]. . . . There were moments when . . . you saw the intimation of a dream of love rising up out of death and the carnal body. And out of this worldwide festival of death, this ugly rutting fever that inflames the rainy evening sky all round—will love someday rise up out of this, too?[33]

It seemed to be a guarded message of hope. This, at least, is how *The Magic Mountain* struck poet Hugo von Hoffmannsthal, who praised the author for confronting the desperate problems of the day as if Mann were steadied somehow by the beauty in Castorp's dream. "What is primarily admirable," he wrote in 1926, "[is] the courage with which the "I" in this book leans far out over the abyss, over chaos, and without getting dizzy."[34]

With its adoption of traditional literary forms, its preoccupation with death and dying, as well as its redemptive overtones, *The Magic Mountain* serves as a bridge to the distinctly non-modernistic postwar culture of mourning and commemoration that has begun to interest historians. In contrast to researchers who discuss only the expansion of modernism from its narrower prewar base, recent investigations have shifted the limelight to the catharsis and healing that traditional rituals and symbols offered to the grief-stricken. These studies look at Europe's religious revival with its consoling commiseration with the passion and suffering of Christ, the sprouting of war memorials and the "laying on of hands" at dedication ceremonies and armistice anniversary gatherings, the focus in film, art, and litertaure on religious themes like the apocalypse and the resurrection of the dead—especially the ghostly return of the slain—and the immense attraction of séances with their promise of hearing soothing words from deceased loved ones taken by the war. "Irony's cutting edge—the savage wit of Dada or surrealism, for example—could express anger and despair, and did so in enduring ways," observes one historian, "but it could not heal." Europe's reliance on older modes of expression to mediate grief is important to keep in mind, for just as modernism represented a first break from dominant conventional cultures before the war, so too after 1918 modernism, for all its deepening significance, was still not the language of loss for most people. We should also remember that in countries like France and Germany, which lost around three percent of their populations in the fighting, typically thirty or more mourners per dead soldier were left behind—grandparents, parents, siblings, cousins, close friends, a wife, and children. "The quasi-totality of the population, virtually an entire society," concludes one study, "formed a community of mourning."[35]

Anti-War and Pro-War Novels

Not long after *The Magic Mountain*'s appearance Europe entered the era of optimism and good feeling created by Locarno. One measure of the popular depth of these sentiments was the rise of the anti-war novel. During early postwar years many readers, still in a state of bereavement, preferred to escape from a horrible recent past. The grim process of mourning and burying loved ones—when bodies could be found at all—seemed to preclude a closer examination of machine combat. In Britain, for example, six novels with war themes appeared in 1922, but sold so poorly that publishers risked only three more in 1923 and a mere two in 1924. After mid-decade, however, a greater willingness to confront the gruesome reality of the Great War manifested itself: Twenty-one war novels were published in Britain between 1925 and 1927, jumping to thirty-five in 1928–1929, and thirty-six in 1930 alone. Works like Robert Graves's *Goodbye to All That* (1929) and *Her Privates We* (1930) omitted all mention of grand politics and concentrated on individual soldiers in the trenches, thus highlighting the meaninglessness, futility, and horror of death. The anti-hero who shrinks from or is victimized by martial tasks made his appearance. This literary phenomenon was clearly linked to a mourning process whose most healthy resolution required survivors to affect a "nonidealization" of the departed person and/or that person's cause.[36]

Erich Maria Remarque's *All Quiet on the Western Front* (1929) epitomized the great anti-war novels, bringing to print the same negative assessment of war that Otto Dix painted on canvas throughout the interwar years. The idealistic Paul Bäumer and his German schoolmates allow themselves to be talked into volunteering for war service by a blindly patriotic schoolmaster whose authority the adolescents trust in their hearts. Surely the teachers had "a greater insight and a more humane wisdom." The first death "shattered this belief," however, and the first bombardment "showed us our mistake, and under it the world as they had taught it to us broke in pieces."

> While they continued to write and talk, we saw the wounded and the dying. While they taught that duty to one's country is the greatest thing, we already knew that death-throes were stronger. . . . We loved our country as much as they . . . but also we distinguished the false from the true, we had suddenly learned to see.[37]

Bäumer's friends and comrades die one by one, and he is finally killed too in late October 1918, just days before the armistice. The book was an instant classic, selling a million copies in Germany and Britain in the first six months.

Not everyone who bought *All Quiet on the Western Front* agreed with its anti-war message, of course, especially in Germany where stridently competing voices were heard. Thus shock troop veteran Ernst Jünger turned out a string of very successful books that bowed to the gods of war: *Storm of Steel* (1920), *War as Inner Experience* (1922), *Fire and Blood* (1925), and *Total Mobilization* (1931). He wanted to spark a "faith in Folk and Fatherland that will flare up like a demon from all classes of society. . . . Everybody who feels differently must be branded with the mark of the heretic and exterminated." Similar nationalistic anger oozed from Ernst von Salomon's *The Outlaws* (1930). "If there is a power whose destruction it is our task to accomplish by any means," wrote Salomon, one of the assassins of German Foreign Minister Walther Rathenau in 1922, "it is the West and the German class that has allowed itself to be alienated by [the West]."[38] German literature's answer to the question of Europe's direction at decade's end was not, therefore, a clear and unmistakable verdict for pacifism.

Weimar Culture

The novels of Mann, Remarque, Jünger, and Salomon were a significant part of that complex and contradictory artistic phenomenon known as "Weimar culture."[39] Even in the category of the novel, however, these works represented only a subset of a remarkable literary flowering that included Franz Kafka's posthumously published *The Trial* (1925) and *The Castle* (1926), Hermann Hesse's *Steppenwolf* (1927), Alfred Döblin's *Berlin Alexanderplatz* (1929), and Robert Musil's *The Man Without Qualities* (1930), classic expressions of

A satiric look at the bourgeoisie: Georg Grosz's **Pillars of Society.** (Bildarchiv Preussischer Kulturbesitz/Art Resource, NY/© Estate of George Grosz/Licensed by VAGA, New York, NY)

doubt or despair for modern man's existential predicament. These novels can be grouped with Hans Grimm's lesser-known *Volk Ohne Raum* (1926), a fictional plea for racial "space" which one scholar dubs "the *Magic Mountain* of the [political] Right."[40] On canvas, similarly, Expressionist Georg Grosz continued in the vein of his shocking wartime caricatures, joining Otto Dix to brand the times uncertain, anxious, cynical, and cold. A whole genre of silent films, moreover, like *Joyless Street* (1925), *The Love of Jeanne Ney* (1927), and *Berlin: Symphony of a Big City* (1927), painted urban life as lonely, indifferent, and without vital energy. In contrast to prewar times when modernists had hammered away from the "outside" at traditional culture, these artists now assumed somewhat more of an "inside" position, for the Great War had discredited the old artistic and political orthodoxies with their confident rationalism, legitimating previously unacceptable but now credible insights and sensitivities to man's unconscious, subjective, irrational, and violent nature.

This is not to say that Weimar culture, like prewar European Modernism before it, was uniformly pessimistic about man's fate. As already noted, Mann's "I" leaned over the abyss without getting dizzy. One does not have to look very far, in fact, for similar kinds of sentiments. Thus Expressionist poets like J. R. Becher and Franz Pfemfert as well as popular novelists like Leonhard Frank and Rudolf Binding wrote about the goodness of men in search of God, while Expressionist stage ventures like Erwin Piscator's *Theater am Nollendorfplatz* in Berlin waxed optimistic in all kinds of innovative plays that sounded the gospel of leftist social revolution. Undoubtedly the most positive statement about Europe's direction in the 1920s came from the so-called Bauhaus school founded in the city of Weimar by the architect Walther Gropius. Believing that the accelerating urban/industrial era needed an architectural style distinct from the defunct classicism and ornamentation of a now discredited past, his team pioneered steel-framed buildings that featured low lines, open interiors, and copious use of glass paneling for walls. Like kindred spirits Frank Lloyd Wright in America and the Franco-Swiss Le Corbusier, they wanted a structure's function to guide its form. Gropius also attracted Expressionist painting talents like Paul Klee and Vassily Kandinsky to help create innovative designs for furniture, fixtures, utensils, and interior décor. They aimed to unite technology, art, and art-as-such into a functional, affordable urban architecture with progressive social vision. Designed to be appropriate for any urban setting, the cosmopolitan "international style" of the Bauhaus buildings in Dessau that Gropius constructed in 1924–1925 seemed to epitomize the contemporary spirit of Locarno.

The giants of continental philosophy also disagreed about what modern man could expect from his world. In March 1929, therefore, the organizers of "University Week" in Davos, Switzerland, the *Magic Mountain* site of Thomas Mann's fictional debate between humanism and authoritarianism, arranged for two of Europe's most prominent philosophers to thrash out their differences. Life's embodiment of Hans Castorp's humanitarian dream was Ernst Cassirer, rector of Hamburg University, while Naphta appeared in the guise of Martin Heidegger, professor at Freiburg University. The notion of their debating bordered on intellectual sadism, for philosophically the two stood poles apart, and Heidegger, some said, wanted to annihilate Cassirer's positions.

The Davos organizing committee had nevertheless chosen wisely. On the one side Cassirer espoused philosophies that positioned him in the moderate middle ground of his discipline.[41] Since before the war he and other modern disciples of Kant, the great eighteenth-century philosopher from Königsberg, had broken with the highly speculative metaphysics of nineteenth century idealistic philosophy to stress more empirical methods of investigating the nature and origins of knowledge. Cassirer's epistemology, however, did not go as far in the direction of empiricism as the highly scientific and mathematical "Vienna Circle" around Rudolf Carnap and Ludwig Wittgenstein, nor did he drift the other way toward more subjective Southwest German scholars like Heinrich Rickert and the fellow-traveling historian Wilhelm Dilthey, who gave somewhat more emphasis to the subtle, immeasurable complexities of feeling and life experience. Uniting the neo-Kantians and the analytical Vienna Circle, which spread to Cambridge University that year in the person of Wittgenstein, was the markedly positive and democratic politics that somehow flowed from their academic pursuits. Cassirer, for instance, had recently traced the intertwining roots of republicanism and peace to the philosophy of Kant.

On the other side of the Davos debate, Heidegger's philosophy represented a complex mix of Southwest German subjectivism, Nietzscheanism, and the kind of patriotic politics that equated Cassirer's defense of the Weimar Republic with defeatism. Catapulting Heidegger to prominence and controversy, *Being and Time* (1927), his first significant work, shone an uncomplimentary light on human existence. Most contemporaries lived in what he termed an "inauthentic state of being" that obscured life's nothingness, its terrifying contingency, its nonexistent alternatives to fear, despair, and especially, death.[42] More authentic, more genuine, more attuned to life's imperatives was a state of angst-like guilt about the bleak nature of human existence that made one receptive to a "call of conscience" that could prompt, in turn, the decisiveness and resolve to overcome the passive submission of the overwhelming majority of people to false realities. To what end such resolute decision making? This real-life Naphta positioned his potential "authentic state of being" between the past of the Folk, with its heroic legacy, and the future of the Folk, with its unavoidable "destiny." Falling back on his mentor of sorts, Friedrich Nietzsche, Heidegger would let "authentic existence"—the elite of those courageous and insightful few who lived it—"choose its hero."

Again one must ask, to what ultimate end? With his comments on the political drift of *Being and Time*, Richard Wolin provides an insightful response:

> 'A dominant race can grow up only out of terrible and violent beginnings,' observes Nietzsche. '*Where are the barbarians of the twentieth century?*' he goes on to declaim in an oft-cited remark [from *The Will to Power*]. That is: where are the 'modern pagans' who are no longer beholden to the decaying cultural paradigms of bourgeois Europe, and who are thus capable

of giving birth to a new set of heroic, life-affirming, *antinihilistic values*? Could it be that Heidegger poses precisely this Nietzschean question in the late 1920s?[43]

Heidegger's extremely pessimistic worldview clearly precluded notions of popular sovereignty and democracy. Indeed, *Being and Time* was inherently fascistic with its philosophical justification of an elitist leadership principle and its call for submission to a joyless world of sacrifice and death. Is it surprising, therefore, that the man from Freiburg avidly read the works of his friend and former storm trooper, Ernst Jünger, or that a few years later he would cement his sympathy for the Nazis by joining Hitler's party? Perhaps the only consolation for friends of humanity—a note of optimism, in fact—was the implicit admission in Heidegger's work that most people were unreceptive to his call for resolute "authentic" action.

No wonder University Week drew the rapt attention of the entire intellectual world during the hopeful spring of 1929. Cassirer and Heidegger gave a number of lectures to an impressive audience of invited international guests, but the week's climax was the debate between the two. Cassirer's *The Philosophy of Symbolic Forms* (1922) had optimistically trumpeted the historical assertion of the creative spirit of mankind. "Culture to him erects man's spacious dwelling, which is more easily destroyed than preserved against a barbarism that, as a permanent possibility, threatens man's culture," writes one scholar.[44] But Heidegger doubted whether it was philosophy's task to allow liberation from anxiety, preferring "to deliver man radically *to* anxiety." Cassirer would not have it, objecting that philosophy's objective should be liberational "in this sense: 'Cast out from yourselves the anxiety of the earthly!'" Heidegger, he accused, wanted to transform "the ground into an abyss." Not surprisingly, the dark spokesman who would liberate mankind for action waved off his accuser with a grand gesture of defiance. "Man exists at the peak of his own potentialities at only a very few moments,"[45] said Heidegger. The implication was obvious: This was such an "authentic" moment—and it was not a moment for peace.

Freud

A few months later, famed Viennese psychologist Sigmund Freud wrote *Civilizations and Its Discontents*. By now four decades of clinical practice, the appearance of numerous volumes on psychoanalysis, and the formulation and perfection of a remarkable body of theory on human behavior stood behind him.[46] In contrast to nineteenth-century assumptions about the mind—namely, that it processed sense experiences rationally, logically, and without inner conflict—Freud argued that mental processes were torn by unconscious urges and the perceived need to control them, an unstable dynamic rooted in a child's conflict-ridden interaction with parents, especially sons with fathers. In Freud's model, behavior emanated from a constant struggle between the mind's feuding parts: the instinctual, unconscious "id," which unleashed sexual, aggressive, pleasure-seeking impulses; the "superego," which induced moral values and societal norms; and the conscious "ego," which tried to mediate and control what a person ultimately did. Largely ignored outside the professional and art worlds before the war, Freud's emphasis on the irrational, precarious side of man caused an explosion of popular interest in his ideas after the great bloodletting of 1914–1918.

Although he did not intend it as such, *Civilization and Its Discontents* rendered a kind of arbitral judgment on the great debate at Davos. Venturing into social psychology, Freud wrote that mankind was profoundly unhappy because of its suppressed, unfulfilled urges, frustrations stemming from erotic desires condemned by society as perverted or immoral, like nongenital, extramarital, and homosexual sex. Even more threatening was man's basic aggressiveness, a constant in human history stretching from the earliest times to the "horrors of the recent World War." Anyone studying history, he wrote, "will have to bow humbly before the truth of this view." Against these innate sexual and violent drives civilization built its restraining wall of "guilt" cemented into the conscience of each individual in the form of the "superego." Thus civilization tried to obtain "mastery over the individual's dangerous desire for aggression by weakening and disarming it and by setting up an agency within him to watch over it, like a garrison in a conquered city."[47]

Despite these safeguards, human existence remained a struggle between "Eros," a force working for the unity of mankind, and love's opponent, "Death." To those arguing that peace and humanitarianism represented "trends which cannot be averted or turned aside" Freud offered little consolation, for he believed that those peaceful forces which many considered "insurmountable" had often been "thrown aside and replaced by other trends." The book's last paragraph finally struck a measured hopeful chord.

> The fateful question for the human species seems to me to be whether and to what extent their cultural development will succeed in mastering the disturbance of their communal life by the human instinct of aggression and self-destruction. It may be that in this respect precisely the present time deserves a special interest. Men have gained control over the forces of nature to such an extent that with their help they would have no difficulty in exterminating one another to the last man. They know this, and hence comes a large part of their current unrest, their unhappiness and their mood of anxiety. And now it is to be expected that the other of the two 'Heavenly Powers,' eternal Eros, will make an effort to assert himself in the struggle with his equally immortal adversary.

The reader gains the impression from Freud's final sentence that he expected the effort to succeed in 1929. Only as bleakness spread with economic collapse in 1931 did he add another sentence: "But who can foresee with what success and with what result?"[48]

Popular Culture

Are there indications from the pastime activity of average men and women that they suffered from Freud's "mood of anxiety"? Would they have agreed with Valéry that "doubt and disorder are in us"? In the absence of today's ubiquitous opinion polling no definitive answers are forthcoming, but on the surface, at least, one observes the opposite kind of behavior. Indeed, the 1920s witnessed a flowering of hectic and frenzied mass culture that would not be entirely snipped short by the Great Depression of the 1930s.[49] Take, for example, sport and recreation. Exploiting the West's increasingly common eight-hour workday and off-time on weekends, people cycled into the country, went hiking, and camped out in much greater numbers. Closer to home they learned to swim in municipal bath houses built by labor-oriented governments eager to provide voters with an experience previously reserved for the wealthy elite. Furthermore, as workers and white-collar employees across America and Northwestern Europe flocked to sporting events colossal stadiums were built to accommodate them: Ohio Stadium in provincial Columbus sat almost 90,000 football fans; Wembley Stadium in London held 126,000 for soccer; and Strahav Stadium in Prague, built for track and gymnastic meets, packed in an incredible 240,000. Berlin's indoor Sport Palace also held huge crowds, especially for the city's beloved bicycle races. Novelist Georg Kaiser brought the excitement of the sprint to the finish to life in *From Morn to Midnight* (1922):

> Look up, I say! It's there, among the crowd, that the magic works. Look at them—three tiers—one above the other—packed like sardines—excitement rages. . . . From boxes to gallery one seething flux, dissolving the individual, recreating passion! Differences melt away, veils are torn away; passion rules! The trumpets blare and the walls come tumbling down. No restraint, no modesty, no motherhood, no childhood—nothing but passion! There's the real thing. That's worth the search. That justifies the price.[50]

It is just possible that Heidegger was right, however, in viewing these "searches" for "recreating passion" as evidence of "inauthentic" existence papering over life's precariousness. Certainly one dominant trend of the postwar years was its driving determination to bury the dead, find some kind of closure, and return to normalcy whatever the odds against finding it. The hedonistic side of mass culture may well have been "a reaction to wartime tension and continuing insecurity," writes one preeminent social historian, "as people sought to escape their nagging fear that the world had gone wrong."[51]

Daily newspapers and frequent cinema visits emerged as other common features of postwar popular culture. Thus circulation for big city papers like the *Daily Express* and the *Petit Parisien* quadrupled and quintupled from prewar times as more than half of the adult population came to read one. Unlike the highbrow *Times* and *Le Temps*, however, the inexpensive mass dailies intentionally lured the man in the street with sports coverage, sensational serialized fiction, and gratuitous stories about heinous crimes, loose morals, and the bizarre. Movies, too, affected much greater numbers of people than before 1914 as the era of silent films came into its own. In both Britain and Germany weekly attendance soared above fifteen million, bringing about one-quarter of all adults into a theater once a week. Entrepreneurs responded by constructing the great movie palaces of the late 1920s, lavish emulations for the common man of the opulent opera houses that went up in earlier decades to entertain the rich and powerful. Similar to the big dailies, typical movie fare tended to be more sensationalist than Expressionist classics like *The Cabinet of Dr. Caligari* (1920), with its beautiful props and wrenching, unappealing choice viewers must make between tyranny and chaos. By the mid-1920s, in fact, more artistic films like this (and other German titles mentioned earlier) were yielding at the box office to whole blocks of American films that Hollywood rented in package deals to British and continental theater owners. Consequently, European audiences also grew fond of the frantic automobile chases of the Keystone Kops as well as the daring exploits and amorous adventures of film stars like Douglas Fairbanks, Rudolf Valentino, Mary Pickford, and Lillian Gish. The greatest movie star of the decade, however, was undoubtedly Charlie Chaplin, an Englishman transplanted in Hollywood whose delightful screen roles combined entertainment with great art. His endearing depictions of the lonely tramp in crumpled top hat seemed to appeal to a "lost generation" of Great War survivors yearning for "the gay spirit of laughter in a cruel, crazy world."[52]

The rapidly maturing second industrial revolution served up another form of popular entertainment and public information in the 1920s—the radio. Made possible by Guglielmo Marconi's invention of transatlantic wireless communication in 1901 and the advent of vacuum tubes in 1904, radio transmission technology advanced quickly with the wartime need to communicate quickly inside mass armies, and then found peacetime uses after the armistice. In June 1920, for example, a European-wide audience enjoyed a special radio performance of British soprano Nellie Melba sponsored by Lord Northcliffe of the mass-circulation *Daily Mail*. By this time private companies in Holland and the United States offered regular broadcasts of programs for entertainment. The British Broadcasting Corporation (BBC) came on the air in 1922 exclusively with newscasts, adding classical music and great plays to its repertoire in 1923, the first address by King George V in 1924, and light music, vaudeville acts, and sports shortly thereafter. The popularity of the new device sent sales skyrocketing into the millions. By 1932 half of all British and German households owned radio sets. French percentages were lower, and Italian and East European lower still—the European average stood at one set per seven or eight households—but the widespread practice of collective listening had made radios the universal conveyor of popular culture across the continent.

Increasingly by the late 1920s radio programs included jazz, the distinctive rage music of the age. Widespread purchase of jazz recordings and record players reinforced this trend. Born among African Americans in New Orleans and other towns of the American South around the turn of the century, and then spreading into the North during and after the war, jazz came to be the catch-all term for a variety of musical styles such as ragtime, the blues, Dixieland, and swing. Famous postwar jazz bands like those of Louis Armstrong, Duke Ellington, and Paul Whiteman incorporated two common elements into their music: syncopation or the accenting of a typically unstressed beat,

Franz Marc, **Fate of the Animals.** (Art Resource, NY)

Art captures industrial energy. Umberto Boccioni, The City Rises (1910–1911). (Digital Image © The Museum of Modern Art / Licensed by SCALA / Art Resource, NY)

Boris Grigoriev, House Under the Trees. (The State Russian Museum, Saint Petersburg)

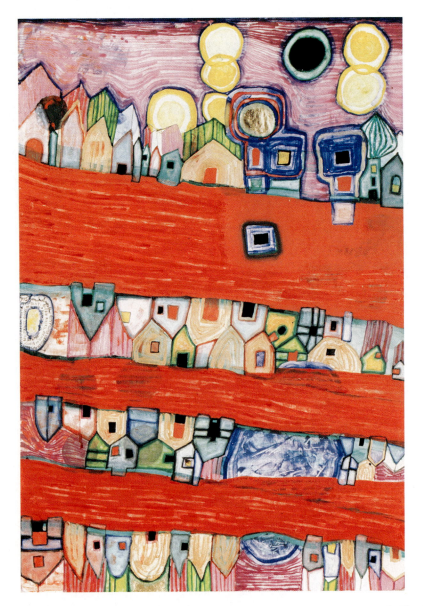

Hundertwasser, 905, Red Rivers Streets of Blood—Red Streets Rivers of Blood.
(Kunsthaus Wien/© J. Harel, Vienna)

Music for the democratic age: Louis Armstrong with his band.   (Library of Congress)

thereby depriving the normally stressed beat of its anticipated emphasis; and an unusual "three over four" polyrhythm that imposed an odd *"one-two-three"* rhythmical element onto the fundamental "one-two-three-four" rhythm. Jazz also featured a great deal of improvisation by performers, even in the more rehearsed arrangements of great swing bands like Benny Good-man's. All of this contrasted with the unsyncopated rhythm of European sym-phonic music and its emphasis, both in the tonal and atonal varieties, on com-posing and conducting. By the early 1920s jazz had established its primary European colony in Paris, where nightclub audiences reveled in *le jazz hot* and learned to dance the crazy "shimmy" and the frenetic "Charleston." Modern art tipped its hat to the new rave music with Pablo Picasso's *Three Musicians* (1921), whose mature cubist deconstructions seemed to praise jazz's broken up sound, its syncopation. By mid-decade Berlin's bawdy cabaret scene had begun to rival Paris as the jazz capital of Europe. German enthusiasts were also drawn to plays like *The Three Penny Opera* (1928) of Kurt Weill and Bertold Brecht, an interesting mixture of jazz, popular music, and leftist criticism of established society.

Jazz seemed to epitomize the spirit of democracy, in fact, at a time when both spread quickly throughout the western world. The new music rose up from the people, not down from the elite conservatories. It also came from America, whose plebian republican institutions had variously fascinated or repelled Europeans for a century. The unorthodox beats and rhythms exuded

Pablo Picasso, **Three Musicians.** (Digital Image © The Museum of Modern Art/Licensed by Scala/Art Resource, NY/© 2004 Estate of Pablo Picasso/Artists Rights Society (ARS), New York)

rebelliousness, furthermore, while the upbeat pace of jazz combined with the wild and wanton dances that it spawned to liberate devotees. The "jazz-fox trot flood," complained one conservative German composer, represented "the American tanks in the spiritual assault against European culture." A German music critic swept up in the frenzy could praise jazz, however, for being "so completely undignified." Whoever feared "making himself laughable cannot dance it." Because jazz allegedly undermined haughtiness and aggressiveness, all public officials needed to hear it. "If only the Kaiser had danced jazz—then all of that [killing] never would have come to pass!"[53] The writer's humorous exuberance touches us today, but it begged many questions as the interwar decades unfolded, for the contagious jazz craze would neither secure the peace nor rescue democracy.

DEMOCRACIES YOUNG AND OLD

Eight democracies existed in Europe before 1914, but only three had fairly deep roots: Switzerland (1847), France (1870), and Britain (1884), states that introduced universal male voting for parliamentary bodies that possessed real

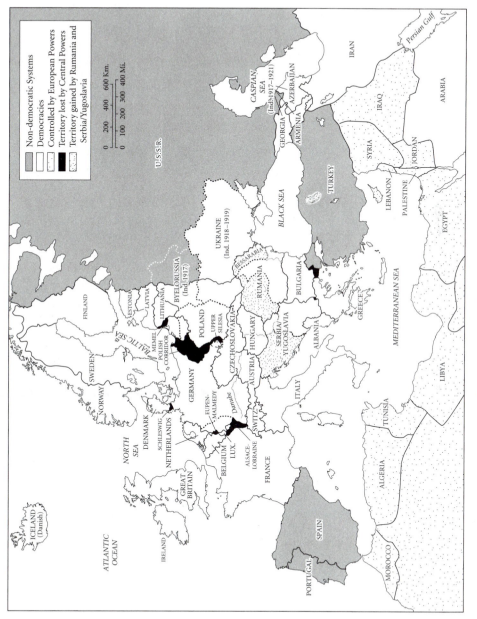

Legend:
- Non-democratic Systems
- Democracies
- Controlled by European Powers
- Territory lost by Central Powers
- Territory gained by Rumania and Serbia/Yugoslavia

0   200   400   600 Km.
0   100   200   300   400 Mi.

ICELAND
(Danish)

ATLANTIC
OCEAN

IRELAND

GREAT
BRITAIN

NORTH
SEA

NORWAY

SWEDEN

FINLAND

BALTIC SEA

ESTONIA

LATVIA

LITHUANIA

MEMEL

POLISH
CORRIDOR

BYELORUSSIA
(Ind.1917)

U.S.S.R.

UKRAINE
(Ind. 1918–1919)

CASPIAN
SEA
(Ind.1917–1921)

GEORGIA

ARMENIA

AZERBAIJAN

IRAN

Persian Gulf

ARABIA

IRAQ

SYRIA

LEBANON

JORDAN

PALESTINE

EGYPT

DENMARK

SCHLESWIG

NETHERLANDS

EUPEN-
MALMEDY

BELGIUM

LUX.

Danube

ALSACE-
LORRAINE

FRANCE

SWITZ.

GERMANY

POLAND

UPPER
SILESIA

CZECHOSLOVAKIA

AUSTRIA

HUNGARY

BESSARABIA

RUMANIA

BLACK SEA

TURKEY

BULGARIA

SERBIA/
YUGOSLAVIA

ALBANIA

GREECE

ITALY

MEDITERRANEAN SEA

TUNISIA

LIBYA

ALGERIA

MOROCCO

PORTUGAL

SPAIN

Democracies after World War One

decision-making powers.[54] The pace of democratization quickened after 1900 as other countries widened their electoral bases. Serbia (1903), Sweden (1911), Greece (1911), and Italy (1913) granted voting rights to all men, and Norway (1913) became the most egalitarian nation in the world by implementing universal suffrage.

The hardship and sacrifice of the Great War unleashed social forces that greatly accelerated the trend toward popular rule. Authoritarian systems, already suffering legitimacy crises before the war, were further discredited and then swept away by the killing and the sacrifice. There were also pressures on Europe's relatively more liberal or democratic states to become more genuinely democratic. All men and women received the suffrage in Denmark (1915) and Holland (1917), for instance, and Sweden (1919) added women to the rolls. Following the British example, Belgium (1919) enfranchised all men but restricted women's suffrage to older females. There was also a quantum leap from semi-autocracy to universal suffrage in the new democratic republics of Germany, Austria, and Hungary as well as Finland, Estonia, Latvia, Lithuania, Poland, and Czechoslovakia, states that had broken away from the Russian and Austro-Hungarian empires. Women's gains did not extend southeast to Rumania, Bulgaria, Yugoslavia, Albania, and Greece, but throughout this region manhood suffrage became the norm as the delegates gathered in Paris in early 1919. Indeed, the Great War had ushered in a new political order—democratic systems of some sort governed twenty-eight of thirty-two European states—88 percent.[55] Democracy, writes one historian, "was the alpha and omega of political wisdom."[56]

Young democracy, however, is a fragile thing. Thus Russia, one of Europe's non-democratic states of 1919, had possessed representative institutions for eight months in 1917 until communist revolutionaries seized power. A short-lived Byelorussian republic similarly fell in late 1917 to the Bolsheviks, who were overrun in their turn by the Germans. The communists seized it again in late 1918 when German troops withdrew. Over the next three years Red armies also conquered the briefly independent republics of Ukraine, Georgia, Armenia, and Azerbaijan. Hungarian democracy succumbed in 1919 to the Bolshevik regime of Béla Kun, furthermore, which then quickly fell to reactionaries. And Italy's near civil war paralyzed the nation's political system, preparing the groundwork for Mussolini's rise to the premiership and subsequent violent consolidation of power. It seemed increasingly obvious that Europe was not yet safe for democracy.

The Successor States of Eastern Europe

Most of the sovereign nation-states newborn or else greatly expanded after the disintegration of the Russian and Austro-Hungarian empires suffered from political and economic weaknesses that threatened their survival.[57] In both the newly emerging republics (Czechoslovakia, Poland, the Baltic states, and Finland) and the victorious states that existed before 1914 (Albania, Serbia/Yugoslavia, and Rumania) the transition from authoritarian to popular rule was often accompanied by severe political fragmentation and polarization as numerous opposition party cliques, previously suppressed or forced underground, surfaced during the first burst of democratic freedoms. The presence of ethnic and religious minorities wanting their own representation exacerbated the basic problem of numerous competing parties. The solution adopted at Paris, namely, constitutional guarantees for minorities with the additional proviso of League of Nations protection, was initially no small consolation to disappointed minorities, but one that quickly faded as Geneva floundered. The unfortunate fact that leaders in many of these nations lacked leadership and administrative experience, having mastered only those skills required in the underground or opposition, heightened still more the turbulence of young democratic rule. "Everyone wants to be in opposition," complained the leader of one of Poland's five peasant parties, "but no one wants to accept responsibility."[58] Making matters worse, these leaders had experienced only oppression, which gave them no opportunity to work in a rule of law environment, but without this experience, respect for laws did not always come naturally. Agrarian problems complicated the problematic mix in overwhelmingly rural Eastern Europe, for recently enfranchised peasants radicalized by wartime deprivations and inspired by peasant gains in Russia demanded more land and a wide range of educational and banking services. Ignoring such demands threatened to inflame the countryside against allegedly uncaring city dwellers, but on the other hand redistribution schemes ran the risk of alienating landowning elites, while the likely result of a plethora of inefficient smaller farms would be the little man's vulnerability to swings in prices, which in fact dropped precipitously after 1926. In facing all of these dilemmas, finally, some of the new democratic regimes failed to ensure the loyalty of existing military establishments—or build adequate military force in the first place—to protect themselves against domestic or foreign enemies. All of these general points come into better focus by considering specific examples of both problematic and successful young democracies in this category.

Poland suffered many of these pitfalls. The constitution granted universal suffrage, proportional representation, a wide range of civil liberties, guarantees for ethnic minorities, and far-reaching citizens' rights to material betterment, but the promise of democracy was never realized. Born in the Great War's violent aftermath, Poland grew up amidst constant warfare with Bolshevik Russia, the Ukraine, Lithuania, Czechoslovakia, and German free corps. Although Warsaw won these conflicts, the army drained away much of the budget and resented parliamentary scrutiny. Indeed, the generals held the people's body, the Sejm, in near contempt. Marshall Joseph Pilsudski, hero of the Russo-Polish War, described parliament variously as a "band of thieves" and a "sterile, jabbering, howling thing."[59] Attitudes like this stemmed from the fact that twenty-five parties contested most elections, including numerous radical factions representing recalcitrant Ukrainian, Jewish, and German minorities comprising a third of the population. Cabinets lasted only five or six months as party feuding blocked legislative compromise. Nor could presidents, granted few constitutional powers by wary legislators remembering tsarist autocracy, do anything to overcome the chaos. Worst of all, perhaps, the Sejm failed to pass land reforms trumpeted in the constitution—and without them, the peasants mocked democracy. Disgusted with the system, Pilsudski seized power with a bloody march on Warsaw in May 1926.

Inspired by the Polish example, conservative colonels in Lithuania took control in December 1926. For years farmer-oriented factions and cliques had looked askance at trade union, socialist, communist, and allegedly Jewish circles in the towns and cities. Indignation at leftward-leaning, pro-Soviet policies, in fact, had triggered the coup, which served as a storm-warning signal for similarly fragmented and polarized democracies in Latvia and Estonia that had been buffeted by high political winds since the Bolshevik Revolution. Contemporaries doubted whether these democracies could avoid Lithuania's fate—a judgment, sadly, that proved correct in the 1930s.

Among the newborn sovereign nations of northeastern Europe, Finland alone implemented a relatively successful democracy. For one thing, the Finns possessed a reservoir of political talent after a century of autonomy inside the Russian Empire. Emerging from the former Grand Duchy of Finland, for instance, was Carl Gustav Mannerheim, an able general who served as Finland's regent in 1918–1919. The tsarist past also provided useful experience with universal suffrage in multiparty Diet elections after 1906. These were turbulent years, filled with party political fighting over language rights, temperance, land reform, and labor legislation. Gaping fissures opened in Finnish society—indeed, rural-urban tensions erupted in a bloody civil war in 1917–1918. Learning from its past, Finland attempted to counteract party political confusion by investing the presidency with strong executive powers. Even though fragmentation and polarization brought down cabinets in Helsinki every nine or ten months, the Finns successfully legislated language guarantees for the Swedish minority as well as land reforms that doubled the percentage of families owning farms. The source of instability in Finnish democracy, however, remained the rural majority's prejudice against urban workers. The government banned the Communist Party, kept trade unions largely without rights, and barely tolerated the moderate Social Democratic Party, which nevertheless earned over a third of the vote in the 1920s.

The most stable democracy in the region, Czechoslovakia, managed to overcome the problems that brought others down. Although seventeen political parties surfaced in 1920 and bitter German and Hungarian minorities created further polarization, a reservoir of Czech bureaucratic talent from the old empire bequeathed some stability. The constitution helped to avert decision-making breakdown by granting American-style executive responsibilities to the president. In that office the Czechs were fortunate to have Thómas Masaryk, a liberal arts professor and prewar opposition leader sensitive to the political needs of struggling classes and rival parties and—born half-Czech and half-Slovak—extremely tolerant of suspicious non-Czech nationalities. Cabinets revolved frequently, but Masaryk presided over a polity that successfully passed impressive labor legislation, including the eight-hour day, old age pensions, and very generous unemployment insurance. The state also redistributed land to poor farmers, introduced bills to stimulate industry, and made clever political concessions to ethnic minorities. Although nothing assuaged Czechoslovakia's small Hungarian minority, Sudeten German leaders with constituents numbering over a fifth of the population soon agreed to join cabinets. Foreign Minster Eduard Benes enhanced the new nation's security, moreover, by signing a military alliance with France, a close diplomatic understanding with Britain, and lucrative trading deals with both democratic powers. The fact that Czech Bohemia included much of the munitions potential of the former empire and, further, that a cadre of returning veterans and officers joined the army seemed to augment Czechoslovakia's security.

Albania is a good bridge to the Balkan states that fought with the victorious allies. The fact that this small principality had come into existence in 1913, only to be overrun and occupied by foreign armies in 1914, meant that the provisional government established in December 1918 had many parallels to newly sovereign states like Estonia and Latvia, which remained battlegrounds until the end of the Russian Civil War. The comparison strengthens when considering that Italian troops were present until 1920, and Greek and Yugoslav units until early 1922. Albania also witnessed the same kind of political turmoil that undermined any chance of stability in the Baltic States and Poland. Indeed, politics soon disintegrated into a struggle between Muslim estate owners who had prospered under the Turks, poorer Orthodox Christians who saw democracy as a chance to redistribute land, and mountain chieftains who distrusted both sides. Ahmed Zog, a chieftain's son who originally backed the liberal land reformers, turned on their leader, Fan Noli, and seized power in December 1924. Only in power seven months, Noli had concentrated on land reform legislation but ignored the pragmatic task of forming an army to defend democracy.

Yugoslavia offers another good comparison. Unlike states in the Northeast, the "Kingdom of the Serbs, Croats, and Slovenes" coalesced around the prewar kingdoms of Montenegro and Serbia. The latter's monarch, Alexander I, became king of the new state, bringing the Serb constitution with him. Like the countries previously analyzed, however, Yugoslavia contained new territories that had known only suppression, like Bosnia-Herzegovina, or limited involvement in government through provincial diets, like Croatia and Slovenia. Yugoslavia had also made the same fortunate progression from wartime defeat and occupation to ultimate victory, thereby experiencing much of the exhilarating rush of freedom characteristic of newborn states. Proportional voting made the new country more democratic than prewar Serbia, furthermore, but spawned nine major parties that made governing coalitions difficult to form.

The Croatian Peasant Party led by Stjepan Radich, a rabble-rousing demagogue who wanted an independent Croatia, emerged as the most troublesome parliamentary faction in Belgrade. His party captured 12 percent of the seats in the Constitutional Assembly of 1920 by campaigning on a program of regional autonomy attractive to countrymen who had learned before 1914 to be suspicious of faraway administrators. When the Serbian parties enticed the Slovenes and Bosnian Muslims to back a constitution that centralized power in Belgrade, Radich protested—and his vote soared to 22 percent. A loose cannon careening between boycotts of parliamentary proceedings, a spewing of verbal abuse on party rivals, and seemingly disingenuous offers of cooperation that invariably ended in a return to obstructionism, Radich damaged Yugoslavian democracy. After a Montenegrin deputy gunned him down in parliament in 1928, the Croatian Peasant Party bolted Belgrade while their constituents rioted in Zagreb for a free Croatia. Weary of the chaos, King Alexander established a personal dictatorship.

Prewar Rumanian monarchs variously tolerated and manipulated a parliament chosen in restricted indirect elections. This undemocratic political culture carried over into the postwar period. Defeated and occupied by the German Army in 1917–1918, Rumania eventually emerged on the winning side, doubling in size at the expense of Russia and Austria-Hungary. These gains affected politics in 1919 when a coalition of peasant parties from the prewar core territories and newly acquired lands in Transylvania succeeded in prodding King Ferdinand into fulfilling a wartime promise of universal manhood suffrage made to boost morale among peasant recruits. Elections returned a huge peasant majority, but before the new leadership could establish itself, Ferdinand ousted them and installed Alexander Averescu, one of his wartime generals, as premier.

The royal coup ushered in years of corruption and intimidation as police interference and ballot box stuffing made a mockery of democratic elections. Averescu was clever enough to muffle rural discontent by pushing through a radical land reform, the most far-reaching redistribution of farmland outside of Soviet Russia. With the peasantry pacified in 1922, Ferdinand dismissed Averescu and turned to Ion Bratianu and his Liberal Party, spokesmen of the urban industrial and financial elite, who furthered their own interests by promoting home industry at the expense of agriculture. High protective tariffs raised the price of farm implements, while export taxes on farm products kept food inside Rumania to feed city workers. When worldwide grain prices plummeted after 1926, Rumania's hard-pressed and exploited farmers began to protest. The deaths of their oppressors, King Ferdinand and Bratianu, in 1927 emboldened the small men still more, culminating in a "march on Bucharest" in 1928. Unnerved, the Liberals allowed Iuliu Maniu, leader of the resurgent peasant movement, to organize free elections. His National Peasant Party swept into power that December. Rumanian democracy had a second chance.

Young Democracies with Nationalist Grievances

Defeated Germany, Austria, Hungary, and Bulgaria also adopted democratic institutions after 1918, but all too quickly, inexperience, lack of respect for the law, outright corruption, political fragmentation, polarization between classes and factions, and economic problems began to take a heavy toll—familiar weaknesses of other young democracies. Making matters worse, however, was the stigma of national defeat, a burden that proved very difficult for these democratic regimes to bear when added to other loads. Allied leaders abandoned Hungary when neighboring states seized territories in 1919, for example, helping to make it Europe's first democracy outside Russia to fall. Readers will also know from previous sections that nationalist grievances fueled the postwar rise of Benito Mussolini. Because similar kinds of problems weakened both rule by the people and the generals in Greece, it will be useful to include it in the discussion here.

Greece democratized its monarchy in 1911. The infant system took its first steps, however, amidst the turmoil of the Balkan Wars and the tremendous strains of the Great War. Much like Italy, Greek entry to the war caused tremendous dissension, for King Constantine favored neutrality while the author of the 1911 constitution, Prime Minister Eleutherios Venizelos, dreamed of using the war to reestablish the ancient Hellenic Empire. With Entente backing in 1917 he overthrew Constantine for Alexander, the king's son, much to the ire of royalist generals and their numerous voters. But Venizelos took no notice. Emboldened by allied victory and eager to realize the "Great Idea"[60] from antiquity, he sent Greek troops to occupy Smyrna in 1919.

Now Greek democracy began to unravel. The fluke death of Alexander, bitten by his pet monkey, turned the 1920 elections into a plebiscite on the return of Constantine. When the royalists won, Venizelos resigned and left the country. Constantine's men had taken their revenge on Venizelos, but, just as enamored with his "Great Idea," they hurled their war-weary country into the caldron of the Anatolian expedition of 1921–1922. Imperialist pride proved their undoing, for republican generals seized power after the debacle of Greek arms, won a plebiscite on the abolition of the monarchy, and executed Constantine's premier and five generals.

The republican generals eventually turned the country back over to civilians, who introduced a new constitution in 1927 that seemed to guarantee stability by granting the president more power. Venizelos returned from his self-imposed exile to a triumph in the 1928 elections. In one of his first acts as premier, he abolished the proportional voting system that had fragmented politics and felled so many cabinets. Thus Greek democracy, like the Rumanian, got a reprieve.

Bulgaria's story followed similar lines. Beaten down by six years of constant warfare in October 1918, the defeated kingdom was so wracked by hunger, labor unrest, and mutiny that unpopular King Ferdinand abdicated to his son, Boris III. The new sovereign grudgingly lifted all male voting restrictions and installed the imprisoned anti-war hero of the peasantry, Alexander Stamboliski, as premier. In the first postwar elections of August 1919, his Agrarian Union won 28 percent of the vote.

Not worried about the methods he used to acquire more power, Stamboliski decreed compulsory voting in March 1920 that enabled the Agrarian Union to mobilize more rural support and capture 109 of 229 seats. By arbitrarily invalidating thirteen opposition mandates, he finagled a majority. Becoming more corrupt now, Stamboliski's cronies received bureaucratic posts and lined their own pockets. The Union's paramilitary organization, the Orange Guard, roughed up and frequently jailed political opponents. Such abusive tactics drove much of the opposition underground by the April 1923 elections, which gave the Union 212 of 245 seats and established a quasi one-party system.

Stamboliski's policies split the country into two antagonistic camps. On his side were small farmers who received impressive benefits like cheaper credit, tax relief, easier access to the courts, and a greatly expanded system of rural elementary education. The dynamic tribune of the folk drove home his advantage in rural Bulgaria, where nearly 80 percent of households worked farms or herds, by praising the virtues of a peasantry allegedly uncontaminated by corrosive urban or western ideas and practices. On the other side waited his many enemies, above all the army, which never forgave Stamboliski's "traitorous" opposition to the war. In league with the generals were Macedonian terrorists who blamed him for kowtowing to the victorious allies and abandoning ethnic brethren ceded to Greece and Yugoslavia. The upper classes, moreover, feared reforms sometimes passed with Communist Party help. These patrician elements presented King Boris with a fait accompli in June 1923 by using the Sofia garrison to move against the Orange Guard and arrest Stamboliski.[61] The army callously handed its prisoner over to the Macedonians, who sadistically tortured and executed the ex-premier. Bulgarian democracy had disintegrated in less than four years.

Austria's revolution also inaugurated democratic rule.[62] Legitimated by universal suffrage in the first postwar elections, a coalition government of Social Democrats and Christian Socialists attempted to salvage the nearly bankrupt republic. This partnership worked fairly well at first for three reasons. First, the Habsburg war effort had been such an abysmal failure that few Austrians of any social class shed tears after its collapse and no extremist party attempted to shift blame for defeat to the new rulers. Second, the Social Democrats demonstrated wise restraint in ignoring pleas from Lenin and Kun to implement a dictatorship of the proletariat, for they knew such action would trigger civil war between paramilitary units in "Red Vienna" and the armed Catholic peasantry. So Vienna's Defense League and its countryside rival, the Home Guards, both warily stood down. Finally, the victorious allies appreciated the economic and financial precariousness of an Austrian rump state severed from the empire it had ruled for centuries. The Treaty of Saint Germain called for reparations, but the victors demanded no immediate payments—on the contrary, the League of Nations lent Austria 130 million dollars to stabilize its inflation-ridden currency in 1922.

Already by this time, however, class tensions mounted in intensity. Disagreements over social welfare and taxation measures broke up the ruling coalition in late 1920. Thereafter Christian Socialist governments ruled at the national level, drawing support from the countryside that made up two-thirds of the Austrian population. The Social Democrats went their own way, legislating largely autonomous federal state status for Vienna in 1921. The capital city initiated progressive welfare programs like government-subsidized housing, free kindergartens, hospital care, and burials, but stiff taxes on the wealthy alienated the urban upper classes. Meanwhile the peasants scoffed at the "parasitic" city dwellers and "Jewish" socialists. By mid-decade rival party armies squared off on a regular basis as political leaders made shrill ideological denunciations of one another. Matters came to a head in July 1927 when the courts acquitted Home Guard members who had ambushed a Defense League column, killing two people. Socialist workers in Vienna protested by assaulting the Ministry of Justice and rampaging through the inner city. When they finished, eighty-nine policemen, rioters, and innocent bystanders lay dead— and Austria hovered on the brink of civil war.

The young German republic had to contend with starvation, disease, communist uprisings, and free corps vigilante justice.[63] Runaway inflation added to the impression created by death and disorder that the new freedoms had somehow caused the country's woes. However, nothing undermined popular support for democratic procedures more than the inability of Germany's left-center parties, the so-called Weimar Coalition, to refute rightist accusations that leftists had betrayed the nation during and after the war. Many middle- and upper-class Germans who believed their army had been winning in 1918 found it hard to understand the government's acceptance of the punitive Treaty of Versailles. Was it true, as many charged, that Socialists, Catholics, and Jews had sold out the nation? Former Field Marshall Paul von Hindenburg gave tremendous credence to these rumors when he testified before parliament in September 1919 that selfish elements on the wartime home front had undercut the army. Newspaper readers already irate over Versailles were left to draw their own conclusions about treason in high places.

These groundless allegations cut deeply into the electoral base of the three parties that had campaigned for democratic republican institutions in January 1919. From 76.2 percent of the vote in that election, the Social Democrats, Center Party, and German Democratic Party slipped to 47.8 percent in June 1920. Subsequent inflation, reparations, and allied incursions into the Rhineland and the Ruhr produced still more defections from the Weimar Coalition. The plea of Chancellor Joseph Wirth of the Center Party in 1922 that these foreign developments were "likely to damage and weaken the core of German democracy"[64] proved correct in May 1924 when the once dominant troika slid farther to 41.8 percent, despite the return to the Social Democratic fold of "independent" socialists who had received an impressive 17.9 percent in 1920. The exaggerated rightist quip that Germany was "a democracy without democrats" rang slightly true. This verdict was confirmed in May 1925 when the democratic presidential candidate, Wilhelm Marx, got only 45.3 percent, the Communist Ernst Thälmann 6.4 percent, and the kaiser's former army chief, Hindenburg, 48.3 percent to capture office.

It seems very doubtful, on the other hand, that most Germans wanted to restore the monarchy after the war had so thoroughly undermined that institution. Because Hindenburg had acquired a legendary status of his own as a military hero, a vote for him meant more likely a non-democratic penchant for militant nationalism or perhaps an army dictatorship. Corroborating this view was the mediocre showing of the two parties most closely associated with the old regime, the German People's Party and the German National People's Party, which together polled no higher than 30.6 percent in 1924, and then slipped to 22.9 percent in 1928.

By 1928, in fact, many Germans seem to have become disillusioned not only with democracy but also with established right-wing parties, for none of these had ousted discredited democrats, restored economic prosperity, or re-built national prestige. Increasing numbers of Germans, in other words, looked for radical new political departures, throwing nearly a third of the 1928 vote to numerous new revolutionary or extremist parties representing communist workers, small businessmen, white-collar employees, farmers, and veterans. Among them: Adolf Hitler's Nazi Party with 2.6 percent. German democracy survived, but only because the anti-democratic majority was too splintered to agree on an alternative.

The Democracies of Northern and Western Europe

Holland, Denmark, Norway, and Sweden experienced a much smoother tran-sition to democratic rule. While all had labor troubles in 1919 as unions struck to bring wages in line with wartime inflation, politics remained comparatively stable. Holland and Denmark responded to worker protests by expanding their social insurance networks. Cabinets rarely fell here before regularly scheduled elections. Even in Norway and Sweden, where party fragmenta-tion and class tension caused cabinets to break up typically after a year or two, none of this seriously jeopardized the survival of the democratic system.

One finds the reasons in an almost total absence of those forces that un-dermined democracy in East-Central Europe. Unlike many of those nations, the northern democracies were not newborn states making turbulent transi-tions from an authoritarian prewar empire, contending with anti-democratic military establishments, and wanting for experienced politicians. On the con-trary, Holland, Denmark, Norway, and Sweden built on prewar parliamen-tary political cultures that featured rule of law, acceptance of compromise, and tolerance for the opposition—albeit within the restricted suffrages common here before the war. None of these countries had absorbed large new territo-ries, furthermore, nor were their mostly homogenous populations plagued by the protests of recalcitrant ethnic minorities. Finally, neither Holland nor the Scandinavian democracies participated in the Great War, thus avoiding the searing controversies faced by all belligerents.[65] To be sure, merchant ships were sunk, economies were disrupted by blockades, and markets were lost during postwar commercial dislocation. Greatly outweighing this, however, the neutrals spared themselves the terrible suffering of military campaigns that lasted into the early 1920s in some parts of Europe. The contrast with de-feated nations whose wounded ethnic pride turned into a tremendous liabil-ity for democracy stands out in stark relief.

Belgium also benefited from a prewar political culture that had respected rule of law and the will of the electorate in a fairly broad-based parliamen-tary system—37 percent of adult males voted before 1914. Although the unfortunate kingdom suffered the ravages of war, the four-year nightmare actually facilitated postwar democratization by accentuating the need for fair dealing. It was not so difficult after 1919, therefore, for the propertied classes to welcome working-class newcomers into coalition governments that lifted restrictions on trade unions, legalized the eight-hour day, and expanded social insurance. Ballot-box imperatives and the spirit of compromise also facilitated a solution to Belgium's ethnic problems. Politically dominant since 1830, the French-speaking Walloons conceded linguistic equality to long-disgruntled Dutch-speaking Flemings comprising 51 percent of the population. The country was divided into two administrative sections in which French and Flemish, respectively, were the official languages. French and Flemish regiments were formed in the army, the school system reorganized, and the University of Ghent reestablished as a Flemish institution. Thus Belgian democracy defused the kind of ethnic issues that had destroyed rule by the people in many other lands.

Switzerland, Europe's oldest democracy, remained neutral during the Great War. These four years nevertheless took their toll economically and financially, prompting the federal government to adopt strict controls over currency, foreign exchange, and banking, and generally to increase its regulatory role and powers vis-à-vis the cantons. Social tremors also mounted, leading finally to a general strike in November 1918. Generally intolerant of disruption and disorder, the Swiss once again called out the army to suppress their workers.

Gender tensions added to the stress and strain on Swiss democracy. Serious protests against women's suffrage by the Catholic Conservative Party, dominant in the Italian and Alpine cantons, undercut support for this reform among the other major parties, the Liberals and the Socialists. Such a controversial change, many feared, might break apart the religiously, linguistically, and politically diverse Confederation. Another issue that tended to divide men and women—prohibition of alcohol—went man's way when voters rejected it twice in the 1920s.[66]

As the postwar years unfolded, Switzerland took significant steps to mend society's fences. The federal government finally legalized trade unions, introduced collective bargaining and compulsory accident insurance, and joined the cantons in subsidizing local unemployment insurance. Swiss men fine-tuned their democracy, furthermore, with the introduction of proportional representation and the extension of initiative and referendum rights to foreign policy issues. One of the most significant uses of the latter came in 1920 when Switzerland put membership in the League of Nations to a vote. Anxious lest joining compromise the nation's century-old policy of neutrality, the electorate barely accepted the League. Despite the lack of female suffrage, direct democracy through referendum did much to bolster Switzerland's reputation as one of the freest countries in the world.

The French people and their established democracy faced an immense challenge as they began the work of reconstruction.[67] The war had almost completely devastated the northeastern quadrant of the country. Thousands of miles of railroad track, highways, bridges, and canals had been ruined, coal mines flooded, factories turned into rubble, homes destroyed, and millions of acres of farmland bombed into a battle-scarred wasteland. There were six hundred thousand widows eligible for pensions, three-quarters of a million orphans, and three million wounded soldiers who needed medical care—many hundreds of thousands permanently. The state had borrowed twenty-eight billion dollars from its own people during the war, another seven billion from the British and Americans, and now faced the prospect of paying reconstruction costs reckoned at twenty billion—nearly three times France's national income in 1913.

Answering the question of how to pay dominated French politics in the immediate postwar period. The coalition of nationalist and conservative parties that captured 64.9 percent in 1919 borrowed money short term to finance the nearly twenty billion dollars in reconstruction, pension, and medical costs paid out by early 1923, but was unable—and also largely unwilling—to increase taxes. But many nay-saying deputies also asked why France should pay for damages inflicted by Germany. Accordingly, Paris exerted its great influence in the Reparations Commission, which decided in 1921 that France should receive seventeen billion dollars or 52 percent of the reparations total. By late 1922, however, Berlin had paid only three hundred million. With French reconstruction costs and national debt soaring, Premier Raymond Poincaré looked askance at Germany's denunciation of reparations and request for a moratorium. He responded with the Ruhr invasion of January 1923.

This move precipitated a domestic financial and political crisis. Germany refused to pay more reparations and the French and their allies exacted less payment in kind from production than the cost of the occupation. With the government on the verge of bankruptcy in the spring of 1924, Poincaré and his supporters levied a 20 percent tax increase. The Socialists and other left-center parties exploited the unpopularity of the taxes and the decline in France's international position during new elections in May, reducing the Right to only 40.2 percent. The succeeding cabinet of Edouard Herriot brought the great task of reconstruction close to completion, but, given the taxpayers' near revolt of 1924, could find no acceptable form of taxation. Herriot's cabinet soon fell in its turn.

France's spending and borrowing continued, however, as inflation worsened, the franc tumbled to a tenth of its prewar value, and seven more cabinets fell in fifteen months. Finally in 1926 the deputies bowed to pressure from the Bank of France, which had refused more credit, by granting emergency powers to Poincaré. His Government of National Union cut expenditures, raised six billion dollars in new taxes, balanced the budget, and restored the franc to a fifth of its prewar value. A steady flow of reparations under the Dawes Plan guaranteed further liquidity. French democracy had weathered another long storm and seemed secure.

But was it? Cabinets collapsed in the 1920s every six months on average, roughly the same degree of governmental turnover as Latvia, Poland, and Yugoslavia. Even in Germany's ailing democracy, cabinets typically lasted twice as long. Such instability was the product of a political culture that valued the rights of individual deputies and small cliques more highly than the need for parliamentary order. French presidents performed a largely ceremonial, ribbon-cutting role, while premiers lacked the considerable leverage over the chamber that came with the power to dissolve parliament and hold new elections. Cabinet ministers normally came from coalition parties, but back-benchers felt little compulsion to support their ministerial leaders or suppress embarrassing interpellations and no confidence votes, for they rested secure in the knowledge that they would not soon face local nominating committees and voters. To be sure, the French political system possessed many advantages that younger democracies to the East did not: a competent bureaucracy, a loyal army, a free and vocal press, an entrenched tradition of the rule of law, and longevity—the constitution of the Third Republic had functioned since 1870. The state had shown strength and resiliency, moreover, in the caldron of the Great War. As the financial crisis of the 1920s demonstrates, however, the near anarchic inefficiency of French democracy could be a great liability in times of domestic crisis.

Class divisions exacerbated the problems of French democracy in the first postwar decade. The "Sacred Union" of 1914 did not survive the war's turbulent final eighteen months as workers, enthused by the Bolshevik example, went on strike. Premier Georges Clemenceau responded with political concessions combined with a swift repression of the wildcat strikers. His approach in 1919 was the same: Parliament sanctioned the eight-hour day and forty-eight-hour week as well as collective bargaining, but the state brutally squashed a spiraling strike wave with tanks and machine gun–toting mounted troopers. Labor's defeat was so thorough that three-fifths of the union membership—nearly a million workers—fled their organizations in 1919–1920.

The alleged Bolshevik menace continued to loom large, nevertheless, in the mind of bourgeois France. Indeed, throughout much of the 1920s educational reforms discriminated against the lower classes, employers widely ignored the eight-hour day and collective bargaining, and a parliament still packed with rural deputies refused to expand social insurance programs for urban "free-loaders." Poincaré's tax increase of 1926, moreover, fell disproportionately on the shoulders of the masses. Given the upper-class bias of legislation, it is not surprising that the Communists and Socialists routinely refused to join cabinets, thereby exacerbating parliamentary inefficiency. On the positive side, the chamber finally passed an expanded package of old age, sickness, disability, death, and maternity benefits in 1928. But this did little to overcome the bitter and sullen mood of blue-collar workers, for the programs only took effect in the depression year 1930. None of this augured well for the long-term health of democracy in France.

Across the Channel, economic and financial problems of a different sort prevented the restoration of stability and "normalcy."[68] Whereas France enjoyed full employment in the 1920s due to the demands of reconstruction, Britain had only a brief postwar expansion in 1919–1920 fueled by pent-up wartime consumer spending. The boom dissolved into a severe recession in

1920–1921 when Britain proved unable to regain export markets lost to the United States, Japan, and other allies during the war. Moreover, whereas France introduced the latest technology in thousands of plants destroyed in the war zone, the former workshop of the world, already slipping technologically behind Germany and the United States before 1914, found such a thorough restructuring blocked by the prudent short-term thinking that makes cost-cutting measures in the old factory or mine seem less risky and more rational than a complete retooling.

The Bank of England exacerbated chances for full economic recovery in the early 1920s by pursuing deflationary measures designed to restore value to Britain's inflated currency, return to the gold standard abandoned during the war, and recapture from New York London's former prestige as financial capital of the world. To conservative, nostalgic financiers like Montagu Norman, governor of the Bank of England, the gold standard was more than a mechanism to bring order to a world plagued by dislocated economies and inflation; it was "a mystical symbol of all that was finest in the struggle of mankind to better its lot on earth."[69] The banking community also felt ethically and morally obligated to repay Britain's debt to the United States, London's only major creditor, at its real or pre-inflation value, hence the need to restore the pound to prewar parity with the dollar. This policy culminated in 1925 with Britain's premature declaration that the pound was once again redeemable in gold at the 1913 rate of 4.86 dollars—about 10 percent more than the pound was currently worth. The overvaluation of the pound further undercut British exports by making them more costly when prices were converted to the currencies of importing nations, thus adding to the problems of technological obsolescence and unshakeable wartime competition. From 1925 to 1926 the volume of British exports fell over 10 percent. By the latter year exports stood 32 percent below the level of 1913.

The social consequence of Britain's export dilemma was high unemployment. When the economy hit bottom in July 1921, over two million hands—more than 12 percent of the industrial labor force—had no work. A coal miners' strike that summer had swollen the numbers, but afterward unemployment still hovered well above anything imaginable in prewar days, dropping to about 9 percent in 1923. From 1924 to 1929 it averaged 8.3 percent, fluctuating in the range of 1.1 to 1.4 million unemployed workers. Prior to 1914 industrial unemployment had never exceeded 5 percent.

Against the backdrop of these swelling ranks, the Labour Party's call for the nationalization of British industry and its trade union wing's increasingly sharp criticism of conservative monetary policy appealed to greater numbers of lower- and middle-class people. Labour's seats in the House of Commons rose from 59 in 1918 to 287 in 1929 and its popular vote increased steadily throughout the decade to 37 percent. The party's rise signified a considerable polarization in British politics, for the Conservatives on the other extreme polled as high as 44 percent in 1924, while the more moderate Liberal Party, the dominant faction in parliament before 1918, declined to a low of 18 percent that year. Of even greater concern was the rebirth of trade union militancy, culminating in a general strike in 1926—the first in British history—affecting three million workers. Winston Churchill of the Conservative Party stated alarmingly in the House: "It is not wages that are imperiled; it is the freedom of our very constitution." The strike was "a conflict which, if it is fought out to a conclusion, can only end in the overthrow of parliamentary government or in its decisive victory."[70] Britain's democracy appeared to be coming apart at the seams.

But it did not. The Trades Union Council (T.U.C.) had called the strike because mine owners locked out their workers, but the public widely perceived the mass walkout as an illegal attempt to force government to coerce management. Although the miners held out in vain for seven months, the T.U.C. canceled the general strike after nine days. The dismal failure of "direct action" clearly strengthened the hand of trade union moderates, for in 1927 they soundly defeated a resolution that condemned industrial peace at the T.U.C. annual congress. British democracy also proved resilient enough to assuage many of the nation's dissidents. Conservative Minister of Health Neville Chamberlain sponsored legislation providing improved unemployment benefits, cheap electricity, and low-income housing. In 1928 the Conservatives also enfranchised all adult women, adding six million voters to the rolls. Furthermore, in stark contrast to the short-lived Labour Government of 1924, which was brought down after ten months by bourgeois fears of communism, the surging party was readily accepted after the elections of 1929 as the next legitimate government. Unemployment had not disappeared, but neither had the British penchant for compromise and concession in stressful times.

Democracy in Ireland

Like so many of the new states in East-Central Europe, Irish democracy drew its first breath amidst violence and death.[71] The situation deteriorated steadily after Irish nationalists attempted to break away from Britain with a badly planned, ill-fated uprising in April 1916, for the British fueled the popularity of the rebels' cause of independence by executing—and thereby martyring—fourteen of the ringleaders. The threat of conscription during the bloody German offensive of 1918 made ties to the British Empire even more unpopular. During British elections that December the pro-independence "Sinn Fein" party won an overwhelming majority of seats in the Catholic south, while Protestant Ulster unionists prevailed in the north. After Sinn Fein leaders Eamon de Valera and Michael Collins proclaimed Irish independence in January 1919, Collins unleashed a campaign of terror that targeted members of the Royal Irish Constabulary (RIC) and British officials. With assassinations and political murders mounting in early 1920, London retaliated by recruiting special auxiliary police units among demobilized soldiers and officers of the Great War—the twisted ones who remained eager, like their counterparts in Germany and Italy, for more combat. The most infamous of these squads, nicknamed the "Black and Tans" because of their khaki army uniforms and black RIC hats and belts, struck back against Collins' volunteer force, the Irish Republican Army (IRA). Before a truce could be established in July 1921, raids, ambushes, hostage killing, revenge shootings, and sectarian mob violence left more than a thousand dead on both sides.

Post-truce negotiations led to a compromise that called for an Irish Free State with Commonwealth status similar to Canada—but excluding Northern Ireland and its substantial Catholic minority. This arrangement was put to a vote in June 1922 that polarized the young Irish Free State. Of the 128 deputies elected, 92 accepted the dominion status negotiated by Michael Collins, while 36 supported Eamon de Valera's bid for complete independence. The diehards around De Valera cried foul, waging a civil war against the new government that proved even bloodier than the war of independence. Four thousand fighters and civilians died, including Collins, shot in an ambush, before the extremists gave up. Peace was not restored until April 1923.

The first elections to the Irish Dáil in August 1923 gave men and women the vote under a highly democratic system of proportional representation, but the campaign could not be called free, for thousands of Sinn Fein republicans sat in jail. When De Valera tried to speak, moreover, he was imprisoned for eleven months. His followers nevertheless managed to win 44 seats out of 153 (28.8 percent), then defied the government by refusing to take their places because it meant swearing an oath of allegiance to the British crown.

The hotly contested legitimacy of the Irish Free State became very evident in 1927. The pro-treaty governmental party, calling itself the "League of Gaels" (Cumann na nGaedheal) won forty-seven seats (30.7 percent) in elections that June, while De Valera's faction, the so-called Soldiers of Destiny (Fianna Fáil), again captured forty-four (28.8 percent), forcing the Gaels to form a minority cabinet supported by splinter parties of the Right. In July, gunmen of the IRA, impatient with the Soldiers' legalistic approach, assassinated the minister of justice, Keven O'Higgins. An outraged Dáil quickly took political revenge on De Valera. The dynamic leader of the Soldiers of Destiny had gathered tens of thousands of signatures on a petition to force a referendum on the oath to Britain. The League of Gaels immediately passed legislation abolishing the constitutional rights of initiative and referendum. Clearly Ireland's political feud now began to gnaw away at democracy itself. September election results confirmed the Free State's crisis of legitimacy: the Gaels 40.5 percent, the Soldiers 37.3 percent.

The situation in Northern Ireland, however, was much worse. The six largely Protestant counties of the Northeast had accepted the British offer rejected by the South in 1920: an autonomous parliament for internal affairs along with House of Commons representation and union with Britain. The border between the two parts of Ireland left a substantial Catholic minority isolated from—but still extremely sympathetic to—the Free State. Because of this, Irish Protestants discriminated against Catholics, regarding them as a subversive and disloyal element not to be trusted with real participation in government. The prejudiced majority routinely voted down Catholics in parliament and normally excluded them from the civil service. A hostile Protestant constabulary, moreover, often victimized Catholics. After the termination of the Irish civil war in 1923 freed up resources, the IRA answered with politically inspired

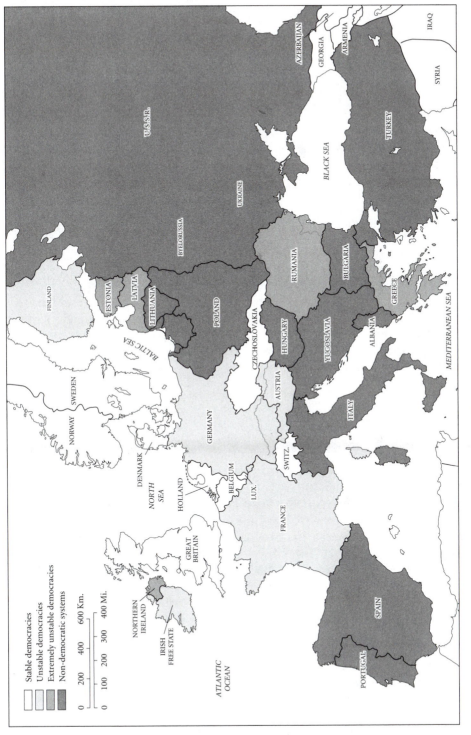

Democracies in 1929

shootings designed to provoke Protestant reprisals, trigger a war with the Free State, and eventually unify North and South. The violence deepened Ulster's siege mentality, twisting and warping its view of Catholics still more. "They were out to defeat Northern Ireland and shoot our people," said one Protestant leader in defense of exclusionary policies against Catholics. "How can you give somebody who is your enemy a higher position in order to allow him to come and destroy you?"[72] The deeply entrenched prejudices of the Protestant majority guaranteed the perpetuation of violence and instability.

The Democratic Balance

The Great War had not created a safe environment for democracy—in fact, just the opposite. Seven former democracies had succumbed to dictatorships of one form or another—Hungary (1919), Bulgaria (1923), Albania (1924), Italy (1925), Poland (1926), Lithuania (1926), and Yugoslavia (1929)—but the total rises to thirteen when adding the Russian Provisional Government of 1917 and the five embryonic democracies overrun by the Bolsheviks. Europe's 88 percent preponderance of democratic states in early 1919 had shrunk to 56 percent a decade later.[73] Of the remaining democracies, however, more than half were unstable or extremely unstable. This overall negative trend raised eyebrows among alarmed advocates of rule by the people, for if it were true that democracies never wage war against one another, what pacifist could find solace after the fall of so many?[74]

COMMUNIST RULE IN RUSSIA

Coming on the heels of the bloody Great War, Russia's ten million deaths in three years of civil war and famine marked a major caesura in its history. It was not just that communism had survived, a victory that shaped the next seventy years. Of significance were also the ways that people—party officials, workers and peasants, parents and children—changed. Contemporary doctors and psychiatrists worried that mass slaughter had decimated society's mainstays, the family and the community; ruined respect for human life; and caused widespread mental illness. For many years subsequent historians concurred that war and civil war brutalized the population and coarsened public life to the point where much worse atrocities—the mass executions of the 1930s—became all but inevitable. More recent researchers adopt a softer determinism, arguing that few people could have survived the civil war's violence, disease, and starvation culminating in sickening cannibalism and infanticide without changing in some way, but that the overwhelming majority of surviving common folk, like counterparts in Western Europe desperately seeking to resolve their grief, nevertheless remade their lives as best they could.[75] "The sword is not fearful," wrote Mikhail Bulgakov in his first novel, *The White Guard* (1924). "Everything passes away—suffering, pain, blood, hunger and pestilence—the sword will pass away too." Although life regained a normalcy of sorts, the past nevertheless bequeathed a heavy burden, for survivors were psychically weaker, emotionally less resilient, less prone to denounce wrongdoing, and more inclined to bury heads in the sand or, as Bulgakov, wrote, "turn our eyes toward the stars"[76] where presumably a better existence awaited. For their part, party zealots exited the civil war eager to build the communist utopia and extremely suspicious of non-communist enemies who might try to wreck this grand social experiment. From the Kremlin leadership down to the rank and file, moreover, cruder Bolsheviks waited for the moment to demonstrate how well they had learned the civil war's brutal "lessons" about dealing with opponents. It would be a tragic mix of popular passivity and official aggression.

The Bolshevik hold on power was initially so precarious that many enactments could not be implemented or, if so, enforced.[77] The constitution promulgated in July 1918, for instance, proclaimed the end of class exploitation and heralded the creation of a "socialist"[78] society and its extension worldwide. The constitution also incorporated early decrees nationalizing all large factories and abolishing private ownership of landed property. Other pronouncements called for a 20 percent wage hike, comprehensive health and unemployment insurance, equality of the sexes, and free coeducational schooling. The truly revolutionary intentions of the Bolsheviks were perhaps most evident in the constitutional clause establishing the right to profess no religion—labeled freedom of conscience—as well as a decree of November 1918 voiding all tsarist laws and legal precedents. Henceforth, socialist consciousness of right would be the sole basis of justice.

While the Bolsheviks had to postpone much of their program as the civil war intensified in 1918, some decrees had more than paper significance. Thus the regime forcefully pursued the fight against religion. Following Karl Marx, Russian communists viewed religion as an "opium" that lulled workers into otherworldly pursuits and diverted them from class struggle on earth. They saw the church as a dangerous institutional agent of the bourgeoisie bolstering an unjust system of class exploitation. Hence shortly after the revolution party fanatics burned and ransacked church buildings, while early decrees separated church and state, confiscated church lands, and abolished religious education. Literature and music that party officials deemed religious was banned—including Plato, Kant, and much of Bach, Mozart, and Rachmaninov. Bolshevik propaganda also mocked the allegedly miraculous nature of religious relics and argued against the existence of God—local functionaries even took peasants on airplane rides to prove that no angels resided in the sky. One especially scandalous poster showed a pregnant Virgin Mary longing for an abortion. Small wonder that thousands of Orthodox priests backed anti-communist forces during the civil war.[79]

As the Bolsheviks' grip on power tightened, so did their underlying confidence in the future of socialism and communism.[80] One measure of this optimism was the "wave of enthusiasm," as Lenin described it, that made them "reckon on being able to organize the state production and state distribution of products on socialist lines in a country of small peasants directly on orders

Leader of the revolution: Vladimir I. Lenin. (Library of Congress)

of the proletarian state."[81] Once again following Marx, they assumed that the distribution of resources, which had been driven under capitalism by the allegedly chaotic market forces of supply and demand, would yield after the revolution to a much more efficient and productive planning of production by workers and peasants who now held all property in common. To Lenin and hundreds of excited party leaders it seemed that civil war conditions were accelerating the fulfillment of collectivism and a socialist command economy, for, unable to trust the "bourgeoisie" to manufacture war materials and sell food, the Bolsheviks expropriated the means of production. From 1918 to 1920 the number of factories nationalized rose eighty-fold to forty thousand. Farms that had been seized and held by the peasants since 1917—despite the first bold communist pronouncements against private property—the Bolsheviks now forced to produce most of their crops for the state. Moscow also began to socialize agriculture, and by 1920 had reorganized ten million acres into thousands of state-run farms (*sovnarkhozy*). Moreover, the world's first socialist/communist state boasted a few genuine communally run "collective" farms (*kolkhoz*), which shared land, work obligations, and revenues from the communal crop among the peasants.

In marked contrast to the deep despair expressed in the culture of Western Europe during the early 1920s, Bolshevik culture mirrored Lenin's "wave of enthusiasm." Not all artists supported the revolution, of course, nor did all benefit from it. Those close to the party, however, especially among the avant-garde, praised Russia's new day. "Like a subterranean quake, smashing everything, the revolution comes," wrote symbolist poet and essayist Andrei Bely. "It comes like a hurricane, sweeping aside forms . . . everything in it gushes, overflows; everything is excessive."[82] Futurism's revolt against the old cultural establishment resonated in these circles, moving poet Vladimir Mayakovsky to proclaim it "time for bullets to pepper museums," and colleague Vladimir Kirillov to shout "in the name of our tomorrow" the need to "burn Raphael/Destroy the Museums, crush the flowers of Art."[83] Filmmaker Sergei Eisenstein added to this impression of a new dawn by memorializing the workers' seizure of power with classics like *Strike*, *Battleship Potemkin*, and *October*. The Ministry of Enlightenment actually restaged the storming of the Winter Palace that went so far as to include actual salvos from the *Aurora*, a battleship that had participated in the historic fight in 1917. The music world also paid tribute to the spirit of revolution by rearranging older works for the new era, like Puccini's *Tosca*, which became *The Battle for the Commune*, and Glinka's *Life for the Tsar*, now performed as *The Hammer and the Sickle*. Composers tried new musical forms, furthermore, in an attempt to penetrate the psyche of workers. The brave new artists held cacophonous concerts in factories using steam engines, sirens, and machines as instruments and creating altogether new sounds electronically.

The excitement among leftist artists for the socialist experiment found its most graphic expression on canvas. One group known as the Association of Artists of Revolutionary Russia saw it as their duty "to record, artistically and documentarily, the revolutionary impulse of this great moment of history."[84] Fairly typical of this school, Mitrofan Grekov's *Heading Toward Budenny* offered a portrait of a Don River peasant making his way to the camp of the Red Army cavalry hero. Like most Association members, Boris Grigoriev also eschewed the abstract for more realistic forms, but one of his paintings, *House Under the Trees*, symbolized the good socialist society arising from the wellspring of the people. The brightly colored trees seem to be alive, their roots reaching down to a submerged, all-encompassing energy source that will revitalize society. Another artistic clique headed by "Constructivist" Alexander Rodchenko glorified Russia's industrial utopia in the making with more abstract representations. His *Density and Weight* emanates optimism for science, engineering, and modern technology. A fellow traveler of the Constructivists, Pavel Filonov, conveyed similar messages with *Formula for the Petrograd Proletariat*. It is a tumultuous scene that we see here: the Red revolutionary destruction of the old order and the geometric forms of a new socialist nation emerging from the fray. *Formula* depicts Filonov's dream of a "universal flowering" born of violence and hard work.

The Bolsheviks soon began arguing about which roads led to communism. Amidst the sheer chaos of civil war and impending societal breakdown, their near millenarian celebration of the coming of the new age seemed destined to collide with awkward realities. Leon Trotsky presented his views at the Central Committee meeting of the Bolshevik party in December 1919. With the transportation system largely destroyed, farmers falling back on subsistence agriculture, and workers deserting the cities for the countryside and a chance of something to eat, only a militarization of the labor force would save the socialist experiment. He wanted to transform Red Army units into labor armies to repair the infrastructure and impose brutal army discipline on factories, for otherwise there would be no goods to sell farmers and no incentive, in turn, for peasants to market crops. "Just as we once issued the order 'Proletarians, to horse!', so now we must raise the cry 'Proletarians, back to the factory bench! Proletarians, back to production!' "[85]

Trotsky's speech triggered fierce opposition from trade union leaders like Alexei Rykov and Mikhail Tomsky, who already disliked the civil war–induced control of production by state-appointed managers, preferring the genuine collectivism of proletarian factory control envisioned by Marx. Trotsky's Draconian policies would depart even more from this ideal. His opponents also criticized the inefficiency of compulsory labor: "You cannot build a planned economy in the way the pharaohs built their pyramids."[86] The trade union position found the backing of the so-called Workers' Opposition, led by Alexander Shlyapnikov and Alexandra Kollontai. This influential leftist faction in the party advocated a sort of proletarian democracy whereby all managerial appointments needed the consent of the unions and "all the cardinal questions of party activity and soviet policy are to be submitted to the consideration of the rank and file."[87]

Lenin and the majority of the party vacillated, first siding with Trotsky at the Ninth Party Congress in March 1920, then, after the termination of war with Poland that autumn, insisting expediently that he mollify his position. Indeed, revolutionary events had forced the Bolsheviks into the storm cellar. A series of political strikes erupted in Moscow, spread quickly to Saint Petersburg and other western industrial cities, and finally reached the ice-bound naval bastion on the island of Kronstadt, which declared independence. The countryside presented greater dangers, for peasants fed up with Bolshevik grain requisition squads began shooting back, killing thousands of "Reds" and eliminating Soviet power in much of the countryside. Lenin drew the appropriate conclusion at the Tenth Party Congress in March 1921: "We are barely holding on," he said, describing the peasant wars as "far more dangerous than all the Denikins, Yudeniches and Kolchaks put together."[88]

But hold on they did with a short-term strategy of brute force. Elite Red Army units assaulted across the ice on March 16–17, 1921, losing ten thousand of their number but crushing the defenders. Later, firing squads meted out communist justice to the prisoners. Massive village-by-village, province-by-province retaliation combined with widespread famine to teach this same steely lesson to the peasants. About fifteen thousand were shot and another hundred thousand jailed or deported in 1921–1922, while an estimated five million starved to death. In the final stage of this crackdown Lenin and his henchmen also ratcheted up their anti-religion campaign. In March 1922 he issued orders for waging "the most decisive and merciless war" against the Russian Orthodox Church. "The more members of the reactionary bourgeoisie and clergy we manage to shoot the better."[89] They "managed" to shoot eight thousand that year and imprison another ten thousand.

The Bolsheviks dubbed their long-term strategy for eliminating the root causes of the strikes and uprisings the "New Economic Policy." Approved as the Red Army prepared to storm Kronstadt, "NEP" featured a partial return to capitalism and a market economy. It stopped grain requisitioning, reduced taxation in kind to 10 percent of the crop, and allowed peasants to market the remainder, hire labor, and rent additional land. It also legalized private trading, which had continued illegally during three years of what was now conveniently called "war communism." In the cities and towns tens of thousands of manufacturing firms returned to private hands. NEP ended labor conscription and restored labor mobility and market wages. Only the so-called commanding heights of the economy—the railroads, the banks, and the largest mines and industrial firms—stayed in state hands. The program aimed to expand light industrial production for farming, induce peasants to increase production and sell their crops, and attract foreign credit and state-of-the-art investment. With the country in revolt and the economy in shambles—overall production in 1921 registered a mere seventh of the 1913 level—no practical alternative existed. Lenin told party members to anticipate at least a decade of the new program.

From 1914 to 1922 apocalyptic riders trampled everything underfoot in Russia, killing over twelve million people. When it was over the Bolsheviks' tightening one-party dictatorship had crushed counterrevolutionaries and opponents of all stripes: "White" Russian nationalists; Constitutional Democrats; ethnic nationalist movements in Georgia, the Ukraine, and elsewhere; clerics; mutinous workers and sailors; peasant rebels; and Socialist Revolutionaries. Only left-wing SRs were tolerated at times during the civil war, but the Bolsheviks finally rounded up the last of these agrarian socialists in 1922 and subjected them to the first of many sham public "show trials." "We might have a two-party system," joked party theoretician Nikolai Bukharin, "but one of the two parties would be in office and the other in prison."[90] "We laugh at pure democracy,"[91] added Lenin. Even the Mensheviks, fellow Marxists, were not safe: Five thousand were arrested in 1921, although they were spared the indignity of a show trial.

Political intolerance spread rapidly within the Bolshevik camp too. The communist art world experienced the beginnings of this crackdown in December 1920 when the party brought "Proletkult," a previously autonomous center for revolutionary culture, under strict control, including censorship of art and expulsion of intellectuals from Russia. "We'll clean up Russia for a long time to come," boasted Lenin to a rising star of the party, Joseph Stalin, in 1922. All of them—throw them out of Russia. This must be done at once. By the end of the SR trial, no later. Arrest a few hundred, and without going into motives—off with you, gentlemen!"[92] Lenin sent nearly three hundred artists and intellectuals packing that year. An amended criminal code permitted immediate execution if they ever returned.

Similarly, the Bolsheviks' Tenth Party Congress imposed a ban on intra-party "factions" in March 1921. Lenin's move targeted mainly the grassroots following of "traitors" like Shlyapnikov and Kollontai. "I maintain that there is a connection between the ideas and the slogans of the petty-bourgeois, anarchic counter-revolution and the slogans of the Workers' Opposition. . . . Why isn't Shlyapnikov being turned over to a court for such statements?"[93] For the "crime" of factionalism Kollontai went into political exile. The Cheka harassed other members of the Workers' Opposition, eventually expelling many of them from the party. Moreover, that year's congress created a special Central Control Commission under the leadership of the apparently unambitious, but actually very ruthless Joseph Stalin. Its mission: to monitor the ban on factions and otherwise ensure party loyalty. In 1921 this security organization struck 30 percent of the rank and file—almost a quarter of a million "anarcho-syndicalists, waverers, doubters, and dissidents"[94]—from party lists.

It would be difficult to exaggerate the degree of disillusionment that descended over the Bolshevik faithful after 1921. Alexander Blok, one of Russia's greatest poets, lost the messianic zeal for communism that earlier allowed poetry to reverberate in his ears. "All sounds have stopped," he lamented shortly before his death in July 1921. Other well-known poets like Vladimir Mayakovsky and Sergei Essenin were driven by political despair to suicide, while the great novelist and close friend of Lenin, Maxim Gorky, left the country "sickened and disturbed by the growing sum of suffering which people have to pay as the price of their fine hopes."[95]

At party congresses party members turned much of this dissent and disgust against Lenin himself. "Why then talk about the dictatorship of the proletariat, about self-initiative of the workers?" cried one courageous delegate. "There is no such initiative—you are turning the party member into a record player." Lenin "rules our Soviet policies," complained another. "Evidently, every movement from whatever direction which interferes with this rule is labeled petty bourgeois in its character and extremely harmful."[96] The fading hopes for intraparty democracy were matched in the depth of emotion they generated by the disappointment many felt for the alleged break from true socialism under NEP. The reappearance of money, markets, and ostentatious profit seeking convinced many party members that the revolution had been betrayed as the country plunged down "the slippery slope that led back to capitalism." Renaming NEP the "New Exploitation of the Proletariat,"[97] tens of thousands of Bolshevik workers tore up their party cards. The bulk of party officials stayed, but there can be no doubt that NEP created a deep reservoir of resentment against capitalist demons and a desire to take revenge with "civil war toughness" on bourgeois class enemies, particularly on perceived worst offenders among the peasantry.

The revolution was not over, however, nor was it time to proclaim the downfall of socialism and communism. By the mid-1920s the regime began to make good on earlier promises of social insurance benefits, medical care, and education. In 1924 communist leaders also initiated a great industrialization debate over the most practical means to build a socialist economy and ultimately attain communism—topics Marx had largely glossed over. On one side argued "gradualists" like Nikolai Bukharin who wanted to proceed slowly within the framework of NEP toward socialized forms of production. Rejecting this opinion, "accelerators" like Leon Trotsky and Evgeni Preobrazhenski, a brilliant young economist, presented their case for a quick and violent buildup of nationalized heavy industry.

Bukharin based his proposals on the need for peace and stability, especially in the countryside. After the scary peasant uprisings of 1920–1921 the party could not afford an abrupt and provocative return to civil war–style socialism. Rather, the party should give NEP time to restore industrial and agricultural output to prewar levels—a position the Soviet Union finally reached in 1927. Only then should they nationalize industry, gearing production to peasant needs like farm implements and consumer items. The presumed efficiency of socialized light industry would prove the correctness of Marxism and gradually convince the peasantry to make a voluntary transition to demonstrably superior collectivized agriculture. Resources of capital and labor accumulated in light industry and agriculture would eventually flow into heavy industry. The whole process would take perhaps fifty years.

The accelerators accused the gradualists of naïveté for refusing to admit that Russian industry was too underdeveloped and burdened with old, nearly worn-out machinery to cater adequately to peasant needs. After waiting for generations to acquire "their" land, moreover, the petty bourgeois enemies of the revolution would never relinquish it. Meanwhile the capitalist nations of Western Europe had recuperated sufficiently from the war to unleash a crusade against communism. Foreign and domestic capitalists would inevitably link arms in this struggle and then "start an economic as well as a military-political offensive," warned Preobrazhenski. "We are building socialism in a situation of a breathing spell between two battles." Accordingly, the party should coerce peasants into collective farms and force them to sell crops to the state at low prices. Proceeds from grain exports at higher world prices would be poured into heavy industry and war-making capacity. Peasants not needed in the countryside would be herded into mines and factories. After perhaps twenty years of this "primitive socialist accumulation"[98] the Soviet Union could defend its revolution.

By the time party leaders adopted a compromise position in December 1927, far-reaching changes had occurred at the top. Lenin suffered two serious strokes in 1922 that limited his capacities and raised immediate questions about his successor. The great revolutionary's death in January 1924 triggered a bitter power struggle among his former henchmen. The heir apparent seemed to be Leon Trotsky, commissar for military affairs and hero of the civil war. Although his impassioned oratory and innovative interpretations of Marx placed him on an intellectual level with Lenin, Trotsky made a series of tactical errors, beginning with his failure to appear at Lenin's funeral. The Red

Army Chief also sorely underestimated his opponents. Three jealous rivals united against him: Gregory Zinoviev, boss of the Saint Petersburg (Leningrad) Soviet and chairman of the Communist International (Comintern); Lev Kamenev, party leader in Moscow; and Joseph Stalin, head of the Central Control Commission (CCC), general secretary of the party, head of the Organization Bureau (Orgburo), commissar of nationalities, as well as chief of Rabkrin, the security apparatus in the bureaucracy. This powerful triumvirate succeeded in denouncing and discrediting Trotsky in 1924. Then Stalin formed a new alliance with *Pravda* editor Nikolai Bukharin during 1925 and 1926. Together they lambasted Zinoviev and Kamenev for siding with Trotsky in the industrialization debate. All three were removed from their posts and expelled from the party in 1926 and 1927. Soon Stalin turned against Bukharin too. While his underlying belief in Marxism appears to have been unshakeable, power, not principles, trumped in each of Stalin's alliances. He had maneuvered himself to the top and would stay there for the next twenty-five years.

Who was Stalin, and how had he obtained so many party positions? Born Joseph Dzhugashvili in rural Georgia in 1879, the future dictator and generalissimo of the Soviet Union had a searing childhood punctuated by frequent beatings at the hands of a drunken father, near death from smallpox that left his face scarred, and a left arm withered by another childhood infection. Expelled from a seminary in Tiflis in 1899, he joined Lenin's Bolshevik Party under the acquired name of Joseph Stalin, the "man of steel." The young Georgian was never the intellectual equal of Lenin, Zinoviev, Kamenev, or later joiners like Trotsky and Bukharin, but Lenin sympathized with Stalin's lower-class background and learned to appreciate the quiet man's eagerness to work. Was it perhaps "the painful sense of intellectual inadequacy that he felt at party congresses as he sat and listened to brilliant speeches being made" that combined with his terrible early life to explain "the deep springs of irrationality, harshness, and cunning"[99] that ran deep in the psyche of Lenin's hardworking lieutenant?

The revolution and civil war created opportunities for Lenin's right-hand man—jobs that more articulate revolutionaries eschewed as mindless bureaucratic drudgery. In 1919 the leader picked Stalin to head the Orgburo, an agency responsible for staffing all local and regional party posts. As chief of Rabkrin (1919) and the CCC (1921), the man of steely nerves kept files—and a close watch—on everyone in the bureaucracy and party. In 1922 Lenin again tapped Stalin as general secretary, the person responsible for setting Politburo agendas and transmitting decisions to the bottom rungs of the party. As the early 1920s unfolded, the Bolshevik's organizational tsar used his authority and personal information to forge a massive party following loyal and indebted to him. In 1922 alone Stalin handpicked ten thousand functionaries at the local and regional level. From this pool of party servers came the delegates to annual party congresses who voted, in turn, for candidates to the powerful Central Committee—candidates selected from a list prepared by the General Secretary. By 1926 Stalin controlled a malleable majority on the Central Committee—the body that successively outvoted and demoted Trotsky, Zinoviev, Kamenev, Bukharin, and many others.

Thus it was Stalin, not any of the men who once appeared more likely to succeed Lenin, who cast final judgments in the industrialization debate. The Fifteenth Party Congress of December 1927 terminated NEP and accelerated planning for the transition to collective agriculture and socialized industry. Economic experts produced a draft Five Year Plan in August 1928, which they fine-tuned prior to the next congress in April 1929. Stalin's planners envisioned a gradual collectivization of agriculture: Only 15 percent of output would be grown on collective farms by plan's end in 1933. This pace still seemed too rapid to Bukharin, whom Stalin and his Central Committee cronies therefore expelled from the Politburo. In contrast to the agricultural goals of the plan, its industrial side bore the unmistakable imprint of Trotsky and Preobrazhenski, whose "accelerator" positions Stalin had once branded "left deviationist." Industrial output, with a particular emphasis on heavy industry, would expand 180 percent by 1933. Projected annual growth rates of nearly 20 percent were unprecedented—four to five times quicker, in fact, than previous rapidly industrializing nations like Germany, the United States, and Japan.

Two years into the plan Stalin explained to party followers the need for heavy industrial buildup at such breakneck speed. "Those who lag behind are beaten," he warned in February 1931.

> We do not want to be beaten. No, we don't want to. In the history of old Russia she was ceaselessly beaten for her backwardness. She was beaten by the Mongol Khans, she was beaten by the Turkish Beys, she was beaten by Swedish feudal lords, she was beaten by Polish-Lithuanian *Pans*, she was beaten by Anglo-French capitalists, she was beaten by Japanese barons, she was beaten by all—for her backwardness. . . . We are fifty or a hundred years behind the advanced countries. We must make good this lag in ten years. Either we do it or they crush us.[100]

Such belligerent assumptions from the Soviet dictator did not augur well for the chances of peace.

Chapter 5

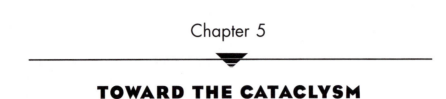

TOWARD THE CATACLYSM

The small town of Northeim braced for another Nazi rally. Although thermometers were dropping in early 1932, political temperatures soared in this rural district seat in North-Central Germany. Local satraps of Adolf Hitler, leader of the National Socialist German Workers Party (NSDAP), mobilized the faithful.

On January 25–26 large throngs packed into the 1910er Zelt, a large meeting hall on the outskirts of town, to hear martial music, patriotic speeches, dire warnings about the Bolshevik threat to the middle class, and inspirational words about the "struggle against Marxism." Over 55 percent of the town and surrounding countryside—and about one in three Germans—needed no convincing that the "Nazis" would be their salvation.

Two days later local organizers of the Social Democratic Party of Germany (SPD) herded their own backers into the 1910er Zelt. The fife and drum corps of the SPD's paramilitary organization, having already provided rousing entertainment as the members arrived, stood at attention beneath the black-red-gold flag of the Weimar Republic. For the next three hours "Sozi" speakers railed against Nazi militarism and accused Hitler's party of capitalist leanings.

On February 2, 1932, came the turn of the SPD-backed War Widows and Industrial Accident Victims Association. Speakers shouted that German democracy had not created all of the widows and orphans, as Hitler claimed—the real culprit was the Great War itself. One thing seemed obvious to the working women of Northeim: If the Nazis had their way the Great War would not be the last world war for poor wives to endure, but rather just the first.[1]

In Geneva, far to the south of Northeim, women also marched on February 2, 1932. They wound their way through the narrow cobblestone streets of the old town and headed toward the lake. Each wore a white armband with "Pax" written on it and a green sash bearing the name of her home country. These "mother-hearts of the world" carried bundles and packages of petitions as if bringing "presents for a Christmas tree," wrote one Geneva newspaper.

The women made their way to a meeting hall near the League Secretariat, where the World Disarmament Conference would open later that afternoon. The opening session had been delayed in order for the Council to hold an emergency meeting over the Japanese invasion of Manchuria. The troubling development in the Far East explained the stern expressions on the women as they filed into the hall. One by one, they placed their bundles near the podium until, swollen even more by extra millions of signatures brought by the delegates themselves, the stacks reached to the shoulders of the opening speaker, Mary Dingman. Representing forty-five million women in numerous women's organizations, she shouted that nations spent far too much money on armaments. Next, a young American college student stepped up and charged that the ten million dead crusaders in the "war to end all war" looked from today's perspective like "victims of an illusion when they fell to earth only a few years ago." His call for world peace was "not a petition but an ultimatum."[2]

Mary Dingman, the American student, and the Sozi women of Northeim all refused to believe that the world's economic doldrums, Mussolini, Hitler, and the first blatant act of aggression in Asia made another war inevitable. They fought against the kind of cynicism that made pundits already begin to call the Great War "World War One" or that made American youth mock the Veterans of Foreign Wars by protesting as "victims of future wars." It was February 1932—and high time for pacifists to step boldly up.

THE GREAT DEPRESSION

The New York stock market crashed on October 24, 1929.[3] For most of the decade America's economy had boomed as the construction and automobile industries provided investment and jobs. Large financial institutions, and the small man too, poured money into Wall Street, believing that the growth in stock prices would never stop. For well over a year before the crash, however, growth in the economy itself had been slowing. As the perception spread that recession neared, stock buying abruptly switched to selling—sixteen million shares on "Black Thursday" alone.

Throughout the winter of 1929–1930 the U.S. recession deepened and widened to the industrialized world, for Japanese and European investors had also speculated on Wall Street. American markets for their goods had shrunk, furthermore, and American banks recalled loans in a frenetic effort to stay liquid. By mid-1930 a new term—Great Depression—had entered journalistic vocabularies. With unemployment soaring above 20 percent that summer in countries particularly hard-hit like Germany, the term seemed very apt.

While it is clear that the Wall Street crash triggered the Great Depression, historians still debate the deeper, underlying causes of this economic disaster.[4] Most investigators turn back to Europe and the Great War for a beginning of the explanation. The last delayed explosion of that conflict, in fact, was an economic one, touched off by the slumping American economy. The war had left European economies enervated and weak. Like tables teetering ominously on three legs, they could not absorb the concussion from New York.

Britain and Germany best illustrate the point. Pillars of Europe's economy before the war, they could not provide this support after 1918. While

British industrialists neglected foreign customers to produce for the war, and investors liquidated overseas investments to finance it, American, Japanese, and Commonwealth firms stole British markets and undercut London's role as world banker. Rigid insistence on returning to the gold standard in 1926 further undercut exports by overpricing these goods. The legacy of the Great War amounted to reduced earnings from overseas investments, a stagnant export sector, and high unemployment—8 percent on the eve of the crash. The world war hurt Germany even more. The loss of colonies and European provinces combined with the punitive aspects of the Treaty of Versailles to keep production low and unemployment high well into the 1920s. The Dawes Plan and American credit created only an artificial recovery. Already in late 1928, in fact, short-term loans from the United States began to be recalled so that banks could speculate in stocks. Without this credit Germany could not simultaneously pay reparations and fuel expansion. Consequently, unemployment rose to 9 percent in the summer of 1929, months before the events on Wall Street.

The fall of the great Austro-Hungarian and Russian empires also had severe economic repercussions. Where a pair of huge free trade blocs existed before 1914 now stood nine struggling states plus the Soviet Union. It would be difficult to exaggerate the disruption and dislocation that this caused. For instance, Poland was plagued by three different railroad systems, each with a different gauge and signaling system. Czechoslovakia's rails radiated north from Vienna and Budapest, whereas the new nation's commercial axis ran east to west. Suppliers of industrial raw materials oftentimes found their customers across a new border, while manufacturers frequently faced the same dilemma for deliveries of coal, ores, chemicals, and other inputs to production. Complicating matters still more, old customers now found themselves behind a new protective tariff wall, for the fledgling states of Eastern Europe wanted to develop their own industries for national security reasons, regardless of the fact that this perpetuated inefficiencies. Reflecting the overall dilemma of the region, trade along the Danube River—which flowed through Germany, Austria, Hungary, Yugoslavia, Rumania, and Bulgaria—sank in the1920s to 17 percent of prewar levels.

These eastern roadblocks to commerce affected the entire continent. Indeed, the tariffs of Poland, Hungary, Rumania, and Bulgaria also hurt Germany, France, Britain, and other nations that had sent a large volume of goods to Eastern Europe before 1914. Trade restrictions in the East contributed to the sluggish growth rate of West European exports in the 1920s—one that did not regain the 1913 pace until 1928. Worse still, the volume of exports, figured as a percentage of overall production in the West, slipped to about 60 percent of the prewar level in 1920—and never climbed above 80 percent before the stock market collapsed.

Perhaps the greatest disequilibrium created by war occurred in European and world agriculture. Farmers in Argentina, Australia, Canada, and the United States expanded food production to meet the voracious demand of the Great War, but, not surprisingly, did not curtail output after 1918. Thus wheat acreage in these countries rose from 87.5 million on the eve of war to 117.4 million in the mid-1920s. By this time, however, Europe's tens of millions of acres of ruined farmland had been restored, and Russian production soared under NEP. Because the demand for food is so inelastic—people eat only so much, and there were fewer people after the war—stockpiles rose by 75 percent and prices cascaded by 30 percent from 1924 to 1929. Farmers' purchasing power dropped proportionately with particularly drastic consequences in countries where a high percentage of the population depended on agriculture: 36 percent of the labor force worked the land in France, but percentages rose to 44 in Italy; 53 in Hungary; 58–66 in Estonia, Greece, Poland, and Latvia; and 71–80 in Finland, Yugoslavia, Rumania, Lithuania, and Bulgaria. Throughout Eastern Europe by the late 1920s, in fact, the ability to import expensive manufactured goods declined precipitously as a result of the worsening agricultural crisis created by the Great War.

In so many ways, therefore, war-weakened Europe was not prepared to absorb the shock waves of the stock market crash and subsequent U.S. recession. Disappearing American industrial markets, investment values, and credit opportunities knocked the third leg out from under the European economy after late October 1929—and it collapsed. Unlike the prewar period when so much of world finance had been controlled in London, moreover, no one hegemonic banking center existed either to prevent the shock from coming or to coordinate international pickup efforts when it hit. European manufacturers already struggling unsuccessfully to regain prewar dominance now panicked, covered declining sales by drawing down inventories, drastically curtailing production, reducing wages, and laying off more workers. Unemployment climbed to 11 percent in Britain and 22 percent in Germany during 1930. Workers who received meager unemployment insurance payments that equaled only 25–35 percent of gross pay, and lasted a mere fifteen to twenty-six weeks, could afford few purchases. Hence factories had to cut back even more on production and lay off even more workers—which worsened the downward spiral of purchasing power and production.

Exacerbating the situation terribly, farmers tried to compensate for falling prices by expanding acreage. This had disastrous results. As food stockpiles continued to rise, overall agricultural prices nose-dived 44 percent from October 1929 to December 1930, then fell another 40 percent through 1931 and 1932. As European farmers—and especially farming nations in Eastern Europe—reduced purchases of industrial goods, industry contracted still more. Percentage declines of manufacturing output in developed industrial economies between 1929 and 1932 were precipitous: 16 in Britain, 28 in France, 31 in Belgium, 36 in Czechoslovakia, and 47 in Germany. Unemployment rates in 1932 ranged from 17 percent in Britain to nearly 40 percent in Germany. It was the worst socioeconomic catastrophe in modern times.

The sheer numbers affected by unemployment speak to the human cost of this industrial crisis. There were almost a million out of work in France, another million in Italy, nearly three million in Britain, six million in Germany—

The Great Depression: hunger march in Britain in 1933. (Hulton/Archive by Getty Images)

but eight million if one counts those no longer looking for work—and a disastrous fifteen million in the United States. Overall numbers in Europe were probably somewhat comparable to the U.S. figure.

Readers can better appreciate the significance to society of these numbers by considering the psychological and emotional distress that unemployment caused to most of these individuals. Two British researchers observed in 1938, for instance, that unemployed persons spiraled emotionally downward from an opening stage of optimistically seeking another job, to a pessimistic and anxious stage when no work was found, and then finally succumbing to a fatalistic stage and "broken attitude." "Us men that's learned to work," said one British laborer, "are lost without it." Another commented more articulately on the "worry and misery" of living on unemployment insurance: "We cannot shake off the general debility, the nervous irritation and bouts of indigestion and headaches, because the main cause—worry—cannot be removed."[5]

Some employers sought to bolster bruised male psyches by firing female employees, even though such assertions of traditional gender roles made no microeconomic sense. More typically businesses reacted rationally by sacking the highly paid men. Women were hardly gainers, however, for they still had to perform household chores during the early morning and evening. Resentful husbands oftentimes vented their depression, moreover, through wifebeating. Male against male violence also increased, especially during the second "anxious" stage of unemployment. In Northeim, for example, thousands of men filed into town and headed for an old army compound housing the district unemployment office. "Inevitably," writes William Sheridan Allen, "there were jostlings, arguments, eruptions of the pent-up energy of idle men."[6]

Like their bourgeois counterparts all across Europe, the upper classes of Northeim reacted anxiously and angrily to the deteriorating situation in their hometown. Seventeen small businesses failed in Northeim during the Great Depression, and farms outside town went bankrupt too. As businessmen and farmers fought to keep solvent, the stress and anxiety level deepened with the fear that one might be next to join the ranks of the destitute. It was perhaps only natural, therefore, that burghers turned their angst against the victims. "Masses of young men stood idle on the corners and made a lot of noise," recalled one, "often insulting people who were passing by." Another recalled that "there were great numbers of unemployed who just stood around—the bulk of them were just lazy and didn't want to work—theirs was a sad case."[7]

What happened in one small town occurred elsewhere too. In Germany as a whole the number of bankruptcies shot up 20 percent from 1930 to 1931. France experienced similar difficulties. With business and farm bankruptcies rising from 6,500 in 1929 to 13,370 in 1935, insecurity swept through the ranks of the French middle classes. This feeling of crisis and impending disaster manifested itself statistically in a declining birth rate, which fell from 18.2 per 1,000 in the period 1926–1930 to 14.8 in 1936–1938. Mothers and fathers did not need extra mouths to feed, nor could they confidently create life knowing that the world, in all probability, would not be spared another war.

What could be said for France and Germany was also true for all of Europe. With each passing year from 1929 to 1932 the continental climate changed from optimism and hope to pessimism and despair. Like the Great Depression itself, this darker mood was a delayed effect of the Great War. Before 1914 most Europeans took the steady advance of European civilization largely for granted. Even the peace movement remained confident of pacifism's ultimate victory until about 1913, when it was forced to concede the necessity of waging a war for peace. The Great War and its violent aftermath seemed to be the very negation of progress and all safe prewar assumptions, but by the mid-1920s much of this disillusionment had been overcome, Europe's optimistic spirit revived, and confidence in peace and democracy strengthened. When in the 1930s, however, the misery of the depression revived the disillusionment of the immediate postwar world it grew harder to refute fascist and Nazi demagogues who had never stopped preaching that war as revealed in the trenches of the first conflagration was the natural order of things.

This is not to say that the Great Depression made another war inevitable, for, as the opening vignettes demonstrate, men and women of peace still resisted the deepening mood of resignation. In many concrete, nonpsychological ways, however, economic collapse accelerated violent, disruptive forces that made pacifists' work increasingly difficult. Above all the Great Depression forced debilitating distractions from the promising peace efforts of the late 1920s. To the excruciating frustration of the champions of peace, national leaders spent less time in Geneva, taken away from the pacifist cause by the pressing need to solve problems at home. The economic theory of that day, however, prescribed no easy solutions for politicians. Operating on the assumption that a recession would right itself by the stimulating effect that low prices and interest rates eventually have on spending and investment, most governments opted to speed recovery with "deflation," that is, by cutting government spending and shrinking the money supply—policies that only worsened economies too shaken to respond to normal stimuli. When the standard solutions failed, leaders redoubled domestic efforts to find a way out, thereby robbing international concerns of their urgent priority.

Meanwhile, peacekeeping work decelerated, eventually slowing to a near standstill. Not until March 1930 did the big three naval powers—Britain, the United States, and Japan—agree on a formula for limiting battleships, cruisers, destroyers, and submarines. Another nine months expired before the League's Preparatory Commission completed work on an agenda for its disarmament conference, and a further fourteen months before that conference convened. Too much time had been lost, for the work of peace would be more difficult in February 1932.

It created considerable bad will in the world, for instance, when leaders of one nation after another turned to the traditional quick fixes. One of the first nationalistic panaceas came in March 1930 with the adoption of higher tariffs in the United States. The notion of protecting jobs at home by undercutting the export industries of other nations offered only temporary improvement, for soon a score of countries retaliated with protective tariffs of their own. Furthermore, when a chain of bank failures swept from Austria and Germany to Britain in the summer of 1931, London terminated the gold standard and devalued the pound, a move designed to recapture markets lost in the 1920s. But now France and many other nations retaliated, devaluing their currencies in the hope of boosting exports. Retaliatory tariffs and currency devaluations worsened a depression that had been triggered, we should recall, by weakened export sectors. Consequently, the value of world foreign trade spiraled farther downward from 2.9 billion dollars in October 1929 to 1.2 billion in February 1932.

Selfish economic nationalism undermined the chances of peace in other ways. France hosted two million foreign workers before the depression struck, the bulk hailing from Italy (30 percent), Poland (19 percent), and Spain (13 percent). Not surprisingly, employers laid off foreigners first. France later deported tens of thousands, and for one reason or another a million went back to their homelands in the 1930s with bitter feelings for this western nation. The United States, Britain, and other West European countries created additional resentments by tightening their immigration policies, with Eastern Europe hurt most by these restrictions. Emigration from Bulgaria dropped from a yearly average of five thousand in the 1920s, for instance, to four hundred in the 1930s. The unwanted peasants of the East soon added exploitation to their list of grievances, for the increasingly adverse terms of trade struck them as malevolent. While the price of Rumanian farm exports fell 62 percent from

1931 to 1935, for example, the price of manufactured goods imported from the West dropped only 33 percent.

As resentments accumulated in the early 1930s, chances for implementing peaceful alternatives to war grew slimmer. Thus Japanese army radicals drew their own conclusions from the Great Depression. Pointing to the fallacy of trading for raw materials vital to national security in a world of slumping trade, they defied democratic rulers in Tokyo and seized Manchuria from China in the autumn of 1931. Exuding a spirit of belligerent autarky, the militants began to transform the stolen province into a military-industrial complex. The seizure of Manchuria was but a twisted logical extension of the tactics of tariffs, currency devaluations, deportations, and immigration quotas—zero sum policies that boosted the home country by taking from others.

Significantly, the world did nothing to punish Japan. The United States and Great Britain had no intention of exacerbating the depression by imposing economic sanctions on Japan, let alone alienating isolationist and pacifist sentiments by going to war in a faraway place. Without British willingness to fight, the League of Nations remained paralyzed. "War is re-enthroned," warned one British newspaper, "a straight road back to 1914 lies open."[8] Would Europe take it?

Author Aldous Huxley had already resigned himself to the worst. In 1931, even before the decade's first shots in Manchuria, he penned one of the interwar years' most pessimistic statements on the destiny of European civilization. *Brave New World* took place in a futuristic society that had largely abolished freedom in order to preserve humankind. Economic collapse and a horrific "Nine Years War" many centuries earlier had triggered revolutionary prophylactic change in the form of a world state divided into regional control zones. People were produced in laboratories with differing degrees of intelligence depending on the work they were designed to perform, but even the genetically most gifted were conditioned from birth to adhere to principles of submission drummed into them by the state. Soma, a benign hallucinatory drug available in unlimited quantities, offered an escape from every form of unpleasantness, and if conditioning and soma failed, controllers rocketed recalcitrant mavericks away to island quarantines.

The only "freedom" permitted in the future—indeed, massively encouraged through conditioning—was unrestricted sexual promiscuity. Contraceptive sex in a world without families became the ultimate diversion of man's destructive or subversive instincts. With *Brave New World*, in fact, Huxley offered a hypothetical solution to the problem of human aggressiveness identified in *Civilization and Its Discontents* two years before. Sigmund Freud "had been the first to reveal the appalling dangers of family life," Huxley wrote. "The world was full of fathers—was therefore full of misery; full of mothers—therefore of every kind of perversion from sadism to chastity; full of brothers, sisters, uncles, aunts—full of madness and suicide."[9]

As readers would expect, brave new world totalitarianism controlled culture as thoroughly as everything else. Monuments and museums as well as art and literature memorializing or mirroring the self-destructive societies of the past have been proscribed. The state feeds its people only multisensory pornographic "feely" films that reinforce the conditioning-induced urge to fornicate and forget. In the book's climactic scene, John, a visitor from a "savage reservation" in the American Southwest who is unfamiliar with and disgusted by this kind of social engineering, protests to one of the world controllers, Mustapha Mond: "But I don't want comfort. I want God, I want poetry, I want real danger, I want freedom, I want goodness, I want sin." "In fact," replied Mond, "you're claiming the right to be unhappy . . . to live in constant apprehension of what may happen tomorrow . . . to be tortured by unspeakable pains of every kind."[10] A tradeoff between unhappiness and stability had become impossible in the brave new world.

THE CRISIS OF DEMOCRACY AND THE FAILURE OF THE LEAGUE

As the Japanese example demonstrates, the most menacing and frightening development for those who desired peace was the havoc the Depression wreaked on democracy. Parliamentary rule by the people, already eroding quickly in the 1920s, lost more ground because of a depression that democratic governments could not solve. The suffering of the 1930s felled six more democracies—Germany (1933), Austria (1933), Estonia (1934), Latvia (1934), Greece (1935), and Rumania (1938). If it is true that established democracies never wage war against one another, then it was certainly tragic that democracies fell, especially so because the people's regimes were replaced by dictatorships advocating violence, not peace.[11] In East-Central Europe only Finland and Czechoslovakia survived into the late 1930s as democracies, and the latter fell to Nazi Germany in March 1939.

Clearly the rise of Adolf Hitler and his jack-booted storm troopers to power did not augur well for peace. Put bluntly, the Nazis exuded hate, worshipped violence, and prayed for war, even though they opportunistically toned down this message after 1928. The story of the fall of German democracy, therefore, becomes a necessary prequel to any analysis of the ultimate failure of the League's disarmament efforts, and of the League itself.

The Rise of the Nazis

The Reichstag elections of May 1928 resulted in tremendous disappointment for Adolf Hitler's NSDAP. Despite three years of organizational buildup and feverish campaigning that spring, the Nazis received a mere 2.6 percent of the vote, enough for only twelve seats. A strategy of targeting mainly industrial workers with extremely nationalistic, anti-Marxist, anti-Weimar, and anti-Semitic propaganda netted over a million votes less than the party's highwater mark of 6.5 percent in May 1924. Determined to reverse fortunes and get into power, Hitler and Nazi Party leaders repaired to party headquarters in Munich for a serious post mortem.

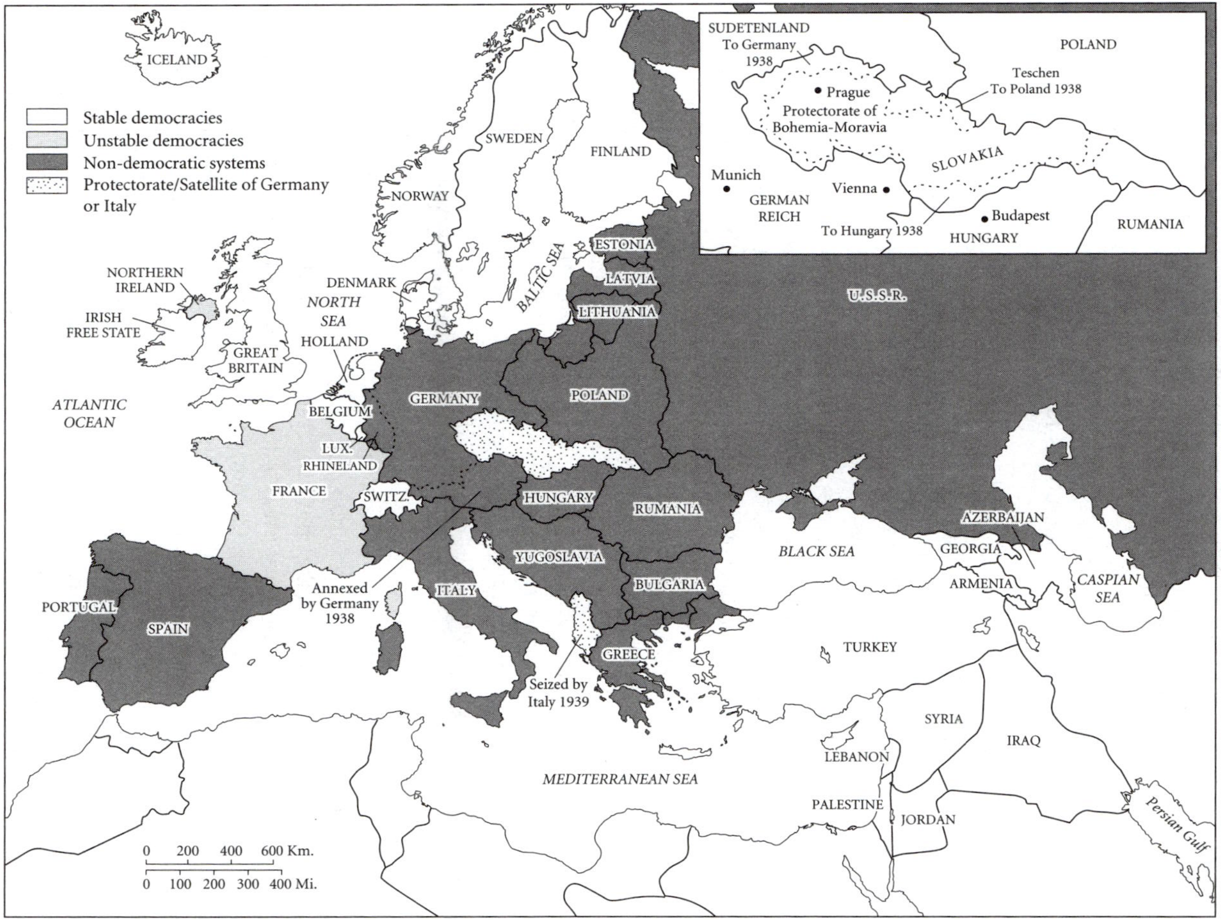

Stable democracies
Unstable democracies
Non-democratic systems
Protectorate/Satellite of Germany or Italy
ICELAND
NORWAY
SWEDEN
FINLAND
ESTONIA
LATVIA
LITHUANIA
BALTIC SEA
DENMARK
NORTH SEA
NORTHERN IRELAND
IRISH FREE STATE
GREAT BRITAIN
HOLLAND
BELGIUM
LUX.
RHINELAND
ATLANTIC OCEAN
FRANCE
SWITZ.
GERMANY
POLAND
U.S.S.R.
HUNGARY
RUMANIA
YUGOSLAVIA
BULGARIA
ITALY
GREECE
PORTUGAL
SPAIN
Annexed by Germany 1938
Seized by Italy 1939
BLACK SEA
AZERBAIJAN
GEORGIA
ARMENIA
CASPIAN SEA
TURKEY
SYRIA
IRAQ
LEBANON
PALESTINE
JORDAN
MEDITERRANEAN SEA
Persian Gulf
0 200 400 600 Km.
0 100 200 300 400 Mi.
SUDETENLAND To Germany 1938
Prague
Protectorate of Bohemia-Moravia
POLAND
Teschen To Poland 1938
SLOVAKIA
Munich
GERMAN REICH
Vienna
To Hungary 1938
Budapest
HUNGARY
RUMANIA

Democracies in 1939

These conferences laid the groundwork for one of the most remarkable turnarounds in political history. While not abandoning the urban working class to the Socialists and Communists, the Nazis would widen efforts to encompass farmers and small townspeople. Auxiliary organizations also came into being to proselytize among engineers, lawyers, doctors, teachers and professors, college students, young people, and, somewhat later, women. A revamped organization extending downward from Munich to local branches in city, town, and country would cater to the grievances of these particular groups by utilizing local party operatives familiar with the neighborhoods, pubs, and social clubs.

Apparently the party also decided to alter the overall propaganda message in one crucial respect: by softening an overt and crude anti-Semitism that had attracted few voters beyond the militant party core.[12] To be sure, anti-Semitic prejudices existed in Germany before 1914, and undoubtedly worsened during the xenophobia of the Great War, but of that segment of the population favoring anti-Semitic measures, which was probably a slight majority, only a small fraction wanted to go beyond limiting Jews' access to governmental and professional positions.[13] While it is true that Hitler had been subtly altering emphases in his speeches already before the 1928 elections, relegating his heartfelt Judeophobia to a secondary role, historians have nevertheless observed a distinct opportunistic change of tactics in campaigns for state elections in 1929. Outright attacks on the Jews were replaced by stepped-up assaults on the Weimar Republic, which was blamed for the Great Depression, the people's suffering, party-political chaos, and German humiliation since 1918. As a result of the new outreach to all groups in society—and also because of the reduced public emphasis on hatred of the Jews—electoral percentages in bi-elections soon leapt up to double, triple, or, in the case of Thuringia, more than quadruple the 1928 national figure.

It would be impossible to exaggerate the brutal cynicism and blatant opportunism of this change of course. Historians disagree about the origins and exact timing of Hitler's deep psychopathic revulsion against the Jews. There can be little doubt, however, that the twenty-five-year-old motorcycle currier who dodged bullets on the Western Front was already convinced that world Jewry was engaged in a clever and complicated conspiracy against the German people to prevent it from realizing its historical destiny. Such irrational, rabid fanaticism led to only one conclusion: the need "to settle scores with that crew, to get at them no matter what the cost," he wrote home in February 1915.

The obsessive drive "to smash Germany's foes"[14] pushed Hitler into politics in 1919. The fledgling Nazi Party that soon saluted him as "leader" was committed to a radical "solution" to the "Jewish Question." Germany had to "combat racial tuberculosis" and end "the poisoning of the people," he shouted in 1920, by "removing"[15] the Jews. That removal meant far more than deportation became clear in an interview Hitler gave to conservative journalist Josef Hell in 1922. When asked what he would do to the Jews if he came to power, Hitler blurted that "my first and foremost task will be the annihilation of the Jews." They would be "hanged indiscriminately" in one city after another "until all Germany has been completely cleansed of Jews."[16] Hell apparently never published the interview, but in his 1925 memoir, *Mein Kampf*, Hitler provided another unambiguous hint about his ultimate intentions. "If at the beginning of the war and during the war twelve or fifteen thousand of the Hebrew corrupters of the people had been held under poison gas, as happened to hundreds of thousands of our very best German workers in the field, the sacrifice of millions at the front would not have been in vain."[17] The fact that few people outside the Nazi Party read *Mein Kampf* certainly facilitated the tactical change of course after 1928.

With its new strategy of toning down anti-Semitism and addressing the grievances and anxieties of all social classes, Hitler's party positioned itself to reap the whirlwind of German politics. Nazi strategists and propagandists seized a major advantage in this campaign by systematically appealing to the traditional, deep-rooted, almost backward-looking nationalism of most Germans.[18] The marching, singing, torch-light processions, and book-burnings made famous by the Nazis, for instance, had all been used by earlier nationalistic movements, while the rousing anthem, *Deutschland über Alles*, composed in the 1830s, similarly anchored Nazism in the respected nationalistic traditions of earlier times. Another good example was the party motto, "Germany Awaken," which tapped into the centuries-old, emotion-charged legend of Barbarossa, the medieval emperor who Germans, particularly during hard times, had always believed would wake from his mountain slumber to restore the nation to greatness. Most important of all, in fact, was the way Hitler blessed the sacrifice of the Great War in an appeal to people's yearning for national restoration. "When he spoke of the disgrace of Germany, I felt ready to spring on any enemy," recalled a young businessman of the Nazi leader:

> His appeal to German manhood was like a call to arms, the gospel he preached a sacred truth. . . . Of course, I was ripe for this experience. I was a man of thirty-one, weary of disgust and disillusionment, a wanderer seeking a cause; a patriot without a channel for his patriotism, a yearner after the heroic without a hero. . . . I felt sure that no one who had heard Hitler that afternoon could doubt that he was a man of destiny, the vitalizing force in the future of Germany.[19]

Thus Hitler and the Nazis commandeered the symbols, language, and culture of nineteenth-century nationalism in a bid to present their movement to voters as traditional and respectable—in short, as legitimate.

One must also appreciate how highly attractive many Germans found the Nazi's nationalistic drumbeat during the nation's economic catastrophe. While the government fumbled and floundered, unsure how to reverse Germany's economic slide, Hitler and a battery of young and dynamic speakers at the local level exhaled confidence about their party's ability to arouse the nation. The lower classes sensed that the Nazis cared about the poor and destitute. They drank deeply of egalitarian propaganda that predicted a comeuppance for the fat cats. For their part the wealthy and established classes preferred to

Militant nationalists: Adolf Hitler with storm troop leader Ernst Röhm.   (Library of Congress)

see the Nazis as a bulwark against Red revolution and the expropriation of their property. Even the brutal street violence of *Sturmabteilung* (S.A.) storm troopers was rationalized as a beneficial phenomenon, for it was directed, after all, at the grasping Communists and Socialists. Professional groups among the middle classes also reacted positively to Hitler's movement, seeing it as a chance to put careers back on track.

Research on non-socialist middle-class women contributes to a fuller picture of Hitler's popularity, for the same issues troubling men in the early 1930s also made women anxious. Without repairing the position of men in society, women could not exert their special womanly influence at home as well as in public through social and patriotic service organizations. "To defend this 'turf' against cultural and economic erosion" they became politically engaged "to protect the patriarchal family upon which, they believed, women's traditional roles depended."[20] These kinds of women were attracted to Hitler, a dynamic, patriotic leader who promised to stand tall where too many German men, broken by the war, whimpered and cried (see Chapter 3). In twenty-seven of twenty-nine districts where men's and women's votes were counted separately in the Reichstag elections of September 1930, both women's turnout and women's support for the Nazis, as compared to 1928, increased faster than the men's.[21] These were the big breakthrough elections that pushed the party's vote from 2.6 percent to 18.3 percent. In July 1932, with unemployment at its high point in Germany, the Nazis captured 37.4 percent of the vote and became the largest party in the Reichstag. Hitler and the Nazis had become all things to all people.

Although the Nazi vote slipped to 33.1 percent in November 1932, Hitler's party still held the most seats in parliament. President Hindenburg, the aristocratic former commander of the kaiser's army, remained extremely reluctant to appoint Hitler, a rabble-rousing former corporal, to the chancellorship. On January 30, 1933, he did so, however, mainly because of worries that without a workable coalition government the army would not be able to contain a likely civil war between the Nazis and Communists or prevent Poland's military regime from intervening to seize territory in eastern Germany. Patrician Conservatives who took cabinet seats next to Hitler also assumed they could manipulate their petit bourgeois puppet.

Within weeks of taking office, however, Hitler began to expand his power. Surrounded by reactionary army compatriots, an aging Hindenburg agreed to his chancellor's request for emergency powers to contain an unsubstantiated threat of communist insurrection in February 1933. The decree suspended freedom of speech and assembly, civil liberties like habeas corpus, and the inviolability of private property. Bolstered by the unruly and thuggish S.A., whose numbers quickly doubled to a million, the Nazis now arrested and imprisoned most Communists as well as many leading Social Democrats. In March the Reichstag, controlled by the Nazis and other nationalistic parties, passed an Enabling Act that extended these emergency powers for the period of Hitler's chancellorship (i.e., for up to four years). Afterward the Communist Party was banned, the trade union movement shut down, and the SPD proscribed. In June and July came the turn of the parties of the Center and the Right to abolish themselves, for by now even conservatives were fearful of the consequences if they did not. Hitler was obviously not the paper tiger that many had thought. By July 1933 only Nazis sat in the Reichstag.

With his position at home consolidated, Hitler turned to foreign policy, withdrawing from the League of Nations Disarmament Conference as well as from the League itself in the autumn of 1933. Simultaneously, the Nazi dictator professed his desire for peace and willingness to sign long-term nonaggression pacts with other countries. Since his first week in office, however, Germany had been secretly rearming. How could champions of peace prevent war when the other side girded for it?

The League Disarmament Conference

The climate of international relations had worsened when the Disarmament Conference opened in February 1932. For two years high unemployment, counterproductive economic warfare, gender tensions, stiffening immigration and deportations, and the surging tide of Nazism had blotted out the idea of a European Union. The author of these plans, Aristide Briand, abandoned them in September 1930. The optimistic era of Locarno, Kellogg-Briand, and disarmament discussions had yielded to pessimism, suspicion, and anxiety by the time Japan seized Manchuria in September 1931. Sensing Europe's mood swing, the French began construction in 1930 of the so-called Maginot Line, a massive chain of fortifications designed to shield the nation from German invasion.

Nevertheless, at the first session France proposed a comprehensive web of arbitration agreements and a standing League of Nations' army to punish aggressors. These proposals had little chance of success. Aside from France and her allies in Eastern Europe, no power wanted to revise the League Covenant in such radical fashion. The United States remained especially reluctant to be drawn out of isolation into a collective enforcement network. When Paris asked Washington merely to consult on possible military action if a nation violated the Kellogg-Briand Pact, President Herbert Hoover waived off consultation as a "political impossibility."[22] Not until December 1932 could Britain, France, Italy, Germany, and the United States agree to a twofold formula for further discussions. First, Germany would have equality of rights in a system providing security for all nations; and second, all European nations would categorically renounce use of force to settle differences. The Disarmament Conference now adjourned until January 31, 1933—one day, as it turned out, after Hitler's appointment as chancellor.

Sensing that opportunities were slipping away in March 1933, the British proposed a five-year timetable for reducing European armies the way Versailles had cut Germany's in 1919. Under this far-reaching plan, France, Germany, and most other powers would maintain troop levels of only two hundred thousand with corresponding limits to artillery, tanks, airplanes, and warships. Britain's proposal "might well have won general acceptance," argues League historian F. P. Walters, "if it had been put forward twelve months earlier."[23] That it took a year to regain some of the momentum of the 1920s was a measure of the damage to international good will wrought by the Great Depression, but failure was not inevitable. In fact, prospects for success actually looked good at first. Italy gave full acceptance, followed by the United States, now under President Franklin Delano Roosevelt. Even Hitler, in a major address on May 17, did not refuse cooperation—in public at least. Negotiations began to bog down, however, when France and the Soviet Union insisted on more rigorous inspections. Paris, in particular, pointed to evidence pouring in from their German embassy about ongoing secret rearmament. During the summer they countered the British proposal, therefore, with one calling for a longer, five-year probationary period for Germany before implementation of army expansion that could not occur until 1941.

France had played into Hitler's hands. The German dictator announced in October 1933 that Germany was withdrawing from the Conference and the League because, as he charged, the heavily armed states intended neither to disarm nor to honor their pledge of German equality of rights. That the Conference had failed became definitely clear in March 1934 with publication of a German air force budget trumpeting a fivefold rise in expenditures.

Germany's withdrawal from Geneva and subsequent open violation of Versailles in 1934 met with no punishment from the three West European signatories at Versailles. Italy, for one, contemplated no action against Berlin. Mussolini had supported German claims for armaments equality during the Disarmament Conference, assuming that revision of the treaty settlement for Germany would advance his own desire to alter Italy's postwar treaty obligations. Although he eyed Hitler warily, knowing what fellow Fascists were capable of doing, the Italian Duce made no move to intervene. Paris, ever on guard against its great historical nemesis across the Rhine, had nevertheless learned a bitter lesson since its invasion of the Ruhr in 1923—namely, that France could not advance its own security by alienating Britain. And London, despite mildly pessimistic dispatches from Berlin, was in no mood to initiate a second world war. British Ambassador Sir Eric Phipps wired the Foreign Office on January 31, 1934, for example, that the "damnably dynamic" Hitler could "at some future date precipitate an international conflict."

> To attain his aims, the first step is obviously to discard the remaining servitudes of the Peace Treaty which stand in his way, namely, the disarmament stipulations. [Hitler's] policy is simple and straightforward. If his neighbors allow him, he will become strong by the simplest and most direct methods. The mere fact that he is making himself unpopular abroad will not deter him. . . . If he finds that he arouses no real opposition, the tempo of his advance will increase. On the other hand, if he is vigorously opposed, he is unlikely at this stage to risk a break.[24]

Phipps had made it abundantly clear that Hitler was no man of peace. The prudent implication of his report was the need to rearm a military establishment that had been allowed to deteriorate since 1919. The British people remained so steadfastly determined to prevent world war and the decimation of another generation of young men, however, that they rejected this conclusion. In the London constituency of East Fulham, for instance, electors who had given the Conservatives a comfortable majority in 1931 swung over to Labour in October 1933 because the Conservative candidate had urged an armaments increase. "One of the perplexities of those statesmen who think we have to rearm is how to bring the country to that point,"[25] noted an adviser to Conservative leader Stanley Baldwin.

The Ebb of Democracy

Meanwhile, democracies—peace's best chance—continued to fall during the Great Depression. In Austria social peace hung by a thread after the "Bloody Friday" riots of July 1927. Both the Christian Socialist national government and the Vienna-based Social Democratic opposition maintained paramilitary units, the Home Guard and the Defense League, respectively. Adding to the explosiveness of the situation, authoritarian regimes in neighboring lands encouraged Chancellor Engelbert Dollfuss of the Christian Socialists to strike out against the Left. Mussolini actually shipped arms to the Home Guard, letting Dollfuss know, however, that Italy would not protect Austria from Hitler and the Austrian Nazis unless Vienna established a Fascist regime and openly supported Italian foreign policy. Hungary's Admiral Horthy also pressured Vienna to eradicate "Bolshevist elements" as he had done. Horthy favored a Fascist confederation of sorts among Italy, Hungary, and Austria.

Dollfuss finally struck in March 1933 after the Socialists voted down a punitive measure against striking workers. Invoking an old act, he closed parliament and banned the Defense League, thus forcing it underground. The Socialists opted not to retaliate, however, "because we wanted to spare the country the catastrophe of a bloody civil war," recalled one of their leaders. "We made a [most fateful] mistake," [26]he later admitted. Indeed, in April 1934 the government attacked Defense League strongholds in Vienna and the provinces. The one-sided shootouts—the government used heavy artillery when machine guns did not suffice—left over three hundred dead and thousands wounded.

Estonian and Latvian democracies fell next. Dependent on agriculture, these two nations suffered terribly in the early 1930s. Exports declined, the terms of trade worsened, German bank failures caused capital to flee, and Britain's currency devaluation undercut these Baltic lands. As a result, Estonia and Latvia witnessed the rise of extreme nationalist movements aiming to overthrow unstable democratic systems on which all problems were blamed. In Estonia the Freedom Fighters, in Latvia the Thunder Cross, associations of veterans from the wars of 1918–1920, railed against Marxists, Jews, and national minorities, embarking on a violent paramilitary style of politics modeled on Mussolini's blackshirts and Hitler's storm troopers. With the voting strength of democratic parties shrinking, parliaments stymied, and fascist-style takeovers imminent, beleaguered democratic leaders in Estonia and Latvia arrested the militants, proscribed democracy, and proclaimed martial law, respectively, in March and May 1934. Democracy had committed suicide for fear of dying.

Similar developments undermined democracy in Greece. The regime of Constantine Venizelos lost popularity quickly as revenues from tourism dried up; exports of wine, olives, and olive oil declined in quantity and value; and sailors grew increasingly idle. Royalists scheming to restore the monarchy blamed the country's woes on Venizelos and liberalism. Politics turned violent again in 1933 as republican and royalist generals exchanged coups. The latter finally prevailed in the spring of 1935.

In Rumania, authoritarian King Carol watched confidently as the peasant movement that had revitalized democracy in the late 1920s lost popular backing during the depression. After the democratic vote slipped below 40 percent, however, two worrisome movements emerged to challenge him with their claims to national salvation. Both the Iron Guard and the National Christians preached a brand of ethnic xenophobia and rabid anti-Semitism that threatened Carol. After asking the allegedly less militant National Christians to form a government in December 1937—only to see them unleash a pogrom against Rumanian Jews—the king disbanded all parties and ruled with the army and police.

THE INTERACTION OF DOMESTIC AND FOREIGN POLICY

During the first three months of 1939 two more democracies fell as the Spanish Republic succumbed to Francisco Franco's three-year military revolt and Hitler's army overran Czechoslovakia (see later in this chapter). Now three antithetical political systems squared off against one another. Fascist, semifascist, or military/dictatorial systems dominated Southern, Central, and Eastern Europe. Democracy prevailed only in Western Europe and Scandinavia, while communism ruled Russia—overall, a volatile and explosive mixture. The Fascists scoffed at democracy, wanted to eradicate Marxism, and were generally prepared to treat foreign countries in the same bullying fashion as they did domestic opponents. For their part, the Communists eliminated alleged class enemies at home by the millions, and, similarly believing in the inevitability of class struggle on a worldwide scale, girded for it, while the democracies, accustomed though they were to peaceful dealings with one another, remained deeply distrustful of both the Fascists and Communists—especially the latter, but increasingly as the 1930s wore on, the former too. In the absence of workable collective security mechanisms, Europe's three-way standoff between incompatible systems resulted in another cataclysmic world war in 1939. The discussion that follows outlines the predictable but tragic connection between domestic and foreign policies in Europe as the decade unfolded toward that cataclysm.

Italy

In 1931 Italy's dictator, Benito Mussolini, penned an article on the nature of fascism. The five-page piece appeared a year later in the *Enciclopedia Italiana*.[27] Although rambling and repetitious, Mussolini's "Doctrine of Fascism," when analyzed, yields frank, sometimes blunt insights to the theory and practice of Europe's "third wave" alternative to democracy and communism.

As a "totalitarian" system, fascism rejected western liberalism and democracy. The latter seemed mere head counting, a false system of choosing leadership "which equates the nation to the majority, lowering it to the level of that majority." If, on the other hand, one conceived the nation "qualitatively and not quantitatively," a purer form of democracy, fascism, raised its head. Under this system a leader emerged from the depths of society to seize power and guide the people with the help of party faithful. Only the leader knew instinctively, however, what was best for the nation. Fascism was "the most powerful idea . . . which acts within the nation as the conscience and the will of a few, even of one, whose ideal tends to become active within the conscience and the will of all." In short, the "leadership principle" advocated rule by one man through one party.

Mussolini was obviously trying to justify what had transpired in Italy since he consolidated power in 1925. Although the Fascist Party numbered only one million, or 2.5 percent of the population, it had gained a monopolistic hold on parliament in 1926 when all non-fascist parties were abolished. Party membership was now a prerequisite for government posts, teaching po-

Fascist tribune: Benito Mussolini. (Library of Congress)

sitions, and most good jobs. The Fascist Party had also infiltrated all aspects of Italian life. Party organizations sprouted up alongside key government structures in order to control and monitor the state. Fascist operatives stood next to each provincial prefect, fascist tribunals functioned alongside ordinary law courts, a secret fascist police force watched the regular police, the fascist militia operated next to the army, and Mussolini himself overlooked the king. Youth groups, cultural associations, leisure time organizations, and the world of press and publishing—all were shadowed by the Fascist Party.

At the apex of this structure stood the Duce himself. Mussolini was leader of the party, head of the government, minister with usually three or four portfolios, and tribune of the people. He assiduously propagated a cult of personality. One compulsory reader for eight-year-olds, for instance, depicted Mussolini as some sort of omniscient god.

> The eyes of the Duce are on every one of you. No one can say what is the meaning of that look on his face. It is an eagle opening its wings and rising into space. It is a flame that searches out your heart to light a vermillion fire. Who can resist that burning eye, darting out its arrows?

"Mussolini," they were told, "is always right."[28]

Fascist society was to be organized by the party along corporate or vocational lines. Mussolini rejected the Marxist notion of class struggle leading eventually to a one-class state of workers. "Fascism is opposed to socialism, which confines the movement of history within the class struggle and ignores the unity of classes established in one economic and moral reality in the state." While he recognized that social problems had given rise to the working-class movements, Mussolini wanted "to bring them under the control of the state" and reconcile them "within the unity of the state." In other words, class struggle would be suppressed.

Corporatist doctrine manifested itself in the 1930s in the National Council of Corporations. This unwieldy body divided gainfully employed Italians into twenty-two job categories, professions, and industries. Although they were supposed to regulate professional life and guarantee workers an equal place in society, the corporations were really "an elaborate piece of humbug,"[29] writes Denis Mack Smith, that forbade strikes and independent trade union activity. Corporatism provided owners with an opportunity "to put into practice the worst kind of monopolistic practices at the expense of the little fellow."[30]

Suppression of the small man was consistent with an ideology that preached the need to sacrifice. Mussolini mocked the western notion of individual liberty. "Fascism is for liberty," he trumpeted, but not the kind of "abstract puppet envisaged by individualistic liberalism," rather "the only liberty which can be a real thing, the liberty of the state and of the individual within the state." And what kind of existence would such "liberty" bring? The Duce wanted Italians to exchange "the flabby materialistic positivism of the nineteenth century" for a more "serious, austere, religious" mode of thinking and living. Fascism "disdains the 'comfortable' life. . . . It does not consider that 'happiness' is possible upon earth." Indeed the unemployment and suffering of the Great Depression struck Mussolini as the right thing for his people. "We must rid our minds of the idea that the days of prosperity may return. We are probably moving toward a period when humanity will exist at a lower standard of living."[31]

Mussolini's Italy also took traditional gender roles to the extreme. The regime extolled man as breadwinner and patriarch, warrior, and maker of children. Women supported their hard-working, battle-hardened husbands, nurtured their young, and gave birth to future workers and fighters sired by men. Fascist policies sought to fashion this ideal with marriage and birth loans, state-paid maternity leaves, and tax breaks for fathers of large families. There were also subsidies and welfare benefits for men whose wives still worked, as many did. On the negative side, bachelors were taxed more heavily, birth control banned, and abortions severely punished— all of this to increase population and buttress the family "as fortress of the state."[32]

Mussolini's male establishment gradually realized that these policies could not succeed without co-opting lower-class women. The same state that mocked democratic voting procedures for men did not seek female backing by promoting women's suffrage, of course, but rather by expanding the network of organizations designed to mobilize and manipulate the masses. In doing so Fascism's class biases shone through, for the party first organized middle-class females, and only years later peasant (1934) and urban working-class women (1938).

The fault cracks of regime failure ran, in fact, along class and gender lines. "One child, professor, one child is all we want," a leading pediatrician heard from working women who resorted to illegal abortions to limit family size. Mussolini's trumpet calls to patriotism left them even colder than many Italian men. "You tell me, professor," the same physician was told, "is it just or humane that we women of the people should have many children, destined for war when they are adults? Oh never! We love our children, we raise them as best we can given our measly means, for ourselves, for an even better future for them, but not for the Fatherland."[33] Such resistance did not augur well for the fulfillment of Mussolini's martial agenda.

Indeed, why was it necessary to have leadership by one man and one party, a society of separate classes whose interests were forcibly "reconciled" by the state, a new Fascist Man who "disdained the comfortable life," and women who went along with all of this? Because, he continued, the new man "conceives of life as a struggle." This held true as much for the individual as for the state in a hostile world, for the state "exists and lives in so far as it develops."

> To arrest its development is to kill it. Therefore the state is not only the authority which governs and gives the form of laws and the value of spiritual life to the wills of individuals, but it is also a power that makes its will felt abroad, making it known and respected, in other words, demonstrating the fact of its universality in all the necessary directions of its development. It is consequently organization and expansion.

Obviously Mussolini had no use for the idea of peaceful coexistence represented by the League of Nations. "War alone," he wrote, "brings all human energies to their highest state of tension and stamps with the seal of nobility the nations which dare to face it."[34] The most important task of fascism, in fact, was to train the people to adopt this new martial mentality. "It wants to remake, not the forms of human life, but its content, man, character, faith." To do this it requires "discipline and authority that can enter into the spirits of men and there govern unopposed."

The year Mussolini's "Doctrine of Fascism" appeared (1932), he gave an interview to German writer Emil Ludwig. The dictator of seven years hinted that his most ambitious goal of remaking Italians into the warriors of antiquity who had converted the Mediterranean into a "Roman lake" was far from fulfillment. "There persists in me a certain feeling of aversion, like that which the modeler feels for the clay he is molding," said the Duce. "Does not the sculptor sometimes smash his block of marble into fragments because he cannot shape it to represent the vision he has conceived?"[35] Such second thoughts did not restrain him, however, when German Nazis supported a coup attempt by their Austrian counterparts in 1934. He rushed Italian divisions north in a clear sign that Italy was making "its will felt abroad" and that Austria lay astride the "necessary directions" of Italian "development." Hitler backed down and the putsch failed. Nor did doubts about the desired martial mentality of Italians cancel plans for the invasion of Ethiopia with airplanes, artillery, poison gas, and half a million soldiers in October 1935. The Abyssinian chieftains who had decimated an Italian army in 1896 would be paid back, and Rome would take the first step toward undermining British—and substituting Italian—dominance in the Mediterranean and Near East.

Doubts and second thoughts about Italian backbone may, in fact, have prompted Mussolini's aggressive course. The king, the army, the church, and much of the middle class still adhered to traditional ways of thinking that did not jibe, argued the Duce, with the militaristic tenor of modern times. The bourgeoisie in particular was riddled with "cowardice, laziness, [and] love of the quiet life," making it necessary, therefore, to harden the character of the Italians "through combat."[36] As MacGregor Knox sees it, "only war, whose uncivilizing effects he well remembered, could help break the old society's resistance to the new paganism, make Italy the 'militaristic' nation he demanded, and further undermine monarchy and church."[37]

The invasion of Ethiopia triggered a world crisis. As the fighting dragged on into the winter, champions of peace sensed the last chance for the League of Nations to redeem itself. The Japanese seizure of Manchuria went unpunished in 1931. The Disarmament Conference failed in 1933. Now the League proved unable to do more than impose partial—and therefore ineffective—economic sanctions on Italy, a boycott that excluded crucial commodities like coal and oil because nonmembers America and Germany did not join the boycott. Geneva was further limited by the Franco-British desire to appease Mussolini, both fearing that a stiffer reaction would push him into alliance with Hitler. London also shrank from action because, as the only country with troops near Ethiopia, it alone would have to shoulder the burden. Italian troops entered Addis Ababa in May 1936. The League was bankrupt.

Germany

There were many similarities between Italian Fascism and its German cousin, Nazism. At the top of party and state stood the Führer, Adolf Hitler, whose instinctive ability and seemingly providential mission to lead were worshipped by followers of his personality cult. "Our Hitler is our savior, our hero," sang the young boys, "he is the noblest being in the whole wide world."[38] The new elite in government, bureaucracy, and society sprang from the Nazi Party, which had forced other parties out of existence and stood watch on state functionaries high and low. The all-pervasive control of the ruling party was even greater in Germany than Italy, extending downward to state and local governments, which the party thoroughly Nazified and subordinated to Berlin, as well as to local club life, which the party also monopolized. Like the Fascists, the Nazis also abhorred class struggles that undermined society's crucial unity. All trade union and working-class organizations were disbanded and forced into a "German Labor Front" that supposedly functioned as a pillar of the restructured corporatist society. While businessmen, farmers, and artisans also possessed their corporate estates, they clearly preserved more privileges and freedom of movement than did the downtrodden proletarians.

Similarly, Nazi Germany, like Fascist Italy, saw life as a fight for existence. "As it is with the individual so it is in the destiny of nations," shouted Hitler in 1928.

> Only by struggle are the strong able to raise themselves above the weak. And every people that loses out in this eternally shifting struggle has, according to the laws of nature, received its just desert. A Weltanschauung that denies the idea of struggle is contrary to nature and will lead a people that is guided by it to destruction.[39]

Moreover, there were obvious "necessary directions" to the development of Germany's national struggle. Whereas Mussolini looked to the Mediterranean basin for conquests, Hitler, preoccupied with the notion that the German people languished because they lacked the necessary land base for sustenance, preached the imperative of overrunning Eastern Europe and Russia to seize "living space" for the race. The views of Duce and Führer on the inevitability and desirability of war represented the most extreme formulation of a doctrine whose roots burrowed deeply into the soil of Europe's long history of ethnic strife and national conflict.

Hitler and Mussolini also agreed on the need to remold the character of their people. "Today nobody can offer us any resistance," claimed Hitler in July 1933, "but now we must educate German man for this new state—a gigantic project lies ahead."[40] In contrast to Mussolini, however, "education" to the German leader meant not only bracing the folk for combat, but also preparing it for the brutal racial and ethnic cleansing that would come in war's wake. Before the German race could achieve its final destiny during a great world conflagration, the Jews, allegedly the great racial nemesis of the Germans, had to be annihilated.

The Nazi "cult of motherhood" also had certain similarities to Fascist Italy. The state encouraged German wives to have more babies, promoting births with anti-abortion laws, family allowances, and marriage loans that withdrew new wives from the work force. The Nazis, however, made the racial and martial context much more explicit—blatant, in fact. Hitler and his henchmen wanted to remake German Woman as well as German Man, toughening her for the murderous times that lay ahead. The Nazi state strove to overcome "the female instinct to care for all those in need of help," declared one official statement, for such "sentimental humanitarianism" and womanly "maternalism," like any "egoism, acts against the race."[41] Women seemed to be able to suppress these instincts when unwanted pregnancies were terminated—as they were by the hundreds of thousands annually in the

1930s—but given Nazism's rabid racial-military agenda, these illegal acts became tantamount to wartime treason. "If these abortions could be prevented," declared one Nazi in 1936, "in twenty years we would have an additional two hundred regiments."[42] This call for fighters would echo in a Nazi wartime ditty: *"Die Räder drehen für den Sieg,"* it exhorted, *"ein Kinderwagen für den nächsten Krieg* !"[43]

One gains a better understanding of Germany's gender policies by viewing them through the morbid prism of Nazi racism.[44] Long-term victory for the Volk would begin with racial regeneration in the present. Purification of the race necessitated both the promotion of breeding among "Aryan" (i.e., German) men and women as well as disallowing it between racial "undesirables." Sterilization of the so-called feeble-minded began, therefore, as early as 1933. In a decade the Nazis performed this irreversible operation on four hundred thousand persons, roughly equally divided among men and women. Further progress toward the stated goal came with the Nuremberg Laws of 1935 (see later), which banned marriage and sexual intercourse between Aryans, on the one side, and Jews, Gypsies, and Blacks, on the other. The most "efficient" method of blocking racially undesirable breeding, of course, was extermination of undesirables. This more determined approach began with euthanasia programs in the late 1930s and led eventually to the Holocaust, which took the same radical anti-natalism to genocidal extremes.

But implementing such an agenda would not be easy for a party that had suppressed the most violent portions of its racial agenda in order to gain votes. Fully aware of the political wisdom of this tactic, Hitler had to be skeptical about demands from Nazi rank and file in early 1933 for harsh measures against Jews. When the party announced a boycott of Jewish shops and businesses that April, in fact, it appeared in the name of the collective party leadership, not of Hitler personally. After the public reacted negatively to the disruption of economic life, moreover, the action was canceled after only one day. Fanatics had to content themselves with a series of laws discriminating against Jews in the legal and medical professions and purging them from the civil service, including schools and universities, unless they had served at the front in the Great War.

Like the boycott, these laws did not appeal to individuals who had accustomed themselves to seventy years of Jewish civil rights emancipation. There was a significant—and probably larger—degree of support for these measures, on the other hand, among segments of the population that regarded Jews as representatives of a non-German culture which did not deserve access to official and professional positions. In these strata one found some of the same Germans who denounced Jews and Jewish supporters when the roundups began a few years later. That those who tolerated Jews did not voice their dissent publicly in 1933, limiting themselves to private words or letters of consolation, made the state's discriminatory task easier—as did arrests earlier that year of leftist political opponents of Nazi fanaticism.[45]

The Nazi crackdown on Communists and Socialists appealed much more consistently to upper and middle classes that yearned for social peace, something they assumed the Marxists had disrupted. The new regime's "get tough" approach to crime as well as its roundup of beggars and vagrants struck the same positive chords. Furthermore, through work creation projects like the new Labor Service—and a fortunate upswing in the economy—Hitler's men could announce in June 1934 that unemployment had fallen more than 50 percent. The Führer added to his growing popularity by a blood purge of the S.A. leadership that same month—a move many Germans applauded as an apparent end to storm trooper violence and a return to law and order. The death of Hindenburg in August 1934 enabled Hitler to consolidate his public relations gains by combining the offices of chancellor and president. What sense did it make, therefore, to push prematurely for radical anti-Semitic measures? "With regard to the Jews," he would say later, "I had for long to remain inactive." There was no point "in artificially creating additional difficulties—the more cleverly you proceed, the better."[46]

As 1934 yielded to 1935, however, the Führer came under increasing pressure from party radicals who insisted that he punish the Jews. Inciting the call for action were Julius Streicher, the party boss of Nuremberg, and Joseph Goebbels, the influential boss of Berlin and minister of propaganda. While a sympathetic Hitler looked the other way, the two whipped up the party faithful into a frenzy of violent acts against Jews as the months drew on to the annual Nazi rally at Nuremberg in September 1935. Once again the public reacted negatively, especially the conservative upper classes that abhorred disorder. Therefore Hitler compromised Nazi radicalism with a series of decrees, the so-called Nuremberg Laws, which removed German citizenship from Jews and forbade marriage and extramarital sexual relations between Germans and Jews. The Führer also instructed party members to abstain from further pogroms.

The Nuremberg Laws failed to placate Nazi radicals, nor did Socialist, liberal, and religious opponents of discrimination accept the stamping out of one ethnoreligious group's civil liberties. One should not exaggerate the extent of dissatisfaction, however, for if anything support for these kinds of anti-Semitic measures had grown since 1933. In January 1936, for instance, the Socialist underground of a notoriously non-Nazi Berlin reported: "the Nazis have indeed brought off a deepening of the gap between the people and the Jews." The feeling "that the Jews are another race is today a general one."[47]

The apparent widening and deepening of anti-Semitism resulted, to some extent, from the constant drumbeat of Nazi propaganda. Even hardened and realistic outsiders like American journalist William Shirer felt the gradual, imperceptible, value-altering effects of the ruling party line.

> It was surprising and sometimes consternating to find that notwithstanding the opportunities I had to learn the facts and despite one's inherent distrust of what one learned from Nazi sources, a steady diet over the years of falsifications and distortions made a certain impression on one's mind and often misled it. No one who has not lived for years in a totalitarian land can possibly conceive how difficult it is to escape the dread consequences of a regime's calculated and incessant propaganda.[48]

Indeed, the Nazis played on most Germans' dislike of communism, opposition to crime, and deep suspicion and resentment of enemy nations by cleverly weaving an anti-Jewish thread into this negative fabric. Germans had to beware of *Jewish*-Bolshevik agitators, *Jewish* criminal elements, and *Jewish* foreign intrigues. Although historians correctly warn against exaggerating the success of Nazi propaganda,[49] there is no doubt that it succeeded with the weak, the insecure, and the impressionable and was particularly effective among the young, whose unquestioning support for the regime spread quickly. The end result, notes Ulrich Herbert, was "a growing lack of moral concern in German society for human rights and the protection of minorities, which grew rapidly during the years of the dictatorship, and which led to a profound moral brutalization in Germany."[50]

Limits existed, on the other hand, to what a population yearning for law and order would tolerate or accept. An unmistakable aspect of the popularity of the Nuremberg Laws, in fact, was their alleged ending, once and for all, of the so-called Jewish problem with its accompanying violence. However, it remained unfortunately true that limits existed to Nazi patience with what seemed to them laughably mild and totally inadequate anti-Jewish measures like the Nuremberg Laws. Indeed, Hitler's henchmen were preparing to solve the Jewish problem their own way, regardless of popular opinion. To brace for any opposition from Jews or Jewish sympathizers, Berlin opened state-of-the-art prisons in 1936–1937 at Sachsenhausen, Buchenwald, and Lichtenberg, which joined the original "model" concentration camp at Dachau. The regime also founded a special "People's Court" to speed up cases of treason, defined as loosely as mere verbal criticism of Hitler. This tribunal, writes Robert Gellately, soon "attained a bloody reputation because of its frequent use of the death penalty."[51] The state's *Schutzstaffel* (S.S.) security organization acquired three regiments of heavily armed motorized infantry, moreover, to maintain internal order in the event of a war. As S.S. officials put it, "good discipline" was necessary "if we want to be immune to the poison of destruction in our own people." The "poisonous" Jews would not undermine the home front as they had allegedly done during the Great War. "It has shown itself to be useful, with those creatures recognized as enemies of the people, to take them into secure custody and to watch them, before a crisis arises and they can become dangerous."[52]

Crises arose with increasing frequency after mid-decade. Faced with the seeming weakness and paralysis of the democracies, Hitler gained confidence—just as Phipps had predicted. With the world preoccupied by Italy's ongoing rape of Ethiopia in March 1936, the Führer sent troops over the Rhine bridges to occupy western provinces that had been demilitarized by the Treaty of Versailles. France and Britain protested but took no punitive action (see later). That summer Mussolini and Hitler gave military aid to Francisco Franco's revolt against the Spanish Republic. The western democracies sat idle. In the following year Mussolini visited Germany and acceded to the so-called Anti-Comintern Pact, an anti-Soviet agreement that Germany and Japan had signed in 1936. The Duce no longer regarded the Führer as an enemy, but rather as a strong and impressive friend.

Hitler drew the appropriate conclusions—for a fascist—from the unfolding situation in Europe. At a meeting of top German officials in November 1937 the dynamic German leader asserted that even in the best of economic times his nation could not depend on world trade for the resources it needed. Survival depended on living space in the East, which had to be seized, beginning with Czechoslovakia, Austria, and Poland. "Germany's problem could only be solved by means of force," read the minutes of the meeting, "and this was never without attendant risk." Britain and France, "two hate-inspired antagonists," would never accept "a German colossus in the center of Europe."[53] Both powers, however, were stymied by internal problems that would prevent retaliation. In fact, Hitler believed France to be on the verge of civil war. And if it broke out, Germany should exploit France's difficulties by embarking immediately on its eastern conquests. The peace of Europe seemed to hang now by a thin thread.

France

When Hitler reoccupied the Rhineland in March 1936, France had just weathered another of its seemingly incessant cabinet crises.[54] A weak interim government that was reluctant to call up troops, further disrupt a struggling economy, and commit the nation to a war that only a few clamored for contented itself with serving out its time until elections the following month. For years the economy had worsened as politicians resorted to budget-slashing measures that not only lengthened unemployment lines but also cut into military preparedness, especially the air force, which France failed to modernize. Therefore, when the army advised the cabinet that France could win a long war with Germany only with British help, and Britain made it clear that none would be forthcoming in a crisis triggered by Germany's essentially moving into "its own back garden," France opted not to challenge the remilitarization of the Rhineland.

For two years prior to the April 1936 elections a handful of fascist and authoritarian organizations with over three-quarters of a million members between them had demonstrated, rioted, and pleaded with Frenchmen to abandon a baneful parliamentary system that allegedly disgraced a proud nation. Worried that one or more of these groups would attempt to seize power, the French Left formed an electoral alliance. Consisting of the Communists, Socialists, and moderate Radicals, this so-called Popular Front captured 62 percent of the seats and advanced Socialist leader Leon Blum to the premiership.[55] The ruling coalition of Socialists and Radicals—backed by the Communists, whose Marxism had prevented them from joining a bourgeois cabinet—now proceeded to introduce its version of the American New Deal. Legislation established the forty-hour week, wage increases, and the right to collective bargaining. Other bills provided for the nationalization of armaments firms and tighter government control of the Bank of France. The majority also appropriated funds for discounted train fares, free leisure-time activities, and inexpensive hostelries for low-income groups. Employers would provide workers, furthermore, with two weeks of paid vacation. Now the small man in France could tap deeper into the rich popular culture of radio, cinema, penny press, sports outings, and day-tripping.

But Blum's coalition did not last. Alarmed by leftist trends in Paris, some employers refused to abide by the new legislation, while others postponed new investments or even cut back on production as a form of protest. Great amounts of capital fled to seemingly safer havens abroad. After Blum failed to confront the business community over these challenges to his authority, Communists and left-wing Socialists urged their rank and file to take direct action. From October to December 1936 an unprecedented twenty-five hundred strikes broke out, involving almost three hundred thousand workers. The crisis turned violent in March 1937 when fascist marchers and leftist counterdemonstrators clashed with police, wounding several hundred people and killing seven. The bloodshed triggered a new wave of strikes. Weary and disillusioned, Blum resigned a few months later. All of this explains Hitler's assumption that France teetered near civil war.

Fear of civil war in France, in fact, determined Blum's policy during the ongoing civil war in Spain. The outbreak of that tragic conflict in July 1936 was accompanied from the beginning by German, Italian, and Soviet intervention (see the following section). In response to the fascist buildup and its clear threat to the survival of democracy in Spain, France stayed neutral. So deep was rightist hatred of Blum that the premier could not be sure of army loyalty if he backed leftists across the border. Nor did he wish to provoke French fascist leagues and their closely allied veterans' organizations, which rallied vociferously behind Franco, into a civil war. "Spain could not have been saved," said Blum later, "but France would have gone fascist."[56] Although the French Communist Party assailed him mercilessly for not following Moscow's example—and despite the fact that his own coalition was coming unraveled—Blum ignored the pleas of democratic Spain.

Spain

The experience of republican Spain provides an extreme example of the inherent problems of young democracy.[57] The experiment began in 1931, much like Germany's Weimar Republic, when the monarchy and army defaulted after years of oppressive and illegitimate rule. But all too soon—again like Weimar—Spain's democracy suffered its own legitimacy crisis. No fewer than twenty-six ill-disciplined political parties won seats in the constitutional assembly. Not only were they divided internally and against each other, but further party divisions along regional lines exacerbated polarization and factionalism, for Basques and Catalonians trusted neither Madrid nor one another. Not surprisingly, the constitution's promise to subordinate private property to the common welfare, even to the point of indemnified expropriation of land, could never be realized in a parliament that agreed on the principles but not on the means of their implementation.

The failure to achieve significant change in the countryside did nothing, however, to calm landlords who were alarmed by the attempt. Similarly, the anti-clericalist bent of the new regime acted as a red flag on the Catholic Church, while army reforms that targeted half of the generals and officers for retirement infuriated men in uniform. Many upper-class interests began to place reactionary hopes in the Falange Party, the Spanish equivalent of Mussolini's blackshirts. Matters worsened when workers struck, rioted, and planted bombs to protest the lack of jobs and unemployment relief, while peasants, alienated by delayed agrarian reforms, began to seize land that they considered rightfully theirs. By early 1936 it seemed merely a matter of time before either Socialists or Anarchists on the Left or Falangists, monarchists, or angry generals on the Right attempted to overthrow the republic.

A rightist coup occurred on July 17, 1936. General Francisco Franco, commander of Spanish troops in Morocco, seized the colony and most of the Balearic Islands. The following morning fellow military conspirators rose up all over Spain, inflicting bloody retribution on leftists wherever they were found. An American journalist entering Badajoz heard of workmen being executed in a bullfighting arena.

> There [in the ring] machine guns await them. After the first night the blood was supposed to be palm deep on the far side of the [entrance] lane. I don't doubt it. Eighteen hundred men—there were women, too—were mowed down there in some twelve hours. There is more blood than you think in eighteen hundred bodies.[58]

Nevertheless, stiff civilian and working-class resistance thwarted the rebellion in Madrid, Barcelona, Valencia, Malaga, and Bilbao, despite the fact that republican forces possessed only a few loyal army units. Initially only a third of Spain was in rebel hands, primarily in the west and northwest.

Both sides realized immediately that they needed foreign aid to win. Franco's rebels moved from Morocco to the mainland in late July, in fact, only with the help of German and Italian planes. Berlin and Rome quickly redoubled efforts by sending arms and ammunition to anti-republican insurgents. Besides the obvious incentive to defeat democracy and install a fascist ally in power, both dictators had rational motives for aiding Franco. Mussolini welcomed another opportunity to harden Italians to the new militant realities, while also cherishing the prospect of undermining Britain's Mediterranean bastion at Gibraltar. Hitler considered the possibility that intervention against "Red" Madrid would recruit London for a wider anti-communist crusade. More likely, however, he simply wanted to distract Britain from Nazi ambitions in Eastern Europe.

Aware of these aggressive possibilities, Stalin shipped supplies to the beleaguered republic in October 1936. The Soviet dictator followed up by ordering communists throughout Europe to form "international brigades." Hitler countered in November by dispatching the infamous "Condor Legion," an experimental combat unit boasting motorized infantry and dive-bombers.

That same month Mussolini contributed his first "blackshirt division," and by March 1937 Il Duce had one hundred thousand troops fighting for Franco.

In May 1937 the Condor Legion dropped a hundred thousand tons of explosives in three hours on the small Basque town of Guernica, killing hundreds of innocent civilians, wounding and maiming many more. The senseless and brutal act moved famed modernist painter Pablo Picasso to protest on canvas. His masterpiece *Guernica* both prophesized tragedy, like so much prewar apocalyptic art had done, and creatively reacted against what was already happening. The painting captured a seemingly endless horror with disjointed cubist forms painted in depressing shades of black and gray. The huge canvas (11 by 25 feet) is littered with dead, dying, or terrified bodies: a crying woman cradling her baby, a suffering man on the ground with outstretched hand, a baying horse, another victim hurtling from a house with her hair on fire. A protest as well as a foreshadowing of worse to come, *Guernica* was destined to become "the twentieth century's most celebrated painting."[59]

The suffering Spanish Republic also inspired Max Ernst's *The Angel of Hearth and Home,* depicting a behemoth that crushes and destroys all that comes in its path. Finished later in 1937, the painting powerfully combines the accusatory with the earlier prophetic genre, for not only was Spain bleeding itself white—over half a million would die—but Japan invaded China that year too. Could even greater slaughter on a horrendous worldwide scale be far removed from a suffering humanity? "That was my impression at the time of what would probably happen in the world," recalled Ernst, "and I was right."[60]

The deep emotional and political support exhibited by Picasso and Ernst for Republican Spain typified the reaction of artists and intellectuals across Europe and America, as witnessed so movingly in novels and accounts like Ernest Hemingway's *For Whom the Bell Tolls*, André Malraux's *Man's Hope*, and

Pablo Picasso, **Guernica.** (Photo Credit: John Bigelow Taylor/Art Resource, NY/© 2004 Estate of Pablo Picasso/Artists Rights Society (ARS), New York)

Max Ernst, Angel of Hearth and Home. (Art Resource, NY/© 2004 Artists Rights Society (ARS), New York/ADAGP, Paris)

George Orwell's *Homage to Catalonia.* A poll of leading British intellectuals in 1937 measured the depth of this wellspring of pro-republican sentiment: Five backed the fascists, eighteen stayed neutral, while a solid hundred spoke out for Madrid. Many on the Left felt seriously enough about Spain, in fact, to volunteer for the republican army or a communist international brigade. Serving the republican cause became the touchstone for one's devotion to human rights, social justice, and progressive political innovation. Indeed, what better time could be found to make sacrifices, especially for something new and untried? Old political ideas like liberalism had been eroded by the Great War and the brutal current of fascism. Capitalistic market economies had been suspended during the war and then buffeted by the Great Depression. Not only had pacifists failed to implement disarmament and arbitration, moreover, but pacifism in general seemed out of touch with reality—how would it stop the behemoth? Thus "Man's hope" lay on the Socialistic/Communistic Left, especially for those unfamiliar with the true face of Stalinism. Others like Orwell and the embittered Arthur Koestler witnessed enough of Moscow's intolerance for anarchists and other leftists in Spain to become disillusioned and disgusted with communism too.

As summer turned to fall 1937, the Spanish Civil War turned into an extremely bloody stalemate. Aid from the Soviet Union and volunteer fighters helped check fascism but could not defeat it. France would not move, so presumably only Britain could make a difference.

Britain

Britain muddled through the Great Depression. With unemployment at 17 percent in 1931, London abandoned the gold standard and allowed the pound to decline in value to boost exports. Currency devaluation was followed by measures that raised tariffs, lowered interest rates, and slashed government expenditures—including a 10 percent cut in unemployment benefits. Joblessness declined to 8.5 percent six years later. Economic historians agree, however, that the private sector (i.e., spending outside of government) did as much or more to stimulate Britain's partial recovery.[61] A long overdue boom in housing construction accounted, largely on its own, for nearly half of employment gains, while the emergence of new industries like automobiles, electrical appliances, and chemical products expanded sufficiently to account for the remainder of new jobs created.

The Labour Party cabinet of Ramsay MacDonald that presided over the first eighteen months of the Depression had yielded, meanwhile, to a "national government." Ostensibly joining Labour, the Liberals, and the Conservatives, the new coalition was backed mainly by the latter, while Labour, for all intents and purposes, went into opposition. The elections of November 1935 maintained this façade of national unity, but the conservative political reality was now even more in evidence. Tories made up 90 percent—385 of 428 seats—of the government's 71.5 percent majority. Conservative leader Stanley Baldwin, who had functioned as a kind of shadow prime minister under MacDonald, stepped forward to head the new government. With the Depression seeming gradually to cure itself, foreign policy took center stage.

In 1935–1936 Britain responded with restraint and moderation during four major international crises. The island nation tried to find an elusive fine line between maintaining its security needs, on the one side, and avoiding provocation and another disastrous European war on the other. After Hitler announced German rearmament in March 1935, for example, London protested the illegality of the move, then negotiated a naval agreement that allowed Berlin submarine parity with Britain and surface warship tonnage equal to 35 percent of the Royal Navy. Next, in response to Italy's invasion of Ethiopia, Baldwin gave public support to the League while privately appeasing Mussolini. "We have never had war in mind," he said frankly. Third, Hitler's remilitarization of the Rhineland in March 1936 triggered more British protests, but the Nazi chancellor's offers to negotiate non-aggression pacts also appealed to a Conservative administration that regarded the Versailles Treaty as overly punitive, even "iniquitous." "It is the appeasement of Europe as a whole that we have constantly before us,"[62] stated Foreign Secretary Anthony Eden. Finally, that summer's widening civil war in Spain found Baldwin unwilling to take action. Britain reinforced Leon Blum's fatalistic attitude, in fact, by adopting a policy of non-intervention. If French aid to the republic triggered a wider war, warned London, France would fight alone.

These policies sparked controversy at home. Months before violence erupted in Ethiopia, for instance, a survey conducted by the League of Nations Union of 11.6 million British voters—38.2 percent of the adult population—found that 58.7 percent favored collective military sanctions against an aggressor, with only 20.3 percent opposed and 20.4 percent abstaining.[63] During the crisis itself Baldwin had said that deliberations in Geneva "may lead to action, at the extreme to coercive action—we mean nothing by the league, if we are not prepared, after trial, to take action to enforce its judgment."[64] When the public learned in December 1935, on the contrary, that Baldwin's Foreign Secretary had joined the French in offering Mussolini territorial concessions in Ethiopia, a dumbfounded and offended press reacted with almost universal condemnation. After Hitler moved troops into the Rhineland four months later, the Baldwin government began to remove its head from the sand and increased military expenditures nearly 38 percent.

In May 1937 Baldwin yielded office to Neville Chamberlain, perhaps the most controversial prime minister in British history.[65] Scion of a wealthy manufacturing family, Conservative minister of health from 1924 to 1929, and chancellor of the exchequer in both national governments after 1931, the new man did not regard the Treaty of Versailles as viable or enforceable, nor was he sanguine about the League of Nations and its failed experiment in collective security. Throughout the crises of 1935–1936 he criticized Baldwin privately for "drifting without a policy." Such negligence could land the nation in another ruinous arms race or, worse, another Great War—an abhorrent fate he wanted to avoid at almost any cost. Accustomed to the gentlemanly world of business dealings, and thoroughly steeped in the democratic political culture of compromise and respect for the loyal opposition, Chamberlain believed that he could defuse Europe's mounting tensions through personal diplomacy with Hitler. Key concessions would right the wrongs of Versailles and fashion an understanding between London and Berlin that would keep other threats to the peace—the Spanish Civil War, the minor annoyances of Mussolini, as well as the greater dangers of communism—in check. Thus Chamberlain pursued "appeasement," which, freed from today's negative connotations, simply meant "to bring peace," a policy that certainly had the potential to resonate with a people that had consistently sought ways to avoid war since 1919. The prime minister wanted to create "the *détente* which would then lead to an Anglo-German *entente.*"[66] It was an approach that tended to work when democrats in one country, conditioned to sit around the table and work out differences peacefully, dealt with democrats from another country. Because Germany's "loyal opposition" had been proscribed, however, prudence mandated policies built on the assumption that Hitler would treat foreign opposition in the same way. Consistently enough, British military expenditure rose 37 percent in 1937 and a steep 54 percent in 1938. With Europeans killing one another in Spain—and Japan launching a massive invasion of China—it seemed wise to hedge bets, stockpile powder, and keep it dry.

Chamberlain's policy of appeasement soon underwent two jolting tests. The prime minister sent a personal emissary, Lord Halifax, to Berlin in November 1937. His mission: to inform the Führer that London would be amenable to peaceful, negotiated border changes in Eastern Europe. "Both Hitler and [Luftwaffe Chief] Goering said repeatedly and emphatically that they had no desire or intention of making war," reported Halifax, "and I think we may take this as correct at any rate for the present." When Hitler proceeded to forcibly annex Austria in March 1938, Chamberlain found it "very disheartening and discouraging . . . that force is the only argument that Germany understands," but absolutely refused to let himself become overly disheartened or discouraged: "I am not going to take the situation too tragically." Indeed, when Hitler rattled his saber that spring and summer over Czechoslovakia's alleged mistreatment of the German minority of the Sudetenland province, Chamberlain traveled to Munich in September 1938 to save the peace. London and Paris abandoned Prague, which was humiliated into ceding the disputed territory to Germany.

Although his own doubts about appeasement were certainly mounting, the prime minister put the best face on the situation to London crowds after his return from Munich: "I believe it is peace in our time." Within weeks, however, he seemed to have convinced himself that it was true. Thus, to a growing list of critics like Winston Churchill, who denounced Munich as a shameful defeat, the supremely confident Chamberlain scoffed that "a lot of people seem to me to be losing their heads and talking and thinking as though Munich had made war more instead of less imminent. . . . The only thing I care about is to be able to carry out the policy I believe, indeed *know* to be right."[67]

Peace in our time? Neville Chamberlain returns from the Munich Conference in September 1938. (Hulton/Archive by Getty Images)

The Neutral States

Switzerland, the Benelux states,[68] and Scandinavia experienced particularly hard times during the early 1930s. Farming sectors that formerly contributed a major portion of national income languished under the impact of dropping prices, while the urban proletariat, desperate for work in times of industrial retrenchment, queued in lengthening unemployment lines. A shocking 43 percent of Danish trade unionists had no jobs, for instance, and percentages were nearly as high in Norway, Sweden, and Finland. The initial social reaction followed the trend of other countries rocked by strikes, riots, and political violence. In the Swedish industrial town of Adalen, for example, police fired on workers protesting the employment of strikebreakers in 1931, killing five people.

All of the small democracies of Western and Northern Europe managed, however, to reverse this unsettling trend by mid-decade. From Denmark to Finland workers' and farmers' parties moderated their antithetical demands, formed parliamentary coalitions, and agreed on impressive legislative programs. The "Red-Green" governments of these northern democracies laid the groundwork for the statist economies and "cradle-to-grave" social services that became the hallmark after 1945. Switzerland and the Benelux did not move as far toward the modern welfare state, but the overall pattern of social insurance and state economic intervention remained the same.

How does one explain this relatively great degree of social and political harmony in especially trying times? Historians point to the rule of law and existence of parliamentary practices before 1914 as well as the absence of bitter wartime disputes during probationary years of young democracy in the 1920s—the dearth, in fact, of "festering animosities"[69] resulting from a Great War that did not involve most of these neutral states. Unlike the new nations of Eastern Europe, moreover, recalcitrant ethnic minorities did not exist to block the path of parliamentary reconciliation—the exception here was Belgium, but these differences did not prove insurmountable. Finally, although no truly great political personality or outstanding historical figure emerged in any of these eight democracies, they nevertheless possessed effective and prudent leadership capable of cementing political relationships and welding together parliamentary compromises. One thinks here of unsung heroes of democracy like Per Albion Hansson of Sweden, Johan Nygaardsvold of Norway, Thorwald Stauning of Denmark, and Hendrik Colijn of Holland, whose governments dominated their respective parliaments in the 1930s and paved the way for Europe's postwar mixed economies.

The foreign policy of these small democracies was much more problematic. With such a wide range of shared values and common political preferences and practices, some form of closer union seemed warranted. As the Great Depression deepened and widened in December 1930, therefore, leaders of Scandinavia and the Benelux signed the so-called Oslo agreements, pledging commercial cooperation and maintenance of the principles of the League of Nations.[70] Within six years, however, the Manchurian, Ethiopian, and Rhineland crises left each of the Oslo signatories scrambling for other means of security after they abandoned the League principle of collective security that had failed so miserably in practice. Holland and Belgium opted for strict neutrality and began constructing frontier defenses. Scandinavia discussed the idea of a Nordic defense pact, but talks led nowhere. Finland, busily rearming, wanted to unite against the Soviet Union, while Denmark, reluctant to arm, was at any rate more concerned about Germany. Sweden expanded her armaments too, but worried that a pact would merely alarm the Great Powers, thereby undermining Nordic security. Last, the Norwegians "believed everyone would leave them alone in the event of a war, and that the British would save them if need be."[71] With the possibilities of agreement slipping farther away, Austria already gobbled up, and the German-Czech crisis escalating, the four northern nations declared neutrality in May 1938. Similarly, Switzerland asked that summer to be released from any potential military obligations under the League of Nations Covenant. Like Belgium, Holland, Sweden, and Finland, she would fall back exclusively on armed neutrality.

The Soviet Union

In stark contrast to the reeling market economies of Europe, state-planned socialism[72] appeared to produce a veritable "Great Leap Forward" of industrialization in the Soviet Union. During the First and Second Five Year Plans (1928–1937), annual industrial growth exceeded 10 percent by *western* estimates—a blistering pace. Coal production increased from 35.4 to 128 million tons, steel from 4 to 17.7 million tons, oil from 11.7 to 28.5 million tons, and electricity from 5.1 to 36.2 billion kilowatt-hours. Workers employed in industry rose from 3,086,000 to 10,110,000.[73] Historians now realize that these huge increases were to some extent "fiddled not only by a central party machine wishing to fool the world," writes Robert Service, "but also by local functionaries wanting to trick the central party machine." They covered up extremely high rates of alcoholism, absenteeism, and job turnover; damage done to machines by illiterate peasants; as well as turnout of "shoddy goods" that became essentially "unusable."[74] However, labor and quality problems diminished during the Second Five Year Plan, and in the end, according to Alec Nove, "a great industry was built."[75] By the late 1930s Russian industrial output stood behind only the German and American.

The Soviet Union also succeeded in finally negotiating the ever steeper technological gradient of the maturing second industrial revolution. Accelerating since the national exertions of the Great War, in fact, western techniques raced rapidly toward their full potentials: America's huge open hearth steel furnaces; Germany's Haber-Bosch process for mass-producing high quality sulfuric and nitric acids; America's ingenious lathes, milling and grinding machines, drills, and gear-cutting devices; and the rapidly evolving metal monoplane, which combined many technologies mastered in every developed western nation and Japan. If the Union of Soviet Socialist Republics (USSR) were to avoid the disasters of the last war Stalin's experts knew they had to adopt these integral, all-pervasive technologies lock, stock, and barrel. Hence the

The USSR enters the second industrial revolution: steel complex at Magnitogorsk in the 1930s. (John Scott, *Behind the Urals: An American Worker in Russia's City of Steel* [Boston, 1942])

First Five Year Plan included special arrangements with western metallurgical, chemical, and engineering firms for incorporating the key parts of the modern technological system in Russia. One researcher concludes that the remarkable technical capabilities actually achieved by the Soviets in the critical areas listed here were "heavily" dependent (i.e., 80 percent of all new capacity) on western borrowings.[76] What is more, much of the nation's industrial/technological effort went into the military machine—a massive 17 percent of gross national product (GNP) in 1932 with continuing high levels throughout the decade. Such martial spending towered ominously above Germany's 12.9 percent, Italy's 11.7 percent, France's 6.9 percent, and Britain's 5.5 percent in the mid-to-late 1930s.[77]

In dreary contrast to Soviet industrial policy, what happened in the countryside proved nothing short of disastrous. Farm policy under NEP allowed peasants to market 90 percent of their crops, the remainder to be procured by Moscow at state prices. As early as 1926–1927, however, radical Bolsheviks alienated by "bourgeois" aspects of NEP succeeded in lowering procurement prices 20–25 percent. General Secretary Joseph Stalin aligned himself with this faction, championing its warped view of peasants as dreaded class enemies of the proletariat as well as its "built-in dislike of market forces." Because Soviet prices now dipped below slumping world levels, peasants reacted logically by hoarding grain in the hope that state prices would rise, or by selling stockpiles to private traders at market rates. The standoff between city and country worsened during the First Five Year Plan, for now private trade was banned, all crops were procured at low state prices, and peasants were pressured to abandon family property for cooperative farming ventures or the full-fledged collective farm (*Kolkhoz*) where farmers shared all work, land, capital, and revenue. Further hoarding and black market sales by those prosperous enough to possess a surplus, mixed with reports of more serious opposition to the state, provoked Stalin and his followers into cracking down on these recalcitrant "tight-fisted" peasants, the so-called kulaks. Determined to wage war against such "sworn enemies of the collective farm movement," the man of steel turned against advocates of a more gradual collectivization process like Nikolai Bukharin, who was removed from the Politburo. "Now we are able to carry on a determined offensive against the kulaks, eliminate them as a class," he told an excited gathering of Marxist agrarians in December 1929. "Now dekulakization is being carried out," he added ominously. "When the head is off, one does not mourn for the hair."[78]

Indeed, terrible developments were proceeding in the peasant world. One recent biographer, Dimitri Volkogonov, describes these events as "the real revolution, or more properly, something like a holocaust from above."[79] The original Five Year Plan targeted four-fifths of peasant households for some type of cooperative farming venture, with only a sixth in actual collective farms. But Stalin frenetically accelerated the pace in the autumn of 1929, whipping local and regional party functionaries into the kind of brutal class warfare some of them had wanted for years. All farm properties deemed by the party's crude and arbitrary definition to be "kulak" were confiscated for redistribution to collective farms. Countless tens of thousands died on the spot resisting communist justice. Far worse, from 1929 to 1931 a criminal regime deported 675,000 kulak families—over three million people—to Siberia or other remote provinces in cattle cars unventilated in summer and unheated in winter. For frightening numbers of people, especially the very young and the elderly, these turned into death rides.

The middle and small peasants, meanwhile, got herded into collective farms. Fierce resistance erupted, sometimes reaching insurrectionary proportions, but was crushed when necessary with Red Army regulars. By 1933 collective farms comprised two-thirds of rural households—four times the original plan goal. Peasants normally did not abandon their private property, however, before slaughtering hard-to-replenish livestock—over 120 million cattle, horses, sheep, and goats were butchered. Collectivization also disrupted grain production, which slipped to 81.5 percent of 1928 output in 1933, remaining at relatively low levels throughout the decade. Despite the food crisis, however, planners callously exported millions of tons of grain to pay for imported machines and machine tools, and continued to requisition grain from the peasantry, turning a blind eye to the outright starvation that devastated some regions, particularly the Ukraine. Volkogonov concludes that over eight and a half million men, women, and children died as a result of dekulakization, collectivization, and famine. A comparable number of Europeans perished, one should recall, in the Great War.

The famine that worsened with every month from the autumn of 1932 into the pre-harvest summer months of 1933, eventually killing several million citizens, seems to have been the final stage in a brutalization process whose origins stretched back to the civil war and Great War years. Human resiliency had limits, and the Soviet people reached these limits in 1933, committing the worst kinds of crimes against one another, and then slipping into a kind of massive collective denial. "That's what the famine did to people," recalled one woman. "Stalin reduced people to such a condition that they lost their reason, their conscience, and their sense of mercy."[80] As Catherine Merridale reminds us, however, the kill-your-neighbor/denial mentality that progressively hardened in the 1930s was not just Stalin's responsibility, but rather "part of a specific Soviet mentality—the product of a shattered culture, of broken communities, a civil war, of misplaced stoicism, the revolutionary mission, utopian hope, and the experience of repeated, massive suffering."[81]

The bloody events of the early 1930s also affected Stalin. Perhaps in 1945 this latter-day Ivan the Terrible thought about the throne-shaking peasant uprisings of earlier times when dismissing Winston Churchill's suggestion that the Great Patriotic War (1941–1945) had produced an incomparable amount of stress. "Oh no," replied the dictator, "the Collective Farm policy was a terrible struggle. . . . It was fearful. Four years it lasted." Always cold, deceiving, mistrustful, and probably psychopathic, Stalin had survived a harrowing trauma that left him willing to crush, ruthlessly and mercilessly, any who opposed him—or any who seemed to have even the remotest incentive to do so,

The man of steel: Joseph Stalin.   (Library of Congress)

at least in the twisted mind of Russia's "maniacally suspicious"[82] ruler. The anxiety that corroded him stemmed not only from the ferocity of peasant resistance, but also from the perceived lack of party toughness in the face of this challenge. Most functionaries did not hesitate to do their duty, muttering "let the lot of them die" as they packed class enemies into cattle cars. But over 850,000 communists, almost a third of the rank and file, were removed from their posts in 1933 for one infraction or another, most, presumably, for failing to carry out dekulakization instructions, while others "were appalled at the slaughter, obeying orders but sickened by their own responsibility."[83] It is probably true, as Merle Fainsod observed in his classic study, that opportunistic considerations of advancing within a rapidly growing state machine in need of reliable servants influenced many who did their duty whatever they may have felt about it.[84]

Suspicions that such opposition could smolder, perhaps igniting a coup, mounted in February 1934 when nearly a quarter of the delegates to the Seventeenth Party Congress voted against Stalin as general secretary. Now the secret police swung into action, arresting about a million people over the next two years, including 1,108 of the 1,225 delegates to the seventeenth Congress. Preceded by the infamous show trials of scores of Bolsheviks like Gregory Zinoviev, Lev Kamenev, and Nikolai Bukharin, who were all executed, about five million additional arrests occurred in 1937–1938. About a million of these innocent detainees were summarily shot, while additional hundreds of thousands died in forced labor camps, the infamous "GULAG," which had been rapidly expanding since the collectivization/industrialization drive of the early 1930s.[85]

The rights of Soviet women also eroded considerably under Stalin's brutal reign. In order to increase a population he had already done so much to destroy, the man of steel banned previously legal abortions, restored the husband's previously attenuated authority as family head, and made the divorce process, heretofore fairly easy, much more cumbersome and complicated. Writing in 1936 after the horrendous rape of the countryside that was collectivization, and just as the bloody purges began, Stalin gave new and frightening meaning to hypocrisy: "abortion, which destroys life, is unacceptable in our country." Soviet women allegedly had the "same rights" as men, "but equality does not exempt her from the great and noble duty that nature bestowed on her: she is mother, she gives life." The family wrecker also made it a crime to be the "relative of a traitor,"[86] a wicked device that police used to compel wives and sisters to denounce husbands and brothers. Failure to do so, even the claim of not knowing about a man's activities, could land women in prison. Or worse—about 15 percent of the people executed in the Great Purge of 1936–1938 were female.

The purges extended into the Red Army as well. One recent study concludes that thirty thousand of eighty thousand officers were imprisoned or executed. Ever suspicious that his generals wanted to overthrow him, especially with Leon Trotsky rashly trumpeting knowledge of such intrigues from exile, Stalin took massive preemptive action after reports came to him—false, as it turned out—that a Red Army plot was afoot. The military bloodletting began at the top with three of the army's five marshals, including Mikhail Tukhachevsky, hero of the civil war, then sliced through the entire officer corps. All deputy defense commissars, all military district commanders, the Navy and Air Force commanders and their chiefs of staff, 14 of 16 army group commanders, 60 of 67 corps commanders, 136 of 199 division commanders, 221 of 397 brigade commanders, and half of all regimental commanders got the axe.[87] Why had Stalin decimated his own army? Besides the obvious goal of staying in power and remaining alive, the insidious dictator probably sought a guarantee of absolute loyalty from his soldiers when the war clouds gathering ominously over Europe finally burst. He reckoned that the "liquidation of the Trotskyites and double dealers"[88] would prove its worth when the tocsin sounded.

For many years, in fact, Stalin had eyed developments in Europe warily and suspiciously. Convinced by mid-decade that Mussolini and Hitler represented the greatest threats to Soviet security, he attempted to rally non-Fascist political forces throughout Europe. This so-called popular front strategy featured Soviet membership in the League of Nations, alliance negotiations with France and Czechoslovakia, French Communist Party support for the first government of Leon Blum, and military backing for Republican Spain. By early 1939, however, the apparent failure of the League, the decision of Britain and France to appease Hitler over annexation of Austria and the Sudeten province of Czechoslovakia, and their refusal to intervene in Spain against Franco, whose forces victoriously entered Madrid in March 1939, had largely frustrated Stalin's popular front strategy. Revival of the old Triple Entente of Britain, France, and Russia remained Stalin's most attractive option, but after the abandonment of Czechoslovakia at Munich in September 1938, Soviet leaders began to consider making a deal with Hitler. "My poor friend, what have you done?" asked a dumbfounded V. P. Potemkin, assistant commissar for foreign affairs, of the French ambassador. "As for us, I don't see any other conclusion than a fourth partition of Poland."[89]

Digression: Culture Under Totalitarianism

The actual totalitarian systems of the 1930s were unenlightened by Aldous Huxley's standards: the problem not the solution, furthering the kind of foreign conquest or international class struggle that Mustapha Mond and company had eradicated in *Brave New World*.[90] Consistently enough, the dictators' militant goals demanded militant cultures quite the opposite of the erotic escapism administered by Mond. Mussolini, Hitler, and Stalin commandeered popular radio culture for these ends, for instance, broadcasting programs and political messages that buttressed the leaders' personality cults, castigated class and foreign enemies, and readied true believers for coming struggles. In matters of high culture all three preferred "realistic" creations that did not distort, twist, or obscure heroic meaning and truth as defined by the state. Art had to glorify rank-and-file willingness to serve the cause and promote loyalty to the selfless leader—or else disappear. Stalin's tastes, for example, were extremely conservative. After Dmitri Shostakovich's avant-garde opera *Lady Macbeth* opened in 1936, the party newspaper, *Pravda*, denounced it. "Snatches of melody, embryos of musical phrases, drown, escape and drown once more in crashing, gnashing, and screeching."[91] Hitler, for his part, put "degenerate art" on display for public ridicule. If contemporary artists produced such works because their eyes actually saw things this way, then the degenerate ones "should be dealt with in the Ministry of the Interior, where sterilization of the insane is arranged."[92] Later, party thugs publicly burned nearly five thousand modernist paintings and drawings.

Italian policy was more tolerant in the 1920s in large measure because of Mussolini's long-time intimate association with Margherita Sarfatti, an advocate of "New Century" (*Novecento*) blending of classical and modern forms. By 1933, however, Il Duce had turned his back on the Jewess Sarfatti in favor of his cruder henchmen's demands for "a simple and easily understood Fascist realist painting." *Novecento*'s "horrible figures with such big hands and feet, with eyes in the wrong places, are ridiculous," blurted Mussolini, "beyond common sense, outside tradition and Italian art—it's time to stop it, I say, stop it."[93] But Mussolini had not completely abandoned fascism's eclectic approach to art. He approved plans in 1934, for instance, for a new train station in Florence that would become "the most daringly modern public building in the country."[94]

In contrast, Nazism snuffed out modernism, leaving behind extensive cultural barrenness. Although cultural oases were rare, Germany did make impressive aesthetic achievements in the medium of film. Leni Riefenstahl's *Triumph of the Will* (1935) remains a classic, especially its opening scene presenting Hitler, god and man, descending from the sky to mingle with mortal party comrades. The brilliant filmmaker even catches a ray of sunlight landing on the upheld palm of the evil genius's hand as he is driven through the medieval streets of Nuremberg. Karl Ritter's films *Hitler Youth Quex* (1933), a sensitive morality tale of political devotion and death, and *Operation Michael* (1937), with its moving representation of selfless soldierly sacrifice in 1918, made tremendous artistic accomplishments while still remaining within the mold of politically correct state culture.[95]

Not even the murderously stifling atmosphere of Stalinist Russia destroyed all trace of good art. Mikhail's Sholokhov's powerful *Quiet Flows the Don* (1928–1940) adhered to Socialist Realism's propagandistic mission of "[showing] the masses positive models of initiative and heroic labor"[96] while also laying claim to epic literary qualities. The four-volume opus follows life in a Cossack village from the eve of World War One through the bitter fighting of the Russian Civil War. Wonderful things also appeared on the silver screen. Thus *Alexander Nevsky* (1938), Sergei Eisenstein's cinematic masterpiece, depicted a grim and perilous medieval world full of Russia's enemies and eerily foretold the slaying of invading Germanic hordes. Sergei Prokofiev's stirring score for the film heightened the artistic achievement, although this piece, like his other compositions of the 1930s, had to depart from an earlier partially modernist style now out of favor. Only when cameras turned to the camp of the evil and decrepit Teutonic Knights did the score incorporate the atonal and off-key sound of modernism. Unlike Italy, in fact, the only means to produce culture that departed from Stalinist dictates were to artfully and ingeniously circumvent them—as in Iuri Krymov's novel *Tanker Derbent* (1938), a tale of tough oil shipping businessmen on the Caspian Sea—or to go underground. The latter alternative applied to Mikhail Bulgakov's novel *The Master and Margarita*, a "bravura performance of truly heroic virtuosity, a carnival of the imagination."[97]

At its most basic level, Bulgakov's work is a searing satire of Soviet literary officialdom. The devil, known as Woland—a metaphor, perhaps, for Stalin—visits Moscow with his four assistants and plays a series of cruel tricks on the in-crowd of poets, writers, and theatrical managers—one is beheaded, another driven into an insane asylum, a third exiled to Yalta in his underwear, and yet another shot dead at Satan's midnight ball. Later, the exclusive dining club of the privileged writers' union is burned to the ground. Bulgakov's characters and plot contradicted the tenets of Socialist Realism in every way imaginable. The hero (the Master) is an anti-hero without resolve and the heroine (Margarita) an adulteress who goes publicly naked. Margarita also concentrates her love on her man, rather than society. The ideal of collective progress yields to expression of contempt for crowds and ordinary people, furthermore, and Soviet atheism is mocked by the appearance of a real devil as well as the telling, in the novel within the novel, of Pontius Pilate's emotional and intellectual engagement with a human Christ figure. "Not a page was publishable,"[98] concludes one expert on Bulgakov.

At a deeper level, the novel attacks all those who lack the courage to pursue truth. It is not just a dictatorial regime and its cow-towing literary establishment, however, that submits to falsehood in *The Master and Margarita*. Bulgakov also condemns the ordinary people of Moscow for their materialism, narrow-minded conformity, hatred of foreigners, callous disregard for fellow citizens, and the relish with which they denounce one another. Thus Woland's reign of trickery and terror can be seen as a well-deserved punishment of the common folk. Before turning one victim's head into a goblet, in fact, he proclaims: "a man will receive his deserts in accordance with his beliefs."[99] The suggestion that many average Soviet people were at least partially responsible for the evil that occurred in their society is given added emphasis by the Sanhedrin's abandonment of Yeshua, the novel's Christ figure, much to the dismay of the more powerful Pontius Pilate. A few hours later, moreover, the crowd roars its approval of the release of Bar-Abba, which dooms Yeshua to crucifixion. Thus Bulgakov, who had undoubtedly observed crowds demanding the death penalty during the show trials, was among the first to charge, between the lines, that Stalin and his henchmen were not the only ones to blame for Russia's tragedy. As Dimitri Volkogonov wrote fifty years later, "the people allowed their own consciences to be driven into a reservation, thus giving the grand inquisitor the opportunity to carry on with his dark deeds. . . . It was not only the leader who was sick, but the whole society."[100]

Arthur Koestler composed his grim, depressing novel *Darkness at Noon* as it became clear for communist insiders in the late 1930s that Stalin's version of the revolution had taken on frightening dimensions not yet fathomed by West European leftists. The author, born in Budapest and educated in Vienna, participated in communist activities in the 1930s, spent time in the Soviet Union, fought against Franco in Spain, escaped imprisonment there, and then broke with the party, eventually settling in Paris to write his anti-Stalinist classic. Only in inner exile, like Bulgakov, or exile, like Koestler, could one feel safe to criticize Stalin. *Darkness at Noon* led the way for others like Englishman George Orwell, whose biting postwar satires *Animal Farm* and *Nineteen Eighty-Four* widened the assault on communist totalitarianism.

As the novel opens Koestler's protagonist, Rubashov, has been arrested. A composite of many of the early Bolshevik leaders whose contributions to the cause of world revolution the Kremlin mocked, he has voiced too many criticisms of "Number One," and consequently hears the cell door slam behind him. Rubashov enters into a long soul-search of his own past, remembering those he has sent to their deaths and gradually questioning whether the ends of the great revolution have been justified by the means. His first inquisitor, Ivanov, has no such inhibitions: "The vice of pity I have managed up till now to avoid. The smallest dose of it, and you will be lost. Weeping over humanity and bewailing oneself—you know our race's pathological leaning to it. Our greatest poets destroyed themselves by this poison."[101] Unfortunately for Ivanov, he is not pitiless enough in his interrogation to avoid getting sacked and executed. An automaton, Gletkin, takes over, gets a confession, and arranges the dramatic show trial. Awaiting execution, Rubashov realizes that the movement, "sailing without ethical ballast" into the mist, has lost sight of its end goal of reducing human suffering. "Perhaps now would come the time of great darkness." And later, much later perhaps, a new movement would arise "with new flags" and a "new spirit"[102] of humanitarian socialism.

As Bulgakov entered the most intense period of work on his masterpiece between 1932 and 1936, and Koestler still drank deeply of communist reality, Thomas Mann completed and published the bulk of his tetralogy, *Joseph and His Brothers*.[103] The reader is taken on a lengthy two-thousand-page journey through the life of Joseph, the talented Israelite who is sold into Egyptian slavery and rises to administrative prominence under the pharaohs. Like Bulgakov, Mann warps time and obscures its passage by weaving the myth of creation and allusions to the Virgin Mary and Jesus into the story of Joseph. This toying with time and place served to reinforce the present-day concerns of the Joseph books, for Mann wanted to show that the legacy of mythic time to succeeding generations was essentially humanist and positive in the person of the humane and strangely modern Joseph, not brutal and violent as the Nazis and their Aryan sagas would have it. Expropriating the power of myth for the good cause of humanity "was like turning a captured cannon around," he wrote, "and firing it at the enemy."[104] Mann saw his salvo as a kind of rearguard action that would not succeed in his lifetime against Nazi violence and anti-Semitism. His conscious choice of an ancient Jewish setting for the Joseph tetralogy therefore amounted to a courageous gesture of solidarity with this troubled and persecuted people—and a not-so-subtle act of defiance. When the first volume appeared in 1933, in fact, the great writer and his Jewish wife had already been forced into exile.

Germany and War Again

Fully prepared to wage war over the Sudetenland in September 1938, Adolf Hitler had no change of heart after Munich. One of the best indications that Chamberlain's hopes for peace had been misplaced, in fact, was Berlin's radicalizing, escalating anti-Semitic policy, for to Hitler and his Judeophobic henchmen the racial enemy could not be allowed to perpetrate a second "stab in the back" during a war. On the contrary, Jews would be neutralized, cowed into submission, prior to that conflict. Not at all coincidentally, therefore, screws had been tightening on German and Austrian Jews throughout 1938. During the spring and summer a series of decrees began to squeeze Jewish businesses out of the economy. In June Nazis torched the synagogue in Munich and threw fifteen hundred Jews into concentration camps. They destroyed the Nuremberg synagogue in August, incarcerated four thousand Austrian Jews in September, and deported eighteen thousand Polish Jews working in Germany in October. When the vengeful son of one of the hapless exiles killed a German official in Paris, the Nazis unleashed a massive pogrom on the night of November 9, 1938. Party thugs set five hundred synagogues ablaze and smashed over seven thousand Jewish shops. Debris from the shattered store windows would give the pogrom its infamous name: *Reichskristallnacht*, the "Night of the Broken Glass." When it was over, ninety-one Jews had been killed, while countless hundreds of others would later die of their wounds or commit suicide. About thirty thousand Jews were forced temporarily into concentration camps.

The night's actions sparked widespread "obloquy and indignation"[105] in the German public, including protests from anti-Semites who had welcomed earlier discrimination, but now realized in horror how much they had contributed to barbarism in their own country. Completely ignoring such criticism, the regime arrested huge numbers of Germans who had expressed criticism of the pogrom or sympathy for Jews. The immediate result of the crackdown, observed the socialist underground, "is that grumbling has become less pronounced. . . . Everybody realizes more and more that after all the Nazis have the power to do what they like."[106] Hitler knew this too, summarizing the lessons of *Reichskristallnacht* for the ever-widening cadre of his radical followers, hard-core Nazis who knew this was just a first step, by blaming the victims. "Today I will once again be a prophet," he told Nazi Reichstag deputies in January 1939. "If the international Jewish financiers . . . should again succeed in plunging the nations into a world war, the result will be not the Bolshevization of the globe and thus victory for Jewry but the annihilation of the Jewish race in Europe."[107]

Like a falling barometer, the Führer's chilling anti-Semitic speech signaled the approaching storm. The danger to Europe from regimes that treated their own subjects in criminal fashion struck Con O'Neill, third secretary at Britain's Berlin embassy, as self-evident. "Such ruthlessness is the essential method of Nazi policy, which they not only prefer," he wrote soon after the great pogrom, "but also *cannot avoid*." Consistently applying the same domestic philosophy to foreign policy, Germany would use "terror in a world full of rabbits" and represented, therefore, a "direct threat"[108] to Britain and the other nations of Europe. But O'Neill's superior in Berlin, Neville Henderson, did not agree. Hitler had no intention of seeking world domination, the ambassador wired home on March 9, 1939. "I believe Hitler to be far too sane to cherish such a chimera." It seemed significant to Henderson that the German leader had given his word at Munich to honor the peace. "Strange though it may sound, he prides himself on keeping his word."[109]

Henderson's superiors in London unfortunately put credence in these overly sanguine dispatches. So much so, in fact, that when Stalin hinted strongly on March 10, 1939, that he favored an alliance with Britain and France over an accommodation with Hitler, Chamberlain opted to persist with appeasement. Besides, how much military value could a Red Army purged of its best generals possess? And what democratic diplomat could trust someone who killed off the domestic opposition? Indeed, Chamberlain distrusted a man whose motives "seem to me to have little connection with our ideas of liberty and to be concerned only with getting everyone else by the ears."[110]

Such an inconsistent application of libertarian principles played into the hands of Hitler and Mussolini. Having acquired the most easily defensible portion of Czechoslovakia at Munich, Germany sent its divisions to occupy the remainder on March 15, 1939. Italian troops seized Albania three weeks later. Afterward Chamberlain appeared ready to abandon appeasement, confessing privately that he could no longer feel safe with Hitler and irritated that Mussolini had behaved "like a sneak and a cad."[111]

During subsequent months Britain tried to send a deterrent message to Berlin and Rome by guaranteeing the independence of Poland, Rumania, Greece, and Turkey and opening negotiations in Moscow for a military alliance. At the same time, however, Sir Horace Wilson, one of Chamberlain's political acolytes, hinted to the Germans that his boss wanted a Polish Munich,[112] a pact that "would enable Britain to rid herself of her commitments vis-à-vis Poland."[113] Always well-informed, Soviet officials assumed from these maneuverings that Britain had already offered Hitler "freedom of movement in the east."[114] Their conclusion was incorrect: Chamberlain's team wanted peace, not war—in fact, Britain wanted Hitler to accept a comprehensive peace plan that went beyond rearrangements in Poland to the point of restoring post-Munich Czechoslovakia.[115] It was nevertheless clear that Chamberlain had not abandoned appeasement despite its embarrassing failures.

Events moved inexorably toward war during the summer of 1939. When the British-French negotiating team arrived in Moscow in early August, Stalin immediately noticed the absence of a high-ranking official like Foreign Minister Halifax. "They're not being serious," he blurted. "London and Paris are playing poker again." Talks soon bogged down over the unacceptability of transporting Red Army units through East European countries if Germany provoked war. "Enough of these games,"[116] said Stalin. He then pulled out a pen and signed the non-aggression treaty his underlings had been negotiating with Berlin. In their unscrupulous pact of August 23, 1939, both sides agreed not to attack one another. The signatories divided Poland and the Baltic on paper between them.

With the ink drying on the pact, Hitler ordered his generals to finish preparations for the invasion of Poland. As recent research demonstrates, the Führer expected war, but probably not a general European conflagration at this point, for his economic preparations for expanding armaments output still had three years to run.[117] That night in his alpine retreat near Berchtesgaden the Nazi leader and his entourage saw Northern Lights of an unusually intense red hue light up the valley. "The last act of *Götterdämmerung* could not have been more effectively staged," recalled one of them. Turning abruptly to a military adjutant, Hitler said: "Looks like a great deal of blood. This time we won't bring it off without violence."[118] With or without the requisite level of armaments and raw materials, he would not turn back now.

Chapter 6

WORLD WAR TWO

A nervous duty officer knocked timidly at Stalin's dacha bedroom door. In a moment the dictator's suspicious pockmarked face appeared, a withering glance all that was required to question the need for middle-of-the-night business. "General Zhukov is asking to speak to you on the telephone on a matter that cannot wait!" Stalin walked to the phone. His impassive eyes and motionless lips did not divulge the shocking news streaming from the receiver into his ears: German airplanes had bombed Kiev, Minsk, Sevastopol, Vilnius, and numerous other sites along the western frontier. Zhukov heard nothing on the other end. "Did you understand what I said, Comrade Stalin?" No response. "Comrade Stalin, do you understand?" Finally Stalin stammered: "Come to the Kremlin with General Timoshenko."[1]

The leader of the Soviet Union had made the pre-dawn drive from Kremlin to dacha many times, staring in thought at the darkened windows of the capital. On June 22, 1941, however, he drove in the opposite direction. Arriving at the red bastion of communist rule Stalin ascended his private stairway to the meeting rooms of the Politburo. "Get the others here, now!" he snapped at his frightened private secretary. After the generals and political satraps assembled, Molotov called the German embassy, reporting back that Berlin "has declared war . . . 'to forestall an attack by the Russians.'" Hours passed in angry confusion. At first Stalin ordered the destruction of enemy forces without violating borderlines, but by evening the Red Army was ordered to decimate the foe with no regard for foreign territory. At 10 P.M. jubilation reigned when word came that most of the German attacks had been beaten back.

Nothing could have been farther from the truth, for enemy spearheads were advancing rapidly along the entire western frontier of the Soviet Union, penetrating in some places over fifty miles during the first twenty-four hours. As the extent of the emergency became clearer in subsequent days, Stalin maintained a semblance of composure until, on June 26, fleeing Red Army units reported that German tanks had reached Minsk, nearly three hundred miles inside Soviet territory. "What was that you said, what's happening at Minsk?" asked the incredulous, unraveling dictator. "Have you got this right? How do you know this?"

Poland 1939–1942

Soon guilt and self-doubt undermined Stalin's ability to lead. "Lenin left us a great inheritance," he said on June 29 as enemy divisions rolled farther East, "and we, his heirs, have [screwed] it all up!" Obviously slipping into depression, he refused to leave the dacha, shocked into inaction by the nightmarish realization that "the Germans were an enemy who could not be conjured away by bracing slogans, tricked by a ruse, or taken charge by the [secret police]."[2] A delegation of cronies drove to see him the next day, but their surprised leader, no doubt fearing arrest or assassination, said only: "What have you come for?" An astonished Molotov recalled that Stalin "had the strangest look on his face, and the question itself was pretty strange, too."

On July 3, however, Stalin recovered enough of his steely nerves to address the nation on radio. Fear—of arrest, of the Germans, of his place in history—had galvanized him into action, but just barely, for he paused often, breathing heavily, to take drinks of water. He seemed sick and at the end of his strength. Nevertheless, drawing on the moving patriotic legacy of the defeat of Napoleon's Grand Army in 1812, Russia's latter-day tsar called on the people to undertake a scorched-earth resistance and, ultimately, to annihilate the new invader.

BLITZKRIEG 1939–1941

Stalin had signed a non-aggression pact with Hitler almost two years earlier.[3] The agreement of August 23, 1939, signaled the Soviet leader's exasperation with British and French appeasement of Germany and his deep, irrational suspicions about western motives. Were they sanctioning a Nazi drive to the East, hiring a surrogate fighting force to eradicate the communist demon? He would do them one better and deal with Hitler. Stalin was willing to gamble that Germany and the West would exhaust themselves as they had in the Great War, leaving the Soviet Union free to continue its military-industrial buildup.[4] Indeed, only days after signing the pact with Hitler Stalin unleashed General Georgi Zhukov, a surviving protégé of purged Marshal Tuchachevsky, on Japanese forces threatening Outer Mongolia. The strike successfully terminated a two-year border war and seemed to guarantee Stalin the time he needed for further rearmament. Once his western enemies had bled themselves white, the USSR could intervene and dictate the future of Europe.

The gamble went badly almost from the beginning. Russian interests favored many months of costly fighting in Poland, a bloody quagmire of a struggle lasting until spring. On September 1, 1939, however, 960,000 German troops massed in five armies crossed the border from three directions, quickly smashing Poland's more than 600,000 defenders. Tanks and motorized infantry assigned to one army in Pomerania sliced across the Polish Corridor to East Prussia in three days. The lead tank corps of the most powerful mobile army advancing from Silesia pierced to the outskirts of Warsaw in one week. These two army contingents, totaling six armored divisions, four motorized infantry divisions, and four combined mobile divisions, represented only a fourth of Germany's strike force. The remainder of the army moved on foot or with horses, as it had in World War One.

Death from above: German dive-bombers. (Getty Images)

Germany's modernized fourteen divisions implemented a new doctrine of lightning warfare—"Blitzkrieg"—ideas that more orthodox German Army (Wehrmacht) commanders still regarded skeptically on the eve of the invasion. All armies of that day, including Poland, treated tanks like artillery, distributing them evenly among infantry divisions. The German innovators, however, massed available tanks in armored "panzer" divisions that punched gaping holes in the Polish line and raced to the rear with no regard for flank protection. The tanks were aided by ground support "Stuka" dive-bombers that rained explosives on frightened defenders, adding considerably to the panic with shrieking wing sirens dubbed by pilots the "Trumpets of Jericho." With an inferior air force—four hundred versus two thousand planes—no comparable number of tanks—six hundred versus twenty-six hundred—and no anti-tank capability, Poland was routed. German armies progressed so quickly, in fact, that on September 17, Stalin, eager to put as much distance between Moscow and the new German frontier in Poland, ordered half a million Red Army regulars to occupy the chunk of eastern Poland allotted to Russia in the Nazi-Soviet Non-Aggression Pact. Warsaw capitulated ten days later.

If Stalin had hoped for immediate military action by Britain and France to aid Poland, or at least quick retaliation against the German victors, he was again disappointed. Indeed, the whole episode demonstrates the inertia, the tragic irreversible momentum of two and a half years of appeasement. Poland could have placed about two million soldiers in the field if she had persisted with efforts to mobilize them after August 23, but relented instead to pressure from London and Paris to stand down lest mobilization provoke Hitler. When Warsaw finally ignored Chamberlain's last-minute peace initiative and gave the order on August 31, less than a third of the army would be ready to defend on the morrow. Tens of thousands were caught in troop trains by enemy fighter planes. The unfortunate chaos contributed to the speed of the German advance. And what of the French Army, which had promised swift air support to the Poles? None came, prompting indignant Polish queries in the French capital. Fear of German retaliatory air raids, however, produced a dumbfounding reply: "[Surely] you don't expect us to have a massacre of women and children in Paris!" said the French foreign minister.[5] When an offensive finally got underway in the Saar on September 17, its desultory probes were called off after a few days. France, with an equally reluctant and inactive Britain at its side, intended to maintain a defensive posture behind the Maginot Line until a few years later when offensive warfare promised more success.

Hitler, on the other hand, had no compunction against massacring women and children, especially if they were of allegedly inferior races and ethnic groups. "Genghis Khan had millions of women and children killed by his own will and with a gay heart," he told his generals on August 22. "Only in such a way will we win the vital space that we need—who still talks nowadays of the extermination of the Armenians [in the last war]?"[6] In Poland Hitler's pilots strafed indiscriminately as hundreds of thousands of terrified civilians clogged roads in a desperate effort to stay alive. On September 25, moreover, four hundred bombers flew repeated sorties over Warsaw, killing at least forty thousand innocents, and demonstrating with shocking brutality the worthlessness, in Nazi eyes, of inferior enemy peoples. The campaign in Poland also witnessed the deployment of the first "S.S. Einsatzgruppen," an innocuous-sounding, sanitized designation for death squads. Their grisly mission: to terrorize the civilian population by executing priests, politicians, intellectuals, and Jews. The squads did their work with dispatch, hanging or shooting about fifteen thousand people.

When hostilities ended the Third Reich annexed western Poland, callously deporting 325,000 ethnic Poles and 330,000 Jews, the first step toward Germanizing these provinces. The deportees were herded into central Poland, where the Nazis established a so-called General Government of occupation. While life for Poles in this massive concentration camp became a day-to-day struggle for survival, Jewish families in the General Government, as well as those remaining in the annexed provinces, received far worse treatment. "Murder, abduction for forced labor, deportations, robbery, abuse, the burning of synagogues, the imposition of fines, the arrest and often murder of hostages all created great insecurity among the Jews," writes Leni Yahil, "and under-

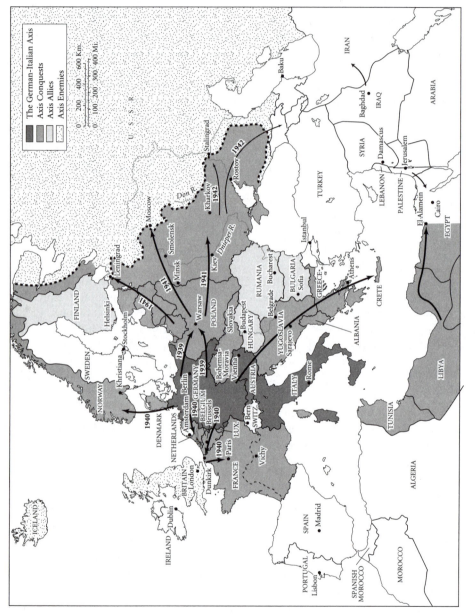

Axis Advances 1939–1942

mined the basic conditions of their existence, which had already been severely shaken by the war." In what seemed in 1940 the final cruel indignity, many of the nearly two million Polish Jews under German control were forced into hundreds of cramped, sealed-off ghettos with little food. The largest ghettos in Lódz and Warsaw accounted, respectively, for 160,000 and 450,000 Jews. In Warsaw 30 percent of the city population lived behind a ten-foot wall surrounding 2.5 percent of the city area. As Nazi ideologist Alfred Rosenberg put it, " 'living space' for the Jews should be *Lebensraum* in the opposite direction." Only the strongest would survive in the long run as the others slowly starved or perished from disease in what Nazi Propaganda Minister Josef Goebbels described as "death caskets."[7]

Stalin added to the toll of suffering and injustice in the eastern third of pre-war Poland and the Baltic. According to their own records the secret police arrested over 260,000 Poles for political reasons and deported them to slave labor camps in the Soviet Union. Tens of thousands died there. About 230,000 prisoners of war were taken too, including 15,000 officers.[8] Many of the latter were executed during the spring of 1940, and then buried in mass graves in the infamous Katyn Forest. By this time Moscow had coerced Lithuania, Latvia, and Estonia into protectorate status, abruptly ending two decades of independence as Red Army units occupied these countries. Over 130,000 "anti-Soviet elements" from the Baltic joined their Polish counterparts in the GULAG.

Seeing this bloody writing on the wall, Finland wisely resisted Soviet blandishments during the autumn of 1939. The small Scandinavian land bravely fought punitive expeditions during the subsequent "Winter War," killing hundreds of thousands of Red Army soldiers before superior numbers forced her to sue for peace in March 1940. Remarkably, Finland remained an independent country at the relatively inexpensive cost of border provinces near Leningrad and the White Sea that she ceded to the Soviet Union. Of all the countries from the arctic to the Caucasus that had broken away from Russia in 1917–1918, Finland alone still flew her own flag.

To the peoples of northeastern Europe the fall and winter of 1939–1940 seemed anything but a "phony" or "sit-down war" (*Sitzkrieg*), those misnomer, play-on-word labels coined by contemporary western journalists. The war seemed brutally real as well to seamen of the merchant marines and navies of Britain and Germany. The latter sunk nearly a million tons of shipping from September to December—and twice this amount in the first half of 1940. The Royal Navy immediately blockaded the German coast, moreover, and in December 1939 managed to destroy the pocket battleship *Graf Spee* in South American waters.

The phony *Sitzkrieg* got its name from the absence of military activity along the Franco-German border. German generals convinced Hitler that bad autumn weather as well as the need to refit depleted panzer divisions necessitated postponement of offensive operations against France. French Commander-in-Chief Maurice Gamelin, meanwhile, positioned a fifth of his troops in a sixteen-division reserve far to the rear near Paris, and over a third, twenty-eight divisions, passively behind the Maginot Line. The massive forts and redoubts of these formidable fortresses guarded the entire stretch between Switzerland and Montmédy near the Belgian border. Gamelin, an old, backward-looking commander, chose an unwired medieval structure in faraway Vincennes as his headquarters, sending messages by motorcycle as opposed to the allegedly less reliable wireless, ignoring hundreds of intercepted—and apparently equally unreliable—German wired messages, which hinted strongly at a bold outflanking strategy. Despite the lessons of Poland, furthermore, the French commander dispersed two-thirds of his 3,250 tanks throughout the thirty-six divisions of his frontline armies north of the forts. The remaining 1,250 he grouped in impressive armored, light mechanized, and light cavalry divisions, but half of this force he held in reserve. The nine-division British Expeditionary Force (B.E.F.) initially left its 300 tanks behind. These were ominous signs.

Nazi Germany lashed out at its democratic enemies in the spring of 1940. Shock divisions overran Denmark and Norway in April, securing Germany's northern flank as well as indispensable deposits of Norwegian iron ore. The bulk of the army struck Holland, Belgium, and France on May 10. Authored mainly by a young operational genius, Erich von Manstein, Germany's plan called for a feinting assault on the weak armies of Holland and Belgium. Manstein hoped to draw France's northern armies, the B.E.F., and most of the allies' armored and motorized units into Belgium where they would be engaged and pinned down by thirty German divisions and seven hundred massed tanks. The main attack would occur simultaneously, surreptitiously, and threateningly farther south. He proposed to pass a huge force through the allegedly impassable Ardennes Forest north and east of Sedan. The powerful impact of forty-five divisions and seventeen hundred tanks would fall on an unfortified sector north of the Maginot Line weakly defended by Gamelin. "As the German and Allied plans worked themselves out," writes Ernest May, "the best French soldiers would be in the wrong places, and the worst-prepared French soldiers would face the best that the Germans had."[9] Once this force penetrated, it could easily cut off allied troops rushing into Belgium, for, with 2,780 aircraft to the allies' 1,660, Germany would control the skies. Germany positioned only nineteen reserve divisions opposite France's mighty fortress barrier.

Manstein's operational planning succeeded far beyond expectations. Holland capitulated on May 15 before the French Seventh Army, fast-charging across northern Belgium, could reach Dutch lines. The murderous bombing of civilians in Rotterdam, whose inner city now smoked in ruins, extorted a panicky surrender from The Hague. German divisions also broke through Belgian lines after the ingenious destruction by commandos of the formidable Eben Emael citadel at Liége. With Holland paralyzed, and panzers racing westward, four Franco-British armies hurried to the East. They left a dangerous gap on their southern flank, where the French Second Army had been left behind to await, unwittingly, its fate around Sedan.

The main armored force struck out of the Ardennes on May 12. Having already seized neutral, democratic Luxembourg, the German juggernaut then quickly broke through Second Army and its northern neighbor, the French Ninth Army, as well as reserve units rushed to help. In one week of terrifying Blitzkrieg the better part of twenty French divisions disintegrated. Hundreds of thousands were killed, wounded, captured, or surrounded in isolated pockets. By May 20 German infantry divisions were pouring into northern France through a seventy-mile hole in French lines, and advanced armored units had seized Abbeville on the Channel, thereby sealing off lines of retreat for the surviving allied field armies. A huge force, totaling around forty-five British, French, and Belgian divisions, was "like a cut rose in a vase,"[10] according to one German officer. Belgium's surrender on May 28 removed further divisions from the line, effectively ending all allied chances. By early June the Royal Navy and hundreds of valiant volunteer boaters had evacuated 338,000 survivors without equipment at Dunkirk, while a few other shattered units escaped to the south—altogether a mere remnant of what, three weeks earlier, had been seven Dutch, Belgian, British, and French armies numbering a million and a half men.

Now nothing could stop the heady conquerors. On June 5 French soldiers stretched thinly between Amiens and Rheims absorbed the impact of fifty German divisions. Outnumbered two to one, the defenders' line finally gave way after three days of bloody fighting. The attackers entered Paris on June 14 forcing France to accept humiliating armistice terms one week later. The northern two-thirds of the country would be occupied indefinitely, France paying the costs. Hitler reduced the army and navy of rump France, with its capital at Vichy, to the same low levels Germany had been forced to accept in 1919. A million and a half French POWs would remain in captivity as hostages to ensure that "Vichy" France fulfilled the terms—which the Führer insisted they sign in the same town, Compiègne, indeed in the same railway car that the sullen Germans had visited twenty-one years before.

Paris's capitulation marked the nadir of government by the people in the twentieth century. Six democracies had fallen that spring, including powerful France, the proud victor of 1919. Isolated Iceland, cut off now from Denmark; uncommitted Ireland; mountainous, neutral Switzerland; intimidated, neutral Sweden; and, for the time being, battered Finland, stayed out of the fray. Great Britain and five small democratic states—this was all that remained of the democratic wave that swept across Europe in 1918–1919. Britain, the surviving democratic combatant, retained, to be sure, its navy. Beyond that, however, less than half an air force and the unequipped remnant of the demoralized B.E.F. were all that stood against "Festung Europa," the continental fortress of fascism and fear.

Britain and France had paid a terrible price for a lack of readiness and incompetent military leadership. It was somehow fitting, therefore, that Neville Chamberlain yielded on May 10, 1940, to the outspoken, controversial advocate of resistance and rearmament, Winston Churchill. Already, however, democratic leaders pondered deeper, more troubling lessons. Nazi Germany had run rampant among a "world full of rabbits," feasting on small states in Northern and Western Europe that had turned coweringly inward after the League's failures, choosing isolated neutrality in the desperate hope that somehow it would protect them from aggression. Manstein's outflanking maneuver was made possible, for example, when Belgium reneged in 1936 on its commitment to France to build Maginot-style forts north of Montmédy—all to assuage Berlin and supposedly avoid a repetition of Belgium's hard fate in the Great War. Worse still, although Hitler had already mocked the territorial rights of Denmark and Norway, Holland and Belgium refused to coordinate defensive plans with one another, or with London and Paris, lest such actions provoke him. The Führer fully exploited the lack of democratic solidarity.

A small measure of hope for democracy flickered from across the Atlantic that bleak early summer of 1940. Having buried its own head deeply in the sand of isolationism for two decades, the American public noticed—with considerable alarm—the extent of Europe's tragedy. As France collapsed, the Republican Party presidential nominating convention dropped isolationism from its plank, substituting mild interventionist language that promised economic assistance to the enemies of fascism, but stopped short of military commitments. Poised to run for an unprecedented third term in the White House that June, Franklin Delano Roosevelt immediately matched the Republicans with rousing words of his own. The United States, which he later dubbed "the arsenal of democracy," would "extend to the opponents of force the material resources of this nation." At least it was something.

But could such help arrive in time? Past its navy shield Britain had only two battle-ready infantry divisions, a portion of its lone armored division, 520 serviceable fighter aircraft, and a defiant populace bolstered in its belligerence by the angry eloquence of Winston Churchill. "The whole fury and might of the enemy must very soon be turned on us," he told radio listeners on June 18.

> Hitler knows that he will have to break us in this island or lose the war. If we can stand up to him, all Europe may be free and the life of the world may move forward into broad, sunlit uplands. But if we fail, then the whole world, including the United States, including all that we have known and cared for, will sink into the abyss of a new Dark Age, made more sinister, and perhaps more protracted, by the lights of perverted science. Let us therefore brace ourselves to our duties, and so bear ourselves that, if the British Empire and its Commonwealth last for a thousand years, men will say, "This was their finest hour."[11]

Hitler believed, in fact, that Britain must be broken, sooner or later. In early July 1940 he probably preferred a temporary end to hostilities under terms tantamount to a British surrender, thereby freeing his forces for their destined seizure of *Lebensraum* in the East. Even while waiting for London to relent, however, Hitler's generals drew up their plans for continuing the hostilities "if necessary," as Hitler put it. "Operation Eagle" would unleash nearly twenty-seven hundred airplanes on England to gain undisputed control of the skies. "Operation Sea Lion" would follow, disembarking twelve divisions for what the Nazis assumed would be mopping-up work. Hitler lost patience with Churchill and ordered his Luftwaffe chief, Hermann Goering, to ready the planes on July 16. Three weeks later Goering told his fliers: "Within a short period you will wipe the British Air Force from the sky. Heil Hitler!"[12]

The most intense period of the so-called Battle of Britain lasted until late September 1940.[13] Contrary to legend, the Royal Air Force (R.A.F.), having built back quickly to over a thousand fighter planes, entered the showdown on fairly equal terms, for German fighter strength—the critical comparison—stood similarly around a thousand. The R.A.F. also possessed more maneuverable fighter planes, the Spitfires and Hurricanes, as well as radar warning and air-to-ground communications systems that facilitated an efficient use of planes and pilots. The Luftwaffe committed an operational error in late August, furthermore, when it shifted its attacks to cities, believing from faulty intelligence that R.A.F. airfields and planes had been largely destroyed. Britain's more concentrated defenses around London and other cities now took such a heavy toll on the Luftwaffe—2,376 lost or damaged planes and 2,500 pilots and crew killed by mid-September—that Hitler "postponed" Operation Sea Lion. He could not put a positive spin, however, on the first stinging defeat for Blitzkrieg. Britain's survival had tremendous strategic significance, for the island could now serve as a launching site for air attacks against Germany and a potential staging ground for invasion of Fortress Europe.

The "Blitz," however, would continue. Londoners' name for the air war against civilians commenced on September 7, 1940. For an uninterrupted fifty-seven nights hundreds of bombers came over the capital, sending the death toll into the many thousands. In November the Luftwaffe turned to the unalerted provinces, killing four hundred people in one night over Coventry, eight hundred in three nights over Birmingham, injuring about three thousand in these cities. On and on went the daily killing and maiming. The Blitz did not let up significantly until the spring of 1941, in fact, when Hitler needed his air force to settle accounts in the East. By this time almost forty thousand British civilians had become victims of terror bombing runs, joining further tens of thousands in Warsaw and Rotterdam whose deaths had already shown what the Nazis thought about older norms of international behavior.

Hitler caught Benito Mussolini off guard in late August 1939 when he let loose his panzers. Not yet prepared to do battle with Britain and France, the Duce nevertheless recovered enough of his martial resolve in June 1940 to seize a chunk of France's Mediterranean coastline around Nice. He was further emboldened in September 1940 by the Tripartite Pact between Italy, Germany, and Japan. The aggressors divided the world into three spheres of interest with Southeast Asia allotted to Japan, most of Europe to Germany, and the Mediterranean and Africa to Italy. Already during the final negotiation stage of the pact Mussolini moved to conquer his sphere, ordering the Tenth Army in Cyrenacia (Tripoli) to attack British Egypt. His divisions advanced quickly to el-Alamein, only sixty miles west of Alexandria. In late October Mussolini hoped to add to the spoils by ordering an invasion of Greece from Italian-held Albania.

This division of strength contributed to the failure of both campaigns. The small but well-equipped and well-commanded Greek Army counterattacked in early November 1940, rapidly turning the Italian invasion into a headlong retreat. In the midst of this debacle, on November 11, Royal Navy torpedo planes hit the Italian fleet in its main base at Taranto, crippling three of Il Duce's six battleships as well as many other capital ships. On December 9, moreover, British troops struck west from el-Alamein, routing the Italians. Over the next ten days Mussolini and Hitler came to the mutual conclusion that Italy's Mediterranean "sphere" needed German bolstering.

Two months later, one German armored and one motorized infantry division arrived in Tripoli. Commanded by General Erwin Rommel, the famed "Africa Corps" counterattacked the British in late March 1941. The "Desert Fox" established his own legend by pushing British forces back hundreds of miles to Egypt in thirty days of lightning advances. German divisions, transported through friendly satellites Hungary, Rumania, and Bulgaria, also attacked Yugoslavia and Greece in early April. Now the people of Belgrade experienced the hallmark Nazi terrorization that had left other cities smoldering, bombed-out graveyards—about twenty thousand people died in one night. Yugoslavian forces surrendered on April 17. Despite assistance from forty-three thousand British troops rushed from Egypt, Athens fell ten days later, forcing the Royal Navy into a Dunkirk-style evacuation of this force. In late May Germany took Crete and once again British troops had to be rescued by an offshore flotilla. This time, however, over two thousand sailors were lost and thirteen capital ships sunk or damaged as the Luftwaffe pursued its enemy into the sea. The pounding of the Italian fleet at Matapan and the sinking of the mighty German battleship *Bismarck* in the Atlantic added only a little good news for Britain during the dismal spring of 1941.

Hitler had welcomed Italy's Mediterranean operations in 1940 for the same reason he sought to rescue them in 1941: namely, the need to secure his Balkan rear flank from the threat of British incursions and air raids as Nazi divisions mounted an attack of unprecedented scale on the Soviet Union. Indeed, during the early stage of the Battle of Britain Hitler had ordered his army to draw up plans for this grand operation. Always preoccupied with the crazed notion of seizing huge territories in Russia in order to provide land for the allegedly cramped German race—"Lebensraum" acquired by cold-blooded ethnic cleansing of Slavs and Jews—the Nazi dictator had grown increasingly anxious about pushing east as 1940 yielded to 1941. Now that Britain had beaten him, she would attempt to pull Stalin into an anti-German alliance, hence the need to eliminate this potential ally with one final Blitzkrieg. The economic and martial stirring of the United States also concerned Hitler. Declaring that "we must be the great arsenal of democracy" in December, a newly reelected and deceptively more belligerent Roosevelt asked Congress in January 1941 to "lend" billions of dollars of military equipment to Britain.[14] Funding was approved in March simultaneously with seizures of

German and Italian ships in American ports. Already during the summer of 1940, moreover, Congress had drafted almost a million men into the army and passed a Two Ocean Navy Act that would place scores of powerful modern warships at sea by 1942–1943. Before any war of attrition with Britain, which was aided now by Americans who seemed determined to stand with their old motherland, Germany had to eradicate the communist enemy at its rear. Eliminating the possibility of another debilitating war on two fronts had the added bonus of securing the USSR's vast supplies of oil and raw materials—the sine qua non of any longer and more protracted struggle against the remaining western democracies.[15]

Over 152 German divisions, reinforced in the south by a small Rumanian contingent, attacked the Red Army on June 22, 1941.[16] Fourteen Finnish divisions joined the Wehrmacht on the northern flank, for democratic Helsinki, attacked by the Soviets in 1939 and feeling itself continually threatened by Moscow, had cast its lot with the perceived lesser of two evils. Although Stalin's 171 western divisions possessed twice as many planes and triple the tanks, their poor leadership, organization, training, morale, and equipment put the defenders at a tremendous disadvantage, which was compounded by the complete surprise of "Operation Barbarossa," begun while Soviet soldiers slept and planes sat on unguarded tarmacs. The Kremlin had received numerous warnings of Hitler's intentions, but Stalin refused to issue an alert lest it provoke an unwanted confrontation. By late August the central army group had taken Smolensk, only two hundred miles west of Moscow. Northern armies besieged Leningrad in early September, and Kiev fell a few weeks later. In three months nearly three million Red Army troops had been killed, wounded, or captured.

This shocking figure climbed above four million as the Germans drove to the outskirts of Moscow in November 1941. Remarkably, however, Soviet resistance did not slacken. In fact it strengthened, bolstered by millions of reservists who had been called up since June and ninety-seven regular divisions that were deployed from other parts of the Soviet Union. German units had also suffered heavy casualties, many fighting that autumn at only a third or half of authorized strength of men, tanks, and trucks. An early and extremely severe winter took an additional toll on enemy men and machines, for Hitler and his staff, anticipating another Blitzkrieg victory, had not provided cold weather uniforms. The Red Army counterattacked on December 5, 1941, driving Germany's once-powerful Army Group Center far away from Moscow before the invaders' lines finally held in January 1942. The two exhausted adversaries burrowed into the frozen earth and redoubled efforts for what would be two more years of fighting on Soviet soil.

In the meantime, warfare deteriorated to levels of criminality and bestiality unprecedented in the annals of military history. Nazism's utter contempt for Slavic peoples, coupled with its irrational belief that communism represented one strong tentacle of an all-embracing Jewish conspiracy against Germans, explains this cold-bloodedness. Almost three million Soviet POWs died in captivity before the spring thaw of 1942. The Wehrmacht shot about a sixth of these victims—half a million people—because they were Red Army political commissars, for Hitler saw them as part of the so-called Jewish-Bolshevik intelligentsia. But most perished from untended wounds, starvation, or subzero temperatures while their German captors did nothing, sometimes mocking the captives by heaving a few loaves of bread into their midst to provoke a hopeless fight for survival. The racial struggle on the Eastern Front also swept civilians into its murderous vortex. As General Staff Chief Franz Halder put it, the army had to brace itself for killing Soviet civilians, for all of them were potential "bearers of the Jewish-Bolshevik world view."[17] Nazi brutality in occupied regions inevitably provoked a backlash by resistance fighters and partisans, which triggered terrible reprisal murders of hostages by the Germans. Even more shockingly, the S.S. had trained its own death squads—the infamous Einsatzgruppen—for systematic slaughter of Jews behind German lines (see later).

World War Two became a completely different kind of conflict after the failure of Operation Barbarossa. The defeat of this ultimate Blitzkrieg forced Germany to make its economic mobilization more effective—methods of attritional warfare honed to perfection in World War One. Somewhat like that previous struggle, in fact, the German Army now faced determined foes on many sides: in the East, the Soviet Union; in the West, Britain; and farther West—suddenly—the United States after the Japanese attack against the American fleet at Pearl Harbor on December 7, 1941. This assault profoundly changed World War Two, for Hitler, hoping to embolden his Japanese allies for a long Pacific struggle that would tie down American troops, declared war on the United States four days later. The gamble backfired when Roosevelt's arsenal of democracy soon committed itself to a "Europe first" strategy. Without the Führer's declaration of war, Washington would probably have pursued a Pacific strategy for the time being, contenting itself with economic and military aid to Britain.[18] Instead Hitler blundered into a multifront war against antithetical communist and democratic systems, whose unlikely—and seemingly unbeatable—alliance his aggressive actions had forged.

THE DECLINE OF THE AXIS, 1942–1944

Economists have dubbed World War Two "the GNP War," a slugfest of attrition whose outcome depended on "gross national product." After December 1941 Nazi Germany's still very powerful army fought against a potentially superior alliance of the United States, the Soviet Union, and Great Britain, nations whose prewar industrial outputs were first, third, and fourth, respectively, in the world—Germany's had been second in 1939.

Since well before the war, in fact, Berlin had attempted to build up an overwhelming material advantage, but the invasion of Poland interrupted programs aiming for maximum armaments production by 1942–1943. Raw materials deficiencies underscored the risky nature of these early campaigns. Before attacking in 1939, for example, Germany produced only 35 percent of its oil needs and possessed stockpiles for a mere three to six months of warfare—and not by design: The notion that cavalier unpreparedness fit with the arrogant short-war assumptions of Blitzkrieg is another myth that recent research has exposed. To be sure, by overrunning most of continental Europe and European Russia by summer 1941 Berlin should have been able to forge a huge armaments advantage, but remarkably enough did not as bureaucratic inefficiencies and army interference hamstrung economic potential. "Nobody would seriously believe," lamented a German engineering team, "that so much inadequacy, bungling, confusion, misplaced power, failure to recognize the truth, and deviation from the reasonable could really exist."[19] Consequently, total German armaments output in 1941 amounted to 70.6 percent of the Soviet Union and only 31 percent of the Grand Alliance countries—and America had just begun to convert to a war footing.

A few weeks after the successful Soviet counterattack of December 1941 Hitler insisted on mass production of tanks and airplanes in order to prevail against economically superior foes in a war of attrition. Technological research should concentrate on conventional weapons that promised victory in the current war. Hitler canceled all scientific and engineering projects of purely postwar interest. The decree of March 1942 forced developers of new weapons like jet airplanes, long-range missiles, and atomic bombs to justify extended funding (see later).

One should not forget, however, that the mighty economic alliance facing Hitler in early 1942 could not benefit from American productivity without control of the sea. Britain was particularly vulnerable, for it had to maintain a supply lifeline in the Atlantic or face defeat by slow starvation. Until early 1943, German submarines appeared to be accomplishing this gruesome task. Since war's outbreak they had torpedoed thousands of allied ships totaling 17,860,000 tons—nearly twice Britain's prewar merchant marine tonnage. Clearly only American ships and joint shipyard construction kept Britain supplied, but net Anglo-American losses at sea (i.e., *after* combined new launchings) amounted to a staggering 7,143,000 tons from 1939 to 1942.

Fighting against time, allied scientists and engineers managed to gain the upper hand during the fall and winter of 1942–1943. Having broken the German cipher machine "Enigma" with the aid of Polish scientists earlier in the war, British code-breakers learned that Berlin had been reading London's convoy routing messages. Now Britain changed her naval cipher and "a curtain slammed down on the window which had given [Germany] a full view of convoy movements."[20] Simultaneously, a series of breakthroughs opened windows on the allied side. The introduction of high frequency direction finders ("Huff-Duff") enabled American and British ships to detect the radio signals of massed submarine "wolfpacks" and determine their location. As convoys were routed around the menace, destroyer escort ships armed with more powerful depth charges that sunk faster and were shot by salvo in patterns took a higher toll of submarines. The allies also devised a new form of radar that could detect surfaced subs without tripping enemy defensive systems designed to warn commanders when their boats were floodlit by radar and give them ample time to dive. Because Germany's "search receiver" devices could not pick up the allies' new "microwave" radar frequency, entire wolfpacks could be surprised from the air while surfaced. Bombers specially fitted with larger gasoline tanks also enabled pilots to range further into the Atlantic to find these easy targets.

Consequently, submarines sunk a mere twentieth of the tonnage in May 1943 that had been destroyed in November. That same month, on the other hand, allied ships and planes sunk 40 of the enemy's 235 operational submarines—twice Germany's monthly production—forcing abandonment of wolfpack tactics. Anglo-American shipyards were producing "liberty ships" at double the 1942 pace, furthermore, sending net tonnage *gains* (i.e., after losses at sea) to 10,974,000 by year's end. The Battle of the Atlantic was won. The allies could now use sea lanes to build up an invasion force for "D-Day," the assault on Fortress Europe.

The eventual victory of the Grand Alliance nudged closer to reality, meanwhile, as the Axis suffered two additional major defeats. The first came in the East. In early 1942 the Wehrmacht still held a fifteen-hundred-mile front stretching from Leningrad to the southern Sea of Azov. But its divisions had suffered such severe losses of men and materiel—well over a million casualties, thousands of artillery pieces, and all but a few hundred tanks—that Hitler ruled against another large-scale offensive. Instead, he concentrated troops and tanks for a risky drive on the massive oil-producing region of the Caucasus and the Caspian Sea. Seizure of these reservoirs would literally fuel Germany's war effort while denying the same to Stalin and immobilizing his forces.

Thus one powerful army group received orders to strike into the Caucasus while a second pushed east to Stalingrad on the Volga to cut off millions of tons of river-bound supplies going north. The southern armies, consisting of a third of a million German soldiers spearheaded by a thousand tanks, squelched a Red Army counterattack near Kharkov in May 1942, and then swung over to the offensive in June. Simultaneously the northern army group, of comparable troop and tank strength, pushed east and southeast from Kharkov and Kursk. By late August the two-pronged attack had reached the northern slope of the Caucasus Mountains as well as Stalingrad, whose people, like those of many other Soviet and European cities, were now terror-bombed by the Luftwaffe.

The German Army had driven four hundred miles, but met stiffer resistance and took far fewer prisoners than 1941. Wehrmacht commanders worried, moreover, that relatively poorly equipped Italian, Hungarian, and Rumanian divisions covered the flanks of the advancing columns—additional warning signs of Germany's overtaxed effort on the eastern front. Indeed, with spearheads approaching Baku in November 1942, and the northern wing engaged in ferocious street fighting in Stalingrad, the man of steel ordered his marshalling forces to strike Rumanian positions northwest of the city while other units swept around the southern side. Within two weeks the Red Army had surrounded 238,000 soldiers. The only ones still alive surrendered in late January 1943—most of the 91,000 prisoners, including 24 generals and 2,500 additional officers, would never see Germany again. The southern army group scurried back out of the Caucasus, meanwhile, in a frantic bid to avoid the same previously unthinkable fate.

The disaster at Stalingrad marked a major turning point in World War Two. Totally eliminated from the German battle order were 24 infantry, armored, or artillery divisions and a huge cache of equipment: 7,074 artillery pieces and mortars, 750 planes, and a depot containing 1,550 tanks and 480 armored cars. The materiel could be replaced with Herculean productive efforts, but not the veteran soldiers, and especially not the sky-high morale that had sustained them and the entire German Army. Even though a million Soviet soldiers had perished in the five-month battle, furthermore, a psychologically recharged Red Army, which had never defeated the Wehrmacht so decisively, knew that their nemesis could be beaten again. Soviet soldiers had demonstrated gritty perseverance and unyielding tenacity—qualities that would eventually carry the Red Army beyond liberated Soviet territory, over Poland and Eastern Europe, to Berlin in 1945. The Germans saw frightening possibilities, too, as both soldiers and civilians began to ponder nightmare scenarios. "There was tremendous danger," one German veteran of the battle remembered thinking at the time, "that the war on two fronts may turn all of Germany into something like Stalingrad . . . and the people would go through the same hell as us."[21]

Simultaneously in North Africa a debacle of nearly equal proportions unfolded. Erwin Rommel and his Italian compatriots had overrun Tobruk in eastern Libya in June 1942, capturing forty-one thousand prisoners, one thousand armored vehicles, and four hundred field guns. As the Africa Corps raced toward Cairo that summer, the British began to evacuate the city. By September, however, the Desert Fox's offensive petered out as Hitler, preoccupied with the Caucasus, denied reinforcements. In late October 1942 a British army under General Bernard Montgomery counterattacked at el-Alamein. On November 6 Rommel's troops began a hurried retreat. Two days later an Anglo-American army evaded German submarines, landed in Morocco and Algeria, and began to race westward. The allied pincers caught up with their legendary nemesis in Tunisia, where significant—but inadequate—German reinforcements finally awaited him in January. By May 1943, with continued resistance futile, 238,000 Italian and German personnel went into captivity. Included in the net were six crack German divisions, tens of thousands of veterans who would not be available for other hard-pressed theaters of war. Hitler had rejected Rommel's advice to withdraw from the trap, but now admitted to the great tank commander, who would soon be charged with preparing Atlantic defenses: "I should have listened to you."[22]

The string of Axis defeats in the East, North Africa, and the Atlantic during the first half of 1943 loosened and threatened to break up Germany's wartime coalition. Italy and Rumania put out peace feelers, and Finland considered doing the same. After vacillating for months, moreover, neutral Turkey opted against attacking Red Army units in the Caucasus. And Japan, which had suf-

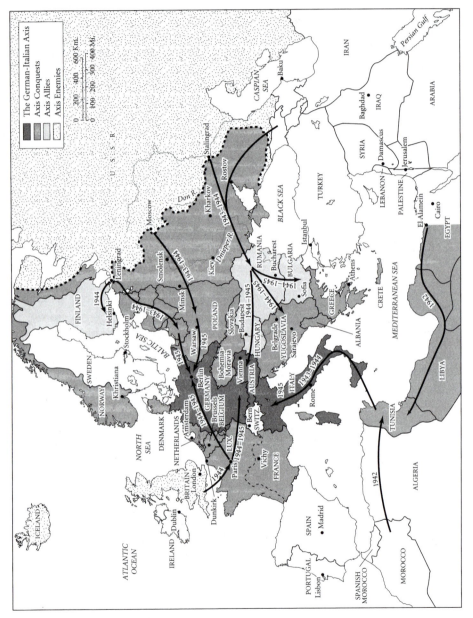

Grand Alliance Advances 1942–1945

fered its own Stalingrad around Guadalcanal in 1942–1943, showed none of the old desire to attack the Soviet Far East. Equally distressing, German popular support for Hitler had begun to wane.[23] Under these alarming circumstances, Hitler and top Nazi leaders knew that no political alternative existed to a third offensive in the East, for surrendering the initiative would be defeatist—worse, it would conjure up dreadful, panicky images of an unstoppable march of vengeful Slavs all the way to Berlin.

In fact, prospects for a limited offensive appeared good. Germany's threatened army group had not only escaped from the Caucasus, but had also punished its pursuers severely in counterattacks led by Erich von Manstein around Kharkov in February and March 1943. Northeast of Kharkov other red armies had overrun German and Hungarian positions, but the subsequent advance left Soviet lines jutting many miles west of Kursk. Hoping to exploit perceived military opportunities, and bolster Germany politically, Hitler opted for an operation designed, first, to encircle scores of Red Army divisions in the seemingly vulnerable Kursk salient. Victory there would shorten Germany's defensive perimeter, facilitating the second goal of shoring up defenses all along the eastern front. To ensure a smashing success, arms production lurched upward. Whereas there had been only five hundred tanks on the entire eastern front after Stalingrad, by July there were nearly two thousand in the Kursk region alone. These included hundreds of heavy "Panthers" or super-heavy "Tigers," new models far better than Red Army tanks.

Wehrmacht columns pierced into the salient on July 5, 1943. The commanders of almost half a million German soldiers in "Operation Citadel" counted on technological superiority and an element of surprise to re-create former victories. They knew the Red Army had prepared rugged defenses, but not that Soviet espionage had alerted Moscow in ample time to amass over a million men, thirty-one hundred tanks, and twenty-five thousand guns and mortars in eight successive defensive lines protected by three thousand mines per square mile. After a week of slow costly advance, the German offensive bogged down. "The armored formations, reformed and re-equipped with so much effort," recalled one Panzer general, "had lost heavily both in men and equipment and would now be unemployable for a long time to come."[24]

Afterward the Red Army swung over permanently to the offensive along a front stretching a thousand miles north from the Sea of Azov. German Army training camps had to hurry half-trained reinforcements to the eastern front, where hard-pressed generals like Manstein patched together a "system of improvisations and stopgaps"[25] with ill-equipped men, too many of whom were unready for combat. By December 1943 the front had been pushed five hundred miles farther west as successive Soviet hammer blows perpetuated the demoralizing cycle of Nazi retreat, retrenchment, and the rushing of more green troopers to the sound of the guns. In the West, Kiev, and in the North, Smolensk, were retaken.

The Soviet people made huge sacrifices during the three years the German Army fought on Soviet soil. The mobilization of millions of men after the German invasion, for instance, sent the percentage of working women to historic highs: from 43 percent of the overall work force in 1941 to 56 percent of blue- and white-collar laborers and 70 percent of agricultural workers by 1944. "I was left with three sons," remembered one Byelorussian widow.

> They were small boys, too young to look after each other. I carried sheaves of corn on my back and wood from the forest, potatoes, and hay. I pulled the plough myself and the harrow too. In every hut or so there was a widow or a soldier's wife. We were left without men. Without horses—they were taken for the army, too.[26]

"In the villages," recalled another overworked woman of the Leningrad region, "they had a very, very difficult time."

> They stopped being women really. They stopped menstruating, of course, but it wasn't just the hard work or the hunger. It was because they weren't really female any more. They said they didn't think about it—about sex, or even about their old lives. They just survived. They were not even like nuns. It was very, very hard.[27]

The destruction of homes made survival even harder. The Germans left an obliterated wasteland behind them as they withdrew in 1943–1944. The heartless invaders destroyed seventeen hundred cities and towns and seventy thousand villages—half of all households in European Russia, twenty-five million people, had no roof over their heads. Many fatherless families burrowed into the earth like soldiers to have rudimentary shelter and avoid hypothermia.

Indeed, the phenomenon of death, already shockingly widespread in early Soviet History, reached depths in the "Great Patriotic War" that are almost impossible to fathom. Between eight and eleven million Red Army soldiers died before the hammer and sickle flew over the Reichstag building in 1945. From the first minutes of Barbarossa, however, civilians made the ultimate sacrifice. Hundreds of thousands died in the first terror bombing raids, and many more as cities came within artillery range—over two hundred thousand men, women, and children in Novgorod alone during a few terrible summer weeks in 1941. The Battle of Stalingrad claimed the lives of even more city dwellers, while the three-year siege of Leningrad was worse still—over a million and a half perished there, most from starvation. The death squads and their auxiliaries shot a further million and a half Soviet Jews (see later). The Wehrmacht executed a roughly equivalent number of hostages, including more Jews, in "anti-partisan" sweeps (see later). Altogether, no fewer than fourteen million civilians—and perhaps as many as seventeen million—died on the Eastern Front.

"The Soviet response," concludes Catherine Merridale, "was sacred vengeance."

> If you haven't killed a German in the course of a day [wrote Ilya Ehrenburg] your day has been wasted. If you have killed one German, kill an-

other: nothing gives us so much joy as German corpses. Your mother says to you: kill the German! Your children beg of you: kill the German! Your country groans and whispers: kill the German! Don't miss him! Don't let him escape! Kill![28]

They would do just that, and more.

By 1943 the German home front had also turned into a nightmare. In contrast to the image conveyed in earlier histories, for instance, women's lives steadily deteriorated as the share of women working full-time rose from 37.3 percent to 53 percent of the overall labor force, and 65.5 percent of workers in the countryside. Now they were forced to do the man's backbreaking farm work, aided during times of peak summer activity by a million city women dragooned from all over the Reich. "Agricultural work was particularly resented," observes Richard Overy, "and conditions for women from the cities were so primitive that many tried to escape from the land as soon as they could."[29] Others had to tend a shop or small business without male assistance, or shift from physically less demanding jobs in consumer industries to harder work in the producer goods sector. "Conditions of nervous depression are piling up," reported one medical official so alarmed by the state of females in the armaments industry that he predicted a "rapid decline in productivity."[30] All of this makes Claudia Koontz's dubbing of German women as "the second sex in the Third Reich"[31] particularly apt.

The real hell began, however, after the intensification of allied bombing in early 1943.[32] It was then that one German POW's vision of Germany becoming "something like Stalingrad" with friends and family going through "the same hell as us" became reality. The so-called Battle of the Ruhr brought major devastation to German industrial cities in the spring of 1943, while the "Battle of Hamburg" wreaked havoc on northern towns that summer and fall. The allied attacks culminated with the "Battle of Berlin" that raged until March 1944. During these aerial campaigns London and Washington gave a horrific and twisted meaning to the old saying that "turnabout is fair play." While forty thousand British citizens died in German air raids during World War Two, over half a million German civilians perished and another eight hundred thousand were badly maimed—forty thousand died in Hamburg alone during four mid-summer raids in 1943. By war's end 40 percent of all German homes had been reduced to rubble—70 percent of dwellings in Cologne, and over 90 percent in Nuremberg, the city so closely identified with the Nazis. The whole nation was "traumatized," recalled one survivor, "by the blast of blockbuster bombs detonating around them; by basement walls cracking open, allowing waves of fire and smoke to roll into cellars full of women and children."

> I remember my family taking an aunt's ring finger to its grave because this was the only identifiable part of her body found in the rubble of her Leipzig apartment building. I recall going to school every morning after a

bombardment—if indeed the school building was still standing—and learning during roll call that Heinz, Ernst, Helmut or Rudi was dead, killed at age seven or eight.[33]

Although German morale did not break down completely, it is significant that the Führer's popularity plummeted to new lows in 1943–1944.[34]

Hitler needed the kind of lucky break that had occurred frequently in his earlier career. Perhaps the tightening ring of powerful enemies would break up, he thought, just as Frederick the Great's foes had fallen out in the 1760s, miraculously preserving victory for Berlin. In April 1943, therefore, Germany's own murderous regime asked Red Cross officials to investigate the mass grave of Polish officers discovered by assaulting Wehrmacht columns in 1941 inside the region overrun by the Red Army in 1939. Perhaps news of the Katyn Forest killings would exacerbate tensions in the uneasy alliance of communists and capitalists.

The Polish government in exile in London played into Hitler's hands by stormily insisting on breaking ties to Moscow. Churchill wisely resisted, but Stalin reacted by denouncing the London Poles, establishing his own Polish Communist government in exile, and repeating earlier demands for postwar border concessions in Eastern Europe, including Eastern Poland. Roosevelt and Churchill curtly refused to discuss these communist annexations, reminding Stalin of the mutual agreement signed in January 1942 to restore sovereignty and self-government to lands liberated from the Axis.[35]

Such rejoinders struck Stalin as treacherous hypocrisy, for the same document pledged signatories not to sign separate peace treaties with the Axis and to commit all means at their disposal to the war effort. The latter promise seemed violated by the allied invasions of North Africa and Italy with a mere twenty-one allied divisions. Why not open a second front in northern France, asked Stalin impatiently and indignantly, that could directly threaten the German heartland with anything like the three hundred divisions he had committed to the Eastern Front? In June 1943 the Soviet leader cancelled a summit meeting scheduled that summer for Alaska and recalled his ambassadors from London and Washington. Stalin's suspicions deepened after Mussolini's ouster (see later) when the West signed an armistice with the new Italian government of Victor Emmanuel and Prime Minister Pietro Badoglio, formerly a general under Mussolini. What were his western "friends" contemplating—a similar deal with Hitler? Two could play this game. Totally without scruples, Stalin would not hesitate to make another deal with the Nazis if it suited him.

Churchill and Roosevelt did not let the Grand Alliance break apart. Already at Casablanca in January 1943 they had issued a controversial demand for "unconditional surrender." They saw their refusal to accept anything but complete Axis surrender as a means to allay Stalin's suspicions about betrayal and to reconfirm their January 1942 agreement not to sign separate armistices. London and Washington redoubled diplomatic efforts in Moscow during the

Democratic solidarity: Churchill and Roosevelt at Casablanca. (Library of Congress)

autumn of 1943, assuring Stalin that it seemed only pragmatic to support Badoglio with German troops rushing into the peninsula, and that they stood squarely behind the principle of unconditional surrender. At Teheran in December 1943 the "Big Three" finally convened their first summit meeting. Churchill and Roosevelt had traveled the longest distance to the conference, a gesture that reflected their willingness to make major concessions. All agreed that the Soviet Union would receive the portion of Eastern Poland seized by the Red Army in 1939. The western allies promised to open another major front in France in the spring of 1944. Hitler's plot had failed.

After nearly five years of war German victory seemed an extremely remote possibility: The Eastern Front was quickly receding, the Mediterranean was falling into allied hands, German cities were being pounded into rubble, the Atlantic was lost to the wolfpacks, American troops were pouring into Britain to prepare to breach the Atlantic Wall of Fortress Europe, and the Grand Alliance seemed politically solid. Nor did Germany's successful armaments buildup hold out hope for winning the GNP War. German airplane production stood 367 percent above the level of early 1942, and tank output an impressive 598 percent—enough to produce 15,000 tanks and 45,000 planes amidst devastating allied air raids in 1944. Allied output of tanks and planes that same year, however, reached 52,000 and 168,000, respectively.

A growing manpower shortage exacerbated Nazi economic disadvantages. In 1944 German industry produced enough armaments to equip 250 full-strength infantry divisions, but Germany had only enough fighting men—around two and a half million—for 150. An early sign of this manpower crisis occurred during the buildup for Kursk with the "manning" of anti-aircraft batteries by hundreds of thousands of Hitler Youth members in order to free up adults for combat. Facing Hitler's Reich were three million men in the East, a third of a million in Italy, and almost three million assembling in Britain. Only a dramatic scientific or technological breakthrough, it seemed, could produce victory when one side so greatly outnumbered and outproduced the other.

LIFE IN OCCUPIED EUROPE

For a thousand years conquests like those made by Germany had been the stuff of dreams for European kings and emperors. But in 1942, at his zenith, Hitler's power was even greater than Napoleon's—a hegemonic base not seen in Europe, in fact, since the days of Roman antiquity. The German core of this truly evil empire extended the hated Versailles borders over Alsace, Lorraine, Luxembourg, and parts of Belgium in the west; Czech Bohemia, Austria, and Slovenia in the south; and portions of Poland in the east. Areas occupied and administered by Germany included a huge part of the Soviet Union, the remainder of Poland, and all of Greece, Serbia, Norway, Denmark, Holland, and Belgium. France, too, was totally absorbed after Germany widened its hold by occupying Vichy territory in November 1942. Hitler also amassed a formidable array of allies (Italy and Finland), satellites (Croatia, Bulgaria, Rumania, Hungary, Slovakia), and friendly neutrals (Spain). Even Sweden and Switzerland, more genuinely neutral, had to respect German power with deferential commercial and financial deals. This survey helps one appreciate how entirely isolated Britain, and later the Soviet Union, remained until the American buildup took effect in 1943–1944.

It is probably impossible with the written word to do justice to what life was really like in occupied wartime Europe, what with its horrible contrasts between the powerful and powerless, exploiters and exploited, perpetrators and victims, and the almost indistinguishable line between hellishly violent fronts and home fronts. The effort is a critical one, however, not only to give readers a fuller picture of the war itself, but also to appreciate the vast lengths required for Europe's moral and material reconstruction after war had run its grisly course.

The Nazi New Order

Nazi propagandist Joseph Goebbels coined the phrase "new order" shortly after the fall of France.[36] Germany was allegedly engaged in a great constructive crusade to unite Europe along autarkical, racial, and authoritarian anti-communist lines. This sleight of hand, combined with the stark reality of Nazi victories, turned many down the "collaborationist" path.[37] These active supporters of the new order included businessmen from all over the continent who tapped into the lucrative market for armaments, construction, and a variety of services to the ruling class. Berlin also benefited from a vast network of people who volunteered for the new order as auxiliary police, propagandists, and informers. There were zealous helpers among the native Nazis, furthermore, the so-called Quislings, named for the Norwegian Vidkun Quisling, who briefly helped Germany rule Norway in 1940. Most remarkable of all, perhaps, were the hundreds of thousands of young men who felt strongly enough about the German crusade—or those who simply saw the writing on the wall—to volunteer for the various special divisions that the S.S. and Wehrmacht recruited during the war. About twenty thousand Frenchmen joined units like the Anti-Bolshevik Legion and the Charlemagne Division. Fifty thousand volunteered in Holland and forty thousand in Belgium. The so-called eastern troops represented a somewhat different phenomenon. As German manpower grew short on the Eastern Front after the 1941 campaign, the army started recruiting auxiliary troops among the Soviet POWs who had not yet perished. About a million served "voluntarily" in this capacity, and beginning in 1944 a desperate Wehrmacht put nearly as many into fighting units that saw, however, little action.

The phenomenon of collaboration lasted throughout the war. Thus eastern troops helped defend Normandy on D-Day, and the Charlemagne Division fought to the finish in the streets of Berlin in 1945. Long before this time, however, the ugly contrast between the propaganda of a Nazi crusade to unify Europe and the reality of Nazi spoilage, exploitation, and murder turned many activists among the hapless populations of occupied Europe down different paths. Estimates of official tributes exacted from defeated nations during the reign of the Nazi New Order, for example, amount to the equivalent of forty billion dollars, almost twice the total of all American loans and Marshall Plan aid to Western Europe from 1945 to 1952 (see Chapter 7). But the spoils of war went far beyond this admittedly huge sum, for the conquerors engaged in outright looting of property on a scale unprecedented in history: Horses, automobiles, art collections, private estates, and entire businesses were ripped from their owners' hands. Human beings, too, became mere confiscated chattel as Germany's manpower shortage grew extreme. By 1945 seven million civilians—a fifth of the Reich's labor force—had been dragged from Poland, France, and other parts of Europe to work like draft animals under miserable conditions in the core regions of the Reich. An additional million Soviet POWs also toiled as slave laborers. The round-ups of millions of Jews and other so-called undesirables for alleged "resettlement" in Eastern Europe after early 1942 added to the desire of thousands of bold Europeans to resist in some way. Despite the Nazis' brutal policy of shooting a hundred hostages for every one of theirs killed by partisans, many people ignored the pleas of community leaders who urged prudent restraint and took to the hills to join those already fighting back.

The Resistance

As the Nazi shadow lengthened across Europe, one people after another fell under a rule so harsh that normal concerns for personal safety often yielded to the felt moral need to strike back.[38] The story of the resistance, therefore, is doubtless for many Europeans a history of "their finest hour." In practical terms, the various resistance movements made no more than a marginal contribution to ultimate victory over the Axis,[39] but this was a margin that Berlin could not afford to lose, for the resistance diverted significant numbers of German divisions from fighting fronts where troops were already spread dangerously thin by 1943–1944. The discussion of Europe's resistance organizations follows the order of Nazi conquests after 1939.

Polish resistance to Nazi rule began before the last isolated pockets of regular army soldiers surrendered in early October 1939. Although the penalty for armed opposition was death followed by reprisal killings of innocent civilians, the conquerors' brutal ethnic cleansing of whole regions left many Poles with no real alternative. A population whose memory of more than a century of Russian suppression was still fresh could fight back in many ways. Some tried to defeat German attempts to eradicate Polish culture by bringing national art treasures to safe haven, organizing clandestine scholarly publications, and teaching classes in underground universities. Others fled to the woods to gather weapons, ambush troop convoys, and derail trains.

A handful of armed partisan bands had coalesced by late 1940 into the so-called Armia Krajowa. Operating on orders from the London-based Polish government in exile, this "Home Army" eventually boasted over three hundred thousand freedom fighters. A smaller "People's Guard" of Polish Communists also fought back after the Nazi invasion of Russia ended Soviet "neutrality" in June 1941, but the two organizations had vastly different postwar visions, and therefore remained hostile to one another.

These groups achieved a number of dramatic successes. In early October 1942 Home Army demolition squads blew up the main marshalling yards of the Warsaw train station, while later that month the People's Guard exploded a bomb in the city's German officer club. As word spread of subsequent German defeats in the Soviet Union, Home Army leaders began to prepare for a major uprising timed to coincide with the anticipated advance of the Red Army.

Northern and Western Europe fell in 1940. This veritable body blow to democracy left defeated populations demoralized and deeply conscious of their own shortcomings. Such a mood of depression, coupled with the lack of any recent tradition of nationwide opposition to conquerors, ruled out resistance at first. Germany's relatively lax occupation policy in the West initially reinforced the tranquility. The bludgeoning of the Luftwaffe over Britain began to revive continental spirits, however, facilitating the mission of London's "Secret Operations Executive" (SOE) to recruit anti-German agents and "set Europe ablaze."[40] Hitler's invasion of the Soviet Union added further reinforcement, for it broke the shackles of the Non-Aggression Pact that had restrained Europe's well-organized communist parties from joining their nations' resistance movements.

A series of assassinations of German officers in France and brutal reprisals in the summer and fall of 1941 marked the beginning of a more dangerous occupation experience. The "Free French" government in exile of General Charles de Gaulle increased the occupiers' dilemma, especially after the allied invasion of Northwest Africa gave De Gaulle a "home" base of anti-German activities in Algeria. The Germans responded by sending troops into the previously unoccupied portion of Vichy France. Deportations for forced labor in Germany followed in early 1943. "Young men faced the choice of taking the train to Germany or the path to the mountains," observes Robert Paxton. "Thousands who could get to remote areas chose the mountains, and encampments of young men, the *maquis*, sprang up in the Alps, the Massif central, and the Pyrenees."[41] The women of France helped these men by spying in government offices, procuring false identity papers, succoring men on the run, carrying messages to the mountains, and, occasionally, cutting their hair and joining the *maquis*. By early 1944 the coalition of French resistance groups under de Gaulle's overall command, which the communists had joined, easily numbered two hundred thousand—and perhaps twice this number. At this time Norwegian, Dutch, Belgian, and French underground groups were disrupting Nazi transportation and communications networks and waiting for their cue to unleash more threatening fifth column assaults on D-Day.

From 1941 to 1943 the Italian Communists represented the country's most significant resistance force. Adopting the slogan "Peace, Independence, and Freedom," they cleverly invoked revolution in the name of democracy rather than of another dictatorship. The strike wave that began to swell in the northern industrial cities during late 1942, and ultimately peaked in March 1943 before arrests and threats backed the workers down, was the first significant disruption of work inside Fortress Europe. It also emboldened a handful of leftist bourgeois and moderate Christian democratic parties to surface and offer opposition to the Duce, thereby ending twenty years of passivity.

On the third day of Germany's Kursk offensive British and American divisions landed on Sicily. The invasion forced Hitler to pull units away from the East to bolster his rear, but despite these reinforcements the island fell in August. Already on July 24, 1943, worried Italian generals and Fascist Party leaders, sensing impending disaster, overthrew Mussolini, reinstated King Victor Emmanuel, and installed General Pietro Badoglio as prime minister. On September 8 Hitler rescued the man he revered as the first Fascist and installed him atop a puppet Italian state in the northern provinces. Simultaneously, Wehrmacht divisions badly needed elsewhere poured into the peninsula to guard against an allied amphibious assault. That month, however, the British and Americans succeeded in establishing beachheads at Reggio and Salerno in Southern Italy. The allies landed farther north at Anzio in January, and by spring 1944 two well-equipped armies plodded north toward Rome against heavy German resistance.

The coup d'état against Mussolini resulted from the intrigues of highly placed officers and Fascist Party officials, not pressure from the resistance movement, but the anti-Fascist underground had contributed to the necessary climate of opinion for action.[42] Now the rescue of Mussolini created the requisite conditions for heightened resistance activity. In the North partisan communist bands fought a guerilla war against Mussolini and the Wehrmacht. The communists managed to build up a combined strength of ninety thousand by early 1944. Italian women also played a "remarkably active" [43]role in this resistance, fighting by the thousands next to their men, serving in various auxiliary capacities, hiding soldiers of the resistance from deportation to forced labor in Germany, and shielding Italian Jewry from persecution. They paid a steep price. The Germans deployed regular divisions against the resistance that were augmented by the notorious "Black Brigades," bloodthirsty anti-partisan units organized by Mussolini's North Italian regime. In order to demonstrate the inability of males in the resistance to protect their women, the Black Brigades singled out female fighters and auxiliaries for especially cruel treatment. Over three thousand were tortured and executed or sent north to death camps.

The resistance retaliated as best it could. Red comrades in the trade union movement added to the Duce's problems with a general strike in March 1944—the largest work stoppage of World War Two. That spring the communists also struck a deal with the bourgeois anti-Fascist bloc, temporarily abandoning their opposition to the monarchy, and agreeing that its future would be decided by postwar plebiscite. The united resistance parties now entered the Badoglio cabinet, forced his resignation, and raised to office a liberal politician from pre-Mussolini days, Ivanoe Bonomi, who surfaced publicly from the Roman underground when Anglo-American columns entered the capital on June 4, 1944.

The German conquest of Yugoslavia and Greece in 1941 triggered almost immediate resistance, for, somewhat like the Poles, these peoples quickly applied underground techniques learned during centuries of hated Turkish rule. Within weeks of Belgrade's destruction, for instance, Colonel Drazha Mihailovich, a royalist and Serb nationalist, began to recruit his "Chetniks," the peoples' name for militia bands that had battled the Turks. Colonel Napoleon Zervas played a similar role in Greece.[44] In both countries, however, communist partisans, thoroughly schooled in clandestine operations against authoritarian governments, quickly eclipsed the colonels in their daring to liberate—and determination to revolutionize—respective homelands. The National Liberation Front of Greece and the Yugoslav "Partisans" of Josip Broz, commonly known as "Tito," emerged as more serious military threats in 1943 when they disarmed Italian units that had surrendered after the ouster of Mussolini.

Tito's forces rivaled the Russian resistance in tenacity, scale of operations, and the killing of Germans—the major criterion for British military aid, and the main reason Churchill switched funding from Mihailovich to the Partisans in 1943. Although born a Croat, Tito's communism enabled him to transcend narrow ethnic politics and appeal to all groups eager to retaliate. These included Serb, Croat, and Muslim workers who rallied against the ruthless "Ustashi," a Croatian fascist organization installed by the Nazis in Zagreb. The so-called Independent State of Croatia went on an ethnic killing rampage in 1941–1942 that "cleansed" the land of around twenty thousand Gypsies, fifty thousand Jews, and over half a million Serbs.[45] The Serbians retaliated whenever they could, but the Nazis answered with brutal reprisal raids that magnified the slaughter—eight thousand Serbs were shot, including several hundred children, for instance, in the industrial town of Kragujevac. In such dire circumstances the life of a resistance fighter seemed to many young men no less dangerous, and certainly much more righteous, than passively doing nothing.

The German Army undertook six campaigns in 1942–1943 to dislodge the Partisans from mountain strongholds in Bosnia, Herzegovina, and Montenegro, attempting thereby to secure the Adriatic coastline from resistance operations during any allied invasion of the area. All efforts failed. By early 1944 Tito had a quarter of a million well-armed men under his command, who succeeded in tying down fourteen German divisions in the region. These units would be unavailable to defend other parts of Fortress Europe on D-Day, or to fight the Red Army as it liberated Russia and pushed into Eastern Europe.

In the summer of 1942 more than a third of a million Jews led an extremely precarious existence in the Warsaw ghetto. A "Jewish Council" made up of community elders attempted the nearly impossible task of ameliorating cruel Nazi policies, on the one side, and facilitating agreement among the fractious and polarized political groups active in the ghetto, on the other. The most heated arguments that year revolved around the Nazis' ultimate intentions for the Jews. Did reports of death squad activity in the German-held portions of the Soviet Union point to genocide as Berlin's ultimate goal? Or were these killings war-related atrocities, crimes of passion that, terrible though they were, might not recur? Knowledge in the ghetto of Jews who worked as slave laborers in work camps supported the somewhat more comforting latter view, while persistent rumors, and then more reliable messages, about actual death camps convinced radical factions of the need to acquire arms for a desperate struggle. "Insofar as possible," writes Leni Yahill, they wanted "to take revenge on the murderers, and to offer personal testimony that the Jews had fought as part of the wider human struggle for freedom." Most residents of the ghetto, "common people, harassed and weary by their concern for themselves and their families and having undergone bitter and humiliating experiences in order to survive—detached and abandoned by the world—could not identify with the call of the fighters."[46] When massive deportations of Jews began that summer, apparently to labor camps, most went passively while only a small minority of the sixty thousand left behind for subsequent "resettlement" hid themselves and readied their consciences for a final fight. One ghetto warrior from Vilnius recalled seeing "the thousands who chose to be dispatched to detention camps and passed by our barricades, casting pitying glances at us."[47]

When the Germans resumed deportations in January 1943 a brief skirmish took place. Although soldiers succeeded in removing over six thousand Jews, and shot down a thousand more in the streets, the apparent cancellation of the deportation "action" emboldened Jewish activists and accelerated the flow of smuggled weapons from the Polish Home Army. The S.S. returned in force with tanks on April 19. They encountered hundreds of lightly armed resistance fighters who fired from attics and rooftops, shifting positions frequently by moving through a network of prepared passageways connecting building strongholds.

The battle continued until May 8, 1943.[48] By this time the last fighters had been killed or committed suicide and the S.S. had burned or exploded most of the Jewish ghetto. The surviving tens of thousands who had supported the struggle by hiding in bunkers, cooking food, and refusing to surrender were packed into cattle cars headed for the death camp at Treblinka—where, in fact, hundreds of thousands of Warsaw Jews had been sent the previous summer. Although the horrific end result had been the same, the freedom fighters of the Warsaw ghetto had achieved certain immortality through their courageous defiance.

By late summer 1941 word had spread throughout the occupied USSR that the Germans had not come to liberate the peoples of the Soviet Union—as many of Stalin's subjects, alienated by the terrible excesses of collectivization, starvation policies in the Ukraine, and the purges, fervently hoped—but rather to enslave or exterminate alleged racial inferiors. By December about thirty thousand partisans had gathered in the forest regions of White Russia and the Western Ukraine, determined to avoid this fate. Loyal Red Army officers, political commissars, and draftees not captured by the Germans; POWs who managed to slip away from their death-by-starvation confinements; civilian refugees from German work details and reprisal raids; Jews who fled before the death squads—all joined a guerrilla war that took an increasingly heavy toll of invaders.

Stalin increased resistance ranks in 1941–1942 by parachuting specially trained soldiers behind enemy lines. His partisan squads also dragooned tens of thousands of helpless villagers at gunpoint. By mid-1944 hundreds of bands totaling about two hundred thousand men and women fought in Nazi occupied territory. The Wehrmacht committed an equivalent number to anti-partisan operations, whole divisions sweeping repeatedly through the worst-infested parts of White Russia and the Ukraine. Because it was German policy to execute a hundred villagers for every one of its soldiers shot in ambush, the army must have exacted a terrible revenge for the thirty-five thousand Germans killed by partisan bands—probably over a million died in these reprisal raids. Soldiers frequently singled out Jewish villages, for Jews were considered partisans by definition even before thousands of them fled the shootings in 1941 to join the Soviet resistance.[49] Soviet partisans living off the land also frequently victimized noncombatants, as did anti-Soviet Ukrainian rebels who likewise took what they needed, both finding it necessary to hang or mutilate peasants for allegedly supporting the wrong side. Life in the countryside behind German lines therefore became a living hell, but big cities suffered their own nightmare when the Wehrmacht seized available food for itself and then let hundreds of thousands of city dwellers starve—one hundred thousand in Kharkov alone. Making matters almost unimaginably worse was the fact that S.S. Einsatzgruppen remained active in 1942 before their bloody shooting expeditions yielded to the much more efficient methods of genocide implemented during the infamous "final solution."

Genocide

Since 1915, if not earlier, Adolf Hitler had spoken about "settling scores" with the Jews, the alleged racial enemy of Aryan Germans.[50] Speeches and interviews from the early 1920s were laced with venom about "Jewish racial tuberculosis" and the need for a Germany "completely cleansed of Jews" who should be "hanged indiscriminately" or "held under poison gas." After restraining his fanatical oratory for political reasons throughout much of the 1930s, the Führer restated the agenda publicly in January 1939: the result of another war "will be . . . the annihilation of the Jewish race in Europe."[51] Despite such statements historians have disagreed about Hitler's real thoughts. Was it his intention from the beginning to unleash genocide? Or did the Holocaust emerge more spontaneously from the structure of events surrounding World War Two? Recent historians like Richard Breitman tend toward a synthesis of the opposing views. The means and timing of the Führer's end goal would be determined opportunistically. "[Hitler] would undoubtedly seek to unleash his rage at the Jews; how, and when he did so depended upon the circumstances, opportunities, and plans presented to him."[52]

The regime's ultimate agendas came into clearer focus during the "Night of the Broken Glass." Nevertheless, there were no signs of an imminent mass killing of Jews in the immediate aftermath of this terrible pogrom. Even though widespread arrests of suspected Judeophiles in November and December 1938 intimidated that sizeable portion of the German populace shocked by the Nazi hardcore of "willing executioners"—murderous cadres that were expanding, to be sure, at an alarming pace—political prudence dictated a delay of radical anti-Semitic action until the rapidly approaching war provided a politically convenient smokescreen.[53]

Convinced of the dangers of Nazi race hatred, meanwhile, the pace of Jewish emigration accelerated: Whereas 130,000 Jews left Germany from 1933 to November 1938, an additional 200,000 had emigrated by war's outbreak. The remaining 170,000 languished as subjects without rights, purged from all but the lowest paying jobs, denied all benefits and social services, forced to leave their homes for special internment houses, even to shop at special times when no Germans could be present. "The Jews must be driven from our residential districts and segregated where they will be among themselves, having as little contact with Germans as possible," wrote one S.S. publication just days after the November pogrom. Because, reduced to poverty, these detention centers would allegedly become "a breeding ground for Bolshevism and a collection of the politically criminal subhuman elements . . . we would be faced with the hard necessity of exterminating the Jewish underworld" and achieving "the actual and final end of Jewry in Germany, its absolute annihilation." After the regime began to consider a "final solution"[54] to the Jewish problem in all of Europe toward the end of 1938 emigration offered Jews only a temporary reprieve—unless, of course, they were among the lucky few to receive permission to enter British Palestine or the United States.

The defeat of Poland in September 1939; the overrunning of Norway, Denmark, Holland, Belgium, and France in the spring of 1940; the fall of Yugoslavia and Greece in the spring of 1941; and especially the occupation of European Russia in the summer and fall of 1941 accelerated planning for a European-wide settling of scores, for this crescendo of conquest brought the bulk of Europe's eleven million Jews, directly or indirectly, into Nazi hands. Initially, a variety of remedies came up for discussion. The ghettos of Poland—"*Lebensraum* in the opposite direction"—impressed some party officials like the head of the General Government of Poland, Hans Frank, as a means to quarantine Jews and reduce their numbers. Thus Warsaw's ghetto of 450,000 suffered terribly in 1941 when 11,000 died of starvation and 43,000 of typhus. Other Nazis favored "cleansing" methods like dumping millions of European Jews on the Island of Madagascar, a cruel ghettoization strategy that would have meant death on a truly massive scale. But Heinrich Himmler of the S.S., the "architect of genocide" who had Hitler's ear—and knew what the Führer liked to hear—preferred other means of "removal." The grisly work of the death squads, first practiced in 1939, and then made more systematic in 1941, pointed toward killing as "the final solution to the Jewish Question."

Building on the experience of Poland, the S.S. organized four battalions of death that swept into occupied territory from the Baltic to the Black Sea. Their specific mission: to exterminate the Jews of the area. Historians reckon that about half of the Jewish population managed to escape the "Einsatzgruppen" in 1941, many thousands joining the resistance, but that about seven hundred thousand unfortunate souls did not. Whole villages met a gruesome end as inhabitants were forced to run, ten to twenty at a time, into anti-tank ditches or pits dug especially for the executions, and then gunned down as they lay upon the warm, bleeding bodies of those previously shot. Another six hundred thousand were similarly butchered in early 1942. As Wehrmacht "anti-partisan" sweeps escalated in 1942–1943 the total number of Jews slain probably exceeded two million—"each one a name, a person, a kin, a soul, a loss,"[55] writes Richard Rhodes. Thus the death squads were not alone. Recent controversial but incontrovertible findings demonstrate that from the beginning, in fact, the Einsatzgruppen received far-reaching, systematic, willing assistance from regular army units, thus destroying the myth of army non-involvement in the Holocaust. Reserve police battalions from Germany also played an important role, while auxiliary killing squads recruited among Baltic, Rumanian, and Ukrainian nationals expanded the ranks of the executioners.[56] Germany had no shortage of shooters.

It is extremely unlikely, however, that Hitler and Himmler ever favored such methods as the ultimate means of destroying European Jewry. They considered shooting appropriate on the eastern front given the harshness of fighting there, especially after Stalin's radio appeal for civilian resistance offered killing squads a convenient anti-partisan justification for anything they did. But this approach lacked the subtlety required in other parts of the continent. Armed peace reigned in Fortress Europe in 1941—an uneasy, forced tranquility that mass executions would surely disrupt as word spread and the bravest Jews and Christians took up resistance. Rather, deportation of Jews from all over Europe to "resettlement camps" in the East provided a clever, convincing cover for what really awaited millions of deportees. As the Einsatzgruppen began their sweep of European Russia in the summer of 1941, in fact, Himmler ordered the conversion of existing POW and work camps in Poland into death camps. Those who could work would become slave laborers until starvation rations eventually killed them. The old and the infirm as well as mothers and children—the so-called nucleus of new Jewish development— would be herded into gas chambers disguised as de-lousing showers, killed, and then cremated in nearby ovens. Heinrich Himmler had discussed these devious death and disposal procedures with subordinates as early as December 1939. An experiment with "Cyclon B" poison gas pellets succeeded in rapidly exterminating nine hundred Russian POWs in September 1941. Therefore, the S.S. gathered all officials who would be involved with the deportations and gassings at Wannsee outside Berlin in January 1942 to inform them about—and guarantee their cooperation in—the "final solution."[57]

The roundups began in Germany and Poland in late 1941 and extended to the rest of occupied Europe in the spring and summer of 1942. Jews were marched out of their neighborhoods and into cattle cars whose ventilation windows had been nailed shut. Each "resettlement" transport carried thousands of persons to the East. Usually 20–25 percent of those who embarked on the long journey collapsed or suffocated before it ended. Those who survived strained their eyes to read camp names that still evoke flesh-crawling terror: Chelmno, Sobibor, Majdanek, Belzec, Treblinka—and Auschwitz. Although the distinctive odor of burning flesh permeated the air, few suspected what it meant as camp doctors "selected" the latest arrivals for either enervating slave labor or immediate death.

The pace of deportations accelerated after 1942, shoving the population of the camps upward from 95,000, as German armies advanced toward Stalingrad, to 525,000 in the summer of 1944. The pace of the killing also accelerated: Witness the transport to Auschwitz and murdering of 417,000 Hungarian Jews from May to July 1944—a daily average of around 7,000 gassings. But all of this was far too slow for Heinrich Himmler. Before the approach of Red Army troops forced the closing of Auschwitz's gas chambers in early November 1944, he intended to greatly expand the veritable hell on earth of this already massive camp complex in order to speed up the final solution.

Almost four million Jews as well as millions of declared "undesirables"— Gypsies, homosexuals, Soviet POWs, resistance fighters, and others—would perish in the death camps before war's end mercifully stopped the killing. The terrible toll would surely have been less had Britain and America opened their doors wider to Jewish immigrants before 1939, or later diverted their

Survivors of genocide: concentration camp inmates liberated in 1945. (Getty Images)

bombers from other operations in 1942–1943 to destroy the killing facilities at Auschwitz. Fewer Jews would have died, moreover, if more Christians had followed the example of those "righteous gentiles" of Denmark, Holland, Finland, and Bulgaria who resisted the Nazi murder program, or modest men and women of the church and of the resistance in Italy who saved 85 percent of Italian Jewry, or young women all over occupied Europe who jeopardized their own lives to save Jewish children from the gas chambers. Whether the Vatican could have saved Jewish lives by more forcefully speaking out against the Nazis remains a subject of immense controversy.[58] In the end it was mainly allied victory that guaranteed a future for the approximately two million Jews of continental Europe who survived the Holocaust.

FROM D-DAY TO V-E DAY 1944–1945

Germany's outlook appeared bleak after nearly five years of war. The Red Army had attacked constantly since Kursk in July 1943, mostly liberating Soviet territory by the following spring. With more than twice as many soldiers on the Eastern Front, Stalin seemed unstoppable. To the South, more unsettling developments: North Africa, Sicily, and Italy as far as Rome were in Anglo-American hands. At home, only bad news: Bombing attacks of German cities and industrial sites mounted in intensity, and civilian morale, already seriously damaged after Stalingrad, continued to sag. Making matters worse in this GNP slugging match, the Grand Alliance turned out nearly four times as many tanks and planes in 1944 despite Germany's feverish efforts to expand output—and the powerful coalition of industrialized nations showed no sign of breaking up over political differences. Furthermore, the North Atlantic had been largely rid of the submarine menace, permitting the build up of thirty-seven battle-ready divisions in Britain. If the amphibious vanguard of these forces established another major front in the West, their sacrifices on D-Day would make V-E Day—the hour of "Victory in Europe"—virtually inevitable.[59]

Hitler remained steadfastly determined to prevent this. About two-thirds of his army—157 German divisions, plus smaller Finnish and Rumanian forces—stood in the East. A further twenty-seven divisions held the line in northern Italy. This left around ninety divisions to occupy Fortress Europe, contain the resistance, and defend numerous possible locations against an amphibious assault. Germany's chances of crushing the invasion were good if they could concentrate a superior force on the targeted beaches, for even a massive armada could land no more than a handful of divisions in twenty-four hours. If he succeeded, another D-Day would take as long as a year to prepare. After a victory Hitler intended to transfer fifty to sixty divisions to the East and defeat the Red Army—or at least buy time for the Grand Alliance to break up, or the completion of "miracle weapons" that would cancel the allies' quantitative economic advantages.

But where would the British and Americans come ashore? Northern France? Southern France? In the Balkans to join Tito? Hitler and his generals assumed that the allies would take the shortest route to the German heartland—over the Pas de Calais region of Northern France—a site which offered the additional significant advantage of the shortest Channel crossing. Hoping to avoid the seemingly obvious, therefore, the team of generals around joint allied commander Dwight D. Eisenhower chose one of the longest crossings farther west: Normandy. To assure the crucial element of surprise and divert defenders, everything was done to convince the Germans of a landing at Pas de Calais: a heavy "pre-invasion" aerial bombardment of this area; construction of an elaborate phantom army base in nearby southern England "commanded" by the brilliant American tank general, George Patton; and espionage misinformation, planted by a double agent, that the invasion would come over Pas de Calais. The ploys worked. Germany placed an entire army group of twenty divisions, including four powerful armored units, opposite Patton's façade force. Only eight to nine second-rate divisions with few tanks defended Normandy, and of these, only three covered the five beachheads.

On June 6, 1944, a gigantic flotilla of seven hundred warships and eighty-three hundred transports and support craft of all kinds took the Anglo-American strike force across the English Channel. This massive effort was required to land six divisions in Normandy. Three smaller airborn divisions preceded them during the pre-dawn hours. Over twelve thousand allied soldiers were killed or wounded on "the longest day," but by nightfall fairly solid beachheads had been established. The worst casualties—four thousand—came on "Omaha" beach, where advance elements of two American divisions encountered an entire German division entrenched on bluffs overlooking the water. The Omaha experience might have occurred on other D-Day beaches if the Germans had guessed correctly that Normandy was the target—indeed, it probably would have been much worse, the kind of turnaround Hitler needed so desperately. As it was, nearby German units, gradually reinforced from other parts of France, converged on the beaches and the adjacent neck of the Cherbourg peninsula to prevent a breakout. On June 17, Hitler, still smelling victory, met his field generals in France and promised further reinforcements from the Eastern Front.

On June 22, 1944, however, the Red Army unleashed "Operation Bagration," a massive offensive against Germany's most powerful force in the East. Well over one hundred divisions backed by four thousand tanks, twenty-four thousand artillery pieces, and sixty-three hundred aircraft smashed into Army Group Center, whose forty-two divisions still occupied salient positions extending almost as far as Smolensk. The Red Army captured Minsk in ten days and Vilnius in three weeks. At the end of July Soviet forces battled German units just east of Warsaw, having advanced over 350 miles. About thirty Wehrmacht divisions had been decimated—over 550,000 German soldiers killed or wounded. The Soviets lost over a million men, but drew on their deep reservoir of manpower to replace them. Germany could not do this, nor could it afford to send divisions westward. After six weeks of stalemate in Normandy, each side had lost over 100,000 men. Receiving few replacements, however, the German defenders finally gave way in late July. Patton, now commanding real soldiers and tanks, broke into Brittany and turned east toward Paris.

On July 20, 1944, a bomb exploded inside the conference room of Hitler's East Prussian headquarters at Rastenburg.[60] Although others in the room were killed or badly wounded, the Führer escaped serious injury. Colonel Claus von Stauffenberg, the tip of an elaborate opposition network inside the German military establishment, had placed the device under the table.

The conspiracy against Hitler dated from the late 1930s when General Ludwig Beck, chief of the general staff, plotted to overthrow the dynamic Nazi leader whose aggressive foreign policy seemed destined to ruin Germany. Although Beck had many top army leaders on his side, this intrigue, as well as others in subsequent years, came to nothing. Hitler's string of successes and coups, beginning with the peaceful acquisition of the Sudetenland and extending to the smashing military victories of 1939–1940, silenced many of his critics in uniform. Others remained passive because they had sworn an oath of allegiance to Hitler in 1934. Further delay and hesitation resulted from the refusal, first of Neville Chamberlain, and then later of Churchill and Roosevelt, to deal with the conspirators lest such contacts arouse the suspicions of a wary Stalin. In 1943 and early 1944, moreover, secret police uncovered one of the nerve centers of the plotters inside the military intelligence community.

Pressure for action mounted nevertheless during these latter years. The opposition's increasing determination did not stem, significantly enough, from the brutal and immoral racist agenda of the Nazis, which grew increasingly murderous after 1939, but rather from escalating fears after Stalingrad of the Draconian consequences of a peace treaty dictated by Stalin. Not until the last hope for overall military victory faded, however, with the allied buildup in Normandy too great to contain any longer, did Stauffenberg make his way to Rastenburg.

The plot went awry from the beginning. The fact that Hitler emerged unscathed was quickly communicated to Berlin, where officers still loyal to the Nazis seized and summarily executed some of the ringleaders, including Stauffenberg. There followed massive arrests of suspected participants by the secret police. Over upcoming weeks about five thousand conspirators met gruesome ends—some of them impaled on meat hooks and filmed for a vindictive and sadistic Hitler. The most prominent person caught up in this dragnet was Erwin Rommel, commander of German forces in Northern France, who had made his criticisms of Hitler as well as his intention to negotiate with the West to forestall a worse fate from the East too tactlessly clear. Agents from Berlin offered Rommel, the popular Desert Fox, the option of suicide, a hero's state funeral, and safety for his family—and he accepted it.

When Stalin's soldiers crossed the pre-1939 border of Poland in January 1944, the Polish Home Army received orders from the London Polish government-in-exile to harass German lines from the rear to aid approaching Soviet forces. After further Red Army penetrations in June, however, disturbing reports began trickling back from Eastern Poland. In all towns Stalin's officials were summarily dismissing incumbent Polish magistrates and ordering resistance fighters to serve with the communist People's Guard or face arrest. "Anyone who showed the slightest disinclination to obey immediately," writes Norman Davies, "was written off as a war casualty."[61] These mounting atrocities forced Polish resistance leaders to reconsider the timing of their great insurrection, for it might be wiser to regain control of the homeland *before* Red Army units arrived, and then "mobilize the entire population spiritually for the struggle against Russia," wired Home Army General Bór-Komorowski urgently to London.[62]

On July 22, 1944, Moscow formed the Polish Committee of National Liberation in Lublin, investing this subservient communist group with full administrative authority in liberated Poland. The announcement rudely jolted the London Poles. In an attempt to force Stalin to admit their representatives to a postwar government, Home Army forces in Warsaw rose up on August 1. Red Army divisions, which were thought to be only a few days' fighting from the capital, would be presented with a fait accompli when entering the city. Hopefully Stalin would recognize Warsaw's liberators if Churchill and Roosevelt pressured him. If the Soviets continued to "violate Poland," however, the Home Army would resort to "an open struggle against them."[63]

The uprising quickly deteriorated into a human tragedy of immense proportions. Rather than join forces with the resistance, Stalin ordered nearby Red Army corps to halt their advance, thereby freeing four German panzer divisions, which proceeded to systematically smash the revolt.[64] About 20,000 resistance fighters died in sixty-three days of Nazi savagery that also killed 225,000 civilians in daily mass executions; shelled and burned occupied homes, businesses, and hospitals; and roped hostages to tanks as protection against snipers—in short, mass murder. Afterward the Nazis dragged an additional 700,000 residents of Warsaw off to concentration camps or slave labor camps in Germany. For many weeks, furthermore, Stalin denied Anglo-American requests for use of Soviet runways to airlift arms and supplies. He also warned Red Army commanders, who had initially complied, against allowing "hostile elements to use these landings to infiltrate Polish terrorists, saboteurs and agents of the Polish government in London."[65] To expect that Stalin "should have made a generous gesture to [Polish] people who were fundamentally opposed to everything he stood for," writes Davies, was "the most tragic mistake in their recent history."[66] Afterward, Hitler ordered Warsaw razed to the ground. His minions had completed 93 percent of the destruction when Red Army units finally entered the bombed-out remains of the city in January 1945.

Meanwhile, American and British forces swept through northern France, having reached a total strength of thirty-four divisions. Hitler committed all available units to an attack on August 7, 1944, including many panzer divisions he had held back in the event Normandy proved a mere diversion from the main assault still anticipated at Pas de Calais. The German counterthrust broke apart quickly, nearly trapping two entire army groups in a constricting pocket around Falaise. Although many German soldiers managed to escape, Hitler now lost his captive French prize: French and American army units liberated Paris with the assistance of resistance groups on August 25, and by early September one allied spearhead crossed into Belgium while another approached the upper Rhine in Alsace. Since June 6 more than thirty-five enemy divisions had been ground to dust, leaving five hundred thousand German men dead or wounded. The dimensions of the debacle matched the Red Army's destruction of Army Group Center during Operation Bagration.

The success of D-Day and subsequent crushing of German armies in France were highly significant, for these campaigns ended the last faint chance of Germany greatly prolonging its struggle. Annihilation of Anglo-American divisions on the beaches would have preserved Hitler's hold on France until another invasion attempt could be mounted, perhaps from southern France, in late 1944 or early 1945. It would also have permitted a strengthening of defensive lines in Italy. Moreover, the transfer of scores of divisions to the East would have delayed collapse on the Eastern Front, but could not have prevented Stalin's steamroller from flattening the Third Reich. When Anglo-American forces met the Red Army, it might very well have been in Eastern France, not Eastern Germany. By speeding Hitler's demise, D-Day assured joint control, not Soviet domination, of Germany. Its success also saved the lives of hundreds of thousands of soldiers who would have died in a longer war. It is safe to assume, finally, that allied sacrifices on Normandy's beaches left unbolstered eastern defenses more vulnerable, thereby accelerating the

Soviet liberation of Nazi concentration camps in Poland. If this eastern campaign had taken six months longer, another million death camp inmates—Jews, Gypsies, Poles, and Russian POWs—would have perished.

On December 3, 1944, an American jeep entered the recently captured Alsatian university town of Strassbourg on the upper Rhine. In the jeep sat Samuel Goudsmit, a Dutch-born Jewish-American physicist who headed a scientific intelligence team investigating Germany's atomic bomb program. Poring over papers that night taken from participants in the German effort, Goudsmit suddenly exclaimed: "We've got it!" "I know we have it," said his partner, referring to U.S. knowledge of atomic bomb-building, "but do they?" "No, no," replied the scientist, "that's it, they don't!"[67] His cursory perusal of the files indicated that the German team had been working on a nuclear reactor. A bomb was many years from realization.

The discovery prompted a huge collective sigh of relief in London and Washington, for, despite the tightening vice of allied armies, all had lived with the frightening scenario of German science snatching victory from the grip of a seemingly certain defeat. There had been good reason to fear. A German team cracked the atom in December 1938, opening the way for creation of atomic explosives, assuming that key theoretical problems such as "critical mass" could be solved. The Third Reich, however, possessed one of the world's leading theoretical physicists in Werner Heisenberg.

Why, then, had Germany achieved so little in six years? Although historians differ hotly over this topic, it appears that Heisenberg and his team were reluctant to proceed with a bomb project. It was dangerous work: Nuclear piles blew up and the allies bombed laboratories. Furthermore, few scientists, proud of the autonomy of their profession, wanted to work under the anxious, angry glare of the army, the S.S., or Hitler. Would there be drastic penalties if experiments failed? More altruistic and moralistic qualms about placing such a weapon in the hands of a maniacal Hitler mixed with these basic concerns of individual safety and professional pride—higher reservations that Heisenberg, when he finally broke silence in the 1960s, self-deceptively believed were the sole reasons. Before army examiners in 1942, therefore, he consistently downplayed the military potential, timeliness, and feasibility of atomic bombs while pursuing the reactor project for scientific reasons. Convinced by the experts that atomic power had no quick potential for miracle weapons, the army pursued other projects. Although Heisenberg probably overestimated the relatively small quantity of uranium actually required for critical mass—another awkward fact that he suppressed psychologically after the war—Germany's top man might have been able to correct his errors if he had wanted to work as assiduously on atomic explosives as the American team at Los Alamos was. On the other hand, scientific shortcomings like overestimation of critical mass may be seen as ironic punishment for Nazi policies that forced more capable minds to leave Germany for Britain and America, where they solved these theoretical and engineering problems for the other side.[68]

Germany invested its major scientific and technological resources in rockets. As a percentage of gross national product, in fact, this program equaled the prodigious Anglo-American project to complete theoretical scientific spadework and engineer atomic bombs. The meager results, however, have moved one historian to describe the Peenemünde rocket base on the Baltic coast as a giant "boondoggle,"[69] for the so-called Vengeance-2, the prototype for all modern missiles, had guidance problems and a militarily insignificant payload. If the V-2 had been fitted with atomic warheads, of course, the rocket effort would have been worthwhile, but, as was just explained, this did not happen.

Germany missed a long-shot chance of utilizing existing technology for victory or stalemate when it poured developmental resources into the V-2 instead of smaller anti-aircraft missile designs. The latter never became operational due to guidance and proximity-to-target detonation problems, but a V-2 type of effort could have overcome the snags to challenge allied control of the skies.[70] Much like missiles, jet airplanes represented another slight opportunity squandered. When Hitler finally dropped his irrational opposition to jets in early 1944, he insisted that they join the V-2 in bombing Britain, even though they had been designed as fighters. If jets had been developed and produced earlier in the war, and then used for defensive purposes to challenge previously superior American fighter planes, perhaps they could have seriously undermined allied air power before D-Day. "To this day," wrote former armaments minister Albert Speer in 1969, "I think that [the anti-aircraft] rocket, in conjunction with the jet fighters, would have beaten back the Western Allies' air offensive against our industry from the spring of 1944 on."[71] That the U.S. Army-Air Force had developed its own jet fighter, and successfully test-flown the prototype in January 1944, however, casts considerable doubt on such scenarios. By summer 1945, moreover, the atomic bomb was operational.

This discussion underscores the fact that neither the preponderant Grand Alliance, much less the economically overwhelmed Axis, believed it could achieve victory by relying solely on the "GNP War." Scientists and engineers on both sides literally "raced against time"[72] to push past the strained, fully exploited capacities of the second industrial revolution. Put differently, ways had to be found, the sooner the better, to improve upon a technological system, born in the late nineteenth century and now fully matured, that could no longer guarantee military survival in the mid-twentieth century. Clearly, the Grand Alliance won this race as well as the GNP punching match. As will be explored in Chapter 10, the United States more than any other nation emerged economically strong enough in 1945 to act on the perceived scientific and technological lessons of this second great war of the century—namely, that scientists and engineers needed to keep racing in peacetime to preclude the possibility of democracy's defeat at the hands of a better-prepared foe in the next conflagration.

Over two million soldiers died in Europe during the final five months of combat leading up to V-E Day on May 8, 1945. Some of the bloodiest fighting began days before Christmas 1944, when Germany unleashed twenty-four divisions from the Ardennes Forest in a desperate offensive. The attackers punched a fifty-mile "bulge" in allied lines—hence the name of the battle—nearly reaching the Meuse River in Belgium before superior reinforcements arrived. British and American forces counterattacked, retook the bulge, and crossed the Rhine in March.

Allied air raids against German cities continued, meanwhile, including one of the worst attacks of the European war at Dresden: Thirty-five thousand civilians died in the night of February 13 as British incendiary ordnance turned the "Florence of the River Elbe" into a fireball. One man searching the next day for his family in a cellar-turned-crematorium preserved nightmarish memories all his life:

> It was fearfully hot and I could only stay inside for a few minutes. It was the most ghastly sight of my life. Several people were cowering by the entrance. Others were on the steps. You could recognize that the corpses had human shapes, but they were without clothes, hair, or eyes, just charred. If you touched one, it fell apart into ash. There was no skeleton, not even individual bones. I recognized a male body as my father-in-law. Nearby, quite distinctly, I spotted the slim form of my mother. The shape of her head left no doubt in my mind. I found a bin and put their ashes in it. With tears in my eyes I took my treasure out of the hellish place.[73]

It was a civilian Stalingrad.

But worse was to come. As the Red Army rolled up German defenses in Poland and Eastern Germany, initiating the war's final, terrible battle for Berlin, almost twelve million terror-stricken Germans in the East attempted to flee. Many of those unlucky enough to miss the last trains and boats to the West died, either as a result of friendly fire or, more likely, of Soviet "kill the German" justice. After the war West Germany documented the deaths of six hundred thousand refugees, while the files of 2.2 million individuals never located—and probably dead—were stamped "unresolved."[74]

Many of the victims were women, either gang-raped and left alive with the bitter memories or brutally raped and killed. Estimates of German women abused—quite often repeatedly—by rampaging Red Army men range from lows of a few hundred thousand to highs of two million. Often these rapes were committed in front of German men who were forced to watch, and shot if they tried to interfere. Clearly, the perpetrators intended the victimization of enemy women as an unmistakable message to enemy men. "The defeat of Nazi Germany by the Soviet Union did not restore the honor of Soviet men," concludes Norman Naimark. "Only by the total humiliation of the enemy, one might hypothesize—in this case, by completely dishonoring him with the rape of his women—could the deeply dishonored Russian nation win the war, with . . . 'the final act of male domination.'"[75] As if to confirm the success of this brutal strategy, thousands of German fathers and husbands committed suicide.

Simultaneously in Italy, American and British armies, having halted south of Bologna the previous autumn, took the city and chased retreating German

Terrible turnabout: Dresden in 1945. (Library of Congress)

divisions north to the Alps. During this campaign communist partisans captured the Duce and his mistress, Clara Petacci, and brutally executed them on
April 28, 1945. That Petacci was shot seems to have been retribution for what
the Black Brigades had done to thousands of the partisans' women. Her killing
was also of tremendous symbolic importance, for how better to demonstrate
the emasculation of Fascism than to shoot the Duce and his woman, and then
hang both bodies heads down in public?

Two days later the Führer and his wife of a few hours, Eva Braun, committed suicide in Berlin. Braun, like Petacci, probably deserved a kinder fate,
but, not receiving it, became part of the greater tragedy of this horrendous
war. For Mussolini and Hitler it was a very fitting end, however, because they
had destroyed Europe and were largely responsible for the deaths of so many
innocent people. After the organized hostilities, reprisal killings, murderous
rapes, and suicides finally ended, in fact, the death toll of World War Two
stood close to sixty million.

Chapter 7

▼

RUIN, RECONSTRUCTION, AND RECRIMINATION

In a self-portrait of 1910 Käthe Kollwitz peers wearily forward, sad eyes shaded from the harsh glare of the future by a consoling motherly hand. Germany's preeminent female sculptress and artist always seemed to know. She was vacationing in Königsberg with husband Karl and sons Hans and Peter when the Great War broke out. People gave hurrahs outside her hotel. Peter cheered too. But Kollwitz sat helplessly on the bed and wept incessantly. Peter would die in Belgium barely three months later.

Kollwitz's prewar works had featured the poor people she found so beautiful. In the interwar years anti-war themes predominated. Her seven-print woodcut, *War* (1922–1923), typified the messages conveyed by this mother-heart of the world. The second in the series, entitled "The Volunteers," shows five young men following the bony-faced drummer, Death. The two trailing youths shout patriotic slogans, but in front of them a volunteer, who has been shot, jerks a tortured face toward the sky. Ahead of him a fourth young man, face upturned, is unconscious, while the last, closest to the drummer, stares with glassy eyes skyward, presumably already dead. The third woodcut, "The Parents," depicts a mother and father totally enveloped by grief.

Years later, after the peace movement had failed, Kollwitz finished a bronze relief known as *The Lament* (1940). The woman's countenance bears a resemblance to its creator. Now the eyes cannot look forward. They are closed and protective hands cover half the face. A close friend had died, and Europe had drifted into another war, but Kollwitz again seemed to know. It would get worse before it would get better.

She spent the final nine months of her life in the secure lakeside resort town of Moritzburg, Saxony. Husband Karl had passed away and a grandson had also perished at the front. Her Berlin home had gone up in flames during an air raid in November 1943. "In days to come people will hardly understand this age," she wrote a relative shortly thereafter. Aside from rare visits by her surviving son Hans, Kollwitz had only two consolations. One was to look skyward, immersing herself in the clouds as they blew by.

Käthe Kollwitz, **Self-Portrait with Hand on Forehead 1910.** (Swarthmore College Peace Collection/© 2004 Artists Rights Society [ARS], New York/VG Bild-Kunst, Bonn)

She had always imagined Peter looking skyward in his last moment, and now he was there. The other was the firm conviction that her troubled epoch would someday seem incomprehensible to future generations that had finally constructed an unshakeable edifice of peace and social justice. "I am dying in this faith," she said in the autumn of 1944. "People will have to work hard for that new state of things, but they will achieve it." Käthe Kollwitz died on April 22, 1945. "The war accompanies me to the end,"[1] she had written her son six days earlier. It would be left to others to try to understand her age.

The incredibly sensitive artist had done her part to resist evil. Her images always pointed the way to saner alternatives in the hope that "the life of the world" might move forward, as Churchill had said, "into broad, sunlit uplands."[2] It would now be left to others, through their art, to try as she had to elevate the dignity of the individual above the power of the state, egalitarianism and free choice above authoritarianism and automatic obedience, ethical behavior above immorality and amorality in politics, and social welfare and justice above continued suffering.

Käthe Kollwitz, **The Volunteers.** (Foto Marburg/Art Resource, NY/© 2004 Artists Rights Society [ARS], New York/VG Bild-Kunst, Bonn)

CULTURE BETWEEN WAR AND COLD WAR

The survivors of World War Two faced an almost unimaginably hard existence. From Cherbourg to Stalingrad homes, businesses, and structures of all sorts had been shelled and bombed into rubble. The countryside was so disrupted and devastated by modern war that food would continue to be scarce for years. The paltry amount of civilian goods manufactured and crops harvested hardly mattered beyond local markets, for the infrastructure of an entire continent—roads, railroad tracks, tunnels, train stations, bridges, port facilities, and airports—lay in ruins. Moving as best they could, mostly on foot, millions of Germans fled or were expelled westward from Eastern Europe, furthermore, while millions of slave laborers, POWs, concentration camp survivors, and other "displaced persons" looked for handouts and huddled in relief stations before trying to return to their homelands. Politics darkened people's prospects in the chaotic aftermath of the century's second catastrophic war, for the political inertia of Fascism and Nazism was already proving difficult to overcome, democracy's recent history of failure was uninspiring, and communism had swept uninvited into Eastern Europe. Understanding reality and coping with life's dilemmas became even more difficult as the Grand Alliance came apart along ideological seams and the far more frightening image of atomic armageddon appeared on the near horizon. In contrast to World War One's grisly aftermath, however, traditional modes of finding solace—the "laying on of hands" at religious services and around recently constructed memorials—was either physically impossible for many years in the rubble that was postwar Europe or else seemed inappropriate in a world apparently abandoned from on high to its earthly fate.

The "existentialist" philosophers made the first attempts to understand Europe's Dark Age. Preeminent among them was Jean-Paul Sartre. The Frenchman challenged Europeans to accept an "authentic state of being" quite different from that described earlier by Martin Heidegger.[3] A schoolteacher most of his early life, Sartre had read the philosopher from Freiburg during a year's sojourn in Berlin in the 1930s. While both men viewed the world as hostile and threatening, urging individuals to shed their blinders and accept life's dangers, Sartre's experience in the army in 1940, and later as a civilian in Paris during the occupation, convinced him that "authentic" existence could never mean submission to an ill-defined destiny controlled from above by heroic Nietzschean leaders, as Heidegger believed, or yielding to a fateful life of racially determined struggle, as Hitler preached. Although both Heidegger and Sartre rejected the existence of God, this insight took the younger man in a different direction. If there were no such thing as a human nature shaped by a creator, then each man determined his own essence—in other words, "existence precedes essence." And if "man is nothing else but what he makes of himself . . . he can't start making excuses for himself. . . . We are alone with no excuses." By forcing Europeans to choose collaboration or resistance, the war accentuated the complexity of human problems and moral dilemmas, but in so doing made it even more obvious that individuals controlled their own destiny by the choices they made. "To live this war is to choose myself through it, and to choose it through my choice of myself. . . . So, I am this war."[4]

Like Sartre, who aided the resistance, men and women should keep faith with themselves by actively seeking out right and wrong, even when the ambiguities of life obscured the difference. To resign oneself to inactivity, rationalizing such paralysis as the product of fate, blaming it on others, or attributing one's do-nothingness to God's will, was "bad faith." Only by opting to act could man be truly free. Nor did it matter whether action led to the defeat of evil, for "success is not important to liberty."[5] As war and liberation yielded to peace and the ever-clearer outlines of an ominous "cold war" between East and West, Sartre urged writers to engage their talents to motivate people to make moral choices through *political* action. By this time France's chief existentialist wanted his countrymen to choose the party recently so courageous in the resistance, the Communists.

Albert Camus, one-time friend and later bitter rival of Sartre, offered readers a more fatalistic brand of existentialism. A French-Algerian with working-class family background, he achieved quick notoriety with The Stranger (1942), a story that featured a violent, remorseless protagonist whose lack of feeling is resented by those around him. Consistent with the depersonalized, indifferent creatures modern men and women have become, however, their own displays of emotion, which they do not follow up on, amount to no more than shallow pretentiousness. Although the novel showcased existentialism's dilemma of action in the face of a meaningless world, a second major piece of writing surpassed the first in many respects. Widely considered to be his masterpiece, *The Plague* (1947) helped Camus win a Nobel Prize for Literature in 1957.

This story of human reaction to catastrophe unfolds in 1940s Oran as an especially virulent epidemic decimates the quarantined town. Some residents go into denial or escape into the bottle, a local priest warns that God is punishing sinners, while others hysterically blame doctors for not finding a cure, selfishly pay to be smuggled past locked city gates, or engage in profiteering. The main character, physician Bernard Rieux, stoically does his job, even though medical treatments fail to prevent death tolls from soaring. Other good men volunteer to help him: Joseph Grand, an aging minor civil servant and struggling writer; Raymond Rambert, an urbane journalist; and the mysterious Jean Tarrou, a self-sacrificing saintly type who has struggled most of his life against injustice. Risking his own life daily, Tarrou organizes "sanitary squads" that transport victims to hospital, bury the dead, and aid the medical community in other auxiliary capacities. Eventually the plague runs its course and Oran tries to return to normalcy.

The Plague is an allegory of war and peace. Like the worldwide conflagration that had come despite its being banned by pacifists, pestilence reappeared from the blue. "There have been as many plagues as wars in history; yet always plagues and wars take people equally by surprise," muses Rieux, the book's narrator, "and the humanists first of all, because they haven't taken their precautions." Like war, the plague sounds its "passionless tocsin," calls a man up to "do his duty," and kills indiscriminately like "some monstrous thing crushing out all upon its path." Before the plague ends innocent people have been shut away in special camps where they die in huge numbers, are buried in mass graves, and later, when the pits are full, are cremated. Finally the plague "abandons its positions" and "retreats," bringing "peace" to the liberated town as the gates open once again. Afterward plans are made for a monument commemorating those who have died. "I could have sworn it!" says one old survivor. "And there'll be speeches."[6]

The raging plague must also be understood symbolically. Camus warns us against a sickness in society that permits an unquestioning acceptance of practices, patterns, and policies that send innocent people to their deaths. Thus the novel's shadiest character, Cottard, welcomes the plague because it prevents the police who are tracking him from following his trail inside the blocked city. "His only real crime," says Tarrou, "is that of having in his heart approved of something that killed off men, women, and children." This contagion of the heart is not limited, however, to a few shady characters. God's creation is flawed, for he does nothing to alleviate widespread suffering on earth, abandoning this task to the few good men who "rise above themselves" in crisis to become healers. But saintliness avails of nothing because men "are more or less ignorant, and it is this that we call vice or virtue; the most incorrigible vice being that of an ignorance that fancies it knows everything and therefore claims for itself the right to kill." The book closes on a note of pathos as the people of Oran celebrate. Rieux knew "what those jubilant crowds did not know but could have learned from books: that the plague bacillus never dies or disappears for good . . . and that perhaps the day would come when, for the bane and the enlightening of men, it would rouse up its rats again and send them forth to die in a happy city."[7]

Existentialist themes also sounded on the stage and screen of Western Europe. One of France's most prolific playwrights of the late 1940s, Jean Anouilh, centered his dramas on the anguish of innocent people who must choose between right and wrong in a cruel world that constantly suppresses these choices. His main characters struggle unsuccessfully, ultimately seeking some form of release by playing a false role, yielding meekly to the hangman, committing suicide, or turning inward. Samuel Beckett, an Englishman transplanted in France, shed a similar light on life's frustrations in his unconventional *Waiting for Godot* (1952). Two tramps wait on a barren stage for a man who never appears. They move from hope to despair, finally resigning themselves to waiting for waiting's sake. Man wastes opportunities, Beckett hints, for creating a better world. Here, at least, was a faint, oblique call to action. Somewhat more hopeful in its final scenes, Ingmar Bergman's allegorical film *The Seventh Seal* (1957) revisits the problem of human choice in dark times. Against the backdrop of plague-ridden medieval Sweden, a knight plays chess with black-robed Death. Although the warrior's soul is at stake, he loses purposely in the end so that a young man and woman may live. Life must—and will—go on.

Western artists grappled with the same dilemmas of existence, crafting both pessimistic and optimistic images of human nature in war's aftermath of rubble and ruined lives. In a fairly typical postwar painting of Frenchman Jean Dubuffet a man is depicted with lion's head and mane. The confused facial expression and hands gesturing as if in despair underscore his helplessness. The so-called *tachisme* school, which took its name from the French word for "stain," sought to symbolize the barbarism of recent times by ripping and scorching their canvases. Similarly, Swiss painter and sculptor Alberto Giacometti presented men and women as fragile skeletal figures, moving about aimlessly, showing no emotion in their apparent exile from one another. The underlying message of sculptures like *City Square*, however, is that people, for all their separation and isolation, exist within the context of a common situation. Viewers can just as easily resolve to reach out to others—no doubt the intended effect—as turn away, resigned fatalistically to man's predicament. English sculptor Henry Moore strove even more overtly to achieve "a stimulation to greater effort of living."[8] His anthropomorphic figures combined forms from the vegetable and lower animal worlds with skeletal-like reclining human shapes that exuded vitality. "When placed in open country," observes Werner Haftmann, these sculptures "impressively assert their character of Pan-like idols." Others in Britain projected more frightening images. Graham Sutherland's "thorn" paintings, for example, placed shocked and frightened anthropomorphic creatures amidst the threatening malevolence of

Alberto Giacometti, City Square. (Digital Image © The Museum of Modern Art/Licensed by Scala/Art Resource, NY/© 2004 Artists Rights Society [ARS], New York/DACS, London)

a prickly tangle of thorns to symbolize man's fear of the sinister forces of nature released by modern science. Similarly, Francis Bacon's *The Magdalen* (1945) depicts Christ's screaming female friend at the base of the cross like "that ancient creature who down the centuries has howled its grief at the violation of man by man."[9]

The immediate postwar period produced another significant contribution to existentialism, and to feminism as well—Simone de Beauvoir's *The Second Sex* (1949). Sartre's longtime lover and life partner pondered with him the meaning of life amidst the ruins that Hitler's extremist biological determinism had bequeathed to Europe. In critiquing and rejecting the Führer's rabid philosophy during and after the war, de Beauvoir eventually extended and modified Sartre's brand of existentialism by applying it to women. Like Jews and other racial and religious minorities, the female sex had been relegated to marginal secondary status by white Christian males who controlled the world for themselves. "There is an absolute human type, the masculine," she wrote. "He is the Subject, he is the Absolute—she is the Other."[10] Women could either choose to accept this state of otherness, surrendering to domesticity, motherhood, and the admitted attractions of a sheltered life, or else reject such socially constructed, allegedly biologically predetermined, inauthentic existences, and then transcend to a more difficult self-defined life of work, freedom, and equality. *The Second Sex* was an immediate best-seller that would have a profound effect on women's liberation movements in both Europe and the United States.

Italy, the first Axis nation to be defeated, did not witness the more pronounced forms of existentialism that appeared in France and other West European nations. Not that Italians were less affected emotionally by the recent violence. The collages of Alberto Burri, for instance, epitomized the *tachisme* school's protests against the destructiveness of modern times. An army doctor who applied his share of gauze bandages to torn bodies, Burri's burlap creations were dressings for the wounds of the world. "Thin threads seek to hold together the irreparable tears through which the somber ground is seen, string binds incongruous things together, here and there tragic color trickles from the torn fabric like blood from wounded flesh."[11] Roberto Rossellini's films *Open City* (1945) and *Paisà* (1946) were also shockingly graphic in their depiction of Italian suffering under the German occupation of 1943–1944. Existentialism's low Italian profile can be explained, rather, by the fact that its focus on dilemmas of the individual retreated before the emphasis that socialism and communism, occupying the moral high ground due to the resistance, placed on *collectivist* efforts to overcome social problems.

Indeed the political Left seems to have largely expropriated Italian postwar culture. Paintings of Renato Guttuso like *Maffia* (1948), for example, displayed the Socialist Realism in vogue among his fellow communists. A noble, muscular peasant bends over his work while evil, well-dressed Mafiosi take aim from behind a tree. In literature Carlo Levi's *Christ Stopped at Eboli* typified the genre of politicized "neorealist" novels that proliferated in the late 1940s. The author, exiled by Mussolini to the rural backwash of southern Italy, turned his experience into a sympathetic call for redress of peasant socioeconomic grievances. Similarly, the protagonist of Elio Vittorini's *Hero of Our Time* murders his mistress, the inevitable end result of assimilating bourgeois values. Postwar Italian filmmakers had no equal in Europe, and here too leftist themes dominated. Thus in Vittorio De Sica's *The Bicycle Thief* (1948) society reacts insensitively as an unlucky man tries to retrieve a stolen bicycle he must have to keep his poster-hanger job. De Sica and other financially strapped directors enhanced their social messages by filming cheaply on city streets, often hiring untrained actors themselves on skid row. Italy's cultural flowering on ground so recently shaken by the quakes of war signaled humanity's gutsy determination to build a new and better order.

The axis running from Rome to Berlin was littered with broken-down machines of war in the spring of 1945. As soldiers of the Third Reich trudged home, women and old men began to pick up the debris of hundreds of cities and towns. The most poignant artistic statement of German despair appeared on the canvasses of Wolfgang Schulze, known as "Wols," himself a survivor of the fire-bombing of Hamburg. "A spontaneous will to expression forces its way on to the surface in an uninhibited psychographic script," writes Werner Haftmann. "Where the surface is damaged and scratched, we see the painter's own feeling of pain; where the forms gesticulate, it is his own emotion that cries out; where the restless lines grope their way over the ground, it is his heart that falters."[12] A spate of war and coming-home writings gave added expression to the bleakness of Germany's immediate postwar years. The best of this "literature of the ruins" are Wolfgang Borchert's play *The Man Outside*

The long road back: German "women of the rubble" in 1945.   (Getty Images)

(1947) and some of the early "Group 47" novels, *Beyond Defeat* (1947) by Hans Werner Richter and *Return to a Foreign Land* (1949) by Walter Kolbenhoff. All three had fought in the war, so not surprisingly their works featured a down-to-earth, sometimes crude soldierly style patterned after the matter-of-factness of Ernest Hemingway.

Group 47's first authors had come out of the POW camps eager to deconstruct Nazi myths about the glories of war, belittle an officer corps that had subjected them to life's worst experience, and commiserate with both the victims and the survivors.[13] Beginning in 1947 this loose-knit organization of writers held annual conferences featuring book readings; frank, often vicious critiques; and the awarding of a modest monetary prize. The 1951 award went to Heinrich Böll, whose latest novel had appeared that year, *Adam, Where Art Thou?* Its author saw enough of war in Poland, France, and Russia to appreciate its absurdities. After an extended absence without legitimate leave that amounted to near desertion, Böll rejoined German units in 1945 and was quickly captured by the Americans.

Like many of Böll's earlier writings, *Adam, Where Art Thou?* borders on pathos. We sense from the beginning that brutal, ineluctable forces will destroy the book's characters, all soldiers and civilians caught up in the crumbling German war effort of 1944–1945. One likeable soldier steps on an unexploded artillery shell in a garden. Another eats bad fruit and wretches so badly that he can't escape Red Army firing. The reader also knows that Finck, holding on to a suitcase of rare wine that his superior has ordered him to deliver, will be blown away before he can execute these selfish, stupid orders. Only when men and women begin to experience love does history's deterministic grind come to a standstill, but there are only momentary reprieves in wartime. Thus the grim reaper ultimately dispatches both of the novel's lover-protagonists, the Hungarian Jewess, Ilona, and the German infantryman, Feinhals.

A world catastrophe can "serve as an alibi before God," wrote philosopher Theodor Häcker in 1940. Thus God asks of his lost and forlorn humanity: "Adam, where were you?" Mankind's feeble excuse for its wretched behavior is a parental nightmare: "I was in the world war." Böll offers Häcker's imaginary exchange with the frontage material of his novel as a key to understanding what follows.[14] Given the twentieth century's egregious level of criminality and tragedy—all so contrary to divine plans—there can be only one reason to pray. Not to ask for help, or get something, or protest, says Ilona, representative of a persecuted people, to the German Feinhals: "We must pray in order to console God."[15] Thus Böll accepts the notion of "metaphysical guilt" advanced by German existentialist Karl Jaspers, namely, that *each human being* is "co-responsible for every wrong and every injustice in the world."[16]

It was not metaphysical guilt, however, but rather *German* guilt that preoccupied and angered Grand Alliance survivors during the first seasons of peace. All over Hitler's former heartland the triumphant allies hung posters with photographs of crimes perpetrated in the Holocaust, captioned with the angry indictment: "You are the guilty!"[17] Harrowing firsthand accounts of the death camps like Ernst Wiechert's *The Forest of the Dead* (1945) and Eugen Kogon's *The Theory and Practice of Hell* (1947) appeared simultaneously in German bookstores. A weary, battered society faced the excruciating choice of confronting, rationalizing, or ignoring what it had done in Europe. Wols's paintings seemed to advocate the first and toughest option. In his *Blue Phantom* (1951) an eerie-looking alien creature stared at Germans as if saying: "Look at me, face the terrible facts, for they will be facing you for generations to come."

Karl Jaspers adopted the same frank and honest philosophy in *The Question of German Guilt* (1946). He distinguished among four concepts of guilt for Nazi crimes. "Criminal guilt" covered prosecutable violations of national and international laws. "Moral guilt" affected a much larger number of Germans: those soldiers who justified the commission of evil deeds by calling it patriotism or following orders; those civilians who remained indifferent to crimes they witnessed, or rationalized the bad by pointing to Nazism's allegedly good accomplishments; those who genuinely hated Hitler but ran with the pack to survive; and those who deceived themselves into inactivity by boasting that later they would resist. Jaspers threw the net of "political guilt" wider still to cover all Germans, for each nation is responsible for the governments and leaders it empowers and must therefore suffer the political consequences of misdeeds—subjugation, occupation, territorial loss, and reparations. And finally he identified "metaphysical guilt" covering all humanity. While Jaspers hinted at the moral guilt of British appeasement and urged the allies not to bring criminal charges against Germans for moral failure—"You are the guilty!" said the posters—he tactfully downplayed this critique, placing almost exclusive emphasis on Germans' own need to face the nature of their guilt. The community of nations would not soon readmit Germany, but the process would take much longer if Germans did not begin a frank dialogue among themselves, especially about moral guilt. This was no time for excuses, denial, or counteraccusation.

This preoccupation with guilt and moral responsibility prompted searches for solutions in the literature and drama of immediate postwar Germany. Novels by Elizabeth Langgässer and Werner Bergengrün served up religious faith as redemption for immoral characters. The works of Group 47 co-founder Alfred Andersch and Swiss-German novelist Max Frisch offered existentialism's tough individualistic credo of making morally correct—albeit excruciating—choices in nearly impossible situations. And the grand old leftist of Weimar theater, Bertold Brecht, answered from American exile with *The Caucasian Chalk Circle* (1948). A corrupt, incompetent judge reverts to an old Chinese test to determine the true mother of a child. He has a chalk circle drawn on the floor, and then orders the contesting women to enter it with the boy, each grabbing hold of an arm. The mother that tugs the hardest will ostensibly win the trial and receive her child, but the real mother refuses to rip her offspring to pieces and lets go, thus revealing the false claims of the other woman. Set in contemporary Soviet Georgia, the play pokes too much fun at officialdom to be seen as Stalinist. Rather, a kind of soft socialist message filters through. Material things should belong to the people who will prosper by them: "Wagons to good drivers that they may be driven/ And the valley to those who water it, that it may bear fruit."[18] In subtle fashion Brecht's play implored society to build a better future by ordering its priorities more appropriately.

Thomas Mann offered answers from American exile too. His audacious, monumental *Doctor Faustus* (1947) brought to anguished conclusion earlier artistic ruminations—*Death in Venice* (1913) and *The Magic Mountain* (1924)—on the historical course of Germany and Europe, for now no intelligent observer could deny that both had been locked on a track to destruction, smashed beyond recognition just as the author's hopes for a humane, Europeanized Germany had been crushed by the satanic alternative of a Germanized Europe. "He was all the more heartsick at Germany's transformation because it was so late in the day that Germany became an enemy of reason, of thought, of man, an anathema," wrote brother Heinrich Mann. "He felt betrayed."[19]

The novel's narrator, Serenus Zeitblom, a university-educated philologist and high school Latin teacher, sits down at his desk in Munich in 1943 to tell the story of his childhood friend, Adrian Leverkühn. As he progresses to the end of the tale in 1945, bombs rattle his building and the iron ring of the Grand Alliance tightens around the fatherland. Zeitblom's hand shakes because of more than the air raids, however, for his friend, a bold and innovative composer, had sold his soul to the devil and forsaken the love of others in order to acquire twenty-four years of musical creativity. Once the great works were written, the devil snatched his payment. Two who have come too close to Adrian, a lovely child and a virtuoso violinist, are killed. Not long thereafter the Meister succumbs to madness and dies a hollow shell of his former self.

Mann wrote *Doctor Faustus* as an allegory of Germany's descent into the hell of Hitlerism, war, and mass death. Like many in his nation, Adrian Leverkühn is inward, brooding, aloof, and largely indifferent to the fate of other peoples. He has turned his back on humanity, but his music is a cultural breakthrough, a Schönbergian leap beyond the sterile compositions of the past. Alas, like Germany, he reaches too far and destroys himself—a fate reflected and foreshadowed in his penultimate work, *Apocalipsis cum figuris*. As described by Zeitblom, Leverkühn's "sonorous painting" drew on Dürer's *The Last Judgement*, re-creating musically the terror of this final reckoning: "One damned fleshy voluptuary, surrounded, carried, dragged by the grinning sons of the pit, takes his ghastly departure, a hand covering one eye, the other staring in horror at eternal damnation, while not far away grace snatches the souls of two other plummeting sinners and lifts them toward salvation."[20]

Literary scholars have continued to excavate *Doctor Faustus*, thereby considerably widening the allegorical layer of Mann's last great novel.[21] Leverkühn and Zeitblom, whose lives and stories are so inextricably entwined, who almost shadow one another throughout the novel, seem to represent two halves of the inwardly conflicted German mind and spirit. Musician versus scholar, avant-gardist versus classical humanist, Dionysian genius versus hard-working Apollonian bourgeois, one sups with the devil while the other does not—the bad German, apparently, versus the good one. Mann tells us, on the other hand, that the two were "protagonists who had too much to conceal, namely, the secret of their being identical with one another."[22] The paradox unravels with a closer examination of Zeitblom, who is not without considerable faults. When Adrian is tempted to send a love message to Marie Godeau of Geneva, a transparent symbol for pacifistic trends in the 1920s, he sends the ill-fated violin virtuoso, not Serenus Zeitblom, a "nunzio of more grave aspect . . . [who] has nothing to do with matters of love." It is Zeitblom, furthermore, who shields the Master from the commercial advances of Saul Fitelberg, a Jewish impresario and symbol for cosmopolitanism and the world beyond Germany. "I did not like to think of him left alone to the mercies of this 'representative,'" brags the narrator. And it is the bourgeois humanist Zeitblom who is both frightened and helplessly mesmerized by Leverkühn's radical music, despite the fact that he realizes it "strangely corresponded to and stood in intellectual congruence with"[23] pre-fascistic political circles in Munich that preached war and anarchy and propagated myths to whip up the masses for their destiny. Thus "good" bourgeois humanism bears moral guilt for Germany's fate.

But it is this half that survives and struggles to find some reason to hope again. Adrian Leverkühn's last masterpiece, *The Lamentation of Dr. Faustus,* is a "dark tone poem" that to the end "permits no consolation, reconciliation, transfiguration," and sounds like "the lament of God for the lost state of His world, like the Creator's sorrowful 'I did not will this.'" It nevertheless "softly touches the emotions" of the friend and narrator. The last mournful, despairing note, a high G of a cello, transcends despair and provides "hope beyond hopelessness" as it trails off to nighttime silence. "But the tone, which is no more, for which, as it hangs there vibrating in the silence, only the soul still listens, and which was the dying note of sorrow—is no longer that, its meaning changes, it stands as a light in the night." And so Zeitblom prays for German forgiveness:

> Today, in the embrace of demons, a hand over one eye, the other staring in horror, [Germany] plummets from despair to despair. When will it reach the bottom of the abyss? When, out of this final hopelessness, will a miracle that goes beyond faith bear the light of hope? A lonely man folds his hands and says, "May God have mercy on your soul, my friend, my fatherland."[24]

The Faust legend obsessed many Germans in the aftermath of World War Two. This tragic story of a pact with the devil played especially well in the makeshift prisoners' theaters of the American internment camps, packed with tens of thousands of Nazi leaders, generals, concentration camp guards, lower-level officials, as well as "erroneous arrestees" caught up in the net of allied group justice that spread over Germany in the spring of 1945. Ernst von Salomon found himself in the latter group until September 1946. An admirer of Mann's novels and devotee of Nietzsche, this former participant in the assassination of Walther Rathenau, gifted right-wing novelist, and reluctant scriptwriter of Nazi "B" movies perfected the role of the dark Mephistopheles before captive audiences preoccupied, understandably, with issues of guilt and punishment. Salomon later turned the mandatory pre-interrogation survey forms completed by all adults in the American zone into an autobiographical account of the German story. *The Questionnaire* (1951) quickly became a best-selling answer to "the question of German guilt" that no doubt left Thomas Mann and Karl Jaspers wondering if Salomon agreed with them or not.

The book unfolds as a point-by-point response to the survey's 131 questions. The nearly seven-hundred-page result is an artistic shuffling of the details of Salomon's life as they intersect at critical junctures of twentieth-century German history. Born in 1902, Salomon was too young to serve in the Great War, but shortly thereafter became embroiled in the Free Corps violence and political turbulence of the early 1920s. A five-year prison sentence after the Rathenau affair yielded to renewed involvement on the Far Right as well as an initial literary foray, *The Outlaws* (1930). Salomon strove to reestablish the state authority that a world war had destroyed. His ideal was an egalitarian military dictatorship, not the totalitarian lawlessness, rabid racism, destructiveness, and nihilism incarnate of Nazism. Rather than return to the path of resistance after 1933, however, rather than reinvigorate himself with the "spirit of the deed," Salomon lapsed into the survivalist mode that had worked well in prison, the sideways detour that the crab takes around obstacles rather than confronting them head on. He lived in the shell of denial, grumbling privately about Nazi crimes, but living the high life in Berlin and Munich, knowing full well that Hitler had to be deposed, but risking nothing to achieve that end. Only in 1945 could Salomon begin to admit before a guilty conscience that his behavior had amounted to the "most terrible corruption"—the "lesser evil" of inaction against the greater evil of Nazism. He would have confessed to a priest were it not for the fear that passivity before Hitler's laws amounted to "sins against the Holy Ghost" [25] that could not be forgiven.

Thus Salomon fit into Jaspers' category of the morally guilty ones, not least because he admitted it and tried to clear his conscience. However, whereas Japsers dodged the issue of *allied* moral guilt—and Mann simply, and wisely, refused to go there—Salomon rushed in. *The Questionnaire* is full of moral indignation at the United States for indiscriminate bombing of women and children, collaborating with Stalin's criminal regime, and then pursuing a blind victor's justice. The Americans lumped "morally" guilty Germans like Salomon together with the "criminally" guilty, subjecting them to beatings, humiliations, and inhumane conditions that made a mockery of the U.S. claim to truth, justice, and rule of law. Although "erroneous arrestees" were eventually released, Salomon never forgave the West. His remarkable narrative sold over a quarter of a million copies in the 1950s, appealing to Germans who felt a deep sense of shame as well as those who sought convenient excuses to avoid the staring "blue phantom" of their consciences. And thus began the unconscionable process, however understandable, of burying and forgetting. Although written by a nationalist who despised Hitler, *The Questionnaire*'s angry, defiant tone also bridged the gap to large numbers of unreconstructed Nazis—perhaps one in five Germans—who were also angry. Although many readers must have misunderstood it, Salomon's popular autobiography clearly reflected the unpleasant fact that a great number of adults in defeated Germany—probably the majority—had not come to grips, and did not want to come to grips, with their recent past.

The exigencies of winning the Great Patriotic War caused Socialist Realism's cultural bans to be lifted. Stalin could tolerate just about anything that contributed to war productivity and the people's willingness to fight Nazism. Jazz, religion, atonal symphonies, realistic war novels, social satire, and lyric poetry all enjoyed official approval in the early years of the struggle. As soon as the Red Army began its long march to Berlin, however, the old cultural dogmas made their comeback. The first sign appeared in late 1943 when the party denounced Mikhail Zoshchenko's collection of satirical autobiographical sketches, *Before Sunrise*, as "vulgar philistinism." With tensions mounting between the Soviet Union and its wartime allies after 1945, Stalin and his loyal watchdog of hack communist culture, Andrei Zhdanov, cracked down on everything that smacked of the "degenerate bourgeois culture of the West."[26] Zoshchenko and lyric poetess Anna Akhmatova were expelled from the All-Russian Union of Writers in 1946. In early 1948 the party extended its ban to the avant-garde compositions of Serge Prokofiev and Dmitri Shostakovich. As they had in the 1930s, artists were faced with the depressing options of kowtowing, ingeniously skirting official dictates, or "writing for the desk drawer."

One of the best literary accounts of the Great Patriotic War, Vasily Grossman's *Life and Fate*, remained in the latter category until its posthumous publication in 1980. The author, a Ukrainian Jew whose mother perished in the Holocaust, narrowly avoided the same fate in 1953 when Stalin's merciful death cut short an escalating series of purges aimed especially at Jews. Not coincidentally, Grossman therefore condemns Nazism and Stalinism in equal measure as oppressive state systems that attempted to crush the spirit of individual free will and human kindness. He achieves this purpose by juxtaposing passages on German death camps and the Soviet GULAG during the Battle of Stalingrad. On the outcome of this climactic struggle rests the fate of Stalin's police state, but it must defeat more than Hitler's minions: The surge to freedom of the Soviet peoples epitomized by the heroic resistance on the Volga must also be terminated once it has served Stalin's ends. Despite the cultural thaw that set in with the tyrant's passing (see later), Grossman's existentialist handling of the theme of freedom determined, according to one irate official, "that there could be no question of *Life and Fate* being published for another two hundred years."[27]

Like Tolstoy's *War and Peace*, the novel portrays an entire society through the experiences of one family during a war's climactic campaign. The extensive clan is that of Alexandra Vladimirovna Shaposhnikov, an aging populist whose network of relatives, friends, and acquaintances forms Grossman's cast. As Stalin's police terror squelches the spirit of soldierly egalitarianism and camaraderie that produced victory over the Germans in 1942–1943, readers are told that only "fate"—the seemingly all-determining force behind the great state establishments—"has the power to pardon and chastise, to raise up to glory and to plunge into need, to reduce a man to labor-camp dust." Individuals who are the victims of evil have a hand, however, in their own destiny: "A man may be led by fate, but he can refuse to follow—he may be a mere tool in the hands of destructive powers, but he knows it is in his interest to assent to this." But despite the unfavorable odds, a man can also choose "life"—the enduring force of human kindness. Over time, in fact, life always prevails, and "in this alone lies man's eternal and bitter victory over all the grandiose and inhuman forces that ever have been or will be."[28]

Thus Alexandra Vladimirovna's son-in-law, Viktor, a Jewish nuclear physicist, refuses to continue work that may benefit evil leaders. A phone call from Stalin initially derails him from the course of life as he returns to his laboratory. Viktor even denounces innocent intellectuals. But soon enough he regains the courage of his convictions: "Every hour, every day, year in, year out, he must struggle to be a man, struggle for his right to be pure and kind. He must do this with humility. And if it came to it, he mustn't be afraid even of death; even then he must remain a man." Similarly, Ikonnikov, an inmate in a German concentration camp whose simple philosophy of human kindness is the philosophical fulcrum of *Life and Fate*, refuses to do construction work on a crematorium—and is shot by the Nazis. Clearly Grossman's brand of existentialism departs from the hopeless fatalism of Camus, joining Sartre's "I am this war" philosophy of sacrifice and resistance, cost what it may. The Jewish pariah Grossman's great plea for the salvaging of humaneness amidst so much contemporary cruelty—"the most complete portrait of Stalinist Russia we have or are likely ever to have," says Robert Chandler—is also quite consistent with Böll's and Jaspers's concept of metaphysical guilt, albeit with no trace of religion: "Everyone feels guilty before a mother who has lost her son in a war," wrote Grossman. "Throughout human history men have tried in vain to justify themselves."[29]

VISIONS OF NEW WORLD AND EUROPEAN ORDERS

The "life and fate" dilemmas that preoccupied existentialist philosophers, artists, and novelists resonated among political leaders too. Indeed, the century's second awful cataclysm, like the first before it, spawned visions of a new world order that would save mankind from destruction. Of the Big Three leaders who met at the summit to coordinate Grand Alliance strategy, Winston Churchill, the idiosyncratic warhorse of Great Britain, first expressed these ideals. His initial draft of the "Atlantic Charter" issued with President Franklin Delano Roosevelt in August 1941 called for an "effective international organization" to guarantee the security of "all states and peoples."[30] Although he would not have gone into detail with the American president during their meeting at sea, Churchill had long pondered the failure of the League of Nations and the 1925 lesson of Locarno, namely, that peace depended on Great Power willingness to enforce it. In 1938 he had called for an alliance of freedom-loving European states buttressed by the armies of the great democracies, whose actions to deter or punish outlaw nations would "rest upon the Covenant of the League of Nations, agreeable with all the purposes and ideals" of that organization and "sustained, as it would be, by the moral sense of the world."[31] This notion of a regional power bloc loosely affiliated with—and legitimated by—a worldwide umbrella organization came into clearer focus with new proposals by Churchill in 1943. "Regional Councils" for Europe, the Western Hemisphere, and the Pacific would undertake policing actions with standing military forces, but "always under the general overriding authority" of a "Supreme World Council."[32] The Soviet Union and Great Britain would sit on the European and Pacific Councils, the United States on all three.

Roosevelt had soured on international organizations. Having campaigned with Woodrow Wilson for the League, the great pragmatist had watched with dismay, and eventual disgust, as Geneva slipped from fiasco to ultimate failure. When Churchill broached the topic of an "effective international organization" in 1941, therefore, Roosevelt declined. "He would not favor creating a new League of Nations, or anything like it, until the United States and Great Britain had functioned as a world police force for a number of years after the war and had effectively disarmed aggressor nations and established a stable international situation."[33] By 1943 Roosevelt had allowed State Department officials like Under Secretary Sumner Welles to convince him that consideration for the legitimate concerns of small nations necessitated creating a central world organization (as opposed to regional councils) replete with general assembly as well as rotating nonpermanent seats for weaker countries on some sort of steering committee. The president insisted, however, that whatever the structural trappings, success depended on the core idea of Great Power control: omnipotent "policemen" consensually walking the world's beat.

Roosevelt and Churchill knew that the gutsy Russian counterattack before Moscow in December 1941 and formation of the Grand Alliance one month later necessitated adding the Soviet Union to the world's posse. But would Stalin join? Moscow's strongman clearly had a different perspective on problems of worldwide law and order. "Everyone imposes his own system as far as his army can reach—it cannot be otherwise,"[34] he said. Territorial expansion around the periphery of the Soviet Union supplied a valuable commodity, namely, security: "The more you've got, the safer you are."[35] Thus membership in an international peacekeeping organization meant maintaining Great Power spheres of control in Europe and the world, deferring, for the most part, to the territorially delimited political prerogatives of each ally, and hunting down any bandit who threatened the peace. Such deals between powerful equals aside, Stalin expected class struggles to erupt in the capitalist bloc and was fully prepared to promote these conflicts surreptitiously, not least because he suspected class enemies would attempt to implant troubles in his sphere.[36] Thus he was ready to formalize the wartime alliance in peacetime, especially in the short term as the country licked its considerable wounds, but his instincts would not allow him to count on cooperation's indefinite survival. Initially drawn to Churchill's plan of regional councils, the man of steel hinted at Teheran in December 1943 that he favored the centralized world organization desired by Roosevelt, a powerful leader "Stalin accepted as a partner . . . with whom he knew he could play a grand game with a good chance of success."[37] Roosevelt counted the Russian's final agreement to participate in the "United Nations" as the greatest success of the Yalta Conference of February 1945.

The United Nations (UN) took final shape at San Francisco during the spring of 1945. The delegates of forty-four founding nations aspired to "save succeeding generations from the scourge of war, which twice in our lifetime has brought untold sorrow to mankind." Members would "establish conditions under which justice and respect for obligations arising from treaties and other sources of international law can be maintained."[38] The basic guarantee of peace and security remained unity among the policemen, grown now to five with the addition of China, which Roosevelt and his successor, Harry

Truman, saw as a democratic beacon for the peoples of the Far East, and France, which Churchill promoted to compensate for the anticipated withdrawal of American forces from Europe. These powers received permanent seats on a "Security Council" of fifteen. The votes of nine—with all five policemen concurring—could send UN standing forces that were envisioned in the charter to any trouble spot. A "General Assembly" of all members could exert influence but wield no power.

Although the new peace enforcement organization definitely restored respect for international law to a world recently abused by outlaw nations, power considerations assumed a much higher profile than the legalistic concerns that had been so prominent in the League of Nations. The difference emerged into plain view over the issue of rights of conquest. Whereas the League sought to squelch the age-old principle that had helped unleash the dragon of world war, its successor condemned aggression but did not "expressly stipulate that the acquisition of territory by force cannot provide legal title," observes Sharon Korman. The blatant absence of "any specific obligation of non-recognition"[39] of lands annexed by force reflected the fact that the victors, after so much sacrifice of human life to defeat the Axis, intended to freely shift territories to guarantee security. Thus the United States made de facto annexations of Japan's Pacific island holdings while the Soviet Union acquired the South Sakhalin and Kurile Islands from Japan as well as the city of Königsberg (Kaliningrad) from Germany. The reemergence of recognition for rights of conquest corresponded with the realpolitik of the Grand Alliance, moreover, for six years earlier the Soviet Union had taken Bessarabia (Moldavia), Eastern Poland, Lithuania, Latvia, Estonia, and portions of Finland. British and American acquiescence in these conquests smoothed relations with Moscow—a turning of a blind eye that was as important to the potential success of the United Nations as it had been for the defeat of Hitler.

The allies intended to undergird the new world order by punishing German political, diplomatic, military, and industrial leaders. Nationwide denazification, disarmament, and democratization efforts would follow. The first step involved dealing somehow with Nazi war criminals, but here, too, considerations of power wrestled for paramountcy with legal concerns. A near consensus existed until late in the war, for instance, that Nazi leaders should be summarily executed for crimes so heinous as to preclude the necessity of trials. Churchill wanted to draw up a list with a hundred names; American Treasury Secretary Henry Morgenthau, who initially had Roosevelt's ear, spoke of killing twenty-five hundred; and Stalin averred in a not so tongue-in-cheek toast at Teheran: "at least 50,000 and perhaps 100,000 of the German Commanding Staff must be physically liquidated."[40] The only champion of due process to step forward was American Secretary of War Henry Stimson, a lawyer who had long held Germany criminally culpable for violating the Kellogg-Briand Pact of 1928, which outlawed wars of aggression. His advocacy of war crimes trials to set a postwar example of rule of law won over Roosevelt shortly before Yalta. That spring the British, French, and Soviets agreed to talk about trials.

Negotiations in the summer of 1945 proved highly controversial and divisive. All sides wanted to prosecute "war crimes" and "crimes against humanity," but both the Soviets and the Americans had nervous qualms about these counts of the draft indictment, the former because they had killed Polish and German POWs—and humanity had not fared well under Stalin's brutal reign—the latter because of lynching and other "regrettable" abuses against racial minorities. The issue was sidestepped by agreeing solely to prosecute *German* crimes arising from Berlin's conspiracy against world peace. "There might come a time," commented A. N. Trainin of the Soviet delegation, "when there will be a permanent international tribunal of the United Nations organization to try all violations of international law." In the meantime, the allies had "a definite purpose in view, that is, to try criminals of the European Axis powers."[41] The American team nearly lost patience with the Soviets, however, over Moscow's attempt to dilute the final indictment, "crimes against the peace," to "fascist aggression," thereby undermining Washington's bid to establish an international legal precedent for the criminality and punishment of aggression. Viewing its own conquests as "just wars, wars of liberation," Moscow had no desire "to condemn aggression or initiation of war in general."[42] The negotiators finally hammered out a compromise in August whereby the charter defining the competence of the war crimes tribunal charged it specifically with prosecution of Nazi crimes while the indictment itself retained the general wording desired by the Americans.

The trials opened at Nuremberg, site of the Nazi Party rallies, in November 1945. In the docket sat twenty-two top level defendants, among them Luftwaffe chief Hermann Goering, army staff chiefs Alfred Jodl and Wilhelm Keitel, Nuremberg Nazi Party boss Julius Streicher, and Foreign Minister Joachim von Ribbentrop. When the judges handed down their sentences, twelve received death penalties, including all of these men. Goering cheated the hangman by taking poison in his cell. Nevertheless, the world's first international war crimes tribunal had successfully completed its work. In successor trials of lesser Nazis the British, French, and Americans carried out 486 executions. The United States also handed over 3,914 internees to the vengeful justice of sixteen European nations liberated from Axis inhumanity. Small wonder that Ernst von Salomon and his captive compatriots wiled away their time nervously producing versions of the Faust legend. Fate proved much harsher, however, for 240,000 Germans held in former S.S. death camps now used by the Soviets: One in three died of malnutrition-induced diseases.[43]

Cold War

Advocates of world peace viewed the Nuremberg precedents and United Nations as support columns for a new world edifice. Already before the UN began operations in January 1946, however, the foundation of allied unity began to crack beneath these twin pillars. Although East-West tensions wracked the Grand Alliance (see Chapter 6), the Big Three had consistently managed to preserve solidarity during a war against dangerous enemies. But as first Germany and then Japan surrendered in the spring and summer of 1945, the cement of common wartime interests crumbled under the stress of changed circumstances and clashing personalities, and the strain of antithetical, conflicting ideologies. Long the subject of controversy and rancor among historians, the origins of the Cold War divide researchers less severely since the fall of communism.[44]

The struggle between opposing politicoeconomic systems, glaring suspiciously at one another through the prism of incompatible worldviews, sped this breakdown as much as any other factor. In the Atlantic Charter Great Britain and the United States proclaimed the goal of restoring self-government to all lands liberated from the Axis. More specifically, the Yalta Conference's "Declaration on Liberated Europe" called for elections at the earliest possible moment of governments responsive to the will of the people. Demands for western-style democracy in Eastern Europe triggered an angry standoff between Truman, Churchill's replacement Clement Atlee, and Stalin at the Potsdam Conference of mid-summer 1945. Washington and London continued to press Moscow for democratic progress at subsequent meetings of the Council of Foreign Ministers (CFM), established at Potsdam to complete peace treaties with Italy, Germany, Berlin's former ally Finland, as well as Axis satellites Hungary, Bulgaria, and Rumania.

Inextricably bound up with British and American insistence on parliamentary elections was their desire for "free entry into the Danube Valley and Eastern Europe for the goods and capital of the Western countries." The connecting rod between democratic governments and market economies appeared obvious to Leo Crowley, director of the Foreign Economic Administration under Roosevelt and Truman: "If you create good governments in foreign countries," he told Congress, "automatically you will have better markets for ourselves."[45]

Stalin agreed to the Atlantic Charter and the Declaration on Liberated Europe. He rejected the underlying principles of these documents, however, for they promoted ideals at complete variance with the personality cult and one-party monopoly of the Soviet Union—and, even more importantly, because they could potentially foster regimes in Eastern Europe hostile to Moscow. East European democracy had broken down in the 1920s and 1930s, yielding to authoritarian systems allied with Hitler like those of Hungary and Rumania. Moreover, the democratic governments of Poland and Finland had also attacked the Soviet Union in 1920 and 1941, respectively. At Yalta, therefore, Stalin exacted a promise that postwar governments in Eastern Europe would be "friendly" to Moscow. At Potsdam this enabled him to waive off western accusations that the USSR had violated the Declaration on Liberated Europe: "A freely elected government in any of these countries would be anti-Soviet, and that we cannot allow." To Polish communists he remarked much more bluntly: "When the Soviet Army has gone, [your countrymen] will shoot you like partridges."[46]

Western economic penetration of Eastern Europe through the "open door" of the market was equally unacceptable to a Soviet establishment eager to integrate conquered territory with the Russian economy and establish a compatible socialist system in this region. Thus when U.S. Secretary of State James Byrnes pressed Stalin in December 1945 to cooperate on postwar treaties with the nations of Eastern Europe "so that we can be in a position to render them economic assistance," the dictator sensed a trap. "An argument less likely to persuade Stalin can hardly be imagined," writes William McNeill. "He must have interpreted Byrnes's words to mean: 'We must have peace treaties to re-establish capitalist exploitation of Rumanian oil wells and Finnish nickel mines.'"[47]

The personal and political landscape of the Grand Alliance had also changed. FDR died on April 12, 1945. Replacing the genial patrician whom the Soviet dictator respected and trusted—to the extent that a Marxist, especially one as wary and suspicious as Stalin, can trust a bourgeois—was the rough-hewn Missourian and blunt anti-communist Harry S. Truman. Only ten days in office, he blurted to cabinet officials that the United States would go forward with the United Nations "and if the Russians do not wish to join us they can go to hell."[48] The ex-artillery officer blasted Soviet Foreign Minister V. M. Molotov later the same day. At Potsdam "Give 'Em Hell Harry" attempted to boss the Soviets, relishing the opportunity to tell Stalin that the United States had successfully exploded a weapon of mass destruction. Although he maintained a placid exterior, the Soviet leader seethed on the inside, ordering his scientists soon thereafter to accelerate work on atomic bombs.[49]

Sensing his back against the wall, Stalin stiffened instinctively. In London for a CFM meeting in September 1945, Molotov received orders from his boss to be "absolutely inflexible. . . . I think we can now tear off the veil of amity." The unfriendly mix of personalities grew more acrimonious that autumn as the new British foreign minister, Ernest Bevin, a former trade unionist "spoke up to the Russians as a great many plain people in pubs and corner drug-stores had often wanted to speak." Fiery American General George Patton exacerbated already tense relations in December with a militant speech to a Sunday School class in Germany. "There will be another war," he assured the children, "there always has been." His commander-in-chief seemed only slightly less bellicose. World War Three was inevitable, said Truman in January 1946, unless the West "faced [the USSR] with an iron fist and strong language." He was "sick of coddling the Soviets." One month later Stalin stated publicly that capitalist countries would resort to war to avert another depression. Although he probably meant war with one another, not against the Soviet Union, the latter interpretation prevailed, leading observers like U.S. Supreme Court Justice William O. Douglas to dub the speech "a declaration of World War Three." Winston Churchill's famous address of March 1946, warning about the "iron curtain" that had descended on Eastern Europe, moved Stalin to label the Englishman "a firebrand of war."[50] The rhetoric could not get any hotter.

Stalin knew, however, that his country was weaker than the West—in fact, far weaker. Invasion and counteroffensive had devastated the USSR and depleted the Red Army, bringing it "ever closer to the bottom of its once-limitless barrel of manpower."[51] Nationalist revolts rocked the western provinces, especially in the Ukraine. Making matters worse, the West had abruptly terminated wartime aid that had provided tens of thousands of machine tools and hundreds of thousands of trucks. Britain and America also rejected Soviet proposals for large-scale reparations from defeated Germany and balked at reconstruction loans for Moscow. And the United States was rapidly expanding its stocks of atomic weapons—from one at war's end to nine by spring 1946. The reality of Soviet weakness compelled Stalin, therefore, to make a series of concessions in the eight months after Potsdam: withdrawing troops from Iran; dropping demands for joint control (with Turkey) of the Dardanelles Straits; withholding direct assistance to communist rebels in China and Greece; accepting reasonably free elections in Austria, Czechoslovakia, Hungary, and Yugoslavia—even though communists prevailed only in Belgrade; and agreeing to balloting in neighboring Poland and Rumania. Bulgaria, whose communist-backed government had been "elected" after widespread fraudulence and police terror in November 1945, would make amends by adding non-communists to the ministries.

The possibility of returning to the relative cordiality of wartime relations, on the other hand, faded away to near impossibility. "Stalin felt that a difficult and unequal confrontation had begun, but he had no thought of yielding," writes Dmitri Volkogonov. "He would turn the country into a fortress."[52] Contact with the West once again grew more difficult—and former contact politically risky—for Soviet citizens. Political controls and censorship tightened; cultural policy rigidified under the policeman of Socialist Realism, Andrei Zhdanov; and the Red Army squashed ethnic rebels in the border provinces. In Rumania and Poland, covering the wide approaches from Central Europe, elections were postponed until November 1946 and January 1947, respectively—ample time for the police to kidnap unreliable politicians, cripple opposition parties, and rig successful communist outcomes. A second Bulgarian "election" in October 1946 confirmed the communists' monopoly. The protests of London, Washington, and native opposition leaders fell on deaf ears.

Conflicting interests and ideologies produced another breakdown in occupied Germany. The Yalta and Potsdam Conferences envisaged a joint administration of the defeated Axis nation, split up again into Germany and Austria, by four powers: the Soviet Union, whose occupation cordons would lie in the east; and the United States, Britain, and France, with zones in the west. Similarly carved into four national sectors, the cities of Berlin and Vienna would serve as headquarters for Allied Control Councils (ACCs) charged with monitoring disarmament, denazification, and democratization. The competence of the ACC also extended to matters affecting interzonal trade and reparations. The first stage of re-educational efforts, the Nuremberg Trials, proved to be the only area of agreement, however, and even here East-West arguments over crimes of aggression almost scuttled the trials.

On other issues, relations deteriorated immediately, especially in Germany. Thus the Soviets accused their wartime allies, especially the British, of

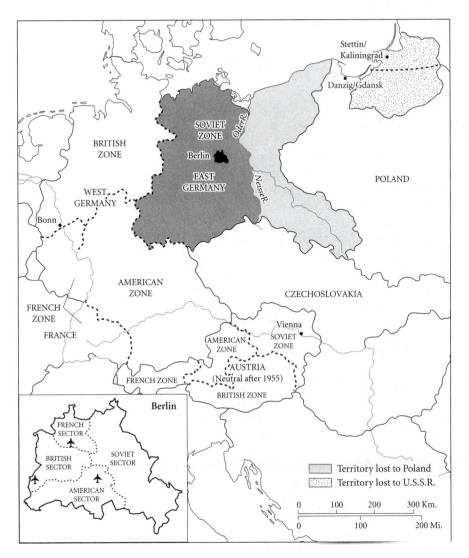

Divided Germany and Berlin

permitting too many ex-Nazis to reenter public life. The West replied that the Soviets staffed offices with German communists returning from Russian exile, which seemed undemocratic, and defended their own actions as an expedient response to manpower shortages. Adding to the acrimony, each side promoted its own political system: political life in the western zones drifting back quickly to electoral practices reminiscent of the pre-Hitler era; politics in the eastern zone dominated increasingly by the Moscow-backed German Communist Party. In response to western cries of foul, the Soviets and German Communists trumpeted their own "socialist" style of democratization that included radical land redistribution and nationalization of industry schemes. Soviet representatives on the ACC prodded their capitalist counterparts to follow suit, adding that Moscow would not complete a peace treaty until Germany possessed a trustworthy "anti-fascist" government. This aggressive set of policies, like communist criticisms of western practices, reflected Stalin's design to bring a united Germany into the Soviet orbit. As recent research demonstrates, he was even prepared to tolerate a "bourgeois" Germany, but fully expected this to be a temporary phase along the way to the ultimate triumph of Marxism.[53] The West, of course, desired as much success for its political system in Germany as well as Eastern Europe. Winning Germany, the former hegemonic power in the center of Europe, could significantly advance the political cause of the victorious side.

The issue of reparations drove the wedge of discord deeper. Aware of their immense reconstruction task, the Soviets insisted at Yalta that Germany pay reparations to defray a portion of the costs. But the British and Americans, wary of repeating mistakes that had weakened Germany's economy and hurt European trade after 1918, refused to commit to reparations. The allies finally arranged a compromise at Potsdam whereby each occupying power could take reparations of current production and equipment removals from its own zone as long as these payments-in-kind were covered by a German export surplus and did not push the Germans below a minimum standard of living yet to be defined. In addition, the Soviet Union could dismantle 25 percent of the stock of industrial machinery in the western zones in return for shipments of food and raw materials from its zone.

These arrangements soon collapsed. By the spring of 1946 the Soviets had dismantled and carted away more than forty-five hundred mid-to-large-size factories—over a third of East Germany's industry—prompting western complaints that living standards were being driven too low.[54] As American representatives on the ACC Reparations Committee recalled, however, Moscow viewed things differently. "The Soviets did not relish the idea of explaining to their people, who had suffered much at the hands of the Germans, that the vanquished were to have a higher standard of life than they, the victors." The same vindictive spirit motivated the Soviets to shift "surplus" food east to the motherland rather than west to the other zones. The absence of shipments from the eastern zone forced western administrators to import food at great expense to prevent starvation in their zones. In what struck the West as a double standard, however, the Soviets continued to insist on major reparations removals from the Ruhr to meet reconstruction timetables at home. For many months the West complied, but the drain of productive capacity eventually cut against the grain of western businessmen responsible for supervising industry, especially the Americans.

> They were affected by their American training in which all efforts are bent toward getting the largest possible production. . . . In fact, the task of deliberately reducing production . . . went contrary to all habits of thought in the Western World, in which it is practically a religion to encourage more and better production and promote higher standards of living. For this task we had to make ourselves think in reverse in many respects.[55]

The desire to stop "thinking in reverse," along with plans to leverage food shipments from the Soviet zone, triggered a halt to equipment removals in May 1946. This unilateral action led to bitter accusations from the Soviets that the West had violated promises made at Potsdam.

Desperate to obtain machinery for postwar rebuilding, Stalin instructed Molotov to repeat demands for reparations at subsequent CFM meetings. The same need for access to the western zones also explains Moscow's insistence that Germany remain one nation, as declared at Yalta and Potsdam, and eventual willingness, after obstructing CFM meetings for over a year, to negotiate a German peace treaty. Frustrated over Soviet intransigence, meanwhile, Washington and London began to drift in the direction of establishing a separate West German state. In January 1947 they fused their occupation zones into one "Bizonia" to reduce the burden on war-weakened Great Britain, and then in December they adjourned the CFM, leaving the ACC in Berlin as the only point of regular diplomatic contact between the two sides. Its meetings, however, had become sterile and meaningless.

Throughout 1946 and 1947, in fact, the West had been taking a different tack. The first democratic leader to tire of the Soviets and recommend a change of course was Ernest Bevin. Convinced that Stalin wanted to exploit Europe's postwar economic and social misery to push his sphere of control as far west as possible, the hard-talking British foreign minister lobbied Washington to overturn Roosevelt's plan to withdraw American troops from Europe at war's end. This pressure succeeded, as evidenced by James Byrnes's comments of September 1946: "We are not withdrawing," declared the American secretary of state. "We are staying here and will furnish our proportionate share of the security forces."[56] Britain's withdrawal from Greece in early 1947 convinced Truman that U.S. resources were required in that country's struggle against communist insurgents aided by neighboring Marxist regimes in Yugoslavia and Bulgaria. That March the president announced the "Truman Doctrine," pledging millions of dollars for the defense of Greece and Turkey, but also for the wider "containment of communism" wherever it might threaten democracy. Bevin's influence contributed, furthermore, to Washington's decision to grant billions of dollars to the economic rehabilitation of non-communist Europe. Announced by Byrnes's successor George Marshall in June 1947, the so-called European Recovery Plan (ERP) aimed to rebuild shattered infrastructures, restore prosperity, and block communism, whose agents, he was convinced, would seek to politically exploit Europe's troubles. To maintain appearances, Moscow received an invitation to participate in the ERP.

What soon came to be known as the "Marshall Plan," however, had a deeper agenda. On this point American "revisionist" historians who took a critical view of later U.S. foreign policy unearthed evidence that led to valuable insights. After the establishment of the Grand Alliance in 1942, market economy ideologues in the State and Treasury departments moved to free the postwar world from the counterproductive economic nationalism of the 1930s. At the Bretton Woods (New Hampshire) Conference of July 1944 they overrode British reluctance to replace its system of Commonwealth tariff and exchange preferences with the "open door" of unrestricted trade and monetary exchange. These "missionaries of capitalism and democracy"[57] watched with increasing dismay and alarm after 1945–1946 as the Soviets shut off Eastern Europe from this new world order—and Western Europe appeared too broken by the war to participate in it. By pumping billions of grant-in-aid dollars into Europe, Marshall's ERP aimed to facilitate reconstruction, stimulate private European investments and intra-European trade, provide dollar liquidity for the purchase of American exports, and, perhaps most importantly, free Europe from social and economic instability so that it could avoid revolution and afford to help the U.S. militarily. In fact, the White House stressed the economic and military complementarities of American policy: The Truman Doctrine and the Marshall Plan "are two halves of the same walnut."[58] In order to ensure the success of these designs, Washington urged nations receiving subsidies to form a customs union and, ultimately, a political federation. Given the fading prospects of the United Nations, a "United States of Europe" inextricably bound, both economically and militarily, to the United States of America, was the best guarantee for capitalism, democracy, and the containment of communism.[59] European representatives, including a large Soviet delegation, assembled in Paris during the summer of 1947 to discuss participation in the ERP.

The Kremlin reacted preemptively to the perceived threat of the Marshall Plan. The Americans wanted to divide Europe "into two groups of states, creating new difficulties in the relations between them." On the front line stood a revived, unfriendly, dangerous Germany "subordinated to the interests of American capital."[60] Interpreting the ERP as a capitalist wedge that would be driven deeply into Eastern Europe, Stalin ordered Molotov to bolt the Paris Conference, and then forced the Poles and Czechs, who were both eager to participate, to decline their invitations. Next the Soviet strongman extended his hold on Eastern Europe beyond Poland, Rumania, Bulgaria, and Yugoslavia. A succession of incremental purges and coups brought Hungary gradually under communist leadership during the summer and fall of 1947. In heretofore democratic Czechoslovakia, furthermore, native communists struck more quickly in February 1948. Both Soviet-backed takeovers reversed the outcome of free 1945 elections. During the late fall and winter of 1947–1948 Moscow also whipped the Communist Parties of Italy and France into massive and violent strike movements designed to disrupt economic recovery, foment political trouble in the class enemy's sphere of Europe—and, ideally, bring communist governments to power.

These threatening actions gave considerable urgency to economic and military negotiations ongoing since 1947. Belgium, the Netherlands, and Luxemburg consummated the Benelux Customs Union in January 1948, then joined Britain and France in the so-called Brussels Pact two months later. The five nations that had been victims or near victims of Nazi aggression in 1940 largely because of insufficient cooperation with one another now agreed to social, economic, and cultural collaboration as well as collective self-defense—an attack on one was an attack on all. Meeting with U.S. officials that spring in London, the Brussels Pact nations also agreed to transform the western occupation zones of Germany into a separate state. The agreement included international controls for the new state's mining and metallurgical industry, West German participation in the Marshall Plan, and a new West German currency. British, French, and American troops would stay in Germany as long as necessary. Shocked into quicker action by the Czech coup, moreover, the U.S. Congress approved an initial five billion dollars of Marshall Plan aid in April 1948. In May, finally, the Senate accepted American entry to the Brussels Pact military alliance.

The clashes of ideology, national interest, and personality that undermined the Grand Alliance after 1945—heightening distrust, sparking disagreements, triggering successive measures and countermeasures—finally brought East and West dangerously close to the brink of war in 1948. Emboldened by their successes in Hungary and Czechoslovakia, Russian officers began to exhibit more confidence on the ACC in Berlin. "I have felt and held that war was unlikely," wrote American commander Lucius Clay in early March, but "within the last few weeks I have felt a subtle change in Soviet attitude which gives me a feeling that [war] may come with dramatic suddenness."[61] Clay's intuition proved keen, for two weeks later his eastern counterparts, aware from espionage about the allies' London discussions on West Germany, protested these secret plans for a new state, then blocked train travel to Berlin for eleven days in April. The so-called baby blockade was followed with a complete cutoff of road and rail access to East Germany in late June 1948. Coming only days after the introduction of a new currency, the "D-mark," in the western zones as well as the allied sectors of West Berlin, the blockade was a blatant bit of Stalinist brinkmanship. The Soviet dictator sought to force a continuation of four-power administration in Germany and a resumption of reparations removals from the Ruhr. "At best, he would achieve a united Germany on his own terms," writes W. R. Smyser, "at worst, he would get all of Berlin."[62] "Perhaps we can kick them out,"[63] Stalin told East German leader Walter Ulbricht. Achieving this minimal goal seemed worth the risk if it eliminated West Berlin's perceived security threat to Communist Europe. The 2.4 million people in the western sectors possessed less than two months supply of food and coal.

The British and Americans responded with risky brinkmanship of their own. Claiming that they deserved to stay in the city by right of conquest, the West attempted to supply it by air. The so-called Berlin Airlift nearly triggered war—it was only narrowly averted, in fact, by the prudence of higher-ups. Thus Clay's ACC counterpart, General Vassily Sokolovsky, wanted to answer the new D-mark with a massive show of armored force around Berlin, but Molotov scotched the idea in favor of road and rail blockage. This was still too much for Clay, who pressed Washington hard for armed transports to force open a lifeline to the city: If the Red Army resisted, it would be war. The chain-smoking general was "drawn as tight as a steel spring." Truman cautiously opted for the airlift, but braced himself for hot war if planes were downed. The gruff chief executive dispatched sixty B-29 bombers designed to carry atomic weapons to Britain, assuring his advisers that they should not doubt his resolve: If the A-bomb had to be used "he would do so." Fortunately, Truman denied the Pentagon's request that the nation's hundred or so bombs be placed at the army's disposal: He would not have "some dashing lieutenant colonel decide when would be the proper time to drop one."[64] Red Army pilots tested western nerves all summer and fall by harassing and buzzing transports, even shooting off their guns at times. The crisis gradually passed when it became obvious that even harsh winter flying weather could not prevent the West from feeding and heating Berlin. Stalin ended the blockade in May 1949.

By this time the West had taken steps to shore up its position. In April 1949 the Brussels Pact allies (Britain, France, and the Benelux states) joined Italy, Portugal, Norway, Denmark, Iceland, Canada, and the United States in the North Atlantic Treaty Organization (NATO). Designed as a deterrent to Soviet aggression, the alliance of twelve transatlantic nations would fight together if Stalin and his satellites attacked any one of the signatories. The catastrophic overrunning of isolated democracies—half of the democracies that failed from 1918 to 1940 fell because of communist or fascist aggression—would not happen again. Simultaneous with the founding of NATO the allies gave birth to the Federal Republic of Germany (FRG). In October, however, the Soviets retaliated by establishing the German Democratic Republic (GDR), thus widening the division of Germany. From the outset, therefore, the still far from sovereign German states became a potential flashpoint for conflict between the armed forces of Europe's two feuding blocs. Indeed, Russia's twenty-two divisions in the GDR squared off ominously against four Anglo-American divisions in the FRG buttressed by America's rapidly expanding arsenal of atomic bombs, which now stood at two hundred.

The nearly yearlong standoff over Berlin marked the beginning of the Cold War. Neither side wanted bloodshed after the years of destruction and death that had just ended, and yet distrust ran so deep that war became a distinct possibility. The Soviet Union, and before it tsarist Russia, had suffered the kinds of invasions predicted by Marxist-Leninist theory. Stalin, a dedicated Marxist-Leninist whose years of political struggle had seared an already troubled soul, unquestioningly assumed that the great capitalist-imperialist powers wanted to subdue him in the latest round of their fight for world domination. A chilling study by the U.S. National Security Council reflected a mindset similarly locked into the notion of struggle. Completed during the Berlin Airlift, "SCN-20" advocated the liberation of Eastern Europe, the dismantling of the Soviet military establishment, and the dissolution of the Communist Party, using peaceful means if possible—and force if necessary—to foil the Soviet design of world domination.[65] With its absence of regular diplomatic contacts, its preference for saber rattling, and its manly readiness to toe the line,[66] the Cold War heightened the chances that these hostile assumptions would trigger war. The level of anxiety ratcheted up in August 1949 when the Soviet Union successfully detonated its own A-bomb, many years before the West believed it possible. "This is now a different world,"[67] said a hawkish but humbled U.S. Senator Arthur Vandenberg.

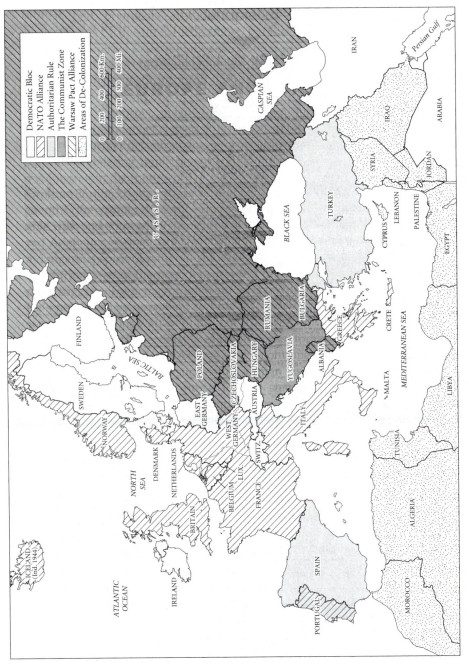

Europe during the Cold War

The deaths of sixty million people in World War Two did not advance the quest to find legal alternatives to war, for the worsening East-West feud of the late 1940s dashed initial hopes that the United Nations would significantly improve upon the League of Nations. To be sure, the UN, like the League before it, unfolded an impressive array of social, economic, and humanitarian agencies that advanced the cause of humankind. In the crucial area of war prevention or, barring that, the "policing" of aggression, however, Europe and the world took a step backward. The Security Council could not function as enforcer of the charter with the world's posse divided against itself in the Cold War. Given the backsliding of the Grand Alliance on the critical issue of rights of conquest, furthermore, the legal environment for waging war had actually improved. It seems reasonable to conclude that a Third World War, hovering like the proverbial Sword of Damocles without any institutional means to keep it from falling, would have eviscerated the UN as quickly as the sharp edge of the Second World War had cut short the life of the League. As explained later, the existence of the United Nations contributed only a little to the fortunate circumstance of the Sword not falling.

COMMUNISM IS EAST

As the Red Army battered and bludgeoned the Wehrmacht in 1943–1944, Soviet power returned to Finland, the Baltic, Byelorussia, the Ukraine, and Moldavia. Stalin's minions subsequently drove through Poland and Eastern Germany and far into Central Europe and the Balkans.[68] Communist parties beholden to Moscow essentially ignored the Yalta agreement as they established hegemonies in Bulgaria and Yugoslavia (1945), Rumania (1946), Poland and Hungary (1947), and Czechoslovakia (1948). The cold reality of Soviet domination in Eastern Europe would last another forty years.

Developments in Eastern Europe

In the first postwar decade Moscow systematically exploited its new European empire to support the gargantuan rebuilding effort underway at home. Thus the Soviet German zone and defeated axis satellites Finland, Hungary, and Rumania made hefty reparations payments to the USSR. Although these transfers covered barely a tenth of Soviet war damage, Moscow also took a portion of current production from these and other countries it dominated in Eastern Europe—even though some, like Poland, had also fallen victim to Nazism, and others, like Bulgaria, had not participated in Barbarossa.[69] Reparations, siphoned-off production, expropriated Nazi assets from Finland to Rumania, and other "unallocated external receipts" from Eastern Europe amounted to 17.6 percent of the final industrial product of the Soviet Union in 1946 and 10.7 percent in 1947—only sinking below 1 percent in 1953.[70] As the Cold War worsened, moreover, Moscow forced the economies of the region into rigid conformity with Soviet planning imperatives. Emphasis on the rapid growth of raw materials and heavy industry—to the detriment of agriculture, consumer goods, housing, wages, and embryonic educational and heath care reforms—meant little or no improvement to already low standards of living. Ideological correctness in the face of perceived Marshall Plan conspiracies to spread capitalism eastward also necessitated the nationalization of factories and collectivization of farms. Native communist leaders, many of whom had fought in the anti-Nazi resistance for national freedom, balked or protested against infringement of their nations' rights to develop flexibly and independently. Many were forced to confess their crimes "darkness at noon" style, and then executed—two thousand in Hungary alone, with hundreds more in Czechoslovakia and Bulgaria. Soviet forces imprisoned additional hundreds of thousands of communists from 1948 to 1952, and expelled over two million people, a quarter of the rank and file in Eastern Europe, from native communist parties. Their more suppliant replacements held correct views about the incorrectness of separate national roads to communism.

Moscow drew prudent limits, however, to what it forced on Eastern Europe. For instance, while Muslim and Orthodox Christian clerics throughout the Balkans put up little resistance to the stark secularism and atheism of the communists, Pope Pius XII refused to recognize the expropriation of church lands, the termination of Catholic education, the dissolution of youth and other organizations, and the imprisonment of bishops. This defiance resonated with the Catholic faithful of Poland, Czechoslovakia, Hungary, and the Croatian portion of Yugoslavia, whose stubbornness convinced these regimes to make many compromises. The hierarchy exacted the most concessions in Poland, managing to preserve an essentially autonomous position there. In a similar—and seemingly closely related—development, it proved impossible to push through collectivization programs according to plan. Launched on a grandiose scale in 1949, they featured Soviet-style disincentives for noncompliance, like higher taxes; the withholding of loans, farm equipment, fertilizer, and seeds; and, frequently, the use of force. Peasant resistance remained so fierce into the 1950s, however, that private farms still comprised 25 percent of the land in Czechoslovakia, 50 percent in Rumania, 67 percent in Hungary, and 75 percent in Poland and Yugoslavia. Only in Bulgaria did collectivization affect nearly all land. These examples demonstrate the underlying instability of the communist East Bloc and Moscow's felt need to avoid unnecessary troubles and the attendant expenditure of military capital.

This phenomenon was more pronounced on the northern and southern fringes of Soviet power. Thus Finland, after suing for peace, had to swallow a treaty with the USSR in early 1945 that reduced the Finnish Army and assigned Moscow responsibility for defense of the land. The Red Army officers that dominated the Allied Control Council took up residence in Helsinki's posh Hotel Torni—whose American-look, art deco interior provided an ironic backdrop to its new residents' mission—and then began meddling in politics. Although the communists received only 25 percent of the vote, one of theirs, Mauno Pekkala, eventually became prime minister with colleagues occupying a third of the cabinet, including the crucial Ministry of the Interior. In 1948, however, the feisty Finnish legislature ousted the interior minister after a no-confidence vote, and later that year when the communist vote declined,

Pekkala also had to resign. Although it kept open the option of a coup, the Kremlin did nothing, desiring no repetition of the bloody Winter War of 1939–1940. "We did the right thing," said Molotov. "It would have been an open wound."[71]

The Soviets demonstrated similar caution in Greece. Throughout the winter of 1944–1945 communist insurgents in the National Liberation Front, the most significant resistance army during three years of Nazi occupation, refused to abandon their weapons. Later in 1946, calling themselves the Democratic Army of Greece (ELAS), the rebels attempted to seize power using bases in Yugoslavia and Bulgaria. Washington poured military aid into the small nation after the British announced their withdrawal in 1947, but communist fortunes continued to rise into early 1948. Implored by ELAS and Bulgarian leader Georgi Dimitrov as well as Tito to intervene, Stalin drew in his claws. "Do you believe in the victory of the Greek rebellion?" he asked one of the Yugoslav emissaries.

> No. They have not the slightest chance of winning. Do you really imagine that Britain and the United States—the strongest countries in the world—that they will tolerate any disruption to their communications artery in the Mediterranean! What rubbish. And we don't even have a fleet. No—the rebellion in Greece must be crushed and the sooner, the better.[72]

Stalin had said no. Zhdanov echoed his boss, rebuking the Yugoslavs for failing to appreciate that the Soviet Union "cannot and should not waste its strength, crucial for bigger battles."[73] ELAS was eventually crushed.

In a bitterly surprising lesson, the Soviets would also learn about the limits of their power in Yugoslavia. Indeed, Stalin had been tempted to help ELAS, even after the announcement of American aid in March 1947: It might have been just the kind of knife twisting in the enemy sphere that he relished. After Tito and Dimitrov began floating plans for some form of Balkan union that summer, however, the Soviet dictator held fast to non-intervention, for with the United States trying to make capitalist inroads into the East with dollars (Marshall Plan) and guns (Truman Doctrine), any kind of Balkan grouping independent of Moscow would make such encroachment that much easier. Dimitrov heightened Stalin's fears by declaring in January 1948 that his confederation would include all of Eastern Europe from Poland to Greece. "It is they who will decide what it shall be . . . and when and how it will be formed."[74] Now Stalin cracked down, forcing Dimitrov to recant and insisting that Tito follow suit. When the Yugoslav refused—the Red Army had entered Sofia in 1944, but not Belgrade—Stalin imposed an economic boycott on Yugoslavia, accused Tito of Marxist heresy, and expelled the Yugoslav Communist Party from the Communist Information Bureau (Cominform), an organization of European communist parties formed the previous autumn to coordinate a struggle against the Marshall Plan. "I will shake my little finger and there will be no more Tito—he will fall."[75] However, backed by hundreds of thousands of veteran resistance fighters, and soon supported by Washington, whose aid eventually reached two billion dollars, Tito did not fall. Stalin fumed, but opted for discretion over military valor. Rather, he unleashed a witch-hunt for "Titoists" and "nationalist deviationists" throughout the East Bloc. The resort to these brutal purges (see earlier) underscored the shaky state of relations behind the Iron Curtain.

Political Life in the USSR

The Red Army soldiers who marched back from Berlin in 1945 had some reason to believe that political circumstances at home would be freer, for Stalin had loosened his grip on society somewhat in order to unleash those popular forces needed to defeat Nazism. As early as 1944, however, the familiar mechanisms of brutal police power began to reappear as the Kremlin cracked down on all forms and signs of resistance. "At first, when they got back, they would bang on the tables with their fists and demand that the administration got things done," remembered the son of one veteran. "But gradually even they were brought into line," he continued, leaving little recourse but homemade vodka and wallowing in self-pity. Another survivor of the Great Patriotic War remembered the pain of realizing that "because we were exhausted, because of the strain of the postwar years, we were not going to be able to maintain the high level of moral development which we had achieved during the war, and which we had created for ourselves, in spite of the soullessness and obstructiveness of our own immoral and criminal leadership."[76]

One consolation for men frustrated by their emasculation before Stalin was their continued domination of the other sex. Indeed, as women cheered returning men's resounding victory over Fascism, life began its struggle to fit back into accustomed gender patterns. Wherever possible the man reclaimed his old job, for instance, a trend particularly evident at the managerial level. Thus the proportion of women serving as directors of collective farms and state industries, which had risen from 2.6 to 14.2 percent from 1940 to 1943, slipped back to 2 percent after the war. It was quite impossible, however, to thoroughly reconstruct gender hierarchies on the job, for the century's shedding of male blood had left twenty million more women than men by 1950. Women's overall share of the labor force remained well above prewar levels at 47 percent. Single women headed around 30 percent of Soviet households, working by necessity, not choice. It would be incorrect to assume that this situation created some sort of a matriarchy, on the other hand, despite the domineering personalities of many of these working women. Simply put, male scarcity meant that "boys were coddled and men honored."[77] It remained a man's world in the USSR—except for the fact that Stalin suppressed everyone, men as well as women.

Historians agree that Iosif Vissarionovich, Comrade Stalin, the man of steel, having imposed order on Eastern Europe and the USSR by 1952, readied another massive purge. In the night of March 1–2, 1953, however, he died under suspicious circumstances, perhaps suffering a stroke.[78] Life slowly ebbed from the body of the man who had taken it from nearly nineteen million of his hapless subjects during a quarter of a century's reign. When Stalin's Kremlin cronies finally released news of his death four days later, the collective reaction of the shocked nation was as complex and mixed as we would expect. Some who harbored no illusions about the meaning of Stalinism, like secret police chief Lavrenty Beria, secured incriminating documents and began the deadly game of maneuvering for power. Few of the over five million inhabitants of the GULAG shed any tears for Stalin either. Thus one woman inmate of the labor camps recalls the cold day when the announcement was made:

> Suddenly some officers appeared and spoke to our guards and told them that father Stalin was dead, which meant such pain, such sorrow, such a loss—all those stupid adjectives. And we stood there and shouted 'Hurrah!' We started to sing, too, we sang lots of songs.[79]

Others close to the brutality of Stalinism reacted in a more confused way. Thus his eventual successor, Nikita Khrushchev, one of the few Old Bolsheviks to survive the purges, "had never forgotten the promise of the Russian Revolution: a decent life for all who did not have it, peace for people tired of war."[80] But, like so many who rose to the top over the bodies of innocent executed comrades, he admitted that he had allowed himself to suppress the revolution's promise and be "infected" by the tyrant. Now he felt ashamed, but also "cheated."[81] These mixed feelings of guilt and anger descended deeply into Soviet society, shared by all who knew that violence against Kulaks, party members, and others had been wrong, but did nothing, or worse, made denunciations of their own. However, for the many millions of Soviet citizens who had been neither perpetrators nor victims in any direct sense, who naively believed that those arrested had been guilty, and that father Stalin had led them to industrial power and military victory, grief and fear were the only emotions felt in March 1953. "Anyone who says they did not cry is lying," one woman insisted to historian Catherine Merridale. "We did not know what was going to happen next—we had never known anything different."[82]

Much the same held true for the successor leadership in the Kremlin. To be sure, they realized that the horrendous abuses of the past had to stop and therefore terminated purge plans and promised all citizens the protection of "Soviet socialist legality." One of Stalin's favorites, Georgi Malenkov, the new premier and chairman of the Council of Ministers, also announced bold plans to expand consumer production. An article that passed the censors in May 1953, moreover, cautiously criticized the sterility of culture under Stalin. But the labor camps remained teeming with millions of mistreated people. When successive GULAG revolts broke out, Moscow answered with the characteristic mailed fist, as it did when violent protests of East German workers against harsh working conditions proved too difficult for East Berlin to contain. And soon enough politics, too, assumed familiar Stalinist patterns. After Beria made suspicious moves in an apparent bid to seize power, Malenkov, Foreign Minister Molotov, Party First Secretary Khrushchev, and Defense Minister Nikolai Bulganin nipped the coup in the bud. They arrested the surprised police chief in June 1953 and executed him after a quick trial in December. With so much blood on Beria's hands, no one could claim that his shooting blatantly violated "Soviet socialist legality." But it did seem very much like business as usual in the Kremlin.

The challenge to residual Stalinism would have to come from a different direction—from the world of culture, whose openness and frankness authoritarian regimes will sometimes tolerate, especially if change is under discussion, or authority breaking down. In November 1953 an article by composer Aram Khachaturian lambasted censors whose constant interference had nearly killed musical culture. "Problems of composition cannot be solved bureaucratically," he wrote. "Let the individual artist be trusted more fully, and not be constantly supervised and suspected."[83] Ilya Ehrenburg stressed the same theme in his novella *The Thaw* (1954), which would give the immediate post-Stalin era its name. By comparing a painter of official "socialist realist" works unfavorably with an innovative and unorthodox artist who must work in secrecy and obscurity, the short tract expressed opposition to a frightening and tyrannical atmosphere that threatened to suffocate creativity and individual human dignity. Vladimir Dudintsev's novel *Not By Bread Alone* (1956) steered through the same narrows of an at least temporarily acceptable criticism: In this case it is an inventor whose creativity is stifled by the heavy hand of the state. All of these works, and many more that appeared in the mid-1950s, met with the determined opposition of conservatives who believed that culture had to remain within the rigid ideological limits set by the late Andrei Zhdanov lest the floodgates of political change be flung open. Indeed, everyone realized that much more than art was at stake: When liberals insisted on artists being "trusted more fully," and conservatives opposed it, each side wanted to achieve this, writ large, for society.

Khrushchev cautiously threw in his lot with the liberals. In what amounted to a political gamble, he denounced the crimes of Stalin at a closed meeting of the Twentieth Congress of the Communist Party in February 1956. The First Secretary charged the former dictator with murdering fellow communists in 1936–1938, nearly losing the war with his incompetence in 1941, and riding roughshod over the legitimate rights of East European communists after 1945. The USSR had to reject Stalinism and its cult of personality, return to the path of intraparty democracy allegedly championed by Lenin, allow for national variations of communism in Eastern Europe, and attempt to live in peaceful coexistence with the West.

Khrushchev's bold, four-hour speech represented the culmination of his own personal struggle with tormenting Stalinist demons from which he now tried to wrestle free. He believed that the country's leadership elite had to make the same liberating effort, if nothing else out of simple pragmatism. "If we don't tell the truth at the Congress, we'll be forced to tell the truth some time in the future," he warned colleagues on the Presidium (Politburo). "And then we shan't be the speech-makers; no, then we'll be the people under investigation."[84] Behind the admonition, however, lay a shrewd calculation that without dirtying himself he could tar Malenkov, Molotov, and other rivals like

Stalin's old henchman Lazar Kagonovich with the brush of the tyrant's crimes, thus weakening them politically in the eyes of party members favoring a full-fledged "thaw." Malenkov and Molotov had slipped in power the previous year, but remained on the Presidium.[85] When his opponents hesitated to approve the speech, Khrushchev cleverly outmaneuvered them: "I'll tell [the Congress] who on the Presidium is for and who against—let the delegates decide, whatever they vote for, that's what we'll do."[86] Shying away from this clearly worse alternative, they let him proceed, only to turn red when he singled some of them out in taunting impromptu asides: "Cut out the lying. . . . Can't you find the courage and conscience to tell the truth about what you saw with your own eyes?"[87]

Khrushchev also hoped to influence the international community, hence his haste in distributing copies of the allegedly "secret" speech to foreign communists present in Moscow—and, through his secret service, the KGB, to the American Central Intelligence Agency (CIA). Would such an unmistakably clear departure from the violent and manipulative past quell the restive mood of the East Bloc? Could serious signs of change in the USSR lure Yugoslavia back into this fold? Khrushchev and Bulganin had made a trek to Belgrade in 1955, but Tito maintained cordial neutrality, refusing, for instance, to join the new Warsaw Pact military alliance between Russia and its satellites, Moscow's answer to NATO.

Indeed, relations with the West needed improvement from Khrushchev's point of view. Washington had won over France to West German rearmament in 1954 provided that the newly forming German divisions possessed no weapons of mass destruction, entered NATO, and remained exclusively under its largely American command. One has to appreciate the alarm that a re-militarized Germany triggered in top circles of the Soviet Union, invaded just thirteen years earlier by Germany. Khrushchev seized the initiative from his colleagues in early 1955, negotiating a neutrality agreement with occupied Austria to which the West acceded in May. Each side withdrew its troops and the once-powerful country joined Switzerland and Sweden in a neutral buffer zone in the center of Cold War Europe. Khrushchev appears to have pushed this arrangement in Vienna as a prelude to a similar neutralization of a reunited Germany. The new man in Moscow moved closer to the goal in September 1955 by establishing diplomatic relations with West Germany. There was no immediate response, however, from Washington. Would news of Khrushchev's speech lead to more summit meetings, an end to the Cold War, and peaceful coexistence at long last? To demonstrate his seriousness, Khrushchev began to empty the labor camps, permitted a further cultural thaw, and initiated a program of cultural exchange with the West.

The "secret speech" accomplished few of its goals. The United States remained too conscious of its vast military superiority to wax conciliatory. Tito stayed aloof, furthermore, because he simply had too much to gain by playing East and West off against each other. And far from calming the East Europeans, the message from Moscow incited them, for it seemed to condone opposition to native leaders who had purged "nationalist" communists after

1948. Labor riots in Poland in June 1956 undermined the old guard Stalinists, for example, advancing former resistance leader Wladislaw Gomulka to power by late October. Caught by surprise, Khrushchev flew to Warsaw and threatened armed intervention, but ordered the tanks to retreat after it became clear that he had not intimidated the Pole, and, more importantly, that Gomulka's colors were indelibly communist.

Events in Hungary took a more tragic course. On October 23, 1956, police fired upon demonstrators who had taken heart from Polish developments to call for their government's resignation. The protests now became so violent and revolutionary that the Stalinists fled, leaving the premiership in the hands of a reform-minded communist, Imre Nagy. The new leader produced a state of near euphoria among his countrymen by convincing the Soviets to pull Red Army troops out of the capital. Nagy soon proved too democratic for his own good, however, by releasing imprisoned Cardinal Mindszenty, agreeing to hold free multiparty elections, and announcing Hungary's exodus from the Warsaw Pact. Predicting rightly that Nagy could not preserve communist rule, Khrushchev sent the tanks rumbling back into Budapest on November 4. That afternoon a Hungarian radio message pleaded to "the civilized people of the world" for assistance.

> Listen and come to our aid, not with declarations but with force, with soldiers, with arms! Do not forget that there is no stopping the wild onslaught of Bolshevism. . . . Light is failing. The shadows grow darker every hour over the soil of Hungary. Listen to our cry. . . . SOS! SOS![88]

The West watched in horror but did not act, however, lest aid to the Hungarian people set off nuclear war. Such was the unpleasant reality in a Cold War that could heat up at any moment. Nagy fled to Belgrade but Tito extradited him to Hungary, where he was later executed.

Khrushchev's embarrassing debacle in Hungary nearly ended his career. Presidium enemies Malenkov, Molotov, and Kaganovich bided their time, and then moved in June 1957, charging the first secretary, among other things, with "a tendency to commit impulsive and ill-planned acts"—which was a very apt description of the man—and removing him by a seven-to-four vote. Khrushchev wisely insisted on a vote of the Central Committee, where the ranks of his supporters had multiplied since the secret speech. With their Central Committee enemies pounding on the locked Presidium door, the troika consented to a new debate—and was overwhelmed in a cacophony of heckling and hooting. In attempting to defend himself Central Committee members interrupted Kaganovich 112 times, Malenkov 117 times, and Molotov 244 times: "Horrors. . . . Executioners. . . . Lies. . . . Don't try to blame it all on the deceased [Stalin]. . . . Shame!" The assembly turned the tables on the three accused, removing them from office lest the apparent alternative—restoration of "the old Stalinist order of things"[89]—threaten everyone's lives. Kaganovich had fed fuel to the fire when he sobbed pathetically: "I loved Stalin and there was something to love, he was a great Marxist." The outcome left Khrushchev the most powerful man in Russia. He owed much of this to the lone success of the secret speech.

Once ensconced in power, Khrushchev avoided the terror methods of his frightening predecessor, demoting his opponents to humiliating minor posts, but not liquidating them. Shocked by the slippery slope experience with reform in Hungary, however, Khrushchev reassessed his commitment to ideological openness and permissiveness at home. The capricious party leader stunned writers at his dacha by blurting out that they were quite expendable. There would have been no revolt in Hungary if only the trouble-making intellectuals had been shot. "My hand will not tremble,"[90] he declared, if bloodshed is required. Thus for a time the thaw ended.

When cultural policy warmed up again somewhat in 1958, Russia enjoyed a flowering of art, literature, poetry, and film not unlike the early 1920s, but certain taboos existed. Boris Pasternak learned this when the authorities refused to publish his great novel, *Dr. Zhivago*, the story of a man who fails at practical things, excelling only as a closet poet. Pasternak's emphasis on human spirituality as the rejuvenating force of life and society undercut the state's paeans to the party and its essentially materialistic goals, and was thus unpublishable. Vasily Grossman's *Life and Fate* ran up against similar obstacles in 1960, for his type of existentialism placed human kindness above the party and communism. De-Stalinization had its clearly demarcated limits, which, as Hungary had also shown, did not include undermining the monopoly position of the Communist Party.

DEMOCRACY IS WEST

The Second World War salvaged rule by the people. Only a few of Europe's representative democracies had survived the rise of the Bolsheviks, the political attrition of the 1920s, the Great Depression of the 1930s, and Nazi and Soviet aggression: Britain, Iceland, the Irish states, Switzerland, Sweden, and Finland were the only frees states left standing in 1940. By V-E Day, however, France, the Benelux states, Denmark, and Norway had been liberated, while Italy, Austria, and West Germany began the process of restoring representative institutions. Democracy—albeit chaotic and unstable—also returned to Greece. The breakthrough to women's suffrage in Belgium, France, Italy, Greece, and parts of Switzerland added a qualitative dimension to these improvements in democratic fortunes, although significant legal and societal barriers still barred the way to genuine gender equality. After the Iron Curtain descended, an arc of seventeen democratic states—most of them united by interlocking cultural heritages and many of them allied in NATO—flanked the Communist Bloc. In the course of the 1950s the democratic core of continental Europe drew even closer together economically and politically by taking the first steps toward today's European Union. The passing of West European imperialism added further credence to the term "Democratic Europe," for decolonization not only terminated the empires but also the political double standard of democracies having them in the first place.

The End of Empire

While the Soviet Union shored up its East European empire, most of the imperial nations of Western Europe were forced to abandon their colonies.[91] Native resistance to European rule began in the late 1800s, gaining intensity after the Russo-Japanese War and World War One, but for all their efforts, anti-imperialists had gained very little ground by 1939. Only the British showed reluctance to fight for every position, withdrawing or conceding autonomy in many areas of the Middle East and Asia. World War Two, however, greatly accelerated the end of the West European imperial era. The Nazi occupation or weakening of Holland, France, and Britain, rulers of Indonesia, Indochina, India, and other Asian colonies, followed by Japan's conquest of much of this area, precluded any turning back of the imperial clock. Seizing the initiative after the defeat of Japan, independence leaders throughout Asia sensed correctly that Europe was now too strapped financially and weak militarily to reestablish itself—and their revolts impressed freedom fighters in the Middle East and Africa.

Britain freed its "jewel" of a subcontinent in 1947 and 1948, giving rise to the independent nations of India, Pakistan, Ceylon (Sri Lanka), and Burma (Myanmar), all but the latter joining the Commonwealth. In Malaysia British administrators defeated communist insurgents before pulling out. By the 1950s Singapore and Hong Kong were all that remained of Britain's Asian holdings.[92] Dutch rulers returning to Indonesia from Japanese-imposed exile first tried to negotiate with nationalist rebels, then reverted to force when talks broke down. Lacking adequate strength for the task, the Dutch had to leave Indonesia in 1949.[93] France freed the Laotian and Cambodian provinces of Indochina that same year, but fought to retain Vietnam. The effort was complicated by the simultaneous rise of Communist China, which backed the three-year-old liberation struggle of Vietnamese leader Ho Chi Minh. A war that cost France 206,000 dead or wounded and 8.5 billion dollars—triple France's Marshall Plan receipts—ended with the defeat of French forces at the stronghold of Dien Bien Phu in 1954. Only 3,000 of the fort's 20,000 defenders returned to France—the worst setback for European arms in the history of colonialism. The sun had set on Europe's Asian empires.

A similar pattern unfolded in the Middle East and North Africa. The French had promised before the war to liberate Syria and Lebanon. With some prodding from Britain and the United States, a reluctant Paris honored these pledges in 1946. Simultaneously the British granted independence to Jordan. Two years later, hard-pressed by conflicting Arab and Jewish demands in Palestine, London asked the United Nations to resolve the dilemma, and then withdrew. This incremental ending of empire continued in 1951 with Great Britain's freeing of Libya, which it had occupied since 1943. The French followed suit in 1956 by liberating Tunisia and Morocco. In 1956 Britain also freed the Sudan and faithfully carried out an earlier promise to evacuate Suez.

Now the charismatic military ruler of Egypt, Gamal Abdel Nasser, precipitated a crisis by wresting control of the Suez Canal from its European stockholders. The nationalization of this important waterway in September 1956 prompted an Anglo-French parachute assault on the canal, timed to coincide with an Israeli offensive in the Sinai Peninsula later that autumn. For Britain and France the Suez expedition was a matter of protecting business interests and soothing offended imperial egos. But more was involved: France wanted to undercut Nasser's moral and material support for Algerian rebels whose insurrection had escalated for two years, and both Paris and London hoped the attack would topple the feisty Nasser. The attack proceeded well enough militarily, but not politically, for the young United Nations roundly condemned the action. The United States found Suez particularly galling, coming at a time when it led the UN's verbal assault against the Soviet invasion of Hungary. Therefore Washington pressured London and Paris to terminate a similarly aggressive—and embarrassing—invasion in Egypt. The expeditionary force was rather ignominiously withdrawn in late December, replaced by the first UN peacekeeping mission. This jolting defeat of eleventh-hour European imperialism further emboldened rebels in Algeria. Although French imperialists and die-hard soldiers vowed never to desert Algeria's million French settlers, not even 350,000 French troops and a brutal regime of counterterrorism sufficed to suppress the independence movement. President Charles de Gaulle finally proclaimed Algerian independence in 1962.

Nationalists in Sub-Saharan Africa watched with growing interest and encouragement as the countries of Asia, the Middle East, and North Africa won their freedom from European rule. The British freeing of Ghana in 1957 also encouraged them. Therefore, after Britain finally suppressed the Mau-Mau rebels of Kenya in 1957, but then opened negotiations that would lead to Kenyan independence, the floodgates of African independence opened wide. No longer willing to bear the high financial and human costs of empire, London, Paris, and Brussels, ruler of the Congo (Zaire), performed midwifery at the birth of twenty-four African states between 1958 and 1963.[94] In the short span of eighteen years since the end of World War Two, West Europe had lost the vast majority of its colonies, and forty-four new states had come into the world. The change was most apparent in the United Nations Assembly in New York City, where representatives from thirty-seven of these new creations had taken seats by 1963.

Democratic Europe would earn handsome long-term returns on its largely forced end to colonialism. Although Britain, France, Holland, and Belgium certainly incurred short-term costs as their economies were dislocated from overseas holdings and specific companies and stock-holders had to write off investments, mother countries gained in the long-term by cutting off the drain of expensive military expeditions and the incalculable losses of human capital. Hundreds of thousands of soldiers deployed abroad, as well as large numbers of returning settlers and former administrators, could now contribute their considerable talents and skills domestically. The political gains, however, undoubtedly exceeded the material benefits. As western imperial states had grown increasingly democratic after the late 1800s, the contradiction of granting more rights at home while suppressing allegedly inferior peoples abroad became more glaringly transparent—and politically awkward, as anti-imperialists mocked the double standard. By leaving the imperial past behind, Western Europe could ascend the moral and political high ground, especially when it began to pour foreign aid money into former colonies—and also to open immigration doors to former colonial subjects whose labor was needed as Europe rebuilt. They began their treks in the 1950s and 1960s in search of work and a better existence: from India, Pakistan, and the Caribbean to Britain; from Indonesia and Surinam to Holland; from North Africa and the Sub-Sahara to Spain, France, Italy, and Germany. West Berlin and other German cities also attracted large numbers from Turkey.

Portugal offered a striking and fitting study in contrasts. It alone among the former colonial powers retained significant holdings, including the largest, Angola and Mozambique in Africa. One of two Iberian dictatorships surviving from the Interwar Period, undemocratic Portugal, this authoritarian carry-over and imperial throwback, possessed, not coincidentally, the lowest standard of living in Europe.

European Integration

Speaking at Zurich, Switzerland, in September 1946, the indefatigable Winston Churchill gave tremendous impetus to European integration by advocating "a kind of United States of Europe" led by France and Germany and befriended by London and Washington. "The fighting has stopped: but the dangers have not stopped. . . . Therefore I say to you: let Europe arise!"[95] It is significant that Churchill did not stand alone with these sentiments—not after the Second World War had nearly terminated European democracy and illuminated the unacceptable costs of continued divisiveness. A subsequent survey of four thousand West European parliamentarians found 64 percent support for Churchill's idea in Italy, 53 percent in Holland, 50 percent in France, Switzerland, and Belgium, 26 percent in Britain, with dwindling 12 percent backing in Denmark and Scandinavia.[96]

Veterans of the anti-Nazi resistance also converged around the cause of uniting Europe. Should it not be possible to gather under the banner of liberty and personal freedom, asked enthusiasts like former Italian partisan Altiero Spinelli, what the Nazis had forced together by evil force? Spearheaded by Spinelli and fellow fighters from Italy and France, the "Union of European Federalists" began agitation in Paris that December, focusing on the goal of unifying democratic Europe. By August 1947 the organization boasted one hundred thousand members in thirty-two associations. Further momentum resulted from a joint meeting of Churchill's "United Europe Movement" and the fellow-traveling "French Council for a United Europe" at Paris in July 1947, and the coalescing of like-minded parliamentarians in the "European Parliamentary Union" two months later.

The simultaneous outbreak of the Cold War gave increased priority to purely military means of security, and in so doing, nearly completely undermined this promising movement for political federation in Western Europe. In May 1948 the various organizations that had been coalescing politically since 1946–1947 sent representatives to The Hague. Under the august chairmanship of Winston

Churchill, over seven hundred members of West European parliaments as well as former and current premiers and foreign ministers, including an especially strong contingent from France, Belgium, and Italy, formulated proposals for the new Europe. There would be a customs union, a European court of human rights, human rights conventions, and, significantly, a partial transfer of member states' sovereignty to a supranational deliberative assembly. As the organizers sought to implement their decisions during the upcoming year, however, they discovered that the political ground had already eroded beneath them, for the national interests of Britain—and eventually France—dictated conflicting policies.

Although he initially favored West European union, British Foreign Minister Ernest Bevin lost enthusiasm in the course of 1948. The State Department in Washington had given strong backing to federalist plans, and London supported America's Europeanist agenda as long as such schemes offered the best guarantee of military solidarity against the Soviet Union. After the Brussels Pact, and later NATO, accommodated national security considerations, however, European unification of any sort, even a customs union, seemed less important. A Board of Trade report warning of the dangers of American and German competition in a Europe of the "open door" also influenced Bevin. The pull of empire and protection guaranteed by imperial tariff preferences proved stronger than the tug of Bretton Woods and a still eager State Department. The Foreign Office made its policy public in January 1949.

French policy initially backed the federalist movement emanating from The Hague. The notion of European unity attracted about half of the Chamber of Deputies in 1946–1947, including most of the Christian Democrats (MRP), the largest party in the ruling coalition. Supporters believed, however, that European formulas necessarily had to include harsh solutions to the "German Question." Although passing a strong resolution in favor of European federalism in March 1947, for instance, the MRP instructed its ministers to ensure that "Germany is made incapable of harmful action."[97] Of the four occupying powers, in fact, France, not at Yalta and Potsdam to be consulted, objected most strenuously to Big Three plans to administer Germany as an economic and political unit. "We love Germany so much," the old joke went round, "we want more than one of them." Consistent with these views, France opposed the creation of "Bizonia" in 1947 and could only be moved to accept a separate West Germany at London in 1948 by America's threat to withhold Marshall Plan funds. Four German zones each going their own way was superior, in other words, to three zones—but even that was better than two German states. In another display of this Draconian mindset, Jean Monnet, head of the country's technological modernization program, proposed that France gain control of German coal mines to enable French industry to displace German competition—and prevent any resuscitation of German armaments potential. Increasingly eager to build up Germany in the face of Soviet threats, Britain and the United States refused this demand at London. They sought to placate France by offering international control of Ruhr coal and steel, but the arrangement did little to constrain German production, which Paris wanted to cap. By the summer of 1948, therefore, the idea of a supranational West European union including the Federal Republic grew even more attractive to Paris: not only as a means to satisfy the wishes of many ruling coalition politicians for a new kind of Europe, but also to hamstring the ominous Anglo-American creation across the Rhine.

London and Paris took opposing stances to the Hague resolutions during the fall and winter of 1948–1949. Increasingly drawn to empire, Commonwealth, and eventually NATO, Britain refused to sacrifice an iota of sovereignty to a European parliament. "We must avoid creating a kind of chamber of echoes where cranks could make their voices heard,"[98] said Bevin, cutting typically to the quick. Paris, by contrast, wanted the European federation "to exercise certain parliamentary functions in order to make it a credible political framework into which West Germany could be inserted—and held."[99]

Not wanting to drive off the British and their Scandinavian sympathizers, leaving only a rump Europe of western continental countries, French Foreign Minister Robert Schuman met Bevin much more than halfway, proposing that the new "Council of Europe" have a bicameral legislature. Its Parliamentary Assembly, consisting of deputies appointed by member states, could do no more than consult the Committee of Ministers, consisting of member states' foreign ministers. The decisions of the ministers' group, however, could not even bind home governments. In accepting this, Bevin clamped the lid on supranationalism and a "Pandora's box full of Trojan horses."[100] The Council of Europe came to life with ten members in May 1949.[101] Efforts by disappointed federalists to revise the charter during the Council's first session at Strasbourg in November failed.

At this point the roles of two key international players helped determine the integrationist course that Europe would take. The first, West German Chancellor Konrad Adenauer, had taken office in Bonn just as the Council of Europe drew its first breath. The Christian Democrat leader believed firmly that his state should seek security and bolster democracy in cooperation with the western democracies, but ongoing allied reparations and other limitations on German sovereignty made political difficulties for him at home. Rumors swirled in the press, for instance, that ex-Wehrmacht commanders plotted to seize power, and in parliament one deputy suggested that the Holocaust had not really happened. Such anti-democratic and anti-Semitic sentiments not only threatened Adenauer's effort to rebuild a democratic German state, but, aimed as they were against the allies, also undermined his western orientation. Without a clear sign from the West that Bonn had some kind of parity, his policy had no political chance. Worried about these developments in the autumn of 1949, the second player, American Secretary of State Dean Acheson, made a personal appeal to his French counterpart Schuman. It was high time for Paris to take the lead in developing "a Western European community in which the Germans can assume an appropriate position as a reasonable and peaceful nation." The lesson of the ill-fated Weimar Republic taught that "we must give genuine and rapid support to those elements now in control of Germany if they are to be expected to retain control."[102]

Schuman and Monnet wanted peace as much as anyone. As someone who had grown up in German Alsace before 1918, Schuman in particular genuinely longed for friendship between his two homelands. Both men reacted with understandable alarm to reports in early 1950, however, that Britain and the United States wanted to strengthen NATO by including a rearmed West Germany. In May, therefore, with Britain backing away from Europe, Washington continuing to press for unification, West Germany responding quickly—and in French eyes, threateningly—to Marshall Plan stimulus, and NATO considering placing weapons back into German hands, the two Frenchmen turned their ship into the prevailing political and economic winds. Their tack was to announce a "European Coal and Steel Community" (ECSC) uniting the mining and metallurgical resources of France, West Germany, Italy, and the Benelux states. The proposed ECSC would guarantee the supply of iron ore, coal, coke, scrap metal, and steel to members on identical terms (i.e., equal prices and transport charges). It created internal customs-free trade in these commodities and a common external tariff. An executive "High Authority" based in Luxembourg would enforce the treaty, initially without interference from national governments. It also managed an investment fund for technological modernization. A Court of Justice settled disputes between member states and the High Authority, and a Common Assembly, either elected or appointed by member states, monitored the High Authority, whose members could be dismissed by a two-thirds majority of the Assembly. Because membership brought parity and a considerably improved international status, Adenauer accepted the deal.

After ratification by member states, the new supranational body began operations in August 1952—with only one modification: A Council of Ministers appointed by member states and functioning as kind of a nationalist legislative check now limited the power of the High Authority to make binding decisions in certain areas of weighty national interest like production levels. With military protection provided by NATO, economic security by the ECSC, Washington cleverly appeased, and the German Question seemingly solved, passions for more extensive European federalism now cooled in Paris.[103]

Thus the Cold War had interrupted the dream of a United States of Europe cherished by resistance fighters as well as a wide array of political organizations and prominent politicians. The next-war phobias of the late 1940s limited the ideal of a European union to the non-communist states outside of the Soviet bloc, and then, after Britain's emasculation of the Council of Europe, to the "Little Europe" of France, West Germany, Italy, and the Benelux states. The significance of what "the Six" accomplished with the creation of Robert Schuman's coal and steel community, however, cannot be underestimated, for the ECSC, a supranational seedling, would spread its spores and grow over fifty years into a proud European forest.

Almost from the beginning the Six planned further integrative steps.[104] With the ECSC beginning to function smoothly and contributing at least marginally to the decade's full-throttled economic expansion (see later), leaders of member nations met at Messina, Italy, in 1955 to discuss additional areas of economic cooperation. West European solidarity grew more urgent during the following year's Suez Crisis, for the debacle interrupted the flow of oil from the region to Europe and highlighted the divergent political interests of Western Europe and the United States. At Rome in 1957, therefore, the Six signed two important treaties. One created the European Atomic Energy Community (Euratom) in order to pool resources for a more rapid development of peaceful nuclear power. The second established the European Economic Community (EEC), commonly known as the "Common Market," to gradually eliminate internal tariffs *on all commodities* as well as facilitate the free movement of labor and capital, stabilize prices, equalize wages, and, eventually, it was hoped, coordinate monetary policies. Modeled closely after the political and administrative institutions of the ECSC, the EEC possessed an influential supranational executive bureaucracy, the European Commission, checked by a more powerful legislative branch, the Council of Ministers, whose members were normally the foreign ministers of the states. The Common Market also shared the ECSC's parliamentary assembly and court of justice. The European Commission's attenuated powers relative to the ECSC's High Authority, which was itself weaker than originally intended, cast considerable doubt on the willingness of national leaders to move from economic integration to the long-term goal of political federation trumpeted in the treaty's preamble. As one French insider at Messina recalled, "one could no longer mention the subject of European defense, nor that of supranationality, European constitution, relinquishment or delegation of sovereignty, or even European institutions, without in most cases eliciting from the listener a wry smile of disappointment, skepticism, or irony, and sometimes even a [hostile] reaction." There can be no doubt, however, that the EEC was at least an exclusively democratic club—one that had no room from the outset for "fascist" Spain and Portugal.[105]

It may help to understand how Europe's new Common Market functioned politically, situated as it was on sometimes hard to discern borders dividing national and supranational competencies, by looking at one very important legislative action of the early years. In 1962 the EEC reached agreement on a Common Agricultural Policy (CAP) that erected tariffs on food imported to the Common Market, guaranteed member-state farmers a minimum price for their produce, bought up surpluses to maintain this price, and paid rebates to farm exporters who had to sell at lower world prices to compete. The idea for the CAP stemmed from France, which insisted on supports for its farmers already during the founding negotiations of the EEC. The actual legislative process began in 1958 when the vice president of the European Commission responsible for agriculture, Sicco Mansholt, convened representatives from the six governments, the farmers, and the Commission to agree on guiding principles. The Commission then formulated a bill over subsequent years, being careful to keep interested parties informed of progress and to consult the European Assembly—later renamed the European Parliament—which it was constitutionally obligated to do. The final details of the CAP were thrashed out at a crucial series of marathon sessions of the Council of Ministers in December 1961 and January 1962.

Britain had opted not to join the EEC. London was wary of supranationalism of any sort, and unwilling to submit to the stiff external tariffs of the

Common Market and thereby forego the benefits of duty free food imports from its Commonwealth. However, Britain responded to the creation of the EEC with a constructive counter idea: an all-West European free trade union that would neither require non-EEC members to surrender sovereignty nor force them to relinquish their own tariff preferences. Paris, unwilling to compete with food moving from the British Commonwealth over London to Europe, squashed the deal. In 1959, therefore, Britain formed a European Free Trade Area (EFTA) with Portugal, Switzerland, Austria, Denmark, Norway, and Sweden. Finland became an associate member in 1961. Both EFTA and the EEC had eliminated their internal tariffs by 1968. The contrast with the counterproductive internecine economic warfare of the 1930s—and the political significance thereof—cannot be overestimated.

Socialist Market Economies

A widespread consensus on the appropriateness of social democracy strengthened the cohesion of Democratic Europe.[106] Like so many postwar trends, the proliferation of social insurance schemes grew out of the suffering and sacrifices of six years of fighting, and the conviction, as a British Labour Party spokesman declared, that "the people deserve and must be assured a happier future than faced them after the last war," and that "the good things of life," in the words of a Conservative, "shall be more widely shared."[107] The new wisdom of academicians like John Maynard Keynes underscored and reinforced the need for these programs. Government expenditure had to stimulate the economy in a time of depression and to sustain it during expansions by distributing income to help the lower classes make purchases.

Belief in the justness and necessity of social welfare programs was not limited to victorious, undefeated Britain: It was just as common and widespread among Axis victims from France to Norway; old and new neutral states like Switzerland, Sweden, Finland, and Austria; and humbled former enemies Italy and West Germany. In every democratic country legislators either expanded prewar social insurance schemes or introduced new ones. Usually these included unemployment insurance, comprehensive health and accident insurance, old age pensions, government housing or rent subsidies, family allowances, school lunch programs, paid vacations, and occasionally day care. As early as 1943 The Times had heralded the opportunity "for marking this decisive epoch" with great social measures "which will go far towards restoring the faith of ordinary men and women throughout the world in the power of democracy."[108] West European leaders seized this opportunity in the late 1940s and 1950s, typically setting a seventh of government outlays aside for social welfare. Britain, West Germany, and Sweden offered the most extensive social insurance and fringe benefits: Government expenditures for these purposes amounted to an impressive 16–20 percent of GDP among these leaders. Placing this in some perspective is the fact that U.S. defense expenditure during this period of escalating Cold War averaged 6–8 percent of GDP.

The remarkable economic recovery of Western Europe made much of this possible. Most of the region reached and surpassed prewar levels of production in 1948. Economies continued to grow at an unprecedented annual pace for the next fifteen years, ranging from the "economic miracles" of Germany (7.6 percent), Austria (5.8 percent), and Italy (6.0 percent), to the slower but still respectable annual growth performance of Britain (2.5 percent), Belgium (3.2 percent), and Scandinavia (3.5 percent). Historians attribute this long-term expansion to many factors: the need to repair or replace war-damaged housing and infrastructure, the presence of an abundant and skilled labor force that swelled even larger as millions of refugees fled communist-controlled Europe, the stimulus of governmental social expenditure, progress toward economic cooperation, and the discarding of colonies. Another significant cause of Europe's turnaround came from Washington—11.2 billion dollars in loans and aid from 1945 to 1947, followed by 12.3 billion in purely economic grants under the ERP from 1948 to 1952.[109] We can better appreciate the immensity of this total aid by keeping in mind that, although spread over seven years, it was roughly equivalent to the 1939 national income of the Third Reich, Europe's economic behemoth.

If the Marshall Plan did not create the political federation of Europe favored in Washington, at least it provided a loose economic structure through the Organization for European Economic Cooperation (OEEC) that distributed the grants. Given the anti-communist agenda of the Marshall Plan, it was not surprising that OEEC membership included sixteen of Europe's seventeen democracies. Finland, which declined to participate to appease Moscow, accepted U. S. loans instead. Nondemocratic Portugal and Turkey also belonged to the OEEC.

In defending the ERP before Congress in 1947, the Truman administration claimed that economic aid would also "eradicate the threat of continued nationalization and socialism by releasing and stimulating the investment of private capital."[110] This it did not do. Although Western Europe retained market economies whose private sectors remained vital to growth and prosperity, its political leaders turned away from Washington's laissez-faire formulas. Anxious memories from the 1930s of the vagaries and uncertainties of market forces combined with the very widespread wish, described earlier, for a superior postwar world, to expand the direct business role of government in most OEEC nations.[111] Three basic variations on this theme emerged. Throughout Scandinavia government-run companies competed with the private sector, especially in housing, energy, utilities, and transportation. The Italian government took a different tack, purchasing controlling shares in companies that commanded key sectors of the economy like banking, metallurgy, utilities, and transportation. Britain, France, and Austria preferred outright nationalization of many of the same critical industries. Only West Germany shied away from such direct government involvement in business due to the weight of American influence in Bonn and the conservatism of the ruling Christian Democrats and their chancellor, Konrad Adenauer. Government in most West European countries accounted for 40–50 percent of persons employed and roughly the same percentages of industrial investment by the early 1960s. The state also played an increasingly important role in economic planning: Witness Swedish use of economic forecasts in nationwide collective bargaining agreements, Norway's development of hydroelectric power in the far north, and French and Belgian efforts to modernize metallurgical plants—designs which carried over into the ECSC after 1953. Together with cultural, military, and commercial ties and the new emphasis on social justice, the shared experience of these "mixed" or "socialist" economies tightened the integration of the democratic bloc.

The Functioning of Democracy

Democratic Europe enjoyed political stability, generally speaking, during these first postwar decades.[112] One found the most smoothly functioning parliamentary institutions in the northern tier of states with long traditions of rule of law, universal suffrage, and peaceful transfers of power—countries that had made democratic breakthroughs in the 1900s and 1910s, or even earlier. Britain provides a prime example. With over a century of incremental progress toward democracy behind it in 1945, the people of the proud island nation turned in overwhelming numbers to the British Labour Party and its agenda of social justice. In 1951 the majority shifted to the Conservatives, whose long tenure in office finally ended with the return of Labour in 1963. Majority parties dominated cabinets in other countries too, for instance, the long Labor Party and Social Democratic runs, respectively, in Norway (1935–1965) and Sweden (1921–1991). Workable two- or three-party coalitions predominated in Denmark, Holland, Belgium, Luxembourg, and Switzerland, usually consisting of a centrist Catholic or Christian Democratic, a leftist Social Democratic, and various other liberal, "radical," or agrarian parties.

The most remarkable turnarounds occurred in Ireland, Finland, and Austria, whose democracies had limped through the 1920s. Politics in Dublin remained turbulent until Eamon de Valera's Fianna Fáil Party began its long period of ascendancy (1932–1959) in the Dail. The key to its success was the popularity of establishing full independence from Britain, which occurred in stages in 1937 and 1948, and its avoidance of foreign entanglements and imbroglios that could lead to war, either over Northern Ireland, World War Two, or the Cold War. The Finns also developed a more cooperative brand of politics after the camaraderie and sacrifice of war enabled younger politicians like Agrarian Party leader Urho Kekkonen, president from 1956 to 1981, and Social Democrat K. A. Fagerholm, who headed many postwar cabinets, to bridge the old class-ideology divide. The constant need to please its powerful Soviet neighbor, moreover, made it impossible for Finland to engage in the kind of anti-communist politics that tarnished democratic cultures in other western states—although, as explained earlier, the Finns did not tolerate communist abuses either. In Austria, similarly, the old feud between the Christian Socialists and the Socialists faded into irrelevance as leaders of both parties suffered at the hands of the Nazis. Under the watchful eyes of the victorious occupying powers, which finally pulled out in 1955 after Vienna pledged its neutrality in the Cold War, the two Austrian parties cooperated to make democracy work.

Representative institutions did not function well everywhere, of course, especially on the periphery of democratic Europe. Political suppression and one-sidedness by Protestants against Catholics continued to be a major problem in Northern Ireland, for instance, eventually exploding into incessant violence in the late 1960s, while authoritarian regimes hung on to power in Portugal and Spain (see Chapter 9). As will be argued later, moreover, the limits to women's rights placed further restrictions on the spread of democracy. Finally, many of Europe's democracies possessed glaring weaknesses: Politics in Greece, Italy, and France continued to be plagued by polarization, fragmentation, and resort to manipulation or force; and even West Germany, so progressive and placid on the surface in the 1950s, had serious problems. Democratization, in other words, remained a very incomplete process.

Gender Relations. Europe's democratic legitimacy had long been faulted along gender lines. More than a century and a half after French revolutionaries proclaimed their "rights of man and citizen" in 1789 few European women had broken through this double standard to register gains toward legal and political equality. In 1945 only Scandinavia and Britain could make such progressive claims.[113] The Protestantism of these countries blended well with concerns for individual rights, while their common law traditions imposed fewer restrictions on women than did the patriarchal Civil Code (see Chapter 1) that had long remained on the books in the core countries ruled by Napoleon.[114] What is more, much of Scandinavia missed the full impact of the world wars, thus avoiding combat's traumatic effect on gender relations and accompanying retardation of women's movements.[115]

Germany offers an instructive comparison with Scandinavia, for here a common law tradition and longtime Protestant establishment worked in one direction while the century's conflagrations led ultimately in another. As one might anticipate, early activism and progress for German women yielded after the Great War to heightened female sensitivity to the need for restored male strength, and finally under Hitler to nadir years of manipulation, discrimination, coercion, and fear.[116] Britain was also spared none of the twentieth century's war-induced male backlash and female retreat, which helps to explain why Sweden and Norway forged ahead of Britain during the 1930s and 1940s in terms of women's rights to equal hiring and pay, day care and paid maternity leaves, nondiscriminatory welfare benefits paid directly to mothers, liberalized divorce laws, and reproductive freedoms like legal abortions, so antithetical to the "women-as-baby-machine" fixation with births of male military establishments.

Indeed, the women's movement of Britain lost considerable momentum after the century's great wars. "Today the spirit of the old pioneers is so dead it seems a miracle it ever existed,"[117] wrote a London journalist in 1956. In contrast to popular memory, however, a few activists had kept the cause alive in the interwar period. The coming of female suffrage in two stages—1918 for thirty-year-olds and women of property, and 1928 for the rest—facilitated improvements in women's status. Thus legislation opened previously all-male professions like the law and removed the last vestiges of wives' legal subordination to husbands.[118] The Great War strengthened hierarchical relations between men and women, on the other hand, by evoking sympathy from women for male suffering and accentuating the frightening and intimidating violence of men. The women's movement largely disintegrated as a result of the dual impact of postwar legislative gains and the war's conservative impact on gender relations—much to the dismay of women's leaders who wanted to make further progress with equality of opportunity and pay. They bemoaned the passage of new laws like the "marriage bar" that forced women to leave teaching and civil service positions when they married. "War to man, like childbirth to women, is simplifying in its emotions" and had "set women back a generation," wrote Pearl Buck in 1941. By this time, in fact, there were few traces of the old activism for women's equality. "Women want equality don't they," recalled a woman worker in 1991, "but fifty years ago it wasn't heard of, you wouldn't have gone into things like that."[119]

Like the First World War, the second great conflagration had a complicated, yet largely conservative effect on British gender relations. Its most immediate and evident impact was to expand the numbers of women working full-time from the historic average of 28–30 percent to around 43 percent during the war's latter stage. Nearly eight million women worked in 1943—and four of five wartime entries to the labor force were female. It is doubtful, however, that this experience represented the "out of the cage" phenomenon that early researchers, critical of women's traditional relegation to private sphere domesticity, emphasized.[120] For one thing, female wartime employment tended to expand in sectors already absorbing more women before 1939: clerical work, food manufacture, and assembly of electrical equipment. Few women moved into "men's" skilled labor or professional jobs, received far less pay when they did, and even fewer remained in such positions when the military services demobilized males.

Protests against women's inequality that had simmered since the 1930s became somewhat more pronounced as a result of these problems. The government established an investigating commission in 1946, but its finding that most women earned about half as much as men for comparable work prompted no remedial legislation out of concern for the country's postwar economic recovery. Further lobbying from "old pioneers" and the trade unions moved the Conservative government to introduce equal pay for women in the civil service, teaching, and local government in 1955–1956, but the private sector lagged behind.

That the old spirit of female emancipation seemed so moribund to contemporaries stemmed no doubt from the longing of many women for security and motherhood after V-E Day. There seems to have been a fairly strong consensus across gender lines at war's end, in fact, that young women of childrearing age should leave the labor force, marry, and attempt to replenish the hundreds of thousands of lives lost in bombed cities and faraway battlefields. The portion of married women working fell to 26 percent, only gradually rising to a more typical 35 percent in 1961. The percentage of women working declined so precipitously below historic levels after 1945 that the government, alarmed by labor shortages, lifted marriage bars and conducted campaigns to encourage older women to return to work.[121] In the meantime Britain enjoyed a baby boom, with births per thousand peaking at a century high in 1947. As the austerity of the late 1940s gave way to increased consumer spending in the 1950s, furthermore, much of British purchasing was done by women who did not seem to mind the domesticity of it all. On the contrary, they took pride in what they were accomplishing for a recuperating nation, their families, and themselves. Consequently, marketing targeted at women proliferated as sales of women's magazines quadrupled to 11–12 million in the late 1950s. As will be explained later, by comparison with her West German counterpart the British housewife kept a less tyrannical grip on the purse strings, reveling in shopping like only a Sixties successor generation would allow itself to do in Germany.

World War Two had a searing effect on German gender relations. Approximately four million soldiers died in combat.[122] Adding to the toll of misery, only a few thousand of the two million Germans captured by the Red Army avoided a slow, terrible death in camps, eventually returning to loved ones, but usually after a delay of five or six years. Those who returned from Europe's combat fronts were often broken from the experience, finding it difficult to work at jobs, if they could find one, preferring usually to drink, forget the war if possible, and otherwise vegetate in what passed for housing in bombed-out postwar Germany. Some women who had shouldered the burden of wartime work reacted with disgust and rapidly waning tolerance, applying for divorces at record rates—nearly fifty thousand in 1946, and almost ninety thousand in 1948, a postwar high. More typically, however, German women who had survived the bombing, the fleeing, and the raping tended to sympathize with their men and the similarly tough times they had been through—not unlike the experience of the Great War, but now emotions cut to the bone. "At first our troops came through: beaten down, worn out, and they had nothing to eat," recalled one woman forty years later. "And then the [Americans] came: beaming faces, the boys were rested, with gloves and not in rags like ours—it pierced me and it still hurts after so many years."[123]

Rather than reject their men, therefore, most German women wanted to help them. In so doing they could help themselves, for by reconstructing a shattered gender hierarchy there was promise of security in a harsh, murderous world. "There no longer existed a social order in which women found their place and protection," recalled Hamburg journalist Edith Oppens in the early 1950s. "All protective measures for health, for life, and for honor as well had proven themselves to be illusory." Most women sought normalcy by making the family—whether they had one or not—an "obligation, a phantom, a project" that would ultimately produce "warmth, understanding and help, simplicity, fairness, and protection." Only 25 percent of married women worked in 1950, far below 1939 levels. Harsh conditions ruled out, however, anything like Britain's baby boom. Circumstances were so bleak, in fact, that some women reacted by taking irrational "flight into the past and better days, with which they mainly mean the Hitler years," noted one researcher in 1947. "Overburdened mothers, who without any significant help from others feel themselves almost crushed by elemental forces in their cold, frequently half-destroyed abodes, are particularly visible in this group. . . . Statements like 'If Adolf were [still here], then there would be order at home' . . . can frequently be heard."[124] As explained below, such sentiments made the task of reestablishing democracy an extra challenge for postwar German leaders.

The memory of Anglo-American bombing, Red Army rape and murder, and the excruciating hard work of rebuilding hung over gender relations well into the postwar period, shaping and molding the attitudes of female survivors in ways that seem contradictory at first glance. On the one hand, women welcomed conservative social policies with fully paid maternity work leaves and family allowances paid to the father, both designed to promote marriage, childrearing, and the man's place. Women also voted in greater numbers for conservative parties and seemed to want even more than men to bury controversies over Nazi crimes. On the other hand, revived women's organizations from across the political spectrum, armed once again with meaningful suffrage rights, fought hard for a well-deserved equality clause in the Federal Republic's Basic Law (1949), which stated simply that "men and women have equal rights," and then continued their pressure for a decade until reluctant legislators and the Constitutional Court wrote legal equality in marriage and parenting into West Germany's civil code. Women trade unionists also fought legal battles against employers—and organized male workers—who were not prepared to accept equal pay for equal work. The courts agreed, although management easily circumvented the judges' interpretation of the constitution by paying more for "heavy" work and less for "light" (i.e., work by females).[125]

The simultaneous striving of German women for legal equality and domestic security seems less contradictory, however, in the light of recent research. Not only were one out of three married women gainfully employed by 1961, but housewives, whether they worked or not, performed vital *public* roles as stingy accumulators of household savings and strict management of family consumption.[126] Representing an important part of German economic recovery after the war, purchases at self-service supermarkets, department stores, and home appliance stores were usually made by women with keen eyes for bargains. Accordingly, magazine, radio, and television advertisements as well as market surveys targeted mainly the woman, not so much the man. Larger household investment items like new cars and homes also tended to be made jointly by husband and wife in West Germany. "In the everyday practices of female consumption, from research interviews to household management," writes one historian, "women were both formed *and actively formed themselves* as the objects and the agents of postwar national reconstruction."[127]

This contribution had an exhilarating, even liberating effect on women, particularly after the harsh times of war and the bleak postwar period prior to the "economic miracle" of the 1950s. A political flier for the conservative Christian Democratic Union (CDU) reflected these female sentiments and emotions in 1953:

> The shelves filled with things the likes of which our children scarcely knew. We could shop again—where we wanted and what we wanted. And if we were sometimes short at the cash register, whatever, we still had the possibility to choose for ourselves once again, to accept or reject, even for a small purchase, what we didn't like. It was as if a door had opened into freedom. The world was brighter, life worth living again. Can a man even begin to sense what the [postwar low point] had meant to us women, a [crisis] which we suffered through in great bitterness, one which broke not only the last measure of our self-consciousness, but also brought us, looking into the imploring eyes of our children, to the edge of despair? . . . We know, in the free play of the market forces of supply and demand, that the housewife is a factor one has to reckon with again—and one *should* reckon with us.[128]

Thus it seems fairly consistent that German mothers of the 1950s should have valued security, which they helped to provide for themselves, while at the same time insisting that the law at least begin to reflect woman's contributions and importance to family, economy, and society.

The political legacy bequeathed by female war survivors to their daughters is difficult to determine, but must have been ambiguous and complex. Erica Carter believes that many young women in the 1960s "began to challenge their mothers' values of parsimony and deferred pleasure and embraced, instead, a domestic ethos of consumerist gratification."[129] The likelihood of feminist activists emerging from this cadre to push for a fuller range of Scandinavian-style women's rights seemed slight—indeed, one could probably expect less from these more materialist daughters. Noting the absence in 1960s Germany of assertive groups like America's National Organization of Women (NOW), Bonnie Smith concludes that lingering Cold War anticommunism, reinforced by a persistent desire for "respectability" after the national blemish of Nazism, made the successor female generation "hesitate to take any step indicating political difference."[130] Moreover, while some daughters undoubtedly derived strength from their mothers' example of hard work and household leadership, eventually carrying these inherited qualities into the women's struggle of the 1970s, maternal strength could be a two-edged sword. This message permeates Jutta Brückner's *Years of Hunger* (1979), an autobiographical film which Carter sees as a paradigm of family life in the 1950s. The mother squirrels away money, fantasizing about the consumer purchases that will someday make all the hard work worthwhile. She is not depicted as the victim of any male plot to relegate women to the home, but rather as a repressive agent in her own right. "In her desire for the ordered commodity trappings of prosperity—tasteful tea parties, plush home furnishings—the mother works throughout the film to erase from family reality the disruptive traces of politics or personal emotion, for these are sources of indiscipline that shatter the stringent order of her commoditized domesticity."[131] This female oppressiveness includes squelching all talk of her husband's role in the anti-Nazi resistance as well as ignoring and stifling her daughter's emotional needs. The bulimic, suicidal teenager will hardly grow up to be a fighter for greater women's equality.

In the last days of the war Italian partisans captured Benito Mussolini and his mistress, Clara Petacci; machine-gunned them; and then strung up the bodies by the feet for public display in Milan. This gruesome image conveyed considerable ambiguity for relations between men and women. By executing Mussolini and Petacci men of the resistance exacted revenge for their own fallen women and paid tribute to women's contribution to victory. Italian males rewarded female comrades in the same magnanimous spirit after the war by granting women voting rights as well as legal equality in the job market. On the other hand, by shooting Petacci men were punishing a woman who had slept with the enemy. With this act they declared their manhood still intact despite the best efforts of the Nazis and Mussolini's infamous Black Brigades—and warned women not to cross lines again.

Indeed, the war did not affect a complete caesura in gender relations, for afterward the same men who overthrew Mussolini and enfranchised women kept the dictator's patriarchal penal codes and family laws and maintained social mores and cultural behaviors carried over from the fascist era.[132] This was mere surface irony, for at a deeper level it represented the predictable continuation of a male-first hierarchy only partially attenuated by the experience of another terrible war. Eventually men wedded to traditional gender roles even suppressed the real story of women's wartime opposition to Fascism, refashioning a tale of heroic all-male resistance.[133] Thus, together with a genuine and complete female emancipation, truth became the final casualty of war.

Similar circumstances existed in France. During the interwar period democrats denied women the suffrage, preserved much of the husband's legal authority in the family, and promoted pro-natalist legislation designed to repopulate a nation decimated by the killing of 1914–1918. These policies hardened under the authoritarian Vichy regime after 1940. When resistance to German occupation flared up in 1942–1943, however, women played an important role. The postwar Fourth Republic recognized this contribution by finally enfranchising women and decreeing equal employment rights: "The law shall guarantee to women rights equal to those of men in all spheres—it shall be the duty of all to work, and the right of all to obtain employment."[134]

But women did not become equal to men "in all spheres" after 1945. Napoleon's Civil Code remained in force, thereby perpetuating married women's subordinate status to their husbands. The Fourth Republic also continued allowance schemes from the Third Republic and Vichy that supplemented the income of men whose wives stayed home, thus buttressing the pro-family aspects of the Napoleonic Code. French women were equal, in

other words, until they married. The same inferior status affected wedded females in Belgium, Luxembourg, and Holland, lands that had once belonged
to Napoleonic France.

Several factors aided the maintenance of gender order. Over a million and
a half Frenchmen went into captivity in 1940, not to be freed until V-E Day. Of
these men, over half left wives behind, 616,200 of them with children. The latter experienced particular hardship, forced to fend for the children alone, console and discipline them alone, and somehow, alone, prepare for the day of the
husband's return. Some wives never really managed or accustomed themselves
to sole parental responsibility. As one mother wrote in 1943: "I will abandon
[these responsibilities] little by little, with pleasure, to my husband as he
readapts." Others grew "a bit used to this independent existence," admitting
that "it took some readjusting" when the man reclaimed his authority. They
chafed as "little by little the hero of the early days [became] a tiresome and
disappointing troublemaker."[135] The intimidating display of male anger that
accompanied liberation kept such complainers in line, however, as considerable numbers of women who had established relationships with German officers and soldiers were paraded naked with shaved heads.[136] In many cases the
retribution was far worse, for the *maquis* and other resistance groups went on
a killing rampage, gunning down about nine thousand collaborators—a figure
that would have climbed far higher had de Gaulle's forces not slapped over
125,000 in protective custody.[137] The percentage of women that had suffered
the fate of Clara Petacci will probably never be known, but it must have been
significant. Like British, German, and Italian women, French women, as well
as those in surrounding small states, would wait until the 1970s and 1980s for
the fuller range of rights enjoyed by Scandinavian women for decades.

Democratic Soft Spots in Greece, Italy, France, and West Germany. The potential for democratic government returned to Greece as Nazi forces withdrew
in late 1944. Any hope for stability soon disappeared, however, amidst bloody
fighting between the government and communist rebels. American military
aid eventually helped "right-wing cliques"[138] in Athens crush the insurgents,
especially after Stalin rejected intervention (see earlier). These same conservative circles, coalescing in 1952 under Constantine Karamanlis in the National Radical Union, rode the political wave of Marshall Plan grants, which
drove a massive economic expansion that pushed agricultural and industrial
production well beyond prewar levels and nearly quintupled per capita national income by the early 1960s. Karamanlis grew increasingly unpopular,
however, as it became obvious to political opponents that Washington manipulated cabinet formation to bolster NATO, which Greece had joined in
1952. When he largely abandoned the volatile cause of Greek union with
Cyprus in 1959, and then rigged elections to stay in power two years later,
democracy in Greece seemed a mere sham.

Italy encountered similar problems. The political fulcrum lay considerably left of center in 1945 as a result of the courageous role in the resistance
played by the Communists, Socialists, and other fellow-traveling groups like
the Party of Action. In the first postwar provisional government the former

parties occupied a number of key ministries, while the latter placed its leader, Ferruccio Parri, in the premiership. They shared cabinet posts with the Christian Democrats of Alcide de Gasperi, a moderate Catholic with populist roots. Italians issued a clear rejection of the past by abolishing the monarchy and exiling the royal family.

Over the next three years, however, Italian politics became badly polarized, beginning with de Gasperi's ousting of Parri from office over the latter's plans to radically purge government of ex-fascists. In late 1946 the Communists and Socialists issued a joint declaration lambasting Italy's "conservative reactionary forces" and advocating "the conquest of power on the part of the working classes."[139] As the Cold War in Europe deepened in 1947, de Gasperi responded by removing Communists and left-wing Socialists from his cabinet, thus setting the stage for a vitriolic election campaign the following year. With massive CIA as well as Vatican support for the Christian Democrats—Pius XII threatened to excommunicate communist voters—the Christian Democrats and their non-communist coalition party allies held onto a solid majority. Moscow's plans for making inroads in the capitalist bloc had failed.

Despite opposition claims, de Gasperi was not a reactionary. However, neither the conservative Pope nor conservative business and landowning elements in the party desired reforms. Consequently, as the 1940s yielded to a new decade the prime minister found himself expending considerable energies just keeping the Communists and Socialists at bay, while leaving important political work desired by Christian Democratic leftists undone. In contrast to unfolding welfare and nationalization efforts in Britain, France, and West Germany, for instance, Italy's social services and state-run firms dated from the fascist era—the government accomplished little new. It also neglected a thoroughgoing solution to the rural poverty of southern Italy. Moreover, civil and criminal practices and procedures unchanged since Mussolini's day—implemented by fascists still on the bench, or sometimes by leftist judges interested only prosecuting the class struggle—abused citizens in ways inconsistent with democracy. Thus arrestees in felony cases were often detained without bail or trial for years, and even automobile accidents could lead to months of questioning and detention. A prominent historian, Gaetano Salvemini, quipped that if he were arrested for raping the statue of the Madonna atop the Milan cathedral he "would think first of escaping and only later of defending himself against the charge."[140]

Democracy in Italy deteriorated further after 1953. Elections that year cut into the Christian Democratic vote and prompted de Gasperi's resignation. The governing coalition produced a series of cabinets over the next seven years—eight unworkable combinations, many without majority backing. When Fernando Tambroni needed twenty-four neo-fascist deputies to put together a government in 1960, however, severe leftist rioting erupted in several cities. Tambroni's opponents, aware of his ties to rightists who railed against the "dictatorship of the parties," quickly brought down his government. "It was difficult to escape the conclusion," writes Denis Mack Smith, "that a quite different grouping of parties was urgently needed if parliamentary democracy were to thrive."[141]

From the moment of liberation in August 1944, French politics was marred by violence as resistance fighters sought instant justice against countrymen who had aided and abetted the enemy.[142] The entire postwar generation would be split asunder over the choices—to resist or to collaborate—which individuals made between 1940 and 1944. Another layer of discord and dissension came with the debate over a new constitution. Head of the provisional government, General Charles de Gaulle insisted on replacing the revolving door ministries of the 1920s with a strong presidency, while most party leaders understandably wanted to retain a powerful Assembly. Defeated on this issue in 1946, de Gaulle resigned from office to conduct a hard-hitting campaign against the new "Fourth Republic." Cold War vitriol mixed into French politics when the governing Christian Democrats and Socialists expelled the Communists from the cabinet in 1947. As governments rose and fell—eleven of them between 1946 and 1954—Gaullist and Communist forces eroded the political center, combining for 47.6 percent in the 1951 elections. Remarkably enough, France embarked on its impressive social insurance and nationalization schemes during this turbulent period.

The Fourth Republic survived a mere twelve years, in fact, brought down by its own ill-fated venture in Algeria. The revolt of the National Liberation Front (FLN) began in 1954 with terrorist attacks against settlers, colonial administrators, and army bases. The victims quickly organized a shocking counterterror of their own, however, and the violence spiraled out of control. Nearly a million Algerians and tens of thousands of French died during the eight-year conflagration. Although politicians in Paris made concessions to the FLN as early as 1958, army hard-liners in Algeria who had not forgotten the "disgrace" of Vietnam rejected peace talks as cowardly. To prevent the unthinkable they seized the island of Corsica, and then drew up plans for a coup on the mainland. The National Assembly reacted by granting six-month emergency powers to de Gaulle, the only politician the conspirators respected and trusted. There would be no coup.

In taking his oath in June 1958, however, the new premier made it clear that he favored another constitution. The founding document of a new "Fifth Republic" won the support of 80 percent of the voters that September. Supported by 78.5 percent of an electoral college controlled by the parties, de Gaulle became the first president. The new system greatly enhanced the presidency at the expense of parliament. The executive could dissolve the assembly for elections, thus terminating the irresponsible practice of undercutting a premier without having to face the electorate. Nor could legislators make backroom deals to unmake a cabinet: This now required a majority vote of no confidence. Moreover, the president appointed the premier and in effect all ministers. Because cabinet members could not simultaneously hold parliamentary seats, de Gaulle had sealed off administrative functions from "the politicians." These changes shifted governmental initiative to the executive branch, which was further strengthened by the practice of "reserving" military and foreign policy decisions for the president. In 1962 de Gaulle also won a referendum calling for the direct election of the president, thus guaranteeing further independence from the legislature. Finally, there was the towering prestige of de Gaulle himself: war hero, man above the parties, and savior of democracy from military caprice—a role he could play all the more convincingly while, for four more years, the war dragged on in Algeria. The president parlayed all of this into an absolute majority for his "Gaullist" party, the Union for the New Republic, which won 250 of 480 seats in 1962. Small wonder that critics accused him of having "created a virtual monarchy, elective to be sure, but in which a misconceived referendum system and the docility of a National Assembly elected on the personal appeal of a single individual reduce democracy to a mere façade."[143]

It may seem odd to include West Germany in a discussion of democratic problem areas, and in fact many historians would not place it here, preferring to emphasize the country's democratic success story. German politicians who formulated a new "Basic Law" (i.e., constitution) in the summer of 1948 made a special effort to avoid the perceived mistakes of the 1920s. They scaled back the presidency to a respectful figurehead position, mindful of the fact that it had drifted in a dictatorial direction under Hindenburg, the man who abused his right to rule by decree—and eventually appointed Hitler. Next, the drafters fine-tuned Weimar's system of proportional representation to prevent extremist elements from disrupting parliament: Unless parties received 5 percent of the national vote, or else won three districts outright, they received no seats. The Nazi Party was officially outlawed. West Germany's postwar leaders also sought to limit obstructionism in parliament by stipulating that governments could not be felled, even with a vote of no confidence, unless opponents presented a working majority coalition behind a new cabinet. Finally, the Basic Law dismantled the problematic political centralization of the Nazi years by giving back to the federal states significant cultural functions as well as the ability to participate on the national stage through an upper chamber, the Federal Council (*Bundesrat*), that shared power with the lower house, the Federal Diet (*Bundestag*). All of these changes paid handsome dividends in the 1950s when the Federal Republic became one of the smoothest functioning democracies in the world. Cabinets had staying power and elections occurred at normal intervals, conducted in efficient Anglo-American style by two or three parties. Konrad Adenauer, chancellor from 1949 to 1963, presided over the whole process. His party alliance, the Christian Democratic Union/Christian Social Union (CDU/CSU), won an absolute majority of the popular vote in 1957.

External circumstances much more fortunate than those of the post–World War One period contributed mightily to the democratic turnaround in West Germany. No one made "stab in the back" accusations, for unconditional surrender had been imposed on Germany's defeated authoritarian rulers, not on a young democracy that allegedly betrayed those rulers. The western allies assumed all political responsibility during bleak postwar years of reparations, rubble clearing, and great hunger, furthermore, thus avoiding the erosion of

democratic support caused by embarrassing foreign policy setbacks and economic collapse in the early 1920s. When Adenauer took the reins of a semi-
sovereign Federal Republic in 1949, Marshall Plan funds began to fuel a rapid
expansion. Finally, the need in Washington and London for reliable allies during the Cold War made it comparatively easy for Adenauer to negotiate an
end to reparations and controls over economic and foreign policy, and thus
return to nearly full sovereignty, again in great contrast to the 1920s.

Circumstances for democracy had been so fortunate that recent historians have begun to ask if the transition had been, in fact, *too easy*. No great revolutionary upheaval like 1789, 1848, or 1917 had empowered and legitimated
the new order; and nothing like the massive, martyr-making defiance shown
by the Italian resistance against Mussolini, the French resistance against Vichy,
or the European-wide resistance to the Nazis had occurred in Germany. To
some historians like Jeffrey Herf the truth of West German democratization is
that it stayed a surface phenomenon for many years because so many Germans refused to come to grips with their Nazi past. Those who spoke out
bravely, like leading Social Democrats Kurt Schumacher and Ernst Reuter, or
the first president of the Federal Republic, Free Democrat Theodor Heuss, remained odd men out:

> The inner German political victims [said Heuss], and on their side the
> hundreds of thousands, yes millions of foreigners who were tortured to
> death speak to the heaviest and costliest sacrifice of National Socialism:
> the honor of the German name, which has sunk in filth. As we say this,
> angered, depressed, and ashamed to have been defenseless contemporaries
> of this dark period of German history, we feel the duty once again to clear
> our name and the name of the German people. The memory of those who
> suffered yet were innocent, and who died bravely, will be a quiet, calm
> light illuminating our path during the dark years through which we are
> going.[144]

Heuss wanted memories of Nazi crimes against the Jews and other peoples
to serve as kind of an unwritten constitution, a mental document against which
all private behavior and public policy could be scrutinized for its moral and
ethical "constitutionality." But the past functioned differently for most of his
countrymen. Surveys of adult Germans in 1946–1947 exposed a broad anti-
Semitic segment of 39 percent, with almost half of these classified as unreconstructed Nazis. Nor did this layer erode quickly. Five years later about 41
percent of respondents saw more good than evil in Nazi ideology, while 42
percent believed they had been better off under the prewar Nazi regime.[145]
Such large numbers of disaffected former Nazis and fellow travelers presented
leaders of West Germany's democracy with a dilemma not unlike that which
had faced Weimar democrats three decades earlier, for voter perception of
governmental "wrong moves" like vigorous prosecution of "patriots" could
trigger a backlash against the new political system.

Adenauer worried, in fact, that Germany's nascent democracy would not
survive another groundswell of "stab-in-the-back" accusations prompted by

West German anti-Nazi trials. As it was, the prosecution and conviction of German detainees by the western allies—nearly six thousand lower-level Nazis by 1951—had provoked "a growing and extreme nationalism" that bitterly rejected the punishment of "harmless followers and soldiers who [only] believed that they were doing their duty." Adenauer believed that it would have been unjust—and thus also a form of political suicide—for the new German government to pursue the many scores of thousands of former officials. Even to condemn the Holocaust, as Heuss had done, ran a political risk. "If Adenauer, as early as 1949, had said [that] what we did in the past was wrong," recalled a key aide to the chancellor, "then certainly the German people would have been against him."[146] Indeed, about 70 percent of survey respondents that same year did not reject Nazism outright. Motivated by a prudent concern for democracy—as well as a fair measure of political expediency that undoubtedly contributed to his party's votes—Adenauer radically cut back prosecutions in the German courts after 1950. The following year he lobbied fairly successfully for an end to allied executions, and rehabilitated 150,000 persons fired from their jobs under allied de-nazification programs. Reflecting the political prudence of the chancellor's refusal to prosecute ex-Nazis was the fact that high school history curricula, which the federal states controlled separately, ignored the twentieth century altogether. By completely burying the recent past, the secondary educational establishment had refused to grapple with the issue of criminal or even moral guilt.

These political realities put into context—and help one appreciate—the steps that West Germany actually took to begin coping with the legacy of Nazism. In 1954, for example, the Federal Republic began restitution payments to Israel that would mount over four decades to 110 billion marks. It had taken three years for Adenauer to move his coalition to take action. One incredulous critic of the opposition to restitution summed up their attitude sarcastically: "No persons were guilty of persecution, and where is it written that persons not guilty of a wrong should make restitution?"[147] It took even more political courage in 1958 for Bonn to begin a vigorous prosecution of Nazi criminals. To delay justice is to deny it, of course, but regardless of the morality or immorality of Adenauer's decade of expediency, the fact that his administration postponed the legal process speaks to the fragility of democracy and the difficulties of effective denazification after Weimar's frustrations and thirteen years of Hitler. In 1960, furthermore, the states finally began to revise their history curricula to take Nazi crimes into account, but reeducation efforts among adults faced the really tough slog. Indeed, well into the 1960s polls showed that a majority of Germans opposed prosecution of Nazi war criminals and harbored considerable resentment against "traitors" who had tried to overthrow Hitler. The obvious danger of such persistent denial of past errors was the lingering potential for the past to return. Would such stubborn refusal to deal with recent history nurture another era of fascism?

Chapter 8

EUROPE AND AMERICA

On June 26, 1963, John Fitzgerald Kennedy flew to Berlin.[1] In office for thirty months, the young, dynamic successor to Eisenhower remained uncomfortable with and somewhat suspicious of Germans. Their aging chancellor, Konrad Adenauer, seemed from the distant White House perspective to embody a dangerous spirit of nationalism. Like many in the West old enough to have fought in the war, the president refused to sanction German fingers on nuclear triggers. Their mayor in West Berlin, Willy Brandt, had put off America's new chief by appealing to him as "a friend" for help two years earlier when the infamous wall went up. Their ambassador in Washington got on his nerves. To be sure, Kennedy and his advisers appreciated the value of West German membership in NATO as well a continued allied presence in Berlin. His team also knew that a successful German visit would counter de Gaulle's efforts to woo Adenauer into a Europe steering its own course between Moscow and Washington. The importance of agreements with Khrushchev still weighed more heavily in American geopolitical calculations, however, than reunifying the two German states—something that de Gaulle warily avoided too, but a policy that was holy writ to Adenauer. All of this residual anti-Germanism trickled down to White House staffers, who began making fun of the Berliners as the crowds gathered around airport exits to catch a glimpse of Kennedy. "Why, they must have cheered the Nazis the same way!" "Won't these Germans just do anything for a parade?"

As the motorcade of black limos escorted by cordons of white-bloused motorcycle policemen pulled out of Tegel Airport and began to slither along a circuitous thirty-five-mile route through the city, the mood of the Americans, especially of the top man, changed dramatically. Over two million West Berliners—just about everyone in town—lined the streets, crowded onto balconies, and thrust heads out of windows, heaving tons of confetti American-style. Kennedy was overwhelmed by this awesome reception. Later on the route he stared angrily at the Brandenburg Gate, rising forebodingly behind East Berlin's concrete wall monstrosity. He was deeply touched by the sight of captive subjects waving kerchiefs at him from the other side. All the while West Berlin worked its unnerving ways on him, as it did on all Yanks who went there in the days of the wall and felt peril. One had left the land of the free "many miles away on the other side of the Atlantic" to journey to this "defended island of freedom,"[2] surrounded and besieged far inside the communist bloc. As a dyed-in-the-wool politician, he sensed that the drab, noncommittal address his staffers had prepared would never do. So he reworked the speech.

By the time Kennedy stepped out onto the balcony of the Schöneberg Town Hall to address a throng of three quarters of a million, the substance and tone of his policy on Berlin, Germany, and indeed Europe had changed. Warned beforehand not to provoke Khrushchev, the president threw down instead the gauntlet of the American challenge. There were those who maintained, said the U.S. commander-in-chief, that we must work with the communists, that their system promotes economic progress, and was the wave of the future. "Let them come to Berlin!"[3] Freedom had many difficulties and democracy was not perfect, "but we have never had to put up a wall to keep our people in, to prevent them from leaving us." He castigated the wall as "an offense against humanity, separating families, dividing husbands and wives and brothers and sisters, and dividing people who wish to be joined together." Then Kennedy went farther than he—or any of his predecessors—had gone:

Tragic symbol of the Cold War: the Berlin Wall at the Bernauer Strasse Subway. (Private Collection)

> When all men are free, then we can look forward to that day when this city will be joined as one, and this country, and this great continent of Europe, in a peaceful and hopeful globe. When that day finally comes, as it will, the people of West Berlin can take sober satisfaction in the fact that they were in the front lines for almost two decades.

Now the crowd was in frenzy, more than a thousand fainting from excitement. JFK's closing remarks completed the process of bonding America and Berlin, cementing a relationship that his successors dared not abandon: "All free men, wherever they may live, are citizens of Berlin, and, therefore, as a free man, I take pride in the words: *Ich bin ein Berliner.*"

BERLIN AND CUBA

Nikita Khrushchev distrusted the Germans too, especially the West Germans, who he believed harbored militaristic designs. His anti-Germanism flared up at a Paris news conference in 1960. Having broken up a summit meeting with Eisenhower over the latter's refusal to apologize for a recent botched spy flight over Russia, Khrushchev took some rough questioning from reporters, and then exploded, shouting he knew that Adenauer had sent agents to disrupt the press conference: "Take a look around when you boo us. We beat you at Stalingrad, in Ukraine and Byelorussia, and we finished you off. If the remnant are going to boo us and prepare another invasion, we'll boo them so hard that . . . " At this point he cut off the interpreter and continued in his native tongue. "These people understand Russian perfectly well—they are Hitlerite predators who were on Soviet territory and who managed to take to their heels and escape."[4]

After the great sacrifices Russia made on the Eastern Front, these irrational phobias are perhaps easier to understand. Adenauer had contributed to Soviet fears, however, by accepting West German membership in NATO, resisting Polish/Soviet proposals after the neutralization of Austria for creation of a wide nuclear free zone in central Europe, and persistently pressing Washington to arm the Bundeswehr with nuclear weapons. Although certainly not a militarist, the chancellor's unshakeable belief that western armed superiority and diplomatic intransigence could win the Cold War and reunite Germany—and that any easing of tensions (détente) between Moscow and Washington might perpetuate German division—carried definite risks in the atomic age. Thus the first full-scale NATO war game after West German adherence to the alliance in 1955 demonstrated that massive nuclear retaliation would prevent the Red Army from reaching the Rhine, but incinerate five million German civilians in the process.[5] Yet shortly before NATO adopted this "new look" policy of reliance on tactical nuclear counterattack in 1957, West Germany calmly ignored Soviet blandishments that Bonn forego such armaments. "If England and other powers have atomic weapons," said the German foreign minister, "why shouldn't the Federal Republic of Germany have them too?" In the end the Pentagon delivered artillery and airplanes capable of being fitted with nuclear devices, but not the shells and bombs. Nevertheless, Soviet leaders were incredulous. Adenauer was as bad as Hindenburg, blurted Khrushchev, and the Americans "may someday pay with their blood for having encouraged such people."[6] Moscow's deepest worry, that Bonn assumed the point position of a western scheme to undermine the admittedly unstable regime of East Germany, and probably Poland too, may seem exaggerated today, but these fears were real at a time when the Soviets, shaken by events in Poland and Hungary in 1956, saw heavily armed capitalists behind every bush.

Khrushchev also distrusted the East Germans. Their leader, Walter Ulbricht, had consistently opposed Moscow's designs for a united Germany in the late 1940s and early 1950s, fearing not unjustifiably that both of the proposed unification arrangements, either the Soviet call for a merger of the two states or the U.S. insistence on free nationwide elections, would weaken, not strengthen, communism in Germany. Pointing to an exodus of over two million disgruntled East Germans into the easily accessible allied sectors of West Berlin by the late 1950s, Ulbricht insisted on forcing the capitalists out of the city. Such pressure tactics, of course, had nearly touched off an explosion in 1948. Thus the Soviet premier laughed during a summit meeting when the U.S. ambassador said that his countrymen "would rather deal with the Russians" over German issues "than leave it to the Germans," adding: "I refuse to believe that your Germans are any better than ours." Khrushchev extended his hand over the table, instinctively replying: "Let's shake on that."[7] To be sure, he did not like the West's outpost in Berlin any more than Ulbricht, worrying that it could serve as the base for the feared economic or, worse, military penetration of the East Bloc. As an old Bolshevik, Khrushchev also believed so fervently in the communist cause that he could not countenance its failure, especially in strategically vital Germany. With his advisers already quipping that the current rate of escape would soon leave Ulbricht all by himself in East Germany, however, the premier knew that the wound had to be staunched. Khrushchev did not shrink from taking risks, but he refused to let Ulbricht have control of events that might trigger war.

Indeed, Nikita Sergeevich had a gambler's streak in his personality that emboldened him to start a dangerous game with the bourgeoisie. The United States possessed an overwhelming advantage in nuclear armaments and delivery capabilities in the late 1950s. With two thousand bombers, six thousand nuclear devices of all sorts, and a ten-to-one lead in warheads, America had given chilling new meaning to Roosevelt's "arsenal of democracy." The Pentagon had also begun to develop intermediate range missiles as well as intercontinental ballistic missiles (IRBMs and ICBMs), but these deadly projectiles had not finished testing in August 1957 when the USSR successfully launched the world's first ICBM, the SS-6, and then deployed the vehicle in October to put a satellite into earth's orbit.[8]

"Sputnik" shocked the West, panicking the CIA into reporting in 1958 that Russia would be able to deploy five hundred ICBMs within three years. Khrushchev encouraged such exaggerations by making wild public claims about turning out missiles "like sausages on an assembly line"[9] when in truth he knew that Soviet missile figures would remain in single digits for years—only four SS-6s would sit on launch pads, for instance, in late 1959. But the maverick premier thought he could fool the West into making concessions, just as he thought U.S. officials had only bluffed with their talk of "massive retaliation." While he worried that allegedly sinister militaristic elements in Germany and America might succeed with their dark intrigues, Khrushchev gambled that he could exploit the rational and responsible desire of western leaders to avert thermonuclear holocaust.

With escapee numbers from East Germany mounting alarmingly in November 1958, therefore, the gambler threw his dice. It was time, he charged, for the victors of World War Two to sign peace treaties with the German Democratic Republic (GDR) and the Federal Republic of Germany (FRG). He accused the latter of Hitlerite tendencies. If within six months the West did not act, the USSR would make peace with the GDR and give East Germany authority over access routes to the city. The western allies had no right to remain in Berlin, which should join the GDR and become a "free city." Khrushchev declared ominously that if the West resisted these arrangements the Soviet Union would defend the GDR. Washington rejected this ultimatum in December, stating that NATO would retaliate "if need be by force"[10] against any move on West Berlin. Khrushchev replied that western force would trigger World War Three.

Sizing up the American Leader: Khrushchev and Kennedy at the Vienna Summit in 1961. (Library of Congress)

The crisis cooled in 1959 when both sides backed away from the brink just as the six-month ultimatum period expired. With no diplomatic solution in the offing for Berlin, however, the people of East Germany pushed matters back to a crisis as 200,000 fled to the West in 1960 and another 155,000 from January to early August 1961. Ulbricht increased pressure on his Russian ally to do something, even to storm West Berlin if necessary. His Socialist Unity Party (SED) drew up lists of individuals west of the Brandenburg Gate to be "purged." Once the peace treaty was completed "the free city of West Berlin" would not be "disturbed by occupation forces, agents' centers, radio stations of the organizers of the Cold War, or by other measures which might serve the preparation of war,"[11] said Ulbricht in June.

But Khrushchev did not want to gamble that summer of 1961, especially with a German pressing him. Sensing this dynamic, perhaps, Ulbricht seized on a series of American hints that a move by the GDR to prevent its own citizens from leaving would not violate western treaty rights. "We will not build a wall,"[12] Ulbricht had said in June, but this is what he convinced Khrushchev to do in August. At first barbed wire cut off West Berlin from the surrounding Brandenburg countryside and eastern parts of the city. After three weeks, once it was clear the West would not retaliate, concrete construction began, which eventually fully encircled West Berlin like a medieval walled city.

The Wall: woman with groceries near the Heinrich Heine Strasse Checkpoint. (Private Collection)

As 1961 yielded to 1962, Khrushchev's gambler's instincts drew his eyes elsewhere. Although the Pentagon now possessed over twenty thousand nuclear devices and a fifteen-to-one lead in warheads, from the communist viewpoint a critical time in world history approached, one that called for bold and dynamic leadership. Scores of new nations had broken away from the imperialist-colonialist camp, fledglings that needed protection from former subjugators and the emergent capitalist superpower across the Atlantic. The strongest among the newcomers, China, openly criticized Moscow's apparent unwillingness to challenge the "paper tiger" in the West. One of the weakest among them, Cuba, had managed to ward off a poorly backed invasion at the Bay of Pigs in early 1961, but would surely fall if the United States returned to the beaches in force. Castro leaned on his Moscow patron for firmer support. Khrushchev sensed the time was ripe for action.

Foreign Minister Andrei Gromyko learned about his chief's intentions in the spring of 1962.[13] "The situation forming around Cuba at the moment is dangerous," asserted Khrushchev. "It is essential that we deploy a certain quantity of our nuclear missiles there for its defense as an independent state." Gromyko paused, screwing up his courage to point out the obvious: "I have to say quite frankly that taking our nuclear missiles to Cuba will cause a political explosion in the United States." But the impetuous leader would not be deterred. "What about putting one of our hedgehogs down the Americans' trousers?" he asked the defense minister.

> According to our intelligence [continued the premier] we are lagging almost fifteen years behind the Americans in warheads. We cannot reduce that lead even in ten years. But our rockets on America's doorstep would drastically alter the situation and go a long way towards compensating us for the lag in time.[14]

As the plan proceeded without much discussion or dissent that summer, Cuba was supposed to receive sixty shorter-range missiles capable of reaching targets over two thousand nautical miles away—that is, all of North America west of the Rocky Mountains and south of the Hudson Bay. Khrushchev assumed that his "hedgehogs" would make it impossible for Washington to contemplate another invasion of Cuba. These "ersatz" ICBMs would also provide valuable geopolitical leverage in the developing "Third World" as well as renewed potential to force the West out of Berlin if another crisis erupted. Thus Khrushchev had come to see the Cuban missiles as a panacea for a whole set of embarrassing problems—a "cure-all," observes William Taubman, "that cured nothing."[15]

Indeed, the plan backfired badly. U.S. reconnaissance flights discovered Soviet IRBM sites in Cuba during the late summer and early fall of 1962. Over two-thirds of the missiles had been unloaded, but the first batch would not be operational until October 25–27. On October 22 Kennedy addressed a startled nation, announcing a naval "quarantine" of Cuba to halt Soviet ships, warning that "further action" would be justified if the existing sites were not dismantled, and pledging that any Soviet missile strike in the Western Hemisphere would trigger "a full retaliatory response upon the Soviet Union."[16] As each side traded harsh words over the next few days, American bomber, submarine, and ICBM crews went on alert—and the world gasped in horror. An incident at sea between Soviet and American ships, or nervous trigger fingers in Moscow, Havana, or Washington, could lead to Armageddon. The crisis began to subside only on October 26–28 when Khrushchev gave repeated assurances that the missiles would be withdrawn if Kennedy foreswore an invasion of Cuba, later adding the need for a dismantling of U.S. missiles in Turkey. The Soviet leader had not even consulted an incensed Castro. Indeed, the risk-taker in Moscow had gone cold with fright: Kennedy, the man he had sized up in Vienna the year before as a young lightweight, stared at him now with steel nerves and did not blink. But the American president had also made the concessions asked of him, lest disaster strike—whose likelihood he placed at "somewhere between one out of three and even."[17] Reason prevailed, and the world let out its breath.

Although relieved that war had twice been averted, Europeans reacted with a mixture of resignation and alarm to the succession of crises over Berlin and Cuba. Throughout Eastern Europe the construction of the Berlin Wall reinforced the lesson of Hungary five years earlier, namely, that Moscow possessed the resolve to suppress freedoms in its sphere and Washington had no

The Wall: American military police at Potsdamer Platz. (Private Collection)

intention of drawing its sword to protect them. "It's not a very nice solution," said Kennedy as the cement slabs went into place, "but a wall is a hell of a lot better than a war."[18] No amount of rhetoric in West Berlin two years later altered the sobering underlying realities for Berliners on the other side. The crisis had also shown how dependent the once-powerful center of Europe had become on power centers either on the periphery—Moscow—or altogether out of Europe—Washington. This became even more evident—and even more frightening—during the subsequent Cuban crisis as Europeans watched helplessly, hoping that reason prevailed but unable to affect the outcome. The unnerving talk from Washington during the Eisenhower administration of "massive retaliation" with nuclear weapons against any Soviet power play had caused the first furrowed brows in Europe. Now the near armageddon over Cuba accelerated grassroots pressure for nuclear disarmament or, barring that, détente, a much-needed "easing of tensions."

Both Khrushchev and Kennedy felt the same imperatives. Thus the Soviet leader sent his American nemesis a letter in December 1962 inviting the president to negotiate a treaty banning all tests of nuclear weapons. In January 1963 the humbled Soviet leader stated publicly that the Berlin Wall had eliminated the need for a separate allied peace treaty with the GDR. Thus the threat of another blockade subsided, and the Berlin crisis simmered down.

A sobered Kennedy responded to these olive branches by avoiding harsh rhetoric, and then making a peace offering of his own during a commencement address in June 1963. "We all inhabit this planet," he declared, "and we are all mortal."[19] If the USSR halted atmospheric tests, so would the United States. The Kremlin reacted favorably on June 20, proposing that each side install a "hot line" teletype link to ensure instant communication between Washington and Moscow during international crises and thereby reduce the threat of nuclear war. Nuclear test ban talks had already begun.

As JFK's Berlin address demonstrated later that same month, however, the ugly realities of East-West standoff could still spark confrontational rhetoric. Indeed, real differences reflecting deep mutual distrust soon barred the way to a comprehensive test ban treaty. The stumbling block was the issue of on-site inspections: Khrushchev agreed to three visits for each side, but Kennedy, surveying suspicious sentiment in the Senate, wanted six. The treaty signed in August 1963 banned tests in the atmosphere, in outer space, and underwater, but not underground. Kennedy's fateful trip to Dallas in November ended further progress toward détente, which froze altogether when the assassinated leader's successor, Lyndon Johnson, escalated a previously covert war against the pro-communist, Soviet-backed regime of Ho Chi Minh in North Vietnam. The mid-1960s saw ever bloodier fighting in Vietnam, Washington striving to overtake the Soviets in space—a race with obvious military implications—and Moscow redoubling efforts to catch up with and pass its adversary in ICBMs.

Obviously the world still confronted the frightening possibilities projected on screen with black "theater of the absurd" humor in Stanley Kubric's *Dr. Strangelove: Or How I Learned to Stop Worrying and Love the Bomb* (1964). In order to protect his "precious bodily fluids" from contamination by communist infiltrators to the water system, an insane American base commander unleashes his B-52s against Russia—and frantic officials in Washington fail to abort all of the bomber missions. Who was to say, theatergoers worried after the last nervous laughs, that it could not come to this hot end?

CAPITALISM, COMMUNISM, AND CONSUMERISM

The United States of America represented more than a military threat to the Soviet Union: It also epitomized the adversarial economic system that true communist believers said their system was destined to overtake. Capitalism, gloated Khrushchev, was "like a dead herring in the moonlight, shining brilliantly as it rotted."[20] It required a deep well of faith to make such statements in the late 1950s, for U.S. productivity and per capita consumer income stood two to three times above the USSR.[21] Production of meat and eggs per head was about three times higher; TV sets and washing machines seven and nine times greater, respectively; refrigerators more than eleven times higher; and per capita output of automobiles eighty-three times greater than in the Soviet Union. Nevertheless, Nikita Sergeevich could point to higher *official* GNP growth rates—7.1 versus 2.9 percent for 1950–1958—and confidently predict: "We will bury you." At the party congress in 1961 he even specified dates, predicting that Russia would pass through the "socialist" building stage and reach the "communist" utopia of material superabundance by 1980. "We are guided by strictly scientific calculations . . . [which] show that in twenty years' time we shall essentially have built the communist society."[22]

The ebullient premier concentrated much of his energy on agriculture—a real dilemma after Stalin's brutal and sustained persecution of the peasantry. Cold weather conditions and their attendant short growing seasons also presented a steep challenge in a state with over half of its territory situated above the latitude of the North Sea coast and the American-Canadian border. To provide incentives to farmers in the mid-1950s, Moscow had almost trebled procurement prices for compulsory deliveries from nonstate collective farms (*Kolkhozy*), absorbed collectives' transportation costs, canceled their debts, reduced taxes and limitations on private garden plots and livestock holdings, and expanded tractor and fertilizer production. One of Khrushchev's pet projects also increased sown areas 28 percent by cultivating over eighty-eight million acres of fallow land in the southeast of European Russia, northern Kazakhstan, and southwestern Siberia. The so-called virgin lands were mind-bogglingly vast, equivalent to the entire cultivated land of Canada or twice that of France. All of these efforts boosted grain harvests 63 percent from 1953 to 1958. Milk production rose 61 percent and meat 38 percent in the same period.[23]

Khrushchev proved sorely unable, however, to sustain these impressive rates of growth.[24] For one thing, the anti-peasant inclinations of Stalin's former underling shone all too clearly through pushing and prodding policies that slowed Russia's agricultural impetus. Thus he made collectives buy their own tractors for the first time, driving many of these farms to the verge of ruin. The new boss also unwisely reimposed restrictions on private plots and pastures, thereby undercutting an important source of produce and undermining peasants' morale as well as what little incentive they had to work hard on collective farms, for despite a sharp rise, procurement prices to the *Kolkhozy* still lagged below farm costs. "They pretend to pay us and we pretend to work," so the joke went round. Moreover, Khrushchev intensified Stalin's program of amalgamating collective farms into ever-larger units. Thus the number of these nonstate communal operations, which had fallen from 235,000 in 1940 to 125,000 in 1953, plummeted below 45,000 in 1960 as land area increased a few million acres. With 445 workers per farm as opposed to 110 in 1940, the causal connection between an individual peasant's extra work and extra share of profit became even harder to see, increasing the tendency to be a free rider. Making matters worse, the top man insisted on bulldozing villages and forcing residents into the drab and often shoddy housing of his newly built "quasi-urban" rural settlements. These policies caused enormous distress and "nearly finished off a peasantry bludgeoned to its knees by Stalin."[25] The virgin lands turned into a near dust bowl, meanwhile, as periodic drought and soil erosion from monoculture—Khrushchev's insistence on the perpetual planting of corn or wheat—took a heavy toll. By 1965 overall farm output stood a mere 14 percent above 1958, and grains a scant 7 percent higher. Production had fallen 9 percent in 1963, prompting embarrassing importation of foodstuffs and the depletion of gold reserves.

Nor did Russia "bury" the West with consumer items. To be sure, their production increased 60 percent from 1958 to 1965, making clothing and appliances more abundant, but such growth percentages can be highly misleading.[26] Thus producer goods expanded during the same period by 96 percent, reflecting the continued top priority assigned to heavy industry and defense. Military expenditure jumped 30 percent in 1961 alone as Khrushchev strained his nation's resources to eliminate the missile gap with the United States. National security needs meant that capital-intensive consumer goods like housing and automobiles took a back seat to refrigerators and washing machines: It was consumerism, in other words, on the cheap.

The USSR had assigned such a low priority to personal consumption historically, in fact, that more production of even this limited range of goods from such low levels looked impressive in percentage terms but made little short-run impact on the average family. From 1958 to 1965, for instance, ownership of refrigerators increased from just a few per one thousand of the population to twenty-nine, which meant that around 10 percent of all households enjoyed the considerable comfort of this commodity. "Now when we have a mighty industry," said Khrushchev in 1964, "the party is setting the task of the more rapid development of the branches that produce consumer goods."[27] Household ownership of refrigerators would climb to 59 percent in 1975, but the comparable American figure had reached 70 percent *already in 1958*. Examples like television sets and automobiles project the same unfavorable comparisons with either the United States or Western Europe. Thus 51 percent of

Soviet families owned TVs in 1970 compared to 90–100 percent in the West, while less than 5 percent had cars, far below Europe's 50–65 percent and America's nearly 100 percent. Clearly the West's consumer challenge had not yet been met.

And there were other problems. The flagship industrial sector, growing impressively at 11.7 percent annually in the rebuilding postwar decade, sank to 9.5 percent from 1955 to 1958.[28] Inflated and padded as these official statistics were, no amount of Khrushchev's gesticulating and posturing could cover up the embarrassing downward direction. The beleaguered party leader blamed Russia's top-heavy planning apparatus, decentralizing it in 1957 by creating a plethora of regional planning agencies (*Sovnarkhozy*) loosely coordinated from Moscow. He intended the move to weaken political opponents like Molotov, Malenkov, and Kaganovich in league with the influential state-ministerial hierarchy, but Khrushchev also sensed instinctively that the economy suffered from a kind of entropy, a progressively disorderly state of affairs caused by the ministerial gurus' inability to understand the dynamics of an ever more complicated industrial system. With 107 *Sovnarkhozy* monitoring plan fulfillment locally in the provinces, Khrushchev strove for more efficiency, better quality, and heightened attention to consumer preferences. The result was near chaos, however, as regional authorities hoarded resources and ignored the supply needs of others. Further tinkering with the system in 1962–1963 failed to improve industrial growth, which fell to 7.3 percent. Agriculture's problems meant that overall GNP growth slowed three points to 4.2 percent—although CIA estimates of 2.5 percent, slower than the slowest capitalist economies of the West, seemed more accurate.

Khrushchev had too many problems and enemies to survive in office. His organizational reforms had created disorganization and badly alienated the old planning establishment. The army bristled because he had drastically cut troop levels to afford the missile buildup. Foreign relations were a shambles after the embarrassing Berlin Wall, the Cuban debacle, and a worsening rift with Communist China. Presidium colleagues winced, furthermore, at his hayseed mannerisms in the world limelight. Even common people knew that his policies had failed, mocking his housing projects as "Khrushchev slums" and joking that America raced to the edge of the abyss—and Russia would overtake them. "It is normal for a leader to be feared or cursed or criticized," writes Dmitri Volkogonov, "but when he is laughed at and made the butt of jokes, his time is up."[29] An alliance of top party conspirators, among them the *primus inter pares* and new chairman of the Central Committee Secretariat, Khrushchev's protégé Leonid Brezhnev, deposed him in October 1964.

One of the most important changes a renewed collective leadership now considered as it strove to catch up with the United States militarily lay in the realm of consumer competition with the capitalist West. "The problem is to create a really modern sector producing consumer goods and services for the population, which meets their demands,"[30] Brezhnev would say later. Tales of quality problems abounded: chandeliers too heavy to hang, sofas too long for cramped housing, clothing too large for most people—all because factories maximized quantitative production targets identified in the plan and callously disregarded other considerations. Khrushchev had sought the solution with planning decentralization, but his reforms still kept production and pricing decisions under party control and out of the hands of factory managers who might possibly have known better what consumers needed and wanted. He had largely rejected a whole range of "firm accountability" experiments tried in Eastern Europe over the past decade: some radical, as in Yugoslavia; some ambitious, as in East Germany; some timid, as in Poland and Czechoslovakia.[31]

Because Yugoslavia's economic reforms represented the greatest degree of innovation in the communist world—and threw down a gauntlet, therefore, to the entire East Bloc—they deserve closer attention. Stung by Stalin's denunciations in 1948, Josip Broz Tito and his colleagues progressed quickly from contrition to a soul-searching reexamination of Karl Marx's writings with an eye on uncovering the essence of communism. The resulting changes, implemented gradually from 1950 to 1965, advanced the notion of worker self-management through democratically elected workers' councils. These profit- or income-sharing industrial collectives possessed the closely monitored autonomy to set some of their own prices, hire and fire laborers, make some of their own investments and long-term plans, and compete not only with one another, but also with all foreign producers. Each firm's freedom of maneuver was fenced in, to be sure, by planning guidelines and special investment priorities established in Belgrade as well as party-political controls at the local, regional, and federal levels, but market forces had become more important than planning bureaucrats in determining the distribution of industrial resources. Yugoslav agriculture also allowed the largely invisible hand of supply and demand to shape decision making on the nation's overwhelmingly privately owned farms, still home to 48 percent of the population. "The field left to the market in Yugoslavia," noted one expert, "differs from that open to a country such as France only on two fundamental points: the statutory limitations imposed on private enterprises and the absence of a stock market."[32] Indeed, the heightened role in Western Europe of state planning, government-owned industries, and socialized welfare programs seemed to blur most distinctions with Yugoslavia's market communism, prompting speculation that capitalism and communism might someday "converge."

Impressed by the potential of market stimuli to rationalize the communist system, Soviet economists like Yevsei Liberman had also proposed reforms that would make each firm responsible for turning a profit. Managers should formulate their own plans based on anticipated sales to stipulated retail outlets, thereby forcing firms to pay attention to consumer preferences and quality complaints. Wary of approving something that smacked of restoring capitalism, Khrushchev agreed only to an experiment in two large clothing firms shortly before his ouster. Its success emboldened his successors to widen the scope of the trial to 400 of the USSR's 350,000 enterprises in the winter of 1964–1965.

The champion of "market socialism" was Alexei Kosygin. An executive with Soviet-style business experience, the new premier had long advocated expansion and improvement of the consumer goods sector.[33] At the Central Committee meeting of September 1965, therefore, Kosygin proposed freeing plant managers from many existing controls so that "their output meets the requirements of consumers, finds a buyer, and corresponds to the world technological level." He also preferred to retain the regional *Sovnarkhozy* as a means of blocking anti-reform efforts by former ministers fighting tooth and nail to revive their old planning prerogatives. To yield to market forces, they claimed, would be "unscientific"; to succumb to "refrigerator socialism" would be "bourgeois." Brezhnev acknowledged the need for communism "to keep pace with the stormy scientific-technological revolution of our day,"[34] but, more interested at this time in outmaneuvering political rivals than consumer issues, he diluted the reforms and brought back twenty-seven of thirty-two "new" ministers from pre-1957 days. Enterprise plans would now target sales and bottom-line profitability as well as propose new investments and technical innovations, but the ministries had to sign off on everything. Product prices, moreover, came from above. Finally, Gosplan, the central planning agency, still established overall levels of output and investment in all sectors of the economy.

Nevertheless, momentum seemed to be on the side of market socialism in 1965–1966 as Hungary, Poland, and Czechoslovakia moved toward the bolder Yugoslav and East German experiments.[35] And in the Soviet Union by early 1967 over twenty-five hundred enterprises operated with greater autonomy under the new incentive system. With official rates of industrial growth accelerating again, Kosygin wanted to intensify his remedies by applying them nationwide in order to overtake the West.[36]

TO AMERICANIZE OR NOT

Russia's economic wrangling with the United States, accompanied as it was by Marxist-Leninist ideological assaults and an escalating military buildup, represented the most extreme form of "anti-Americanism" in Europe. As the Soviet-American rivalry intensified with Yankee military intervention in Vietnam, other quarrels simmered among the western democracies—not so much feuds as internal squabbles in the democratic family. Readers have already encountered this milder type of tension in the late 1940s and 1950s over American preference for open door commerce, political union in Europe, and free market solutions to social problems. To Washington's considerable annoyance, the Europeans went their own way instead, advancing socialist societies, limiting political union to the ECSC and EEC, and tending to favor trade protection: the British within the Commonwealth, the European "Six" behind their common external tariff wall.

An even greater threat to harmonious transatlantic relations emerged in 1958 with the ascent to power of Charles de Gaulle. The new leader wanted to preserve the western alliance after a fashion, but not, to be sure, at the expense of enervating his homeland. De Gaulle believed that a revitalized France could lead continental Western Europe to a position of parity in western counsels—boost it, in fact, to a kind of sane third force between the feuding parties in Moscow and Washington. His attempts to realize this agenda provoked the increasing ire of Presidents Eisenhower (1953–1961), Kennedy (1961–1963), Johnson (1963–1968), and Nixon (1969–1974).

De Gaulle's first step came in 1959 with the removal of France's Mediterranean fleet from the integrated command structure of NATO. Still resentful of perceived wartime snubs by the Americans and British, he wanted complete freedom of action for the military forces of the new Fifth Republic—free, that is, from Pentagon influence. The Atlantic fleet was similarly withdrawn in 1963. The army followed three years later, thereby terminating all French participation in NATO and forcing its headquarters to move from Paris to Brussels. France also ignored Washington's policy on nonproliferation of nuclear weapons, exploding its own atomic bomb in 1960 and a hydrogen device six years later. The French president had stood loyally by Kennedy during the Cuban Missile Crisis, but he felt an understandable revulsion at Europe's helplessness as life-and-death matters were decided in faraway capitals.

Meanwhile, de Gaulle pursued an ambitious foreign policy designed to lure Konrad Adenauer and the Federal Republic of Germany into the Franco-European camp. Visits by the chancellor to France in 1958, 1960, and 1962 led to the French president's successful tour of Germany in September 1962, highlighted by his addressing crowds in German, calling them "a great people." "Having personally seen their nations try to destroy each other twice in half a century," writes W. R. Smyser, "the two old men wanted to set those nations on a new and unalterable course."[37] Germany and France should lay the foundation for a more independent Europe less dependent on Anglo-Saxon power.

In keeping with this agenda, de Gaulle vetoed Britain's bid to join the EEC in January 1963. British leaders, reversing previous policies directed more toward the Commonwealth, had wanted to overcome relatively sluggish economic performance and participate in the continent's boom. While he feared the threat to French agriculture from British Commonwealth food imports, de Gaulle also dreaded the prospect of Britain serving as a kind of Trojan horse for U.S. business interests. The EEC would become "a colossal Atlantic Community dependent on America and directed by America," which could quickly and easily "absorb this European Community."[38] Adenauer also snubbed London because he resented what he perceived as Britain's "occupation mentality toward Germany."[39]

A few days after the veto Paris and Bonn signed a special treaty of friendship, thereby putting even more distance between a past of enmity and tragedy and a present of cordiality and peace. Although the West German Bundestag performed a responsible diplomatic feat by passing a parallel resolution that stressed the importance of maintaining integrated NATO forces and expressed its support for British entry to the EEC, the motion did not have the desired effect of softening the Franco-German treaty's impact in Washington. Indeed, it had stunned Kennedy, who saw only an embarrassing rejection of his "Grand Design" for drawing the United States, Britain, and Western Europe into a closer

Former enemies, political friends: Adenauer visits de Gaulle in 1963. (Hulton/
Archive by Getty Images)

economic partnership. Hence the president's trip to Berlin in June 1963 sought
to repair American prestige and influence in Germany without provoking
Khrushchev. As long as de Gaulle remained president of France, however,
Britain's attempts to enter the EEC failed. Thus a second bid in 1967 foundered
once again against a French veto. Not until 1973, in fact, did de Gaulle's successors admit Britain, Ireland, and Denmark to Europe's common market.

This long and persistent defense against allowing Englishmen into the
citadel—and with them, those carpetbag capitalists, the Americans—demands
further explanation. Indeed, de Gaulle, for all his interest and success in modernizing the military and promoting economic and technological development, remained wedded to a traditional notion of society that could not accommodate what he perceived as American ways. Looking back on the 1960s
in his memoirs, he bemoaned the coming of a consumer society that allegedly
did not bring the happy faces of Madison Avenue advertisements. "Despite

the variety and quality of food on every table and the clothes everyone wore, the increasing numbers of appliances in homes, of cars on the roads, of [television antennas] on the roofs, everyone resented what he lacked more than he appreciated what he had." De Gaulle also regretted the passing of "the individualistic way of life that many generations [of Frenchmen] had followed as farmers, craftsmen, merchants, and rentiers," and its replacement by drearily uniform lifestyles.

> [Now commerce] was carried out in identical supermarkets, with rows of shelves and imperious advertising. Everyone's house now resembled a cell in some nondescript block. Gray anonymous crowds traveled in public transportation. . . . Even leisure now was collective and regimented: meals efficiently served in canteens; cheers in unison from the grandstands of sports stadia; holidays spent in crowded sites among tourists, campers, and bathers laid out in rows; day or evening relaxation at fixed hours for families in identical apartments, where before bedtime everyone simultaneously watched and heard the same broadcasts on the same wavelengths.[40]

Obviously the modern drift of things displeased the French president. In fact, de Gaulle's rejection of American-style consumerism strengthens the impression that all was not well with French and European democracy (see Chapter 7), for such attitudes, shared by many French as well as European elites on the political right as well as the left, reflected an underlying unease with the coming of age of the people.

Indeed, to the alarm of some, democratic Europe seemed increasingly like America, outwardly at the very least. Thus one of the hallmarks of the American shopping experience, the self-service store, became much more prevalent in Europe, increasing in quantum leaps from 1,200 in 1950 to 45,500 in 1960. Beginning in the early 1950s and accelerating rapidly into the 1960s, furthermore, material possessions rarely encountered in a European home in the early postwar years increasingly revolutionized lifestyles. By the mid-1970s in France and Great Britain 90 percent and 68 percent of respective households owned a refrigerator, 75/67 percent had washing machines, 60/50 percent drove a car, while 90 percent of families watched their own televisions.[41] The percentages in Italy, Switzerland, West Germany, the Benelux states, and Scandinavia fell mainly between Britain and France, with Italy trailing slightly behind and Sweden a bit ahead. But even wealthy Sweden had fewer material things than the United States—283 motor vehicles per 1,000 of population in 1970, for instance, to America's 532. De Gaulle could complain that the dominant issues of the day turned less on "victory or annihilation" and more around "living standards,"[42] but as Cold War yielded to détente international rivalries were being waged increasingly on this mundane battlefield. "The war we face will be an industrial one,"[43] wrote French journalist Jean-Jacques Servan-Schreiber in his 1967 bestseller, The American Challenge. He had stated a basic truth—one that the Soviets admitted alarmingly to themselves.

Contemporary observers, followed by historians, have debated whether a process of "Americanization" was actually underway, or, rather, a kind of "modernization" driven by the self-generated desires of European consumers largely independent of outside influences. Thus French intellectual Raymond Aron wrote in 1953 that the Marshall Plan "accelerated a historically signifi-cant trend—the spread of American products, customs, and ideas," adding that "even without the Marshall Plan this certainly would have occurred."[44] Writing in 1967, historian Andreas Dorpalen was less sure about the allegedly ineluctable march of America, discounting the impact of self-service stores, Coca-Cola, and other American products as "at best superficial." As for chang-ing values that placed more importance on individual gratification and real-ization of individual potentialities, the extent to which Americanization ac-counted for these changes "and how much of it was simply the result of an inevitable adjustment to changing [European] conditions was and would al-ways remain an unanswerable question."[45]

More recently researchers have tended in the one direction or the other. Thus Victoria de Grazia points to the persistence in Europe of "small retail-ers alongside the big, the reworking of old types of cooperation such as retail buying groups, and the establishment of voluntary wholesale chains," con-cluding that "a European narrative of the rise of mass consumer society could doubtless be told such as to diminish, if not exclude the influence of the United States."[46] An excessive emphasis on the Americanization of Europe also runs

British invasion: The Beatles.   (Library of Congress)

the risk of ignoring the ways that the old world simultaneously Europeanized the new. Nowhere was this more evident than in the world of pop music. American rock-and-roll rhythms resonated and then mutated in Britain, flooding back to America in the contagious new sound of groups like The Dave Clark Five, the Rolling Stones, and, of course, The Beatles. Any American teenager watching their television debut in 1963 was fixated only on the British invasion of the United States, not the parental discussion in the next room about "the American challenge" to Europe. *Time* magazine tipped its hat to the phenomenon of Britain's vibrant youth culture in 1966, dubbing London "the city of the decade."[47]

Other historians still like the concept of Americanization, positing causal connections between American initiatives and European change. In a classic sentence, Richard Kuisel captures the sense of how Americanized European shopping shelves had become:

> To the familiar names of Gillette razors, Singer sewing machines, Carnation milk, Frigidaire, Johnson wax, Simmons' mattresses, Columbia records, Addressographs and IBM office machines, Hoover appliances, Mobil petroleum products, Colgate toothpaste, and Kodak cameras that date from before the war came jeans by Levi Strauss, Coca-Cola, Tide soap powder, Camay bath soap, Quaker Oats, Q-Tips, Ronson lighters, 3M Scotch tape, Black and Decker electric drills, Hollywood chewing gum, Marlboro cigarettes, Jantzen swimsuits, Playtex brassieres, Firestone tires, Timex watches, Libby's canned foods, computers from Texas Instruments, Tupperware, Tampax, Polaroid cameras, Culligan water softener, and Formica kitchen counters.[48]

Trade, of course, was a two-way street that also brought European goods to America: British toy soldiers; Guinness ale; Swedish Lego blocks; Swiss watches; French wines, perfumes, and fashions; Michelin and Pirelli tires; and the increasingly evident European automobiles—Citroens, Fiats, Mercedes, BMWs, and especially the Volkswagen "Beetle," which began to pop up everywhere in the United States after 1960, including the driveway of this author's boyhood Cincinnati home. The dominant flow of commerce, however, went the other way. Obviously it had taken a gargantuan marketing and advertising blitz to have struck "made in America" so ubiquitously on the face of Europe.

This campaign began officially—quite literally so—with Marshall Plan funding (1948–1952). West Europeans received the message, propagated through a variety of media, that arduous labor had to displace absenteeism, spending come before saving, and borrowing take precedence over a bank balance. As one skeptical Frenchman observed, it sounded like "the art of making someone buy something that he doesn't want with money he doesn't yet have."[49] Beneath the productivity and production and "you can be like us" propaganda lay intensifying Cold War worries. Thus an Economic Recovery Program (ERP) memo urged staffers to spread the word that "productivity must increase because more food, more machines, more of nearly everything is needed to make Europe so strong it will be unassailable." A vigorous productivity program was "so essential," noted another memo, "both to permit improvement in the standard of living and to support the requisite military defense effort."[50]

And spread the word they did—through documentary films, newsreels, radio programs, mobile cinema shows and traveling exhibitions, pamphlets, and other publications. In 1950, for instance, fifty ERP documentaries and newsreels circulated in Europe, drawing altogether forty million viewers. In West Germany special "*Amerika* Houses" gave over twelve million annual visitors an idea of the good life across the ocean. ERP programs also transported about twenty thousand select European workers and managers to the United States for a closer inspection. Although the defense message seems to have dissipated amidst the European desire for "social justice,"[51] and few failed to see through the widely trumpeted altruism of the Marshall Plan to the self-serving of American interests, the overall result was positive, mainly because the Americans' media approach proved highly effective at conveying to Europeans "what the U.S.A. was," as one British historian put it. America's "economic strength, her output and productivity, her technological achievements and ever-mounting prosperity provided Europeans with an object of emulation." Then, as European economies took off, "the American myths kept their promises and won through,"[52] concluded a leftist Italian intellectual.

After the ERP and its follow-up programs phased out in the mid-1950s, American business picked up the propagandistic slack. The Yankees founded three thousand new operations or subsidiaries in Europe between 1958 and 1965—a third of these in Britain alone. U.S. investments in Europe rose from two billion dollars in 1950 to fourteen billion in the mid-1960s—with six billion in the United Kingdom. Small wonder that de Gaulle worried about the "colossal Atlantic Community" that could "absorb" the EEC. What the Frenchman had dubbed "imperious advertising" also followed the flag of U.S. business abroad, typically altering the message little for America's new customers. "We've found that the desire for a more attractive complexion or a drier baby," said a spokesman for detergent, paper and consumer products giant Proctor & Gamble, "[does not] vary much from geography to geography." Other companies simply sold their products, cleverly or not so cleverly, with ads selling America: Jeeps parked in front of cabins, beer commercials set in Wisconsin, and cowboys in jeans or dragging on a cigarette. "This effort to associate American . . . merchandise with American values was precisely why many parents in Europe worried that their Pepsi-drinking, Marlboro-smoking . . . children were becoming 'Americanized.'"[53]

Such paternalistic anti-Americanism was not uncommon in democratic Europe. On a visit to Stockholm in 1960, for instance, American writer James Baldwin heard complaints about the Americanization of Sweden. Jukeboxes played rock-and-roll hits; the "jazz joint" was ubiquitous, as were posters of Hollywood idols like James Dean. In Norway patriots like Sigmund Skard bemoaned an American-style modernity that threatened to "devour what I appreciate most in our own old [Nordic] civilization."[54] Recently Volker

Berghahn has probed deeper into the origins of these animosities, finding a long-standing historical fear among European elites of the people pushing their way into government. Post-1945 trends only exacerbated these deep-seated conservative anxieties, for now the masses purchased automobiles and other goods previously restricted to the upper classes. The people also undermined classical forms of art with a crude "lowbrow" culture of radio melodramas, television soap operas, and the primitive beat of rock music.[55]

Consistent with these findings among the elite are signs of the inverse below in society: that average Europeans actually liked what was happening to them. From the world of art, for instance, came a celebration of consumerism with Richard Hamilton's *Just What Is It That Makes Today's Homes So Different, So Appealing?* (1956). By incorporating previously denigrated examples of kitsch into his painting, this leader of Britain's "Independent Group" conveyed the message, somewhat tongue-in-cheek, that candy, comic books, cleaners, canned foods, commercials, and cars were all right. And in France opinion polls from the 1950s showed that while elites from politics, business, and the professions complained that "American influence in Europe endangers good taste," average French men and women welcomed popular culture and consumer products.[56]

By opposing what was crossing the ocean, therefore, enlightened Europeans exhibited more than a justifiable pride in their own rich traditions and cultures, for a faint element of political hypocrisy mixed in. "When they speak of the excesses of 'the consumer society,'" wrote Servan-Scheriber, many intellectuals were really attacking "a small but precious aspect of economic democracy," namely, the "consumer's right to determine his own needs."[57] French leftist Jean-Marie Domenach went even farther in 1960 when he confessed that "ten years ago we could still look down on the snack bars, the supermarkets, the striptease houses, and the entire acquisitive society," but that now "all [of this] has more or less taken hold in Europe" and should be accepted if one claimed to be progressive: "Try a left-wing critique of American society and in the end you realize that it becomes a right-wing critique; that you attack democracy, popular culture, [and] mass consumption ... and that you call into question your own ideology."[58]

An even profounder degree of Americanization came with the adoption of Yankee production and business methods. The big U.S. firms emphasized managerial teamwork, market research to predict mass sales potential, advertising to boost sales, and high wages to encourage labor productivity and fuel mass consumption. American corporations also poured billions of dollars into their laboratories to develop new products and create virgin markets. These practices "made their great contribution to the economic prosperity of Western Europe and guided it toward a consumer civilization on the American model,"[59] wrote Andreas Dorpalen in 1967.

But this transformation did not come smoothly or easily. European businessmen accustomed to cheaper labor, higher investment costs, smaller markets, and reliance on a firm's reputation, not advertising, to make sales, ini-

Richard Hamilton, Just What Is It That Makes Today's Homes So Different, So Appealing? (Kunsthalle Tübingen/© 2004 Artists Rights Society [ARS], New York/DACS, London)

tially balked at the Americans' radical ways. As one New York journalist quipped in 1949, a genuine capitalist mentality, willing to take risks and enthusiastic about individual initiative, was "as rare in Italy as a communist on Wall Street." In France, similarly, sympathetic bureaucrats complained about the "immense frozen ice field, which has characterized the French economy for thirty years, with its network of false protections, costly routines ... and outmoded, traditional outlays." And in Germany even use of the word "manager" met opposition from conservative business leaders who adhered to old-fashioned learning-by-doing. "Insofar as these opponents believed in any management training at all," writes Volker Berghahn, "they would send their employees to Reinhard Höhn's Harzburg Academy, where they would be taught an authoritarian model of leadership inspired by the Prussian General Staff."[60]

Change would necessarily come slowly, resulting at first from the enterprising efforts of businessmen who had grown curious enough to visit U.S. factories for the first time or attend Harvard Business School, and then returned as converts to American methods. In other instances European businessmen who had good relations with Yankee firms in the prewar period reestablished these ties and learned business approaches that had evolved considerably since the 1920s and 1930s. One German executive with Henkel who revisited Proctor & Gamble in 1951, for instance, took note of housewife surveys and home product trials done by P & G's special marketing department on scented dish liquids, returning with a recommendation "that we won't be able to get around a scenting of our own products."[61] The Marshall Plan accelerated this transition by bringing thousands of European managers over the Atlantic to inspect America's biggest manufacturing sites, as well as providing "training within industry" programs for thousands of businessmen back home in Europe. The most enthusiastic pro-Americans among them founded proselytizing institutes in the 1950s that spread the word through seminars, publications, and networking contacts. European demand for knowledge about American business methods literally took off in the early 1960s: Witness the U.S. consulting firms with European branches whose staffs expanded thirty-fold in five years, the typical want ads for Europeans with training and experience in American firms, and European companies, oftentimes aided by their governments, that sent executives to American universities to study business administration—a subject not taught on continental campuses. In ways like these borrowers could filter American methods through European sieves to ensure the most practical application.

Nothing did more to promote the unmodified, undiluted Americanization of European business, however, than the coming of American business to Europe—three thousand companies between 1958 and 1965, including the biggest and wealthiest corporations. Thus Standard Oil of New Jersey (Esso) opened European headquarters in London, IBM established command operations in Paris, while Monsanto and P & G came to Brussels, Dupont to Geneva, and Union Carbide to Lausanne. These offices administered scores of regional branches and manufacturing plants that sprouted up throughout the EEC. In 1965 alone American companies invested four billion dollars in Europe—but earned dividends on the continent that year in excess of this amount. "Fifteen years from now," Servan-Schreiber warned, "it is quite possible that the world's third greatest industrial power, just after the United States and Russia, will not be Europe, but *American industry in Europe*." The impact of this invasion on the European approach to business is difficult to measure, but it must have been immense given the trend-setting personnel policies of Dupont and P & G—followed by many other American corporations in the late 1960s—of bringing their executives home after they had trained native Europeans in American practices. Additional ripple effects occurred as European companies hired away compatriots from American corporations, or Europeans in Yankee firms left to found consulting services. Thus directly or indirectly "the Americans are creating a 'market consciousness' in their wake,"[62] observed Servan-Schreiber.

The ship of American business carried more with it to Europe, however, than managerial science and an intense market orientation—it also brought

American technology. In 1965, for example, 71 percent of new computers installed in Europe bore American labels—most sold by IBM, which had cornered 62 percent of the European market. The dominance of U.S. computers was just one aspect, in fact, of a wider technological lead. Thus of 140 major innovations in the world between 1945 and 1969, one study identified 85 of these breakthroughs—almost 61 percent—as American. From 1957 to 1961 the United Stated earned 175 million dollars annually from Europe in royalties, fees, and licenses for new products and processes while paying out only 41 million to the continent—more than a four-to-one ratio. As will be explained later, a "third industrial revolution" was underway whose country of origin and propagation was undoubtedly the United States of America. Reaping the benefits of this ongoing transformation in 1960, U.S. manufacturers turned out 51 percent more output per unit of total factor input than companies in the EEC did. By 1965 American "state-of-the-art" had pushed the country's share of world automobile production to 76 percent, its portion of global machinery output to 70 percent, and its claim on worldwide electronics manufacture and chemicals production to 68 percent and 62 percent, respectively.[63]

THE CONTEMPORARY TECHNOLOGICAL SYSTEM BETWEEN WEST AND EAST

The third industrial revolution germinated during the Interwar Years and World War Two. For three quarters of a century prior to that conflict the technologies of the second industrial revolution had developed, matured, and aged. Old "King Coal" from the first industrial revolution, supplemented increasingly by oil and electricity from dynamos and generators, provided energy. Reciprocating steam engines from the earlier system, increasingly replaced, however, by steam turbines and internal combustion gasoline engines, provided power. Highly precise electric machine tools like turret lathes, universal milling machines, grinders, and stampers shaped steel, the dominant material that had replaced iron for most uses. Other materials included aluminum, reinforced concrete, natural and synthetic rubber, and sulfuric and nitric acids produced ingeniously in sophisticated laboratories. Lending these technologies their systemic character was their ubiquitous use throughout the economy.[64] Modes of transportation, for example, combined many component parts of this "modern" technological system: At sea, steamships incorporated oil, steam turbines, and steel, and on land and in the sky, automobiles and propeller airplanes used internal combustion engines, electric ignitions, precision-cut/stamped metal, and rubber tires. Communication devices like the radio and telephone could also be more accurately described as "technological clusters" drawing on a variety of techniques like precision parts and electronics.

These technological combinations had their frightful side, too: Witness the tens of thousands of alloy steel tanks and aluminum fighters and bombers equipped with radio communications and precision-cut metal weapons fir-

War spawns another technological revolution: captured V2 rocket, jet fighters, atomic bomb, early giant computer, proximity fuse plastic miniaturization. (Photo by Peter Groesbeck/James Phinney Baxter III, *Scientists Against Time* [Boston, 1946)

ing nitrogen-based ordinance, plus other engines of destruction that drove the war machines of the Axis and the Grand Alliance. However, neither side could afford to gamble that the struggle would be won by expanding armaments production solely along existing lines. Frantic research efforts therefore accelerated development of embryonic interwar technologies, or else plowed new ground.[65] Scientists and engineers unleashed the awesome energy of the atomic bomb and made practical military use of powerful new engines like the jet turbine and the rocket/missile launcher. Communications technology leaped forward with radar and sonar as well as ingenious devices like radio-self-detonated "proximity fuse" shells and television-sighted bomb-steering mechanisms. Many of these gadgets, especially proximity fuses, prompted the first large-scale use and production of miniaturized plastic components. Born into a category unto itself, moreover, was the first generation of computers. The belligerents had crossed the threshold into a new technological era.

Vannevar Bush commented on the military-technological lessons of World War Two in a report to President Truman in July 1945. With an eye on the worsening Cold War, the director of the Office of Scientific Research and Development, the government agency that had coordinated the nation's scientific effort, argued forcefully that the West might not enjoy the considerable benefits of superior technology in the next war unless it made a permanent peacetime commitment to research. Future work should continue the wartime practice of giving universities and industrial labs wide-ranging freedom to pursue applied as well as basic scientific research—the kind of policy that came naturally in a democracy, and exactly opposite to the approach taken in dictatorial Germany.[66] Acting on this recommendation, Washington began to set aside billions of dollars annually for research and development grants to American companies as well as university science and engineering departments. Big business followed suit, with 350 of 378 large corporations investing heavily in organized "R & D" by 1958. Together the U.S. government and private sector ploughed back twenty-one billion dollars in 1963—over 3 percent of the gross national product. The United Kingdom and EEC added another seven to eight billion that year—about 1.5 percent of combined European product—bringing the West's annual R & D total to almost ten times any given year of Marshall Plan funding. By 1968 the U.S. total had jumped 67 percent to thirty-five billion dollars, roughly evenly divided between government and business.[67] "In America today the government official, the industrial manager, the economics professor, the engineer, and the scientist have joined forces . . . [to stimulate] what amounts to a permanent industrial revolution,"[68] noted Servan Schreiber.

Indeed, the dominant techniques of the pre-1939 period yielded increasingly to the familiar outlines of our "contemporary" technological system as the 1950s unfolded into the 1960s and 1970s.[69] Coal receded before the continued advance of oil as well as newer sources of energy like natural gas and electricity generated in giant atomic reactors—both especially important in oil-poor Europe. The automobile, one of the hallmark engines of the modern technological system, played an even greater social and economic role in the contemporary system as more families in the United States and Europe could not cope without one. Preprogrammed "numerically controlled" (NC) machine tools made huge productivity breakthroughs in machine shops. On the rails during these decades, steam locomotives finally took a sidetrack to diesel-generated electric engines, while in the skies, propeller planes yielded to jet aircraft and rockets took men into earth's orbit and eventually to the moon with the aid of seemingly futuristic computers and satellite transmissions. Materials developments maintained an equally torrid pace with the advent of metals like titanium, advancements in plastics, man-made fibers, and a host of chemically induced synthetics. Plate glass and steel buildings pushed up past the older steel-skeletoned, reinforced concrete skyscrapers that had dazzled onlookers in the Interwar Period. The steel was produced, moreover, with ingenious new methods: reduced directly from ore with blasts of oxygen (as opposed to air), and then rapidly and continuously rolled in wider mills. The quarter century after 1945 also witnessed the coming of television to the masses. Entertainment, the media, and politics were altered radically as families stayed home to relax, heard news from all over the world and even outer space instantaneously, and studied politicians' messages and mannerisms with a new facility. Telephone-generated opinion polls affected politics immensely in the 1960s, first in America, but before the end of the decade in Europe too.

But no technology would change military, industrial, and societal relations as much, and as quickly, as the computer. First-generation vacuum tube machines appeared during and after the war in Germany, Britain, and the United States for use in code breaking, ballistics, and census taking. IBM introduced its 704 and 705 models designed specifically for scientific calculations and commercial computing in 1955. State-of-the-art at this time meant 8K of memory, a thousand circuits per cubic foot, and up to ten thousand instructions per second. IBM forged a second generation of transistorized computers in the late 1950s that would make possible more sophisticated jet airliners and spacecraft as well as rudimentary computer-aided design and manufacturing (CAD/CAM). The newer computer models were 1/200 the size, one hundred times as fast, and had eight times more memory than the older vacuum tube varieties. During the mid-to-late 1960s a third generation of computers began to facilitate more complex CAD/CAM operations, computerized machine tools and robotics, and space travel to the moon. These integrated circuit designs boasted 4,000K (i.e., four megabytes) of memory, ten million circuits per cubic foot, and performed up to ten million operations per second—ten times faster than the transistor models. In the early 1970s large-scale integrated circuits and microprocessors spawned a fourth generation of smaller computers, with even more memory, which would eventually be able to process ten billion instructions per second—a thousand times faster than third-generation computers. Now the remarkable little machines could begin to enter homes, offices, and schoolrooms. In 1958, about twenty-five hundred computers operated in the United States; in 1967, around forty thousand; in 1985, over ten million. The contemporary technological system had come into its own.

By the 1970s, therefore, a new system of technologies unfolded that bore increasingly less resemblance to its predecessor—a stage reached by the previous system perhaps around 1900. In the most interesting and significant passage of his oft-cited *The American Challenge* (1967), Servan-Schreiber attributed the largely American origins of this techno-scientific revolution to the country's democratic traditions. For nearly thirty years after the practice started in World War Two, Washington had given universities free rein to pursue liberally funded pure and applied research. The research professors of 1941 taught students who became professors with students and future researchers of their own two decades later. Some stayed in the academy, but the bulk of their graduates left, taking scientific, engineering, and business expertise as well as inquisitive minds into corporate offices and labs. Benefiting from the relative egalitarianism of the United States, lower-class Americans had a three to five times greater chance than in any West European nation of advancing into college. With roughly the same population as the EEC in 1965, the United States turned out more than three times the science graduates, and over four and a half times the overall graduates. "There is no miracle at work here," noted the Frenchman. "America is now reaping a staggering profit from the most profitable investment of all—the education of its citizens." With such an immense outlay on its own people—thirty-nine billion dollars for education in 1965, even more than the national R & D total—no wonder America displayed more "virtuosity in management" and a greater "talent for accepting and mastering change."[70]

There was every reason to believe, however, that the American challenge would be met. As free and open societies allied to America, no barriers existed to technological borrowing like the defense-related bans that limited western technology's flow into communist Eastern Europe and the Soviet Union. That Western Europe took four times as many patents, processes, and product recipes from the United States as it sold, in other words, could not be seen exclusively as a detriment or cost of America's preponderant technological lead, for the new devices and machines came to Europe all the same. This helps to explain the impressive growth in its manufacturing productivity—a statistic usually reflective of technological progress—which grew catch-up style at 5–7 percent annually after 1960, more than double the American rate. The nearly two-point gap in R & D expenditures as a percentage of GNP slowly narrowed over the next decade and a half as Europe pulled to less than a point and West Germany actually caught up with its industrial role model. Successfully borrowing from America as well as ambitiously developing indigenous techniques, the expanded Common Market of the 1970s briefly enjoyed a five hundred million dollar trade surplus in such high-tech exports as computers, digital telecommunications systems, computerized machine tools, and robotics.[71] Europe's entry into the era of the contemporary technological system did not come, however, without a high social price. As will be explored in the next chapter, technological modernization in newly emerging sectors usually meant a shriveling up of older industries from the second industrial revolution. The result was unemployment, social protest, and, all too frequently, violence.

A more pressing question at this time was not whether Western Europe could compete with the United States in promoting the system of technologies driving the third industrial revolution, but whether the USSR and Eastern Europe could do so too. The issue had become urgent for a politicoeconomic system whose ideology trumpeted the inevitability of advancing rapidly to conditions of material abundance. The rate of growth of industry amounted to much more, in other words, than the mundane blackboard chalking of economics professors: Growth rates measured the superiority of communism itself. For decades Soviet industries had grown *extensively* by forcibly shifting labor resources out of agriculture as well as *intensively* by massive injections of foreign state-of-the-art machinery that increased labor productivity. By the 1970s, however, this formula for industrial expansion had nearly exhausted its potential to produce positive returns. Incremental labor inputs plummeted toward zero, for instance, as a largely emptied countryside offered no more assistance and population growth decelerated in accordance with parents' preferences for only one or two children in crowded urban housing. Continued growth could occur in just one way—intensively—but the challenge of scaling this particular growth curve had greatly increased. The Soviet Union kept up with the maturing technologies of the *second* industrial revolution by massive borrowing of turnkey installations in the 1930s and wartime acquisitions in the early 1940s (see Chapters 5 and 6). Once on line, Soviet metallurgical plants, machine tool facilities, chemical works, and armaments factories contributed mightily to the final smashing victory over the Wehrmacht. After 1945 the USSR rebuilt and developed its industries largely along technological lines purchased from abroad and mastered before the war. Although atomic weapons, jet aircraft, and ballistic missiles represented major military forays into the new era, here too borrowing or scientific espionage played a major role. As the West accelerated scientifically and technologically in the 1950s and 1960s, however, Soviet leaders grew increasingly worried about their own inability to generate indigenous techniques while America tried, not without success, to block technological transfers to the East, for communism would not overtake capitalism by investing in antiquated machinery. The USSR had not yet introduced state-of-the-art "closed loop" NC machine tools, for example, when new wave computerized machine tools and robots began to appear in the West. Russia had almost completely neglected computers, furthermore, and even when policy changed in 1965 Soviet research institutes contented themselves with "reproducing innovations which were created long ago abroad," bemoaned Alexei Kosygin, "and which, incidentally, are far from the best." Thus Russian and East European cloned transistor computers "reverse-engineered" from surreptitiously acquired western models accommodated maximally a few hundred thousand instructions per second, while the West, racing through the next generation of integrated circuit devices, pushed speeds to ten million—and soon much higher with fourth-generation models.[72]

Already in 1965 the Soviets took controversial steps to reverse this adverse trend. The planning and incentive changes introduced that September as part of the "firm accountability" movement gaining momentum in Eastern Europe (see earlier) would not only make enterprise managers more attuned to consumer wants and needs, hoped reformers like Kosygin, but also induce the creation and adoption of machinery that "corresponds to the world technological level." The retention of considerable oversight of individual enterprises by the restored central ministries undercut the desired technical rejuvenation, however, by forcing managers to meet quarterly sales quotas.[73] Because only the boldest enterprise heads wanted to disrupt production to retool, fewer and fewer did so. As one Soviet journalist put it to his American counterpart, Hedrick Smith, the largely unattenuated powers of the ministries allowed the overall industrial plan to be "a brake on its own growth, on improving the efficiency of the economy."

> In a planned economy, a man with a new and more efficient machine is dangerous to everyone. . . . If you introduce new machinery, you have to shut down the plant, or part of it. That means that the Plan will not be fulfilled. That is bad for the factory director and the workers. They will not get the bonuses that sometimes comprise 20–30 percent of their pay. It is bad, too, for the ministry in charge of the factory, because it will not fulfill its Plan. And if you stop the plant to install new machinery and that takes several months, you have to stop delivery of steel and other output from that plant which goes to other plants. And they will have trouble fulfilling their Plans. That is the problem with the planned economy.[74]

Ministerial pricing policies created additional disincentives to invest in new technology, for, unable to stay abreast of myriad changes in the business world, bureaucrats often priced goods produced with expensive new machines too low to turn requisite profits. Many enterprise managers found it more rational to produce bottom-line profits by using older, cheaper technologies. Because of these and other problems, the rate of growth of new industrial technology actually decreased in the late 1960s: Witness the percentage share of new products in machine building output, which dropped steadily from 13.8 in 1965 to 8.3 in 1968.[75] Only a loosening of ministerial controls would have produced the intended effect, which explains why Soviet reformers pushed hard for a tougher second stage to the 1965 guidelines. A "full commercial accounting" by factories "competing for the best satisfaction of the demands of consumers," argued one of the renegades, would guarantee the adoption by lagging firms of those modern technologies "being applied at more advanced enterprises."[76]

Meanwhile, Soviet technological reformers tried to build momentum for their cause, partly by emulating American-style education, but mainly, in good communist fashion, by attempting to supersede the Yanks. In late 1966 came a new college-like high school curriculum developed by the elite Academy of Sciences that featured five years of physics, two years of geometry, two years of calculus, four years of chemistry, and five years of biology—all mandatory. At the end of the decade an impressive 50 percent of Soviet eighteen-year-olds were finishing this grueling ten-year program, one that left even the most affluent American school districts far behind in math and science. The Soviets also departed from the traditional European model of sending only a small fraction of high school graduates to college. Stealing a page from the Americans, Russian institutions of higher learning had opened their doors to 4.5 million full- and part-time students by 1970—over 25 percent of the college-age population, an accomplishment second to none in Europe at the time.[77]

Efforts were also underway to somewhat Americanize the research establishment, the targeted recipient of all this educated manpower. In early 1967 reformers managed to loosen the hold of the ministries over the conduct of applied research in the ministerial institutes, which also received encouragement to increase the proportion of their research under direct contract with industrial enterprises. In the following year, then, a decree mandated that several research institutes and design bureaus work simultaneously on identical problems. Breaking the practice of one research group attempting to fulfill ministerial directives would create a "competition of ideas" and permit an evaluation of scientific work "on the basis of a comparison of several solutions." It was this type of research autonomy and scientific spontaneity that the United States had put to dramatic effect since World War Two. As the USSR implemented these reforms its labs and institutes attempted to accommodate the impressive influx of technicians from the educational institutions. Within a decade of implementing these changes the USSR employed 873,500 scientists and engineers in R & D, more than the United States in both absolute and percentage terms.[78]

For a number of years, however, market reformers eager for a Soviet technological renaissance had been fighting a tough uphill battle. Chances of success faded rapidly after the late 1960s, in fact, as developments in Eastern Europe undermined and discredited reform factions in the USSR. Problems began in Czechoslovakia with the ascent of Alexander Dubcek to power in January 1968. His Stalinist predecessor had toyed with market reforms while economic growth ground to a halt, a failure that prompted Dubcek to emulate the compromise incentive measures that Kosygin had introduced three years earlier. The economic portions of the Slovak's "Action Program" of April essentially echoed the arguments of Soviet reformers:

> Methods of direction and organization hitherto used in the national economy are outdated and urgently demand changes, that is, an economic system of management able to enforce a turn towards intensive growth. It will be necessary to prepare the country for joining in the scientific-technical revolution in the world, which calls for especially intensive cooperation of workers . . . with the technical and specialized intelligentsia, and which will place high demands upon the knowledge and qualifications of people, and on the application of science.

That there were *democratic* prerequisites for economic success, however, no Soviet reformer had dared to say:

> A broad scope for social initiative, frank exchange of views and democratization of the whole social and political system becomes virtually the condition for the dynamics of socialist society—the condition for us being able to hold our own in competition with the world.[79]

Throughout the spring and summer the Czechoslovak Communist Party tried desperately to preside over an increasingly unruly situation as censorship was abandoned, new political groupings sprang to life and voiced demands, and old parties suppressed since 1948, like the Social Democrats, returned to politics. Moscow now began to worry that democratization would embolden dissident movements to surface and challenge authority. "Liberalization and democratization are in essence counterrevolution,"[80] blurted Brezhnev to the Politburo in May. Given these dynamics, big brotherly patience did not last much longer. On August 21, 1968, armored divisions from the USSR, Poland,

Birth of the Brezhnev Doctrine: Red Army tanks enter Prague in August 1968.   (Getty Images)

Hungary, and Bulgaria crossed into Czechoslovakia to restore communist order. The "Prague Spring" of democratic reform had been terminated.[81]

These tragic developments presented a brilliant opportunity to opponents of economic reform in the Soviet Union. Since the early 1960s it had been fashionable among western academicians, journalists, and politicians to argue that economic reforms in the East Bloc would lead inevitably to a relaxation of Bolshevism's rigid system of political controls. The apparent liberalization of communism, coupled with the evident socialization of democracy—even standoffish America seemed part of this trend with the 1960s Great Society programs of Lyndon Johnson—convinced many pundits that the two systems were "converging" in the political middle.[82] One side's dream, however, was the other's nightmare. After the Czech experience of 1968 conservative communists, whose genuine belief in centralized direction of the economy as the true Marxist-Leninist path to utopia was reinforced by their vested interest in maintaining ministerial controls, could argue persuasively that market socialism played into the hands of western imperialists who wanted to wreck the communist political system. Concepts like enterprise profitability and accountability, in short, were the slippery slope to political disaster.

Throughout the Bloc that autumn reformers began to backpedal before the conservative counteroffensive. Thus Günther Mittag, the East German Central Committee member most identified with his nation's five-year economic experiment, recanted as early as October 1968, criticizing colleagues who still favored a socialist market economy. East Berlin had canceled all vestiges of firm accountability by 1970. Dubcek's successors in Czechoslovakia cracked down even earlier, reestablishing central economic controls during the spring of 1969. Hungarian reformers also relented to mounting criticisms of their "petty bourgeois" attitudes by scaling back their programs after 1972. In Yugoslavia by this time, furthermore, parallel developments had weakened the boldest market experiment of all. Forced to tighten central political controls to counteract centrifugal nationalist tendencies, above all in proud Croatia, Tito began to substitute political pressure and negotiation for market mechanisms in determining the overall direction of the economy.[83]

Kosygin's reforms, meanwhile, had been subjected to scathing public indictments from Soviet conservatives eager to finish off the opposition.[84] Proponents of further decentralizing reforms lashed back at their attackers, accusing the overbearing ministries of trying "to cram the scientific-technological revolution into the framework of old methods and forms of organization" and thereby running the considerable risk of "putting the brakes on the development of our economy." But Brezhnev had made up his mind before the Central Committee plenum of late 1969. He dismissed market reforms, which "naturally could not fully solve" the pressing dilemma of declining efficiency. "Victory in the economic competition of the two world systems" would come, rather, from central planning improved by econometrics and cybernetics, new sciences that would create solutions based on "the Marxist-Leninist line." Deviationist thinking, warned the premier, would be punished. Seeing the writing on the wall, Kosygin finally dissociated himself from the reforms in 1971. The Soviet Union had probably missed its best opportunity to avoid eventual economic collapse.[85]

Chapter 9

▼

THE WIDENING AND DEEPENING
OF DEMOCRACY

Darkness slowly enveloped a passenger train darting across the Swiss border into France. Destination: historic Avignon and the wine country of the Provence. As hungry travelers, the present writer among them, made their way through the compartments to the dining car, conductors began to spread the word that service this particular Sunday evening would be bare bones: A general strike was set for midnight, and many employees saw logic in stopping work a few hours early. Pundits aboard the express who had been following French events of recent days predicted, ominously, that things were likely to get worse before they got better—indeed, that it might prove easier to get into France this spring than to get out. They were right. It was May 12, 1968, and the whole country was about to grind to a halt.

1968

French history has witnessed many revolutions, coups, failed coups, and riotous disturbances. As late as 1962, in fact, military rebellion brewing over the colonial war in Algeria had threatened French democracy. While few anticipated a return to this pattern of instability in early 1968, storm-warning signals blared elsewhere across the West. Assassins' bullets cut down American civil rights leader Martin Luther King Jr. and presidential candidate Robert Kennedy, touching off riots, while in Germany a crazed assailant badly wounded student activist "Red" Rudi Dutschke, which triggered angry marches and violence. University students in Madrid struck against the oppressive regime of Francisco Franco: "Political action" took the form of "violent demonstrations, commandos breaking windows, stopping the traffic, setting up barricades, hurling Molotov cocktails," recalled one participant. "It looked like the Nevski Palace in 1917,"[1] commented another, alluding to the Bolshevik Revolution. Their compatriots in Italy struck scores of universities that spring, immobilizing many campuses, and then battled with police in Rome after occupying the buildings of aloof university administrators. "We ripped up the wooden park benches and used the planks as clubs." The so-called Battle of the Valle Giulia became the norm in 1968: Witness London, *Time*'s "city of the decade" two years earlier, where now thirty thousand demonstrators, marching against America's war in Vietnam, clashed violently at the U.S. Embassy with men in blue determined to uphold public order.

Indeed, for all of the diverse issues that mobilized European students, opposition to the escalating fighting in Southeast Asia served as a common stimulus to action. Young people who had watched older siblings or parents campaign for nuclear disarmament or protest French oppression in Algeria focused their anger on the new colonial oppressor; earlier efforts to "ban the bomb" faded in significance as nuclear weaponry came to be seen more as "a symptom, not a cause"[2] of everything wrong with world capitalism and western hegemonic politics. In early 1968 the ugly hegemon's war took a surprising turn with Hanoi's "Tet" offensive, rattling U.S. military confidence up the chain of command to President Lyndon Johnson himself, who startled the world by renouncing a bid for reelection. As winter turned to spring, European and American students redoubled their efforts, sensing, perhaps, a weakening of resolve in Washington—and a better chance for peace.

The Zeitgeist was clearly troubled. But would this spirit spawn another French revolution? The answer throughout much of the early spring of 1968 was a clear *non*, for such turmoil seemed impossible in the land of Charles de Gaulle. "Practically no radical over the age of twenty-five," writes Eric Hobsbawm, "believed that revolution in an advanced industrial country was possible in conditions of peace, prosperity and apparent political stability."[3] Flare-ups at the University of Paris's austere annex at Nanterre did not really alter this relatively placid picture. Angered by crowded classes, poor facilities, Olympian professors, insensitive administrators, perceived worldwide social and political injustices, as well as the Vietnam War, radicals like Daniel Cohn-Bendit briefly took over the suburban campus in late March. Further sit-ins and disturbances in April led to the indefinite suspension of classes on Friday May 3, 1968. University magistrates summoned Cohn-Bendit to the Sorbonne for a Monday hearing.

In so doing, however, they opened Pandora's box, for as students assembled in ever greater numbers to hear the charged oratory of "Danny the Red," officials, fearing their authority threatened, summoned riot police. Arrests and the appearance of paddy wagons triggered student retaliation, to which the police responded with appalling brutality. The shocking scene repeated itself with escalating ferocity in the evening of May 6 and the night of Friday May 10–11. Students fortified the Latin Quarter with makeshift barricades in conscious symbolic remembrance of 1848, hurling cobblestones and Molotov cocktails at shielded charging police swinging nightsticks and shooting tear gas. In the span of eight days almost fifteen hundred were arrested and *at least* as many injured. The students issued furious calls for de Gaulle's resignation—demands that began to resonate in the wider world of French politics on Saturday morning when leaders of the Communist Party (PCF), surveying the human and physical damage, called for "vigorous protests" against the "Gaullist power's launching of unheard of violence."[4] The move surprised many observers, for Cohn-Bendit had shown no respect for the old men of the PCF. Nevertheless, Communist and non-communist trade unions agreed to a twenty-four-hour general strike for midnight, May 12–13.

Finally realizing the seriousness of the political threat to de Gaulle, Premier Georges Pompidou promised to withdraw police from the Sorbonne and review all student arrests and convictions. The president himself, the father of his nation who had led the people back from defeat in the last war, responded ominously a few days later with a terse mixture of political hope and barrack room slang and contempt for politicized students, sons of the nation who he thought were having trouble growing up: "Reform, yes; shitting the sheets, no."[5] Although many workers looked with similar disdain at would-be bourgeois revolutionaries who had never calloused a hand, rank-and-file proletarians soon flung their own problems in de Gaulle's face—and defied their own leaders—by continuing to strike. Within a week around ten million workers— 50 percent of the labor force—had walked wildcat-like off the job.

Meanwhile, the students proclaimed the Sorbonne a liberated area and began to debate how to proceed with their revolution. The young men in charge presided over a politically intense but socially and sexually "laid-back" polity that represented a kind of microcosm for the radicalized wing of the younger generation. A number of circumstances specific to the decade of the 1960s shaped these young people as well as their relationship to the older generation.[6] Like teenagers and college students throughout Western Europe, the inhabitants of the Sorbonne were products of a postwar era whose economic prosperity put more money in young people's pockets, whose welfare states provided youth with more leisure time to spend it, and whose technological revolution enticed spenders with hand-held transistor radios, mass-produced vinyl records, and ever-cheaper television sets, all of which propagated an increasingly standardized and internationalized youth culture of fashion and rock music that sometimes led to experimentation with sex, alcohol, and marijuana. If there was sometimes an element of irreverence and protest to youth culture, however, it certainly stemmed from a problematic interaction with (and inability to relate to) a parental generation that had perhaps enjoyed some of these things, only to see most of it cut short by the Great Depression and World War Two. Young teenagers in Britain and America reacted with a mixture of awe and intimidation, and later more frequently with annoyance, to parents' repeated references to the superiority of classical music and/or jazz, to what they had done without in the 1930s, and to the depth of discipline and hardness that had been required to win—or just survive—the war. In countries like France, where pointed questions of collaboration or resistance were asked, or Germany, where complicity in aggression and the Holocaust became extremely awkward topics of conversation, an extra element of anger entered cross-generational relationships. In many European families the threat of nuclear destruction, followed by the hugely controversial Vietnam War, sent some angry students along the path from youth culture to radical leftist politics.

The Grand Amphitheater, recently site of crammed lectures for the first hundreds lucky enough to find a seat, now housed the plethora of action committees that sought to remake society. The historic countenances on placards and posters glued to walls and pillars testified to the fragmented, leftist political scene: Marx, Mao, Trotsky, and slain guerilla fighter Ché Guevara appeared everywhere. "In the grand auditorium, where we had a general assembly every night, each announcement of a new strike, of support from foreign movements, of sympathy from people outside the university raised immense and endless applause in the room," recalled one organizer. "The Sorbonne was the site of coherent and mature contestation against a disastrous society."[7]

This student's observation reflects the influence of an intellectual who was extremely popular among French, and indeed among European students in 1968: Rudi Dutschke's mentor, Herbert Marcuse. The German-born professor from UCLA had studied under the great Martin Heidegger from 1928 to 1932. As a Marxist, and as a Jew, Marcuse could never accept his professor's backing of Hitler in 1933, but Heidegger's earlier critique and rejection of the paralysis of modernity's "inauthentic existence" permeated Marcuse's own later writings. In *Eros and Civilization* (1962) and *One-Dimensional Man* (1964) he lambasted developed society's weapons of mass destruction, rape of the environment, exacerbation of world poverty, and especially its peoples' soma-like acceptance of such unworthy conditions. "I certainly wouldn't deny that authenticity is becoming increasingly difficult in the advanced industrial society of today," said Marcuse. Through a manipulative process he dubbed "repressive desublimation" the natural instincts for goodness of whole societal strata were being diverted into a frenzy of getting and spending:

> People recognize themselves in their commodities. They find their soul in their automobile, hi-fi set, split-level home, kitchen equipment. . . . This identification constitutes a more progressive stage of alienation . . . [whereby] the subject which is alienated is swallowed up by its alienated existence. There is only one dimension, and it is everywhere and in all forms.

Because genuine democracy, theoretically preferable, had allegedly also been subverted, Marcuse favored a "dictatorship of intellectuals"[8] that would return to authentic existence and harness the true potential of technology to utopian ends. Through its creation of leisure time, technology's ever-greater productivity should make possible widespread individual self-realization and gratification. Hence the students' determination to banish "alienation" from society and their angry rejection of everything "bourgeois" or "fascist," especially in their classrooms. Cohn-Bendit lambasted the modern university system, for instance, as a "sausage machine, which turns people out without any real culture and incapable of thinking for themselves, but trained to fit into the economic system of a highly industrialized society."[9]

For a few weeks it appeared that the rebels in the Sorbonne would find common cause with the strikers, for some of the wildcat actions were motivated not by traditional wage demands, but rather by the desire for *autoges-*

tation: more workers' control in the form of self-managing cooperatives, participatory decision making, and, hence, job enrichment. The proletarian version of revolution against alienation dissipated by early June, however, as government promises of wage hikes convinced most to return to work. Government force finished the job on June 7–8 when thousands of police ejected workers who had occupied the Renault and Peugeot automobile plants. Two were killed, prompting student rioting in Paris on June 10–11, hundreds of injuries, and another fifteen hundred arrests. Police retook the Sorbonne a few days later. The voters rendered their judgment on the spring violence on successive Sundays in late June 1968, returning 358 Gaullists to the assembly out of a total of 485 seats—nearly a 74 percent majority for de Gaulle's renamed "Union for the Defense of the Republic." The "almost revolution" was over.

Assessing its impact and significance is no mean task. The police clearly succeeded in restoring order to campuses and factories, while students and wildcat strikers, demoralized and broken, won none of their radical demands. On the other hand, students received a partial redressing of their grievances that fall when Education Minister Edgar Faure announced reforms. To overcome crowding as well as enable higher education to serve democratic purposes and meet America's challenge, the state would triple the number of universities by 1972. Faure also weakened ministerial control over university administration, gave students meaningful participation in this more autonomous university policy-making process, and curtailed the arbitrary and hated authority of chaired professors. For their part, workers received a 10 percent pay raise and 30 percent hike in the minimum wage. As something of a weak concession to demands for *autogestation*, moreover, trade union leaders got representation on the executive boards of selected industries. With French democracy demonstrating its resiliency, flexibility, and responsiveness, the political system seemed healthier.

Determining the extent to which protestors and strikers succeeded in their increasingly shrill demand for de Gaulle's resignation also presents a challenge to historians. For one thing, the general's standing had suffered before the May events as his regal posturing and controversial decisions to build a nuclear force and block British entry to the EEC alienated moderate and leftist voters. Thus Socialist François Mitterand forced him into a humiliating run-off in the 1965 presidential elections, and by 1967 the Gaullist majority in parliament had shriveled to a mere two seats. The police abuses of 1968 fueled further opposition, and, for a few days in late May, brought the president within a hair's breadth of resignation. In one of history's most dramatic reversals, however, de Gaulle drew strength from the loyalty of his generals, and then called for elections allegedly to preserve democracy from street subversives and communists. As noted earlier, the second run-off election of late June produced a "law-and-order backlash" as voters, alarmed by the violence and destruction, cast ballots for de Gaulle's party. Far from removing him, the "almost revolution" seemed to have revived his fortunes. The June turnaround would prove to be only a temporary reprieve, however, for nine months later

Democratic action: anti-de Gaulle protest in Paris in June 1968. (Getty Images)

the proud president resigned after 53 percent of the electorate rejected a referendum package that included reduced powers for the upper house. It seems likely that the events of 1968 had left de Gaulle hypersensitive to what was, after all, only a minor rebuff. A year earlier the students had "exploded the major obstacle—the myth that no one could do anything to shake the regime," boasted Cohn-Bendit. "We've proved that this isn't true."[10] By shaking de Gaulle the demonstrators had certainly contributed to taking him down.

Whatever the main cause of de Gaulle's departure, there can be little doubt that French democracy improved without him. The president had returned France to a plebiscitary or Napoleonic half-democracy (see Chapter 7), ruling above the parties and at times even above his own ministers. Gaullism, the alleged cure for an admittedly ailing democracy, threatened to kill the patient. The general's successors, Georges Pompidou (1969–1974) and Valery Giscard d'Estaing (1974–1981), did nothing to weaken the presidency or the image of France abroad, to be sure, but they dropped much of the pretense to grandeur on the world stage, concentrating instead on extending the suffrage to eighteen-year-olds, improving women's rights, and attempting to shore up democracy by creating a measure of economic security in severe recessionary times (see later).

The eruption of 1968 stamped not only French political history, but also that of Europe. Indeed, one should view the French events in a wider context in order to appreciate their long-term import, for, as the climactic episodes in a year that saw much of the continent in turmoil—Italy, Spain, West Germany, and Britain were convulsed by violent protests—they marked a significant watershed in European politics and both advanced and undercut democracy.[11] As the generation of 1968 grew to middle age over the next two decades, this new Left and the established Social Democratic and Communist parties, so far apart during the year of unrest, tried to engage and accommodate one another. So healthy for democracy, the so-called Eurocommunist trends of the 1970s cannot be fully understood outside this context. Leftist establishments did not always succeed in cooperating with maturing "68ers," however, as new parties and movements with new definitions of democracy broke away— for instance, the environmental "Greens" and the anti-NATO protesters of the early 1980s, both striking out against leftist establishments, both continuing the irreverent politics and grassroots protests of the late 1960s, but both also benefiting from the spadework of pre-1968 predecessors. Generation 68ers would make two additional indelible marks on the European political scene of the late twentieth century. Thus the modern women's liberation movement, like the Greens and the peaceniks, inherited momentum from early pioneers but then took off during that year of unrest as young females, resentful of male insistence on leading the revolts, began to do more for themselves, and with positive results. In this way, especially, the experience of 1968 enriched and deepened democracy in the West. Unfortunately, dissatisfaction among some of the protesters with the unacceptable outcome of their youthful efforts also emerged tragically in the form of terrorist acts—political crimes that marred West European democracy, especially in Italy and West Germany. As will be described later, the "Irish Troubles" were a related negative phenomenon.

HARD TIMES

The impressive economic growth and prosperity enjoyed by Democratic Europe from the late 1940s into the 1960s made it possible to support the welfare state establishments that finally gave the lower classes their due. As the new decade dawned, however, these good times were fading away—and would never really return. In order to understand why this happened one must examine and appreciate the social consequences of the technological transformation sweeping across the West after World War Two. Put simply, as new techniques and industrial groupings emerged in the third industrial revolution, industries that had driven the second shrank.[12] To take an extreme example, British coal mining sustained 690,000 workers in the 1950s, but by the 1980s, after oil and nuclear power had grown as energy sources, only 60,000 miners had jobs. Over the same decades the fraction of the overall British labor force employed in the industrial sector fell from 49.2 percent to 30.2 percent as coal, iron, and steel; railways, shipping, and docking; automobiles and machine tools; and textiles each put hundreds of thousands fewer people to work. Belgium's industrial sector experienced a similar fall from 48.3 to 28.7 percent, while France, Holland, Scandinavia, West Germany, and Austria suffered ten- to eleven-point drops. To be sure, oil, nuclear, computer, electronic, aerospace and pharmaceutical companies rising with the new industrial wave created jobs, but far fewer than those lost—and these positions typically required special training or higher education lacked by the unemployed. The same held for new careers in business and information services or other service sector slots opening with the expansion of West European welfare and social insurance programs. Making adaptation to the new labor scene harder and harsher, many of the remaining job opportunities with old technology firms shifted to the suburbs or countryside—approximately half of Britain's inner-city industry fled—while often declining qualitatively from full- to part-time and employing women rather than men, a zero-sum game that helped women but hurt men. The result: Trade union strikes and labor demonstrations gained momentum across Europe after the late 1960s as angry workers tried to preserve wages and jobs.

Events in the Middle East complicated Europe's painful structural adjustments. The Arab-Israeli War of 1973, resulting in the fourth victory in a quarter-century for the struggling Jewish state, triggered an angry—albeit economically rational—response from the oil-producing states of the region. In order to maximize profits from their highly sought-after natural resource, as well as punish the United States and Western Europe, Israel's patrons in the industrially developed "North," the Middle Eastern members of the Organization of Petroleum Exporting Countries (OPEC) exacerbated their cartel's stiff 70 percent price hike of that year with a temporary oil embargo.[13] Tantamount to economic warfare, the retaliatory move sent a shock wave throughout the North by doubling oil prices almost overnight. Western Europe, whose dependency on oil had tripled from 20 percent of energy needs in 1955 to 60 percent in 1972, was particularly hard hit. OPEC continued to squeeze its customers throughout the decade, sending prices to ten times the 1973 level by 1979. The subsequent surge of "cost-push" inflation worsened the dilemma of older industries, which had been struggling to adjust to reduced demand; dampened the dynamism of newer high-tech firms, which were engaged in an intense international competition for market shares; and created unwanted hardships for lower class consumers, who already faced the prospect of layoffs. OPEC added a layer of politically induced cyclic disruption, in other words, to an ongoing structural/technological crisis.

The labor disruptions that shook Europe in the 1970s and early 1980s cannot be fully understood outside this dual structural-cyclic context. Strikes that had brought down one British Labour government in 1969–1970, for instance, felled a Conservative government in 1974 and another Labour government during the so-called winter of discontent in 1978–1979. Accompanying the labor disruptions, rock-and-roll metamorphosed into "punk rock." Angry antiestablishment groups like The Sex Pistols, The Poison Girls, and Crass spat out songs with "feed the five thousand" lyrics that made even the Rolling Stones and The Doors look tame by comparison.

In West Germany, moreover, normally disciplined workers also struck more frequently—at three times the rate of the 1960s, in fact, forcing the loss of nearly four times as many days worked.[14] They announced sarcastically and impatiently: "We are waiting for the next 'economic miracle,'" a mocking reference to Adenauer's economic recovery of the 1950s. The situation was even worse in France and Italy, where trade unions nearly paralyzed their nations. Cabinets in London, Paris, Bonn, and Rome tried to convince unions to accept deals with moderate wage increases. These so-called social contracts ameliorated conditions somewhat in the mid-1970s before breaking down a few years later, but even limited wage hikes hurt the economy as employers passed their increased costs along to consumers in the form of higher prices. Consumption and inflation received additional fuel from social insurance and welfare programs that regularly pumped money into the economy.

Now both Europe and America struggled to combat the unprecedented scourge of "stagflation," a disturbing new term for high unemployment coexisting, against all previous economic logic, with double-digit rates of inflation. Each side dealt with the challenge differently. Washington increased the money supply in a bid to stimulate economic growth amidst worsening inflation, thereby holding increasing costs down as a percentage of rising prices. Congress also passed a wise piece of legislation in 1978 that cut long-term capital gains taxes from 49 to 28 percent in order to fuel investment in new ventures and stimulate technology-related productivity gains. The move, which reversed an earlier bill, spiked such investments from ten million dollars in 1975 to 1.3 billion in 1981, facilitating the founding or expansion of hundreds of enterprise gambles—among them Apple Computers Incorporated, the pride of "Silicon Valley," the California microprocessor chip production center whose name became synonymous with American computer prowess. The pro-business, tax-cutting environment ushered in with the election of Ronald Reagan in 1980 helped to increase overall *private sector* R & D from thirty-seven billion dollars in 1977 to an unprecedented forty-four billion in 1983.

Western Europe, on the other hand, pursued more conservative policies. Always more sensitive to foreign trade needs than the near-autarkic United States, which relied much more on its huge domestic market, they sought to preserve currency values and stabilize exports with deflationary programs designed to gut inflation, reduce interest rates, energize investment in technology, and stay abreast of the new industrial revolution. The first major spokesmen for ignoring the seemingly rash, short-term mentality of the Americans were moderate French President Valéry Giscard d'Estaing and German Social Democrat Helmut Schmidt, both coming to power in 1974, but the election of Margaret Thatcher's Conservative government in Britain in 1979 took inflation fighting to extremes. The "Iron Lady" introduced Draconian cuts in government services and attempted to bust the militant miners union, all in the name of economic revitalization. Successive reelection in 1983 and 1987 led to far-reaching privatization programs—two-thirds of Britain's state-owned industries were sold into private hands before she left office. Even the Socialist governments of François Mitterrand in France and Olof Palme in Sweden, entering office in 1981–1982, felt the need to pursue varying degrees of austerity in the hope of eventually stimulating investment. Because American interest rates stayed higher as a hedge against inflation, however, much of

Europe's capital gravitated rationally enough to the greater returns available in the United States and was therefore not available for domestic ventures. German portfolio investment abroad, for example, rose from 2.7 billion dollars in 1981 to 40.8 billion in 1988, most of this to purchase American treasury bills.[15]

Transparent economic nationalism further hampered European efforts to compete technologically with the Americans. Thus Common Market members, increasingly desperate to overcome stagflation and bail out sinking older industries, postponed plans for monetary union (see later) and turned instead to a plethora of so-called non-tariff barriers (NTBs) designed to curb imports from neighboring countries. Thus Italy used safety regulations that called for laminated automobile windshields to shut out West German cars built with toughened glass. Contrasting public health and environmental standards provided convenient arguments for NTBs in other areas. Member nations also gave national companies preferential treatment on government contracts, which helps to explain why the ten-member Common Market had nine different telecommunications switching systems in the early 1980s. Experts equated the decelerating economic effect of NTBs to an 8–12 percent tax on foreign goods. "You can imagine what would have happened to Apple Computer if it had to fight such barriers in different American states,"[16] lamented one official of the European Commission in Brussels. Plagued by stagflation, strikes, capital flight, proliferating NTBs, and other competition-restricting measures, Western Europe saw the brief 1978 surplus in high-tech trade goods it had enjoyed with the United States turn into a forty-billion-dollar shortfall in 1991.

Long-term potential nevertheless remained bright. For one thing, Western Europe still held on to many niches of scientific and technological superiority: Swiss pharmaceuticals and electric-generation equipment, British precision instruments, West German engine technology and machine tools, and Swedish robots. In 1986, moreover, Common Market leaders agreed to abolish NTBs by 1992 and return to scrapped plans for monetary union as the only way to enhance transatlantic competitiveness. The potential to meet America's growing challenge seemed assured, finally, as Western Europe embarked on a very tortuous acceleration of democratization (see later), for one byproduct of the continent's heated politics of the late 1960s and 1970s was the emulation of American-style mass education and a meteoric rise in the percentage of young people entering college.[17] French journalist Jean Jacques Servan-Schreiber would certainly have agreed that "daring more democracy"[18] made good business and technological sense.

EUROCOMMUNISM AND THE SPREAD OF DEMOCRACY IN SOUTHERN EUROPE

In Italy the violent student demonstrations of 1968 led, as they had in France, to serious labor unrest. This turmoil worsened in the "hot autumn" of 1969 as both groups protested the unfulfilled and long overdue social promises of the nation's political leadership. Five years earlier the so-called opening to the left had finally brought Christian Democrats and moderate centrist parties into a governing coalition with Pietro Nenni's Socialists, who throughout the 1950s had preferred stubborn opposition alongside the Communists to cooperation with the bourgeoisie. By 1962–1963, however, the ardor for class struggle of many Socialist deputies had cooled as industrial advances brought undeniable consumer benefits, and Moscow's heavy-handed politics in Hungary in 1956 discredited the extreme Left. For their part, moderate Christian Democrats like party leader Aldo Moro realized that Italian democracy could not survive another "opening to the right" that included making deals with neo-Fascists (see Chapter 7). But this center-left collaboration produced only a few significant results—namely, the nationalization of the electric power industry—before both coalition partners slowed the pace of reform in 1964, apparently to avert the imminent threat of a right-wing coup aimed at blocking the Left. This intrigue, associated with secret service chief Giovanni De Lorenzo, broke into the headlines in late 1967, adding extra fuel to the protests of 1968–1969. Like French legislators the previous year, coalition leaders in Rome moved forward with reforms like enhanced old age pensions to demonstrate to workers that Italian democracy was no sham.

By doing this, however, the cabinet unwittingly precipitated a spiral of terrorist violence from both extremes of the political spectrum. In December 1969 four bombs exploded in Milan and Rome, killing sixteen people. The explosives had been planted by shadowy Masonic conspirators hoping to lay the murders at the Left's doorstep, trigger a crackdown, and scuttle the government's legislative initiatives. The truth soon emerged, and the government, to its credit, actually quickened the pace of reform, introducing the so-called Workers' Charter, which improved job safety, strengthened trade union rights, and gave workers legal recourse against unfair dismissal. The ruling coalition also attempted to fine-tune democracy by establishing autonomous regional governments and amending the constitution to provide for popular referenda.[19] But none of this satisfied a minority of disgruntled leftist protesters who did not want to repeat the French experience of coming close to revolution only to see it frustratingly slip away. "The myth of imminent revolution was a direct emanation from '68," writes Paul Ginsborg. "When the revolution did not arrive, it was not surprising that some militants decided that a final, supreme voluntarist act would provide the necessary short cut."[20] Disgusted by the inactivity of the entire establishment—stretching in their definition past the Christian Democrats to the Socialists and Communists, both of whom had allegedly ignored their historic revolutionary mission—the so-called Red Brigades began their own criminal campaign in late 1970. "Political violence, armed confrontations, and conspiracies to overthrow the republic continued unabated over the next years," observes Spencer Di Scala, as "Italy seemed to fall apart."[21]

Amidst the greatest challenge to Italian democracy since 1945, Communist Party (PCI) leader Enrico Berlinguer made a tough decision for "historic compromise" with bourgeois democracy. This meant a rallying of all popular forces—Communists, Socialists, and Christian Democrats—to defend the republic. The strategy entailed an acceptance of rule of law and parliamentary give-and-take as well as a rejection of Marxism-Leninism's provocative credo of proletarian revolution. The seemingly unnecessary invasion of Czechoslovakia in 1968 facilitated Berlinguer's ultimate acceptance of democratic procedures. The Soviets' brutal suppression of political pluralism and embryonic democracy exposed the political bankruptcy of Moscow's ideology in the eyes of many western communists who had grown accustomed to election campaigns and parliamentary debates. As recent developments in Chile also seemed to prove, socialism in Western Europe would have to advance gradually, peacefully, and democratically, or not at all, for the reactionary dangers that struck down the Socialist government of Salvador Allende in 1973 clearly threatened Italy too. Moreover, the military coup in Greece six years earlier against an even less threatening center-left coalition (see later) reinforced this wisdom. Therefore, after local elections in 1975 gave his party over 33 percent, and national balloting the following year pushed the PCI vote above 34 percent, Berlinguer offered parliamentary support for a cabinet headed by Christian Democrats. In 1976 a Communist, Pietro Ingrao, presided for the first time over an Italian parliamentary body. The historic compromise had been made, but it remained unclear what would come of it, especially amidst the technological restructuring dilemmas and OPEC-induced economic recession of the mid-1970s (see earlier).

Developments in Spain, meanwhile, heightened the mood of tension and apprehension across the continent, for Francoist oppression seemed to be weakening, if ever so slightly. Eager to catch the wave of economic boom sweeping into Europe in the late 1950s, technocrats appointed by Francisco Franco began to dismantle the autarkic regime so typical of 1930s-style Fascism and transform Spain into a market economy institutionally compatible with neighboring EEC nations. In 1962 Spain formalized its priority goal of joining the Common Market by applying for membership. Reformist voices within Spanish Fascism already advocated an accompanying political liberalization, both for idealistic as well as pragmatic, EEC-related reasons. The wisdom of this advice became apparent at a meeting in Germany of scores of Spain's non-communist opposition, many of them living in exile, who argued adamantly against admitting non-democratic Spain into Europe's democratic club. Also rebuffed in Brussels, Franco's men had extra incentive to proceed with the new "liberal" regime. Their flurry of bureaucratic decrees included a collective bargaining process freed from central ministerial controls. The result: fifteen hundred illegal strikes from 1963 to 1967, culminating with one hundred thousand laborers marching in the capital for higher wages, followed by the ringleaders' arrests. In 1966 came a measure of press freedom; in 1968, greater freedom of association. The result: a barrage of criticism and honest reporting, followed typically by the seizure of newspapers and magazines, with worse insults to Fascist legitimacy in 1968 when student radicals shut down the University of Madrid. As in France and Italy, student riots led to escalating labor unrest, punctuated by fifteen hundred strikes in 1970 and almost two thousand in 1974. "Spain was an anti-liberal state yet desperately searching for some form of democratic legitimacy,"[22] write Raymond Carr and Juan Pablo Fusi, but few inside or outside the country were impressed. Terrorists assassinated Franco's handpicked president, Carrero Blanco, in 1973, prompting a wave of arrests as well as mass demonstrations by Fascist hard-liners demanding an end to reforms lest this alleged sign of weakness beget more terrorism. Franco's death in 1975 left skeptical Europeans asking whether the troubled nation would suffer another bloody civil war. During the first two months of 1976 alone, in fact, workers struck 2,377 firms. Could Franco's successor, Juan Carlos, son of the last king, coroneted soon after the dictator's funeral in a prearranged restoration of the monarchy, keep the peace?

The Spanish Communist Party (PCE) headed by Santiago Carrillo had positioned itself at the center of these events. Heavily involved with the workers' and students' strikes of the late 1960s and early 1970s, his highly disciplined party strove to end Francoism and found a democratic republic in close association with other progressive anti-Fascist groups. Indeed, Carrillo, like Berlinguer, had rebuked the Soviets after Czechoslovakia, insisting that Moscow could not dictate which single road led to socialism—for there were many roads, one being genuine participation in government, "popular front" style, with non-communist parties. This "Eurocommunist" appeal did not resonate initially with other Spanish parties of the Left, primarily because memories lingered from the Civil War of the PCE's bullying, autocratic behavior. By early 1976, however, two coalitions had formed demanding some form of democratization: the Democratic Junta, led by Carrillo, pressing for a referendum on a republic; and the Democratic Convergence, grouped (from Left to Right) around the Socialists, Social Democrats, Christian Democrats, and various centrist parties, which did not reject monarchism outright (except for the Socialists), but expressed skepticism that King Juan Carlos could produce the desired democratic reforms. These doubts, and the common longing for democracy, brought the two coalitions together on a loosely united platform as the "Democratic Coordination" in March 1976. The government quickly arrested five leaders of this united opposition.[23]

Indeed, Juan Carlos appeared initially to be more of the problem than the solution. His speeches sounded Francoist, and his prime minister, Carlos Arias Navarro, would not yield to mounting pressures from Democratic Coordination. Appearances were deceptive, however, for privately the king sympathized with the democrats, lambasting Arias as a "complete disaster" and an "immobilist"[24] who blocked reforms. By June 1976 Arias had been replaced by Adolfo Suárez, a Fascist reforming insider. Over the next ten months Juan Carlos and Suárez made clever use of referenda to outmaneuver Franco's rubber stamp parliament, the Cortez, and appeals to personal loyalty to finesse another key Francoist institution, the army. These efforts produced widespread agreement on changes that heretofore seemed impossible: amnesty for political prisoners, including terrorists; legalization of trade unions and political parties, including the PCE; and parliamentary elections based on universal suffrage. Carrillo underscored his seriousness about working within the establishment—one that would continue as monarchy—by holding a Eurocommunist conference in Madrid in March 1977. With campaigns already beginning for Spain's first free elections in forty-one years, Berlinguer and PCF leader Georges Marchais joined their Spanish colleague in renouncing Marxism-Leninism and professing commitment to democracy.

The Madrid conference was the high-water mark of Spanish communism. The elections of June 1977 yielded a mere 9 percent for the party that had done so much to undermine Fascism. Suárez's Union of the Democratic Center, riding the prime minister's coattails, garnered over 34 percent, and the newly revitalized Socialist Party of Felipe González took a surprising 28.5 percent. The Socialists, the group most identified with the martyred republic of the 1930s, had retained an impressive backing among unionized industrial workers and also received heavy subsidies from foreign Social Democratic powerhouses like the West German SPD. González and his followers stole 68er backing from the communists, moreover, by spouting "revolutionary rhetoric on the platform," and in this way cutting militant figures "beside the tired appearance of the old men of politics . . . like Carrillo."[25] The Communist leader further damaged his party by maintaining a Stalinist internal discipline that, by tolerating no dissent, hurt recruiting among leftist youth while also disillusioning many recent joiners. The party angered some backers, furthermore, by accepting Suárez's "Pact of Moncloa," which limited wage increases and imposed fiscal and monetary discipline on Spain's limping economy in return for a further dismantling of Francoist repression. For all of these reasons the coopted PCE lost over half its membership from 1977 to 1983 and declined to marginal importance in Spanish politics.

Carrillo's bold commitment to Eurocommunism is nevertheless highly significant, for it smoothed the transition to Spanish democracy by eliminating the pretext for counterrevolution from the army and aging Fascist movement. Despite the impressive roles played by Juan Carlos and Suárez, it is difficult to imagine a scenario without bloodshed if the PCE would have adhered to revolutionary Marxism-Leninism. As for González and the Socialists, who finally took power in 1982, their revolutionary bark proved worse than their political bite, for, like Mitterrand in France and Palme in Sweden, they cut budgets and restrained labor in order to generate an investment wave that was slow to gather momentum.

French communism also passed its apogee in the 1970s. Distrusted by the students in May 1968, and shunned by the voters in June, Georges Marchais maneuvered followers into an electoral alliance with the Socialists designed to capture leftists and forge an "advanced democracy." Still leery of what this meant in practice, run-off voters gave only 15.4 percent to the PCF and 18.8 percent to the Socialists in 1973, thus preserving Pompidou's hold on power. The disappointing results helped convince Marchais to sign a "declaration of principles" endorsing Eurocommunism with Berlinguer in 1975. While this move alienated the French Stalinist old guard still devoted to Marxist tenets like the dictatorship of the proletariat, it contributed to a 50 percent jump in new members, many of them 68ers enthused by the possibilities of "advanced democracy." Pressures from old and new guard factions explain Marchais's subsequent attempt to force the Socialists further left by accepting more nationalization of industry. His bitter public attacks on the reluctant Socialists during the 1978 elections, however, probably ruined the coalition's best chance for victory since 1936. The Socialists and Communists got only 22.6 and 20.6 percent in the initial balloting, respectively, capturing a disappointing 199 of 485 seats in the run-off as electoral pacts broke down amid mutual acrimony.

With only eighty-six seats to show for his party, Marchais came under fire, which he suppressed self-destructively "in time-honored Stalinist style," observes Geoff Eley. "As the generations of 1968 entered the PCF—salaried and technical workers, women, and those aged 16–25—its political culture had to change."[26] However, when no attempt was made to democratize by providing these cadres with a meaningful voice, they exited, leaving the PCF with huge gaps in membership and voting ranks by 1981. The Left finally captured the presidency that year, but it was Francois Mitterand and the Socialists who took power, not the increasingly irrelevant party of old men around Georges Marchais.

By this time the Eurocommunist phenomenon had also run its course in Italy. With eighteen-year-olds voting in June 1976, Berlinguer's PCI captured 34.4 percent of the vote, subsequently agreeing to support a Christian Democrat coalition headed by Guilio Andreotti. The Communist leader wanted his "historic compromise" to protect democracy from reactionaries, but also to implement a succession of socialist measures so that gradually Italy's depressed economy would advance beyond capitalism. This "profound change in social and economic structures" would pave the way for "a more just society, with greater equality, more real freedom, more democracy, and more humanity."[27] Announcement of such great expectations was bound to disappoint backers, however, for a cautious, suspicious Andreotti, and behind him the political "master weaver" Aldo Moro, had more control over the pace of change—the Christian Democrats did not consent to PCI equality in the coalition and an *eventual* cabinet seat until January 1978. Consequently, ameliorative reforms came within the existing structures of society: public housing construction, fair rent laws, town planning, and a national health system. In addition to parliamentary support for these impressive yet moderate measures, Berlinguer's trade union allies agreed to limit wage increases and promote greater labor productivity in Italy's "stagflationary" environment. Increasingly tired of "swallowing toads,"[28] however, the rank and file grew restless.

Cooperation with Andreotti and Moro proved problematic in another respect, for it saw the PCI sever ties with many of the student backers who had provided critical electoral support. To be sure, many factions of 68ers had already broken with the Communists and their trade unions after the original revolts. A plethora of revolutionary groups like "Workers' Vanguard," "Workers' Power," and the most influential, "Unceasing Struggle," attempted unsuccessfully to carve out a political space between the PCI and the terrorist Red Brigades until most of these groups lost heart after the 1976 elections. Their places were taken in the late 1970s by two communal factions, the irreverent yet peaceful "Metropolitan Indians" and the violence-prone "Workers' Autonomists." Although both groups rejected contemporary bourgeois society, many PCI-run municipal governments looked askance at their antics, unorthodox living styles, and occasional violence. Berlinguer was also less than amused, referring to the young rebels as "plague-bearers"[29] in 1977. Unfortunately for the PCI, this vocal anti-youth stance, combined with the party's seemingly compromised political cooperation in Rome, convinced many young party members that their party had sold out. One woman who resigned put it this way:

> I understood that our strategy of opposition to the student movement was absurd, dictated by a policy of conciliation towards the [Christian Democrats] which would inevitably lead us to accept repression. One can't hide behind the trite analysis that calls the students 'fascists,' paid *provocateurs*, because [the truth is that] this movement—the Autonomists, the Metropolitan Indians—expresses real anger, real social disintegration. . . . We [Communists] are supposed to represent 'social-democratic' order, good for the shopkeepers and bosses big and small, while [the Autonomists and Metropolitan Indians allegedly] represent subversion, extremism—the wicked wolf in fairy tales.[30]

The party's overall crisis among the rank and file caused a 4 percent decline in the 1981 elections—1.5 million fewer voters than 1976—highlighted by a drastic ten-point drop among eighteen- to twenty-one-year-olds. Many former PCI voters had abandoned politics altogether, but some embittered Autonomists lurched leftward to the more systematic terror of the still-active Red Brigades.

The nearly unthinkable happened on March 16, 1978, the very day of official PCI entrance to the ruling coalition: A Red Brigade assault team ambushed Aldo Moro, killing all five bodyguards and kidnapping the Master Weaver. Eight weeks later his body was dumped on the Via Caetani, a street midway between Communist and Christian Democratic party headquarters, the murderers' brutal way of expressing their seething contempt for "historic compromises." While the Socialists and Christian Democrats close to Moro had wanted to negotiate his release, Andreotti, backed by the PCI, refused lest the precedent of dealing with terrorists embolden them to further outrages. Thus the Brigades failed to spark a revolution or bring about a general collapse of law and order, but, oddly enough, they may have succeeded in terminating the Christian Democrats' opening to the Left, for the episode "helped to persuade Andreotti against continuing Moro's attempt at consociation with the extreme Left," writes Denis Mack Smith. "The suggestion was even made that some conservatives had not been altogether sorry to see Moro removed from the political scene."[31] Be that as it may, Andreotti never offered cabinet seats to the PCI, and a frustrated Berlinguer, concerned about the dwindling state of his "army,"[32] withdrew from the government in January 1979.

The health of Italian democracy in the early 1980s was certainly not good. Prime ministers still had great difficulty fashioning working majorities for governments, and, worse still, graft, corruption, scandals, and inefficiency undercut much of the reform legislation introduced since 1968. But democracy had survived. Years of police crackdowns, investigations, and clever use of guilt-ridden Red Brigade informers had rooted out their five operating columns in Venice, Milan, Genoa, Turin, and Rome. Nor had the Damocles Sword of right-wing reaction fallen on the republic. And for this fortunate circumstance the PCI, like its counterpart in Spain, deserved much credit for ending its intransigent class struggle and thereby bolstering democratic institutions.

Portuguese developments provide an instructive contrast to Eurocommunist trends in Italy and Spain. After decades of mind-numbing authoritarian rule, the dictatorship fell to a military coup in April 1974. Heading the new "junta of national salvation" was Antonio de Spínola, the popular former deputy chief of staff, sacked by previous rulers for advocating democratization and wanting to end the country's seemingly hopeless colonial wars. Plans to seize power had gestated for years, in fact, among younger army officers defending the Portuguese colony of Angola against better-equipped Soviet- and Cuban-backed communist insurgents. Given insufficient support and shown little respect by superiors in Lisbon, the beleaguered officers had fallen under the influence of leftist university graduates, serving involuntarily in the colonies, who railed against imperialism and authoritarianism and articulated the justice of revolution. Imprisoned communist guerillas with influence on their captors reinforced these revolutionary propositions. Once in power, the "Supreme Revolutionary Council" of the Angolan conspirators fronted the more conservative Spínola due to his popular backing.

Although the junta consisted of numerous leftist factions, one clique headed by Colonel Otelo de Carvalho, an impetuous revolutionary with avowed communist sympathies, soon gained prominence. In league with the Portuguese Communist Party of Alvaro Cunhal, the radical colonel insisted on a fellow pro-communist officer as prime minister, and then quickly pushed through measures that alienated Spínola and many of his followers. When the president balked at the collectivization of landed estates, the establishment of elected workers' councils in factories, and proclamations of independence for Angola and Mozambique, Carvalho and Cunhal forced him to resign. In May 1975, however, electors rejected the junta: 40 percent went to the moderate Socialist Party of Mario Soares, 27 percent to the Democrats, and only 12.5 percent to the Communists.

That free elections had been held at all underscores the difficulty of pinning political labels on a Napoleonic personality like Carvalho—and certainly reflected the complex politics in the military. Now, however, events turned violent. Spínola's replacement in the presidential palace, a pragmatic political survivor, General Costa Gomes, eyed the election results, weighed the mounting American and European Community (EC) criticism of Carvalho, and then dismissed the junta's communist prime minister. Carvalho answered the challenge in November 1975 with a second rebellion, but Gomes triumphed, killing five of the rebels. Afterward he removed Carvalho and the "Angolans" in a bloodless purge. To his credit, however, Gomes realized on which side the bread of politics was buttered: The Portuguese people wanted moderation, West European leaders wanted democracy, and Washington wanted all of this as well as a reliable member nation of NATO. The Portuguese constitution of April 1976 featured the checks and balances of a strong presidency, a multiparty legislature, and an independent judiciary. Soares's Socialists headed the first series of governments from 1976 to 1979 as Portugal embarked on the first leg of its democratic journey.

Democracy returned to Greece after World War Two, but many of the old problems continued to hamper its effectiveness (see Chapter 7). Leftist and rightist party blocs emerged, polarized from one another by seemingly unbridgeable ideological differences that a weak, almost nonexistent tradition of rule of law could not ameliorate. Civil war against communist insurgents in the postwar years yielded in the 1950s to corrupt rightist governments propped up and manipulated by the CIA to secure non-communist rulers loyal to NATO. By 1964, however, Greece seemed to be on a path to more democratic rule. Prime Minister Karamanlis, who had rigged elections to stay in power, resigned over disagreements with King Constantine and went into exile. The monarch turned to George Papandreou of the moderate Progressive Center Union, which captured a majority in subsequent elections. But on the eve of another apparent electoral triumph in February 1967 an army clique headed by Colonel Giorgios Papadopoulos showed its disdain for rule of law by seizing power. The conspirators regarded the alleged "shameless and wretched horse-trading of the parties" and "ceaseless inflammatory declarations of conscienceless demagogues"[33] as a threat to army authority. The prime minister and his center-left supporters fled the country, followed shortly by the king himself.

Democratic Europe roundly criticized and ostracized the Greek colonels. Arbitrary arrests, torture, and censorship—students could not even read Plato's *Republic*—made the regime unpopular at home and abroad, but the soldiers' grip on power did not loosen. Feeling invulnerable, General Dimitrios Ioannides, who in the meantime had pushed out Papadopoulos, succumbed to the ancient Greek temptation "to walk on purple carpets" by attempting to seize control of Cyprus in July 1974. The ill-considered move triggered an immediate Turkish retaliation that forced Ioannides to surrender the Turkish part of the hotly contested island, which soon returned to its partitioned status under UN peacekeepers. So great was the humiliation, and so loud the Greek outcry against the blundering of the colonels, that they meekly let themselves be shoved aside.

Constantine Karamanlis returned as prime minister, winning a majority in November 1974 elections. During his exile the former premier had reflected deeply on the need to replace rule of force with genuine democracy, and consequently was widely respected in Greece as a man of principle and integrity. He would remain the elected leader until Papandreou's son, Andreas, succeeded him as prime minister in 1981. That year the younger man's leftward-leaning Pan-Hellenic Socialist Movement won 172 of 300 seats, a 57 percent majority.

CLOSER UNION

In 1967 the European Economic Community (EEC), or Common Market, merged with its predecessor, the European Coal and Steel Community (ECSC) as well as the European Atomic Energy Community (Euratom) to become simply the European Community (EC). A decade and a half along the path of European integration it was one sign of what one historian has labeled Europe's "ever closer union."[34] Generally speaking, however, the 1960s saw little progress toward a closer union—and the main reason, for better or worse, was Charles de Gaulle. The chauvinistic French president had not only twice exercised his right of veto[35] to block Britain's otherwise acceptable entry to the Common Market, but he also snuffed out efforts of European enthusiasts in Brussels who wanted to revive earlier dreams of a more "federal" European union. Walter Hallstein, the zealous federalist president of the European Commission, the executive and bureaucratic branch of the EEC, expected to take rapid steps toward a more genuine supranationalism with a two-thirds majority voting system on the EEC's powerful legislative body, the Council of Ministers. When the pre-arranged measure took effect in 1966, any four nations on the Council would be able to override the other two.[36] Hallstein made his agenda even more unpalatable to nationalists like de Gaulle by announcing plans first to secure most EEC tariff revenues for commission use, thereby giving Brussels financial autonomy from member states, and then attempting to undercut countil power to control budgets. Incensed, the French President ordered his foreign minister to boycott council meetings for seven months, bringing EEC work to a halt. This so-called empty chair policy effectively established broader rights of veto for council members claiming overriding national interests—the "Luxembourg Compromise." Majority voting, commission revenues and budget controls—and, for the time being, federalism itself—had been squashed.

De Gaulle's resignation in 1969 advanced the cause of European integration. Already that December his successor, Georges Pompidou, called heads of member states and governments to a conference at The Hague, which consented to the transfer of tariff revenues to Brussels, set up a committee to prepare for a European monetary union by 1980, and agreed to open negotiations with Britain and its non-EC European trading partners, Ireland, Denmark, and Norway, for community membership. The financial uncertainties triggered by the Yom Kippur War of 1973 and subsequent founding of OPEC (see earlier) disrupted and postponed any chance of quickly establishing a common European monetary and financial policy. The admission of Britain, Ireland, and Denmark to the EC in 1973, however, established a pattern of "enlargement" that has continued to the present day.

In the short span of a few years in the mid-1970s European democratization accelerated as reactionary dangers subsided in Italy and authoritarianism ended in Spain, Portugal, and Greece. Not coincidentally, the latter transitions to democratic rule facilitated another round of EC enlargement. Since its founding in 1957, the Common Market had given members the right to veto applicant nations, primarily to calm the fears of West European socialists adamantly opposed to the entry of "fascist" Portugal and Spain.[37] Both were shunned, in fact, as the "historical and political tradition" deepened, as one council resolution put it, that the EC "can only give support to democracies of a pluralist nature,"[38] as had happened with the admission of Britain, Ireland, and Denmark. Once the Iberian pariah regimes fell, however, established EC democracies regarded enlargement as an excellent means to stabilize these young democratic states, while for their part the newcomers appreciated the opportunity to fertilize democracy with expanded western contacts. As one Greek observer noted, the EC, clearly more than a set of economic arrangements, "also represents a political culture and a way of thinking which, through a process of osmosis, may be transmitted to a new member country."[39] Thus Greece rushed to apply in 1975, while Portugal and Spain followed suit in 1977.

Accession did not proceed, however, without complicated negotiations that delayed membership for Greece until 1981 and Portugal and Spain until 1986. All three nations had less national income than existing members— except for Ireland and Southern Italy—and every applicant specialized in agricultural and other primary products, meaning that each would receive aid from the EC's already strained Regional Development Fund as well as force up the costs of the so-called Common Agricultural Policy (CAP). Under the latter arrangement, farmers received high prices and a guaranteed market through expensive measures to store or dump surpluses—the CAP consumed 80 percent of the EC budget in the late 1970s. Spain clearly created the most difficulty, for its population was much larger than the other newcomers and its fishermen, already notorious for putting down nets illegally in EC waters, would expand the community's fleets by 50 percent. Portugal, Europe's weakest economy, also generated worries that it could not compete in the EC's free internal market. Negotiators finally resolved regional aid- and CAP-related problems as well as fears of Portuguese collapse by phasing in full compliance with EC regulations over a five- to seven-year transition period for Greece and seven to ten years for Portugal and Spain—all done "to protect the EC from Spain and to protect Portugal from the EC."[40] CAP budget pressures had also declined in 1981 with an agreement to establish farm production quotas among members, thereby reducing subsidized surpluses. The fishing controversy lessened in 1983, furthermore, when EC leaders substituted national catch quotas for the previous policy of members' equal access to (and unlimited fishing in) EC waters. In 1986, finally, the EC agreed to reduce CAP spending to 60 percent of the budget by shifting monies to regional aid funds desperately needed by the prospective new members. With these problems resolved, "The Nine" became "The Twelve."

Aside from the cementing factors of economic cooperation and common democratic values and procedures, the EC showed other signs of becoming a more integrated union at this time. Beginning with Pompidou's conference at The Hague in December 1969, for example, EC heads of state and government began to meet frequently to coordinate community business as well as respond to a variety of European and world problems. European leaders formalized these gatherings in 1975 with the first session of the so-called European Council. Over subsequent years these semi-annual summit meetings of EC heads of state and government undercut the executive influence of the commission, especially when weak presidents administered in Brussels, which tended to be the case after Hallstein's resignation in 1967. Although the federalist cause suffered as sovereign heads gradually encroached on commission business, the advent of the European Council nevertheless furthered integration as national leaders devoted more attention to common European issues. Advocates of federalism insisted, however, on concessions for their side. First, in 1975, the European Parliament, which had played a marginal consultation role since 1957, began to codetermine budgets with the Council of Ministers, the latter actually crafting the budget, the former with right of approval. Federalists hoped that such an infusion of popular participation in EC affairs would strengthen supranational impulses. Similar motivations prompted the first direct elections to the European Parliament in 1979. Although low by national standards in Europe, the decent 63 percent voter turnout kept hopes of furthering supranationalism alive.

Little noticed at the time, federalism struck even deeper roots with the behind-the-scenes work of the European Court of Justice (ECJ) in Luxembourg. Active since the inception of the Common Market, the Court's legal competency covered disputes between individuals and the EC, between EC institutions themselves, and between member states and the EC, with the bulk of significant cases coming in this latter category. Although the court cannot interpret national laws outside its bailiwick of commercial and labor law, decisions in these areas are binding on EC members. In an important case in 1971, for example, the ECJ held that member states had no right to sign treaties with non-member states that undercut EC rules. That same year the court ruled that the provision in the Common Market's founding treaty calling for equal pay applied to all citizens, not just men. Empowered with this judgment, the commission issued a number of directives forcing member states to end discrimination against women. And in 1974 the ECJ found for an individual who had claimed the right to take up employment in any member state under the same conditions as nationals of those states. As these latter cases demonstrate, the European Court of Justice sees its primary mission as the protection of human rights and freedoms. Because of the binding nature of a growing body of case law dealing with such fundamental issues, one legal expert believes that the court's persistent hammering away equates to "the making of a constitution for Europe."[41]

THE IRISH TROUBLES

Amidst heartening successes for advancing West European democracy and integration, events in Northern Ireland certainly gave reason for pause, reflection, and redoubled efforts.[42] The root of the difficulty lay deeply embedded in Early Modern Europe's interethnic power struggle, in this case the sub-jugation of Catholic Irish by Protestant English in the 1650s. The emergence of the Irish Free State in 1922, and eventually an independent Republic of Ire-land, solved the ethnoreligious problem for most of the island, but not for the six counties of Northern Ireland, which split off in 1922 as an autonomous Ul-ster Province united with Britain and tightly controlled by the Protestant ma-jority of a parliament sitting in Stormont. The large Catholic minority in the North protested its discriminatory plight over the decades, sometimes em-ploying violence, most notably the IRA's unsuccessful armed struggle of 1956–1962 to compel unification with the South.

The failure of this revolt greatly weakened the IRA and took it down a Marxist path toward an anticipated uprising of Catholic and Protestant pro-letarians that would finally unite Ireland in revolution. These developments allowed a peaceful student-led movement to the fore that drew inspiration from the American civil rights cause, the youth culture of the 1960s, and the protests that rocked other parts of Europe in 1968. With the IRA looking in other directions, the new movement concentrated on achieving social and po-litical equality for Catholics. Its first major protest march at Derry on October 5, 1968, however, triggered a brutal backlash from police and Protestant ex-tremist groups. The attacks against marchers grew even worse at Burntollet Bridge on January 4, 1969. With the IRA leadership refusing to help— abandoned young people wrote "IRA = I Ran Away" on the walls of Derry— one faction, naming itself the Provisional IRA, broke away to defend the hard-pressed protesters. Now marches, confrontations, and retaliations escalated uncontrollably into the summer of 1969, culminating in four days of violence at Derry and Belfast (August 12–15) that forced the British to send troops to Northern Ireland.

London also insisted that Ulster revamp its exclusively Protestant police force, reverse unfair gerrymandering of electoral boundaries, end discrimi-nation in housing and public employment, and restructure local government to include better minority representation. Before these reforms could mollify Catholics, unfortunately, clashes between soldiers and crowds of civilians sparked worse violence in 1970, which prompted internment of protest lead-ers and the adoption of terrorist tactics by the Provisional IRA in 1971. These tensions escalated to "Bloody Sunday," January 30, 1972, when British troops fired into a throng, killing 13 people. That March the British imposed direct rule from London as the Stormont parliament went into a kind of political re-ceivership. The Provisional IRA answered with a series of bombings in Belfast on "Bloody Friday," July 21, 1972, which killed 9 and injured 130. And so it went in 1973 and 1974. In five years of "the troubles," over a thousand peo-ple had died.

Britain tried unsuccessfully over the next decade to restore peace and or-der. Although the civil rights reforms of 1969–1970 represented long-term progress, they had exacerbated matters in the short run by alarming militant Protestants unwilling to loosen majority control of Ulster. What these ex-tremists feared, in fact, was what both the Provisional IRA and the more mod-erate Social Democratic and Labor Party, founded in 1970, wanted by the early

1970s, namely, union with the Republic of Ireland. British efforts focused, therefore, on finding a formula for "devolving" governing authority to Ulster on the basis of a broad consensus that North-South institutions might be created to administer matters of common interest, but no outright union would take place without the consent of the people of Northern Ireland—which was diplomatic language for the Catholic minority admitting and accepting that union would probably never occur. Repeatedly, however, extremists from both sides scuttled promising arrangements and compromises. While London, Dublin, and eventually Washington might agree on a deal, recalcitrant politicians on both sides in Ulster and pro-Catholic supporters in the American Irish community did not.

DEMOCRATIZATION IN WEST GERMANY

Konrad Adenauer, West Germany's first postwar chancellor, resigned in October 1963. The octogenarian, known by friend and foe alike simply as *Der Alte* ("the old man"), had won the hearts and votes of many West Germans by rebuilding the country, restoring much of Bonn's sovereignty, and taking a bold, controversial, but largely popular stand against criminal pursuit of most ex-Nazis. After a decade in office, however, critics inside the political establishment longed to see him retire. Both the SPD opposition and cabinet coalition partner Free Democrats (FDP) bemoaned a high-handed "chancellor democracy" that isolated decision making to a narrow circle of close advisers, relegated ministers to secondary importance, and reduced parliamentary deputies to negligible quantities. Tolerable in the early 1950s when economic times were hard, parliamentary experience just beginning to rebuild, and memories of the Weimar Republic's tragic party-political divisions still keen, Adenauer's authoritarian leadership style seemed less appropriate as circumstances changed. The chancellor angered his own party by promising to run for president in 1959, and then reneging when he realized that CDU/CSU colleagues wanted to appoint Minister of Economic Affairs Ludwig Erhard, whom Adenauer disliked, to the chancellery. The bullying three years later of *Der Spiegel*, a national newsmagazine that had been critical of Defense Minister Franz Josef Strauss, did even greater political damage. The arrest of the magazine's publisher and ten journalists for treason after allegedly betraying national security secrets triggered a media and public outcry against this abuse of press freedom. Adenauer eventually sacked the main culprit, Strauss, and, when public criticism did not fully subside, announced his own intention to step down within a year. By showing the democratic system to be so clearly alive and well, this resolution of the *Spiegel* affair offered some reassurance to those who had doubted the durability of German democracy. The popular architect of Germany's "economic miracle" of the 1950s, Ludwig Erhard, succeeded Adenauer in office until November 1966.

Well into the 1960s, however, skeptics still found good reason to worry. The main problem remained an adamant denial of moral or criminal guilt by the bulk of the German populace for the crimes of World War Two and, worse, an overt sympathy for the fallen regime that was hard to square with fundamental support for democratic values. In a 1962 poll, for example, only 20 percent of West Germans agreed that the 1944 plot against Hitler had been justified, while over half of respondents branded the conspirators "subversive traitors." Small wonder that wartime physicist Werner Heisenberg kept to himself any attempt he may have made to deny Hitler the atomic bomb (see Chapter 6). In 1965, moreover, two-thirds of men and three-fourths of women demanded an end to further trials against Nazi criminals, percentages that flew in the face of that year's extension by the Bundestag of the statute of limitations on such crimes.[43] High school curricular reforms underway since the early 1960s provoked just as much controversy. "I keep hearing the opinion that we shouldn't burden the younger generation with the so-called guilt question," stated a pro-reform Hans Graf von Lehndorff.

> Youth, it is said, should have the privilege of being able to think and act without prejudice. . . . Life is hard enough, and we shouldn't make it harder for the young. And whenever I hear that sort of thing, I always ask myself: in whose interest is this really being said? Do the young really resist this burden? Or is it not really we older people who would like to hide behind the young in order not to have to admit our own mistakes?[44]

As younger Germans started to learn the truth in school a serious rift opened, in fact, between children and their parents. "If somebody had told me earlier that my father's generation tortured human beings to death merely because they were Jews, I would have slapped his face," confessed one shocked eighteen-year-old. "How can it be that there are still people today who approve of the crimes of that period?"[45] Another fifteen-year-old returned home from school in 1963 upset and wanting reassurances, but got none:

> Without explanations, my father responded by talking about the Communists after 1945. He simply refused to deal with the Nazi past. The East is now, the past is past, he was saying in effect. I never heard him voice any concern about the past. I took that very badly, something broke between us, and later it led to a split between the rest of the family and my brother and me.[46]

Throughout the West in the 1960s, youth preference for rock music, longer hair, alternative dress styles, and experimentation with alcohol and marijuana opened up a "generation gap," but nowhere did angry confrontations split young and old as deeply and bitterly as in West Germany.

Two especially gifted novelists stepped forward to deal fictionally with the recent past, thereby helping the SPD opposition and embattled high school teachers cure "the prevailing collective amnesia"[47] that afflicted older Germans. The first was Günter Grass, who emerged from "Group 47" baptism by fire with his first novel, *The Tin Drum*, in 1959. Other related works, *Cat and Mouse* (1961) and *Dog Years* (1963), followed in quick succession, but the sequels in this self-styled "Danzig Triology" have resonated less among readers and critics than the 1959 overture, the satiric story of a little boy named Oscar who protests against the crude petit bourgeois world of Interwar Danzig by deciding not to grow up. With the rise of the Nazis as backdrop, the permanent three-year-old seems to long for the protective warmth of the womb by hiding in closets, under tables, and inside women's skirts, but there are other, aggressive sides to Oscar. When confronted by life's adult banalities, he emits an ear-piercing, glass-shattering shriek. And while telling the tale of his adventures years later in a mental institution, tum-tumming on a toy drum, we learn that Oscar has led many to untimely deaths. "He has never killed with his own hands," writes Peter Demetz, "but he is nevertheless a vicious killer." *The Tin Drum* depicts a pre-fascistic Danzig that could nevertheless just as easily be Germany's present, for Nazism can always issue forth from the right societal conditions, damaging parents and children alike. Such readings of Grass "made him the favorite author of the younger West German intelligentsia challenging the Adenauer establishment."[48] As the near future would reveal, however, some leftists failed to heed *The Tin Drum*'s underlying warning about the possibilities for tragedy in protest.

The other tribune of German remembrance was Heinrich Böll. Already known by the late 1950s for his haunting stories of war's destructiveness (see Chapter 7), the still-evolving and experimenting novelist produced a series of notable new works. In *Billiards at Half-Past Nine* (1959) the meek and mild strike back at those who have run with the Nazi beasts, while *Absent Without Leave* (1964) deals once again with the composite tragedy of a world war that kills indiscriminately. Böll turned to more overtly contemporary themes in *The Clown* (1963) and *End of a Mission* (1966). The former tells of a man who paints his face white and plays a guitar at the Bonn train station as a form of protest against the establishment, the latter of father-and-son carpenters acquitted in court for ceremonially burning a West German army jeep. "Obsessively returning to May 1945, the time of liberation, Böll tells us . . . that it was a marvelous chance irretrievably lost, and thereafter, as narrator, satirist, and public figure, tackles the question whether or not the new Federal Republic of Germany really differs from the Wilhelmine Empire or the 'Third Reich.'" His answer "is not always in the affirmative."[49]

During the late 1960s the prolific author buried himself in another project, a fictional investigation of the life of a forty-eight-year old woman, Leni Pfeiffer, née Gruyten, who had survived Germany's times of trouble. *Group Portrait with Lady* (1971) introduces readers to a disparate set of average people and the various means they employed—some noble, most not—to get through the war and rebuild their lives. Center stage is Leni, an odd woman to be sure, but one who exudes a kind of primeval innocence, goodness, and sensuality that touches all those around her. Böll seems to offer his strange protagonist as a latter-day Madonna who extends hope for national redemption if Germans will just follow her example. Never known to shrink from sending a political message, the Nobel Committee awarded its Literature Prize to the extremely worthy Böll in 1973.

In the meantime German politics had experienced considerable flux. Ludwig Erhard resigned in November 1966, his popularity sapped by a severe economic recession. For the next three years a "Grand Coalition" of Christian Democrats, Free Democrats, and Social Democrats ruled in Bonn. This marked the first time since the waning years of the Weimar Republic that the SPD held governmental portfolios, most prominently the Foreign Ministry headed by the dynamic former mayor of West Berlin and current party chairman, Willy Brandt. Two generations of reformist thinking, reinforced by the Christian Democrats' electoral landslide in 1957, had motivated moderate party leaders around Brandt to steer a pragmatic centrist course. The SPD deleted all reference to Marxism from its program in 1959, banned the leftward-leaning Social Democratic Student's League from party membership in 1961, and finally stepped into the government in 1966. The calculus of compromise coalition politics prevented Brandt from taking bold reform initiatives, but his party's influence was felt in June 1969 when parliament voted to extend the statute of limitations on Nazi era crimes for another ten years. Buoyed by the campaign support of students disappointed with the failure of the previous year's street violence, the SPD gained twenty-two seats in the September Bundestag elections. Brandt entered the chancellery as head of an SPD-FDP coalition. Now numerous 68ers flocked expectantly to the new man, excited by his challenge to Germans "to dare more democracy."[50]

Willy Brandt's greatest accomplishment during five years in office came undoubtedly in the realm of foreign policy. *Ostpolitik*, his bold "eastern policy" of reconciliation and bridge-building to Communist Europe, both contributed to and capitalized on the unfolding détente between Washington and Moscow (see Chapter 10). Although the Nixon administration initially looked askance at Brandt, suspecting him of trying to play East and West against each other, his strategy aimed to reduce tensions with the USSR and Poland in the hopes that such progress would improve relations, in turn, between East and West Germany (including West Berlin), ameliorate living conditions for average East Germans, and improve the long run chances of some sort of reunification. His strategy "was to alter the status quo by accepting it formally," observes David Calleo. "Once communication and trade were reopened, he thought time could be expected to do the rest."[51] *Ostpolitik* registered its first successes in talks with Moscow and Warsaw in 1970. Each side made nonaggression pledges and gave de facto recognition to all existing borders pending final resolution of frontiers in formal war-ending peace treaties.[52] Brandt followed up these breakthroughs by negotiating a treaty normalizing relations with East Germany. In late 1971 the SPD chancellor received the Nobel Peace Prize.

In presenting this package of treaties, Brandt was asking West Germany's representatives to discard two decades of refusing all diplomatic dealings with East Germany—as well as Bonn's long-standing refusal to have relations with any state, with the exception of the USSR, that recognized the GDR. More than this, the Nobel recipient implored his countrymen to expand their horizon of historical memory to include the unprovoked German aggression of World

Ostpolitik: *Willi Brandt (left, holding glasses) meets with East German leaders in 1970.* (Getty Images)

War Two, which was responsible for current Polish and Russian suspicions of Germans and had caused nearly three decades of East-West divisions in Europe as well as the accompanying irretrievable loss of Germany's former eastern borderlands. The Federal Republic, in other words, should take responsibility in the present for ameliorating problems Germany had created in the past. Still more, Brandt urged fellow Germans to learn from his example: Cold War anti-communism could not be allowed to function as a convenient mechanism for burying all recognition and contrition for crimes against humanity committed by Germany. In one of the century's most poignant moments in December 1970, he demonstrated the integral connection between *Ostpolitik* and Holocaust remembrance by kneeling in Warsaw at the memorial to the victims of the 1943 Jewish uprising.

A full understanding of the protracted controversy during ratification of Brandt's treaties in 1972–1973 is impossible without appreciating the underlying tension and bitterness over *Vergangenheitsbewältigung*—"coming to grips with the past." The CDU/CSU initiated a no-confidence vote in April, accusing the government of violating its constitutional obligation to emancipate East Germans from communist oppression, charging it, moreover, with acceptance of the "unacceptable" borders of 1945. The motion failed by the razor-thin margin of two votes. In November Brandt precipitated new elections, gambling that Germans would support him and break the near-deadlock in parliament. Voters returned the government to power with 54.3 percent—an overall gain for the coalition of six points. The CDU/CSU polled 44.8 percent, only one point less than 1969. However, with many Christian Democrats refusing to campaign against Brandt's *Ostpolitik*, a policy, they realized, whose time had come, the 1972 election has to be seen as a major caesura in postwar German politics: the time for *Vergangenheitsbewältigung* had also come. The Soviet and Polish treaties passed in December 1972, the East German accord in May 1973.

The Brandt years did not provide German democracy watchers with much of a respite, however, for the German Left was soon engaged in a nasty squabble. Within the SPD, for instance, tensions mounted in 1970–1971 over the demands of the "Jusos." The "Young Socialists," many of them 68ers, bemoaned the party's centrist course and dumping of Marxism. Reacting in Eurocommunist fashion to Brandt's challenge to "dare more democracy," they called for a "strategy of system-transcending reforms" that would produce "a stronger humanization of social and political life,"[53] Party leaders initially ignored the Jusos, but eventually took steps to muzzle or expel them for jeopardizing the party's continued cooperation with Free Democrats who wanted no radical experiments. Extremely sensitive to opposition charges of being "soft on communism," in fact, the SPD went even farther in January 1972 by agreeing to a "Decree Against Radicals." Aimed at Marxist-oriented university graduates in the civil service, the measure prohibited government employment for anyone found to be disloyal to the state. Its enactment led to 256 dismissals, rejection of 2,250 applicants for political reasons, and a massive loyalty check of 3.5 million existing state employees. "This sorry episode of abusing state power to enforce an allegedly threatened law and order was arguably one of the most ignominious acts committed by the German Social Democrats since 1945,"[54] conclude two recent historians. It was the height of irony, therefore, that Brandt had to resign in May 1974 after he discovered that one of his top aides, Günther Guillaume, was a spy planted by the GDR. Brandt's pragmatic SPD colleague, Helmut Schmidt, replaced him as chancellor and chaired the coalition until 1982.

But all too soon a real threat to democracy arose to replace the phantom danger that lay behind the Decree Against Radicals. Just as they had in Italy, certain factions of 68ers, angry that their protests had failed, redoubled efforts to force a revolutionary settlement of society's problems. In February 1972 the so-called June 2nd Movement, named for a student demonstrator killed on June 2, 1967, bombed the British yacht club in Berlin. In 1974–1975 they shot a Berlin judge and kidnapped the chairman of the Berlin CDU, Peter Lorenz, releasing him when police met demands. Their even more callous compatriots in the so-called Red Army Faction (RAF) showed greater disregard for human life. Bursting into public view in May 1972 with a daring triple bombing of the American Army base in Frankfurt, the RAF followed up by murdering innocents with bombings in six other cities. Over the next five years this group perpetrated numerous other explosions, bank robberies, airplane hijackings, and notorious kidnappings and killings of prominent West Germans like Jürgen Ponto, chief executive of the Dresdner Bank, and Hanns-

Martin Schleyer, president of a powerful employers' lobby. The government greatly weakened (but never completely broke) the RAF by resorting to informers and penitent turncoats, as in Italy, but also to a series of controversial laws that curtailed the civil liberties of individuals suspected, accused, or convicted of terrorism. While a large majority in the SPD justified these measures as a defense of democracy, some members saw such steps as more of their older colleagues' abuse of power, especially coming after the Decree Against Radicals and crackdown on the Jusos. Now the "SPD's lost children"[55] began their exit.

The departure of Jusos and 68ers quickened as the decade drew to a close. Helmut Schmidt's response to the skyrocketing cost of oil in the 1970s seemed to many a logical enough economic response to the gauntlet thrown down by OPEC: Germany needed to build more nuclear power plants. For many environmentally conscious Germans, however, his decision threatened disaster to neighboring towns and cities if the installations proved unsafe. The chancellor's inherent commitment to continued economic growth, furthermore, contradicted recent challenges from environmental think tanks, most notably the Club of Rome, whose alarming report, *The Limits to Growth* (1972), forecast a millenarian disaster triggered by pollution, overpopulation, and depletion of natural resources (see later). Protests turned violent in 1977 when two thousand demonstrators broke away from a larger anti-nuclear rally outside Brokdorf in Northern Germany, overran police lines, and occupied an atomic power plant construction site. Schmidt's 1979 decision to approve the stationing of a new generation of NATO missiles in West Germany to counter the perceived threat of Soviet SS-20s (see Chapter 10) exacerbated worries over the constraints to economic growth. Now environmental concerns merged with fear of nuclear holocaust on German soil to produce the largest demonstration in West German history—some three hundred thousand chanted "no more nukes" at an anti-nuclear march through Bonn in October 1981. In the meantime this "eco-pax" alliance took more concrete political form as numerous local environmental protection citizens' initiatives, most of them breakaway movements from the SPD, coalesced into an "alternative" or "Green" party list at the federal level. Once loosely organized as a national party in 1980, the SPD's "lost children" captured 7.2 percent of the vote in West Berlin in 1981 and 7.7 percent in Hamburg in 1982.

Helmut Schmidt's coalition collapsed in September 1982. For two years the chancellor had faced mounting pressure from the Left, not only from "eco-pax" rebels, but also from trade unionists pushing for expanded social benefits in recessionary times. On the Right, however, his coalition partners balked at more deficit spending. Realizing that cooperation with the FDP could not endure, Schmidt rejected their demands for reduced spending, knowing full well they would turn to the CDU/CSU to form a new government. Christian Democrat Helmut Kohl became the new chancellor and soon found a pretext to hold new elections. In March 1983 the SPD's inability to overcome the recession or patch over internal splits became embarrassingly evident as its returning delegation sank to 191 (38.2 percent), while the Greens captured a startling 27 seats (5.6 percent). Kohl's CDU/CSU coalition with the FDP would preside over Germany for the next fifteen years.

West German democracy seemed fundamentally sound under Kohl's regime, mainly because genuine democratic values, as measured by Germans' willingness to reject the crimes of the Nazis, now undergirded the surface efficiency and stability already evident in the 1950s. Gone was the bristling, indignant opposition to men like Theodor Heuss, the FRG's first president, whose appeal for memory of Nazi atrocities had fallen largely on deaf ears. "West Germany as a society and polity had changed in this regard,"[56] writes Jeffrey Herf. Polls from the mid-1980s showing only 20 percent of adults proud to be Germans provide some sense of this change, for they point to an underlying national shame.[57] Alarmed by such data, conservative historians sparked a heated debate by attempting to shift focus away from Nazi genocide to the crimes of Stalin and the alleged validity of Germany's combat against communism on the eastern front. If anything, however, the "historians' controversy" (*Historikerstreit*) only deepened Germans' appreciation for studying past mistakes. A few years after this heated debate, for instance, polls found over 93 percent of West Germans believing that knowledge and understanding of the Holocaust was essential or important.[58] Although this penitent national mood was very evident in Helmut Schmidt's speech on the fortieth anniversary of the Night of the Broken Glass in 1978, Kohl's dedication

Anselm Kiefer, **Shulamite.** (The Saatchi Gallery, London)

at the Bergen-Belsen concentration camp memorial in 1985, and especially that year's Bundestag address by President Richard von Weizsäcker, nothing captured the nation's painful coming to grips with the past better than Anselm Kiefer's apocalyptic painting *Shulamite* (1983). The artist uses the expressionist style damned by the Nazis to damn their crimes: Dark, ominous vaults hover broodingly over tracks leading to the fires that destroyed Jewish men, women, and children. As much as anything else Kiefer's creation functioned as Heuss's "quiet, calm light illuminating our path in the dark years through which we are going."[59]

WOMEN'S EQUALITY

The modern European women's liberation movement surfaced first in Britain. Its common law traditions, Protestant roots, and persistent pressure from pioneers of the early twentieth-century movement for women's emancipation kept hope and progress alive for women's betterment despite the patriarchal influences of two world wars.[60] It is also possible that the return of prosperity and consumer spending in the 1950s, especially among materialist-minded mothers, affected daughters in ways that factored into later political activism. Historians of Britain draw a causative connection, in fact, between the spending spree on clothing and appliances in that postwar decade and the emergence of "women's lib" in the 1960s, but disagree about the specific reasons why. Thus some researchers believe that daughters rebelled against the domesticated consumer world of their mothers, turning instead to the public sphere of women's politics, while others see more positive impulses emanating from the motherly lessons of hearth and home. "It can be argued," writes Pat Thane, "that the possibility of dressing well and looking good which opened up for many more women after the war than before, as family incomes rose and many more mass produced consumer goods were available, strengthened the confidence of many women, gave them a greater sense of control over their own lives, which they passed on to their daughters who perhaps took this sense of control and independence in different directions."[61] Regardless of which view is correct—and there is likely truth on both sides—the implications may shed light on West Germany too, for feminist activism did not occur until later in the 1970s, partly in response, perhaps, to the more materialist mothers who first came on the scene in the 1960s.

Indeed, a complex mix of factors lay behind the far-reaching changes in sex legislation and gender relations that occurred in Britain at the end of the 1960s. In addition to continuing pressure from old pioneers and their successor organizations, as well as the sociofamilial trends discussed earlier, activist impulses emerged from Peggy Duff's Campaign for Nuclear Disarmament (CND), founded in 1958, and its more radical offshoot, the Direct Action Committee. Both brought women into a new world of protest marches, civil disobedience, and unorthodox oppositionist politics in the early 1960s. With its protest against French brutality in Algeria and its clarion call for the overthrow of European imperialism in Africa, Frantz Fanon's *The Wretched of the*

Earth (1961) reinforced this tendency to show irreverence to the establishment. Stimuli also came from abroad: Simone de Beauvoir's *The Second Sex* (1949); Betty Friedan's *The Feminine Mystique* (1963), which castigated middle class female domesticity; and the founding of NOW in 1966. Two years later female employees at Ford's Dagenham plant struck for equal pay to the applause of sympathetic women MP's in the Labour Party. Simultaneously, sit-ins and flare-ups at numerous British universities, escalating into the violent student demonstrations of 1968, lit new fires for the improvement of women's rights. Indeed, many female protesters broke with their male colleagues that year, incensed that men had assumed total leadership of the revolt while relegating women to typewriters, kitchens, and beds. Within two years of the spring uprising the first National Women's Liberation Conference attracted over five hundred participants to Oxford University, where they issued the movement's famous "Four Demands" of equal pay, equal education and opportunity, twenty-four-hour nurseries, and free contraception and abortion on demand. "I'd always been a socialist, anti-nuclear marcher, anti-apartheid, that sort of thing," said one women's libber, "but this was different because it was our own struggle."[62]

Britain's second postwar Labour government (1964–1970) tried to deal with all of these changing attitudes and escalating demands. The party, obviously very sensitive to trade unionist and leftist pressures, found itself in a better position to respond after an unscheduled general election returned a larger governmental majority in 1966. Over the next three years came a spate of legislation legalizing abortions on medical or psychological grounds, allowing local authorities to provide birth control advice, liberalizing divorce laws, and securing wives an equal share of family assets. The Equal Pay Act of 1970 capped this first wave of parliamentary efforts by eliminating gender discriminatory wage and salary rates for women of comparable age with equivalent training and experience who performed the same work. Compliance was voluntary for five years, afterward compulsory. Returning to office again in 1974, Labour introduced bills banning sex discrimination in hiring and promotion, mandating paid maternity leaves and protection from unfair dismissal during pregnancy, and strengthening the legal rights of battered wives and rape victims.

Britain's upsetting of hierarchical relations between men and women combined with the almost equally impressive accomplishments of America's NOW to produce a powerful demonstration effect across the Channel, where women were just beginning to stir again. This greater degree of assertiveness started as a reaction against the "leftist misogyny" of male 68ers. Thus one female Parisian who had experienced politics á la Sorbonne recalled that "when they are involved in 'serious men's talk' we really have to battle to have a turn to speak, and then when we've finished we might as well not have bothered, they haven't even been listening."[63] Italian women also encountered chauvinism from male colleagues during the 1968 student strikes and intense labor actions of 1969's "hot autumn." Drawing further inspiration from the contagious examples of their Anglo-American counterparts,

French and Italian women founded organizations in 1969–1970 to push for greater female rights. They employed the same kind of bold and irreverent shock tactics first used by CND and NOW, and then perfected by 68ers: chaining themselves to the gates of the Vatican to protest birth control, or placing a wreath at the Arc de Triomphe dedicated to someone even more unknown than the Unknown Soldier—his wife. Women by the hundreds also signed petitions admitting that they had had illegal abortions, and marched by the thousands to demonstrate their resentment of legal discrimination dating from Napoleon's time.

In France, home of the Civil Code, legislative results came slowly but steadily. Men's sole claim to head families fell in 1970; divorce was legalized and adultery decriminalized in 1975; abortion through the tenth week of pregnancy, subject to medical approval, was legalized in 1977; and wives' right to co-administer family wealth finally passed in 1985. In Italy, where Napoleon's Code survived only in attenuated form after 1815, advances were greater despite the Vatican's conservative pull. Divorce, first passed in 1970, was confirmed by referendum in 1974. Over the next four years came free preschool nurseries, paid maternity leaves, gender equality in family law, and legal abortions. Italian women also received legal parity with men in the workplace, including equal pay—rights won on paper after the war, but never realized in practice.

The drive for women's equality—and thus a fuller measure of democracy—spread to other parts of Western Europe in the 1970s. Luxembourg, where women had voted since 1919, was among the last Napoleonic Code countries to grant wives their civil rights in 1972. Iberia's dramatic political turnaround brought similar legal breakthroughs as well as voting rights to the women of Spain and Portugal in 1975–1976. And Switzerland, Europe's first democracy for men, finally granted women's suffrage in 1971 after three years of agitation by female 68ers. The country's male hierarchy now succumbed to unrelenting pressure from the inside: The Federal Council established a commission to investigate gender inequality in 1975, the end result of which came in the form of a 1981 constitutional amendment guaranteeing men and women equal rights in the family, in schools and universities, and on the job, including equal pay for equivalent work. The necessary cantonal referenda passed easily.

Meanwhile, young women in West Germany had become more vocal. In contrast to France, Italy, and Switzerland, however, the impetus did not come mainly from 68ers. To be sure, a revolt from male control occurred that year within the Socialist German Student's League (SDS), highlighted by Sigrid Röder's now-famous hurling of a tomato at a male leader for scoffing at women's lib. But this rebellion remained an isolated leftist phenomenon that did not spread among German women. This passivity began to change in 1971 when a marginal group of activists, inspired by "pro-choice" calls from America, Britain, and France for abortion on demand as a woman's right to control of her own body, drew up a similar petition for legislators in Bonn. When, instead of meeting this demand, the SPD-FDP coalition confirmed the ban on abortions, adding British-style exceptions only for psychological or medical reasons, female protest increased, for here was an issue that potentially touched all women, not just SDS ideologues. But in its attempts to circumvent the criminal code's controversial Article 218, the nascent women's liberation movement quickly encountered difficulties as the government spread the net of its Decree Against Radicals (see earlier) to punish pro-abortion groups that offered lists of willing doctors. "Without being directly named," writes Bonnie Smith, "feminists, socialists, and lesbians were singled out as being among the politically suspicious."[64] Further pressure from feminists emboldened by America's *Roe v. Wade* court decision ending all abortion bans in 1973 finally moved the governing coalition to present a compromise bill in early 1974 permitting abortions during the first three months of pregnancy. Although women mobilized and marched against the limits of the legislation—*Der Spiegel* dubbed it an "uprising of the sisterhood"[65]—passage of the act later that year thinned the ranks of the young West German women's movement, much to the chagrin of radical American feminists who desired German progress on many other fronts.

But appearances could be deceptive. For one thing, although less active organizationally both before and after 1974, German women had already made considerable gains—more in some respects than their American sisters (e.g., equal rights under the constitution). German feminists took an inward turn after the pro-abortion bill, moreover, immersing themselves in "consciousness-raising" groups, opening women's bookstores, founding homes for battered women, and organizing innovative "take back the night" marches against rape. The movement seemed to be groping for a sense of its own distinct identity and political focus, appearances that gradually strengthened as various women's groups became more overtly politically engaged. In 1979, for instance, the new Democratic Women's Initiative condemned all forms of male violence, drawing a connection between rape, the arms race, and environmental destruction. The dovish "greening" of the women's movement came into even clearer focus that year with the political emergence of feminist, peace, and ecological activists like Petra Kelly, who joined hands with disillusioned SPD youth and former 68ers in the coalescing Green Party. Within a decade, furthermore, the "mixed-gendering" of the environmental movement projected its silhouette in the Bundestag: twenty-five of forty-two Green deputies (60 percent) were women in 1987, far above the thirtieth percentiles of the highly mixed-gendered parliaments of Scandinavia.[66]

The merging of these causes was not an isolated West German phenomenon. Denmark's "Eurocommunist" Socialist People's Party, for instance, opened its doors to anti-war, ecological, and women's activists in the 1970s. Women soon made up nearly half of SPP committee membership, helping to push the party's vote to 14.6 percent in the 1987 elections. In Iceland a separate women's environmental party, Kvennalistinn, also mobilized for the country's elections in 1983, taking 5.5 percent of the vote that year and 10.1 percent in 1987. In Britain the strong women's movement that had organized the first Women's Conference at Oxford in 1970 had factionalized and broken up by 1979, but it produced offshoots like the Women's Peace Camp, founded in 1981 after the "Women for Life on Earth Peace March." The encampment sought to block the stationing of NATO cruise missiles at the U.S. air base at Greenham Common. In 1982 and again in 1983 tens of thousands of female activists linked hands around the facility in "embrace the base" protests.[67] Indeed, across Western Europe in the early 1980s the feminist revolt that had given the 1970s a distinctive stamp—and advanced the democratic cause by expanding women's rights—merged with eco-pax protest and, increasingly as the decade unfolded, with more exclusively environmental political action.

ENVIRONMENTALISM

The 1968 student protests ushered in a new era of environmental activism in Europe and the United States. So many of that year's demonstrators, having drunk deeply of Herbert Marcuse's allegations against modern technology, became later fighters for environmental safeguards. Daniel Cohn-Bendit, now a prominent French Green in the European Parliament, personifies this causal link. The 68ers benefited, to be sure, from the intellectual and legislative work of their predecessors. As early as 1941, Swedish feminist Elin Waegner had warned about the poisoning of nature, and within a decade her countryman, Georg Borgstroem, railed against untrammeled industrial expansion and predicted environmental disaster. In 1961, moreover, the Swiss branch of the Worldwide Fund for Nature began to make ecological protests CND-style. Soon the voices of these European Cassandras echoed loudly from America with Rachel Carson's *Silent Spring* (1962), a moving condemnation of the havoc wreaked by pesticides.

Although most scientists, politicians, and common people in the early 1960s wrote off the Waegners and Carsons as cranks, historians can point to a few signs that environmental attitudes had begun to change. Thus Britain became the first nation to enact clean air laws in 1956, followed by the United States in 1962 and the West German state of North Rhine-Westphalia in 1963. The spiritual message of materialism, the economic imperative of consumption, and the philosophical call to conquer nature still reinforced one another in a "dominant ideology" as the 1960s yielded to the 1970s, but alternative views had clearly gained more credence: Witness the controversial arguments of E. J. Mishan's *The Costs of Economic Growth* (1967), Farley Mowatt's *Canada North* (1967), Paul Ehrlich's *The Population Bomb* (1968), and the Club of Rome's *The Limits to Growth* (1972). Another indication of growing concern came in 1972 with the UN "Conference on the Human Environment" in Stockholm, the first worldwide meeting of this sort. Meanwhile, clean air legislation had been tightened in the United States (1967) and Britain (1968), while the Ruhr's safeguards became standard in West Germany. Gathering in scores of American cities, furthermore, hundreds of thousands of college students joined this growing international chorus with the first "Earth Day teach-in" (April 22, 1970). Over the next two years Congress responded with legislation promoting cleaner air and safer drinking water and banning pesticides like DDT. In

Europe similar laws were enacted by the "Green Troika" of West Germany, Holland, and Denmark.[68]

European 68ers began their struggle amidst this general environmental awakening. Typically eschewing orthodox political arenas, alternative lifestyle groups like Flemish Belgium's *Anders Gaan Leven* ("Go Live Differently") and similar "new social movements" from France and Switzerland to West Germany and Scandinavia engaged in direct action demonstrations aimed at protecting a river from pollution; reducing poisonous automobile traffic in cities; blocking road, railway, or canal building in the undeveloped countryside; or shutting down construction of nuclear power plants. Anti-nuclear protests grew particularly angry in Holland, West Germany, Switzerland, and France in the late 1970s. Traditional political activity was rarer, but not completely shunned: Witness the Norwegian EC referendum (1972), the founding of Britain's fledgling Green Party (1973), and Réné Dumond's unspectacular run for the French presidency (1974). The Norwegian case assumed greater historical significance when a phalanx of youth and student organizations determined to preserve Norway's recent precedent-setting ecological safeguards[69] joined in protest with farmers and fishermen worried about the depletion of natural resources that would allegedly come with Europe's "monopoly capitalism" to solidly reject EC membership.

As the decade drew to a close, however, mainstream politics acquired greater urgency. The death of a French anti-nuclear demonstrator in 1977 convinced many young people that direct action was too costly, especially when such battles with police only rarely curbed plant construction. Sweden's national debate and referendum on nuclear power in 1980 strengthened the arguments of those favoring long-term parliamentary strategies, for, much to the dismay of anti-nuclear activists alarmed by the near-meltdown at Pennsylvania's Three-Mile Island the previous year, the Swedish vote produced a moderate pro-nuclear majority. Developments in Switzerland also helped "realists" in the movement overcome "fundamentalist" prejudices against participating in politics. Thus a decade of hearings in Bern culminated in 1983 with one of Europe's most comprehensive environmental protection laws. The legislation would shield "mankind, animals, and plants, their group associations in life, and their living space, against dangerous or undesirable substances and effects, and preserve the fruitfulness of the soil."[70]

Although it did not appear so at the time, therefore, the eco-pax demonstrations and "embrace the base" actions against deployment of NATO missiles in 1981–1983 masked the ongoing transformation of the environmental movement from tactics of confrontation to a politics of left-wing opposition within the established system. The founding of the West German Green Party and Belgium's Ecolo in 1980 initiated a trend that accelerated with the coming of Ireland's Green Alliance, Sweden's Environmental Party, and Belgium's second environmental party, Agalev, in 1981–1982. Additional "Green" or "Green Alternative" foundings occurred in Iceland, Denmark, Holland, Switzerland, and France in 1983–1984. The European Parliament elections of 1984 brought further gains as the West German Greens won 8.2 percent, Belgium's Ecolo and Agalev 9.8 percent and 7.1 percent, respectively, and the Greens of Holland and Luxembourg 5.6 percent and 6.0 percent, respectively. As noted earlier, many of these fledgling organizations had close links to women's group's branching out from their struggle, as illustrated dramatically by Iceland's Kvennalistinn but also by environmentally active leftist parties like Denmark's Socialist People's Party, both of which scored impressive victories in national elections.[71]

The deepening environmental consciousness in Western Europe found graphic representation in the art of Friedrich Stowasser, a Viennese Jew who had adopted the name of "Hundertwasser" as a young man in 1949. Works decades later bore the stamp of early traumas—he escaped the Holocaust with family help, but scores of his relatives did not—as well as the influence of postwar existentialism and the suffering canvasses of tachism (see Chapter 7). Even though some of Hundertwasser's first paintings contained aesthetic warnings about cities and the banal direction of modern architecture, his artistic-political commitment to environmental and ecological causes strengthened in the turbulent decades of leftist and youth protest: Witness his *Red Rivers Streets of Blood—Red Streets Rivers of Blood* (1987), a damning of urban ills of crowding, congestion, pollution, aggression, introversion, and indifference.

Hundertwasser, 847A, **Peace Treaty with Nature.** (Kunsthaus Wien/© J. Harel, Vienna)

Peace Treaty with Nature (1986) contains the same overt political message and distinctive bold color (blue, red, yellow, green) as well as his trademark use of spirals. Hundertwasser wanted to employ art to motivate viewers politically—they should not "escape from the world, but escape into the world and the wish to change the world," writes one art critic. The spiral allowed artist and viewer "to live in the painting," for this pattern's line possessed both inward and outward directions, one that "incorporates the world," the other "only winding about itself, protecting itself." Thus citizens of the world are given a choice. "As easily as we can enter [Hundertwasser's] world, as seductively as it appeals to us, as open as its paths are to us, its intentions are all-embracing, the demands it places on us are huge—we can try to do justice to it, or we can shirk the task."[72]

Unfortunate events of the mid-to-late 1980s magnified the resonance of Hundertwasser's message, enhanced environmental awareness, and strengthened the leftist base of Europe's Green parties. Scientists discovered, for instance, that air pollution was destroying the ozone layer in the atmosphere over Antarctica. The spilling of eleven million gallons of oil in the wreck of the *Exxon Valdez* triggered a more evident ecological catastrophe in Alaska's Prince William Sound. Far worse, the leak of poison gas from a pesticide plant in Bhopal, India, killed over two thousand people. A terrible accident at the Chernobyl nuclear power station in the Ukraine brought this kind of tragedy closer to home for Europeans in 1986. The meltdown and explosion released more curies of toxic radionuclides into the atmosphere than the bombings at Hiroshima and Nagasaki combined. Over five thousand people died and thirty thousand were disabled, but nearly five million in surrounding European Russia received unhealthy doses of radiation, while crops as far away as Eastern Europe, Scandinavia, and Britain were contaminated.[73] The political fallout from all of these alarming incidents became evident in the 1989 elections to the European Parliament. Belgium's Ecolo and Agalev captured a combined 28.7 percent, while the British (14.9 percent), French (10.6 percent), West German (8.4 percent), and Dutch (7.0 percent) Greens made significant gains.[74]

Green political strength was actually greater than these percentages indicate, for the established parties were now forced to respond to the greater environmental consciousness of their constituents by introducing comprehensive Swiss- and Norwegian-style environmental legislation, or else lose votes to the eco-challengers rising on the Left. The greatest progress came in Austria, West Germany, Holland, the Nordic lands, and Britain.[75] Many of these nations also cooperated with one another in regional agreements to reduce air and water pollution. The disparity between the record of these countries and the rest of Western Europe increased the urgency, in fact, of finding EC solutions to environmental problems, particularly with industrial and automobile emissions drifting with weather patterns in the form of acid rain. Throughout the 1970s and 1980s, however, EC members had shown a marked tendency to favor national solutions in hard economic times. The European Commission in Brussels had drafted four "environmental action programs"

(EAPs), each more ambitious than the last, but these remained largely paper accomplishments.

Different circumstances in the early 1990s—the fall of communism, the end of the Cold War, and the creation of the European Union (see Chapter 11)—augured well for a fifth EAP's chances of success. Completed in 1992, "Agenda 21" called for "sustainable" economic development that "meets the needs of the present" without depleting resources or impinging on environmental quality and thereby "compromising the ability of future generations to meet their own needs."[76] Notable successes at the European-wide level included the establishment of a European Environmental Agency (EEA), mandatory environmental impact assessments for many industrial and infrastructural projects, introduction of catalytic converters on new cars, stringent recycling policies, and expansion of forests as well as lands reserved for natural habitats. Air quality problems remained particularly vexing, however, as new roads and the volume of car and truck traffic increased. Repeated attempts by EU bureaucrats to solve the problem with stiff taxes on energy and carbon dioxide emissions were opposed by national governments on economic grounds. What is more, many EU members not only continued to lag considerably behind North-Central Europe but also fell far below the union's own standards. Heading the "shaming by naming" list were Ireland, France, Portugal, Spain, Italy, and Greece. While aware of the progress it has made, the EEA tends to emphasize its admonitory Cassandra role.[77]

THE DEMOCRATIC BALANCE

Europe's democratization process—so promising in the 1920s, so disappointing in the 1930s, so frustrating with the onset of the Cold War in the 1940s—accelerated in Western Europe after World War Two. It is possible to identify two distinct phases in this advance. The first came with the liberation of France, the Benelux countries, Denmark, and Norway; reinstatement of popular rule in Italy, Austria, and West Germany; and the introduction throughout Western Europe of governmental insurance programs that finally provided the lower classes with an impressive measure of social justice. Decolonization reinforced democratic legitimacy in Europe, moreover, by ending the double standard of expanding rights at home while denying them to colonial peoples (see Chapter 7). The second phase gained momentum with 1968, inducing both a deepening, widening, and maturing of democracy despite the dark side of that year's legacy: its terrorist threats to democracy. In the 1970s de Gaulle fell, Italian democracy held, and the Germans came to grips with their Nazi past, thereby scrubbing political values that sooner or later would have undermined democratic structures. Military rule disintegrated in Greece, furthermore, while authoritarianism crumbled in Portugal and fascism's long reign ended in Spain. Simultaneously, West European women revitalized struggles for greater legal and political rights, efforts that had been suppressed or deflected by the world wars. That women, representing over half of the population, finally approached equality with men meant the beginning of the end of decades of hypocrisy and double standards and a chance for democracy to reach its full potential. The political effects showed up in the 1980s as greater percentages of women than men voted for leftist parties—the so-called gender gap. "Over the past forty years women's lives have undergone a silent revolution," writes Mariette Sineau, "and their voting reflects this."[78] Perhaps the clearest manifestation of women's political arrival, however, has been the boost this gave to the environmental movement and the greening of political values underlying many of the far-reaching party-political changes described earlier.

Chapter 11 looks again at the widening and deepening of European democracy, making it clear that Europe, for all its progress, has not completely overcome the dangers of terrorism witnessed in the 1970s or the heritage from earlier centuries of ethnic and religious prejudice, discord, and violence. The contemporary history of Northern Ireland, Basque Country, the Balkans, Chechnya, and tense majority relations with growing Muslim minorities—not to mention the wrenching environmental and political transformations in the post-communist East—are sobering reminders of the need for democratic perseverance and more hard political work.

Chapter 10

THE FALL OF COMMUNISM

A long line of black limousines sped past the open gate of the Tashkent air-craft factory. In the third car, concealed by tinted, bullet-proof glass from a nervous welcoming delegation, sat a pained, stone-faced Leonid Brezhnev. On this gray wintry day in March 1982 the fourth Soviet leader since the Revolution, the soldier who had fought in the Great Patriotic war, the cagy politician who had maneuvered his way to the top of the Communist Party in the 1960s, the statesman who had built détente with the West and then watched it crumble, did not feel well. An overweight ex-smoker who craved being "fumigated" with second-hand smoke, the first secretary also suffered from insomnia, which he combated with sleeping pills washed down routinely with flavored vodka. Not surprisingly he had already suffered several strokes and heart attacks. A slowly dying man, Brezhnev stepped grimacing from his seat with the help of a fawning entourage, shook hands with the greeters, and awkwardly shuffled into the plant.[1]

Inside, as if on roll call, the management gathered the entire work force along the main assembly line. To his left and right, and above him on a bridge-like gantry used for assembling giant craft, Brezhnev saw the proletarian grandsons of the revolution. What were they thinking? Did they pity the man who had become the pathetic butt of a nation's cruel jokes—or did crowd psychology take over, imposing awe and respect on simple people now so close to a very important person? Whatever the thoughts, suddenly thoughts changed as the gantry collapsed from the weight of too many onlookers. Brezhnev's aides tried to shield him from the falling girders, but one struck him, breaking a collar bone and sending the decrepit old man into shock. As soon as possible the broken leader was removed to his limo and speeded out of the gate he had entered only moments earlier. On the hastily arranged return flight to the more reliable hospitals of Moscow, the airplane's VIP passenger suffered another stroke. Amazingly, he survived the journey.

Time, however, clearly worked against Leonid Brezhnev. Only eight months later he died in his pill-induced sleep. Within three years two aged successors, Yuri Andropov (1982–1984) and Konstantine Chernenko (1984–1985), in fragile health when they took office, followed him to the grave. Seven years after Brezhnev's death communism fell in Eastern Europe. And

Chief of the Soviet gerontocracy: Leonid Brezhnev in April 1981.   (Hulton/Archive by Getty Images)

only nine years after his passing the Soviet Union itself disintegrated. A bad omen of things to come, the ill-fated visit to Tashkent seemed to presage the end of an era. Like the girders of the faulty gantry, it would all come crashing down.

THE DÉTENTE INTERLUDE

Détente was the first to fall. Its roots extended back to the 1950s when fears of nuclear destruction mounted with the Eisenhower administration's threat of "massive retaliation." The era of easing tensions came into its own in the aftermath of the frightening Cuban Missile Crisis, and then intensified with reactions to the unfortunate Prague Spring of 1968. Realists had cautioned against the rosy predictions of convergence theorists, but no doubt remained about the impossibility of Western-style economic and political liberalism establishing itself behind the Iron Curtain after the tanks of the Warsaw Pact rolled into Czechoslovakia. As policy-makers in the West soberly assessed the meaning of these events, Soviet spokesmen took pains to communicate their view that a lessening of tensions, although highly desirable, did not alter historical inevitabilities. The threats and dangers of nuclear and conventional war necessitated peaceful coexistence, including diplomatic give-and-take as well as scientific, cultural, and athletic exchanges, but ideological struggles between antithetical worldviews would continue, just as Marx and Lenin had prescribed. Indeed, these tensions would at times necessitate struggle, especially in the Third World as downtrodden classes fought for social justice against the forces of imperialism. While equally confident about the eventual victory of democracy and the market economy over what was seen as an unnatural system, the administration of Richard Nixon (1969–1974) and Secretary of State Henry Kissinger, resigned to communism's apparent staying power, entered into lengthy negotiations that finally produced the first significant breakthrough since the days of Kennedy and Khrushchev. With the so-called Strategic Arms Limitation Treaty (SALT) of June 1972, Washington and Moscow agreed to an approximate parity between the long-range missile capabilities of each side.[2] West German Chancellor Willy Brandt (1969–1974) contributed to the growing hopes for peace by improving relations with the Soviet Union, Poland, and East Germany (see Chapter 9). The capstone to détente came with the Helsinki "Final Act" of 1975. The United States, Canada, and thirty-five states of Eastern and Western Europe brought a formal end to World War Two by recognizing all existing European borderlines and agreeing to resolve disputes peacefully. Further accords called for enhanced East-West cooperation in economics, science, technology, and the environment; free movement of people and ideas across frontiers; respect for human rights; and subsequent meetings to discuss compliance. While the Soviets believed they had purchased security cheaply with promises on human rights and freedom of emigration and travel they had no intention of keeping, the West gambled that it had obtained some long-term political leverage.[3]

During this first half-decade of détente the Soviets, increasingly aware of their own sluggish economic performance, redoubled efforts to accelerate growth. Although none of these remedies gave early indications of success (see later), it is important to keep in mind that Moscow's confidence remained fairly high, mainly because the West's problems appeared comparatively greater. Not only had the United States withdrawn from Vietnam after failing to achieve battlefield victory, but aghast Americans—and nervous European allies—watched impotently in 1975 as forces of communist North Vietnam overran Washington's ally in the South. Within months communist rebels had also seized power in Laos and Cambodia. Angola followed the next year, and soon Ethiopia and Yemen accepted client status with the Soviet Union. The Nicaraguan Sandinistas climaxed this string of Marxist victories by taking power in 1979. With every passing year after 1973, furthermore, OPEC demonstrated the vulnerability of western economies to Third World solidarity. The escalating strike movements that disrupted Western Europe as recessions worsened added to the Soviet impression that things were spinning out of control in the enemy camp—a perspective strengthened by the irreverent "alternative politics" of women's and environmental groups, the spiral of left-wing terrorism in Italy and West Germany, and the fall of authoritarian regimes in Portugal, Spain, and Greece, all of which stood in marked contrast to the enforced law and order of the East Bloc after 1968.

Two developments of the late 1970s brought a rather abrupt and unanticipated end to détente. The first came shortly after mid-decade when the Soviets began to replace obsolete intermediate range SS-4s and SS-5s positioned in Eastern Europe and European Russia with upscale SS-20s. This otherwise routine technological upgrade had acquired somewhat more urgency when the American Tomahawk Cruise and Pershing II missiles came on line in the mid-1970s. Neither could reach Russia from North America, nor did NATO employ them yet in Europe, but adoption of a new Soviet system seemed to be a prudent defensive response. Presumably the SS-20 would also prove valuable along the long border with a hostile China while not upsetting détente, because this missile did not threaten the continental United States. Indeed a continued easing of East-West tensions loomed increasingly important in Soviet economic calculations by the late 1970s, for Moscow finally yielded to the imperative for systemwide technological modernization of the civilian sector by halving the annual growth of military spending from 4–5 percent to 2 percent.[4] Thus there was every reason to believe Brezhnev—at least for the foreseeable future—when he said in early 1977, "it is nonsense and completely baseless to argue that the Soviet Union is doing more than what is necessary for defense or that we are striving to gain military superiority." To be sure, the SS-20 and its big brother, the intercontinental SS-18, were impressive weapons, but both had been built with computer, metallurgical, and machine tool technology obtained through espionage.[5] Long-term survival in the arms race depended on self-generated technologies—and, paradoxically, only a respite from the arms race would allow the USSR the opportunity to develop this capability. Not long before his death in 1971 a retired Khrushchev had written that "vast military expenditure is all very well for the Americans who can sustain it and profit from it, but it spells the ruin of the communist world."[6] Now his successors seemed willing to concede that there was at least some truth to this.

Installation of the first SS-20s triggered consternation in West Germany, however, for this NATO country, a likely first target, stood well within range. Worse still, the new missile used reloadable mobile launchers, making it a permanent threat—the SS-4 and SS-5 launchers could not be reloaded—and nearly impossible to hit with NATO's existing Lance and Pershing I technology. Equipped with such weapons, Moscow might bully or "Finlandize" West European nations, forcing them to do the bidding of the powerful neighbor. Helmut Schmidt sounded the alarm publicly in November 1977. His warnings fared no better at first than earlier private entreaties, eliciting only annoyance from American President Jimmy Carter (1977–1981), who had entered into intricate SALT II negotiations that might break down if another complicated issue were added. In 1978 Schmidt pulled first Giscard d'Estaing and then Margaret Thatcher over to his view, however, thereby forcing Carter to listen. NATO decided formally in mid-December 1979 to install hundreds

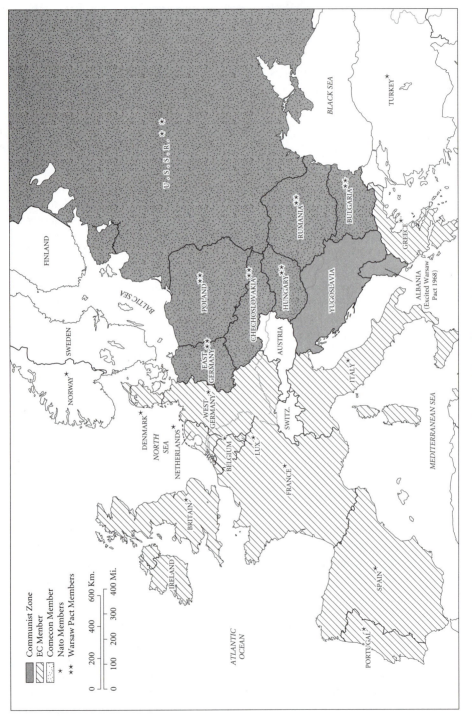

The East and West Blocs in 1986

of Pershing II and Cruise missiles unless Moscow removed the SS-20s beyond the Urals. Brezhnev, who had threatened in October to target any European city that accepted the new NATO weapons, now refused to negotiate until NATO reversed its missile decision. The breakdown of diplomacy smacked more of the Cold War than détente.

Two weeks after NATO's vote the Soviet Union invaded Afghanistan— the second development that terminated détente. The expedition sought to buttress a young communist regime in Kabul that had nearly succumbed to a fierce Islamic fundamentalist rebellion. Even though it was perfectly consistent with the post-1968 "Brezhnev Doctrine" of taking the offensive to uphold communism in neighboring states, Carter found this kind of interference in the affairs of an independent nation completely unacceptable. His state-of-the-union address in January 1980 asked for a huge 1.2-trillion-dollar defense budget over five years. The shocked president also asked Congress to delay ratification of SALT II, which subsequently wilted on the vine. The election of Ronald Reagan in November 1980 finished what little remained of détente, for a gargantuan 1.6-trillion-dollar military budget presented to Congress in early 1981 for defense against the "evil empire" bristled the hair of the Russian bear. Brezhnev demanded more military spending for the post-1981 quinquennium and the Politburo obediently approved a massive 45 percent increase. "A lag in this [arms] struggle is inadmissible,"[7] asserted the dying leader in 1982. Suspecting it would be "the ruin of the communist world," Khrushchev turned over in his grave.

ECONOMIC DOLDRUMS

After the Prague Spring discredited market socialism in the USSR, Brezhnev gambled that cybernetically improved planning would restart the growth process. Rationalized management and top-down rejuvenation of the economy never materialized, however, as the 1970s dragged drearily onward. The grandiose scheme of a "Fifteen-Year Plan" for accelerating scientific and technological change deteriorated into bureaucratic in-fighting between Gosplan, the central planning ministry, and enthusiastic scientists in the Academy of Science and their allies on the State Committee for Science and Technology. The squabbling lasted a decade without producing a plan. Computational deficiencies certainly stretched the odds of ever achieving rational administrative success. The Soviets intensified efforts in this area in 1972, amassing fifty thousand technicians in a village near Moscow to create a Russian version of Silicon Valley. But the "Ryad-2" machine they produced with help from the East Europeans disappointed, holding *maximally* two megabytes of memory and attaining top speeds of only 1.3 million operations per second.[8]

With neither a computer breakthrough nor a Fifteen-Year Plan, economic management grew ever more top-heavy, ossified, and incapable of combating entropy. "Our economy is gigantic," complained Brezhnev. "Take any ministry—it's almost the size of an army. The government apparatus has proliferated. And we have far too many miscalculations and misunderstandings."

His solution? "Perhaps the key problem for us today is to tighten discipline."[9] Fresh out of real solutions, the leader was returning to coercive Bolshevik roots.

Perhaps the greatest potential for reversing the USSR's relative technological decline in the 1970s lay within the burgeoning scientific and engineering establishment itself, which grew impressively in numbers as the new education reforms turned out more technicians (see Chapter 8). Here too, however, the system failed. Part of the problem stemmed from the huge drain of financial and human resources into military research. Thus while civilian research institutes responsible for creating new types of machines, equipment, and apparatus turned out prototypes at a 30 percent *slower* rate of growth from 1965 to 1980 relative to the early 1960s, their military counterparts actually *increased* their rate of growth by 62 percent. No surprise here, for the servants of Mars claimed the best scientific talent, paid the best salaries, and boasted the best facilities. Although the numbers of civilian researchers grew rapidly, their lower pay meant lower status, which hurt morale and productivity. What was worse, "expenditures on buildings and equipment also lagged behind the growth of employment," writes Vladimir Kontorovich, "producing hordes of researchers without a desk, much less instruments for the conduct of research."[10]

Not all the problems with civilian R & D, however, could be laid at the military's doorstep. Although the reforms of the late 1960s created a degree of research institute autonomy from the ministries, bureaucratic paperwork imposed from above still consumed valuable time and wasted talent. State planners with limited knowledge of scientific lab realities still established research priorities, moreover, while below, senior scientists heading research institutes often used what autonomy they had to run tyrannical operations that stifled younger researchers with daring ideas. "In our society, ideas boil to the surface more than they do in the Soviet Union," commented Yale physicist D. Allan Bromley in 1980. "There is no intellectual ferment [there], no give-and-take."[11] Consequently, with civilian R & D producing less technology, and industrial managers less than eager to risk installing what was produced (see earlier), small wonder that the percentage of products in the vital machine-building sector built with new technology continued its slide from 8.3 in 1968 to 2.9 in 1980. It had stood at 13.8 in 1965.

Overall economic growth (including troubled agriculture) kept to the same downward trajectory, dipping below 1 percent in 1979. Official rates of industrial growth remained higher that year, around 4 percent, but this represented less than half the growth rate of the late 1960s, and well-informed western skeptics suggested that industries, like farms, were not really growing at all.

Injurious jokes began to circulate. One, told privately amidst much back-slapping in Moscow, involved Stalin, Khrushchev, and Brezhnev aboard a special train. "When the engine breaks down," said the jokesters, "Stalin has the crew shot. Nothing happens. After a while, Khrushchev rehabilitates the engineers. Still no movement. Finally, Brezhnev pulls down the shades and sighs,

"Well, let's pretend we are moving."[12] In the early 1960s, jokes had been directed more against Khrushchev, hurting him politically more than the system. Cynical mockery like the train joke, however, cut to the quick of communism's flaws. Economic problems had become seriously political, and political problems threatened to exacerbate the economy—and so the vicious cycle would continue unless innovative efforts were undertaken to reverse it.

Unable to generate computer, electronic, and telecommunications technology comparable to the rapidly evolving capabilities of Western Europe and the United States, the USSR resorted in the early 1980s to expedients such as importation of nonbanned high-tech items from the West. In many hundreds of cases of mismanagement, disorganization, and sheer technical incompetence, however, expensive machinery purchases lay rotting in shipping crates or languished half-installed, incorrectly assembled, or otherwise unproductively employed.[13] The KGB's efforts at industrial espionage produced better results, as witnessed by the components it pilfered for the SS-18 and SS-20 missiles, but such spy coups were mere stopgaps that could not sustain Russia in the gauntlet-throwing arms race begun by Washington.

The Red Army emerged as one of the most outspoken critics of these technical shortcomings. As early as 1973 American journalist Hedrick Smith learned of martial dissatisfaction with conservative ministerial micromanaging that stifled technological innovation in the factories and research institutes.[14] By the late 1970s top brass like Chief of the General Staff Nikolai Ogarkov were prepared to accept budget cutbacks as long as such military belt-tightening cured an ailing Soviet economy thus far incapable of producing all of the army's technological needs. During the early 1980s, however, an exasperated Ogarkov lost faith in the aging party leadership's ability to jumpstart economic and technological growth. Brezhnev did nothing to free enterprises from the ministries' choke hold, and his successor Andropov quickly dashed initially high expectations that he would undertake bold "market socialist" reforms: "First try it out at a few plants and factories,"[15] he ordered in March 1983. Returning to timid pre-1965 levels of experimentation would not allow the USSR to catch up with the United States and its threatening space shuttle missions, "star wars" missile defense programs, and vastly expanded arsenal of high-tech conventional weaponry. "The reality was that the Soviets were falling further behind," writes Dale Herspring, "and the only hope Ogarkov saw was in the allocation of increasingly greater amounts of rubles to the military—in essence, throwing money at the military's technological problems."[16]

This Andropov did in 1983, spiking military outlays 10 percent above the 45 percent increase already worked into the plan by his predecessor. The acceleration of growth rates of military spending from 2 percent annual increases in the late 1970s to nearly 10 percent yearly hikes after 1981 did not satisfy the worried general staff chief, but civilian leaders feared that any greater military allocations would end all chance of righting the economy, especially the agricultural and consumer goods sectors. As it was, military spending would shoot up from 22 to 27 percent of GNP, necessitating a freeze in outlays for civilian machinery in the Eleventh Five Year Plan (1981–1985). In contrast, the United States increased defense expenditures to a mere 6.5 percent of GNP during Ronald Reagan's armaments buildup, while West European countries expended between a high of 5.2 percent in Britain and a low of 2.3 percent in Italy.[17] It was as if the Soviet Union was arming herself against a hostile phalanx of the entire capitalist world.

Toward the end of his life Brezhnev struggled with the vexing "guns versus butter" dilemma, for unmistakable evidence accumulated during these years that the nation's poor economic performance had taken on disturbing *political* dimensions. "The ruinous super-militarization of the country is getting worse," wrote famed nuclear physicist and leading dissident Andrei Sakharov to the first secretary in 1980. Two decades of feverish efforts to achieve nuclear parity with the West meant "vitally important reforms in the consumer economy and social spheres are not coming into being."[18] Brezhnev left the letter from Sakharov, recently forced into internal exile, unanswered, but he could not ignore the message. "The store, the cafeteria, the laundry, the dry cleaners are places people visit every day," he warned subordinates in 1981. "What can they buy? How are they treated? The people will judge our work in large measure by how these questions are resolved."[19]

These were questions, however, that the Soviet Union left unresolved. The "consumer economy" Sakharov mentioned had made advances, to be sure, as increasing numbers of families acquired watches, television sets, refrigerators, and washing machines, but for all the progress so evident to children of parents who had possessed few of these things in the bleak 1940s and 1950s, lengthy waiting time for delivery, sometimes stretching into years, created frustrations, while poor workmanship and service oftentimes forced buyers to improvise makeshift repairs and modifications. Moreover, few households owned automobiles, and housing, although inexpensive, was cramped with no alternatives. Even those fortunate few who managed to climb professionally and acquire a fuller range of material goods were sapped by the obstacle course they had run, like Vadim Glebov, main character of Yuri Trifonov's *The House on the Embankment* (1976), who had dreamed in youth "of all the things that later came to him—but which brought him no joy because achieving them used up so much of his strength and so much of that irreplaceable something called life."[20] Expending small amounts on rent and finding little in stores worth buying, average consumers voted negatively with their feet, so to speak, by depositing hard-earned monies they preferred not to spend. As annual per capita consumption growth declined from 4 percent in the 1950s and 1960s to under 1 percent in the 1980s, personal savings grew quickly in the early 1970s, rose significantly in the late 1970s, and then took off during the renewed arms race of the early 1980s—overall a quintupling of savings deposits from 1970 to 1986.[21] The poor productivity of collective farms exacerbated consumer morale, for shoppers found a limited selection of often unappealing foods in state stores, and then complained about the absolute necessity of going to farmers' markets where peasants sold a much better selection of produce from their private garden plots, but at exorbitant prices.[22]

Communism's problems cut deeper, however, than grocery store grumbling and increasing unwillingness to make consumer purchases. Indeed, many observers noticed a politically and economically induced societal malaise in the late 1970s. Public health deteriorated as a result of rampant alcoholism, excessive reliance on abortions, and a flagrant official disregard for levels of air, water, and ground pollution, but as life expectancy declined and infant mortality increased, Moscow, understandably preoccupied with defense, allocated less for public health, whose GNP share declined from 9.8 percent in 1955 to 7.5 percent in 1977—far less than Western Europe (11–20 percent) and America (11 percent).[23] Thus Sakharov had every reason to issue his warning about the dangers of neglecting vital "social spheres." Related problems compounded the regime's worries as the great dissident penned his letter to Brezhnev, for divorce rates, suicide, bribery, corruption, black-marketeering, absenteeism, theft, teenage drinking, "hooliganism," and violent crimes rose in 1980. There were even strikes, demonstrations, and riots in cities bordering on a rebellious Poland that year (see later), prompting a team of western journalists to forecast "stormy weather ahead"[24] for the Soviet leadership.

With the Eleventh Five Year Plan devoting so much additional effort to defense, however, the best guarantees of social order remained the army, the police, the KGB, and a vast web of ten million *Stukachi*, or "squealers," transgressors of one sort or another promised freedom from prosecution for informing on fellow citizens. "Everything and everyone was being inspected, monitored, and checked, and yet the standard of living was falling lower and lower," [25]recalls Dmitri Volkogonov. Thus the widely observed submissiveness of the Soviet people seemed to prove Shakespeare's wise line identifying discretion as the better part of valor. "One reason for the man in the street's aversion to dissent is that political trouble makers have very often ended up in prison, or dead," concluded a team of reporters.[26] While death at the hands of interrogators was now the exception, the prospects of a jail cell were nevertheless real enough. Yuri Andropov's report to the Politburo for KGB activities in the single month of March 1981, for example, boasted that "1,512 authors and distributors of anonymous anti-Soviet and slanderous documents have been identified; 15,527 Soviet citizens have been cautioned, 433 arrested for hostile activity."[27]

DISSENT AND THE COMING OF GORBACHEV

The dissident "slanderers" of Soviet officialdom never represented a majority, probably between 2 and 6 percent of the population.[28] At the tip of the iceberg, emboldening the others, stood a few prominent members of the intelligentsia like Andrei Sakharov. A young and talented nuclear scientist when Stalin died in 1953, he had not yet begun to doubt the legitimacy of a political system that had purged so many citizens, assuming unquestioningly that ends justified means. "Somewhere in the back of my mind the idea existed, instilled by propaganda, that suffering is inevitable during great historic upheavals: 'When you chop wood, the chips fly.' "[29] His oppositionist spirit grew after the late 1950s, however, as he observed the cold indifference of military and political superiors to the threat to humanity of nuclear weapons. During the Prague Spring of 1968 a Sakharov manifesto leaked out to the West warning both sides to avoid nuclear war, worldwide pollution, and global over-population. He reserved special criticism for Soviet stifling of intellectual freedom and civil rights and "almost serf-like enslavement of the peasantry." Hopeful that East and West would someday converge as democratic socialist systems, he urged Moscow to democratize, come to grips with its Stalinist past, and "wash off the blood and dirt that befouled our banner."[30] During the post-Dubcek crackdown Sakharov founded a human rights movement to compel official observance of freedoms guaranteed in the Soviet constitution, but cynically ignored for decades. When Brezhnev made human rights promises at Helsinki in 1975, this movement expanded, but the "Helsinki monitors" fared only slightly better than the Czechs as Moscow arrested hundreds and staged trials on trumped-up charges. Finally in 1980 an embarrassed Kremlin attempted to muzzle Sakharov, a 1975 recipient of the Nobel prize, by forcibly relocating him to Gorky (Nizhniy-Novgorod), a city off-limits to western visitors.

In 1974 the Soviets expelled Nobel prize–winning novelist Alexander Solzhenitsyn, another indomitable dissident spirit. The talented writer gained initial notoriety with *One Day in the Life of Ivan Denisovich* (1962), a story of ugly labor camp reality that closely paralleled the author's brutal eight-year confinement in the GULAG for referring to Stalin as "the man with the moustache."[31] The novella's publication benefited from Khrushchev's more tolerant mood as he swung from freezing cultural freedoms to another season of "thawing." When policy refroze under Brezhnev, censors blocked the author's next two books, *The First Circle* (1968) and *Cancer Ward* (1968). The latter surfaced in the West against the will of Solzhenitsyn, for he knew this could mean political difficulties—it did, as officials soon expelled the socalled leper from the Writer's Union. Shortly before his exile the first volume of another devastating anti-Stalinist exposé, *The Gulag Archipelago* (1973), appeared in Paris. By now the fearless writer openly criticized Marxist-Leninist ideology as "decrepit and hopelessly antiquated." That he simultaneously rejected western liberalism could not save him from deportation, mainly because he opposed an unrestrained industrial growth that Moscow sought just as much as the West.[32]

Some consider *Cancer Ward* Solzhenitsyn's best novel, comparing it to Thomas Mann's metaphoric *The Magic Mountain*. The book opens in the late winter of 1955—a time of climactic and political thaw. The scene: a hospital crowded with cancer patients, including Rusanov. Solzhenitsyn uses this obnoxious Stalinist apparatchik for such blatant communist bashing from page one that censors hardly needed to read on—Rusanov has denounced his neighbors and climbed coldly upward through the Soviet hierarchy, so high, in fact, that he disdains having to rub elbows with commoners in the ward. His antagonist there, Kostoglotov, serves the same literary-political purpose of condemning communism, for he loves freedom and wants desperately to cure himself and salvage his life after fifteen harsh, debilitating years in the army and GULAG.

Like other great works of literature, *Cancer Ward* contains deeper and richer veins of meaning and message. Thus Solzhenitsyn brings Kostoglotov into contact with three women: the head diagnostician; her assistant, Vera; and a nurse who studies medicine, Zoya. Unlike Rusanov, these representatives of Soviet officialdom are thoroughly likeable: All are extremely hard-working professionals dedicated to curing their patients. There are few happy endings, however, as operations take legs, breasts, and digestive tracks; most suffer through radiation treatments; and Kostoglotov must face the added indignity of hormone therapy that will sterilize him. "All in all, I feel I've been doctored to death," he says shortly before book's end. "I want you to let me go."[33] As the ex-prisoner boards a crowded train, having been unable to bring himself to respond to the welcome advances made by Vera and Zoya, he is obviously too beaten down by life and the cancer ward to survive for long.

At this more deeply embedded level Solzhenitsyn lodges his most damning statement on communism. Stalinism is obviously morally wrong, but look not for cures from well-meaning reformers who are zealously committed to a system that, whatever form it takes, kills off the freedom that the human spirit must possess in order to breathe, grow, and prosper.

The third leading dissident was historian Roy Medvedev. As a teenager in 1938 he witnessed police drag his father away, three years later learning cruelly from GULAG officials that money the family had sent to prison was being returned "on account of the death of the addressee."[34] With these searing experiences buried in the deep recesses of his memory over two decades later, Medvedev found himself drawn increasingly into research on a massive history of Stalinism. Khrushchev's 1956 revelations about the dictator's "mistakes," followed by renewed calls for "de-Stalinization" at the 1961 Party Congress, seemed to sanction such a project. As the manuscript neared completion in 1966, however, party policy was changing. Two critics of Soviet life who had regularly smuggled their satires and parodies abroad received five to seven years hard labor, and when this injustice stirred outcry from intellectuals, four of the protesters got even harsher sentences. Finally in 1968, after an official journal defended Stalin, Medvedev wrote a critical letter and was expelled from the party. It took considerable courage in 1971, therefore, to arrange foreign publication of his magnum opus, *Let History Judge*, a scathing indictment of Stalin, at a time when Brezhnev, more worried about dissent and the potential for more Prague Springs, had partially rehabilitated the reputation of the man responsible for millions of deaths.

Authorities did not expel Medvedev, however, or force him into internal exile. Knowledgeable journalists and historians associated this modest good fortune with the study's limited critique of communism, always phrased in a reasonable way to cater to reformers within the party.[35] Mixed with accusations of criminality against Stalin, in fact, one finds almost universal praise in *Let History Judge* for Stalin's great predecessor. "He constantly appeals to

Lenin's dicta as unquestionable truth,"[36] writes Joseph Joravsky. Indeed, Medvedev's plea for a return to Lenin's supposedly more humane communism not only distinguished his wing of the dissident movement from those around Solzhenitsyn, but also from the followers of Sakharov. "I am skeptical of [communism] in general,"[37] said the scientist. This pragmatic willingness to try something new seems to have been the majority view among dissident intellectuals. "By itself, [communism] is meaningless—no call it worthless," asserted a physician claiming to be mainstream.

> Divorced from the other aspects of society, private or public ownership of the means of production is neither good nor bad. In fact, no general theory of society holds water. The only question is, what *works*. . . . In Russia, certainly, [communism has] caused as much harm as good—and if you include agriculture, far more harm than good.[38]

Because of Medvedev's belief in the economic and political viability of a communism shorn of its bureaucratic top-heaviness, police abuses, and stifling of intellectual freedom, his relationship with many of his fellow dissidents suffered, some even charging that he had betrayed the cause to the KGB. The accusations were unfounded, but nevertheless persisted.

It was probably true, however, that a certain amorphous faction of younger generation party leaders, to whom Medvedev was in fact appealing, did not wish the dissident any harm—on the contrary, they harbored a deep respect for him. These were the *shestidesyatniki*, the "people of the Sixties," who responded enthusiastically to Khrushchev's thaw and later advanced up through party ranks to become leading journalists, academicians, plant managers, agricultural specialists—even members of the Central Committee. Although they refused to jeopardize their careers by crossing the line to dissidence, these children of the thaw privately disapproved of Brezhnev's refreeze, the junking of economic reforms, and the suppression of the Czechs. Like Medvedev, they wanted communism to work, but unlike him, they kept reform opinions to themselves and a few friends. One of these so-called double-thinkers, journalist Len Karpinsky, described the mental blocks they all had to communism failing some day. "You were simply incapable of thinking that way—to think that way was not only career suicide, it was a form of despair."

Interestingly enough, Karpinsky saw the possibility in the late 1960s of an "alliance" between his own "layer of party intellectuals" and the likeminded dissident intelligentsia, arguing that Communist Party *shestidesyatniki* already constituted "an arm of the intelligentsia, its 'parliamentary fraction.'" This alliance would be consummated "if favorable conditions arose." Another enthusiast for change in the 1970s, KGB technology expert Nikolai Leonov, bemoaned the country's "half-dead leaders" in private conversation with close colleagues. They all assumed with near-religious zeal that all would be well with their "higher and more humane system" if only "a new, young, anointed generation of party and state leaders"[39] came to the fore.

These circumstances materialized in March 1985 when fifty-four-year-old Mikhail Gorbachev, an advocate of returning to what he saw as Leninist communist purity, succeeded Konstantin Chernenko as first secretary of the Communist Party. On the eve of his promotion the new man confided to wife Raisa that all previous reform efforts had failed miserably, and that "we can't go on living like this any more." Thirty years earlier, as new head of the Communist Youth League (Komsomol) of the northern Caucasus, Gorbachev embarked on the career that would eventually lift him to the top. Intelligent and observant as well as hard-working, he realized early on that changes were needed, but after hopes ignited by Khrushchev's secret speech faded under Brezhnev "he kept quiet about these thoughts, except amidst his family and with his most trusted friends." Karpinsky, for example, remembers the future reformer privately complaining in the 1960s about communist agriculture's lack of incentives. Another close aide, Georgi Shakhnazarov, admitted that "Gorbachev, me, all of us, we were double-thinkers, we had to balance truth and propaganda in our minds all the time." And later Foreign Minister Eduard Shevardnadze trusted in sympathetic reactions when he told Gorbachev on a Crimean beach in 1984: "Everything's rotten—there must be change."[40]

But where to begin? Reflecting his political savvy, the new leader began to replace a suspicious and self-interested old guard with fellow *shestidesyatniki*, most from his personal circle.[41] Beyond this partial clearing away of conservatives, however, it is not at all clear that Gorbachev wanted to risk much of a solution. Regime insiders have even expressed doubts that he had "a well thought-out alternative model . . . still less specific methods for moving toward it."[42] As an answer to problems of industrial productivity, for instance, he stressed police order and factory discipline like his most recent mentor, Andropov, including drastic price rises on alcoholic beverages to discourage excessive drinking. Apparently Andropov's 1983 experimental decree slightly increasing the autonomy of some plant managers would suffice. To revive agriculture Gorbachev instituted a new super-ministry (Gosagroprom) to coordinate the cultivation and processing of foodstuffs without addressing the problem, familiar to him, of incentives for collective farm workers. One indication of deeper insights and altered priorities showed up, however, in revisions of the Twelfth Five Year Plan scheduled to begin in 1986: investment in light industrial, consumer-oriented machine building, including personal computers, would increase. A truly radical change, moreover, came in a spring 1985 speech to Warsaw Pact leaders sanctioning independence in the domestic politics of these nations. Apparently the East Bloc audience dismissed Gorbachev's talk as ceremonial rhetoric.

The nuclear accident at Chernobyl, Ukraine, in April 1986 (see Chapter 9) seems to have jolted Gorbachev into greater systemwide reform activity, for the disaster that officials vainly tried to cover up had resulted from shoddy workmanship, lack of proper training, and carelessness—a microcosm, in short, of the USSR's decline. Already in June officials received instructions to relax censorship in the printed media and permit greater freedom of expression in art and film. Impossible for decades, criticism of the state got a green light. A team of journalists headed by one of the chief's liberal aides, Alexander Yakovlev, took the initiative with a barrage of articles examining the system's social and economic shortcomings, even hinting at the need for political changes. Behind the scenes Gorbachev told other close associates to draft legislation restructuring the USSR's command economy into something like market socialism. Indeed, glasnost—the new political openness and airing of grievances—aimed at prodding recalcitrants within the Communist Party of the Soviet Union (CPSU) into perestroika—the revamping of the economic system. Anticipating opposition from conservative elements with a stake in the status quo, Gorbachev tried to forge an alliance between party *shestidesyatniki* like himself and progressive forces in society, thereby "cutting off" hardliners in the party and bureaucracy and "inducing all those who were capable of fresh thinking to participate in the transformation."[43] In December the reforming first secretary placed his political cards on the table by personally informing Andrei Sakharov that he could return to Moscow. "Go back to your patriotic work,"[44] he told the dissident.

In January 1987 the CPSU Central Committee heard Gorbachev's first official sketch of perestroika. This body approved a detailed version in June of two bills that took effect in early 1988.[45] The main reform, a "Law on State Enterprises," aimed to free firms from many of the stifling ministerial controls over prices, wages, production, and planning, but also pushed industry out of the nest by ending central subsidies. Now each enterprise manager would have to pay attention to profits as well as consumer preferences. Mindful of Poland's turbulent experience with price hikes (see later), however, the freeing up of prices would wait for three years. In a related move, banks, the suspicious bourgeois engine of past industrial revolutions, would not operate autonomously in the republics and provinces until 1991. Reinforcing the fact that firms in the USSR would remain socialized or collective, not private or capitalist, workers received the right to elect enterprise directors. "We are going to a new world—to the world of communism," said Gorbachev. "From this path, we will never turn."[46] But he "protested too much" for the skeptics: A sister reform legalized small-scale privately owned businesses—euphemistically called cooperatives—in the service and retail sectors. Western Europe had succeeded in adding an element of socialism to capitalism, but could the Soviets add a degree of capitalism to socialism after six decades of entrenched bureaucratic practices and hostility to everything bourgeois?

By the time these laws went into force, significant changes had occurred in East-West relations. Soon after his ascent to power, Gorbachev extended an olive branch to Washington, concerned, for one thing, that an escalating arms race imperiled the environment as well as humanity. In a more self-centered way, however, he worried that runaway military spending also threatened his economic agenda. On the eve of Gorbachev's first encounter with Reagan at Geneva in November 1985, for instance, the U.S. embassy in Moscow described the Soviet economy after four years of accelerated martial expenditures as practically "on a war footing." Russian economists were predicting that without a significant reduction in military budgets "only half the increase

East meets West: Mikhail Gorbachev and British Prime Minister Margaret Thatcher in 1987.   (Hulton/Archive by Getty Images)

in [civilian] production sought by the leadership can be achieved."[47] Although the Geneva Summit produced no agreements, Reagan also wanted peace. The following October at Reikjavik, Iceland, both men spoke of far-reaching nuclear disarmament, and in December 1987 they signed a treaty in Washington eliminating all short- and medium-range missiles from NATO and Soviet arsenals. In April 1988, furthermore, Gorbachev announced that he intended to withdraw all forces from Afghanistan. And finally, during an address before the United Nations General Assembly later that year, he revealed plans for a unilateral 50 percent downsizing of the Red Army and the removal of six armored divisions from Eastern Europe. He also repeated his earlier claim that Bloc members could make internal economic and political changes. The writing was now clearly on the wall: If East Europeans went once again down the path of reform, no Soviet tanks would stop them. The daring first secretary had eliminated every source of tension that had destroyed détente—and one of the most important barriers to the success of perestroika.

As 1988 yielded to 1989, however, Gorbachev's economic reforms sputtered to a halt—sliding backward, in fact, as industrial production declined

4–5 percent annually.[48] Some of the trouble stemmed from the program's initiation in the middle of the Twelfth Five Year Plan (1986–1990), creating firm-level confusion over whether to formulate independent output targets and pursue new consumer-oriented product lines or continue to take orders from the top. Many enterprise managers chose the latter option, a decision reinforced by force of habit, pressure from anti-reform bureaucrats, and lack of credit facilities to finance new ideas. The fact that prices had not been emancipated from ministerial control also perpetuated all of the old incentives to use old technology and turn profits at the expense of outlays for technological change (see Chapter 8). Moreover, adherence to the old ways meant no interference with lucrative corruption: kickbacks and bribes as well as a limousine, dacha, or vacation on enterprise money. The new small businesses that quickly proliferated with perestroika exacerbated the productivity problem, for their owners often had to bribe skeptical local officials to obtain a license, lacked all bank credit, and survived without a network of middlemen and suppliers. Clothes-kiosks and other retail mini-outlets therefore had to grease palms at state factories to obtain supplies and consumer items for resale at marked up—albeit more realistic—prices. Thus co-ops did not promote the healthy competition with the state sector that Gorbachev had envisioned. They also did little for consumers except erode savings, which caused great resentment among lower paid unskilled workers and retirees and veterans on fixed pensions. In the name of fighting graft and venality, furthermore, enemies of reform in the CPSU and KGB tried to smother the new ventures, calling them "a social evil, a malignant tumor." Vigilantes got the message, actually torching many co-ops in the late 1980s.[49]

Collective agriculture progressed from bad to worse, meanwhile, as Gorbachev finally realized the mistake of his super-ministry, Gosagroprom. He dismantled it in October 1988, but could not convince party conservatives to adopt a seemingly radical plan to make a gradual transition to free market collective farming without subsidies—allowing farms to fend for themselves, that is, but providing incentives to do so. Western skeptics doubted, however, that a Soviet agriculture abused by Stalin, bullied by Khrushchev, and neglected by Brezhnev would respond rapidly to any stimuli. Complicating matters immeasurably was the decades-long siphoning of labor away from farms to maintain industrial growth. "Who is going to save the countryside?" asked one elderly farm woman of journalist David Remnick. "One generation should hand down what it knows and what it has collected to the next. But all that is broken. Everyone has long since left for the cities. The collective farms are a disaster. There's nothing left. It's all lost." As for Gorbachev's talk of revitalizing agriculture, she had a simple question: "Who's going to do the work?"[50]

Facing accumulating problems, Gorbachev and his closest advisers reacted instinctively by pushing further into the uncharted waters of perestroika. They knew, however, that more economic restructuring of industry—not to mention a shake-up of agriculture—would necessitate progressing deeper into the foggy regions of glasnost. The vehicle they chose for this uncertain journey were the Soviets, those councils of workers and peasants that had emerged with the revolution in 1917 only to be shunted aside by the Bolshevik Party after 1920. The first secretary wanted to reinvigorate these formally function-less governing bodies and use them to outmaneuver his opponents. During the second half of 1988, therefore, Gorbachev formulated the ground rules for electing 2,250 representatives to a new Congress of Peoples Deputies of the USSR, the institutional descendant of the 1917 Soviets. One-third of the dele-gates would be selected by "public organizations" like the Communist Party, the official trade unions, and other groups controlled by the party. Gorbachev handpicked about a hundred of these parliamentarians to have some ab-solutely reliable backers in the plenary sessions. However, although the con-stitutional ban on parties other than the CPSU remained in force, the final fif-teen hundred seats were openly contested on the basis of universal suffrage.

The elections of March 1989, Russia's first reasonably free balloting in seventy-two years, seemed to produce acceptable results for Gorbachev. Pres-suring him on the left wing were about three hundred delegates grouped around Sakharov and former Moscow party leader Boris Yeltsin, who had bro-ken with the first secretary over the allegedly slow pace of political and eco-nomic reform. This faction called for multiparty elections, with Yeltsin's back-ers adding a demand for more radical market reforms. On the right sat a somewhat larger group of die-hard opponents of Gorbachev from the CPSU. In the massive center gathered his hand-picked loyalists and an amorphous grouping of delegates from the lower ranks of the party, many of whom had defeated CPSU bigwigs to get their seats. These party neophytes were inde-pendents for all intents and purposes, looking neither left nor right but prob-ably capable of being cajoled if the man at the podium used all of his con-siderable communication skills. In May 1989 the Congress elected Gorbachev chairman, and then later appointed him to a new position: president of the USSR. His tiger ride had begun.

Ethnic tensions within the USSR contributed to the leader's stress and strain during the first half of 1989. Various forms of nationalist protest man-ifested themselves in the Estonian, Latvian, and Lithuanian Soviet Socialist Republics (SSRs), lands that had never really resigned themselves to losing independence in 1940. Similar difficulties occurred in the Moldavian SSR, the Ukrainian SSR, and the Georgian SSR. Throughout the USSR, moreover, a his-torically curious people—starved for history in fact—began to use glasnost to dig deeper into communist abuses, even under Lenin, and, like Solzhenitsyn, to turn against communism in any form. While Gorbachev remained almost naïvely confident, many began to doubt whether he could stay on top of the tiger.[51]

EAST BLOC TROUBLES AND THE 1989 REVOLUTIONS

The rebelliousness that prompted Red Army tanks to enter Berlin in 1953, Bu-dapest in 1956, and Prague in 1968 moderated but did not fully dissipate af-ter the most recent outrage in Czechoslovakia. With western "Eurocommu-

Keeping democratic hope alive: Pope John Paul II visits Poland in June 1979. (Getty Images)

nists" condemning eastern varieties of Marxism-Leninism, and the Soviets themselves signing off in 1975 on western notions of human rights, small wonder that the spirit of the times in Eastern Europe promoted open dissent. Soon after the ink dried on the Helsinki Final Acts, for instance, a storm of protest erupted from Polish intellectual and church circles over publication of a draft constitution praising the "leading role" of the Communist Party and hailing Poland's "unshakeable fraternal bonds"[52] with the USSR. The election of Karol Wojtyla, Cardinal Archbishop of Krakow, as Pope John Paul II in 1978, followed by the new pontiff's triumphal procession through his homeland a year later, left no doubt about the people's state of unrest. Czech intellectuals also showed their political mettle after the imprisonment of the controversial "Plastic People of the Universe." The popular rockers had provoked officials because of alleged degenerate bourgeois values that attracted thousands of young people to each show, but the band's arrest struck the intelligentsia as a violation of freedom of expression, supposedly legalized after Helsinki. Appearing on New Year's Day 1977, the petition of a brave monitoring group, "Charter 77," called the government to account for a whole range of human rights abuses. "We believe that Charter 77 will help enable all the citizens of Czechoslovakia to work and live as free human beings,"[53] they concluded, but the authorities responded by proscribing hundreds of drafters and signers alike, including Czechoslovakia's leading writer, Václav Havel. Even East Germany, home of the infamous "Stasi" security policy, experienced troubles as news reports of western protests against the stationing of NATO missiles appeared on TV in 1981. While the government painted westerners as villains, groups of pacifist seminary students operating from the tolerated autonomous political space of the Evangelical Church drew a different picture.

> In our society, images of the enemy are constantly being created in order to arouse hatred and readiness to engage in violence. This hinders a positive attitude towards peace. Thoughtlessly going along with all this for reasons of fear or for personal advantages furthers this trend and makes us all accomplices.[54]

While this type of "tightrope walking" between blatant and subtle critique seems tame, the distribution of an open letter of this sort in the land of the dreaded Stasi exhibited tremendous courage and moral responsibility.

Economic difficulties in Eastern Europe exacerbated the persistent legitimacy crisis of the region's police states. The same oil-related problems that destabilized the economies of the United States and Western Europe in the 1970s, in fact, sent shock waves reverberating throughout communist lands from Poland to Yugoslavia. Tito's fiercely independent country felt the sharpest pinch, for it bought most of its oil from OPEC at hyperinflated world prices, unlike members of the Council of Mutual Economic Assistance (COMECON), the integrating economic community of the East Bloc, which drew its supplies at somewhat friendlier prices from the USSR. Because Soviet prices also rose significantly above levels of the 1960s, however, huge financial resources were siphoned away from funds used to replace worn-out machinery, maintain R & D, and provide a wider range of consumer items. Rapidly rising oil expenditures also diverted monies from purchase of those more sophisticated western machines and household goods that the East Bloc, having rejected market socialism at Moscow's bidding as too dangerously bourgeois (see Chapter 8), could not produce for itself. In effect they had cut themselves off from one potential solution being tried fairly successfully in America— somewhat less so in the EC—of fueling economic growth as a means of rising out of the crisis.

Rather than accept a politically dangerous fall in their living standards, however, the East Europeans began to borrow large sums from West European and American banks whose governments were only too eager to gain a leveraging upper hand. The "net debt"[55] of Poland, East Germany, Czechoslovakia, Hungary, Bulgaria, Rumania, and Yugoslavia rose tenfold in the 1970s to seventy-four billion dollars. As oil costs shot upward debt levels rose to 20–25 percent of the value of annual gross production in Yugoslavia, Rumania, and Poland, and nearly 50 percent in Hungary. With the eventual exception of Rumania (see later), each country began to divert a portion of production from home consumption to export sales in Africa, Asia, and the West in a desperate bid to earn "hard" or "convertible" currencies from noncommunist countries, thereby reducing net debt. Petroleum problems allowed no respite or escape, however, for Rumania, East Europe's largest producer,

finally exhausted its oil fields in 1979, while the Soviets, increasingly preoccupied with their own industrial slowdown, cut back deliveries to COME-
CON countries in 1981 by as much as 12 percent. Worsening terms of trade
heightened the crisis as western inflation spiked the price of key imports to
Eastern Europe. The result: near zero growth and more East Bloc indebtedness, which soared over one hundred billion dollars as the decade wore drearily on.[56] Consequently, 5–8 percent of the region's GDP drained away annually in the form of interest payments on loans. All of this came at the politically
risky expense of falling living standards; poorly maintained, increasingly di-
lapidated, pollution-spewing industrial plants; and high-tech development
plans canceled for lack of R & D funds.

Political problems had erupted, meanwhile, in unruly Poland. Twice in
the 1970s Warsaw tried to right its foundering economy by increasing food
prices—attempting to make the people pay, in essence, for rising oil costs and
debt payments—and twice workers struck, marched, and demonstrated, effectively backing the government down. When prices were raised in the summer of 1980, laborers again took to the streets. This time strikes coalesced into
an independent trade union, Solidarity, whose leader, Lech Walesa, demanded
freedom of association, including the right to strike; freedom of speech and
publication, including greater political rights for the Catholic Church; and
amnesty for political prisoners. The government conceded the main demands
provided that Solidarity recognized the "leading role" of the communists. The
ensuing year witnessed a feverish jockeying for position by Solidarity and its
considerable reformist allies within the party, on the one side, and government hard-liners backed by conservatives throughout the Warsaw Pact, who
insisted on a crackdown. When it became clear during the following summer
that the party would not make changes, Solidarity threw political caution to
the wind, demanding in October 1981 that central planning be dropped for
"radically increased independence of enterprises" and the one-party monopoly for "self-government, democracy, and pluralism."[57] General Wojciech
Jaruzelski established martial law two months later, arresting Walesa and other
leaders of Solidarity. Brezhnev had made it clear that the alternative would
come, as it had in 1968, in the form of Warsaw Pact tanks. "The Polish winter confirmed the lessons of the Prague Spring," writes Geoff Eley. "Reform
would never come from governing Communist parties while Soviet rule
survived."[58]

Nicolae Ceausescu responded to the crisis of communism with even more
extreme measures. In power since 1965, Rumania's megalomaniacal dictator
relied on the terror of his security force, the frightening Securiate, to deal with
problems when they first arose in the late 1970s. Whether miners on strike or
dissidents sending him open letters, all learned quickly that Ceausescu did
not lack the resolve to employ brutal methods. Rumanians relearned this lesson after the International Monetary Fund insisted on fiscal discipline in 1982
to rein in the country's ballooning debt. Ceausescu obliged, drastically curtailing imports of consumer items, diverting farm production to export, and
forcing his people to follow a so-called rational eating program that reduced

calories to near starvation levels. "In the bleak city center, the markets offered a few rotten potatoes and carrots," observed a British journalist in Bucharest. The cruel leader also forced down electricity consumption levels 80 percent by turning off the power for most of the day. "I recall visiting apartments where families were wrapped from morning till night in coats and blankets, teeth chattering in dark rooms."[59] The Draconian policies succeeded in eliminating Rumanian debt in seven years, but at the cost of reducing the nation to poverty—and spawning the desire for violent revenge.

As the economic crises of the Soviet Union and Eastern Europe deepened in the 1980s, the pace of East Bloc disintegration quickened. The process had begun, to be sure, decades earlier. Yugoslavia had maintained an independent communist status since 1948 (see Chapter 7). Albania followed suit in the early 1960s after taking China's side in the nasty Sino-Soviet feud. Emboldened by Chinese aid as well as the fact that Yugoslavia would never allow Soviet-led armies to cross borders despite Belgrade's own improved relations with Moscow, Tirana soon exited COMECON and the Warsaw Pact. Rumania similarly defied Soviet leaders by refusing to accept their 1962 proposal for a closer coordination of COMECON economies. Bucharest rejected a division of labor that prescribed a more intensive development of its agriculture and raw materials while East Germany, Czechoslovakia, and Hungary could advance their industries. Despite Ceausescu's flirtation with de Gaulle, refusal to invade Czechoslovakia in 1968, and his unbecoming regal pretentiousness, Rumania avoided Prague's fate by strictly adhering to communist institutions and prudently maintaining membership in COMECON and the Warsaw Pact.

The oil-induced problems of the 1970s and 1980s greatly strengthened these centrifugal tendencies, forcing East Bloc members to increase exports to non-communist countries that paid with convertible currencies in order to acquire hard money for western imports and stay abreast of debt payments. Thus the intra-COMECON commerce of Rumania, Hungary, and Poland slid from 66–75 percent of total trade before the crisis to 40–44 percent as indebtedness increased.[60] Well before communism fell, in other words, the economies of the region were gravitating back to the traditional westward-leaning trading patterns of the pre–World War Two era. The need for hard currency became so intense by the mid-1980s that certain COMECON members began pushing for payment in convertible monies for intra-COMECON trade. Hungary, with the highest per capita foreign debt in the East Bloc and interest payments alone absorbing 40 percent of export earnings, was particularly keen to change the system, but Soviet interests also dictated reforms. Eager to reduce East Bloc subsidies that diverted billions of rubles annually from pressing home needs, expending huge sums on food and high-tech imports from the West and consequently sinking farther into debt—needing, in short, to build up its own reserve of bourgeois currencies—the USSR notified COMECON partners in November 1985, just months into the Gorbachev era, that "the present model of cooperation has no future."[61] Over the next year world oil prices plummeted as Saudi Arabia increased production in return for American arms, thereby eroding Soviet hard currency earnings from their oil exports by as much as eighteen billion dollars annually.[62] While Moscow did not reduce its oil exports to COMECON countries in order to boost world sales and recoup hard currency losses, the temptation to do so grew. However, the Soviets kept their intra-COMECON oil prices the same (i.e., well above world levels), causing considerable resentment in the Bloc.

In 1988 East European leaders heard Moscow assert that "the historic division of labor among our countries has exhausted its possibilities."[63] The USSR preferred hard money payment for intra-Bloc commerce and wanted to let the market, not complicated bilateral contract negotiations, determine trade flows. Ideally these changes should take place in the near future. East Germany made the most vehement objections because it paid for Soviet oil with rubles earned from manufactured items sent eastward at favorable negotiated prices, and then "cracked" or refined the crude oil into petrochemicals for resale in the West. Even a cursory examination of the lopsided Soviet–East German relationship would have sufficed to show, however, that East Berlin's protests would not restrain Moscow in the long run from pursuing its own interests.

The dramatic developments in the Soviet Union culminating in the election and convening of the Congress of Peoples Deputies in the spring of 1989 represented a radical departure from the communists' long practice of dictatorial control of politics. Some sense of this historic caesura and the controversy it generated can be gleaned from the sudden, angry resignation from the CPSU Central Committee of seventy-four hard-liners—a quarter of the membership—in protest over Gorbachev's opening up of the political process. Within twelve months, however, these remarkable Soviet events would pale in comparison to the breathtaking revolutionary changes wrought throughout Eastern Europe, for communist regimes fell there in rapid succession, epitomized by the electrifying fall of the Berlin Wall in November 1989 and the crumbling of East German communism shortly thereafter. These events, so much the focus of rapt world attention, sent shock waves back to the East that the USSR's great reformer would not survive politically.[64]

Before proceeding with the narrative readers need to appreciate how surprising all of this was at the time. Most westerners, conditioned by seven decades of Soviet survival and resilience in Russia, and four decades of oppressive Soviet rule in Eastern Europe, assumed that communist institutions were permanent fixtures on the world stage. In these circumstances it was impossible to interpret warning signs when they occurred. A personal anecdote may help to explain. In the autumn of 1987 this writer spent a month in the GDR. In stark contrast with observations made on research trips in 1976 and 1983, common people complained angrily on train platforms, cursed publicly at government officials, and invited the American to private gatherings where criticism of the system continued in the same vein. Subsequent discussion with West German friends of these remarkable goings-on led to the usual platitude that such an unfree system could not last, but nobody really believed this—no one really expected anything to change. What was true at our level was also true among western statesmen and intelligence analysts, for they too were accustomed to communism's persistence—to the point sometimes of criticizing East European dissidents for irresponsibly threatening a status quo on which the peace of the world seemed to depend. Even East European communist leaders did not take Gorbachev seriously in 1985 when he announced different Soviet policies for the Bloc. And when the Berlin Wall came down, dragging communism down with it, Gorbachev himself was as surprised as everyone else. "I would be less than sincere," he later wrote, "if I said that I had foreseen the course of events and the problems that the German question would eventually create."[65]

The troubles began in Poland, where General Jaruzelski's crushing of Solidarity proved only a temporary reprieve from resistance and unrest. The regime attempted to pacify society in the 1980s by inducing economic prosperity, but the reforms failed badly. Seemingly more radical than the later Soviet variant, Poland's perestroika featured a legalization of private enterprise alongside state firms and a freeing up of prices and bank loans. Continued bureaucratic control of wages, supplies of fuel and raw materials, and prices again when inflation flared up had a constraining effect on private firms, whose share of industrial production never exceeded 6 percent.[66] Although greatly weakened by the coup, Solidarity maintained an underground organization throughout this time, contributing to a mood of sullen defiance. John Paul's second visit to Poland in 1983 led in subsequent years to amnesty decrees for Lech Walesa and other union leaders, setting the stage for renewed strikes in May and August 1988.

Hoping in vain that somehow his economic reforms would succeed politically in creating social peace, Jaruzelski finally agreed to open "round table" talks with Solidarity in February 1989. The general knew that Poland's army could not contain the popular tide indefinitely, that Gorbachev would send no tanks to help him, and that forestalling such a now unlikely incursion had been the sole reason Poles had shown even a degree of restraint in opposing his military government. It was clear, furthermore, that western countries would make no additional loans without political liberalization. In April, therefore, regime and Solidarity negotiators agreed to a historic "pact" calling for carefully structured June elections to a two-chamber legislature. The government assumed it could cleverly co-opt Solidarity by reserving 65 percent of the seats in the decision-making lower house (Sejm) for the communists' Polish Workers Party and two nominally independent parties, the Democratic Party and the United Peasants Party, which had been tolerated after 1945 to create the illusion of democratic pluralism but were in fact lackeys of the communists.[67] Solidarity's vote was so great, however, that the lackeys turned on their masters, refusing to form a coalition with anyone but Solidarity.[68] Having essentially outfoxed themselves into a 37.9 percent minority, the communists had no alternative but forming a coalition government with Solidarity. One of the union's leaders, Tadeusz Mazowiecki, became prime minister in August 1989, marking the beginning of the end of the communist era in Poland.

By this time Hungary was poised to go even further—all with Gorbachev's blessing. Like Moscow and Warsaw in the 1980s, Budapest reverted to the type of economic measures that had been discarded as politically risky and incorrect after 1968. Dubbed "goulash communism" by journalists because of its spicy mixture of economic ingredients, Hungary's reforms emphasized decentralized operation of state firms and banks, prices for most goods allowed to float freely with the world market, and legalization of private businesses. The latter accounted for a third of GNP by the end of the decade. This package neither resuscitated the economy nor inspired consumers, however, for it remained a radical half-measure that did not significantly alter Hungary's command economy. "Autonomous" state firms were not only subsidized when weak and raided of their profits when strong, but also forced frequently to export their goods for convertible currencies. Private firms had a different set of problems like extremely high taxes and severe labor force restrictions—no more than thirty workers to guard against exploitation of the proletariat. Unlike West European countries that introduced social programs, state planning, and nationalization of key industries in order to curb the most glaring sociopolitical abuses and shortcomings of capitalism without stifling a market economy that still claimed usually more than two-thirds of GNP, even the most ambitious communist reformers tended to expand the space for private business to maximally a third of GNP, stifling market flexibility in the process, but also without solving the most serious economic *and political* shortcomings of communism. Well aware of these realities by May 1988, reform factions in the Hungarian Communist Party forced their aging chairman since 1956, János Kádár, out of the Politburo, and then began to push political changes designed not only to redress basic human rights grievances, but also to establish the kinds of links between democratization and economic growth identified in 1968 by Dubcek in Czechoslovakia and Servan-Schreiber in France (see Chapter 8). "The basic field of reforms is not the economy," said one of them. "The barriers have to be swept away first in the political arena."[69]

Having debated these issues inside the party for nearly a year, the Central Committee took the plunge in February 1989 by deciding to prepare the way for free multiparty elections. Consulted, Gorbachev assured Hungarian leaders that he approved. That spring an independent trade union organization and a plethora of new or former political entities established themselves: the Smallholder Party and the Social Democratic Party from the Interwar Period, along with newcomers like the Free Democratic Alliance and the Federation of Young Democrats. Eager for years to break loose from COMECON trade restrictions and integrate its economy with the West, Hungary was now westernizing its political system. Two events demonstrated the irreversible momentum of Budapest's democratization process. In May border guards dismantled the ugly barbed-wire barriers on the Austrian border and ceased patrolling adjacent countryside. This hole in the infamous Iron Curtain epitomized both symbolically and practically Hungary's opening to the West. With two hundred thousand people watching reverently in June 1989, moreover, the new leadership reburied Imre Nagy and other leaders executed in 1956, this time as Hungarian national heroes. When the Hungarians finally held their first free elections since 1945 in March 1990, the former communists polled less than 10 percent of the vote and quietly joined the parliamentary opposition.[70]

Erich Honecker's austere police state disapproved of developments in Poland and Hungary in 1989—and the Soviet Union too. Unwilling to recognize, let alone admit, that his country suffered from mounting debt, stagnating economic growth, deferred capital maintenance and related environmental hazards, increasing consumer frustrations and aggravations, and an ever bolder dissident movement, the East German leader seemed to be in denial when he told a visiting Gorbachev that Soviet problems "were significantly worse than ours." Honecker spoke more bluntly to the Soviet ambassador about glasnost and perestroika. "For years we educated GDR citizens about the example of the CPSU and the heroic struggle of the Soviet people, [but] now we learn that it was all a string of failures."[71] At meetings of COMECON countries Honecker argued and intrigued for punitive actions against the Poles and Hungarians, but constantly found Gorbachev blocking the way.

At home, meanwhile, signs of unrest grew harder to ignore. Omniscient Stasi agents knew the worst. A plethora of peace, environmental, feminist, human rights, reform communist, and pro-democracy political cliques and factions emerged publicly in the mid-1980s from the highly politicized space of private friendship circles and the semi-public arena of the Evangelical Church. Tensions peaked in January 1988 during the state's annual remembrance march for martyred communists Rosa Luxemburg and Karl Liebknecht, executed by free corps thugs in 1919. One dissident managed briefly to unfurl a banner with a politically awkward Luxemburg quotation: "Freedom is always the freedom to think differently." Arrests and crackdowns followed, with leading protestors deported to the West. "This was in fact the beginning of the end," observes Mary Fulbrook. Numbers of the politically involved grew larger as church vigils, candlelit meetings, prayer services, and protest concerts became regular events. "All over the GDR, there was a growing sense that, somehow, there would have to be changes; and that people were increasingly willing to organize, discuss, and pressurize for change." The regime's legitimacy crisis worsened in May 1989 when it shamelessly rigged the outcome of elections purporting to show overwhelming support for Honecker's ruling Socialist Unity Party (SED). Closely monitoring this "manifest dishonesty,"[72] coalescing opposition groups openly called foul.

By the early summer of 1989 average East Germans had discovered novel ways to "vote"—as they had before the wall went up in 1961—with their feet. For years some had protested in order to be arrested and deported: the quickest route, in other words, to the forbidden West. When Hungary began its highly publicized opening of the border to Austria, however, East Germans by the thousands went to vacation spots in western Hungary and chose the right moment, usually in the middle of the night, to simply walk to Austrian freedom. Others vacationing in Poland and Czechoslovakia stepped into West German embassies and claimed political asylum. Altogether about thirty-three thousand left for the West in July and August.[73] As the exodus continued, dissidents who opted to stay home and struggle for change held monthly marches to protest the May elections. And then in September 1989 the coming of political pluralism that had rankled Honecker so much about Poland and Hungary came—openly, illegally, defiantly, courageously—to the GDR. Within three weeks, New Forum, Democracy Now, the Social Democratic Party, and Democratic Awakening issued public proclamations.

The GDR's final act played itself out mainly in the streets. The surfacing "citizens' movement" held one march after another in October 1989 for a more humane and democratic form of communism. East Berlin and numerous cities were affected, but the largest demonstrations that month, eventually swelling to around 300,000, took place in Leipzig. "We are the people," they chanted. The civil disobedience of New Forum and allied groups lent urgency to Lenin's old query: "What is to be done?" An aging and ill Erich Honecker wanted to answer with the mailed fist as Chinese communists had done that spring at blood-spattered Tiananmen Square, but cooler heads in the SED prevailed after Gorbachev's spokesman told reporters in Helsinki that "the Brezhnev doctrine is dead."[74] Indeed, with the Red Army ordered to stay in its barracks—without the overwhelming Soviet force, in other words, that had formerly imposed order on the East Bloc—Honecker's more prudent colleagues deposed him and pushed a former protégé, Egon Krenz, into the top position. And then on November 9, 1989, the unimaginable happened: With the stream of East Germans who had illegally exited their country widening to about 120,000, the inexperienced new leader, aided in no way by his panicky and disorganized colleagues, announced the lifting of travel restrictions to West Germany. East Berliners by the tens of thousands flooded past confused border guards for a surreal evening of revelry and celebration in western parts of Berlin walled off for twenty-eight years. As the scene repeated itself all over East Germany in the following days—nine million visited the Federal Republic in one week, 50,000 stayed—the marchers continued to pressure Krenz for meaningful political change. Observers noticed a mood swing in the swelling crowds, however, for now they chanted: "We are *one* people."[75]

Events progressed quickly now toward the end of the GDR. Lacking all credibility because of his association with Honecker, Krenz yielded the reins in early December 1989 to a reform-minded prime minister, Hans Modrow, former party leader of Dresden. Nearly half his cabinet represented noncommunist parties that East Germany, like Poland, had allowed to exist for window-dressing, but which now reversed roles to play meaning parts. Modrow also opened so-called round table meetings with leaders of New Forum and other opposition groups, agreeing in their first meeting to multiparty elections in May 1990. Increasingly, however, angry, impetuous voices from the street demanded immediate elections whose sole purpose should be deciding on the unification of East and West Germany. And many continued to pack bags: The total passed 350,000 in January with no end in sight. This pressure for unity, supported heavily by politicians from West German political parties like Helmut Kohl's ruling CDU, caught the government and round table opposition off guard, for both had come rather quickly to the common ground of reforming the GDR—seeking a "third way" between Stalinism and capitalism—and neither wanted to abandon their state by essentially merging it with the Federal Republic of Germany (FRG). With calls for reunification growing shriller after New Year, Modrow actually invited the receptive round table groups into his government. They both went down together during elections that had been pushed up to March. The communists, renamed the Party of Democratic Socialism (PDS), received 16.4 percent, while New Forum and two other round table groups, running on an "Alliance 90" (Bündnis 90) ticket, got a mere 2.9 percent. The brave citizens' movement of the previous autumn "had created a public space for the articulation of its feelings," writes Konrad Jarausch, only to see "the silent majority fill it with clamor for unity."[76] Within two months the FRG and the GDR had agreed on a reunification process and hammered out a unifying State Treaty. The East German parliament's 302 to 82 ratification vote in May 1990 reflected the clamorous sentiments of the "we are one people" majority.

Elsewhere in Eastern Europe during the autumn and winter of 1989–1990 the largely death-free overthrow of communism ran its remarkable course. The turnaround in Bulgaria came quickly and surprisingly a day after the Berlin Wall fell. The country's dictatorial party boss since 1954, Todor Zhivkov, was deposed from the Politburo by colleagues who declared it high time for glasnost and perestroika. In December they announced the holding of free elections in June 1990. Shedding itself of orthodox party "dinosaurs" from the Zhivkov era and stressing its wealth of administrative experience, the former communists, running as the Bulgarian Socialist Party, won an impressive 47 percent of the vote. Czechoslovakia's bloodless "velvet revolution" followed East Germany's pattern. After police roughed up hundreds of protesting students on November 17, 1989, strikes and demonstrations erupted throughout the country. Now the party that had suppressed Charter 77 in the knowledge that Warsaw Pact power stood behind Prague lost all resolve to use further force. First they dismissed hardliner Stalinists like Gustav Husák, in power since the Prague Spring, and when this failed to quell demonstrations, the panicky communists brought formerly impotent non-communist party representatives and a few leading dissidents into the government. Nothing sufficed, however, and the paralyzed regime finally collapsed under public scorn in late December. Alexander Dubcek returned as president of a heretofore rubber stamp assembly, which elected Vaclav Havel president of Czechoslovakia. Parliamentary elections in June 1990 produced a 53 percent landslide victory for the Civic Forum Party and its Slovak partner, the Public Against Violence, both organized by Charter 77 activists. The former communists polled only 14 percent.[77]

For many months it seemed that Nicolai Ceausescu's police state would avoid Eastern Europe's spreading revolution. Wary of Moscow after the Warsaw Pact invasion of Czechoslovakia in 1968, the Rumanian dictator did not want the Soviet tanks that other leaders in the region yearned to receive for protection: Resolute use of the feared Securiate would suffice. When Hungarian subjects in the border town of Timisoara became unruly on December 15, 1989, therefore, the cold-blooded security troops opened fire on a crowd, killing a hundred people and wounding hundreds more. The massacre sparked disturbances and clashes in other parts of Transylvania as the Hungarian minority, emboldened by courageous acts in neighboring states, refused to be cowed. On December 21 Ceausescu organized a pro-government demonstration in Bucharest to rally the Rumanian majority, but the crowd shouted him down. The Tiananmen-style clearing of the square only made the situation worse. That night violence erupted between the Securiate and insurgents aided, apparently, by disgruntled army units that exploited the situation to strike against Ceausescu. Over two thousand people on both sides died, but the once-untouchable tyrant fled the capital, only to be hunted down, tried in a hastily organized people's court, and shot along with his wife. In May 1990 anti-Ceausescu communists, reorganized in a so-called National Salvation Front, won a startling 67 percent of the nation's first truly free vote.[78]

Two weeks after the execution of the Ceausescus, Yugoslav communists agreed to hold federal multiparty elections before the end of 1990.[79] The voting never took place because the multiethnic state was drifting by then toward another civil war, a conflict that distinguished Yugoslav from other East Bloc developments that year. Although the desire for self-determination characterized all events of the *annus mirabilis*, developments in the north featured suppressed citizenries taking back civil and political rights from frightened regimes, while in the south Yugoslav fighters believed they were struggling for the ethnic or national rights of Serbs, Croats, Slovenes, and Bosnians— peoples desiring separate states after decades of increasingly unhappy federal union. Behind the scenes, unfortunately, ambitious, unscrupulous politicians stoked the flames of these problematic beliefs.

Tito had always known that ethnic chauvinism could rip communist Yugoslavia apart, for it had almost done so in the democratic 1920s before finally reaching this tragic end in the dark days of World War Two. When centrifugal tendencies grew too strong in Croatia during the early 1970s, therefore, the aging leader snuffed them out. He also introduced constitutional changes in 1974 designed to counteract secessionist impulses. The six federal republics (Serbia, Montenegro, Slovenia, Croatia, Bosnia-Herzegovina, and Macedonia) and two Serbian provinces of Kosovo and Vojvodina received greater independence. There would be a collective presidency, moreover, rotating annually among representatives of the six republics and the two newly autonomous provinces. Decision making in the party also devolved largely to the states/provinces. These measures took effect after Tito's death in 1981, creating an unusual kind of political pluralism as government and party figures

The Federal Republic of Yugoslavia

at subfederal levels began to fight among themselves for influence and power. The decade's oil- and debt-related crisis exacerbated fractiousness, for communism's version of "stagflation" and the accompanying consumer woes could be blamed on the alleged machinations of rival federal peoples. Complicating the situation still more was the fact that Yugoslavia's different regions had continued to develop very unevenly despite Tito's efforts of the early 1970s to curb the very market forces he had unleashed (see Chapter 8). By the late 1980s, for example, Slovenia, comprising a mere twelfth of Yugoslavia's population, accounted for a fifth of its production and a third of all exports—with Croatia not far behind. While their living standards approached those of neighboring Austria, per capita income in Kosovo stood six times lower, literally at Third World levels. Proud Serbians could not compete with the Slovenes and Croats either, prompting conspiracy charges and accusations that Tito, himself of mixed Croat-Slovene heritage, had sold out the other peoples of Yugoslavia with his ill-advised constitutional changes. Slobodan Milosevic, the power-hungry, demagogic leader of Serbia after 1986, manipulated these tensions by encouraging Serbians throughout Yugoslavia to advance their cause at the expense of other ethnic groups.

Milosevic pushed things closer to the breaking point in 1989. That February he rescinded the constitutional autonomy of Serbian Kosovo and Vojvodina, triggering strikes that he brutally suppressed. Unrest and tension increased as the opportunistic Serb president purged Albanian Kosovars from administrative positions and replaced them with ethnic loyalists. On June 28, a Serb national holiday commemorating the Turks' defeat of a Serb army at Kosovo Polje, Milosevic visited the site and stirred up emotions on this six hundredth anniversary of the battle by talking provocatively about a "reunification of Serbia."[80] He also used rallies of his supporters to grasp control of largely Serbian Montenegro. With four of eight votes within the collective presidency in Milosevic's pocket, Slovene President Milan Kucan complained that his rival wanted to turn Yugoslavia "into Serbo-slavia."[81] Kucan and his counterpart in Croatia, Franjo Tudjman, gave tit for tat, eliminating Serbs from government posts and police forces in their states. By the autumn of 1989, as developments elsewhere in the East Bloc accelerated, the Slovenes and Croats spoke ominously of national self-determination and the right to secede. Demagogues on both sides evoked bitter memories of the world war, furthermore, a time when Croatian fascist "Ustashi" and Serb partisan "Chetniks" had slaughtered one another. "Day after day," recalls journalist Misha Glenny, "RTY Belgrade and Croatian Television (HTV) emitted images of atrocity, while historical documentaries and movies about the Second World War romanticized each nation's soldiery."[82]

In January 1990 the League of Yugoslav Communists rejected a Slovene motion to restructure Yugoslavia into a looser federal state—the same meeting that announced nationwide elections for the upcoming year. Kucan's followers walked out. As the year progressed, the replacement of East European communist regimes with young democracies embarking on radical market experiments sweetened the economic prospects of secession for Kucan and Tudjman, for enlargement of the EC had now surfaced as an agenda item (see Chapter 11) and their states represented the most highly developed regions in Yugoslavia, areas that might receive a more favorable hearing in Brussels if shorn of their impoverished or economically weaker sister states.[83] Slovenia held a successful referendum on secession in December 1990, identifying June 26, 1991 as the day of independence. The Croatians voted to follow suit. These decisions made civil war in Yugoslavia virtually inevitable, for Milosevic had no intention of abandoning the substantial Serbian population in these states to their probable fate as persecuted minorities.

THE DISINTEGRATION OF THE SOVIET UNION

Mikhail Gorbachev's bold and controversial initiatives to create a more democratic form of communism and accelerate economic growth in the USSR did not—and could not—remain immune from the revolutions sweeping Eastern Europe. Although he and his liberal advisers had initially given only cursory thought to extending their new electoral system downward to the USSR's fifteen republics as well as the numerous regions, districts, and locales, already in December 1989 the Congress of Peoples Deputies hurriedly accepted a proposal for spring elections at these levels. For years, moreover, Gorbachev had rejected Alexander Yakovlev's advice to hold western-style multiparty elections. The indignant leader called the suggestion "rubbish" in early 1989 as he prepared for upcoming elections to the Congress. A few months after the Berlin Wall fell, however, the idea of ending the constitutional party monopoly of the CPSU made sense: "I don't see a tragedy in a multiparty system if it serves the people."[84] The Central Committee and the Peoples Deputies approved the plan. After the spring of 1990, communists would have to compete for their seats.

As the turbulent year progressed, however, Gorbachev's ability to stay in control of events diminished, for political demands multiplied faster than he could adjust to them. Lithuanian nationalists held demonstrations for independence in January 1990, prompting a hastily arranged visit by the harried man from Moscow. Stopping in front of one demonstrator, Gorbachev asked threateningly what the man's placard meant by "total independence." "I mean what we had in the 1920s," he answered proudly, "because no nation is entitled to dictate to another nation." Completely incredulous, the author of glasnost shot back: "What kind of exploiters are we if Russia sells you cotton, oil, and raw materials—and not for hard currency either?" "Lithuania had a hard currency before the war," interrupted the protester. "You took it away in 1940."[85] Acting on these sentiments in March, the government of the Lithuanian Republic voted unanimously to secede from the USSR. Moscow imposed economic sanctions until the unruly Baltic republic agreed to "postpone" its secession in July. A month earlier Gorbachev had promised that the Soviet Union's republics would receive fuller freedoms in an upcoming reform measure, but this could not stop the governments of Estonia, Latvia, the Ukraine, Armenia, Turkmenistan, Tajikistan, and immense Russia—congresses of deputies recently elected in Gorbachev's republic-level elections—from declaring that republican legislation super-ceded Soviet decrees. Russia's sovereignty decision had to be particularly galling for the first secretary because it had been introduced by the new chairman of the Russian Congress of People's Deputies, Boris Yeltsin, a popular, ambitious, rising politician who had broken bitterly with Gorbachev—Yeltsin also bolted the CPSU that summer of 1990 to pull the strings for a competing party, Democratic Russia, which he never joined formally. One step removed from secession, the sovereignty votes represented in the best-case scenario a radical decentralization of the USSR, but at worst, they threatened a total breakup of the Soviet Union.

The Soviet economy deteriorated, meanwhile, as miners struck for back pay; industrial output stagnated; consumer goods grew scarcer; collective farms, largely unchanged by perestroika, sputtered; prices at private markets soared, and the first secretary's popularity plummeted. Representatives from the camps of Gorbachev and Yeltsin tried throughout the autumn of 1990 to negotiate a "500-Day Plan" to turn things around, but found no middle ground. Thus while Yeltsin intransigents spoke behind the scenes of moving quicker with market reforms, even of introducing full-fledged capitalism, the Soviet side held to the original goals of perestroika. "The transition to the market certainly does not mean abandoning socialism," said one of Gorbachev's men. "On the contrary, it means impregnating socialism with new qualities and emancipating its potential—economic, social, and spiritual."[86] Although Gorbachev knew what was at stake—failure to compromise would strengthen the forces of Russian sovereignty, which is what Yeltsin intended—the Soviet leader stuck to his principles and terminated the talks.

He also knew, however, that anti-reform extremists in the Soviet and Russian congresses, the KGB, and certain quarters of the Red Army had coalesced on his right, ready to strike if he moved left, or perhaps sooner to preempt secessionist tendencies. Gorbachev's closest aides warned him about these dangers, a few of the most prominent like Foreign Minister Eduard Shevardnadze even resigning to protest the looming threat of "dictatorship," but the top man evidently felt a more pressing need to assuage the right than an allegedly more threatening left, for as liberal advisers left willingly or unwillingly that fall he replaced them with conservatives. And then in January 1991 KGB operatives attempted to purge the Lithuanian government of nationalists. Although the plot failed as a result of further demonstrations and international pressure, shots had been fired into a crowd, killing fourteen people. Gorbachev claimed he had not ordered the attack, which may have been true, but the bloodshed caused him tremendous political damage. "After the bloody Sunday in Vilnius, what is left of our president's favorite topics of 'humane socialism' [and] 'new thinking'?" asked shocked and offended *shestidesyatniki* like Len Karpinsky. Alexander Yakovlev worried that he and fellow liberals would end up in Siberia "against a wall somewhere."[87] Still more worried about the extremism of his erstwhile supporters, however, Gorbachev stationed fifty thousand riot police in Moscow to deal with potential unrest during a mass rally staged by Yeltsin in March. Over two hundred thousand Muscovites turned out, but no incident occurred to trigger a massacre.

As if coming to his political senses, Gorbachev now veered away from the conservatives. Yeltsin, sobered by the possibility of a rightist backlash, also agreed to multilateral talks on the sovereignty issue. In April 1991 Gorbachev hammered out an agreement with Yeltsin and the leaders of eight other Soviet republics. The so-called Nine plus One (i.e., Yeltsin and the others plus Gorbachev) accord granted far-reaching autonomy to these governments while keeping responsibility for defense, foreign policy, and interrepublic trade in the hands of Soviet central authorities. Still not trusting one another, both men sought to reinforce their positions that spring: Gorbachev by holding a purportedly successful referendum on preserving the USSR, which five republics boycotted; Yeltsin by holding presidential elections in the Russian Republic, which he won easily.

Gorbachev's willingness to compromise infuriated extremist opponents like Colonel Victor Alksnis, founder of Union (Soyuz), a strong party in the Soviet Congress determined to use every means to hold central authority together and preserve the USSR's dwindling Great Power status. "The tragedy is that Gorbachev hates to use violence," said the black-leather-clad officer elected by the Red Army bases of Latvia. "Such a person can follow the teachings of Lev Tolstoy, but he cannot be engaged in politics."[88] As spring turned to summer, negotiators from the "Nine plus One" republics finalized a new Union Treaty scheduled for signing in Moscow on August 20, 1991.

One day before the ceremony conspirators placed a vacationing Mikhail Gorbachev under house arrest in the Crimea, and then seized power in Moscow. The ringleaders included KGB chief Vladimir Kryuchkov, Gorbachev's Vice-President Gennady Yanayev, Defense Minister Dimitry Yazov, Defense Council chief Oleg Baklanov, and commander of Soviet ground forces Valentin Varennikov. Their ominously contradictory proclamation presaged some kind of a purge against everyone to their left: "We intend to restore law and order straight away, end bloodshed, declare a war without mercy on the criminal world, and eradicate shameful phenomena discrediting our society."[89] Almost from the beginning, however, things went wrong with the badly planned putsch. No orders were issued for the arrest of Yeltsin, who immediately rallied popular opposition to the coup among his many supporters in the capital. Moreover, despite the impressive number of top military and security chiefs in the conspiracy and intimidating appearance of tanks in the streets, the army did not close ranks, as witnessed by an armored cordon that quickly formed around Yeltsin's headquarters in the Russian parliament building. The putschists' situation deteriorated further when supposedly loyal units refused to fire on crowds as ordered. The coup collapsed ignominiously on August 21. Some of its leaders committed suicide, while others fled Moscow but could not avoid capture.

The Soviet Union had begun its death throes. Gorbachev flew to Moscow early in the morning of August 22, but he enjoyed no triumphal return. Once it became clear that his appointees in the party had betrayed him, Gorbachev resigned as CPSU first secretary. Yeltsin, the people's man of the hour, banned the party altogether from the Russian Republic in November. He then rudely circumvented the Soviet president by negotiating a treaty with Belarus and the Ukraine on December 8, 1991, that terminated the USSR, establishing in its place a loose confederation of independent, fully sovereign states. After the coup attempt of August, Yeltsin wanted nothing to do with communism or the Soviet Union. Eight additional former Soviet republics joined the so-called Commonwealth of Independent States (CIS) two weeks later. The Baltic republics and Georgia declined to join.[90] It was the end of an era.

Chapter 11

▼

CONTEMPORARY HISTORY

Snow floated down on the Berlaymont, the avant-garde structure in central Brussels that housed the European Commission, the executive and bureaucratic branch of the European Community (EC).[1] It was January 1991, a new time in Europe—and the dawn of another, as yet imperceptible order in the world.

Inside a spacious thirteenth-floor room overlooking the city and neighboring offices of the Council of Ministers, the EC's powerful legislative branch, Jacques Delors, president of the commission since 1985, got up from a desk still cluttered with the work of a long day. He moved sprightly to the lounge area of his posh workplace to welcome an American professor from Harvard. A zealous fighter for greater European integration, the elderly, energetic president did not allow much time for polite conversation with his visitor before launching into an animated monologue. With the wave of a hand Delors dismissed much of the history of his organization since its founding in 1957: "Europe has had ten years of success, five years of crisis, and seventeen years of stagnation." It was high time for the EC to make something of itself, but "at any moment now we could be brought down by crisis."[2] Taking no questions, the Frenchman talked nonstop for an hour.

Despite his having said so, Delors's early years at the Berlaymont had hardly been a time of "stagnation" for the European Community. In 1986–1987, for instance, the EC's Single Europe Act moved to eliminate nearly three hundred trade-inhibiting "non-tariff barriers" before the end of 1992 (see Chapter 9). Delors also pushed through an extension of "qualified majority voting" on the Council of Ministers. All routine market-related, so-called harmonization issues would now be decided by a two-thirds majority, permitting detours around recalcitrant member nations when normal consensus modes of operating broke down.[3] Significant increases to commission budgets followed in early 1988. All of these measures enhanced executive as well as supranational "federalist" impulses, giving notice to "confederal" nationalist adherents in the EC that a new force was building in Brussels.

At its thirty-two-year mark, however, the EC clearly passed a turning point. Exhilaration and anxiety permeated the air in June 1989 when the

Council of Ministers heard Delors's detailed proposals for moving toward a European monetary union with its own currency and banking institutions, both of which necessitated a common monetary policy. Only in this way could Europe avoid currency destabilization, establish an environment for productive investment and technological modernization, and remain competitive with America and Japan. The ministers agreed to allow the first stage of this bold design, liberalization of capital markets, to take effect in the New Year, while the rest would be negotiated at a so-called intergovernmental conference of EC states. In July 1989, furthermore, the Organization for Economic Cooperation and Development, the successor agency to the original Marshall Plan, asked the European Commission to coordinate billions of dollars of joint aid to the democratizing regimes of Poland and Hungary, adding Czechoslovakia to the list in late 1989, and Rumania, Bulgaria, and Yugoslavia in mid-1990.[4] The pledged infusions, if made, would be tantamount to a second Marshall Plan. In 1990 Delors's staffers also began negotiating special EC "association agreements" with Poland and Hungary that envisioned better access to community markets in return for "actual accomplishment of political, economic, and legal reforms"[5] in Warsaw and Budapest. Although the EC had long pursued such overtly political pro-democratic agendas (see Chapter 9) and had taken occasional stands during times of international crisis, Brussels wielded more of an actual foreign policy now than ever before. Eager to accelerate these trends, Delors applauded the decision of France and a reunifying Germany in April 1990 to consider greater political and diplomatic competencies for the European Community. By January 1991 one ad hoc intergovernmental conference had begun discussions on monetary union while a second wrestled over political union, the latter including one of the president's hobby horses since 1989: a common European foreign and security policy.

As the snowfall thickened outside his picture windows, Delors turned back to one of those troubling developments that "could stop us tomorrow"—the unfolding Gulf War against Saddam Hussein's Iraq. Despite its largely unquestioned legitimacy and UN backing, the conflict had nevertheless whipped Europe's horses in different directions. The pacifically inclined Belgians and Germans balked at military action on principle, while the British eagerly rushed army corps to the Americans' side, supported firmly by the Dutch and Portuguese. France sent troops too, but mainly to avoid diplomatic isolation. Paris wanted to organize a West European military force around the largely defunct West European Union, founded in 1948 but then quickly superceded by NATO. Delors took a similar stand, warning that "the Gulf War has provided an object lesson—if one were needed—on the limitations of the European Community," for once it became obvious that "armed combat" would resolve matters in Kuwait, "the [EC] had neither the institutional machinery nor the military force which would have allowed it to act as a community." One question above all others tugged at the man from Brussels: "Are the Twelve prepared to learn from this experience?" His worst nightmare: an economically mighty but politically impotent European Community—a "big Switzerland."[6]

THE VIEW FROM BRUSSELS

The reunification of Germany played into Delors's hands. He realized almost presciently in September 1989 that the precariousness of communist rule could lead to the fall of the communist East Germany, its incorporation into West Germany, and hence into the EC. As early as January 1990 he advocated reunification publicly, the first major political figure outside of Germany to do so.[7] With terrible memories of World War Two still fresh, however, the prospect of a larger German state alarmed surrounding countries. The former wartime allies would have to approve, moreover, especially if they were to abandon occupation rights in Berlin. In December 1989 French President François Mitterrand offered German Chancellor Helmut Kohl a bargain. Paris would support reunification if Germany agreed to the final stages of monetary union. By sacrificing an element of economic and political sovereignty to the EC, in other words, Germany would be less threatening to France, which could exert a comforting measure of indirect control over its historically problematic neighbor. Already avidly behind European integration, Kohl accepted the deal. A similar combination of French anxiety and German Europeanism, mixed with post–Cold War security jitters, soon extended the understanding to include support for a new EC acronym: CFSP, the Common Foreign and Security Policy.[8] Small wonder, therefore, that Delors had taken the lead in promoting German reunification, for it seemed to make "Europe" stronger. East and West Germany united in effect with the introduction of the West German mark in the GDR that summer, and formally on October 2, 1990, with the accession to the Federal Republic of five new states from what had been East Germany.[9]

These developments set the stage in 1991 for the EC's hard year of bargaining over closer economic and political union. Both intergovernmental conferences finished work in the fall, and then heads of state and government made final adjustments at their semi-annual "European Council" meeting in December, thereby paving the way for ratification of a new EC treaty at Maastricht, Holland, in February 1992.[10] "Maastricht" quickly became a household word throughout the West, for it envisioned a bold restructuring of the European edifice. The document identified monetary union as the first priority area, or "pillar," setting forth a timetable for achieving this greater measure of integration with all its accompanying economic and institutional changes. Underscoring the federalist goals of the first pillar was the fact that some form of qualified majority voting on the Council of Ministers would guide political progress toward fuller economic union. The treaty raised common foreign and security policy as a second pillar amidst much applause by federal enthusiasts like Delors who wanted Europe "to speak with one voice" in the new world order. Reflecting unresolved differences over the appropriateness of federalist voting in this area, however, Maastricht left many of the "devil-ish" details to an intergovernmental conference scheduled for 1996. The EC's foreign policy and military reforms would eventually stand alongside a third column whose lesser-priority erection also awaited later deliberations. In this crowded category one found commitments to a new European citizenship, harmonized immigration policies, a social contract for labor, and a more federal and democratic "European Union." The "EU" also agreed to undertake negotiations in 1998 with select former communist states for a first round of enlargement to the East.[11] After Maastricht the twelve member states began a controversial ratification process (see later). The treaty took effect in late 1993.

The rise of the EU in the 1990s, although not without its controversial side among Europeans themselves, represented one of the most positive developments in the history of twentieth-century Europe. After centuries of warfare and authoritarian governing systems, friendly democracies had formed a closer, politically proactive union. That Europe's edifice of peace and democracy still remained a work in progress, however, became frightfully obvious during the course of the same decade as ethnic and sectarian violence of the worst sort erupted in lands that had already seen too much of it in their histories. The remainder of this chapter analyzes contemporary Europe's mix of the positive and the negative, beginning with the ugly disintegration of the former Yugoslavia.

The Croatian and Bosnian Tragedies

The Common Foreign and Security Policy "pillar" wobbled from the discussion stage onward. The Gulf War exposed serious differences in Europe over whether to develop a military arm of the EC, paralyzing intergovernmental negotiations throughout 1991 and necessitating postponement of any real decision. A thinly papered-over compromise at Maastricht resurrected the old West European Union (see earlier) as "an integral part" of the European Union, and then called for "the eventual framing of a common defense policy, which might in time lead to a common defense."[12] The can had been kicked down the road, as diplomats say.

Balkan imbroglios sparked further disagreements that year over foreign policy. With Slovenian and Croatian secession from Yugoslavia drawing near in June 1991 (see Chapter 10), Germany pressed for diplomatic recognition of both states while Britain and France wanted to prevent Yugoslavia's breakup. Events, not consensus, decided the issue. The day of independence soon arrived, sparking a brief war between Yugoslav forces and the Slovene militia. Showing its new foreign policy profile, the community mediated an end to the violence on July 8 when Belgrade agreed to withdraw its units and recognize Slovenia. "This is the hour of Europe,"[13] boasted Jacques Poos, foreign minister of Luxembourg. Hoping to forestall irredentist bloodshed in the region, however, the EC somewhat contradictorily ignored the outcome of the mediation—and German wishes—by refusing to grant diplomatic recognition to either Slovenia or Croatia.

The mediation represented only a minor and temporary victory for peace. Indeed, the deteriorating situation in Croatia, harboring a much greater Serb population than Slovenia, reflected the true face of the impending Yugoslav tragedy.[14] In August 1991 regular and paramilitary units from Serbia moved into Croatia to secure provinces for Orthodox Serbs—and cleanse them of Catholic Croats. Amidst terrible atrocities of the sort not seen in Europe for fifty years, Slobodan Milosevic's men deported 170,000 non-Serbs from enclaves that comprised about a third of Croatia, sending additional hundreds of thousands of refugees fleeing in all directions. The accompanying torture, shooting, and rape of thousands of people can be explained in part as payback for Croat atrocities against Serbs in World War Two, events that were real enough for demagogic politicians like Milosevic and state-controlled media in Belgrade to easily generate a racist, xenophobic hysteria, which was then whipped forward by local Serb leaders whose fighters took a crude "kill or be killed" approach. As one scholar writes, however, "pure old-fashioned thuggery"[15] likely entered the mix, which helps to explain later crimes against neighboring peoples with no record of violence against Serbs.

The European Community responded by initiating peace talks at The Hague. Milosevic accepted a cease-fire, but not until the Croatian enclaves had been seized. In January 1992 about fourteen thousand British and French peacekeepers deployed under UN auspices along cease-fire lines separating the newly forged Croatian and Serbian parts of the country. In February the new European Union finally granted formal recognition to both Slovenia and Croatia. The EU's resolution of the crisis planted the seeds of future trouble, however, for by doing nothing to reverse conquest by aggression its spread had been encouraged. What is more, the union had now legitimated secession, thereby tempting Bosnia-Herzegovina to follow suit, which invited in its turn more Serbian aggression to "save" the substantial 30 percent Serbian population of Bosnia from the alleged threat of persecution. Fearing such an outcome, Britain and France had opposed Germany before finally bowing to Bonn's threat of unilateral recognition. Looking "feckless and divided," writes one expert on the EU, Europe "had been quite unable to act in its own backyard and limit the suffering."[16] The foreign policy promise of Maastricht seemed shallow.

The Common Foreign and Security Policy became even more of a disappointment in March 1992 when Bosnia seceded from Yugoslavia, triggering assaults from Serbian army units and militia groups of the Bosnian Serbs. Within weeks they controlled about 60 percent of the land. Croat militia in Bosnia also attacked, taking another 20 percent of the country inland from the Adriatic coast. The young state had been reduced to a series of landlocked pockets of Bosnian Muslims desperately trying to defend themselves. The Muslim-Croat fighting was fierce, with both sides committing atrocities, but the Serbs committed far worse crimes against humanity, shelling Sarajevo and other Muslim enclaves, killing innocent pedestrians with sniper fire, and blocking humanitarian aid. Hapless Muslims overrun in Serb-controlled areas fell victim, meanwhile, to "ethnic"[17] cleansing actions more outrageous and egregious than those in Croatia. Some 200,000 men, women, and children would become victims of genocide before the war ended, while over a million became refugees, pouring into neighboring countries and all over Europe—generous Germany admitted 220,000 "asylum seekers" in seven months.

In early 1993 the EU and UN proposed a peace plan envisioning a decentralized multiethnic Bosnian state. Only the Bosnian Croats readily accepted it, however, and no power risked sending ground forces to impose order—not America, wary of another Vietnam; not Britain, anxious about another Northern Ireland; not France, unwilling to fight alone; and certainly not Germany, mindful of its militarist past. The UN sent six thousand lightly equipped European peacekeepers to monitor periodic cease-fires, ensure the delivery of humanitarian aid, and protect some of the worst-hit enclaves, but the Serbs ignored them or, worse, captured the brave blue helmets as hostages. And so the killing continued into 1993, 1994, and 1995, including 149 UN peacekeepers.

Peace did not come to Bosnia until December 1995. Earlier that year Mitterrand's successor, President Jacques Chirac, threatened to withdraw France's UN contingent, hinting that NATO must be authorized to use greater force on the ground. U.S. President Bill Clinton, heretofore willing to approve only air strikes, agreed.[18] American, British, and French NATO forces struck from the land and air in August, inflicting heavy losses on Bosnian Serb forces. Simultaneously, Croatia assaulted Krajina, one of the provinces seized by the Serbs in 1991. Successful military force permitted a diplomatic breakthrough with the so-called Dayton Accords in November. All warring parties accepted a loosely united republic split into two autonomous halves: a Federation of Bosnia and Herzegovina for the Muslims and Croats and a so-called Republika Srpska for Bosnian Serbs. Positioned as buffers, sixty thousand heavily armed NATO troops enforced the peace.

The EU had hard lessons to draw from the Balkan tragedies. The diplomatic debacle of the first year, which saw Europe unable to agree on how to put out early fires—and many West Europeans unwilling to take seriously a supposedly hopeless feud of allegedly "ancient" origins—gave way to an impressive united peace effort for Bosnia in late 1992. But this admirable "common" foreign policy failed in the implementation stage. While France had argued earlier for an EU defense arm, nothing very concrete materialized after Maastricht or during the Balkan crises, leaving existing NATO structures as the only viable military solution. "After Bosnia not even die-hard Gaullists wanted a NATO-free Europe," writes a recent historian of the EU. The intergovernmental negotiations of 1996, adopted in the EU Treaty of Amsterdam in June 1997, drew similar conclusions. Joint actions in the foreign policy/security realm leading to military engagement by an as yet unrevitalized West European Union (WEU) would have to be unanimous and therefore confederal, for all intents and purposes, even though Amsterdam's opaque and Byzantine procedures paid proper respect to federalist ideals.[19] The accession of three neutral states, Austria, Sweden, and Finland, to the European Union in 1995 (see later) strengthened Europe's reluctance to engage in military conflicts. The EU would probably be hamstrung in any future crisis, in other

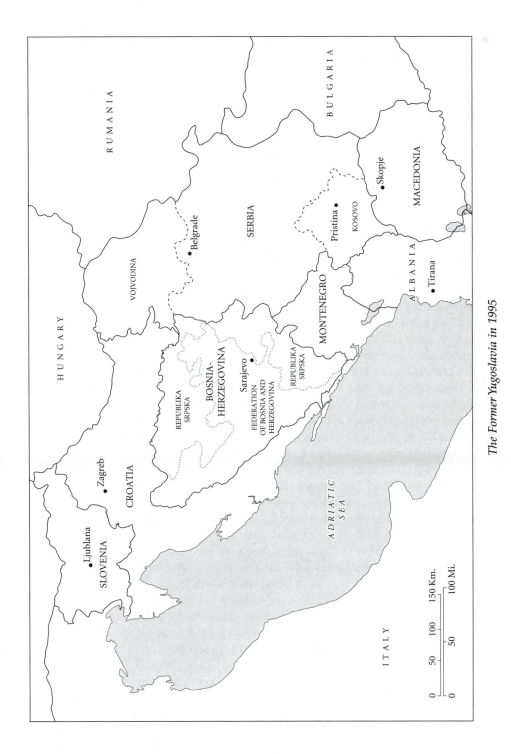

The Former Yugoslavia in 1995

words, relegating police action to America and the biggest European powers working through NATO, which had impressive financial and military resources as opposed to the UN, which did not. The West would seek UN sanction if possible, but not regard it as a sine qua non.[20] NATO's Madrid summit sealed the deal in July 1997 by recognizing the legitimacy of WEU but explicitly stating the primacy of NATO.

The Young Democracies of Eastern Europe

The EU's "third pillar" relationship with Eastern Europe grew controversial quickly after the fall of communism. Already during the intergovernmental negotiations of 1991 an irate Lech Walesa, president of Poland since the previous year, appeared in Brussels to rail against the discriminatory approach taken by Europe's "rich man's club," which merely wanted to protect its own markets while also insisting on difficult political and economic reforms before completing trade deals with Poland and other young democratic states. "We would not like the iron curtain to turn into a *silver* curtain separating a rich West from a poor East," he said. Playing on current phobias in Western Europe, the former revolutionary warned that such exclusiveness would undermine economies all the way to Moscow and set in motion "a rush of ten million Soviets to Germany."[21] Under pressure of this sort the EU made its first commitment at Maastricht to eventual eastern memberships.

The diplomats had kicked another can down the road, however, for the promise of enlargement was for the time being an exercise in public relations. This became clearer in the spring of 1993 after Poland, Hungary, and the Czech and Slovak Republics[22] announced their aspirations for membership. In June the EU heads of government responded at their European Council[23] meeting at Copenhagen. The so-called Copenhagen criteria stated that "membership requires that the candidate country has achieved stability of institutions guaranteeing democracy, the rule of law, human rights and respect for and protection of minorities, the existence of a functioning market economy as well as the capacity to cope with competitive pressures and market forces within the union."[24] It would be another two years, however, before the EU drew up a provisional list of the myriad regulations, divided into economic, social, environmental, administrative, and judicial categories, on which candidate countries would have to pass muster before admission.

EU delays sparked controversy, to be sure, but only reflected the unpleasant reality of East European unpreparedness for Europe's club. Thus eastern economies tailspinned throughout much of the early 1990s as industrial production dropped 36–40 percent, inflation skyrocketed, and unemployment soared to official rates of 13–16 percent. Actual joblessness rose to much higher levels, however, as millions of downsized workers went into involuntary retirement and other discouraged laborers stopped looking for work. Economists debated—and still debate—the reasons why communism's transition to capitalism proved so excruciating,[25] pointing to the fact that three-quarters of western grants promised in the euphoric moments of 1989 vanished as once-eager backers shied away from uncertain property rights,[26] political turbulence, an allegedly slow pace of privatization,[27] the seemingly unending military chaos in the Balkans, and that conflict's potential to spread. Continued debt payments to western countries, left over from the communist era, also drained away huge amounts of capital—and all this at a time when war in the former Yugoslavia shrunk markets for Bulgaria, Rumania, Hungary, and Slovenia; the collapse of COMECON disrupted economies from the Balkans to the Baltic to the Urals; and young industries throughout the East struggled with marginal success to compete in unsympathetic western markets. Attempts to control inflation, mandated by western politicians and creditors, made a bad situation worse, furthermore, as high interest rates and government spending cuts dragged the region deeper into recession. Eager to shed the remnants of communism, in fact, the leaders of many East European countries proved very amenable to the advice of overzealous pro-market academicians from America whose "quasi-religious"[28] recommendations extended well past "Reaganomics" to a near gutting of government welfare and social services. Where this led to extremes, as in Poland, the Czech Republic, Hungary, and Slovenia, recessionary drag worsened as governments put less money in consumers' hands. The unfortunate social consequence of economic crisis in the early 1990s could be measured in alarming poverty levels, which hit 25 percent in the Czech Republic, 30 percent in Hungary, 34 percent in Slovakia, 44 percent in Poland, and 52 percent in Rumania.[29]

The region's problems reminded historically knowledgeable observers of the 1920s, a time of crisis when so many young democracies foundered. Would it happen again? Optimists cautioned against making gloomy historical comparisons based on the collapse of contemporary Yugoslavia, citing the quick adoption by almost every East European state of constitutions guaranteeing human rights, rule of law, multiparty pluralism, and freedom of press, assembly, and association. But naysayers pointed to widespread evidence of political instability as voters turned against parties in power. In Poland, Solidarity fell apart during the 1991 elections, its factions commingling with dozens of parties in an unwieldy parliament that accomplished little business. Protesting their economic woes in 1993, voters gave 37 percent of the seats to former communists who formed a new cabinet. A similar phenomenon occurred in 1994 in Hungary, where a communist successor party captured a 54 percent majority in ousting Democratic Forum. In Czechoslovakia Civic Forum and its Slovakian sister party, Public Against Violence, both disintegrated, and then the country itself split into separate Czech and Slovak republics in 1993 over the issue of rapid market reforms, which Prague wanted and Bratislava did not. Elections favored new centrist parties in the Czech Republic and newly established left-center parties in Slovakia. In the Balkans, reshuffled communist parties on top after 1990 elections took beatings in subsequent polling: Witness the Rumanian Front for National Salvation, which plummeted from 77 to 12.6 percent of parliamentary seats, and the Bulgarian Socialist Party, which nosedived from 88 to 25 percent but held on to power. And in Albania the lone communist regime that had survived the "year of miracles" finally relented to violent university student demonstrations in the winter of 1990–1991, holding multiparty elections that it won after considerable manipulation in March only to resign amidst more demonstrations and strikes in June. New elections in March 1992 gave the opposition Democratic Party a 62 percent majority.[30]

Some continued to caution against panic, seeing East Europe's turbulence as within the range of normal democratic give-and-take, especially downplaying the risk associated with governments of former communists who had no intention of reverting to the old discredited system. But many East European insiders were appalled by the situation, particularly what they saw as a superficial democratization. Estonia and Latvia celebrated independence and the return of democracy, but disenfranchised their 30 percent Russian minorities. Poland proclaimed rule of law, said one legal expert, while exploiting the law in practice "as a tool of the existing politics or policies." Vaclav Havel, president of the Czech Republic, bemoaned his country's "hatred among nationalities, suspicion, racism . . . [and] general lack of tolerance, understanding, taste, moderation, [and] reason."[31] And Slavenka Draculic, a Croatian writer familiar with Eastern Europe, complained that "most people have the wrong notion of democracy as a kind of natural calamity that has descended on us, not something one has to understand, develop and work for." She was particularly critical of Croatia's Franjo Tudjman because of his tendency to rehabilitate the history and followers of the dreaded fascist Ustashe. With such men in power it is small wonder that average Croatians, unlike Germans, had not even begun to come to grips with their own crimes and moral guilt from the World War Two era. Before crossing the threshold to true democracy and the eventual "bright future" of EU membership, therefore, "Croatians will be forced to live not in the present, but in the past."[32]

Thus as Brussels initiated intergovernmental talks in advance of the Amsterdam Treaty, whose main purpose was to reform EU institutions before eastern enlargement, it was high time for the commission to investigate the eligibility of all applicant states. Published in 1997 as *Agenda 2000*, the resulting study concluded positively—and charitably—that democracy and rule of law had made adequate progress in most East European countries, but that their economies remained far from ready despite clear signs of turnaround or bottoming-out at mid-decade. Environmentally many aspirants also faced disastrous conditions. The report identified Estonia, Poland, the Czech Republic, Hungary, Slovenia, and Cyprus as the strongest candidates. When a screening process began in early 1998, screeners possessed an intimidating checklist of thirty-one categories or "chapters" (e.g., democracy, rule of law, minority rights, labor law, business law, market reforms, the environment, educational policy, etc.) that would have to be satisfactorily scrutinized or "closed" before admittance. Negotiations between the EU and applicant nations over the first seven chapters began in November 1998. Over two years later only Hungary and Cyprus approached the end goal, having closed twenty-two chapters.[33]

Eastern enlargement was clearly going to be a slow process, but Europe's Fifteen were themselves unprepared to move any faster. The addition of many comparatively poor farming regions to the EU, for instance, would drastically increase agricultural subsidies under the Common Agricultural Policy (CAP)—to the point, in fact, of bankrupting the union. Reducing the degree of protection, on the other hand, would spark EU farmer opposition. Secondly, the union's "structural" and "cohesion" funds for underdeveloped industries and infrastructures, heretofore spent largely on Portugal, Spain, Greece, and Ireland in a kind of internal EU Marshall Plan, were also inadequate for extension to Eastern Europe. Thus enlargement would necessitate either unwanted budget increases or reduced levels of structural support—hardly an acceptable option for current recipients.[34] Germany's experience since reunification offered further disincentives in this area, for the former GDR had turned into a financial sink hole, absorbing far more investment than anyone had imagined necessary—over a trillion marks in the 1990s, or more than *twenty times* greater per capita than EU aid to Ireland[35]—which in turn triggered inflation, high interest rates, economically regressive and politically unpopular tax increases, and higher unemployment in western Germany without lowering it in the new states.

Finally, neither the preliminary intergovernmental negotiations nor the Amsterdam deliberations produced agreement on those "constitutional" reforms considered necessary prerequisites to enlargement.[36] These issues included reducing the number of seats on the European Commission to make it less unwieldy and a new weighting of votes on the Council of Ministers to compensate the larger states for losing seats on the commission. Amsterdam also did very little to eliminate the so-called democratic deficit in the EU.[37] Germany and Italy, supported by smaller states like Belgium and Holland, argued during the pre-talks leading to Maastricht that the transfer of larger degrees of sovereignty to the union under its monetary union could only be legitimated by simultaneously increasing democratic controls through the European Parliament, since 1979 the only popularly and directly elected EU institution. They argued that eastern enlargement made such reforms more urgent, for how could the EU democratize Eastern Europe without first democratizing itself? While Maastricht and Amsterdam expanded federalist practices like qualified majority voting on the council as well as introducing and then extending "co-decision" of certain issues by commission and parliament, these first few steps hardly constituted democratization, which most EU states, led by confederalist France and Britain, opposed as a loss of national sovereignty.

Political momentum nevertheless pushed eastward expansion relentlessly forward: Witness the extension of accession negotiations in late 1999 to Latvia, Lithuania, Slovakia, Rumania, Bulgaria, and Malta, making for a potential EU of Twenty-Seven. As one skeptic pointed out, European integrationists sensitive to criticism of EU weaknesses "will be drawn irresistibly to presenting the admission of Eastern Europe's new democracies as a sign of the union's vitality."[38] One historian agreed: "The EU cannot afford to let the accession negotiations languish or fail," adding on a more positive note, however, that "promoting democracy and prosperity in Central and Eastern Europe is the EU's primary foreign policy goal, and enlargement is the primary means of

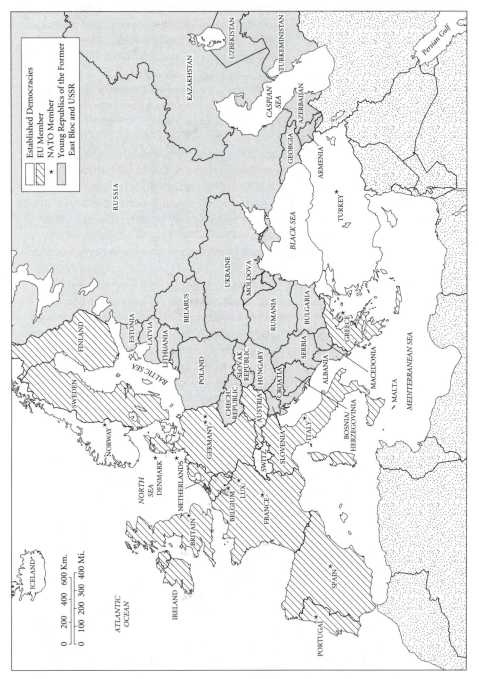

The European Union in the New Europe, 1995

achieving that goal."[39] It is a democratic agenda as old the community itself, but this time Europe, dangling entrée to its rich club tantalizingly above the heads of the East Europeans, possesses tremendous leverage. Thus Slovakian reformers, stung by *Agenda 2000*'s censoring of their country's weak democracy, mustered the strength to defeat strongman Vladimir Meciar in the 1998 elections.[40]

The accession of Austria, Sweden, and Finland to the union in January 1995 provides another example of the seemingly unstoppable momentum of the EU. Negotiators had to resolve problems, to be sure, related to agricultural supports, fishing rights, truck pollution, and existing trade agreements between the Scandinavian and Baltic states that were more liberal than EU treaties with these states.[41] In great contrast to former communist lands, however, Austria, Sweden, and Finland had enjoyed democratic political cultures, the rule of law, and institutions of civil society for much of the twentieth century. Further smoothing the admission process, these states possessed strong market economies that would add to, not detract from, EU budgets and economic stability. In even starker contrast with Eastern Europe, furthermore, the newcomers' environmental standards were actually tougher than the Europe of Twelve. Ratifying the agreements with solid majorities, the people of the new member nations confronted the prospect of European Monetary Union and the new European currency, the Euro. They did so with the same ambivalent mixture of pride, anxiety, and rejection felt by other Europeans.

The European Monetary Union (EMU)

Maastricht's first pillar, EMU, was not as shaky as its second, the Common Foreign and Security Policy (CFSP), or as oft-postponed as its third, which included goals like elimination of the democratic deficit and absorption of Eastern Europe's young, unstable democracies. On the contrary, the high priority politicians put on achieving full monetary union translated into a dogged, decade-long effort to keep this sacrosanct construction project on schedule— even though it became clear almost from the beginning that a high social and political price would be paid for cementing this goal into place.[42]

In 1989 Jacques Delors had proposed a three-stage approach to EMU spread over six or seven years: first, free movement of capital between member states; second, a new European institution to coordinate national monetary policies, nudging each country into line; and third, a permanent fixing of EU exchange rates before substituting a new currency, which a central financial institution of some sort would manage by controlling money supply and interest rates. When Kohl and Mitterrand agreed to proceed with EMU in early 1990, however, the German side, pressed by the wary and conservative German Federal Bank (Bundesbank), insisted on harsh "convergence" criteria that became part of the Maastricht Treaty two years later. Before moving to Stage III, each EMU aspirant had to produce low inflation and interest rates, low budget deficits and government debt, and a stable exchange rate— criteria no EU member met fully in 1992. Bringing economies into line would require imposition of deflationary fiscal and monetary policies at a time when recessionary impulses already reverberated throughout the EU after German reunification. These dismal economic prospects, reinforced by fears of allegedly sacrificing too much power to Brussels, moved a 50.7 percent majority of Danes to reject ratification of Maastricht in a constitutionally mandated referendum in June 1992. Only when European leaders meeting at Edinburgh devised a "variable geometry" scheme that exempted Denmark from the last stage of EMU (as well as military participation in CFSP) did a majority of Danes ratify the treaty. The so-called Edinburgh opt-outs established a clever precedent of pragmatic flexibility that allowed most of Europe to proceed on this and other issues without being restrained by recalcitrant nations, but it would also be an "*à la carte* EU," writes one scholar, "in which, depending on their leverage and negotiating power, member states could pick and choose whatever policies suited them."[43] Later, both Britain and newcomer Sweden opted out of Stage III.

The others, led by resolute France and Germany, put faces to the wind and stayed the course. Fulfilling the Bundesbank's strict convergence criteria proved to be even more painful than the critics of Maastricht had assumed, for deflationary, pump-emptying policies slowed EC-wide annual growth from the already sluggish 2.4 percent of the 1980s to 1.9 percent in the 1990s.[44] As the slowdown sent unemployment percentages to 7.3 in Germany, 11.5 in France, and 10.7 in Italy, organized laborers protested that they were being crucified on the bankers' cross of gold. Voters responded accordingly, casting Mitterrand out of power in 1994 and Kohl in 1998. Three months after Kohl's defeat Europeans learned of graft and corruption in European Commission agencies responsible for stimulating scientific and technological progress— programs whose top-down, almost Soviet-style methods and lack of notable success were already controversial. The public outcry, supported by pressure from the European Parliament, prompted mass resignations from the Commission in early 1999.[44] But Mitterand's and Kohl's successors in office, Jacques Chirac and Gerhard Schröder, forged straight ahead with their pro-Europe course. Stage II of EMU culminated with the opening of a European Central Bank, modeled largely after the U.S. Federal Reserve and headquartered, appropriately enough, in Frankfurt am Main, Germany. When the euro replaced national currencies for accounting purposes on New Year's Day 1999, Stage III began. New coins and paper money entered continental cash registers three years later.

What explains the rugged persistence of EU leaders? That federalist ideals prospered in Europe five decades after the founding of the European Coal and Steel Community and the Common Market is part of the explanation. Jacques Delors, retired from the European Commission in 1995, and many like him in the capitals of Europe's small states, where diplomats had abandoned war as a means of settling disputes long before the larger states shared this vision, had obvious incentives for integration. It seems equally clear, on the other hand, that federalism does not provide a full answer. Indeed, confederalist advocates had compelled EU enthusiasts repeatedly to respect states' rights and sovereignty, which the complex of treaties, regulations, and informal practices that made up the union carefully guarded.[45] That the semi-annual European Council meetings of heads of state gradually enervated the executive functions of the commission in Brussels, especially after Delors's retirement, served as another clear sign that nations retained key decision-making prerogatives in the EU. One need not be jaded or cynical to detect pursuit of national interest, therefore, behind much of the EU's momentum, in Mitterrand's nervous offer to Germany at the time of reunification, for instance, and in the Bundesbank's hard-bargaining response, which Kohl, an integrationist, backed almost entirely. When examining the area of national economic interests more thoroughly one finds the best clues to integrationist motivation, in fact, for EMU had been on Europe's agenda since the late 1960s as a means of meeting the American—and Japanese—challenges.[46] In sum, it was squarely in the interests of every European nation to keep the peace and avoid past horrors while pooling resources to protect the value of their currencies and promote the kinds of investments that would keep Europe abreast of developments in the rapidly evolving contemporary technological system of the third industrial revolution.

As indicated earlier, however, what heads of state and influential figures on the European Commission in Brussels defined as the best interests of their nations, and of Europe, did not always coincide with popular sentiments. Already at the time the Maastricht Treaty was made public in 1991, for instance, 29 percent of the citizens of EU states objected to their country's membership in the union. This disgruntled segment increased over the decade as EU-driven deflationary policies took a social toll and as Balkan collapse highlighted EU weaknesses and unloaded hundreds of thousands of asylum-seekers on countries whose unemployment lines were already growing longer. All of this would pale in comparison to the hordes of job-seekers flooding across borders looking for a better life if Russia followed the Balkan pattern. That Brussels had adopted a common EC external border control under Delors's administration, the so-called Schengen agreement, made little impression on people more worried about the wide open movement of labor *inside* the EU. Faraway bureaucrats seemingly unaccountable to anyone were engaged, critics charged, in a huge irresponsible giveaway of jobs and resources better controlled by elected governments back home. By 1997 the share of citizens in the fifteen-member EU who rejected participation in the union had ballooned to a shocking 54 percent. Because such polling numbers undermined EU legitimacy—and seemed somehow to threaten the ideal of peace and harmony among peoples—European leaders faced a massive public relations challenge as the decade drew to a close.

POST-COMMUNIST RUSSIA

The early post-communist era in Russia proved far more turbulent than the comparable experience in Eastern Europe—with the sole exception of the former Yugoslavia.[47] The underlying cause of this time of trouble was an economic free fall that witnessed GDP plummet an alarming 83 percent over a decade.[48] The person most responsible for exacerbating an economic crisis whose origins dated from the late 1980s, the impetuous, overconfident opposition critic of those days, Boris Yeltsin, had no more grounding in western economic principles than the ousted Gorbachev, while the president's circle of advisers, led by thirty-five-year-old Yegor Gaidar, somewhat naively trusted that price liberalization and property privatization, if introduced simultaneously, could cure economic ills within a year. The young man freed up most prices in January 1992, sending inflation skyrocketing 245 percent *that month* in a kind of universalization of the long-established black market. Inflation hit 1,000 percent before year's end, and then "slowed" to 300 percent over the next two years, but not before destroying much of the people's pent-up savings from the communist era. Yeltsin's team also managed to push through an industrial privatization scheme, but not until late 1992. The bill granted ten thousand ruble vouchers to all citizens for purchasing shares in the bulk of state enterprises at auctions running until mid-1994. Privatization began haltingly with small shops and restaurants, mainly due to recalcitrant "red directors" in the middle and large-scale enterprises who used their remaining influence to block auctions that brought unfamiliar, unwanted change. The same men also joined forces with the anti-reform Russian Congress of Peoples Deputies to dilute Gaidar's economic "shock therapy" by continuing state subsidies with newly printed money, thereby worsening inflation. This support softened the social effects of Russia's industrial nosedive by keeping unproductive businesses open and slowing down the rise of joblessness, but technological change lagged, and wages, in rare instances when paid on time, could not keep pace with inflation. Russia's poverty level soon exceeded Rumania's, the worst in Eastern Europe. Organized crime quickly proliferated, moreover, ensnaring a third of all economic activity in its violent net and making a mockery of any definition of rule of law. In the third year of the reforms gangsters assassinated fifty bankers in Moscow.[49]

All too quickly, politics turned equally violent. Yeltsin's own vice-president, Alexander Rutskoy, mocked his boss's team of "young boys in pink shorts, red shirts, and yellow boots," calling angrily for an end to their "crime against the people." Congress President Ruslan Khasbulatov condemned the "Americanization" of Russia's economy and insisted on a more "socially oriented market."[50] Khasbulatov represented a formidable roadblock to rapid marketization, for he commanded a majority of deputies elected under Gorbachev's rules in 1990, moderate communists who had granted Yeltsin emergency powers to right the economy in October 1991 but now wanted to rescind these powers and cushion the economy from Gaidar's "shocks." As 1992 yielded to 1993, each side upped the ante: Yeltsin, buoyed by a remarkable 53 percent vote of confidence in a March referendum, calling for new elections and a new constitution; the opposition, disappointed in March by barely missing a two-thirds vote needed for impeachment, refusing to pass legislation presented to it—which led to more presidential emergency decrees. When Yeltsin exceeded his constitutional powers by dissolving Congress on September 21, 1993, armed Rutskoy-Khasbulatov supporters seized the parliament building, the so-called White House. The tense standoff continued until the opposition attacked other parts of Moscow on October 3, prompting Yeltsin to send army units into action against the White House the next day. The shocking bombardment and shoot-out killed more than 150 people and wounded over 1,000 before Rutskoy and Khasbulatov capitulated.

By December 1993 Yeltsin had his constitution, approved by 58.4 percent of the voters in a low turnout. The new "super-presidential"[51] rules of the game reflected Yeltsin's frustrations with the old Congress as well as the emboldening outcome of the October events, for the chief executive now possessed greater constitutional powers than both the strong French and American presidents. The crushing of White House opposition also resolved the issue of privatization. This process had slowed to a trickle in the summer as "red directors" waited for Khasbulatov's "socially oriented market," but now accelerated during the last months still open to auctions as factory managers and enterprise chiefs bought up their workers' vouchers and became the new captains of industry. A second phase of privatization known as "loans for shares" began by presidential decree in mid-1994. Under this arrangement banks temporarily received controlling numbers of shares in a dozen huge gas, oil, and mining conglomerates in return for loans to keep government running. Because Moscow did not repay the loans, whose amounts represented a miniscule fraction of the enterprises' net worth, the shares became bank property. "In one year," writes one scholar, "the Russian government essentially gave away some of Russia's richest companies."[52] In late 1994 about 90 percent of the industrial labor force worked in privatized firms.[53]

These controversial giveaways quickened Yeltsin's popularity slide from the highs of the early 1990s. But there were other problems. Inflation, for instance, still raging at 130 percent in 1995, continued to undermine living standards at a time when private businesses, adjusting to the cold realities of market competition and the need to be "lean," pushed unemployment ever closer to 10 percent. Many Russians also felt more than a twinge of nostalgia for the days when their nation had been a superpower respected and feared throughout the world, not a deteriorating has-been. As levels of dissatisfaction rose, two parties made big political gains: the revitalized Communist Party of the Russian Federation (CPRF),[54] led now by an uncolorful Gennadi Zyuganov, who leaned cautiously toward resetting the clock to the 1980s, and the Liberal-Democratic Party of Russia (LDPR) led by Vladimir Zhirinovsky. Ominously and dangerously eccentric, this neo-fascist wanted to take back the East Bloc and resume the old nineteenth-century expansion to the south so that Russian soldiers could "wash their boots in the warm waters of the Indian Ocean."[55] Both maintained a withering criticism of Yeltsin.

Although the power of parliament, renamed the Duma in 1993, was clearly lessened, the people's representatives still exerted considerable influence from the podium and through the media. Yeltsin responded, therefore, by moving closer to the popular positions of Zyuganov and Zhirinovsky. He dismissed Gaidar and other liberal ministers, hesitated to privatize ownership of land, and pointedly spoke out for Serbia and against NATO in Bosnia. The president also sent troops into the breakaway Caucasian republic of Chechnya in December 1994. While the origins of the crisis were highly complex, the move certainly reflected his need to present a tough profile to right- and left-wing critics.

The troops moved into Chechnya to root out the reputedly criminal, terrorist, white-slaving regime of secessionist President Dzhokhar Dudayev.[56] As armored and infantry units advanced toward the Chechen capital of Groznyy, they encountered stiff resistance from well-armed Muslim clans that set aside old rivalries to unite against the alien intruders. When bloodied federal forces entered the city, the defenders fought for every street. So the embarrassed Russian command ordered carpet-bombing, which continued for a month and killed many thousands of civilians. The Chechens withdrew into the hills, however, and the war dragged on, costing by recent estimates 180,000 lives and creating 400,000 refugees before the exhausted and demoralized Russians agreed to a truce and withdrew in August 1996. The conflict illuminated the obvious weaknesses as well as the potential strengths of young democracy in Russia: On the one hand, Yeltsin began the war on his personal authority without needing to consult the Duma, without even bothering, in fact, to issue a decree; on the other hand, the sensible people of Russia opposed the war in overwhelming numbers, preferring a negotiated settlement.[57]

How do we explain this tragic war? In many ways the Chechen story is a microcosm of Europe's story—albeit an extreme variation thereof—one that begins with the inescapable fact of ethnic diversity. This blunt reality of original differences that has shadowed Europe for millennia was particularly pro-

Europe's skeleton exits the closet: the ruins of Groznyy in 1995.   (Getty Images)

nounced in the former USSR, a multinational state that fragmented in 1991 amidst much tension and friction, not only among the new states, but also between them, and with the old imperial center. The new Russian Federation, moreover, was itself a complex mix of different nationalities. "They all have their specific traditions, divergent from and incompatible with the Russian," observes one student of the Chechen conflict, "nonetheless they do not necessarily go to war with each other, that is to say, mutual animosities do not always escalate into bloodbaths."[58] So what made the Chechen-Russian relationship so explosive? A long history of hostility certainly played an incendiary role. From the famous Shamil's failed twenty-year jihad against Moscow in the mid-1800s to the Bolsheviks' suppression of a brief Chechen breakaway in the 1920s, and especially Stalin's near genocidal deportation of the entire people in cattle cars in 1944,[59] bad blood has remained fresh on the Chechen side. Thus Dudayev's bolting from both the USSR and Russia in 1991, coupled with Yeltsin's immediate declaration of a state of emergency, triggered ugly violence against Russians in Groznyy, including selling a few thousand into slavery. The Russian president's apprehension and anxiety about Chechnya's demonstration effect, that is, its potential to promote additional ethnic secessions from his multinational republic, ratcheted tensions higher, especially after Zhirinovsky's LDPR won 22.9 percent in the 1993 elections by lambasting Yeltsin's record on national security issues. But these grand political concerns were surpassed by even weightier geopolitical considerations under discussion behind closed doors in Moscow. For one thing, Yeltsin and his personal circle wanted Caspian Sea oil to flow through projected pipelines westward *over Russian soil*—and this meant Chechnya. Furthermore, Moscow's centuries-old security on its southern flank—important earlier against Iran and Turkey, later against western powers Britain and America—had vanished since 1991 with the independence of Georgia, Armenia, and Azerbaijan. Chechnya, by virtue of its location, became a kind of Russian line in the sand. So the origins of the war, like the history of so many ethnic tragedies of old and recent vintage, lay buried under many twisted layers of emotional and political causation. The same complex of factors almost guaranteed a second Chechen War.

Bungled military efforts, mounting casualties, and high numbers of Chechen civilian deaths created even more political headaches for Yeltsin. Consequently, the CPRF emerged from the chaotic tussle of 43 parties in December 1995 to capture 157 of 450 Duma seats, while Zhirinovsky's LDPR took 52, only five less than "Our Home Is Russia," the party of Yeltsin's prime minister. With presidential elections scheduled for June 1996, the beleaguered Yeltsin now faced a stressful dilemma. A few of his personal friends counseled postponing the balloting and once again banning the rising CPRF. "Why risk everything just to have some people put pieces of paper into something called a ballot box?" asked one of them. The chief, who hated communists from long and bitter personal experience, leaned in this direction as spring due near. On the other side of this tug of war, daughter Tatyana urged him to observe the constitution and run for reelection. Her advice was seconded by a faction of liberals that included Gaidar and his privatization specialist,

Anatoly Chubais, as well as security advisers unsure of army loyalty. Furthermore, the president himself had a concern for the judgment of posterity. "If there is one factor that is still capable of pushing Yeltsin in the right direction," a former minister told journalist David Remnick, "it's history itself—he desperately wants to be thought of as a force for good in history." In the end Yeltsin threw his hat into the ring, and then proceeded to use all of the considerable financial and media resources available to him—and unavailable to Zyuganov—in a campaign that "gave new meaning to the phrase 'the advantages of incumbency.'" That Yeltsin took the constitutional route was fortunate for Russia's nascent democracy, but considerations of rule of law probably meant little to him as election time approached. "I will not allow the communists into power,"[60] he said, forgetting, at least temporarily, what historians might say of him. That he defeated Zyuganov handily in the decisive run-off spares historians from much of the speculation about what might have happened to Russian democracy had Yeltsin lost.

The victor stayed in office until his health, declining throughout the decade as a result of stress and increasingly heavy drinking, forced him to step down in December 1999. His legacy will not be easy to assess. Economic conditions slowly improved after the 1996 election as inflation finally dipped below 10 percent, industrial deceleration halted, and modest economic growth began. It was far too early for claims of long-term success, however, for Russia's foreign debt had doubled since 1991 without contributing significantly to technological modernization or even necessary replacement of worn-out capital, especially in the aging infrastructure. Unemployment had risen to 10 percent, moreover, and worsened when a financial crisis spreading from Asia triggered a severe recession in 1998 that sent monthly earnings plummeting until growth resumed a year later.[61] Even before the crisis, however, some western experts pointed to low income, hunger, malnutrition, and declining levels of public health as signs of "a tragic 'transition' backward to a premodern era.'"[62]

Given Yeltsin's mixed record and the checkered performance of his young democracy it should come as no surprise that the people of Russia expressed extreme ambivalence. When the new president, Vladimir Putin, took office in December 1999, almost 25 percent of the electorate had recently cast ballots for the CPRF, but in polls 46.6 percent identified the pre-Gorbachev political system as the most appropriate for Russia, while 78.7 percent were dissatisfied with the development of democracy.[63] It stood to reason, on the other hand, that a people who had suffered so egregiously under Stalin and spent the recent decade and a half excruciatingly coming to grips with the abuses of the communist era would have no illusions about the drawbacks of police state authoritarianism.[64] Indeed, the same polls showed 85.7 percent in favor of electing leaders, 79.4 percent behind a free press, 70.5 percent against the idea of army rule, 62.9 percent supporting "the idea of democracy," and only 15.2 percent wanting to bring order to Russia "at all costs," while 51.3 percent believed that this must happen "without violating rights." It had to be taken as another positive sign, finally, that Zhirinovsky's LDPR vote had slipped steadily from 22.9 percent in 1993 and 11.4 percent in 1995 to 5.98 percent in 1999. As the century turned it seemed that Russia's glass was half full, not half empty.

TERRORISM AND SECTARIAN VIOLENCE

While an unstable truce, interpreted differently by each side, went into effect on Chechnya in 1996, negotiators at the other end of Europe tried doggedly to achieve at least that much in Northern Ireland. With the death toll from a quarter-century of ethnoreligious and political violence nearing the three thousand mark in August 1994, the Irish Republican Army (IRA), the paramilitary arm of the movement to unite Northern Ireland with the Irish Republic to the south, had agreed to a cease-fire, to which the Ulster Defense Association and other Protestant paramilitary groups adhered. The agreement stimulated some hope that London's long-standing efforts to "devolve" rule back to Ulster and end two decades of military occupation would finally succeed (see Chapter 9). By late 1995, however, mutual tensions and suspicions were rising again, prompting a visiting American President Bill Clinton to issue a warning in Belfast: "Between those who are in the ship of peace and those who are trying to sink it, old habits die hard."[65] He was right, for in February 1996 the IRA broke the cease-fire by exploding a massive thousand-pound bomb after work hours in the London wharfs—which nevertheless killed two workers—claiming that peace talks over Ulster were not "inclusive" (i.e., had not included Sinn Fein, the political arm of the movement). That Britain's Conservative government had also insisted on "decommissioning" IRA and Protestant paramilitary weapons without reforming a police force that still leaned toward the Protestant side seemed to be the underlying cause of the returning troubles. In October 1996 the IRA exploded two more bombs in British Army barracks near Belfast. The scuttlers of "the ship of peace" seemed to have the upper hand.

Something of a breakthrough occurred with the election of Tony Blair's Labour government in May 1997, for the new cabinet reduced emphasis on immediate disarmament. The IRA renewed its cease-fire in July and London brought Sinn Fein on board in September. These concessions facilitated the "Good Friday Agreement" of April 10, 1998, which devolved authority to Ulster after elections to a new assembly but allowed for Dublin and London to exert influence, respectively, through a "North-South Council" and a "British-Irish Council." In important ways, however, the arrangement had kicked a can down the road. For one thing, recognition of Catholic rights of self-determination, that is, to join the Irish Republic, were delayed indefinitely by recognition of Protestant rights of consent, that is, majority veto of unification. The agreement also postponed decommissioning of weapons for two years. Each side committed itself to nonviolence and pledged to work in good faith for this eventual disarmament.

Unfortunately, within three months Protestant fanatics petrol-bombed a Catholic home located in the Protestant neighborhood of Ballymoney, killing three young boys. And then on August 15, 1998, a group calling itself "the Real IRA" exploded a five-hundred-pound car bomb in a street crowded with holiday shoppers, killing twenty-nine people and wounding seven hundred. With the IRA obviously unable to control its militants, the convening of Ulster's new assembly could not occur that year. It would not convene until December 1999.

In September 1998 Sinn Fein leader Gerry Adams visited Bilbao, Spain, hoping to promote a peace process similar to the Good Friday Agreement in Northern Ireland. His interlocutors were Basque separatists in Euzkadi ta Azkatasuna (ETA) and Herri Batasuna (HB), the military and political arms, respectively, of the movement that had waged a thirty-year struggle for Basque separation from Spain.[66] Utilizing its main weapon of terror, the car bomb, ETA operatives had killed eight hundred people in a long campaign of fear that one western journalist described as "a bloody relic of Europe's past."[67] Recently, however, they had kept a close eye on developments in Belfast. Was it not perhaps time to try dialogue?

The Basques are an ethnic amalgamation of ancient tribes that gathered in the region of northern Spain and southern France known today as *Euzkadi*, or "Basque Country." The major claim to nationality is the unique native language of this area, *Euskera*. In 1492 the Spanish crown ended many centuries of independent statehood, whose memory Basque ideologues revived in the early 1800s. Although the ruthless dictatorship of Francisco Franco tried to stamp out all vestiges of Basqueness after 1939, many Basque groups, including the leftist ETA (Basque Homeland and Liberation) founded in 1959, struggled to restore nationhood. The ETA turned to violence in Europe's hot summer of 1968, but it combined nationalism with a hybrid Marxist credo influenced by the theories of Mao Tse-tung and Ho Chi Minh. The death of Franco and the ascension of Juan Carlos led to major concessions to regional autonomy in 1979. The regional parliament elected in 1980 and restored use of the Basque language, together with the ETA's adoption of more indiscriminate terrorism in 1987, gradually undercut popular support for HB (Popular Unity) from 17–18 percent of seats in the Basque parliament in the 1980s to 12 percent by the mid-1990s. But still the violence continued—until the Irish example of 1998. A cease-fire finally went into effect that autumn.

Fourteen months of calm ended on December 3, 1999 when the ETA exploded a car bomb in Madrid. Both the government and Basque militants blamed one another for the breakdown of talks. Over the next two years thirty more died in the ETA's escalation of terror. "It is very clear what we want," said one HB leader referring to complete independence. "If you don't accept their theories," countered a Bilbao journalist, "they kill you."[68]

On April 22, 1996 masked hitmen of the Kosovo Liberation Army (KLA) gunned down three Serbs in a café. Compatriots murdered two more Serbs in other Kosovo towns that same evening. Coming at a time when violence marred Northern Ireland, the Basque Country, and Chechnya and the ink had barely dried on the Dayton Accords over war-ravaged Bosnia, the killings precipitated another round of ugly ethnic conflict in Europe.[69] Further execution-style shootings followed in late 1996 and 1997, all triggering arrests and crackdowns, but after another KLA squad shot two Serb policemen on February 28, 1998, Milosevic flew into a rage, unleashing paramilitary units that killed three hundred and left sixty-five thousand homeless. Later that year as more hits and reprisals sent the death toll over one thousand, he drew up "Operation Horseshoe," a plan for brutal ethnic cleansing in Kosovo.

Did longstanding "racial hatreds" cause the escalating bloodshed, as frequently reported in the press? Yes and no. Kosovar Albanians had not forgotten grandparents' stories about terrible Serb atrocities during the Balkan Wars of 1912–1913, but KLA shootings were mainly motivated by the politics of recent events. Milosevic had purged Albanians from all positions of responsibility in Kosovo seven years earlier and Dayton had neither addressed this discrimination nor recognized the desire of Kosovars to break from Serb-dominated Yugoslavia—worse, in the eyes of Kosovars the West's peace accord had legitimated the oppressor by dealing with him. For these reasons the KLA broke with moderates around Ibrahim Rugova, a pacifist academician justifiably apprehensive about violence given what the Serbs had done in Bosnia, and began their terrorist campaign. History played a somewhat greater role on the Serbian side, for the Balkan Wars rampage was seen as retribution against Albanians who had enjoyed a relatively privileged position during six centuries of Turkish rule, an oppression that began with the Ottomans' crushing defeat of the Serbs in Kosovo in 1389. Once Serbia reacquired Kosovo, anointed with Albanian blood in 1912, nationalists in Belgrade loathed giving it up. That the cynical Milosevic was moved emotionally by the memory of these ancient events has to be discounted, but he certainly realized the political potential of old myths systematically cultivated and sustained in the media.

On January 15, 1999 Serbian army and paramilitary units entered the Kosovo town of Racak and massacred forty-five people. Ethnic cleansing had apparently begun. NATO leaders, having assumed the responsibility of peacekeeping in Bosnia, insisted that Belgrade negotiate an end to the conflict with the KLA or face air strikes. The talks at Rambouillet, France, broke down quickly over Serb refusal to make even the slightest concessions to Kosovar demands. Far from negotiating, in fact, Milosevic amassed troops in the captive province and perpetrated further atrocities. Consequently, NATO struck Serb columns in Kosovo on March 24. The alliance reckoned on a quick buckling under of soldiers lacking air cover, but rugged terrain provided sufficient protection for regular and irregular units to accelerate Operation Horseshoe. That spring they murdered ten thousand Kosovars, deported additional hundreds of thousands, and frightened many more into flight—well over a million of Kosovo's nearly two million inhabitants fled to Albania, Macedonia, or other countries.

NATO soon expanded its bombing to Serbia proper, destroying roads, bridges, and government buildings. For eleven weeks Milosevic refused to yield, however, still hoping to win as a result of pressure to end the strikes from NATO dissenters Italy and Greece, or more promising protests from Russia, a traditional ally and fellow Slav nation. Indeed, Boris Yeltsin, angry that NATO had neatly sidestepped the UN and a certain Russian veto on the Security Council, nearly fell out with the West over the attacks. Determined to do what he could to help Serbia, the Russian president severed his liaison ties with NATO and sent its two representatives in Moscow packing. But NATO persevered. With his country in shambles, fifteen hundred Serb civilians dead, and fifteen thousand military casualties by June, Milosevic finally yielded to the joint peace efforts of the United States, Russia, and EU envoy Martti Ahtisaari of Finland.

The final peace deal went through the UN Security Council in order to reassure Serbia, smooth Russian feathers, and shore up the organization's marginalized legitimacy. The plan brought forty thousand NATO and a few thousand Russian peace enforcers into Kosovo after Serbian troops withdrew. The UN established an interim political administration that guaranteed eventual autonomy and self-government to Kosovo but stopped short of granting independence. Although the KLA soon surrendered its weapons, there were still unfortunate but predictable reprisal killings by Kosovar Albanians against hundreds of Kosovar Serbs, setting in motion a large-scale Serb exodus. Meanwhile, NATO, the EU, the UN, and the World Bank pooled financial resources to facilitate the return of the refugees and the reconstruction of the province.

Although Russia had reason to feel gratified by its participation in the war-ending negotiations and inclusion in the peacekeeping arrangements, the Kosovo crisis had raised dander in Moscow because of Chechnya. Yeltsin's team had neither forgotten the lost war nor recognized Groznyy's repeated claims to independence. All of the grand and geopolitical motivations for intervening in 1994 remained strong—indeed, if anything they had grown stronger as a result of the army's desire for revenge and redemption. Thus Yeltsin's support for Serbia's attempt to discipline an unruly Kosovo was reinforced by Russia's need to do the same in its breakaway province—throughout the spring of 1999, in fact, preparations seem to have been underway in Moscow for a second incursion. Strengthening Yeltsin's opposition to NATO's bombing campaign, and heightening the anxiety, furthermore, were concerns that the West might apply its new peacekeeping principles in Chechnya if Russia attacked again.[70]

The Chechens simplified matters by unleashing their own attack in August 1999. Dudayev had been killed in the first war and his successor, Aslan Maskhadov, could not keep a grip on the many different factions in his disrupted society. So it was that two hardened veterans of the first war, Shamil Basayev and his Jordanian lieutenant, Khattab, invaded a portion of Russian Dagestan where many Chechens had fled in 1994–1996. The popular heroes boldly proclaimed an "Independent Islamic Republic of Chechnya and Dagestan." The alarmed Russian public began to veer away from earlier non-interventionist views, especially after four mysterious explosions in various Russian towns that month killed nearly three hundred innocents in what many believed to be a Chechen terrorist campaign.[71] Better organized and prepared than before, the army moved methodically into Dagestan, securing it in September before crossing over into Chechnya. As civilian casualties soared and hundreds of thousands of Chechens became refugees, Russian forces pushed to Groznyy by December. The city fell in February 2000, but the new Shamil and his rebel band escaped into the mountains to pursue jihad. There would be no halt to the killing.

TOURING EUROPE'S HORIZONS IN THE EARLY TWENTY-FIRST CENTURY

Bosnia, Northern Ireland, Basque Country, Kosovo, and Chechnya, the hotspots of Europe in the late twentieth century, exploded because decades- or centuries-old animosities among rival peoples combined with current politics to produce critical mass. Throughout the post–World War Two period, however, new streams of immigrants had been coming to Europe, generating friction and tension with "indigenous" groups and creating the potential for new layers of trouble laid down over the old.[72] Most of the newcomers worked at low-paying jobs, most were darker-skinned than Europeans, and most were Muslim. With second- and third-generation descendants, some thirteen million ostensible followers of Islam lived in EU countries in 2001, or 3.4 percent of the population. Furthermore, while the number of older European peoples steadily decreases—it could be two-thirds today's level by 2050—the Muslim contingent continues to grow rapidly. At present rates of respective population decline/growth, for example, France's four million Muslims, currently 7.5 percent of the whole, would reach 50 percent by the mid-twenty-first century.[73]

The disintegration of the Soviet Union, the implosion of the East Bloc, and the explosion of the former Yugoslavia sent additional waves of people heading toward "Café Europa," that imagined community of the good life in the West. For the vast majority this meant Germany: Over two million ethnic Germans, who spoke no German after generations in the East but received German citizenship, crowded in, joined by a great influx of "asylum seekers" from the Balkans—over a million between 1989 and 1993.

European governments could not help but react to these quickly escalating immigration trends, especially as early post–World War Two labor shortages gave way to sluggish growth and high hovering unemployment after the 1970s. Britain restricted immigration as early as 1971, France and Germany followed suit in 1993, and the EU sought to make labor more mobile within the community in the 1990s while simultaneously pressuring lax gatekeeper states like Spain, Italy, Greece, and Austria to get tougher at the border. Deportation of illegal aliens also became more frequent as politicians responded to public demands for action. After one controversial ejection of hundreds of African asylum seekers in 1995, Jacques Chirac expressed a common European sentiment: "France cannot accept all the wretched of the earth."[74]

Much of the EU public does not seem impressed with the action or the rhetoric, however, as great numbers of people have lurched in extremist directions. An across-the-board survey of the Europe of Fifteen in 1997, for instance, found 33 percent of respondents labeling themselves as "quite racist" or "very racist." A twisted fraction of these "racists" were also ready to act on their views: Police reported 2,363 ethnic hate crimes in neutral, placid Sweden in 1999, including 281 assaults; almost 7,000 xenophobic incidents annually in Britain, including about 1,500 assaults per year (1997–1998); and many thousands of racially motivated infractions in Holland, including about 3,000 assaults per year since 1997. German figures, considering this nation's moral disintegration in World War Two, were even more shocking: 10,037 hate crimes in 1999, including 746 assaults, which rose to 998 in 2000.

After the turn of the century public opinion polls still registered strong anti-outsider views: 52 percent of Europeans thought that foreign minorities abused welfare systems and undermined the quality of education in public schools; 51 percent were certain that immigrants exacerbated unemployment problems—this figure climbed to 61 percent in beleaguered Germany; and 39 percent of EU respondents wanted to expel *legally established* foreign residents to their countries of origin. While transatlantic critics of this "Fortress Europe" mentality needed to recall the proverb about people living in glass houses not throwing stones, the high incidence of intolerant or xenophobic attitudes that contradicted minority rights policies espoused by the EU as it proceeded with eastern enlargement was cause for alarm.

But have these developments threatened European democracy? It is clear that a certain percentage of respondents use polls to let off steam while refusing to "waste" votes on extreme leftist or rightist parties with no chance of electoral victory. Consistent with this pattern, recent elections in European countries strengthened anti-immigrant parties, but none came close to the high opinion poll survey percentages just cited. Thus Jean-Marie Le Pen's Front National rose to 18 percent of the national vote in France, the right-wing Swiss People's Party to 23 percent, and Jorg Haider's Freedom Party to 28 percent in Austria. Germany, having done much more than Austria to deal with its Nazi past, resisted the lure of the far right more effectively: Only the xenophobic German People's Union raised eyebrows, capturing 12.9 percent in the depressed eastern state of Saxony-Anhalt. Italy, with its own fascist skeletons in the closet, has also contained the far right fairly well. The early post–Cold War era proved turbulent, to be sure, as both the PCI and the Christian Democrats fell apart, reshuffling with other groups into two new fractions, the Democratic Party of the Left and its rival, the bizarre Forza Italia ("Come on, Italy!") of Silvio Berlusconi. The neo-fascist Italian Social Movement, later renamed the National Alliance, rose only as high as 15.7 percent nationally but has entered governments under Berlusconi.[75] Anti-immigrant parties have also sprouted lately in other parts of Europe: Vlaams Blok (Flemish Bloc), which took 15.5 percent of seats in Belgium's Flemish parliament; Leefbaar Nederland (Livable Netherlands), which seized 35 percent of the Rotterdam City Council, and later Pim Fortuyn's "List Fortuyn," which rose to 17 percent of the national vote after the charismatic figure's assassination; the People's Party, which won 12.3 percent of parliamentary seats in Denmark; and the Party of Progress, which captured 15.2 percent in Norway. Surveying the entire spectrum of West European politics, one recent scholar estimates that 80–90 percent of electorates have ignored rightist Sirens and steered a centrist democratic course through difficult political narrows. "Perhaps there is some small comfort in that,"[76] he concludes.

Another recent work makes a convincing case, in fact, that the danger for Europe and the West comes less from the hostile reaction of some Europeans to immigrants than from the related jihadist backlash of a few dangerous splinter groups operating within Europe's Muslim community.[77] The peril does not stem from mainstream organizations that have concentrated on orthodox religious instruction or politics in the homeland, an orientation especially strong among recent emigrants to the Diaspora, or from groups that have shifted focus from old country issues to secular ethnocentric welfare and patronage efforts in the new land: Witness the exclusive German orientation of the longstanding Turkish Association of Berlin-Brandenburg. Rather, problems stem from certain second- and third-generation *Arab* Muslims who have received western educations, learned western languages from birth, and sometimes married European women—men who might have become fully integrated and assimilated into western cultures were it not for a lack of upward economic mobility, a path blocked by the poverty of the surrounding Muslim community and the hostility of the native people, which sometimes meant jail time. Disconnected from and uninterested in traditional Islam, but frustrated in the West, some angry young men experience a "radicalization of the uprooted" and turn to organizations espousing a "universal Islam" that reject both allegedly outmoded homeland Islam as well as the West, the former "as un-Islamic and polluted by superstitions, folklore and accretions from non-Islamic sources,"[78] the latter as aggressive, materialist, alien, and threatening. One such organization founded in Britain that has spread to Sweden, Holland, and Germany, Hizb ut-Tahrir (Liberation Party), aspires to reestablish the long-lost Muslim caliphate and convert the world to Islam. It is allegedly nonviolent. The other, Al-Qaeda (The Base), is clearly violent, having years ago proclaimed its belligerence "against America and against the West in general." Its leader, Osama bin Laden, blamed "western regimes and the government of the United States"—in advance, significantly enough—"for what might happen."[79] From a European base of underground cells, Bin Laden's operatives and recruits organized the suicide assaults on September 11, 2001, against the Pentagon and the World Trade Center, one a symbol of the West's military power, the other of its business, finance, and ingenious technology. In one shocking half-morning of terror they snuffed out three thousand lives.

The attacks of "9/11" ushered in a period of intense cooperation on security and defense between Europe and the United States. A plethora of police and special investigatory units from both sides of the Atlantic began the arduous

Terror from the skies: the World Trade Center towers in New York City on September 11, 2001. (Getty Images)

task of finding the plotters and seizing the vast hidden assets of Al-Qaeda and its front organizations. For the first time NATO invoked Article 5 of its charter, whereby an attack on one meant an attack on all—indeed, 104 Europeans from eleven different countries had also died during the fiery collapse of the gargantuan towers in Lower Manhattan. President George W. Bush declared a "war against terrorism," warning that governments harboring terrorists would incur the wrath of the United States. American military efforts soon focused on the Taliban regime of Afghanistan, known to sympathize with and provide haven for the core training operations and leadership of the Arab Afghans of Al-Qaeda, including Osama bin Laden himself. Assisted in many ancillary respects by its NATO allies, but drawing mainly on its own resources, the United States crushed the Taliban and dealt a severe blow to the terrorists without, however, eradicating Al-Qaeda or seizing its leader or preventing further guerilla-style warfare in Afghanistan.

Soon, however, the transatlantic partnership began to weaken. In January 2002 Bush identified an "Axis of Evil" in Iraq, Iran, and North Korea, countries that were apparently the next "targets of American justice." With an angry eye on Saddam Hussein's Iraq, the outraged president issued a new doctrine of preemptive self-defense in June, asserting before West Point cadets the need to remove in a timely way authoritarian regimes that supported terrorists, allegedly possessed weapons of mass destruction (WMD) long banned by nonproliferation treaties and anti-WMD accords, and seemed to be poised, as an alarmed Washington saw it, to use these weapons in another even more horrific 9/11. Iraq and Iran had also been singled out for their monetary support of suicide bomber families in the bloody Palestinian Intifada against Israel. European leaders, in the meantime, pulled away from what seemed to them an exaggerated emphasis on force that ignored the lessons of Europe's long and costly history of warfare. Berlin and Paris believed, furthermore, that Bush's escalation of the war against terrorism confused acknowledged rights of self-defense with issues of collective security reserved under the UN Charter for decision by the Security Council. They warned that such a doctrine of preemption would embolden allegedly "imperialist" hard-line Israelis or encourage potential aggressions like China against Taiwan or India against Pakistan. Supported by street demonstrations on a scale not seen since the antimissile marches of the early 1980s, leading EU countries insisted on diplomatic solutions in the short run, underpinned by long-term foreign aid programs to address root causes of terrorism.[80]

Privately, European leaders castigated the American president as a unilateralist "cowboy" and the United States as a rogue "hyperpower," while the men around Bush scoffed at "Eurowimps" from "Venus" who had allowed military establishments to go underfunded for decades. American advisers relished drawing denigrating contrasts between the "Old Europe" of Paris, Brussels, and Berlin and the other Europe of Warsaw, Prague, and Budapest, NATO's newest members.[81] Indeed, these and other states in Eastern Europe, torn between mutually exclusive needs to please the wealthy EU and the mighty United States, backed Washington, seen as the best guarantor of the national rights these countries could not protect in the 1940s.[82] Their support incensed Chirac of France, who dubbed it "infantile" and accused them of missing "a great opportunity to keep quiet,"[83] which prompted the East Europeans to question his commitment to democracy. Unable to obtain UN sanction for coercive measures against Baghdad because of French, German, Russian, and Chinese opposition, the United States and Britain, backed diplomatically by Spain and the so-called New Europe of the former East Bloc, ignored those protesting against an internationally unsanctioned war and attacked anyway in March 2003. America and Britain defeated regular Iraqi forces and toppled Saddam Hussein in early April—but killed and wounded thousands of civilians. The conduct of the war exacerbated European-American relations, for the West Europeans, including the British, had come over recent decades to advocate a domestic police model of warfare that sought to minimize civilian deaths at all costs, while the Americans, following the traditional rules and norms of warfare, pursued operational objectives and sought to minimize combatant casualties (i.e., "force protection").

Although the Pentagon also strove to minimize "collateral damage," avoidance of civilian deaths was clearly not the top priority. The chasm between Europe and America grew so wide that some authors, pointing additionally to longer-standing transatlantic contrasts of culture and worldview, warned that more was at stake than "just a friendly disagreement.[84]

The diplomatic crisis and the Iraqi War certainly damaged American-European relations in the short run, but they also spawned longer-lasting changes in European defense policy. The French had long desired a military capability free from Washington. Nothing substantive had come of this agenda, even after the war in Kosovo demonstrated how far the United States had pulled ahead technologically, and how dependent Europe remained on American muscle to solve continental problems.[85] While the European Council announced bold plans in June 1999 for an EU rapid reaction corps of fifty to sixty thousand soldiers, these efforts soon bogged down amidst Greek-Turkish bickering.[86] In December 2002, however, just as the quarrel appeared settled, the so-called Anti-War Four that had most vehemently opposed invading Iraq—France, Germany, Belgium, and Luxembourg—announced much more ambitious plans for EU military independence. A summit meeting of the four nations in April 2003 presented a detailed blueprint for a "European Security and Defense Union" (ESDU), replete with its own defense college, training centers for helicopter and long-range aircraft crews, special WMD civil/military defense and humanitarian first aid units, as well as an agency to promote "inter-operable" (i.e., standardized) military technologies and facilitate competitive European defense industries. Because the drafters did not want to bolt from NATO, an alliance they insisted would always remain beneficial to Europe, and had no intention of forcing ESDU participation on all EU members, which could "opt out" as Britain and others had done with EMU, the significance of the proposed new union lay in the *political* as much as the military arena. Simply put, the Anti-War Four wanted the expanded EU, including the "misbehaving" East Europeans, "to speak with one voice" during subsequent disagreements with overbearing America. Nor could Europe's voice be heard without high military cards in the EU hand. "Europe must be able to fully play its role on the international scene, [but] diplomatic action is only credible if it can be based on real civilian and military capabilities."[87] The Four wanted their ESDU to be part of the new EU constitution under debate in preparation for eastern enlargement (see later).

Although Europe's own military presence seemed destined to increase, pessimistic pundits' predictions of the collapse of a long-established friendship among transatlantic allies who shared democratic cultures seemed premature. Throughout the diplomatic crisis over Iraq and subsequent invasion, for instance, fifty-one thousand American and European NATO soldiers policed Bosnia and Kosovo while thirteen thousand jointly patrolled a still volatile Afghanistan—half of the allies' troops there were non-American, including units from France and Germany. Seeking to mend fences with European friends who felt snubbed when Washington originally circumvented the alliance, in fact, NATO officials formally proclaimed Afghanistan a NATO operation in April 2003. Eight months later the United States, hard-pressed by Iraqi insurgents who had killed hundreds of American soldiers, first broached the topic of a similar arrangement for Iraq. Since the latter half of 2002, furthermore, representatives from the United States, Russia, the UN, and the EU—the very same antagonists of the Iraqi crisis—had united on a "road map to peace" in the intractable Arab-Israeli crisis. Getting Palestinian and Israeli extremists to follow the projected route became the next transatlantic challenge, especially with Europe leaning toward the Palestinians and America toward the Israelis.

What does the future hold for European-American relations? Although Europeans of the aging 68er generation scoff moralistically at the American hyper-power and Americans of conservative stripe return the gibes with trendy anti-European jokes, none of this mutual alienation appears to be very deep—probably not deep enough to outlast the eventual end of the Bush/ Republican Party tenure in the White House. As it stood in early 2004, much of the official post-9/11 discord between Europe and the United States had dissipated as allied nations which had quarreled realized "that we went too far in the divorce." Both sides will no doubt continue to squabble, but it would be prudent to recall what President Kennedy, quoting Winston Churchill, said in 1963: "The history of any alliance is the history of mutual recrimination among the various people."[88]

Europe had all hands full, meanwhile, dealing with its own extremists, some indigenous, others of recent Arab provenance. By summer 2002, British, French, Belgian, German, Italian, and Spanish police had detained hundreds of suspects and made a few hundred arrests in connection with 9/11, including two of the three European ringleaders of Al-Qaeda. While most of the arrestees had to be released for lack of proof and few were actually brought to trial, the key people remained in detention. Germany also moved against Hizb ut Tahrir for disseminating anti-Semitic propaganda, banning the organization in January 2003 and then raiding eighty underground sites in April. Recently the Lebanese Shiite, Iranian-backed Hezbollah militia began recruiting heavily in Europe's Arab communities, adding to the tension and anxiety. "We still have a lot more work to do," conceded the chief of German counterterrorism intelligence. Could EU countries suffer jihadist attacks? "Yes, most definitely,"[89] concluded another expert.

Older terrorist problems represented an additional drain on European energies. In Northern Ireland, for example, the long-delayed devolution of governing authority to Ulster in December 1999 soon broke down. In three years London suspended the assembly four times lest it collapse due to Protestant anger stemming from the IRA's refusal to disarm without further police reforms and guarantees. That IRA and Protestant violence had also been suspended, for the most part, was some consolation. No similar claims were heard in Basque Country, where the ETA had returned to its violent ways almost two years before 9/11, prompting the government of conservative Populist

Party leader Jose Maria Aznar to adopt an even tougher stance, arresting ETA operatives and banning HB from politics. "The only possible position on terrorism is to wipe it out," said Aznar. HB spokesmen, pointing to the yet unsolved root problem of Basque independence, responded, ominously, that "there's going to be more killings."[90] But Aznar's war on terrorism ground on: Nearly five hundred ETA soldiers sat in prison in mid-2003.

When ten bombs exploded simultaneously on Madrid commuter trains on 11 March 2004, killing nearly two hundred and badly wounding fourteen hundred, millions of angry fingers pointed initially at ETA. Others questioned, however, whether the decimated Basque group was capable of the worst terrorist attack in Europe's history. Indeed within days it became known that an Al-Qaeda affiliate had perpetrated the grisly deed as punishment for Spain's support of the war in Iraq. Almost from the beginning Spaniards dubbed the horrific mass killing "our 9/11."

Their political response was noticeably different than across the Atlantic, however, for only days later Aznar was turned out and the Socialists returned to power. The new leadership proclaimed the Iraq War a disaster and announced the pullout of Spanish troops unless the UN became more involved. Further "mutual recrimination" in the alliance sounded from Poland, where leaders hinted that London and Washington had been less than forthright about the supposed threat of Iraqi WMD, which remained unfound by the victors' inspection teams a year after the capture of Baghdad.

Somewhat better news came from the southeastern corner of Europe once known as Yugoslavia, where representative institutions slowly established shallow roots. The death of Croatian President Franjo Tudjman in December 1999 allowed reformist impulses to surface in elections a few months later. His successors were determined to steer the country into both NATO and the EU. The democratic opposition in Serbia finally felled Milosevic in October 2000, extraditing the infamous ethnic cleanser to the UN special tribunal at The Hague in June 2001 after a brief shootout at his villa. He still stands trial there in early 2004, with a growing list of Croatian, Bosnian, and Serbian war criminals. The extradition of Serbs to The Hague remains an unsettling factor, however, in Serbia's young democracy. This controversy triggered the assassination of pro-reform Prime Minister Zoran Djindjic, for instance, in March 2003.

Kosovo, policed by western troops and administered by the UN, turned in November 2001 to Ibrahim Rugova, the moderate alternative to the KLA, as president of an autonomous province of Serbia. The rebel group resisted the voters' verdict, holding things up for months, but finally relented to a UN/NATO quid pro quo that advanced one of their own to prime minister. "We will jointly work for a free, democratic, peaceful, prosperous and independent Kosovo,"[91] said Rugova. The fact that tens of thousands of ethnic Serbs have fled the area may save Kosovo from an intractable majority-minority standoff like Northern Ireland, but ethnic relations remain a source of considerable tension as witnessed by massive rioting in March 2004.

Kosovo's problems spilled over into Macedonia in February 2001, unfortunately, when a KLA-linked "National Liberation Army" (NLA) protesting abuses against ethnic Albanians, which comprised a third of the population, revolted against government forces. After six months of killing, NATO and EU negotiators managed to broker a ceasefire and disarmament of the NLA. Macedonia agreed to make Albanian another official language, raise the number of Albanian policemen, and remove discriminating anti-minority passages from the constitution. Elections in September 2002 brought hopeful signs that democracy and rule of law can function in an ethnically divided state, but a regiment of NATO troops stayed in the country, replaced in April 2003 by a smaller EU force drawn from twenty-six different European countries—the first mini-battalion of the long-awaited Euro-corps.

Only Bosnia refuses to register much democratic progress. Six elections since the 1995 Dayton Accord produced nothing but three-way gridlock between parties representing strident Croat, Muslim, and Serbian constituencies. NATO troops and UN police had to remove elected officials for trying to subvert Dayton. They also had to shut down radio stations for spewing racist hate. "National parties will continue to win until the so-called national question is solved," writes one observer, "but the national question cannot be solved while the nationalist parties remain in power."[92] It was perhaps some consolation in this dilemma that Europe persevered in the cause of peace, sending a five-hundred-man EU police force to Bosnia to help other units there. Assessing the prospects for "the tender plant of Balkan democracy," one recent historian sees the need for continued western commitment. "But if this garden grows, will not the harvest be more bountiful for all the blood that has watered the soil?"[93]

It seems doubtful, however, that any such mildly optimistic assessments will soon be drawn on Chechnya. Four years after the Russian capture of Groznyy, fighting continued. The Second Chechen War had claimed the lives of about four thousand Russian soldiers and fourteen thousand rebels by Russian admission, and tens of thousands of civilians according to outside observers. Almost one hundred thousand refugees waited to return to the hapless country. Public opinion in Russia favoring negotiation dropped in the aftermath of the unexplained 1999 bombings from 52 to 39 percent, but some who voted for Vladimir Putin in March 2000 and backed the war still had their doubts, like a young man living near one of the worst explosions: "Maybe a big war was not necessary," he said with an eye on a century of previously unimaginable bloodshed. "War never brought any popularity, especially in Russia." Not surprisingly, sentiments favoring negotiation soared to 57 percent as the war dragged on.[94] In March 2003 Moscow relented somewhat, holding a referendum inside Chechnya on a plan to provide a relatively small measure of autonomy. Although it passed, the Chechen opposition scoffed, claiming that it was rigged. "The separatist forces will continue to conduct their partisan war—[meaning more] bombings, attacks,"[95] commented a separatist leader dryly in late March 2003. Seven weeks later, in fact, a rebel truck laden with 1.3 tons of TNT exploded in the northern Chechen town of Znamenskoye, destroying a complex of eight government buildings and many nearby homes, killing sixty, and wounding hundreds. As 2003 yielded to 2004 the news was filled with similar terrorist attacks, Russian retaliations, and Chechen counterattacks.

The controversial war remained a good measure of the limits of Russian democracy: Most people opposed the conflict, but were not consulted; the government responded to public opinion, but only with half-measures aimed at assuaging and manipulating. During his years in office, in fact, Putin had not advanced democracy in obvious ways.[96] Although reforms to party finance, the upper house, regional government, and the criminal code may have helped in the long run, other trends struck democracy watchers as an ominous "going backwards." Thus Putin made a more effective use of his constitutional prerogatives than Yeltsin, amassing and centralizing power in the presidency, cultivating a kind of mini personality cult, and bullying the media, whose reporters were spied on, censored, and arrested. The president's crudely contemptuous attitude toward a free press burst forth in full view while he answered western reporters' queries on Chechnya in November 2002, hinting to one pesky questioner that a castration could be arranged for him in Moscow.[97] The most optimistic observers agreed that a weak civil society, a shaky rule of law, and an embryonic democratic political culture slowed democracy's maturation process.

Social and economic factors presented additional challenges. Pollution, heavy drinking and smoking, frequent abortions, and rapidly spreading venereal and other infectious diseases, AIDS/HIV in particular, undermined public health and life expectancy and contributed to a comparatively steep population decline—numbers could reach two-thirds of the 2003 level as early as 2025. Economic growth averaged nearly 6 percent from 1999 to 2002, but by Putin's own calculations when taking office 8 percent growth for fifteen years would be necessary for Russia to catch Portugal—assuming this poor West European country stood still. Nor will current rates of investment rid the nation of its extremely aged and perilous infrastructure and capital base. Only one recent year (2000) registered increases in fixed investment above the 10 percent level required annually over the long term merely to replace worn-out capital. Without greater foreign direct investment (FDI), the productive system faced some sort of breakdown, but FDI remained low for telling reasons. Foreign investors shied away from a country that does not insure deposits, has no guarantees against abuse of minority shareholders, fails to handle commercial disputes in a "transparent" manner, and in general does not protect property rights, all of which left investors unconvinced "that their investments are safe from expropriation."[98] In short, the same kinds of rights dilemmas that limit democracy in 2004 also hamper the economy. It may be the plain practical imperative of solving the latter, in fact, that adds momentum to the solution of the former, for public opinion alone will not suffice.

Political tendencies elsewhere in the former USSR break down into three categories. The first grouping of states, Estonia, Latvia, and Lithuania, drifted into the democratic orbit of NATO and the EU during the 1990s, "although even here," writes one expert, "it is premature to speak of democratic consolidation." States in the second category include Russia, Ukraine, Moldova, Georgia, and Armenia. All have adopted representative institutions and implemented market reforms, but, like Moscow, have made incomplete, uncertain, and indeed questionable transitions to capitalism and democracy. Ukraine was rocked by scandal and protests in November 2000, for example, when tapes surfaced from a security officer implicating President Leonid Kuchma and his advisers in the murder of an outspoken journalist, Heorhiy Gongadze. To the anger, shame, and embarrassment of most Ukrainians, the crime remains unsolved. Kuchma still held office in 2004. Georgia, by contrast, resolved its issues of corruption more impressively and successfully. The remarkable protest movement of Mikhail Saakashvili, a young lawyer educated in the United States, ousted President Eduard Shevardnadze in November 2003, and then voted Saakashvili into the presidency in early 2004. In the third group are Belarus, Azerbaijan, and the five central Asian republics, countries that have reverted to Soviet-style authoritarian politics "or even openly sultanistic regimes."[99]

On the eastern border of what will soon be the EU, Belarus is of particular interest in this tour of Europe's horizons. Its plebiscitary dictator, Alexander Lukashenko, won presidential elections in 1994 and then quickly renationalized industry, abolished parliament, and instituted repression. Opposition leaders and critical journalists were harassed, imprisoned, beaten, and kidnapped—four leading adversaries have disappeared since 1999. Somewhat like Serbia, however, the critics would not be stilled. One of them, Vladimir Goncharik, had the temerity to challenge Lukashenko's "reelection" bid in September 2001. "There will be no Kostunica in Belarus," said the president, referring to the man who ousted Serbia's dictator. "I will not be sitting in a bunker like Milosevic—I am not afraid of anybody." Lukashenko declared victory before counting the ballots. Hoping somehow to embolden the opposition, the EU has shunned "the last dictator in Europe."[100]

Thus democracy in the early twenty-first century remained a precarious phenomenon in Russia and the Ukraine, and nonexistent in Belarus, three of the four countries bordering on the EU and NATO. The fourth, Moldova, wallowed in post-communist poverty, a "land that time forgot," writes *The Economist*, whose governmental system "is too often hopelessly underfunded or corrupt, or both."[101] Combining the Freedom House ratings on the presence of political rights and civil liberties with Transparency International's measures of corruption, one author writing in 2000 devised a "democratic rule of law index," which placed Belarus at 19, Russia at 31, Ukraine at 37, and Moldova at 46, far below the EU minimum of 66, not to mention the "control" 100 of Finland.[102]

Despite the slowly waning controversy surrounding the unpopularity of the European Union—only in 2003 could it finally boast a 54 percent approval rating—the EU certainly remained the brightest spot on Europe's horizon. Soon after the disappointing intergovernmental conference at Amsterdam in 1997, European leaders realized that they needed to accelerate institutional reforms, for accession negotiations began in 1998–1999 with twelve applicant nations of Eastern Europe and the Mediterranean. The Nice Conference of December 2000 finally confronted these imperatives, tacitly agreeing on a target of spring 2004 for expanding the membership from fifteen to twenty-seven.[103] Significantly enough, all twelve aspiring countries were represented at Nice, the first time the EU had taken applicants into its counsels. In order to guarantee a more effective operation of the European Commission, bigger states with two seats in Brussels agreed to the idea of one seat per member, thus preventing further unwieldiness after enlargement. As compensation France, Germany, and Britain got greater voting strength on the Council of Ministers. The latter accord, as seen later, would not last.

Germany and Italy also demanded the convening of a special convention to draft a "European Constitution." Both nations had long favored more democratic legitimacy in the EU and saw the convention as a means to advance this cause. Even the minimal gain of a simplification of the EU's complex web of treaties and agreements would enhance legitimacy by enabling the people of Europe to better understand their opaque institutions. And with understanding would come higher percentages of Europeans willing to support the EU. The European Council agreed to this constitutional agenda in December 2001, charging the convention with finding ways to bring citizens closer to their European institutions, improving political efficiency in the enlarged EU, and better positioning the EU to serve as "a stabilizing factor and a model in the new world order."[104] The latter charge reflected the changed global situation since the horrifying events of September 2001 and subsequent war in Afghanistan. The constitutional convention began its deliberations in March 2002.

As noted earlier, attention shifted after the Nice Conference to the highly complex accession negotiations as applicant nations attempted to negotiate the steep grade of all thirty-one chapters of the *acquis communautaire*, the EU's eighty thousand pages of rules, regulations, laws, and treaties. The timetable set at Nice created its own sense of urgency, for the closing of all chapters, a tough business by itself, had to be completed allowing enough time for ratifying referenda among old and new members. The 9/11 attacks, followed by President's Bush's alarming "Axis of Evil" address, generated added incentive at least to put Europe's house in order in ominous, dangerous times. These pressures pushed negotiations to closure in October 2002, when the council announced its recommendation that ten of the applicants—Estonia, Latvia, Lithuania, Poland, the Czech Republic, Slovakia, Hungary, Slovenia, Malta, and the Greek portion of Cyprus—had made the grade for admission in May 2004.[105] Falling back on the precedents of earlier enlargement rounds, however, the EU approved a host of "transitional agreements" phasing in full compliance with the *acquis* over a number of years. After decades of environmental abuse by communist regimes, for example, none of the East European newcomers could hope to reduce air pollution from large combustion plants to EU levels, arrange for acceptable recovery and recycling of packaging waste, and build water treatment plants to improve the quality of drinking water—

not to mention the expensive cleanup of polluted sites—until in some cases 2015. For its part the EU avoided potentially disastrous budget increases by phasing in full payment of the expensive CAP subsidies and supports until 2013. Even with these transitional limitations EU spending would probably shoot up thirteen to fourteen billion dollars per year—about an eighth of the annual budget. In the course of 2003 all twenty-five existing and applicant nations ratified the accession agreements.

That summer, meanwhile, the European Convention presented EU leaders with a draft constitution. Its preamble highlighted values common to all progressive reformers since the days of Bertha von Suttner and the peace movement at The Hague a century earlier:

> Conscious that Europe is a continent that has brought forth civilization; that its inhabitants, arriving in successive waves from earliest times, have gradually developed the values underlying humanism: equality of persons, freedom, respect for reason,
>
> Drawing inspiration from the cultural, religious and humanist inheritance of Europe, the values of which, still present in its heritage, have embedded within the life of society the central role of the human person and his or her inviolable and inalienable rights, and respect for law,
>
> Believing that reunited Europe intends to continue along the path of civilization, progress and prosperity, for the good of all its inhabitants, including the weakest and most deprived; that it wishes to remain a continent open to culture, learning and progress; and that it wishes to deepen the democratic and transparent nature of its public life, and to strive for peace, justice and solidarity throughout the world,
>
> Convinced that, while remaining proud of their own national identities and history, the peoples of Europe are determined to transcend their ancient divisions and, united ever more closely, to forge a common destiny,
>
> Convinced that, thus "united in its diversity," Europe offers them the best chance of pursuing, with due regard for the rights of each individual and in awareness of their responsibilities towards future generations and the Earth, the great venture which makes of it a special area of hope . . . the citizens and States of Europe . . . have agreed as follows[106] . . .

The preamble and subsequent clauses of the constitutional document fulfilled the convention's first charge of explaining the mission of the European Union to doubters and skeptics. Reducing the many shelves of tomes containing EU laws, treaties, and regulations to a readable 265 pages, the manuscript introduced the core institutions of the union—commission, council, parliament, and court—and delineated their competencies. To comply with the charge that twenty-five—and soon twenty-seven—member-states be capable of making timely European Council/Council of Minister decisions on "first pillar" issues (i.e., monetary, business and labor, immigration, citizenship, and border control), resolutions would now require a so-called double majority. At least 50 percent of member states—casting, significantly enough, only one vote apiece—were necessary, but the collective populations of these resolution-

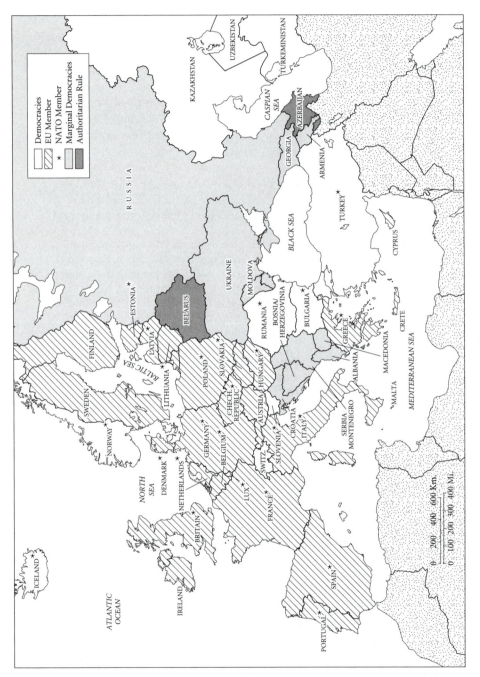

Present-day Europe

approving states had also to represent 60 percent of the EU population. The draft constitution met the third charge—raising the EU profile in a dangerous world—by proposing the creation of an EU foreign minister with his own ministerial staff. The conferees also accepted the need to enhance union security and defense capabilities somewhat along the lines of the European Defense and Security Union (ESDU) suggested by the Anti-War Four in April (see earlier). On such "second pillar" defense and security issues, however, the Council needed to vote unanimously in order to act—another telling sign that the EU reserves a strong measure of sovereignty for member states. Furthermore, the document emphasized the importance of maintaining a strong NATO, an alliance especially dear to the East Europeans—Estonia, Latvia, Lithuania, Slovakia, Slovenia, Rumania, and Bulgaria had joined Poland, Hungary, and the Czech Republic as NATO's newest members only a few months earlier. An intergovernmental conference of the pre-enlargement Fifteen fine-tuned this constitutional draft during the fall and winter prior to submitting it to the Twenty-Five for ratification after June 2004 elections to the European Parliament.

The EU and NATO expansions bring together more than thirty states in a largely interlocking web of democracy, economic integration, and common security.[107] Of the remaining countries of "Europe," as the term has been used in this study, a handful of Balkan countries struggle to implement the system of popular rule of law,[108] while most Eurasian republics of the former USSR are also nascent, borderline democracies.[109] Only Belarus, Europe's last dictatorship, remains blatantly undemocratic. Nevertheless, with the overwhelming majority of states either democratic or else making a transition to democracy, the democratization and pacification of Europe seem to have entered an exhilarating stage of fulfillment. Certainly when compared to the era of the world wars when the continent bled itself white and perpetrated crimes against humanity on a shockingly massive scale—when the present, even with its threat of terrorism, is held up to times when any democratization and pacification appeared next to impossible—one can reasonably conclude that Europe has reversed direction.

Some had never given up hope for this course change, even in the darkest of times. Speaking in beleaguered Berlin, John F. Kennedy looked "forward to that day when this city will be joined as one, and this country, and this great continent of Europe, in a peaceful and hopeful globe." Before him Winston Churchill had spoken of an era when "all Europe may be free and the life of the world may move forward into broad, sunlit uplands." And his Great War/World War contemporary, Käthe Kollwitz, sensed that someday her murderous epoch would appear incomprehensible to future Europeans who had finally built a house of peace and freedom. "I am dying in this faith," she said. "People will have to work hard for that new state of things, but they will achieve it." Although it is clearly too early to celebrate the ultimate victory Kollwitz believed in, what has been achieved thus far is perhaps enough to soften her mournful countenance.

NOTES

CHAPTER 1

1. Bertha von Suttner, *Memorien* (Bremen, 1965), 410. Although these memoirs are not available in translation, readers should see Brigitte Hamann, *Bertha von Suttner: A Life for Peace*, translated by Ann Dubsky (Syracuse, New York, 1996), 134–64; and Barbara Tuchman, *The Proud Tower: A Portrait of the World Before the War 1890–1914* (New York, 1962), 229–88.

2. Cited in William I. Hull, *The Two Hague Conferences and Their Contributions to International Law* (New York, 1970), 36, 7.

3. Citations in Suttner, *Memorien*, 407–08, 409–10, 426; and Hamann, *Life for Peace*, 140.

4. See Robert L. O'Connell, *Ride of the Second Horseman: The Birth and Death of War* (Oxford, 1995); Lawrence H. Keeley, *War Before Civilization: The Myth of the Peaceful Savage* (Oxford, 1996); John Keegan, *A History of Warfare* (New York, 1993); Paul Kennedy, *The Rise and Fall of the Great Powers: Economic Change and Military Conflict from 1500 to 2000* (New York, 1989); and William H. McNeill, *The Pursuit of Power: Technology, Armed Force, and Society Since A.D. 1000* (Chicago, 1982).

5. St. Augustine as cited in Thomas L. Pangle and Peter J. Ahrensdorf, *Justice Among Nations: On the Moral Basis of Power and Peace* (Lawrence, Kansas, 1999), 80.

6. Russian-born sociologist Jacques Novicow. See Sandi E. Cooper, *Patriotic Patriotism: Waging War on War in Europe, 1815–1914* (New York, 1991), 143.

7. Cited in Sharon Korman, *The Right of Conquest: The Acquisition of Territory by Force in International Law and Practice* (Oxford, 1996), 73. Also see Pangle and Ahrensdorf, *Justice Among Nations*, 98, 177–83.

8. David Gates, *Napoleonic Wars 1803–1815* (London, 1997), 272.

9. See the discussion of this principle in Korman, *Right of Conquest*, 12–16.

10. Ibid., 38–39.

11. See Benedict Anderson, *Imagined Communities: Reflections on the Origin and Spread of Nationalism* (New York, 1991); and Eric J. Hobsbawm, *Nations and Nationalism Since 1780: Programme, Myth, Reality* (Cambridge, 1992).

12. For these developments, see David S. Landes, *The Unbound Prometheus: Technological and Industrial Development in Western Europe from 1750 to the Present* (Cambridge, 1969), 41–123; Bertrand Gille, *The History of Techniques*, translated by P. Southgate and T. Williamson (New York, 1986), 2 vols.; Margaret C. Jacob, *The Cultural Meaning of the Scientific Revolution* (New York, 1988); and Eric Dorn Brose, *Technology and Science in the Industrializing Nations 1500–1914* (Atlantic Highlands, New Jersey, 1998).

13. Cited in Eric Dorn Brose, *The Politics of Technological Change in Prussia: Out of the Shadow of Antiquity 1809–1848* (Princeton, New Jersey, 1993), 225.

14. See Dennis E. Showalter, *Railroads and Rifles: Soldiers, Technology, and the Unification of Germany* (Hamden, Connecticut, 1975); and Eric Dorn Brose, *The Kaiser's Army: The Politics of Military Technology in Germany During the Machine Age, 1870–1918* (New York, 2001).

15. See Theodore H. von Laue, *Sergei Witte and the Industrialization of Russia* (New York, 1963).

16. For European imperialism, see Eric Hobsbawm, *The Age of Empire, 1875–1914* (New York, 1989); Daniel R. Headrick, *The Tools of Empire: Technology and European Imperialism in the Nineteenth Century* (Oxford, 1981); Herbert Feis, *Europe the World's Banker 1870–1914* (New York, 1965); Bernard Porter, *The Lion's Share: A Short History of British Imperialism, 1850–1970* (New York, 1975); Thomas Pakenham, *The Scramble for Africa: White Man's Conquest of the Dark Continent from 1876 to 1912* (New York, 1991); Peter Hopkirk, *The Great Game: On Secret Service in High Asia* (New York, 1990); and David MacKenzie, *Imperial Dreams, Harsh Realities: Tsarist Russian Foreign Policy, 1815–1917* (Fort Worth, Texas, 1994).

17. See the older studies on imperialism by John A. Hobson, *Imperialism: A Study* (London, 1902); V. I. Lenin, *Imperialism: The Highest Stage of Capitalism* (London, 1916); and especially Wolfgang Mommsen, *Theories of Imperialism*, translated from the German by P. S. Falla (New York, 1982). Also see Ronald Robinson and John Gallagher, *Africa and the Victorians* (London, 1967).

18. See Benny Morris, *Righteous Victims: A History of the Zionist–Arab Conflict, 1881–2001* (New York, 2001).

19. See David McClellan, *Karl Marx: His Life and Thought* (New York, 1978); Isaiah Berlin, *Karl Marx: His Life and Times* (New York, 1959); and Sidney Hook, *Marx and the Marxists: The Ambiguous Legacy* (Princeton, New Jersey, 1955).

20. Citations in James J. Sheehan, *German History 1770–1866* (Oxford, 1989), 601; Jean-Paul Satre, *The Words* (New York, 1966), 15; and Louise Blakeney Williams, *Modernism and the Ideology of History: Literature, Politics, and the Past* (Cambridge, 2002), 8.

21. See Arno J. Mayer, *The Persistence of the Old Regime: Europe to the Great War* (New York, 1981).

22. See Juergen Kocka and Allen Mitchell (eds.), *Bourgeois Society in Nineteenth-Century Europe* (Oxford, 1993); and Pamela M. Pilbeam, *The Middle Classes in Europe, 1789–1914* (Chicago, 1990).

23. See Renate Bridenthal, Susan Mosher, and Merry E. Wiesner (eds.), *Becoming Visible: Women in European History* (Boston, 1998); Francoise Thébaud (ed.), *A History of Women in the West* (Cambridge, Massachusetts, 1993–1994), vols. 4 and 5; Bonnie G. Smith, *Changing Lives: Women in European Society Since 1700* (Lexington, Massachusetts, 1989); and Martha Vicinus (ed.), *Suffer and Be Still: Women in the Victorian Age* (Bloomington, Indiana, 1972).

24. Norwegian playwright Henrik Ibsen's *A Doll's House* (1879) featured a repressed housewife who rebels against her husband.

25. For these points, see Mariette Stineau, "Law and Democracy," in Thébaud (ed.), *History of Women*, 5: 501–07.

26. Cited in Ann Taylor Allen, *Feminism and Motherhood in Germany 1800–1914* (New Brunswick, New Jersey, 1991), 101.

27. Citations in Edith F. Hurwitz, "The International Sisterhood," in Bridenthal and Koonz, *Becoming Visible*, 331; Cooper, *Patriotic Pacifism*, 79, 98; and Anne-Marie Kaeppeli, "Feminist Scenes," in Thébaud (ed.), *History of Women*, 4: 494.

28. Cited in Hamann, *A Life for Peace*, 268–69.

29. Communism and socialism are terms that have caused confusion. Marx used them mainly in reference to the post-revolutionary period: Socialism was a building stage toward the eventual communist utopia. Consistent with this, socialism, both of a Marxist and non-Marxist variety in nineteenth-century Europe, meant a system of collective as opposed to private property rights. However, the gradual splitting of the socialist movement between advocates of violence and advocates of parliamentary tactics to achieve goals, culminating in the Bolshevik Revolution in Russia in 1917 and later abuses of the system there, led many in the West to distinguish between nonviolent "socialists" or "social democrats" as opposed to nondemocratic communists. The Bolsheviks of Russia also changed the party name to "communist"

in order to distinguish between Russian and West European socialist parties. At the same time, however, Russian communists also referred to the socialist stage of their revolution, that is, the building stage toward the communist utopia. See also Chapters 3 and 4.

30. For these trends, see Paul M. Hohenburg and Lynn Hollen Lees, *The Making of Urban Europe 1000–1994* (Cambridge, Massachusetts, 1995); Carlton J. H. Hayes, *A Generation of Materialism, 1871–1900* (New York, 1983); Charles, Louise, and Richard Tilly, *The Rebellious Century 1830–1930* (Cambridge, Massachusetts, 1975); and Peter N. Stearns, *European Society in Upheaval: Social History Since 1800* (New York, 1967).

31. Cited in Carl E. Schorske, *Fin De Siècle Vienna: Politics and Culture* (New York, 1981), 116.

32. For early industrial conditions, see the exchanges between Eric Hobsbawm and Robert Hartwell in the *Economic History Review* 10 (August 1957): 46–68, 13 (April 1961): 397–416, and 16 (August 1963): 119–46.

33. Discounted for inflation, real wages are an accurate measure of purchasing power.

34. Cited in Eugen Weber, *France Fin de Siècle* (Cambridge, Massachusetts, 1986), 127–28.

35. See Marcelline J. Hutton, *Russian and West European Women, 1860–1939: Dreams, Struggles, and Nightmares* (Lanham, Maryland, 2001); Smith, *Changing Lives*; Barbara Taylor, *Eve and the New Jerusalem: Socialism and Feminism in the Nineteenth Century* (New York, 1983); and Werner Thoennessen, *The Emancipation of Women: The Rise and Decline of the Women's Movement in German Social Democracy 1863–1933* (Frankfurt, 1969).

36. See Wolfgang Mommsen and Hans-Gerhard Husung, *The Development of Trade Unionism in Great Britain and Germany, 1880–1914* (London, 1985); and José Harris, *Unemployment and Politics: A Study in English Social Policy 1886–1914* (Oxford, 1972).

37. See Gordon Wright, *France in Modern Times: From the Enlightenment to the Present* (New York, 1995); and David Thomson, *Democracy in France Since 1870* (Oxford, 1969).

38. See Michael Burns, *Rural Society and French Politics: Boulangism and the Dreyfus Affair* (Princeton, New Jersey, 1984); and Douglas Johnson, *France and the Dreyfus Affair* (London, 1966).

39. Citations in Tuchman, *Proud Tower*, 184, 188–89, 204.

40. Cited in ibid., 185.

41. For Germany and Austria-Hungary, see David Blackbourn, *The Long Nineteenth Century: A History of Germany, 1780–1918* (Oxford, 1998); Volker R. Berghahn, *Imperial Germany 1871–1914: Economy, Society, Culture and Politics* (Providence, Rhode Island, 1994); and Arthur J. May, *The Habsburg Monarchy 1967–1914* (New York, 1968).

42. Cited in Oscar Jaszi, *The Dissolution of the Habsburg Monarchy* (Chicago, 1966), 177.

43. See Eric Dorn Brose, *Christian Labor and the Politics of Frustration in Imperial Germany* (Washington, DC, 1985).

44. See Teodor Shanin (ed.), *Peasants and Peasant Societies: Selected Readings* (New York, 1987).

45. For Russian trends, see Orlando Figes, *A People's Tragedy: The Russian Revolution 1891–1924* (New York, 1997); Michael T. Florinsky, *Russia: A History and an Interpretation* (New York, 1970), vol. 2; Geroid Tanquary Robinson, *Rural Russia Under the Old Regime* (Berkeley, California, 1969); and Adam Ulam, *The Bolsheviks: The Intellectual, Personal and Political History of the Triumph of Communism in Russia* (New York, 1965).

46. Cited in Florinsky, *Russia*, 2: 1147.

47. For Italy, see Denis Mack Smith, *Italy: A Political History* (Ann Arbor, Michigan, 1997); Clara M. Lovett, *The Democratic Movement in Italy* (Cambridge, Massachusetts, 1982); and Salvatore Saladino, *Italy from Unification to 1919: Growth and Decay of a Liberal Regime* (New York, 1970).

48. Citations in Nunzio Pernicone, *Italian Anarchism 1864–1892* (Princeton, New Jersey, 1993), 19, 38.

49. See James Joll, *The Second International 1889–1914* (London, 1955); and Geoff Eley, *Forging Democracy: The History of the Left in Europe, 1850–2000* (New York, 2002).

50. See Note 29.

51. Citations in Hamann, *A Life for Peace*, 245, 247.

52. Förster's article of 1896 is cited in ibid., 247.

53. The document is printed in Cooper, *Patriotic Pacifism*, 221–22.

54. Citations in Tuchman, *Proud Tower*, 239, 241; and Hamann, *A Life for Peace*, 139.

55. Cited in Hamann, *A Life for Peace*, 250.

56. Citations in Tuchman, *Proud Tower*, 259; and Suttner, *Memorien*, 427.

57. Cited in Tuchman, *Proud Tower*, 258.

58. Cited in ibid., 104.

59. Cited in Hamann, *A Life for Peace*, 155.

CHAPTER 2

1. See Norman Del Mar, *Richard Strauss: A Critical Commentary on His Life and Works* (Philadelphia, 1962), 1: 434; and Michael Kennedy, *Richard Strauss: Man, Musician, Enigma* (Cambridge, 1999), 129.

2. Cited in Kennedy, *Richard Strauss*, 103.

3. Citations in Hans Kohn, *The Mind of Gemany* (New York, 1960), 218; and Hajo Halborn, *A History of Modern Germany 1840–1945* (New York, 1969), 398.

4. Citations in Tuchman, *Proud Tower* (Chapter 1, Note 1), 312; and Kennedy, *Richard Strauss*, 115.

5. For wars, crises, and the approaching war of 1914, see Laurence Lafore, *The Long Fuse: An Interpretation of the Origins of World War I* (Philadelphia, 1971); Jack Snyder, *The Ideology of the Offensive: Military Decision-Making and the Disasters of 1914* (Ithaca, New York, 1984); Volker R. Berghahn, *Germany and the Approach of War in 1914* (New York, 1993); David G. Herrmann, *The Arming of Europe and the Making of the First World War* (Princeton, New Jersey, 1996); Antulio J. Ecevarria II, *After Clausewitz: German Military Thinkers Before the Great War* (Lawrence, Kansas, 2000); and Brose, *Kaiser's Army* (Chapter 1, Note 14). Also see Notes 23–30 and 86 in this chapter.

6. Cited in George L. Mosse, *Fallen Soldiers: Reshaping the Memory of the World Wars* (New York, 1990), 55.

7. Citations in Andrew N. Porter, *The Origins of the South African War: Joseph Chamberlain and the Diplomacy of Imperialism, 1895–1899* (New York, 1980), 166; and Thomas Pakenham, *The Scramble for Africa: White Man's Conquest of the Dark Continent from 1876 to 1912* (New York, 1991), 565.

8. The term came from the *reconcentrado* camps set up by Spain to hold Cuban guerrillas.

9. Cited in Herrmann, *The Arming of Europe*, 68.

10. Cited in Cooper, *Patriotic Pacifism* (Chapter 1, Note 6), 87.

11. Between 1899 and 1908 nations signed seventy-seven arbitration agreements. See ibid., 105, 115.

12. Bertha von Suttner, *Memorien* (Bremen, 1965), 427.

13. Citations in Hull, *Two Hague Conferences* (Chapter 1, Note 2)), 315, 337.

14. The eleventh recalcitrant nation was Japan, which abstained from most of the voting.

15. Citations in Roger Chickering, *Imperial Germany and a World Without War: The Peace Movement and German Society 1892–1914* (Princeton, New Jersey, 1975), 221–22; and Cooper, *Patriotic Pacifism*, 107.

16. Citations in Lafore, *The Long Fuse*, 148, 152.

17. Citations in Berghahn, *Germany and the Approach of War*, 96.

18. Citations in Report of the International Commission to Inquire into the Causes and Conduct of the Balkan Wars, Carnegie Endowment for International Peace, 1913, printed in: *The Other Balkan Wars: A 1913 Carnegie Endowment Inquiry in Retrospect* (Washington, DC, 1993), 47, 71.

19. Weber, *France Fin de Siècle*, 237.

20. Thomas Mann, *Doctor Faustus*, translated by John E. Woods, originally published in 1947 (New York, 1997), 385.

21. Cited in Joll, *Second International* (Chapter 1, Note 49), 154.

22. Cited in Cooper, *Patriotic Pacifism*, 184.

23. Citations in Samuel R. Williamson, Jr., *Austria-Hungary and the Origins of the First World War* (New York, 1991), 174–75.

24. For the best overall analysis and summary of causes, see James Joll, *The Origins of the First World War* (New York, 1992). Also see Joachim Remak, *The Origins of World War I, 1871–1914* (Fort Worth, Texas, 1967).

25. See works cited in Chapter 1, Notes 4 and 7.

26. See works cited in Chapter 1, Notes 16–17. Also see David S. Landes, *The Unbound Prometheus: Technological Change and Industrial Development in Western Europe from 1750 to the Present* (Cambridge, 1969), 248. Landes sees war's outbreak as the end result of economic and technological dynamism and accompanying national rivalry, in contrast to the Marxist view (e.g., Lenin), which stresses the crisis and contradictions of a dying capitalism. "The most determined efforts of the wisest men did not avail to appease the resentments and enmities that grew out of the [rise of Germany]," he writes. Those historians who see the resultant war as "the thrashing out of a [capitalist] system in the process of decline and dissolution" are wrong. "The fact is that these were the growing pains of a [technological] system in the process of germination."

27. For the alliance system in general, see the discussion and additional sources in Joll, *Origins of the First World War*. For the Balkans in particular, see Lafore, *Long Fuse*, and Williamson, *Austria-Hungary*, Notes 5 and 23 in this chapter, respectively.

28. For the extent of pro-war and anti-war feeling on the eve of the war, see Roger Chickering (as cited in Note 15); Robert Wohl, *The Generation of 1914* (Cambridge, Massachusetts, 1979); Sandi E. Cooper (Note 10); Hamann, *A Life for Peace* (Chapter 1, Note 1); and Jeffrey T. Verhey, *The Spirit of 1914: Militarism, Myth, and Mobilization in Germany* (New York, 2000).

29. In general, see Joll, *Second International*; Oron J. Hale, *The Great Illusion, 1900–1914* (New York, 1971); Mayer, *Persistence of the Old Regime* (Chapter 1, Note 21); Eric Hobsbawm, *The Age of Empire 1875–1914* (New York, 1989); and Eley, *Forging Democracy* (Chapter 1, Note 49).

30. For the primacy of domestic politics argument, see mainly Mayer, *Persistence of the Old Regime* (Chapter 1, Note 21); and Hans-Ulrich Wehler, *The German Empire 1871–1918* (Dover, New Hampshire, 1985). Also see the discussion and other sources in Joll, *Origins* (Note 24).

31. R. C. K. Ensor, *England 1870–1914* (Oxford, 1936), 557.

32. Cited in George Dangerfield, *The Strange Death of Liberal England 1910–1914* (New York, 1961), 236. The book was originally published in 1935.

33. See Peter Wardley, "Edwardian Britain: Empire, Income and Political Discontent," and Tony Mason, "Sport and Recreation," in Paul Johnson (ed.), *20th Century Britain: Economic, Social and Cultural Change* (London, 1994), as well as the literature discussed here, 57–78, 111–26.

34. Cited in Dangerfield, *Strange Death*, 235, 307, 394.

35. See James F. McMillan, *Twentieth-Century France: Politics and Society 1898–1991* (New York, 1992), 3–61.

36. Cited in Ernst Nolte, *Three Faces of Fascism: Action Française, Italian Fascism, National Socialism*, translated by Leila Vennewitz (New York, 1965), 105. Also see Mazgaj, *The Action Française and Revolutionary Syndicalism* (Chapel Hill, North Car-

olina, 1979); and Eugen Weber, *Action Française: Royalism and Reaction in Twentieth-Century France* (Palo Alto, California, 1962).

37. Citations in Louis Levine, *The Labor Movement in France* (New York, 1912), 176.

38. For overviews, see Blackbourn, *Long Generation* (Chapter 1, Note 41), 400–59; and Berghahn, *Imperial Germany* (Chapter 1, Note 41). For workers' subculture, see Vernon L. Lidtke, *The Alternative Culture: Socialist Labor in Imperial Germany* (New York, 1985).

39. Cited in Blackbourn, *Long Generation*, 360.

40. See Jonathan Dunnage, *Twentieth Century Italy: A Social History* (London, 2002); and Spencer M. Di Scala, *Italy from Revolution to Republic: 1700 to the Present* (Boulder, Colorado, 1998).

41. Cited in Saladino, *Italy from Unification to 1919* (Chapter 1, Note 47), 98.

42. For Russian developments, see David MacKenzie and Michael W. Curran, *Russia and the USSR in the Twentieth Century* (Stamford, Connecticut, 2002) as well as sources from Chapter 1, Note 45: Figes, *People's Tragedy*, 213–41; Florinsky, *Russia*; and Robinson, *Rural Russia Under the Old Regime*.

43. Cited in Figes, *People's Tragedy*, 113.

44. Cited in ibid., 168.

45. Dangerfield, *Strange Death*, 159.

46. For a discussion of these problems and a reference to further sources, see Pat Thane, "The Social, Economic, and Political Status of Women," in Johnson (ed.), *20th Century Britain*, 94–110.

47. See the sources cited in Chapter 1, Note 23, and Ute Frevert, *Women in German History: From Bourgeois Emancipation to Sexual Liberation*, translated by Stuart McKinnon-Evans (Oxford, 1989); also Steven C. Hause, *Women's Suffrage and Social Politics in the French Third Republic* (Princeton, New Jersey, 1984).

48. Cited in Renate Bridenthal and Claudia Koonz (eds.), *Becoming Visible: Women in European History* (Boston, 1977), 335.

49. Citations in Smith, *Changing Lives* (Chapter 1, Note 23), 359; and Cinzia Sartini Blum, *The Other Modernism: F. T. Marinetti's Futurist Fiction of Power* (Berkeley, California, 1996), 31.

50. Citations in Smith, *Changing Lives*, 360; George L. Mosse, *The Image of Man: The Creation of Modern Masculinity* (New York, 1996), 70; and Diane Joan Trosino, "Anti-Feminism in Germany, 1919–1920: The German League for the Prevention of Women's Emancipation," Unpublished Ph.D. dissertation, Claremont Graduate School, 1992, 89, 94–96, 102.

51. Cited in Bridenthal and Koontz (eds.), *Becoming Visible*, 337.

52. Oscar Jaszi, *The Dissolution of the Habsburg Monarchy* (Chicago, 1929), 127.

53. For these fears, see Raymond Pearson, "Hungary: A State Truncated, a Nation Dismembered," in Seamus Dunn and T. G. Fraser (eds.), *Europe and Ethnicity: The First World War and Contemporary Ethnic Conflict* (London, 1996), 92.

54. David S. Landes (Note 26 in this chapter).

55. See poet Kasimir Edschmid (Note 6 in this chapter).

56. Cited in Blum, *The Other Modernism*, 30.

57. Cited in Tuchman, *Proud Tower*, xv.

58. For good introductions to modernism, see Norman F. Cantor, *Twentieth-Century Culture: From Modernism to Deconstruction* (New York, 1988); Marshall Berman, *All That Is Solid Melts into Air: The Experience of Modernity* (New York, 1982); Robert Hughes, *The Shock of the New* (New York, 1981); George L. Mosse, *The Culture of Western Europe* (Chicago, 1974); John Willett, *Expressionism* (New York, 1970). Also see Peter Conrad, *Modern Times, Modern Places: How Life and Art Were Transformed in a Century of Revolution, Innovation and Radical Change* (New York, 1999).

59. Messer, former director of the Guggenheim Museum in New York, is cited in Piri Halasz, "German Expressionism: Explosive Art Movement in a Troubled Age," *Smithsonian* 11/10 (January 1981): 94.

60. Conrad, *Modern Times, Modern Places*, 29; and Tuchman, *Proud Tower*, 323.

61. For the musical analysis, see Bryan Gilliam, *Richard Strauss's Elektra* (Oxford, 1991).

62. Cited in Tuchman, *Proud Tower*, 334.

63. For this interpretation, see Charles Rosen, *Arnold Schoenberg* (Princeton, New Jersey, 1975), 17.

64. Citations in Richard Sheppard, "German Expressionism," in Malcolm Bradbury and James McFarlane (eds.), *Modernism: 1890–1930* (New York, 1978), 278–79.

65. The poems are printed in (and translated by) Richard Sheppard, *Ernst Stadler (1883–1914): A German Expressionist Poet at Oxford* (Oxford, 1994), 31–32, 34–35, 35–36.

66. Printed in Roger Cardinal, *Expressionism* (London, 1984), 46.

67. Sheppard, "German Expressionist Poetry," in Bradbury and McFarlane, *Modernism*, 384.

68. Cited in Sheppard, "German Expressionist Poetry," in Bradbury and McFarlane, *Modernism*, 384.

69. See T. J. Reed, *Death in Venice: Making and Unmaking a Master* (New York, 1994).

70. Thomas Mann, *Death in Venice and Other Tales*, translated from the German by Joachim Neugroschel (New York, 1998), 287.

71. Citations in Reed, *Death in Venice*, 98.

72. Citations in Carnival, *Expressionism*, 77; and Alessandra Comini, "When Form Followed Feeling: German Expressionism, 1905–1920," *Portfolio* 2/5 (November/December 1980): 65.

73. Cited in Frederick S. Levine, *The Apocalyptic Vision: The Art of Franz Marc as German Expressionism* (New York, 1979), 79–80.

74. For this argument, see Modris Eksteins, *Rites of Spring: The Great War and the Birth of the Modern Age* (New York, 1990), 80–89.

75. For Musil, see Russell A. Berman, *The Rise of the Modern German Novel: Crisis and Charisma* (Cambridge, Massachusetts, 1986), 183, 186–87.

76. See Ivan T. Berend, *Decades of Crisis: Central and Eastern Europe Before World War II* (Los Angeles, 1998), 97, 99; and Schorske, *Fin-De-Siecle Vienna* (Chapter I, Note 31), 322–64.

77. Citations in Eksteins, *Rites of Spring*, 50–51; Berend, *Decades of Crisis*, 95; and Smithsonian Institution, *Russian and Soviet Paintings 1900–1930* (Washington, DC, 1988), 34.

78. Citations in Eksteins, *Rites of Spring*, 51, 52, 10, 54.

79. Cited in Blum, *The Other Modernism*, 43.

80. Citations in ibid., 31, 30; and *Futurismo 1909–1919: Exhibition of Italian Futurism* (Newcastle upon Tyne, 1972), 75.

81. Cited in Michael C. C. Adams, *The Great Adventure: Male Desire and the Coming of World War I* (Bloomington, Indiana, 1990), 87.

82. Cited in Williams, *Modernism* (Chapter I, Note 20), 74.

83. Adams, *Great Adventure*, 74.

84. Cited in Peter Paret, *Imagined Battles: Reflections of War in European Art* (Chapel Hill, North Carolina, 1997), 98.

85. See Thomas Nipperdey, "Nationalidee und Nationaldenkmal in Deutschland im 19. Jahrhundert," *Historische Zeitschrift* 206/3 (1968): 529–85.

86. For surveys of the July Crisis, see David Fromkin, *Europe's Last Summer: Who Started the Great War in 1914?* (New York, 2004); William Jannen, Jr., *The Lions of July: Prelude to War, 1914* (Novato, California, 1996); and Joll, *Origins* (Note 24 in this chapter), 9–32. For assessments of each Power's contribution to the coming of war, see Berghahn, *Germany and the Approach of War* (Note 5 in this chapter); Williamson, *Austria-Hungary* (Note 23 in this chapter); D. C. B. Lieven, *Russia and the Origins of the First World War* (New York, 1983); John F. Keiger, *France and the Origins of the First World War* (New York, 1983); and Zara S. Steiner, *Britain and the Origins of the First World War* (New York, 1977).

87. Cited in Cameron Hazlehurst, *Politicians at War* (London, 1971), 32.

CHAPTER 3

1. See the memoir sketch of American nurse Laura Smith, printed in Peter Jennings and Todd Brewster, *The Century* (New York, 1998), 86, and especially the graphic descriptions in Susan Kingsley Kent, *Making Peace: The Reconstruction of Gender in Interwar Britain* (Princeton, New Jersey, 1993), 51–73.

2. For World War One, see Martin Gilbert, *The First World War: A Complete History* (New York, 1994); Jay Winter and Blaine Baggett, *The Great War and the Shaping of the 20th Century* (New York, 1996); Spencer C. Tucker, *The Great War 1914–18* (Bloomington, Indiana, 1998); John Keegan, *The First World War* (New York, 1999); Ian F. W. Beckett, *The Great War 1914–1918* (Harlow, 2001) Hew Strachan, *The First World War* (Oxford, 2001), Vol. 1, *To Arms* (Vols. 2 and 3 forthcoming); and Stéphane Audoin-Rouzeau and Annette Becker, *14–18: Understanding the Great War* (New York, 2002).

3. See Terence Zuber, "The Schlieffen Plan Reconsidered," *War in History* 6/3 (1999): 262–305; and Brose, *Kaiser's Army* (Chapter 1, Note 14), 69–84, 183–216. Also see Zuber's book-length *Inventing the Schlieffen Plan: German War Planning 1871–1914* (Oxford, 2002).

4. Cited in Gilbert, *First World War*, 153–54.

5. Citations in Maria Tatar, *Lustmord: Sexual Murder in Weimar Germany* (Princeton, New Jersey, 1995), 119; and Winter and Blaggett, *The Great War*, 100–01.

6. Cited in Holger H. Herwig, *The First World War: Germany and Austria-Hungary 1914–1918* (New York, 1997), 153.

7. Cited in Gilbert, *First World War*, 245.

8. L. L. Farrar, *Arrogance and Anxiety: The Ambivalence of German Power, 1848–1914* (Iowa City, 1981), 39.

9. For wartime politics, see Trevor Wilson, *The Myriad Faces of War: Britain and the Great War, 1914–1918* (Cambridge, 1986); John Turner, *British Politics and the Great War: Coalition and Conflict, 1915–1918* (London, 1992); John N. Horne, *Labour at War: France and Britain 1914–1918* (Oxford, 1991); McMillan, *Twentieth-Century France* (Chapter 2, Note 35), 65–76; Di Scala, *Italy from Revolution to Republic* (Chapter 2, Note 40), 193–210; Saladino, *Italy from Unification to 1919* (Chapter 1, Note 47), 134–64; Roger Chickering, *Imperial Germany and the Great War, 1914–1918* (Cambridge, 1998); Herwig, *The First World War*; Ulam, *The Bolsheviks* (Chapter 1, Note 45), 314–81; and Figes, *People's Tragedy* (Chapter 1, Note 45), 253–551.

10. Winston S. Churchill, *The World Crisis* (New York, 1931), 28.

11. Cited in D. George Boyce, *Ireland 1828–1923: From Ascendancy to Democracy* (Oxford, 1992), 88.

12. Citations in Sandra M. Gilbert, "Soldier's Heart: Literary Men, Literary Women, and the Great War," in Margaret Randolph Higonnet et al., *Behind the Lines: Gender and the Two World Wars* (New Haven, Connecticut, 1987), 197; and Kent, *Making Peace*, 75, 77.

13. Citations in Steven C. Hause and Anne R. Kenney, *Women's Suffrage and Social Politics in the French Third Republic* (Princeton, New Jersey, 1984), 191, 197, 196.

14. Citations in May, *Hapsburg Monarchy* (Chapter 1, Note 41), 1: 308, 395.

15. Citations in ibid., 1: 428, 2: 638.

16. Citations in Brose, *Christian Labor* (Chapter 1, Note 43), 333; and Richard J. Evans, *Comrades and Sisters: Feminism, Socialism and Pacifism in Europe 1870–1945* (New York, 1987), 128.

17. Cited in Brose, *Kaiser's Army*, 234.

18. See Owen's "The Parable of The Old Man and The Young," in *The Collected Poems of Wilfred Owen*, edited by C. Day Lewis (New York, 1964), 42, 55.

19. For discussions of these problems, see Chickering, *Imperial Germany* (Note 9 in this chapter); Brose, *Christian Labor* (Note 16 in this chapter); and Jay Winter and Jean-Louis Robert, *Capital Cities at War: Paris, London, Berlin, 1914–1919* (Cambridge, 1999).

20. See Robert K. Massie, *Nicholas and Alexandra* (New York, 1967); and especially Edvard Radzinsky's definitive *The Rasputin File,* translated by Judson Rosengrant (New York, 2000).

21. Cited in Florinsky, *Russia* (Chapter 1, Note 45), 2: 1373.

22. For recent research trends, see Edward Acton, *Rethinking the Russian Revolution* (London, 1990), 107–128.

23. Cited in Figes, *A People's Tragedy*, 323.

24. Acton, *Rethinking*, 164.

25. Cited in Figes, *People's Tragedy*, 444.

26. See ibid ; and Acton, *Rethinking*.

27. Kornilov's opinion of Kerensky, cited in ibid., 446.

28. For Lenin, see Ulam, *The Bolsheviks* (Chapter 1, Note 45); Dmitri Volkogonov, *Lenin: Life and Legacy,* translated by Harold Shukman (London, 1994); and Robert Service, *Lenin: A Political Life* (London, 1985, 1991, 1995), 3 vols.

29. Cited in Acton, *Rethinking,* 139.

30. Citations in Marilyn Shevin-Coetzee and Fran Coetzee, *World War I and European Society: A Sourcebook* (Lexington, Massachusetts, 1995), 262, 276.

31. See Rod Paschall, *The Defeat of Imperial Germany 1917–1918* (New York, 1994), 53.

32. Citations in Saladino, *Italy from Unification to 1919,* 158.

33. Citations in May, *Passing of the Hapsburg Empire,* 2: 667–69.

34. Citations in ibid., 2: 692, 677.

35. See Chickering, *Imperial Germany*; and Herwig, *First World War* (Note 9 in this chapter). For a recent discussion of the "Zimmermann Telegram," see David Paull Nickles, *Under the Wire: How the Telegraph Changed Diplomacy* (Cambridge, Massachusetts, 2003), 137–160.

36. Martin Kitchen, *The Silent Dictatorship: The Politics of the German High Command Under Hindenburg and Ludendorff, 1916–1918* (New York, 1976).

37. Cited in Kent, *Making Peace,* 65.

38. For the Paris settlement, see the recent works of Margaret MacMillan, *Paris 1919: Six Months That Changed the World* (New York, 2002); Manfred F. Boemeke, Gerald D. Feldman, and Elizabeth Glasser, *The Treaty of Versailles: A Reassessment After 75 Years* (Cambridge, 1998); and David Stevenson, *The First World War and International Politics* (Oxford, 1991). Also see Gerhard Schulz, *Revolution and Peace Treaties 1917–1920* (London, 1972); and Arno J. Mayer, *Politics and Diplomacy of Peacemaking: Containment and Counterrevolution at Versailles, 1918–1919* (New York, 1967).

39. For the aftershocks in Germany, Austria, Hungary, Italy, and the Middle East, see F. L. Carsten, *Revolution in Central Europe 1918–1919* (Berkeley, California, 1972); Richard Bessel, *Germany After the First World War* (Oxford, 1993); Paul Lendvai, *The Hungarians: A Thousand Years of Victory in Defeat*, translated by Ann Major (Princeton, New Jersey, 2003); Barbara Jelavich, *History of the Balkans: Twentieth Century* (Cambridge, 1983); Misha Glenny, *The Balkans: Nationalism, War and the Great Powers 1804–1999* (New York, 2000); and David Fromkin, *A Peace to End All Peace: The Fall of the Ottoman Empire and the Creation of the Modern Middle East* (New York, 1989).

40. Initially called the Kingdom of the Serbs, Croats, and Slovenes.

41. Cited in Fromkin, *Peace to End All Peace,* 437.

42. Citations in Morris, *Righteous Victims* (Chapter 1, Note 18), 75–76; and MacMillan, *Paris 1919,* 380.

43. Cited in MacMillan, *Paris 1919,* 70.

44. Figes, *People's Tragedy,* 660.

45. Cited in ibid., 672.

46. Ibid., 773.

47. Cited in Louis P. Lochner, *Herbert Hoover and Germany* (New York, 1960), 33.

48. Renzo De Felice, *Mussolini* (Turin, 1966–1993); Denis Mack Smith, *Mussolini* (New York, 1982).

49. Cited in Glenny, *The Balkans,* 387.

50. Cited in Smith, *Changing Lives* (Chapter 1, Note 23), 374.

51. Gail Braybon and Penny Summerfield, *Out of the Cage: Women's Experiences in Two World Wars* (London, 1987).

52. For a discussion of earlier and more recent interpretations, see Francoise Thébaud, "The Great War and the Triumph of Sexual Division," in Thébaud (ed.), *History of Women* (Chapter 1, Note 23), 5: 21–75.

53. Cited in Mariolina Graziosi, "Gender Struggle and the Social Manipulation and Ideological Use of Gender Identity in the Interwar Years," in Robin Pickering-Iazzi (ed.), *Mothers of Invention: Women, Italian Fascism, and Culture* (Minneapolis, 1995), 28.

54. On France, see Paul Smith, *Feminism and the Third Republic: Women's Political and Civil Rights in France, 1918–1945* (Oxford, 1996); and James F. MacMillan, *Housewife or Harlot: The Place of Women in French Society, 1870–1940* (Brighton, 1981).

55. Cited in Ilana R. Bet-El, "Men and Soldiers: British Conscripts, Concepts of Masculinity, and the Great War," in Billie Melman (ed.), *Borderlines: Genders and Identities in War and Peace, 1870–1930* (New York, 1998), 87.

56. Thébaud, "Triumph of Sexual Division," in Thébaud (ed.), *History of Women*, 5: 39.

57. Cited in Gilbert, "Soldier's Heart," in Higonnet, *Behind the Lines*, 199.

58. Citations in Clara Orban, "Women, Futurism, and Fascism," in Pickering-Iazzi, *Mothers of Invention*, 56, 59.

59. See Max Bauer's late 1917 manuscript in NL Bauer (22), 1c, Bl. 202, Bundesarchiv Koblenz.

60. Cited in Gilbert, "Soldier's Heart," in Higonnet, *Behind the Lines*, 209.

61. Cited in Tatar, *Lustmord*, 120.

62. Cited in Thébaud, "Triumph of Sexual Division," in Thébaud, *History of Women*, 5: 21.

63. Cited in Gilbert, "Soldier's Heart," in Higonnet, *Behind the Lines*, 204.

64. Citations in Kent, *Making Peace*, 68.

65. Citations in Lynne Layton, "Vera Brittain's Testament(s)," and Gilbert, "Soldier's Heart," in Higonnet, *Behind the Lines*, 75, 200.

66. Citations in Kent, *Making Peace*, 95, 101.

67. For this argument, see ibid.

68. Citations in ibid., 95, 138.

69. Citations in ibid., 69–70.

70. Cited in George L. Mosse, *Fallen Soldiers: Reshaping the Memory of the World Wars* (Oxford, 1990), 165.

71. Marie Elisabeth Lüders, *Das Unbekannte Heer: Frauen Kämpfen fuer Deutschland* (Berlin, 1936), 77–78, 6.

72. See Mary Louise Roberts, *Civilization Without Sexes: Reconstructing Gender in Postwar France, 1917–1927* (Chicago, 1994). For emphasis on the wartime roots of reconstruction, see also Susan R. Grayzel, *Women's Identities at War: Gender, Motherhood, and Politics in Britain and France During the First World War* (Chapel Hill, North Carolina, 1999).

73. Erich Maria Remarque, *All Quiet on the Western Front* (New York, 1968), 175–76.

74. Siegfried Kracauer, *From Caligari to Hitler: A Psychological History of the German Film* (Princeton, New Jersey, 1947), 9, 135.

75. Cited in Catherine Elaine Boyd, " 'Natonaler Frauendienst': German Middle-Class Women in Service to the Fatherland, 1914–1918," unpublished Ph.D. dissertation, University of Georgia, 1979, 221.

76. Gertrud Bäumer, *Die Frau im neuen Lebensraum* (Berlin, 1931), 251.

77. Lange to Beckmann, March 4, 1922; June 1923; August 14, 1923; printed in Helene Lange, *Was ich hier geliebt: Briefe von Helene Lange* (Tübingen, 1957), 82, 143, 150.

78. Citations in Claudia Koonz, *Mothers in the Fatherland: Women, the Family and Nazi Politics* (New York, 1981), 80, 81–82.

CHAPTER 4

1. Harold Nicolson's memoirs are cited in Macmillan, *Paris 1919* (Chapter 3, Note 38), 86. For other works on Paris and the League, see Gary B. Ostrower, *The League of Nations from 1919 to 1929* (New York, 1996); Elmer Bendiner, *A Time for Angels: The Tragicomic History of the League of Nations* (New York, 1975); George Scott, *The Rise and Fall of the League of Nations* (New York, 1973); Mayer, *Politics and Diplomacy* (Chapter 3, Note 38); and F. P. Walters, *A History of the League of Nations* (London, 1967).

2. Cited in Bendiner, *Time for Angels*, 164.

3. For works on the League, see Note 1.

4. Cited in Scott, *Rise and Fall of the League*, 32.

5. Quotes in John Morton Blum, *Woodrow Wilson and the Politics of Morality* (Boston, 1956), 159, 169.

6. See Korman, *The Right of Conquest* (Chapter 1, Note 7), 180–92.

7. Cited in James Barros, *Office Without Power: Secretary-General Sir Eric Drummond 1919–1933* (Oxford, 1979), 29–30.

8. Cited in Blum, *Politics of Morality*, 159.

9. Walters, *History of the League*, 137.

10. Quotes in Ostrower, *League of Nations*, 48.

11. Cited in Barros, *Office Without Power*, 271.

12. The treaty is cited in Sally Marks, *The Illusion of Peace: International Relations in Europe 1918–1933* (New York, 1976), 68.

13. Cited in Raymond J. Sontag, *A Broken World 1919–1939* (New York, 1972), 120.

14. Cited in Smith, *Modern Italy* (Chapter 1, Note 47), 323. On Italy, also see De Felice, *Mussolini* (Chapter 3, Note 48) and Smith's *Mussolini* (Chapter 3, Note 48).

15. Cited in ibid., 332.

16. Marks, *Illusion of Peace*, 69.

17. Walters, *History of the League of Nations*, 365. Also see the sources cited in Note 1.

18. Ibid., 383.

19. Cited in Piri Halasz, "German Expressionism: Explosive Art Movement in a Troubled Age," *Smithsonian* 11/10 (January 1981): 94.

20. In general, see the works cited in Chapter 2, Note 58.

21. Citations in Paul Valéry, *Variety*, translated by Malcolm Crowley (New York, 1927), 27–28; and Eksteins, *Rites of Spring* (Chapter II, Note 74), 266.

22. Cited in Berend, *Decades of Crisis* (Chapter 1, Note 76), 105.

23. Citations in Gordon Wright, *France in Modern Times: 1760 to the Present* (Chicago, 1960), 569.

24. Cited in Schorske, *Fin De Siècle Vienna* (Chapter 1, Note 31), 345.

25. Conrad, *Modern Times, Modern Places* (Chapter 2, Note 58), 180.

26. *The Wasteland*, printed in Michael North (ed.), *The Waste Land: Authoritative Text Contents Criticism* (New York, 2001), 7, 17–18.

27. See Wilson's review of December 1922, printed in ibid., 144–45, and his *Axel's Castle* (New York, 1931), 106.

28. Citations in Jay M. Winter, *Sites of Memory, Sites of Mourning: The Great War in European Cultural History* (Cambridge, 1995), 223; Paul Valéry, *Variety* (New York, 1927), 27–28; and Wilson, *Axel's Castle*, 66, 87.

29. Charles Loch Mowat, *Britain Between the Wars 1918–1940* (Boston, 1955), 217. For the Ulysses quote: Conrad, *Modern Times, Modern Places*, 128.

30. Cited in Williams, *Modernism* (Chapter 1, Note 20), 207.

31. Henry Hatfield, *From* The Magic Mountain; *Mann's Later Masterpieces* (Ithaca, New York, 1979), 34.

32. Thomas Mann, *The Magic Mountain*, translated by John E. Woods (New York, 1995), 487.

33. Ibid., 706.

34. Hofmannsthal to Mann, March 14, 1926, cited in Hatfield, *From The Magic Mountain*, 41.

35. Citations in Winter, *Sites of Memory, Sites of Mourning* (Note 28 above), 115, and Audoin-Rouzeau and Becker, *14–18: Understanding the Great War* (Chapter 3, Note 2), 212. For the contrasting emphasis on the growth of modernism as a result of the war, see Paul Fussell, *The Great War and Modern Memory* (Oxford, 1975). Also see George L. Mosse, *Fallen Soldiers: Reshaping the Memory of the World War* (Oxford, 1990).

36. Citation in Audoin-Rouzeau and Becker (Note 35), 223. Also see Martin Ceadel, "Attitudes to War: Pacifism and Collective Security," in Johnson (ed.), *20th Century Britain* (Chapter 2, Note 33), 229–34; and Eksteins, *Rites of Spring* (Chapter 2, Note 74), 242–99.

37. Erich Maria Remarque, *All Quiet on the Western Front* (New York, 1968), 12.

38. Citations in Hans Kohn, *The Mind of Germany: The Education of a Nation* (New York, 1960), 339, 341.

39. See John Willett, *The New Sobriety 1917–1933: Art and Politics in the Weimar Period* (London, 1978); Walter Laqueur, *Weimar: A Cultural History 1918–1933* (London, 1974); Peter Gay, *Weimar Culture: The Outsider as Insider* (New York, 1968); and Siegfried Kracauer, *From Caligari to Hitler: A Psychological History of the German Film* (Princeton, New Jersey, 1947). Also see Gordon A. Craig's chapter on "Weimar Culture" in *Germany 1866–1945* (New York, 1978).

40. Lacqueur, *Weimar*, 97.

41. In general, see Fritz K. Ringer, *The Decline of the German Mandarins: The German Academic Community 1890–1933* (Cambridge, Massachusetts, 1969).

42. For the following discussion as well as citations from *Being and Time*, see Richard Wolin, *The Politics of Being: The Political Thought of Martin Heidegger* (New York, 1990), 1–66.

43. Ibid., 22.

44. Rüdiger Safranski, *Martin Heidegger: Between Good and Evil*, translated by Ewald Osers (Cambridge, Massachusetts, 1998), 187.

45. Citations from ibid., 187–88.

46. On Freud, see Anthony Storr, *Freud* (Oxford, 1989); and Peter Gay, *Freud: A Life for Our Times* (New York, 1988).

47. Sigmund Freud, *Civilization and Its Discontents*, translated by James Strachey (New York, 1962), 59, 71.

48. Ibid., 92.

49. In general, see Stearns, *European Society in Upheaval* (Chapter 1, Note 30); and Norman Cantor, *The History of Popular Culture Since 1815* (New York, 1968).

50. Georg Kaiser, *From Morn to Midnight*, translated by Ashley Dukes (New York, 1922), 88, 91. Also see Craig, *Germany*, 497.

51. Peter N. Stearns, *The European Experience Since 1815* (New York, 1972), 265.

52. Robert Graves and Alan Hodge, *The Long Weekend: A Social History of Great Britain, 1918–1939* (New York, 1941), 131.

53. Citations in Peter Jelavich, *Berlin Carbaret* (Cambridge, Massachusetts, 1993), 170.

54. Spain introduced universal manhood suffrage in 1890, but the system was so corrupt that it can hardly be described as democratic.

55. The non-democratic states were Portugal, Spain, Byelorussia, and Russia. The two Irish states enter the total only after 1922.

56. V. Stanley Vardys, cited in Berend, *Decades of Crisis* (Chapter 1, Note 76), 162.

57. For these countries, see Matti Klinge, *The Baltic World* (Helsinki, 1994); Georg von Rauch, *The Baltic States: The Years of Independence 1917–1940*, translated by Gerald Onn (New York, 1974); Philip Longworth, *The Making of Eastern Europe* (New York, 1992); Paul Lendvai, *The Hungarians: A Thousand Years of Victory in Defeat*, translated by Ann Major (Princeton, New Jersey, 2003); Berend, *Decades of Crisis* (Chapter

1, Note 76); Glenny, *The Balkans* (Chapter 3, Note 39); L. S. Stavrianos, *The Balkans Since 1453* (New York, 2000); and Jelavich, *History of the Balkans: Twentieth Century* (Chapter 3, Note 39).

58. Cited in Longworth, *Making of Eastern Europe*, 73.

59. Quotes in Waclaw Jedrzejewicz, *Pilsudski: A Life for Poland* (New York, 1982), 185.

60. Cited in Jelavich, *History of the Balkans: Twentieth Century*, 172.

61. For the noninvolvement of the king, see Stephane Groueff, *Crown of Thorns: The Reign of King Boris III of Bulgaria 1918–1943* (London, 1987), 88–101.

62. For Austria in the 1920s, see David Clay Large, "The Death of Red Vienna," in his *Between Two Fires: Europe's Path in the 1930s* (New York, 1991), 60–74.

63. See Peter Fritzsche, *Germans into Nazis* (Cambridge, Massachusetts, 1998); Gerald D. Feldman, *The Great Disorder: Politics, Economics, and Society in the German Inflation 1914–1924* (New York, 1993); and Detlev J. K. Peukert, *The Weimar Republic: The Crisis of Classical Modernity*, translated by Ricard Deveson (New York, 1992).

64. Cited in Feldman, *The Great Disorder*, 431.

65. The situation in Luxembourg was similar. Although the Germans violated this state's neutrality, the Battle of the Frontiers in August 1914 took place farther west and the occupation experience was not as brutal as in Belgium. After the war Luxembourg's constitutional monarchy quickly democratized, including the implementation of women's suffrage. Thus its experience is more compatible with that of Holland and Scandinavia.

66. Not coincidentally, women voted in every nation that passed prohibition after the war: Finland, Norway, and the United States, as well as the country that only narrowly rejected it, Sweden.

67. Thomson, *Democracy in France* (Chapter 1, Note 37), 170–210; and McMillan, *Twentieth Century France* (Chapter 2, Note 35), 89–100.

68. Mowat, *Britain Between the Wars*; and Jon Lawrence, "The First World War and Its Aftermath," and Bernard Harris, "Unemployment and the Dole in Interwar Britain," in Johnson (ed.), *20th Century Britain* (Chapter 2, Note 33), 151–68 and 203–20, respectively.

69. Andrew Boyle, *Montagu Norman* (New York, 1967), 128.

70. Cited in Mowat, *Britain Between the Wars*, 319.

71. D. George Boyce, *Ireland 1828–1923: From Ascendancy to Democracy* (Oxford, 1992), 94–108; and Donal McCartney, "From Parnell to Pearse: 1891–1921," Patrick Lynch, "The Irish Free State and the Republic of Ireland: 1921–1966," and J. L. McCracken, "Northern Ireland: 1921–1966," in T. W. Moody and F. X. Martin, *The Course of Irish History* (Lanham, Maryland, 2001), 245–59, 272–87 and 262–71, respectively.

72. Cited in Seamus Dunn and Thomas W. Hennessey, "Ireland," in Seamus Dunn and T. G. Fraser, *Europe and Ethnicity: The First World War and Contemporary Ethnic Conflict* (London, 1996), 193.

73. The thirteen states identified above, plus Portugal and Spain, were not democratic. The nineteen democracies in the total of thirty-four include the two Irelands. Northern Ireland was not a sovereign state or, like the Irish Free State, an autonomous dominion, but rather part of the United Kingdom. Because London rarely interfered in matters falling under the jurisdiction of the parliament in Belfast until the 1970s, however, it is included among the sovereign states.

74. For this argument, see Spencer R. Weart, *Never at War: Why Democracies Will Not Fight One Another* (New Haven, Connecticut, 1998).

75. Catherine Merridale, *Night of Stone: Death and Memory in Twentieth Century Russia* (New York, 2001), 111. For the following, also see pp. 112 and 160.

76. Mikhail Bulgakov, *The White Guard*, translated by Michael Glenny (Chicago, 1987), 297.

77. For the Soviet Union in the 1920s, see the works cited in Chapter 3, Note 28; Merridale, *Night of Stone* (Note 75 in this chapter); as well as works drawn on and cited later in this chapter.

78. Socialism in Marxist parlance refers to the period after the revolution when the proletariat introduces collective forms of ownership and begins to expand production. Socialism lasts until a time of material superabundance, known as "communism," is attained. Lenin preferred to use the name "communist" for organizational purposes—Communist International, Communist Party, and so on—in order to distinguish his party from the pre-war Socialists, whom he believed had betrayed Marxism by supporting the war. For differing western uses of "socialism," also see Chapter 1, Note 29.

79. Figes, *People's Tragedy* (Chapter 1, Note 45), 746, 745.

80. See Note 78 as well as Chapter 1, Note 29.

81. Cited in Alexander Erlich, *The Soviet Industrialization Debate, 1924–1928* (Cambridge, Massachusetts, 1967), 4.

82. Cited in Bernice Glatzer Rosenthal and Martha Bohachevsky-Chomiak (eds.), *A Revolution of the Spirit: Crisis of Value in Russia, 1890–1924* (New York, 1990), 273. For early Soviet culture, also see Orlando Figes, *Natasha's Dance: A Cultural History of Russia* (New York, 2002), 434–88.

83. Cited in Figes, *People's Tragedy*, 737.

84. Cited in Smithsonian Institution, *Russian and Soviet Paintings 1900–1930* (Washington, DC, 1988), 40.

85. Cited in Isaac Deutscher, *The Prophet Armed: Trotsky, 1879–1921* (New York, 1965), 493.

86. Cited in ibid., 500.

87. Cited in Ulam, *The Bolsheviks* (Chapter 1, Note 45), 69.

88. Figes, *People's Tragedy*, 758 (both citations).

89. Cited in ibid., 749.

90. Cited in Deutscher, *Prophet Armed*, 518.

91. Cited in Ulam, *Bolsheviks*, 461.

92. Cited in Alexander N. Yakovlev, *A Century of Violence in Soviet Russia*, translated by Anthony Austin (New Haven, Connecticut, 2002), 108.

93. Cited in Ulam, *Bolsheviks*, 472–73.

94. Isaac Deutscher, *Stalin: A Political Biography* (New York, 1967), 233.

95. Citations in Figes, *People's Tragedy*, 785, 773.

96. Citations in Ulam, *Bolsheviks*, 462, 472.

97. Citations in Figes, *People's Tragedy*, 771.

98. Citations in ibid., 37, 44.

99. Dmitri Volkogonov, *Stalin: Triumph and Tragedy*, translated by Harold Shukman (London, 1991), xxii.

100. Cited in Deutscher, *Stalin*, 328.

CHAPTER 5

1. For Northeim in early 1932, see William Sheridan Allen, *The Nazi Seizure of Power: The Experience of a Single German Town 1922–1945* (New York, 1984), 88–89, 93, 103.

2. For the events of February 2, 1932, in Geneva, see Elmer Bendiner, *A Time for Angels: The Tragicomic History of the League of Nations* (New York, 1975), 271–272.

3. See John Kenneth Galbraith, *The Great Crash: 1929* (Boston, 1988). For studies covering the 1930s, see the sources in Chapter IV, Note 1; Raymond J. Sontag, *A Broken World: 1919–1939* (New York, 1971); David Clay Large, *Between Two Fires: Europe's Path in the 1930s* (New York, 1991); Piers Brendon, *The Dark Valley: A Panorama of the 1930s* (New York, 2000); and Eley, *Forging Democracy* (Chapter 1, Note 49).

4. For a variety of arguments about the origins of the Great Depression, see W. Arthur Lewis, *Economic Survey: 1919–1939* (London, 1966); Charles P. Kindleberger, *The World in Depression, 1929–1939* (Berkeley, California, 1986); Gerold Ambrosius and William H. Hubbard, *A Social and Economic History of Twentieth-Century Europe*

(Cambridge, Massachusetts, 1989); Gilbert Ziebura, *World Economy and World Politics, 1924–1931: From Reconstruction to Collapse* (Oxford, 1990); Barry Eichengreen, *Golden Fetters: The Gold Standard and the Great Depression, 1919–1939* (New York, 1996); and Charles H. Feinstein et al., *The European Economy Between the Wars* (Oxford, 1997).

5. Citations in Bernard Harris, "Unemployment and the Dole in Interwar Britain," in Johnson (ed.), *20th Century Britain* (Chapter 2, Note 33), 217–18; and Large, *Between Two Fires*, 187.

6. Allen, *Nazi Seizure of Power*, 42.

7. Cited in ibid., 42.

8. Cited in Charles Loch Mowat, *Britain Between the Wars 1918–1940* (Chicago, 1955), 420.

9. Aldous Huxley, *Brave New World* (New York, 1969), 25.

10. Ibid., 163.

11. Weart, *Never at War* (Chapter 4, Note 74).

12. Ian Kershaw prefers a more gradual phasing-in of this tactic after 1922–1923, with increasing emphasis after the 1928 elections. See *The Hitler Myth: Image and Reality in the Third Reich* (Oxford, 1989), 231–33. For Nazi opportunism in this regard, also see Ian Kershaw, *Hitler 1889–1936: Hubris* (New York, 1998), 308–09, 330; and Sarah Gordon, *Hitler, Germans, and the "Jewish Question"* (Princeton, New Jersey, 1984), 67–69. A recent prominent historian, Richard J. Evans, *The Coming of the Third Reich* (New York, 2004), 257, finds this tactic fully employed by 1930: "Anti-Semitic slogans would be used when addressing groups to whom they might have an appeal; where they were clearly not working, they were abandoned."

13. Voting statistics provide a measure, admittedly very crude, of anti-Semitic activism in Germany. Votes cast for anti-Semitic parties and the Conservative Party, whose agrarian lobby, the Farmers' League, employed anti-Jewish propaganda, totaled 11.6 percent and 10.1 percent, respectively, in 1907 and 1912. Conservative votes cast by tolerant types were probably balanced by votes cast for other parties by anti-Semites. Applying the same method for the postwar period—counting now the Nazis, German National Peoples' Party, and other splinter groups—the percentage jumps to 30.3 in June 1924 and 25.2 in 1928. The fact that subsequent elections saw the figure rise steadily from 35.8 in 1930 to 53.4 in 1933 probably reflected a latent anti-Semitism becoming more active—Germans, in other words, who had never thought of Jews as Germans but were tolerant of Jewish legal equality, now concluding because of the war or hard economic times, however, that the experiment had failed and these rights should be rescinded. For the statistics, see Koppel S. Pinson, *Modern Germany: Its History and Civilization* (New York, 1966), 602–04.

14. Hitler to Hepp, February 5, 1915, printed in Werner Maser, *Hitler's Letters and Notes* (New York, 1976), 88.

15. Cited in Kershaw, *Hitler*, 152.

16. Cited in Gerald Fleming, *Hitler and the Final Solution* (Berkeley, California, 1982), 17.

17. Adolf Hitler, *Mein Kampf*, translated by Ralph Manheim (Boston, 1971), 679.

18. See George L. Mosse, *The Nationalization of the Masses: Political Symbolism and Mass Movements in Germany from the Napoleonic Wars Through the Third Reich* (Ithaca, New York, 1991).

19. Cited in Jackson J. Spielvogel, *Hitler and Nazi Germany: A History* (Upper Saddle River, New Jersey, 1996), 132.

20. Claudia Koonz, "Some Political Implications of Separatism: German Women Between Democracy and Nazism, 1928–1934," in Judith Friedlander et al. (eds.), *Women in Culture and Politics: A Century of Change* (Bloomington, Indiana, 1986), 274.

21. See Helen L. Boak, " 'Our Last Hope': Women's Votes for Hitler—A Reappraisal," *German Studies Review* 12/2 (1989): 289–310.

22. Cited in George Scott, *The Rise and Fall of the League of Nations* (New York, 1973), 259.

23. F. P. Walters, *A History of the League of Nations* (London, 1967), 515.

24. Phipps to Simon, November 21, 1933, and January 31, 1934, Documents on British Foreign Policy, Second Series, Vol. VI, No. 60, pp. 90–91, 363, 365.

25. Cited in Alfred F. Havighurst, *Twentieth-Century Britain* (New York, 1962), 241.

26. Cited in Large, *Between Two Fires*, 80.

27. The article is printed in Thomas G. Barnes and Gerald D. Feldman (eds.), *Breakdown and Rebirth 1914 to the Present* (Boston, 1972), 102–06. Unless otherwise noted, quotes that follow are from this translation.

28. Cited in Smith, *Modern Italy* (Chapter 1, Note 47), 365.

29. Ibid., 342.

30. *The London Economist*, 1935, is cited in Gordon A. Craig, *Europe Since 1815* (New York, 1966), 606.

31. Cited in Smith, *Modern Italy*, 349.

32. Victoria de Grazia, "How Mussolini Ruled Italian Women," in Thébaud (ed.), *History of Women* (Chapter 1, Note 23), 5: 135.

33. Citations from ibid., 134, 138–39.

34. Cited in ibid., 355.

35. Cited in ibid., 343–44.

36. Citations in MacGregor Knox, *Common Destiny: Dictatorship, Foreign Policy, and War in Fascist Italy and Nazi Germany* (Cambridge, 2000), 100, 97.

37. Ibid., 96.

38. Cited in Spielvogel, *Hitler and Nazi Germany*, 130.

39. Cited in ibid., 138.

40. Cited in ibid., 82.

41. Cited in Gisela Bock, "Nazi Gender Policies and Women's History," in Thébaud (ed.), *History of Women*, 5: 154.

42. Cited in Koonz, *Mothers in the Fatherland* (Chapter 3, Note 78), 187.

43. Translated as: "The wheels are turning for the victory—A baby carriage for the next war."

44. For much of the following, see Bock, "Nazi Gender Policies," 149–76; and Richard Overy, *War and Economy in the Third Reich* (Oxford, 1992), 303–11.

45. For public response to Nazi measures in 1933, see David Bankier, *The Germans and the Final Solution: Public Opinion Under Nazism* (Oxford, 1992), 69, as well as the selections by Heide Gerstenberger, Otto Kulka, and Richard Breitman in David Bankier (ed.), *Probing the Depths of German Antisemitism: German Society and the Persecution of the Jews, 1933–1941* (New York and Jerusalem, 2000), 27–33, 273–74, 506–08. Also see Notes 12 and 13 in this chapter.

46. Cited in Kershaw, *Hitler*, 559.

47. Cited in ibid., 573.

48. William L. Shirer, *The Rise and Fall of the Third Reich: A History of Nazi Germany* (New York, 1960), 247–48.

49. See Bankier, *Germans and the Final Solution*, 67–81.

50. Cited in Robert Gellately, *Backing Hitler: Concent and Coercion in Nazi Germany* (Oxford, 2001), 263. Also see Gellately's discussion on pp. 125–26.

51. Ibid., 48.

52. Cited in ibid., 65, 205.

53. Printed in Barnes and Feldman (eds.), *Breakdown and Rebirth*, 132–33.

54. For French inaction in 1936, see Stephen A. Schuker, "France and the Remilitarization of the Rhineland, 1936," *French Historical Studies* 14/3 (Spring, 1986): 299–338; and P. M. H. Bell, *The Origins of the Second World War in Europe* (London, 1990), 208–12.

55. See McMillan, *Twentieth Century France* (Chapter 2, Note 35), 101–23; and J. Jackson, *The Popular Front in France: Defending Democracy 1934–1938* (Cambridge, 1988).

56. Cited in Paul Preston, *The Spanish Civil War 1936–1939* (Chicago, 1986), 70.

57. See ibid (Preston, *Spanish Civil War*); Raymond Carr, *Modern Spain 1875–1980* (Oxford, 1980); Robert Payne, *The Civil War in Spain 1936—939* (New York, 1970); and Gerald Brenan, *The Spanish Labyrinth: An Account of the Social and Political Background of the Spanish Civil War* (Cambridge, 1943).

58. Cited in Preston, *Spanish Civil War*, 59.

59. Large, *Between Two Fires*, 265.

60. Cited in ibid., 265.

61. See Dudley Baines, "Recovery from Depression," in Johnson (ed.), *20th Century Britain*, 188–202.

62. Cited in Havighurst, *Twentieth-Century Britain*, 248, 251. Also see Mowat, *Britain Between the Wars*.

63. The survey was conducted between November 1934 and June 1935. See Martin Ceadel, "Attitudes to War: Pacifism and Collective Security," in Johnson (ed.), *20th Century Britain*, 236–37.

64. Cited in Havighurst, *Twentieth-Century Britain*, 248.

65. For Chamberlain and his policy of appeasement, see the articles in Patrick Finney (ed.), *The Origins of the Second World War* (London, 1997); and Gordon Martel (ed.), *The Origins of the Second World War Reconsidered: A. J. P. Taylor and the Historians* (London, 1999).

66. Citations in Sidney Aster, " 'Guilty Men': the Case of Neville Chamberlain," excerpted in Finney, *Origins*, 63.

67. All citations are from ibid., 66, 71, 72.

68. *B*elgium, *N*etherlands, and *Lux*embourg.

69. Byron J. Nordstrom, *Scandinavia Since 1500* (Minneapolis, 2000), 281.

70. Finland adhered to the accord in 1933.

71. Nordstrom, *Scandinavia*, 297.

72. For Marxist, Soviet, and Western uses of the terms "socialism" and "communism," see Chapter 1, Note 29, and Chapter 4, Note 78.

73. See Stanley H. Cohn, *Economic Development in the Soviet Union* (Lexington, Massachusetts, 1970), 2; and Alec Nove, *An Economic History of the U.S.S.R.* (Middlesex, 1972), 191, 225.

74. Robert Service, *A History of Twentieth-Century Russia* (Cambridge, Massachusetts, 1997), 186.

75. Nove, *Economic History of the U.S.S.R.*, 223.

76. Anthony C. Sutton, *Western Technology and Soviet Economic Development, 1917–1930* (Palo Alto, California, 1968), 336–39.

77. For Soviet figures, see David R. Stone, *Hammer & Rifle: The Militarization of the Soviet Union, 1926–1933* (Lawrence, Kansas, 2000), 212, 214; for the others, Williamson Murray, *The Change in the European Balance of Power, 1938–1939* (Princeton, New Jersey, 1984), 20–21. For an assessment of Soviet success in overcoming the weaknesses and nationalist failures of Imperial Russia, see Theodore H. von Laue, *Why Lenin? Why Stalin? A Reappraisal of the Russia Revolution, 1900–1930* (New York, 1971).

78. Citations from Nove, *Economic History of the U.S.S.R.*, 141, 166.

79. Volkogonov, *Stalin* (Chapter 4, Note 99), 161.

80. Cited in Merridale, *Night of Stone* (Chapter 4, Note 75), 172.

81. Ibid., 160.

82. Volkogonov, *Stalin*, 318.

83. Merridale, *Night of Stone*, 168.

84. Merle Fainsod, *Smolensk Under Soviet Rule* (New York, 1958), 451–54.

85. GULAG is the Russian acronym for "main camp administration." See Anne Applebaum, *GULAG: A History* (New York, 2003), 50.

86. Citations from Francoise Navailh, "The Soviet Model," in Thébaud (ed.), *History of Women*, 5: 244–45.

87. David M. Glantz and Jonathan M. House, *When Titans Clashed: How the Red Army Stopped Hitler* (Lawrence, Kansas, 1995), 11.

88. Cited in Volkogonov, *Stalin*, 344.

89. Cited in Adam Ulam, *Stalin: The Man and His Era* (New York, 1975), 499.

90. For overviews of cultural trends in Interwar Europe, see Sontag, *Broken World*, 209–35; Eric Hobsbawm, *The Age of Extremes: A History of the World, 1914–1991* (New York, 1994), 178–98; and Berend, *Decades of Crisis* (Chapter 1, Note 76), 358–95.

91. Cited in MacKenzie and Curran, *Russia and the USSR* (Chapter 2, Note 42), 203.

92. Cited in Mina C. Klein and H. Arthur Klein, *Käthe Kollwitz: Life in Art* (New York, 1972), 132.

93. Cited in Philip V. Cannistraro and Brian R. Sullivan, *Il Duce's Other Woman: The Untold Story of Margherita Sarfatti, Benito Mussolini's Jewish Mistress, and How She Helped Him Come to Power* (New York, 1993), 379, 395.

94. Ibid., 392.

95. See Jay W. Baird, *To Die for Germany: Heroes in the Nazi Pantheon* (Bloomington, Indiana, 1990).

96. The 1930 *Pravda* editorial is cited in MacKenzie and Curran, *Russia and the USSR*, 198.

97. See Simon Franklin's introduction to *The Master and Margarita*, translated by Michael Glenny (New York, 1992), xix.

98. Ibid., xiii.

99. Ibid., 308.

100. Volkogonov, *Stalin*, 581, 574.

101. Arthur Koestler, *Darkness at Noon* (New York, 1941), 124.

102. Ibid., 210–11.

103. The four volumes appeared in 1933, 1934, 1936, and 1943.

104. Cited in Henry Hatfield, *From the Magic Mountain: Mann's Later Masterpieces* (Ithaca, New York, 1979), 69.

105. Detlev J. K. Peukert, *Inside Nazi Germany: Conformity, Opposition, and Racism in Everyday Life*, translated by Richard Deveson (New Haven, Connecticut, 1987), 58. Also see Bankier, *Germans and the Final Solution*, 86–87, who notes that for the first time "there were large displays of shame" and that the pogrom "aroused disapproval among many who had hitherto endorsed 'moderate' anti-Semitic measures."

106. Cited in Gordon, *Hitler, Germans, and the 'Jewish Question,'* 178.

107. Cited in Leni Yahill, *The Holocaust: The Fate of European Jewry* (Oxford, 1990), 115.

108. Cited in Brendon, *Dark Valley*, 626.

109. Henderson to Halifax, March 9, 1939, printed in *Documents on British Foreign Policy*, Third Series, Vol. IV, No. 195, 215–16.

110. Cited in Gordon A. Craig, *Europe Since 1815* (New York, 1966), 722.

111. Cited in Brendon, *Dark Valley*, 629.

112. Britain was angling for Polish concessions to Germany over the free city of Danzig and the Polish Corridor. See Anna M. Cienciala, *Poland and the Western Powers, 1938–1939* (1968), excerpted in Finney, *Origins*, 420–23.

113. Cited in ibid., 630.

114. Cited in Volkogonov, *Stalin*, 348–49.

115. Gerhard L. Weinberg, *The Foreign Policy of Hitler's Germany: Starting World War II, 1937–1939* (Chicago, 1980), 618–19.

116. Cited in ibid., 349, 351.

117. Overy, *War and Economy*, 233–56.

118. Cited in Albert Speer, *Inside the Third Reich* (New York, 1970), 162.

CHAPTER 6

1. Citations in Volkogonov, *Stalin* (Chapter 4, Note 99), 402, 405, 410–11.

2. Adam Ulam, *Stalin: The Man and His Era* (New York, 1974), 540.

3. For the historiography of the war, see John Keegan, *The Battle for History: Re-Fighting World War II* (New York, 1996). For general histories of the war, see Gordon Wright, *The Ordeal of Total War 1939–1945* (New York, 1968); B. H. Liddell Hart, *History of the Second World War* (New York, 1971); M. K. Dziewanowski, *War at Any Price: World War II in Europe, 1939–1945* (Englewood Cliffs, New Jersey, 1991); Gerhard L. Weinberg, *A World at Arms: A Global History of World War II* (Cambridge, 1994); Richard Overy, *Why the Allies Won* (New York, 1997); and Williamson Murray and Allan R. Millett, *A War to Be Won: Fighting the Second World War* (Cambridge, Massachusetts, 2000).

4. Williamson Murray, *The Change in the European Balance of Power, 1938–1939: The Path to Ruin* (Princeton, New Jersey, 1984), 305.

5. Cited in Edward Spears, *Assignment to Catastrophe: Prelude to Dunkirk July 1939–May 1940* (New York, 1954), 17. The French statement reflected a growing international consensus against the blatant targeting of innocent civilians. Despite a League of Nations resolution in 1939, however, such bombing was not yet anchored well in international law. See Ward Thomas, *The Ethics of Destruction: Norms and Force in International Relations* (Ithaca, New York, 2001), 87–146.

6. Cited in Richard Breitman, *The Architect of Genocide: Himmler and the Final Solution* (New York, 1991), 43.

7. Citations in Leni Yahil, *The Holocaust: The Fate of European Jewry* (Oxford, 1990), 153, 167.

8. For the figures in this paragraph, see Volkogonov, *Stalin*, 359–60.

9. Ernest R. May, *Strange Victory: Hitler's Conquest of France* (New York, 2000), 388.

10. Cited Dziewanowski, *War at Any Price*, 101.

11. Cited in Winston Churchill, *The Second World War: Their Finest Hour* (Boston, 1949), 225–26.

12. Citations in Dziewanowski, *War at Any Price*, 121, 124.

13. The latest history is Richard Overy, *The Battle of Britain: The Myth and the Reality* (New York, 2001).

14. Despite appearances, Roosevelt was probably content merely to aid Britain short of actual war. See Weinberg, *A World at Arms*, 239–45.

15. See Andreas Hillgruber, *Germany and the Two World Wars*, translated by William C. Kirby (London, 1981), 78–89.

16. For the eastern front, see Glantz and House, *When Titans Clashed* (Chapter 5, Note 87).

17. For the orders, see Hannes Heer, "Killing Fields: Die Wehrmacht und der Holocaust," in Hannes Heer and Klaus Naumann (eds.), *Vernichtungskrieg: Verbrechen der Wehrmacht 1941 bis 1944* (Hamburg, 1995), 58.

18. Harold Deutsch and Dennis Showalter (eds.), *What If? Strategic Alternatives of WWII* (Chicago, 1997), 99–102.

19. Cited in Overy, *Why the Allies Won*, 201–02. Also see Overy's *War and Economy in the Third Reich* (Oxford, 1995), 175–315.

20. Deutsch and Showalter, *What If?*, 198.

21. Interviewed in the History Channel documentary *War of the Century*, Part 3: "Learning to Win."

22. Cited in David Fraser, *Knight's Cross: A Life of Field Marshal Erwin Rommel* (New York, 1995), 432.

23. See Kershaw, *Hitler Myth*, 189–99.

24. Heinz Guderian, cited in David M. Glanz and Jonathan M. House, *The Battle of Kursk* (Lawrence, Kansas, 1999), 277.

25. Cited in ibid., 277.

26. Cited in Merridale, *Night of Stone* (Chapter 4, Note 75), 244.

27. Cited in ibid., 245.

28. Cited in ibid., 222.

29. Overy, *War and Economy*, 309.

30. Cited in ibid., 309.

31. Koonz, *Mothers in the Fatherland* (Chapter 3, Note 78), 175.

32. For the air war, see Overy, *Why the Allies Won*, 101–33.

33. Uwe Siemon-Netto, "*Sonderweg*: The Closing of the German Mind," *The National Interest* 70 (Winter 2002/03): 34.

34. See Kershaw, *Hitler Myth*, 200–03.

35. The so-called Declaration of the United Nations, not to be confused with the later international organization of the same name. For "Big Three" relations during the war, see William Hardy McNeill, *America, Britain, and Russia: Their Cooperation and Conflict 1941–1946* (Oxford, 1953); Herbert Feis, *Churchill-Roosevelt-Stalin: The War They Waged and the Peace They Sought* (Princeton, New Jersey, 1967); and Weinberg, *World at Arms*, 722–49.

36. See Norman Rich, *Hitler's War Aims: The Establishment of the New Order* (New York, 1974).

37. See Werner Rings, *Living with the Enemy* (London, 1982); Gerhard Hirschfeld and Patrick Marsh, *Collaboration in France: Politics and Culture During the Nazi Occupation, 1940–1944* (Oxford, 1989); Martin Conway, *Collaboration in Belgium* (New Haven, Connecticut, 1993); Werner Warmbrunn, *The Dutch Under German Occupation, 1940–1945* (Stanford, California, 1983), and *The German Occupation of Belgium 1940–1944* (New York, 1993); and Hans Fredrik Dahl, *Quisling: A Study in Treachery* (Cambridge, 1999).

38. For the European resistance, see Henri Michel, *The Shadow War: European Resistance, 1939–1945*, translated by Richard Barry (New York, 1972); Jorgen Haestrup, *European Resistance Movements (1939–1945): A Complete History* (Westport, Connecticut, 1981); and Jacques Sémelin, *Unarmed Against Hitler*, translated by Suzan Husserl-Kapit (Westport, Connecticut, 1993).

39. In 1937 Mussolini had referred to the "axis" running between Rome and Berlin, a label used subsequently to describe their alliance as well as the military tie to Japan.

40. Churchill's orders to SOE are cited in Wright, *Ordeal of Total War*, 146.

41. Robert O. Paxton, *Vichy France: Old Guard and New Order 1940–1944* (New York, 1972), 292–93. Also see H. R. Kedward, *In Search of the Maquis* (Oxford, 1993).

42. Charles F. Delzell, *Mussolini's Enemies: The Italian Anti-Fascist Resistance* (Princeton, New Jersey, 1961). Also see Richard Lamb, *War in Italy: A Brutal Story* (London, 1993).

43. Victoria de Grazia, "How Mussolini Ruled Italian Women," in Thébaud (ed.), *History of Women* (Chapter 1, Note 23), 146.

44. On Greece, see Mark Mazower, *Inside Hitler's Greece* (New Haven, Connecticut, 1993).

45. Alex N. Dragnich, *Serbs and Croats: The Struggle in Yugoslavia* (San Diego, 1992), 103. Estimates of the number of Serbs massacred vary from three-hundred thousand to one million, but a "generally accepted figure" is five-hundred thousand to seven-hundred thousand. Also see L. S. Stavrianos, *The Balkans Since 1453* (New York, 2000), 772.

46. Yahil, *Holocaust*, 463.

47. Cited in ibid., 463.

48. See Yisrael Gutman, *Resistance: The Warsaw Ghetto Uprising* (Boston, 1994).

49. See Hannes Heer, "Killing Fields," and "Die Logik des Vernichtungskrieges: Wehrmacht und Partisanenkampf," in Heer and Naumann (eds.), *Vernichtungskrieg*, 65–69 and 104–31, respectively.

50. On genocide, see Raul Hilberg, *The Destruction of the European Jews* (Chicago, 1961), 3 cols; Yahil, *Holocaust*; Breitman, *Architect of Genocide*; Henry Friedlander, *The Origins of Nazi Genocide: From Euthanasia to the Final Solution* (Chapel Hill, 1995); Saul Friedlander, *Nazi Germany and the Jews: The Era of Persecution, 1933–1939* (New York, 1997); Marion A. Kaplan, *Between Dignity and Despair: Jewish Life in Nazi Germany* (New York, 1998); Christopher Browning, *The Origins of the Final Solution: The Evolution of Nazi Jewish Policy, September 1939–March 1942* (Lincoln, Nebraska, 2003); and other sources cited below.

51. Cited in Yahil, *Holocaust*, 115.

52. Breitman, *Architect of Genocide*, 65. For historical debates about the Holocaust, see Christopher Browning, *The Path to Genocide: Essays on Launching the Final Solution* (Cambridge, 1992); Abraham J. Peck, *The Holocaust and History: The Known, the Unknown, the Disputed, and the Reexamined* (Bloomington, Indiana, 1998); and Omer Bartov (ed.), *Holocaust: Origins, Implementation, and Aftermath* (London, 2000).

53. Daniel Jonah Goldhagen, *Hitler's Willing Executioners: Ordinary Germans and the Holocaust* (New York, 1996), argues that anti-Semitism was so deeply engrained in German society that most ordinary Germans were capable of participating in Judeocide. Although his thesis is greatly exaggerated, there were nevertheless an alarming number of willing executioners. The numbers of Germans ready to execute Jews in 1932 was at least as high as the S.A. membership of four-hundred thousand, or about 1 percent of the eligible electorate. The fact that S.A. marching songs glorified spilling Jewish blood meant that members, whether they joined for this reason or not, would soon be willing to shoot. If we take S.A. membership in 1934 as the more appropriate measure, the nearly three million storm troopers represented about 6.6 percent of the over forty-five million voters. Immediate postwar surveys of German attitudes toward the Jews conducted by the U.S. Army, however, determined that 18 percent were unreconstructed Nazis exhibiting intense anti-Semitism—and this 1946 poll probably underestimated the wartime peak. Such figures offer only approximate measurements, but it seems reasonably certain that radical Judeophobia worsened greatly over the thirteen years of Hitler's rule. There occurred a "profound moral brutalization in Germany," writes Ulrich Herbert. [Cited in Robert Gellately, *Backing Hitler: Concent and Coercion in Nazi Germany* (Oxford, 2001), 263.]

54. Citations in Breitman, *Architect of Genocide*, 58–59.

55. Richard Rhodes, *Masters of Death: The SS-Einsatzgruppen and the Invention of the Holocaust* (New York, 2002), 257. Also see Yahill, *Holocaust*, 254–60.

56. See Hannes Heer, "Killing Fields," in Heer and Naumann (eds.), *Vernichtungskrieg*, 57–77. Also see Christopher R. Browning, *Ordinary Men: Reserve Police Battalion 101 and the Final Solution in Poland* (New York, 1992); Omer Bartov, *The Eastern Front 1941–45: German Troops and the Barbarization of Warfare* (London, 1985); and Goldhahen, *Willing Executioners*, 167–68.

57. The minutes of the Wannsee Conference that decided on the final solution are on display in the lakeside villa where sessions were held. For the quote, see *House of the Wannsee Conference: Permanent Exhibit Guide and Reader* (Berlin, 2000), 58.

58. Walter Lacqueur, *The Terrible Secret* (Boston, 1980); Martin Gilbert, *Auschwitz and the Allies* (New York, 1981), and *The Righteous: The Unsung Heroes of the Holocaust* (London, 2002); Susan Zucotti, *The Italians and the Holocaust: Persecution, Rescue, Survival* (New York, 1987); and Deborah Dwork, *Children with a Star: Jewish Youth in Nazi Europe* (New Haven, Connecticut, 1991). For contrasting viewpoints on the controversy over the Vatican and the Holocaust, see John Cornwell, *Hitler's Pope: The Secret History of Pius XII* (New York, 2000); David Kertzer, *Popes Against the Jews: The Vatican's Role in the Rise of Modern Anti-Semitism* (New York, 2001); and José M. Sánchez, *Pius XII and the Holocaust: Understanding the Controversy* (Washington, DC, 2002).

59. For D-Day and the Normandy campaign, see Carlo D'Este, *Decision in Normandy* (London, 1983); John Keegan, *Six Armies in Normandy: From D-Day to the Liberation of Paris* (New York, 1994); Samuel W. Mitcham, Jr., *The Desert Fox in Normandy: Rommel's Defense of Fortress Europe* (Westport, Connecticut, 1997); and Adrian R. Lewis, *Omaha Beach: A Flawed Victory* (Chapel Hill, North Carolina, 2001).

60. For the German resistance, see Hermann Graml et al., *The German Resistance to Hitler* (Berkeley, California, 1970).

61. Norman Davies, *God's Playground: A History of Poland* (New York, 1982), 2: 471.

62. Cited in ibid., 2: 473.

63. Cited in ibid., 2: 473.

64. The latest historian to make this claim is Edvard Radzinsky, *Stalin*, translated by H. T. Willetts (New York, 1996), 499. Also see George Bruce, *The Warsaw Uprising* (London, 1979).

65. Cited in Volkogonov, *Stalin*, 491.

66. Davies, *God's Playground*, 2: 478.

67. Cited in Thomas Powers, *Heisenberg's War: The Secret History of the German Bomb* (New York, 1993), 369.

68. This paragraph is an attempt at a synthesis of the antithetical arguments of Powers, *Heisenberg's War*, and Paul Lawrence Rose, *Heisenberg and the Nazi Atomic Bomb Project: A Study in German Culture* (Berkeley, 1998). My interpretation is closer to Powers than Rose because of primary evidence presented by Powers, which he corroborates from contemporary primary sources, that a member of Heisenberg's team, Fritz Houtermans, informed the Americans in March 1941 that his boss was delaying work on bombs as long as possible. See Powers, 93–109. Although there is much worth to Rose's book, he does not succeed, in my opinion, in discounting this evidence.

69. Michael J. Neufeld, *The Rocket and the Reich: Peenemünde and the Coming of the Ballistic Missile Era* (Cambridge, Massachusetts, 1995), 273.

70. Neufeld, *Rocket and the Reich*, 233–38, 252–54, describes the missile's problems. However, it is clear from Albert Speer, *Inside the Third Reich*, translated by Richard and Clara Winston (New York, 1970), 364–65, that the effort was underfunded. Thus 2,210 scientists worked on long-range missiles while only 355 were assigned to anti-aircraft projects.

71. Speer, *Inside the Third Reich*, 366.

72. See the classic study by James Phinney Baxter III, *Scientists Against Time* (Boston, 1946).

73. Cited in Jonathan Steele, "Tangled Memories of the Inferno," *Guardian Weekly*, February 19, 1995, 5.

74. Pierre Aycoberry, *The Social History of the Third Reich, 1933–1945*, translated by Janet Lloyd (New York, 1999), 231.

75. Norman M. Naimark, *The Russians in Germany: A History of the Soviet Zone of Occupation, 1945–1949* (Cambridge, Massachusetts, 1997), 114.

CHAPTER 7

1. For the preceding citations, see Hans Kollwitz (ed.), *The Diary and Letters of Käthe Kollwitz*, translated by Richard and Clara Winston (Evanston, Illinois, 1988), 183, 198, 196.

2. Winston Churchill's radio address of June 1940, cited in Churchill *The Second World War: Their Finest Hour* (Boston, 1949), 225–26.

3. See Mary Warnock, *The Philosophy of Sartre* (London, 1965); and Ronald Hayman, *Sartre: A Biography* (New York, 1987).

4. Citations in Jean-Paul Sartre, "Existentialism Is a Humanism," printed in James P. Sterba (ed.), *Ethics: Classical Western Texts in Feminist and Multicultural Perspectives* (New York, 2000), 320, 322; and Hayman, *Sartre*, 192–93.

5. Cited in Hayman, *Sartre*, 192.

6. Albert Camus, *The Plague*, translated by Stuart Gilbert (New York, 1968), 34–35, 144, 152, 163, 243, 277.

7. Ibid., 120–21, 278.

8. For the citation, as well as the preceding discussion, see Andreas Dorpalen, *Europe in the 20th Century: A History* (New York, 1968), 450.

9. Werner Haftmann, *Painting in the Twentieth Century* (London, 1965), 2: 326, 327.

10. Simone de Beauvoir, *The Second Sex*, translated by H. M. Parshley (New York, 1961), xvi.

11. Ibid, 2:331.

12. Ibid., 2: 331.

13. For Group 47, see Peter Demetz, *After the Fires: Recent Writing in the Germanies, Austria and Switzerland* (San Diego, 1986), 1–17.

14. Heinrich Böll, *Adam, Where Art Thou?* translated by Mervyn Savill (New York, 1955). Häcker's "Adam where were you?" ("Adam wo warst Du?") makes more sense in the God/Adam exchange than the publisher's translation for the book title.

15. Ibid., 172.

16. Karl Jaspers, *The Question of German Guilt*, translated by E. B. Ashton (New York, 1947), 32.

17. For the posters, see ibid., 47.

18. Bertold Brecht, *The Caucasian Chalk Circle*, printed in Ralph Manheim and John Willett (eds.), *Bertold Brecht: Collected Plays* (New York, 1974), 7: 229.

19. Cited in Gunilla Bergsten, *Thomas Mann's Doctor Faustus: The Sources and Structure of the Novel*, translated by Krishna Winston (Chicago, 1969), 133.

20. Thomas Mann, *Doctor Faustus: The Life of the German Composer Adrian Leverkuehn*, translated by John E. Woods (New York, 1999), 377.

21. Bergsten, *Thomas Mann's Doctor Faustus*, 162–63, 190–91; and Henry Hatfield, *From the Magic Mountain: Mann's Later Masterpieces* (Ithaca, New York, 1979), 117.

22. Mann's *Story of a Novel* (1961), cited in ibid. (Bergsten), 190.

23. Citations from *Doctor Faustus*, 459, 418, 391.

24. Ibid., 515, 534.

25. Ernst von Salomon, *Der Fragebogen* (Hamburg, 1961), 635, 6.

26. Citations in MacKenzie and Curran, *Russia and the USSR* (Chapter 2, Note 42), 200, 202.

27. According to a party ideologist cited in Robert Chandler's introduction to Vasily Grossman, *Life and Fate: A Novel*, translated by Robert Chandler (New York, 1985), 9.

28. Ibid., 862, 537, 862.

29. Ibid., 841, 9, 150.

30. Cited in Winston S. Churchill, *The Grand Alliance* (Boston, 1950), 434.

31. Cited in R. A. C. Parker, "Alternatives to Appeasement," in Patrick Finney (ed.), *The Origins of the Second World War* (London, 1997), 218.

32. Churchill's proposals are cited in Townsend Hoopes and Douglas Brinkley, *FDR and the Creation of the U.N.* (New Haven, Connecticut, 1997), 72.

33. Ibid., 39.

34. Milovan Djilas, *Conversations with Stalin* (New York, 1962), 114.

35. Moscow insider Maxim Litvinov's description of Stalin's views is cited in Vladislav Zubok and Constantine Pleshakov, *Inside the Kremlin's Cold War: From Stalin to Khrushchev* (Cambridge, Massachusetts, 1996), 37–38.

36. See ibid., 11–19, 36–37; and Alvin Z. Rubinstein, *Soviet Foreign Policy Since World War II: Imperial and Global* (New York, 1992), 62–63.

37. Zubok and Pleshakov, *Inside the Kremlin's Cold War*, 39.

38. Charter of the United Nations, printed in Hoopes and Brinkley, *FDR*, 223.

39. Korman, *The Right of Conquest* (Chapter 1, Note 7), 242.

40. Cited in Gary Jonathan Bass, *Stay the Hand of Vengeance: The Politics of War Crimes Tribunals* (Princeton, New Jersey, 2000), 195.

41. See Justice Robert H. Jackson's pre-trial comments of July 23, 1945, and Trainin's reply, printed in Michael R. Marrus, *The Nuremberg War Crimes Trial 1945–46: A Documentary History* (Boston, 1997), 45–46.

42. Cited in Bass, *Stay the Hand*, 200.

43. For all numbers here, see Jeffrey Herf, *Divided Memory: The Nazi Past in the Two Germanys* (Cambridge, Massachusetts, 1997), 72–73, 206.

44. For the most recent discussions of the Cold War, see William I. Hitchcock, *The Struggle for Europe: The Turbulent History of a Divided Continent 1845–2002* (New York, 2002); W. R. Smyser, *From Yalta to Berlin: The Cold War Struggle over Germany* (New York, 1999); Ronald E. Powaski, *Cold War: The United States and the Soviet Union,*

1917–1991 (Oxford, 1998); John Gaddis, *We Now Know: Rethinking Cold War History* (Oxford, 1997); and Zubok and Pleshakov, *Inside the Kremlin's Cold War* (Note 35). Also see the other sources cited in this chapter.

45. The London *Times* and Crowley, respectively, are cited in William Appleman Williams, *The Tragedy of American Diplomacy* (New York, 1972), 257, 241.

46. Citations in William Hardy McNeill, *America Britain and Russia: Their Co-operation and Conflict 1941–1946* (New York, 1970), 700 (note 2), and Norman Davies, *God's Playground: A History of Poland* (New York, 1982), 2: 558.

47. McNeill, *America Britain and Russia*, 698 (note 3).

48. Cited in Williams, *Tragedy*, 240.

49. For Stalin's alarmed reaction, see Zubok and Pleshakov, *Inside the Kremlin's Cold War*, 40–46, and Edvard Radzinsky, *Stalin*, translated by H. T. Willetts (New York, 1997), 512–15.

50. Order of citations in Radzinsky, *Stalin*, 511; Powaski, *Cold War*, 68, 69; Walter LaFeber, *America, Russia and the Cold War 1945–1990* (New York, 1991), 29; Williams, *Tragedy*, 260; Smyser, *Yalta to Berlin*, 28; and Edward H. Judge and John W. Langdon, *The Cold War: A History Through Documents* (Upper Saddle River, New Jersey, 1999), 18.

51. Glanz and House, *When Titans Clashed* (Chapter 5, Note 87), 232.

52. Volkogonov, *Stalin* (Chapter 4, Note 99), 531.

53. Gaddis, *We Now Know*, 116. Also see Wilfried Loth, *Stalin's ungeliebtes Kind* (Berlin, 1994), 29.

54. Naimark, *The Russians in Germany* (Chapter 6, Note 75), 169.

55. B. U. Ratchford and William D. Ross, *Berlin Reparations Assignment* (New York, 1947), 89–89, 69.

56. Cited in Smyser, *Yalta to Berlin*, 45.

57. Williams, *Tragedy*, 231.

58. Cited in LaFeber, *America, Russia, and the Cold War*, 62–63.

59. See ibid., 58–63; and A. S. Milward, *The Reconstruction of Western Europe 1945–1951* (London, 1984), 467, 476.

60. The Soviet reactions are cited in LaFeber, *America, Russia, and the Cold War*, 60, 69.

61. Cited in ibid., 72.

62. Smyser, *From Yalta to Berlin*, 82.

63. Cited in ibid., 82.

64. Citations in LaFeber, *America, Russia, and the Cold War*, 77.

65. For NSC-20, see Powaski, *Cold War*, 75–76.

66. For an analysis of masculinity's contribution to the Cold War, focusing on the gendered language of a famous dispatch from Moscow in 1946, see Frank Costigliola, "Demonizing the Soviets: George F. Kennan's Long Telegram," in Robert J. NcMahon and Thomas G. Patterson (eds.), *The Origins of the Cold War* (Boston, 1999), 157–74.

67. Cited in LaFeber, *America, Russia, and the Cold War*, 84.

68. For overviews, see Philip Longworth, *The Making of Eastern Europe* (New York, 1994), 38–63; and Zubok and Pleshakov, *Inside the Kremlin's Cold War*, 110–37.

69. Naimark, *Russians in Germany*, 168–69, estimates total reparations taken from East Germany at 10 billion dollars. The others paid jointly less than 1 billion dollars. Soviet war damage may have been as high as 128 billion dollars.

70. Abram Bergson and Simon Kuznets (eds.), *Economic Trends in the Soviet Union* (Cambridge, Massachusetts, 1963), 179. The totals include hundreds of mines, factories, and war-related operations that the Nazis had commandeered in their zone of control and that were now expropriated and operated directly by the Soviets.

71. Cited in Zubok and Pleshakov, *Inside the Kremlin's Cold War*, 118.

72. Cited in Glenny, *The Balkans* (Chapter 3, Note 39), 543–44.

73. Cited in Zubok and Pleshakov, *Inside the Kremlin's Cold War*, 134.

74. Cited in Eley, *Forging Democracy* (Chapter 1, Note 49), 310.

75. Cited in MacKenzie and Curran, *Russia and the USSR*, 240.

76. Citations in Merridale, *Night of Stone* (Chapter 4, Note 75), 247, 248.

77. Francoise Nevailh, "The Soviet Model," in Thébaud (ed.), *History of Women* (Chapter 1, Note 23), 5: 247.

78. Vladimir P. Naumov and Jonathan Brent, *Stalin's Last Crime: The Plot Against the Jewish Doctors, 1948–1953* (New York, 2003), advance some evidence that Stalin's police chief, Lavrenty Beria, poisoned the dictator.

79. Cited in Merridale, *Night of Stone*, 266.

80. Zubok and Pleshakov, *Inside the Kremlin's Cold War*, 178.

81. Khrushchev is cited in ibid., 179.

82. Cited in Merridale, *Night of Stone*, 259. For the relieved versus grief-stricken reactions, respectively, of the daughter-in-law and grandson of Stalin's ex-foreign minister, Maksim Litvinov, see also David Remnick, *Lenin's Tomb: The Last Days of the Soviet Empire* (New York, 1994), 13–15.

83. Cited in MacKenzie and Curran, *Russia and the USSR*, 343–44.

84. Cited in Service, *Twentieth-Century Russia* (Chapter 5, Note 74), 338. According to recent biographer William Taubman [*Khrushchev: The Man and His Era* (New York, 2003), 103, 276], Khrushchev was never quite honest with himself about what he had known in the 1930s, mixing "deception and self-deception" in trying to deal with Stalin's crimes.

85. Malenkov's program of expanded consumer production had run afoul of the military and heavy industrial managers. Molotov had lost a struggle with Khrushchev over the latter's desire to reconcile differences with Tito (see later).

86. Cited in Dmitri Volkogonov, *Autopsy for an Empire: The Seven Leaders Who Built the Soviet Regime,* translated by Harold Shukman (New York, 1998), 206.

87. Cited in Taubman, *Khrushchev*, 273–74.

88. Cited in Hitchcock, *Struggle for Europe*, 211.

89. Volkogonov, *Autopsy for an Empire*, 251. For the citations here, see pp. 248, 250, 251.

90. Cited in MacKenzie and Curran, *Russia and the USSR*, 345.

91. For decolonization, see Raymond F. Betts, *Uncertain Dimensions: Western Overseas Empires in the Twentieth Century* (Minneapolis, Minnesota, 1985); and Franz Ansprenger, *The Dissolution of the Colonial Empires* (London, 1989).

92. The former until 1965, the latter until 1997.

93. Except for Dutch New Guinea, which joined independent Indonesia in 1962.

94. Senegal, Guinea, Sierra Leone, Ivory Coast, Togo, Benin, Nigeria, Mauritania, Mali, Burkina Faso, Niger, Chad, Central African Republic, Cameroon, Gabon, Congo, Zaire, Rwanda, Burundi, Uganda, Somalia, Madagascar (Malagasy Republic), Tanzania, and Kenya.

95. Cited in Walter Lipgens, *A History of European Integration 1945–1947*, translated by P. S. Falla and A. J. Ryder (Oxford, 1982), 1: 319–20. For European integration in the 1950s, see William I. Hitchcock, *France Restored: Cold War Diplomacy and the Quest for Leadership in Europe, 1944–1954* (Chapel Hill, North Carolina, 1998) as well as his *Struggle for Europe* (Note 44), 147–55. Also see Derek W. Urwin, *The Community of Europe: A History of European Integration Since 1945* (London, 1991); John Gillingham, *Coal, Steel and the Rebirth of Europe, 1945–1955* (Cambridge, 1991); and Milward, *Reconstruction* (Note 59) and his *The European Rescue of the Nation-State* (Berkeley, California, 1992).

96. Ibid (Lipgens), 1: 440.

97. Cited in ibid., 1: 499.

98. Cited in Milward, *Reconstruction*, 393 (note 59).

99. Ibid., 393.

100. Cited in Martin J. Dedman, *The Origins and Development of the European Union 1945–1995: A History of European Integration* (London, 1996), 27.

101. Ireland, Britain, France, Italy, the Benelux states, Denmark, Norway, and Sweden.

102. Cited in Hitchcock, *Struggle for Europe*, 151.

103. See Arnold J. Zurcher, *The Struggle to Unite Europe 1940–1958* (New York, 1958), 95–126.

104. For the history of European union, see Dedman, *Origins and Development* (Note 100); Andrew Moravcsik, *The Choice for Europe: Social Purpose and State Power from Messina to Maastricht* (Ithaca, New York, 1998); Desmond Dinan, *Ever Closer Union: An Introduction to European Integration* (Boulder, Colorado, 1999); and John Gillingham, *European Integration 1950–2003: Superstate or New Market Economy?* (Cambridge, 2003). Also see the sources cited in Note 95.

105. Dedman, *Origins and Development*, 115. See Gillingham, *European Integration*, 44, for the citation.

106. For various distinctions between social democracy/socialism and communism, see Chapter 1, Note 29, and Chapter 4, Note 78. For the welfare states, see Douglas Ashford, *The Emergence of the Welfare States* (Oxford, 1987); and Gosta Esping-Andersen, *The Three Worlds of Welfare Capitalism* (Princeton, New Jersey, 1990).

107. Cited in Alfred F. Havighurst, *Twentieth-Century Britain* (New York, 1962), 367, 374.

108. Cited in ibid., 325.

109. For growth rates, see M. M. Postan, *An Economic History of Western Europe 1945–1964* (London, 1967). For the Marshall Plan, see the excellent discussion in Hitchcock, *Struggle for Europe*, 133–47, 475–76 (note 6).

110. The administration's arguments are paraphrased in LaFeber, *America, Russia, and the Cold War*, 61.

111. For the managed economies of Western Europe, see Philip Armstrong, *Capitalism Since 1945* (Cambridge, Massachusetts, 1991).

112. For overviews, see Maurice Crouzet, *The European Renaissance Since 1945* (London, 1970); Donald Sassoon, *One Hundred Years of Socialism in the Twentieth Century* (London, 1996); and Eley, *Forging Democracy* (Chapter 1, Note 49).

113. Legal competency for married women dates from 1882 in Britain, followed by Norway (1888), Finland (1919), Sweden (1920), Iceland (1923), and Denmark (1925). Full female suffrage came first in Finland (1906), followed by Norway (1913), Denmark and Iceland (1915), Sweden (1921), and Britain (1928). See Mariette Sineau, "Law and Democracy," in Thébaud (ed.), *History of Women*, 5: 500.

114. The patriarchal clauses of Napoleon's law code restricted civil competency for married women until 1956 in Holland, 1958 in Belgium, 1970 in France, and 1972 in Luxembourg. See ibid., 500, 503–08. Family law was also very conservative in Italy.

115. Holland, Denmark, Iceland, Norway, and Sweden were neutral in World War One. Finland participated marginally as a province of tsarist Russia. Iceland and Sweden saw no combat in World War Two, moreover, while Holland, Denmark, and Norway were quickly overrun in 1940, languishing until 1945 under Nazi occupation.

116. Limited legal competency for married women was granted in 1896; higher education opportunities followed in 1908; the vote and equal rights "in principle" in 1919.

117. Cited in Smith, *Changing Lives* (Chapter 1, Note 23), 524.

118. Stineau, "Law and Democracy," in Thébaud (ed.), *History of Women*, 5: 501.

119. Cited in Penny Summerfeld, *Reconstructing Women's Wartime Lives* (Manchester, 1998), 131.

120. See the discussion in ibid., 2–5.

121. Pat Thane, "Women Since 1945," in Johnson (ed.), *20th Century Britain* (Chapter 2, Note 33), 393–95, 409.

122. Pierre Ayçoberry, *The Social History of the Third Reich, 1933–1945*, translated by Janet Lloyd (New York, 1999), 344, estimates the total at between 3.3 and 4.3 million.

123. Cited in Annemarie Troeger, "German Women's Memories of World War II," in Higonnet et al. (eds.), *Behind the Lines* (Chapter 3, Note 12), 294.

124. Citations in Robert G. Moeller, *Protecting Motherhood: Women and the Family in the Politics of Postwar West Germany* (Berkeley, California, 1993), 34, 33, 14.

125. See ibid., 152–53, 155; Sineau, "Law and Democracy," in Thébaud, *History of Women*, 5: 514; and Lewis J. Edinger, *Politics in Germany: Attitudes and Processes* (Boston, 1968), 75, 77.

126. Nearly 33 percent of married women worked in 1961. See Moeller, *Protecting Motherhood*, 217. Calculated as a percentage of the female work force, married women made up 35 percent of all working women in 1950 and 45 percent in 1960. See Erica Carter, *How German Is She? Postwar West German Reconstruction and the Consuming Woman* (Ann Arbor, 1997), 37 (note 54).

127. Carter, *How German Is She?*, 104.

128. Printed in ibid., 74.

129. Ibid., 240.

130. Smith, *Changing Lives*, 529.

131. Carter, *How German Is She?*, 106.

132. See Victoria de Grazia, "How Mussolini Ruled Italian Women," in Thébaud (ed.), *History of Women*, 5: 146, 148.

133. See, for instance, Charles Delzell's *Mussolini's Enemies*. The 1961 publication makes no mention of women in the resistance.

134. Cited in Jane Jenson, "The Liberation and New Rights for French Women," in Higonnet et al. (eds.), *Behind the Lines*, 274.

135. Citations in Sarah Fishman, "Waiting for the Captive Sons of France: Prisoner of War Wives, 1940–1945," in Higonnet et al. (eds.), *Behind the Lines*, 193, 192.

136. Vichy's Family and Health Secretary bemoaned the "considerable development of prostitution by women and minors . . . and the numerous births of children with German fathers." Cited in ibid., 186.

137. For these numbers, see McMillan, *Twentieth Century France* (Chapter 2, Note 35), 151.

138. Glenny, *The Balkans*, 616. On Greece, also see Jelavich, *History of the Balkans: Twentieth Century* (Chapter 3, Note 39), 306–14, 406–38.

139. Cited in Shepard B. Clough and Salvatore Saladino, *A History of Modern Italy* (New York, 1968), 544.

140. Cited in W. Laird Kleine-Ahlbrandt, *Europe Since 1945: From Conflict to Community* (Minneapolis/Saint Paul, 1993), 116.

141. Smith, *Modern Italy* (Chapter 1, Note 47), 440. Also see Di Scala, *Italy from Revolution to Republic* (Chapter 2, Note 40), 289–305.

142. On France, see Thomson, *Democracy in France* (Chapter 1, Note 37), 237–74; and McMillan, *Twentieth Century France*, 153–67.

143. Crouzet, *European Renaissance*, 180.

144. Heuss's speech of November 1945 is cited in Herf, *Divided Memory*, 234.

145. For the surveys, see ibid., 205, 274, and Edinger, *Politics in Germany* (Note 131), 74.

146. Citations in Herf, *Divided Memory*, 217, 226. For additional discussions of the pressures on Adenauer, see Hitchcock, *Struggle for Europe* (Note 44), 147–49; and Hans-Peter Schwartz, *Adenauer*, translated by Louise Wilmot (London, 1995), 1: 475–503.

147. Cited in Herf, *Divided Memory*, 285.

CHAPTER 8

1. For Kennedy's visit, see Richard Reeves, *President Kennedy: Profile of Power* (New York, 1993), 531–37; and Smyser, *From Yalta to Berlin* (Chapter 7, Note 44), 193–99.

2. From Kennedy's speech at the Schöneberg Town Hall, June 26, 1963, printed in GPO, *Public Papers of the Presidents: John F. Kennedy, 1963* (Washington, DC, 1976), 524–25.

3. All citations from the speech in ibid.

4. Cited in Volkogonov, *Autopsy for an Empire* (Chapter 7, Note 86), 223.

5. See Allan R. Millett and Peter Maslowski, *For the Common Defense: A Military History of the United States of America* (New York, 1984), 524.

6. Citations in Zubok and Pleshakov, *Inside the Kremlin's Cold War* (Chapter 7, Note 35), 196, 198.

7. Cited in ibid., 247.

8. For missile figures, see Millett and Maslowski, *For the Common Defense*, 515–16.

9. Cited in Zubok and Pleshakov, *Inside the Kremlin's Cold War*, 192.

10. Cited in LaFeber, *Cold War* (Chapter 7, Note 50), 205.

11. Citations in Zubok and Pleshakov, *Inside the Kremlin's Cold War*, 250; and Smyser, *From Yalta to Berlin*, 155.

12. Cited in Smyser, *From Yalta to Berlin*, 155. For a recent argument that Ulbricht consistently prodded Kruschchev over the years to build the wall, see Hope M. Harrison, *Driving the Soviets Up the Wall: Soviet East German Relations, 1953–1961* (Princeton, New Jersey, 2003).

13. For the Cuban Missile Crisis, see the valuable discussions in Volkogonov, *Autopsy for an Empire*, 235–47; Zubok and Pleshakov, *Inside the Kremlin's Cold War*, 258–71; Smyser, *From Yalta to Berlin*, 183–92; William Taubman, *Khrushchev: The Man and His Era* (New York, 2003), 529–77; and especially Aleksandr Fursenko and Timothy Naftali, *"One Hell of a Gamble": Khrushchev, Castro, and Kennedy, 1958–1964* (New York, 1997).

14. Citations in Volkogonov, *Autopsy for an Empire*, 236.

15. Taubman, *Khrushchev*, 532.

16. Printed in Edward H. Judge and John W. Langdon (eds.), *The Cold War: A History Through Documents* (Saddle River, New Jersey, 1999), 120–21.

17. Cited in Powaski, *Cold War* (Chapter 7, Note 44), 144.

18. Michael R. Beschloss, *The Crisis Years: Kennedy and Khrushchev, 1960–1963* (New York, 1991), 278.

19. Cited in Powaski, *Cold War*, 144.

20. Cited in Service, *Twentieth-Century Russia* (Chapter 5, Note 74), 356.

21. For the figures and growth rates that follow, see Janet G. Chapman, "Consumption," in Abram Bergson and Simon Kuznets (eds.), *Economic Trends in the Soviet Union* (Cambridge, Massachusetts, 1963), 252, and Stanley H. Cohn, *Economic Development in the Soviet Union* (Lexington, Massachusetts, 1970), 61.

22. Cited in Volkogonov, *Autopsy for an Empire*, 209.

23. For the figures, see Alec Nove, *An Economic History of the U.S.S.R.* (Middlesex, 1972), 331, 334.

24. For statistics in this paragraph, see MacKenzie and Curran, *Russia and the USSR* (Chapter 2, Note 42), 280; Service, *History of Twentieth-Century Russia*, 375; and Nove, *Economic History of the USSR*, 362.

25. Quotations from Service, *History of Twentieth-Century Russia*, 372, 358.

26. For statistics in this paragraph, see Nove, *Economic History of the U.S.S.R.*, 353; Chapman, "Consumption," in Bergson and Kuznets (eds.), *Economic Trends*, 252; Peter Howlett, "The 'Golden Age', 1955–1973," in Johnson (ed.), *20th Century Britain* (Chapter 2, Note 33), 321–22; Richard Kuisel, *Seducing the French: The Dilemma of Americanization* (Berkeley, California, 1993), 150; MacKenzie and Curran, *Russia and the USSR*, 281; and Service, *Twentieth-Century Russia*, 409.

27. Cited in MacKenzie and Curran, *Russia and the USSR*, 257.

28. Cohn, *Economic Development in the Soviet Union*, 28.

29. Volkogonov, *Autopsy for an Empire*, 247.

30. Cited in MacKenzie and Curran, *Russia and the USSR*, 281.

31. M. C. Kaser (ed.), *The Economic History of Eastern Europe 1919–1975* (Oxford, 1986), 3: 21–24, 97–111, 185–88.

32. For Yugoslavia, see ibid., 3: 117–21, 163, 165–74, and for the quote, 170.

33. For the 1965 reforms, see Bruce Parrott, *Politics and Technology in the Soviet Union* (Cambridge, Massachusetts, 1983), 210–19.

34. For the quotations, see ibid., 213, 187; MacKenzie and Curran, *Russia and the USSR*, 278; and Charles S. Maier, *Dissolution: The Crisis of Communism and the End of East Germany* (Princeton, New Jersey, 1997), 86.

35. Kaser, *Economic History of Eastern Europe*, 3: 165–216.

36. MacKenzie and Curran, *Russia and the USSR*, 278.

37. Smyser, *From Yalta to Berlin*, 194, 196.

38. Cited in LaFeber, *America, Russia, and the Cold War*, 228–29.

39. Smyser, *From Yalta to Berlin*, 195.

40. These excerpts from De Gaulle's memoirs are cited and translated by Kuisel, *Seducing the French*, 146.

41. Peter Howlett, "The 'Golden Age,' 1955–1973," in Johnson (ed.), *20th Century Britain*, 321; Kuisel, *Seducing the French*, 150.

42. Cited in Kuisel, *Seducing the French*, 150.

43. Jean-Jacques Servan-Schreiber, *The American Challenge*, translated by Ronald Steel (New York, 1968), 274.

44. Cited in Richard Pells, *Not Like Us: How Europeans Have Loved, Hated, and Transformed American Culture Since World War II* (New York, 1997), 57.

45. Andreas Dorpalen, *Europe in the 20th Century: A History* (New York, 1968), 507.

46. Victoria de Grazia, "Changing Consumption Regimes in Europe, 1930–1970: Comparative Perspectives on the Distribution Problem," in Susan Strasser et al. (eds.), *Getting and Spending: European and American Consumer Societies in the Twentieth Century* (Cambridge, 1998), 83.

47. *Time*, April 15, 1966. Thanks to Louise Blackeney Williams for pointing out this article.

48. Kuisel, *Seducing the French*, 150–51.

49. Cited in ibid., 89.

50. Cited in ibid., 72, and the previous quote in D. W. Ellwood, "The Impact of the Marshall Plan on Italy; The Impact of Italy on the Marshall Plan," in Rob Kroes et al. (eds.), *Cultural Transmissions and Receptions: American Mass Culture in Europe* (Amsterdam, 1993), 115.

51. Cited in ibid., 116.

52. Cited in ibid., 123, and the previous quote in M. M. Postan, *An Economic History of Western Europe 1945–1964* (London, 1967), 49.

53. Pells, *Not Like Us*, 299, and for the previous quote, 299.

54. See ibid., 195, and for the quote, 202.

55. Volker R. Berghahn, *America and the Intellectual Cold Wars in Europe: Shepard Stone Between Philanthropy, Academy, and Diplomacy* (Princeton, New Jersey, 2001), 77–107.

56. Kuisel, *Seducing the French*, 34–35.

57. Servan-Schreiber, *The American Challenge*, 257.

58. Cited in Kuisel, *Seducing the French*, 109, 130.

59. Dorpalen, *Europe in the 20th Century*, 507.

60. For the citations, see Ellwood, "The Impact of the Marshall Plan on Italy," in Kroes et al., *Cultural Transmissions*, 105; Kuisel, *Seducing the French*, 99–100; and Volker R. Berghahn, "West German Reconstruction and American Industrial Culture, 1945–1960," in Reiner Pommerin (ed.), *The American Impact on Postwar Germany* (Providence, Rhode Island, 1995), 75–76. Also see Berghahn's *The Americanisation of West German Industry 1945–1973* (Cambridge, 1986).

61. Cited in Christian Kleinschmidt, *Der produktive Blick: Wahrnehmung amerikanischer und japanischer Management-und Produktionsmethoden durch deutsche Unternehmer 1950–1985* (Berlin, 2002), 237.

62. Servan-Schreiber, *The American Challenge*, 3, 8.

63. Ibid., 56; Harvey Brooks, "What's Happening to the U.S. Lead in Technology," *Harvard Business Review* (May–June 1972), 110–18.

64. For the concept of technological systems, see Gille, *The History of Techniques* (Chapter 1, Note 12), 2 vols.; and Brose, *Technology and Science* (Chapter 1, Note 12).

65. See James Phinney Baxter III, *Scientists Against Time* (Boston, 1946).

66. Ibid., 3–25, 449.

67. F. M. Scherer, "Technological Maturity and Waning Economic Growth," *Arts & Sciences* (Fall 1978), 7–11; and Robert H. Hayes and William J. Abernathy, "Managing Our Way to Economic Decline," *Harvard Business Review* (July–August 1980), 67–77.

68. Servan-Schreiber, *American Challenge*, 27.

69. See Landes, *Unbound Prometheus* (Chapter 1, Note 12), 468–537.

70. Ibid., 67, 71, 74.

71. Hayes and Abernathy, "Managing Our Way to Economic Decline," 69–70; "Falling Back in a Critical Race," *Time*, August 13, 1984.

72. For the quotations, see Parrott, *Politics and Technology*, 189. For computers in the communist bloc nations in the late 1960s, see David A. Wellman, *A Chip in the Curtain: Computer Technology in the Soviet Union* (Washington, DC, 1989), 87.

73. For the preceding quotation, see Parrott, *Politics and Technology*, 213. For problems associated with the 1965 reform, see pp. 218, 226–28.

74. Cited in Hedrick Smith, *The Russians* (New York, 1976), 309–10.

75. See Vladimir Kontorovich, "Technological Progress and Research and Development," in Michael Ellman and Vladimir Kontorovich (eds.), *The Disintegration of the Soviet Economic System* (London, 1992), 222, 233.

76. Cited in Parrott, *Politics and Technology*, 280.

77. See Servan-Schreiber, *American Challenge*, 73–74; Mervyn Matthews, *Education in the Soviet Union: Policies and Institutions Since Stalin* (London, 1982), 40–41, 206; and Jessica Tuchman Mathews' two-part article, "The Decline of Education," *Philadelphia Inquirer*, October 21–22, 1981.

78. Parrott, *Politics and Technology*, 219–25, 278–80 (p. 221 for the quote). The United States employed 534,800 scientists and engineers in R & D in 1975, or 61.5 per 10,000 of the work force. The Soviet figure was 66 per 10,000. See Trevor Buck and John Cole, *Modern Soviet Economic Performance* (Oxford, 1987), 120.

79. The Action Program of April 5, 1968, is printed in Philip Windsor and Adam Roberts, *Czechoslovakia 1968: Reform, Repression and Resistance* (London, 1969), 147.

80. Cited in Stephen Kotkin, *Armageddon Averted: The Soviet Collapse 1970–2000* (New York, 2001), 58.

81. See Eley, *Forging Democracy*, 357–60.

82. See Windsor and Roberts, *Czechoslovakia 1968*, 5.

83. Maier, *Dissolution*, 91; Ivan T. Berend, *The Hungarian Economic Reforms 1953–1988* (Cambridge, 1990), 201, 206; and Kaser, *Economic History of Eastern Europe*, 3: 172–74.

84. Windsor and Roberts, *Czechoslovakia 1968*, 72.

85. For this argument, see Maier, *Dissolution*, 59–107. For Kosygin's retreat, see Parrott, *Politics and Technology*, 249–50, and for the preceding quotations, 288, 239–40.

CHAPTER 9

1. Citations in Jose Maravall, *Dictatorship and Dissent: Workers and Students in Franco's Spain* (London, 1978), 157, 116.

2. The words of Peggy Duff, Secretary of the Campaign for Nuclear Disarmament, are cited in Sheila Rowbotham, *A Century of Women: The History of Women in Britain and the United States* (London, 1997), 345.

3. Eric Hobsbawm, *Uncommon People: Resistance, Rebellion, and Jazz* (New York, 1998), 213.

4. Cited in Allan Priaulx and Sanford J. Ungar, *The Almost Revolution: France 1968* (New York, 1969), 42. This account by two journalists covering May 1968 is a fairly reliable contemporary firsthand account. Also see Eley, *Forging Democracy* (Chapter 1, Note 49), 341–57; Hobsbawm, *Uncommon People*, 213–22; and Alain Touraine, *The*

May Movement: Revolt and Reform (New York, 1971). Touraine taught Danny the Red at Nanterre.

5. Cited in Priaulx and Ungar, *Almost Revolution*, 75, with discussion of the meaning of de Gaulle's crude expression.

6. See Michael Mitterauer, *The History of Youth* (Oxford, 1992); Richard Maltby, *Passing Parade: A History of Popular Culture in the 20th Century* (Oxford, 1989); and Anthony Sampson, *The New Europeans* (New York, 1971).

7. Cited in Priaulx and Unger, *Almost Revolution*, 58.

8. Citations are from Richard Wollin, *Heidegger's Children: Hannah Arendt, Karl Loewith, Hans Jonas, and Herbert Marcuse* (Princeton, New Jersey, 2001), 164, 168, 169, 172.

9. Cited in Claire Duchen, *Feminism in France: From May '68 to Mitterand* (London, 1986), 5.

10. Cited in Duchen, *Feminism in France*, 6.

11. That 1968 advanced democracy is the thesis of the post-1968 chapters of Eley, *Forging Democracy* (Chapter 1, Note 49). The discussion that follows places somewhat more emphasis than Eley on continuity between pre- and post-1968 developments and finds 1968's legacy moer ambiguous and harder to discern.

12. For an overview, see Eley, *Forging Democracy*, 384–404.

13. Formed in 1960, OPEC's core members—eight out of twelve—were from the Middle East: Iran, Iraq, Kuwait, Qatar, Saudi Arabia, the United Arab Emirates, Libya, and Algeria.

14. For the figures, see Volker R. Berghahn, *Modern Germany: Society, Economy and Politics in the Twentieth Century* (Cambridge, 1987), 305.

15. For contrasting American and European responses to stagflation, see David P. Calleo, *Rethinking Europe's Future* (Princeton, New Jersey, 2001), 158–71.

16. Cited in "Falling Behind in a Critical Race," *Time*, August 13, 1984.

17. In 1966 an impressive 43 percent of college-age Americans attended universities and graduate schools, while in Europe France trailed with 16, Sweden with 11, and Italy, West Germany, and Britain with 7 percent (Servan-Schreiber, *American Challenge*, 73). Almost thirty years later Finland and Norway led Europe with 51 and 45 percent in tertiary education, respectively, followed by France (43 percent), Germany (36 percent), Sweden (34 percent), Italy (32 percent), and Britain (28 percent). The United States, in the meantime, had advanced to 76 percent [*Der Fischer Weltalmanach 1995* (Frankfurt am Main, 1994), 139, 255, 321, 464, 543, 649].

18. The 1969 campaign challenge of West German Chancellor Willy Brandt is cited in Eley, *Forging Democracy*, 418.

19. For the reforms of 1969–1973, see Paul Ginsborg, *A History of Contemporary Italy: Society and Politics 1943–1988* (London, 1990), 326–31.

20. Ibid., 362.

21. Di Scala, *Italy from Revolution to Republic* (Chapter 2, Note 40), 298–99.

22. Raymond Carr and Juan Pablo Fusi, *Spain: Dictatorship to Democracy* (London, 1981), 194.

23. The Democratic Junta was founded in July 1974, the Democratic Convergence in July 1975. For these developments, see ibid., 195–213.

24. Cited in ibid., 215.

25. Ibid., 229, 228.

26. Eley, *Forging Democracy*, 414. Also see McMillan, *Twentieth Century France* (Chapter 2, Note 35), 188–90, 197–98.

27. Cited in Ginsborg, *History of Contemporary Italy*, 394, 356.

28. Cited in ibid., 402.

29. Cited in ibid., 383.

30. Cited in ibid., 381.

31. Smith, *Modern Italy* (Chapter 1, Note 47), 462.

32. Cited in Ginsborg, *History of Contemporary Italy*, 402.

33. Cited in Glenny, *The Balkans* (Chapter 3, Note 39), 620–21.

34. For European integration, see Desmond Dinan, *Ever Closer Union,* and other sources cited in Chapter 7, Notes 95 and 104.

35. According to Article 237 of the original Treaty of Rome (1957), EEC members had to unanimously approve applications of new members. See Dedman, *Origins and Development* (Chapter 7, Note 100), 115.

36. The Common Market's founding treaty of 1957 called for council majority voting in 1966.

37. See Dedman, *Origins and Development,* 115.

38. The July 1975 Council of Ministers' resolution is cited in Christopher Preston, *Enlargement and Integration in the European Union* (London, 1997), 66.

39. Cited in Loukas Tsoukalis, *The European Community and Its Mediterranean Enlargement* (London, 1981), 1.

40. Cited in Preston, *Enlargement and Integration,* 84.

41. Cited in Dinan, *Ever Closer Union,* 302.

42. For Ireland's "Troubles," see J. H. Whyte, "Ireland: 1966–82," and Richard English, "Ireland: 1982–94," in Moody and Martin, *Course of Irish History* (Chapter 4, Note 71), 288–97, 306–15, respectively; Bruce Arnold, *What Kind of Country: Modern Irish Politics, 1968–1983* (London, 1984); and Henry Patterson, *The Politics of Illusion: A Political History of the IRA* (London, 1997).

43. See Edinger, *Politics in Germany* (Chapter 7, Note 131) 75, 77. The latter poll was 1965.

44. Cited in Hannah Vogt, *The Burden of Guilt: A Short History of Germany 1914–1945,* translated by Herbert Strauss (New York, 1964), xiii.

45. Cited in ibid., v.

46. Cited in Eley, *Forging Democracy,* 418.

47. Henry Ashby Turner Jr., *Germany from Partition to Reunification* (New Haven, Connecticut, 1992), 116.

48. Peter Demetz, *After the Fires: Recent Writing in the Germanies, Austria and Switzerland* (San Diego, 1986), 371, 365.

49. Ibid., 92.

50. Cited in Eley, *Forging Democracy,* 418.

51. Calleo, *Rethinking Europe's Future,* 104.

52. The Helsinki Accords of 1975 (see Chapter 10) satisfied this latter condition.

53. Cited in Andrei S. Markovits and Philip S. Gorski, *The German Left: Red, Green and Beyond* (Oxford, 1993), 96–97.

54. Ibid., 99.

55. The lament of Willy Brandt is cited in ibid., 81.

56. Herf, *Divided Memory* (Chapter 7, Note 43), 362.

57. Richard J. Evans, *In Hitler's Shadow: West German Historians and the Attempt to Escape from the Nazi Past* (New York, 1989), 21. Also see Charles S. Maier, *The Unmasterable Past: History, Holocaust, and German National Identity* (Cambridge, Massachusetts, 1988).

58. Hermann Kurthen, "Antisemitism and Xenophobia in United Germany: How the Burden of the Past Affects the Present," in Hermann Kurthen et al. (eds.), *Antisemitism and Xenophobia in Germany After Unification* (Oxford, 1997), 46, 71.

59. Heuss's 1945 speech is cited in Herf, *Divided Memory,* 234. For synopses of the speeches of Schmidt, Kohl, and Weizsaecker, see pp. 346–47, 353, 355–59.

60. See the discussion in Chapters 1, 3, and 7.

61. Pat Thane, "Women Since 1945," in Johnson (ed.), *20th Century Britain* (Chapter 2, Note 33), 409.

62. Cited in Eley, *Forging Democracy,* 368–69.

63. Cited in Duchen, *Feminism in France,* 7.

64. Smith, *Changing Lives* (Chapter 1, Note 23), 530.

65. Cited in Markovits and Gorski, *The German Left,* 90.

66. Ibid., 92–93; Sineau, "Law and Democracy," in Thébaud (ed.), *History of Women* (Chapter 1, Note 23), 5: 500, 521.

67. For this paragraph, see Eley, *Forging Democracy*, 464–65, 485–86.

68. For environmental legislation in Europe, see Martin Jaenicke et al. (eds.), *National Environmental Policies: A Comparative Study of Capacity-Building* (Berlin, 1997).

69. The government of Labor Party leader Trygve Bratteli introduced a series of reforms in 1971, including far-reaching powers for local government to curb environmental hazards of all sorts.

70. Cited in James Murray Luck, *A History of Switzerland* (Palo Alto, California, 1985), 817.

71. For these trends, see Eley, *Forging Democracy*, 484–86.

72. Wieland Schmied, "Hundertwasser and His Painting," *Hundertwasser: Kunsthaus Wien* (Cologne, 2002), 42.

73. See Mike Edwards, "Lethal Legacy: Pollution in the Former USSR," *National Geographic* 186/2 (August 1994), 102–08.

74. Eley, *Forging Democracy*, 484.

75. See the separate national chapters in Jaenicke et al. (eds.), *National Environmental Policies*.

76. Cited in Dinan, *Ever Closer Union* (Chapter 7, N. 104), 409.

77. See the EEA reports of June 24, 1999, http://reports.eea.eu.int/SPE19990625/en/page002.html, and February 23, 2001, http://org.eea.eu.int/documents/speeches/stockholm_2001.

78. Sineau, "Law and Democracy," in Thébaud, *History of Women*, 5; 517.

CHAPTER 10

1. See Volkogonov, *Autopsy for an Empire* (Chapter 7, Note 86), 324–25.

2. SALT consisted of two documents. One limited each country to two sites protected by anti-ballistic missile systems (ABMs), thus preserving retaliatory capabilities and providing an incentive not to strike. The second document limited each side to the number of long-range missiles in existence or under construction in 1972: 1,710 American versus 2,328 Soviet. The United States accepted this disparity because its ICBMs possessed multiple warheads (MIRVs). See Powaski, *Cold War* (Chapter 7, Note 44), 183–84.

3. For Helsinki, see ibid., 198–99.

4. For the SS–20 story, see ibid., 221–22, and Helmut Schmidt's memoirs, *Men and Powers*, translated by Ruth Hein (New York, 1989), 63–78. This above passage relies mainly, however, on Dale R. Herspring, *The Soviet High Command 1967–1989: Personalities and Politics* (Princeton, New Jersey, 1990), 119–65, which provides insight into the general imperative of détente and into technological modernization in the Soviet military in a climate of general economic decline and budget cutbacks. According to the CIA it was around 1977 that the Soviets halved the rate of growth of military spending, which remained low until the early 1980s (p. 154). For the Brezhnev quote, see p. 129.

5. For technical details and the espionage coup, see Miles M. Costick, "Military Aspects of Technology Transfer," in Hans-Joachim Veen (ed.), *From Brezhnev to Gorbachev: Domestic Affairs and Soviet Foreign Policy* (New York, 1984), 85–88. The SS-20 possessed three independently targetable warheads (MIRVs), the SS-18 between twelve and eighteen. "Everything from the skeleton to the metallurgical parts, from the technology of the electronic sub-systems to the inertial guidance systems, MIRVing mechanism and so on, originated in the West," writes Costick (p. 86).

6. Khrushchev is cited in Peter Schweitzer, *Reagan's War: The Epic Story of His Forty-Year Struggle and Final Triumph over Communism* (New York, 2002), 155–56.

7. Cited in ibid., 218. For the figures, see 218–19.

8. Parrott, *Politics and Technology* (Chapter 8, Note 33), 281–84; Wellman, *Chip in the Curtain* (Chapter 8, Note 72), 87, 92–93.

9. Brezhnev's 1982 remarks are cited in Volkogonov, *Autopsy for an Empire*, 321.

10. Kantorovich, "Technological Progress and Research and Development," in Ellman and Kantorovich (eds.), *Disintegration* (Chapter 8, Note 75), 231. For the statistics, see pp. 222, 226.

11. Cited in "Closing the Gap with the West," *Time*, June 23, 1980, 60.

12. Cited in "Pitfalls in the Planning," ibid., 48.

13. Volkogonov, *Autopsy for an Empire*, 404, 426.

14. Smith, *Russians* (Chapter 8, Note 74), 316–17.

15. Cited in Volkogonov, *Autopsy for an Empire*, 355.

16. Herspring, *Soviet High Command*, 167.

17. For the figures in this paragraph, see LaFeber, *Cold War* (Chapter 7, Note 50), 303; Schweitzer, *Reagan's War*, 218–19; and Calleo, *Rethinking Europe's Future* (Chapter 9, Note 15), 115, 303. In absolute budget terms, the United States increased defense spending 40 percent from 1980 to 1985, the Soviets 55 percent during the 1981–1985 plan years.

18. Cited in Volkogonov, *Autopsy for an Empire*, 281.

19. Cited in MacKenzie and Curran, *Russia and the USSR* (Chapter 2, Note 42), 281.

20. Yuri Trifonov, *The House on the Embankment*, translated by Michael Glenny (Evanston, Illinois, 1999), 197.

21. See MacKenzie and Curran, *Russia and the USSR*, 330, and Charles S. Maier, *Dissolution: The Crisis of Communism and the End of East Germany* (Princeton, New Jersey, 1997), 96.

22. See Smith, *Russians*, 266, citing Soviet sources. Farming less than 1 percent of arable land, private plots accounted for 27 percent of the value of Soviet agricultural output in 1975, comprising an especially high percentage of potatoes (62), eggs (47), meat and milk (34), and fruit and vegetables (32).

23. For these figures, see MacKenzie and Curran, *Russia and the USSR*, 282, 307, 330; and Calleo, *Rethinking Europe's Future*, 159.

24. "After Brezhnev: Stormy Weather," in *Time*'s special "Inside the USSR" edition, June 23, 1980.

25. For *Stukaci* numbers, see Volkogonov, *Autopsy for an Empire*, 346, 420 (quote). Also see "Big Brother is Everywhere," *Time*, June 23, 1980.

26. "A Fortress State in Transition," *Time*, June 23, 1980.

27. Cited in Volkogonov, *Autopsy for an Empire*, 340.

28. According to "An Observer," *Message from Moscow* (New York, 1969), 197. The anonymous author was a foreign intellectual who had lived for many years in Moscow.

29. Sakharov's memoirs are cited in Remnick, *Lenin's Tomb* (Chapter. 7, Note 82), 166.

30. Cited in MacKenzie and Curran, *Russia and the USSR*, 277.

31. See the discussion of Solzhenitsyn's life and works in ibid., 352–54.

32. See his *Letter to the Soviet Leaders* (New York, 1974), 21–31, and for the quote, 55. The letter dates from fall 1973.

33. Alexander Solzhenitsyn, *Cancer Ward*, translated by Nicholas Bethell and David Burg (New York, 1968), 459.

34. Cited in Remnick, *Lenin's Tomb*, 112

35. See Hedrick, *Russians*, 596, 600, and Service, *Twentieth-Century Russia* (Chapter 5, Note 74), 414.

36. See his introduction to Roy A. Medvedev, *Let History Judge*, translated by Stefan Brecht (New York, 1971), xii.

37. Sakharov's 1973 interview with Swedish journalist Olle Stenholm, cited in Hedrick, *Russians*, 593.

38. Cited in "An Observer's" *Message from Moscow*, 238.

39. Citations in Remnick, *Lenin's Tomb*, 168, 174, 176; and Kotkin, *Armageddon Averted* (Chapter 8, Note 80), 53–54.

40. Citations, respectively, in Volkogonov, *Autopsy for an Empire*, 445; Service, *Twentieth-Century Russia*, 436; Remnick, *Lenin's Tomb*, 168; and Service, *History*, 438.

41. By March 1986 there were 125 new members on the 307-member Central Committee and 38 of 100 new ministers. By summer 1987 three-quarters of all republic and regional first secretaries had been replaced. See MacKenzie and Curran, *Russia and the USSR,* 317.

42. Vladimir Mozhin of the Economic Department of the Central Committee, cited in Michael Ellman and Vladimir Kontorovich (eds.), *The Destruction of the Soviet Economic System: An Insiders' History* (New York, 1998), 121.

43. Gorbachev's memoirs are cited in Michael McFaul, *Russia's Unfinished Revolution: Political Change from Gorbachev to Putin* (Ithaca, New York, 2001), 46–47.

44. Cited in Remnick, *Lenin's Tomb,* 163.

45. Service, *History of Twentieth-Century Russia,* 451–52; MacKenzie and Curran, *Russia and the USSR,* 331–32.

46. Cited in McFaul, *Russia's Unfinished Revolution,* 43.

47. Cited in Schweizer, *Reagan's War,* 246.

48. For the 9 percent slide of industrial production in 1988–1989, see Service, *Twentieth-Century Russia,* 469.

49. Ibid., 471–72; MacKenzie and Curran, *Russia and the USSR,* 333; and Remnick, *Lenin's Tomb,* 196–97 (quote on 196).

50. Cited in Remnick, *Lenin's Tomb,* 211. Also see MacKenzie and Curran, *Russia and the USSR,* 329–30.

51. Service, *History of Twentieth-Century Russia,* 457, 473–74, 481; MacKenzie and Curran, *Russia and the USSR,* 321–29; Volkogonov, *Autopsy for an Empire,* 500–09; Remnick, *Lenin's Tomb,* 277–356.

52. Cited in Neal Ascherson, *The Polish August: The Self-Limiting Revolution* (New York, 1982), 112.

53. "Charter 77" is printed in H. Gordon Skilling, *Charter 77 and Human Rights in* Czechoslovakia (New York, 1981), 209–12. For the politics of rock and roll behind the Iron Curtain, see Timothy W. Ryback, *Rock Around the Bloc: A History of Rock Music in Eastern Europe and the Soviet Union* (New York, 1990).

54. Cited in Mary Fulbrook, *Anatomy of a Dictatorship: Inside the GDR 1949–1989* (Oxford, 1995), 205.

55. Net debt equals gross debt minus the value of assets held in "hard" or "convertible" currencies. After Stalin imposed autarky on the Soviet Union and Eastern Europe in the late 1940s, trade between East and West shriveled up. During the post-Stalinist period East-West trade increased slightly, but the West insisted on payment for its exports in western currencies. Rubles and East European currencies were rejected as a means of payment because there was little in COMECON countries that the West wished to purchase and no reason, therefore, to exchange or convert these currencies into western money. Because of the low, largely one-way volume of trade, in other words, banks refused to exchange Soviet rubles or East German marks for dollars or francs or other so-called convertible currencies.

56. The total approached 140 billion dollars if the USSR is included. For the figures cited in this paragraph, see Maier, *Dissolution,* 63, 66; Jelavich, *History of the Balkans: Twentieth Century* (Chapter 3, Note 39), 401; and Ivan T. Berend, *Central and Eastern Europe 1944–1993* (Cambridge, 1996), 229–31.

57. Citations in Geoff Eley, *Forging Democracy* (Chapter 1, Note 49), 433, and Philip Longworth, *The Making of Eastern Europe* (New York, 1992), 29.

58. Eley, *Forging Democracy,* 434.

59. Glenny, *The Balkans* (Chapter 3, Note 39), 607.

60. Berend, *Central and Eastern Europe,* 224, 231.

61. Cited in Maier, *Dissolution,* 64.

62. See Schweizer, *Reagan's War,* 239–41. According to Reagan's secretary of defense, Caspar Weinberger, the Saudis "knew we wanted as low an oil price as possible. Among the benefits were our domestic economic and political situation, and a lot less money going to the Soviets" (p. 240).

63. Cited in Maier, *Dissolution,* 67.

64. The best recent survey is William I. Hitchcock, *Struggle for Europe* (Chapter 7, Note 44), 288–310, 347–379. Good journalistic accounts of "the year of miracles" are Timothy Garton Ash, *The Magic Lantern: The Revolution of 1989 Witnessed in Warsaw, Budapest, Berlin, and Prague* (New York, 1990); Misha Glenny, *The Rebirth of History: Eastern Europe in the Age of Democracy* (London, 1991); and Gale Stokes, *The Walls Came Tumbling Down: The Collapse of Communism in Eastern Europe* (New York, 1993). Also see the valuable collection of articles in Lyman H. Legters (ed.), *Eastern Europe: Transformation and Revolution, 1945–991* (Lexington, Massachusetts, 1992); and Berend, *Central and Eastern Europe* (Note 56), 254–99.

65. Mikhail Gorbachev, *Memoirs* (New York, 1996), 516.

66. Berend, *Central and Eastern Europe*, 263–64.

67. Norman Davies, *God's Playground: A History of Poland* (New York, 1982), 2: 549, 572, 609.

68. For Poland in 1989, see Wlodzimierz Wesolowski, "Transition from Authoritarianism to Democracy," in Legters (ed.), *Eastern Europe*, 302–04. In the less important upper house, Solidarity won 99 of 100 seats. In the *Sejm*, Solidarity took the entire 35 percent bloc of 161 seats not allotted to the government "coalition," while the Communist Party won 173 seats—or 37.9 percent—the United Peasants Party 76 seats, the Democratic Party 23 seats, and lay Catholics cooperating with the communists 23 seats.

69. Cited in Berend, *Decades of Crisis* (Chapter 2, Note 76), 271. Also see Gábor Révész, *Perestroika in Eastern Europe: Hungary's Economic Transformation, 1945–1988* (Boulder, Colorado, 1990), 108–20; and William Echikson, "Bloc Buster," in Letgers (ed.), *Eastern Europe*, 427–34.

70. See Timothy Garton Ash, "Budapest: The Last Funeral," in his *Magic Lantern*, 47–60.

71. Citations in Maier, *Dissolution*, 155, 220.

72. Fulbrook, *Anatomy of a Dictatorship*, 238, 239, 240.

73. For numbers of refugees here and later, see Konrad H. Jarausch, *The Rush to German Unity* (Oxford, 1994), 62.

74. Cited in Hitchcock, *Struggle for Europe*, 366.

75. For East Germany in 1989 and early 1990, see Jarausch, *Rush to Unity*, 1–134; Maier, *Dissolution*, 108–214; and Fulbrook, *Anatomy of a Dictatorship*, 243–65. Also see Barbara Donovan's Radio Free Europe report, "East Germany in 1989," printed in Legters (ed.), *Eastern Europe*, 411–16.

76. Jarausch, *Rush to German Unity*, 87.

77. John D. Bell, " 'Post-Communist' Bulgaria," and Jiri Pehe, "Czechoslovakia: An Abrupt Transition," in Legters (ed.), *Eastern Europe*, 488–97 and 346–51, respectively.

78. Vladimir Tismaneanu, "In Romania: Between Euphoria and Rage," and Dan Ionescu, "The Communist Party Re-Emerges Under a New Name," in Legters (ed.), *Eastern Europe*, 467–73, 480–86, respectively.

79. Robin Alison Remington, "The Federal Dilemma in Yugoslavia," in ibid., 553, 561.

80. Cited in Berend, *Central and Eastern Europe*, 296.

81. Cited in Glenny, *The Balkans*, 628.

82. Ibid., 629–30.

83. For this point, see Berend, *Central and Eastern Europe*, 294.

84. Citations in Remnick, *Lenin's Tomb*, 302.

85. The exchange is cited in ibid., 301.

86. Cited in McFaul, *Russia's Unfinished Revolution*, 102.

87. Citations in Remnick, *Lenin's Tomb*, 389, 399.

88. Cited in McFaul, *Russia's Unfinished Revolution*, 104–05.

89. Cited in MacKenzie and Curran, *Russia and the USSR*, 370.

90. Relevant documents from summer and fall 1991 are printed in William E. Watson, *The Collapse of Communism in the Soviet Union* (Westport, Connecticut, 1998), 136–41.

CHAPTER 11

1. For the evolution of the so-called Common Market or European Economic Community (EEC) into simply the European Community (EC), see Chapter 9. For EEC to EU literature, see Chapter 7, Notes 95 and 104.

2. See George Ross, *Jacques Delors and European Integration* (New York, 1995), 39–52, 78–79, 92–97.

3. Decisions required eight of twelve member states or fifty-four of seventy-seven votes. Luxembourg had the smallest number of votes (two), Germany the greatest (ten).

4. In 1961 the Organization for European Economic Cooperation, founded in 1948 to coordinate Marshall Plan aid, was reorganized as the OECD. The restructuring of the East Bloc, however, was easily the largest project of the so-called G-24. Based on Marshall Plan guidelines that had provided support to recipient nations of up to 5 percent of their GNP, the new projections called for ten to fifteen billion dollars of annual aid to Eastern Europe. Pledged OECD/EC aid totaled forty-five billion dollars over the first three years, but amounted to far less (see later). See Berend, *Central and Eastern Europe* (Chapter 10, Note 56), 335.

5. Cited in Preston, *Enlargement and Integration* (Chapter 9, Note 38), 198.

6. Cited in Ross, *Jacques Delors*, 97, 92.

7. Ibid., 49–50, 264 (note 107).

8. Washington readily agreed to reunification, as did Moscow after NATO pledged that it had no aggressive designs on the USSR, which was also granted liaison status in the western alliance. For all of these developments, see Smyser, *From Yalta to Berlin* (Chapter 7, Note 44), 351–96.

9. Konrad H. Jarausch, *The Rush to German Unity* (Oxford, 1994), 137–76.

10. Since the 1970s heads of member states and governments met twice a year to coordinate and clarify EC business. Their gatherings became known as the European Council. Also see Chapter 9.

11. Calleo, *Rethinking Europe's Future* (Chapter 9, Note 15), 185.

12. Cited in Dinan, *Ever Closer Union* (Chapter 7, Note 104), 515–16.

13. Cited in ibid., 521.

14. For the Balkan tragedy, see ibid., 518–22; Stanley Meisler, *United Nations: The First Fifty Years* (New York, 1995), 312–29; Glenny, *The Balkans* (Chapter 3, Note 39), 634–52; and the cogent analysis of Hitchcock, *Struggle for Europe* (Chapter 7, Note 44), 385–402.

15. Hitchcock, *Struggle for Europe*, 380.

16. Ross, *Jacques Delors*, 238.

17. Most of the Muslims were ethnic Slavs who had converted to Islam during the centuries of Turkish rule, putting an ironic stamp on the tragedy.

18. Calleo, *Rethinking Europe's Future*, 306–07.

19. Dinan, *Ever Closer Union*, 522–26, clarifies these complex arrangements.

20. The UN revivalist euphoria of the Gulf crisis (1990–91) had largely dissipated by 1993 as a result of an underfunded and overstretched UN's inability to enforce peace in Bosnia and Somalia (see Meisler, *United Nations*, 294–329). The Dayton talks reflected these new realities. Represented (aside from the Balkan participants) were the United States, France, Britain, Germany, the EU, and Russia because of its liaison rights in NATO. The UN, which had essentially stepped aside in Bosnia in 1995, was "quietly but deliberately left out" (see Hitchcock, *Struggle for Europe*, 401).

21. Cited in Ross, *Jacques Delors*, 139–40.

22. Czechoslovakia split peacefully into two states in January 1993. See later in this chapter.

23. See Note 10.

24. Cited in Preston, *Enlargement and Integration*, 201.

25. For this paragraph, see Berend, *Central and Eastern Europe,* 321–63.

26. For a number of years it remained unclear whether firms and properties nationalized by communist regimes would be returned to previous owners or whether previous owners would receive compensation for holdings that could be sold to others. The means of privatizing firms founded by communist states also remained unclear for a time.

27. By 1993–1994 the Czech Republic had radically downsized its former state-run economy, with private businesses now producing 65 percent of GDP. The figure was 55 percent for Poland and Hungary, 40 percent for Bulgaria, and 33 percent for Rumania.

28. Berend, *Central and Eastern Europe*, 358.

29. Poverty is defined here as wage levels that sunk to 35–45 percent of 1989 levels.

30. For the statistics here, see *Der Fischer Weltalmanach* (Frankfurt, 1994), 49, 247, 407, 502, 512, 571, 618.

31. Citations in Berend, *Central and Eastern Europe*, 314, 362.

32. Slavenka Drakulic, *Café Europa: Life After Communism* (New York, 1996), 37, 169.

33. For this paragraph and much of the passage that follows, see Dinan, *Ever Closer Union*, 175–99, 418–19; Calleo, *Rethinking Europe's Future*, 250–64; and Ross, *Jacques Delors*, 98–101.

34. Greece, one of the poorest EU members, receives annual aid from the union amounting to 5–6 percent of GDP, well above the old Marshall Plan targets of 3–5 percent. See Preston, *Enlargement and Integration*, 208.

35. Berend, *Central and Eastern Europe*, 337.

36. The other applicant nations were Latvia, Lithuania, Slovakia, Rumania, Bulgaria, Malta, and Turkey.

37. For an excellent discussion of this problem, see Andrei Muntean, "The European Parliament's Political Legitimacy and the Commission's 'Misleading Management': Towards a 'Parliamentarian' European Union?" *European Integration Online Papers* 4 (2000) N-5: 1–16 (http://eiop.or.at/eiop/texte/2000-005.htm).

38. Christoph Bertram, *Europe in the Balance: Securing the Peace Won in the Cold War* (Washington, DC, 1995), 70.

39. Dinan, *Ever Closer Union*, 199.

40. Jacques Rupnik, "The International Context," in Larry Diamond and Marc F. Plattner (eds.), *Democracy After Communism* (Baltimore, Maryland, 2002), 141–43.

41. See Preston, *Enlargement and Integration*, 87–109.

42. For detailed analyses of EMU in the 1990s, see Peter Henning Loedel, *Deutsche Mark Politics: Germany in the European Monetary System* (Boulder, Colorado, 1999), 93–235; Dinan, *Ever Closer Union*, 454–79; and Calleo, *Rethinking Europe's Future*, 185–206.

43. Dinan, *Ever Closer Union*, 155.

44. Calleo, *Rethinking Europe's Future*, 191, 187; Gillingham, *European Integration* (Chapter 7, Note 104), 337–49, 317–29.

45. See Andrew Moravcsik, "Federalism in the European Union: Rhetoric and Reality," in Kalypso Nicolaidis and Robert Howse (eds.), *The Federal Vision: Legitimacy and Levels of Governance in the United States and the European Union* (Oxford, 2001), 161–87.

46. See Calleo, *Rethinking Europe's Future*, 192–205.

47. See Karen Dawisha and Bruce Parrott, *Russia and the New States of Eurasia: The Politics of Upheaval* (Cambridge, 1995); David Remnick, *Resurrection: The Struggle for a New Russia* (New York, 1998); Stephen F. Cohen, *Failed Crusade: America and the Tragedy of Post-Communist Russia* (New York, 2000); Leon Aron, *Yeltsin: A Revolutionary Life* (New York, 2000), 494–633; and McFaul, *Russia's Unfinished Revolution* (Chapter 10, Note 43), 121–371.

48. Hitchcock, *Struggle for Europe*, 457.

49. Remnick, *Resurrection*, 185.

50. Citations in McFaul, *Russia's Unfinished Revolution*, 164, and Aron, *Yeltsin*, 510, 501.

51. McFaul, *Russia's Unfinished Revolution*, 212. The president controlled foreign policy and the armed forces, made declarations of war, could dissolve the Duma for new elections, and ruled by decree. Ministers, including the prime minister, were appointed by the president with very difficult procedures for the Duma to block appointments. Similarly, impeachment was made extremely cumbersome. An upper house, the Council of the Federation, acted as a check on the Duma, furthermore, because many of its members were federal officials appointed by the president (see pp. 212–14).

52. Ibid., 252.

53. For the statistics here and following, see MacKenzie and Curran, *Russia and the USSR* (Chapter 2, Note 42), 400–01.

54. Yeltsin had banned the CPSU in 1991, but a decision of the Russian Constitutional Court in November 1992 allowed the party's Russian followers to reestablish themselves in the new state.

55. Cited in Service, *Twentieth-Century Russia* (Chapter 5, Note 74), 532.

56. For the Chechen Wars, see Remnick, *Resurrection*, 260–91; John Dunlop, *Russia Confronts Chechnya: Roots of a Separatist Conflict* (Cambridge, 1998); Anatol Lieven, *Chechnya: Tombstone of Russian Power* (New Haven, Connecticut, 1998); and Carlotta Gall and Thomas de Waal, *Chechnya: Calamity in the Caucasus* (New York, 1998). The following passage also relies heavily on the cogent, balanced analysis of Olga V. Kucherenko, "Explaining the War in Chechnya," Unpublished M.Phil. thesis, Cambridge University, 2000.

57. For polls showing 70 percent opposition to the war in January 1995, with 52 percent wanting to negotiate, see McFaul, *Russia's Unfinished Revolution*, 257–58, and Kucherenko, "Explaining the War in Chechnya," 24. For casualties, see Ustina Markus, "Russia: The Second Chechen War," in Ustina Markus and Daniel N. Nelson (eds.), *Brassey's Eurasian & Central European Security Handbook* (Washington, DC, 2000), 371.

58. Kucherenko, "Explaining the War in Chechnya," 53.

59. The two-thirds of the Chechens who survived were allowed to return after Stalin's death.

60. Remnick, *Resurrection*, 335, and for the quotes, 331, 333, 338. For the election, also see McFaul, *Russia's Unfinished Revolution*, 289–304.

61. For these statistics, see MacKenzie and Curran, *Russia and the USSR*, 400–01, 416–17.

62. Cohen, *Failed Crusade*, 159.

63. For the statistics in this paragraph, see McFaul, *Russia's Unfinished Revolution*, 286, 314, 332–33.

64. On this point, also see the recent analysis of Merridale, *Night of Stone* (Chapter 4, Note 75).

65. Cited in Dermot Keogh, "Ireland at the Turn of the Century: 1994–001," in Moody and Martin, *Course of Irish History* (Chapter 4, Note 71, also for other sources), 330.

66. For Basques and ETA terrorism, see Stanley G. Payne, *Basque Nationalism* (Reno, Nevada, 1975); Jean Grugel, "The Basques," in Michael Watson (ed.), *Contemporary Minority Nationalism* (London, 1990); and Daniele Conversi, *The Basques, the Catalans, and Spain: Alternative Routes to Nationalist Mobilisation* (Reno, Nevada, 1997).

67. Trudy Rubin, "Basque Guerrilla Campaign Fueled by Emotions of the Past," *Philadelphia Inquirer*, 18 May 2001.

68. Cited in Andrea Gerlin, "Basque Separatists Resume Campaign of Terror in Spain," *Philadelphia Inquirer*, August 21, 2000.

69. For Kosovo, see Glenny, *The Balkans*, 652–62; Tim Judah, *Kosovo: War and Revenge* (New Haven, Connecticut, 2000); Gary Jonathan Bass, *Stay the Hand of Vengeance: The Politics of War Crimes Tribunals* (Princeton, New Jersey, 2002), 271–75; and Hitchcock, *Struggle for Europe*, 402–09.

70. Kucherenko, "Explaining the War in Chechnya," 56; Markus, "The Second Chechen War," and Stan Markotich, "Yugoslavia: Serbia's Self-Induced Insecurity," in Markus and Nelson (eds.), *Brassey's Eurasian and East European Security Yearbook*, 377, 158, respectively.

71. The fact that no evidence was found proving Chechen involvement, when combined with suspicious behavior by the security police, led others to believe that Russia planted the bombs and blamed them on Chechnya.

72. For the discussion and statistics that follow, unless noted otherwise, see the excellent chapter in Hitchcock, *Struggle for Europe*, 410–34.

73. See James Kurth, "Migration and the Dynamics of Empire," and Olivier Roy, "EuroIslam: The Jihad Within?" in *The National Interest* 71 (Spring 2003): 9, 65, respectively.

74. Cited in Hitchcock, *Struggle for Europe*, 420.

75. For Italy in recent years, see Paul Ginsborg, *Italy and Its Discontents: Family, Civil Society, State: 1980–2001* (New York, 2003), 285–324. For other trends, see Daniel Rubin, "Targeting Immigration, Europe's Far Right Gains," *Philadelphia Inquirer*, April 26, 2002.

76. Hitchcock, *Struggle for Europe*, 430.

77. Roy, "EuroIslam" (Note 73). Also see his *L'Islam Mondialisé* (Paris, 2001), forthcoming in English translation.

78. Ibid., 68, 69.

79. See the September 1998 interview with Bin Laden printed in http://www.pbs.org/wgbh/pages/frontline/shows/binladen.html.

80. For excellent discussions of the deep underlying differences between American and European approaches in the post-9/11 crisis, see Michael Elliott, "Children of the Holocaust: Why Do So Many Europeans Reject America's View of the Middle East:" *Time*, April 29, 2002; Steven Chapman, "U.S.-European Opinions Diverge on Israel's Place in the World," *Philadelphia Inquirer*, May 5, 2002; Michael Howard, "What Are Friends For?" *The National* Interest 69 (Fall 2002): 8–10; Michael Farley and Doyle McManus, "U.N. Members Worry: Threat from the U.S.," *Philadelphia Inquirer*, November 3, 2002; and Philip H. Gordon, "Bridging the Atlantic Divide," *Foreign Affairs* 82/1 (January–February 2003): 70–83. Also see Calleo, *Rethinking Europe's Future*, 337–74.

81. Poland, the Czech Republic, and Hungary were admitted to NATO in 1999.

82. Jacques Rupnik, "The International Context," in Diamond and Plattner (eds.), *Democracy After Communism*, 138–39.

83. Cited in "A Continental Divide," *Philadelphia Inquirer*, February 2, 2003.

84. See Mathew Schofield et al., "Civilian Deaths in Baghdad," *Philadelphia Inquirer*, May 4, 2003; David B. Rivkin Jr. and Lee A. Casey, "Leashing the Dogs of War," *The National Interest* 73 (Fall 2003): 57–69; and for the final quote, Russell A. Berman, *Anti-Americanism in Europe: A Cultural Problem* (Stanford, 2004), xvii.

85. For the background, see Charles G. Cogan, *The Third Option: The Emancipation of European Defense, 1989–2000* (Westport, Connecticut, 2001); and Calleo, *Rethinking Europe's Future*, 299–336, esp. 319–20.

86. Because the EU would have access to NATO military equipment, NATO member Turkey worried that EU and NATO member Greece could use NATO weapons against Ankara.

87. The May 1, 2003 "Joint Statement: Germany, France, Luxembourg, Belgium," is printed in http://www.scoop.co.nz/mason/stories/W00305/S00006.htm.

88. Kennedy is cited in Warren Bass, *Support Any Friend: Kennedy's Middle East and theMaking of the U.S.-Israel Alliance* (New York,2003), 6.The earlier quote is Dominique Moisi of the French Institute for International Relations, *Philadelphia Inquirer*, 3 March 2004.

89. Citations in Pepe Escobar, 'Tracking Al-Qaeda in Europe," *Online Asia Times*, July 13, 2002, http://www.atimes.com/atimes/Middle East/DG13Ak02.html; and Roy, "EuroIslam," 72.

90. Cited in "Basque Conflict: Violence in Spain," http://europe.cnn.com/SPECIALS/2002/basque/. Also see related articles on this web site.

91. Cited in "Kosovo's New President Vows Independence," *Philadelphia Inquirer*, May 3, 2002.

92. Djordje Latinovic of the pro-democracy Bosnian Institute, "The Bosnian Elections," October 19, 2002, in http://www.bosnia.org.uk/news/news_body.cfm?newsid=1676.

93. Hitchcock, *Struggle for Europe*, 409.

94. The cited comments were made to Trudy Rubin, "Cloud Hangs over Putin," *Philadelphia Inquirer*, April 2, 2000. For opinion trends, see Kucherenko, "Explaining the War in Chechnya," 24, and *Izvestia*, No. 199, October 31, 2002.

95. Cited in Georg Feifer, "Chechnya," March 24, 2003, http://www.rferl.org/nca/special/chechnya/intro.html.

96. For trends under Putin, see MacKenzie and Curran, *Russia and the USSR*, 413–26; Richard Sakwa, *Russian Politics and Society* (London, 2002), 246–47, 291–96, 331–35, 463–74; and the articles by Lilia Shevtsova, M. Steven Fish, Grigory Yavlinsky, and Michael McFaul in Diamond and Plattner (eds.), *Democracy After Communism*, 246–69.

97. See Gregory Feifer, "Russia: Putin's Statements on Chechnya," November 13, 2002, in http://www.rferl.org/nca/features/2002/11/13112002160541.asp.

98. Pyotr Aven and Christopher Weafer, "Chasing Portugal or Following Venezuela?" *Moscow Times*, January 14, 2003.

99. For the citations, Lilia Shevtsova, "Russia's Hybrid Regime," in Diamond and Plattner (eds.), *Democracy After Communism*, 240. Also see the article by Nadia Diuk, "Sovereignty and Uncertainty in the Ukraine, ibid., 232–39; Karen Dawisha and Bruce Parrot (eds.), *Democratic Changes and Authoritarian Reactions in Russia, Ukraine, Belarus, and Moldova* (Cambridge, 1997); and Paul D'Anieri, Robert Kravchuk, and Taras Kuzio, *Politics and Society in Ukraine* (Boulder, Colorado, 1999).

100. Citations in Peter Baker and Susan B. Glasser, "Tug-of-War in Belarus: Dictator vs. Democracy," *Philadelphia Inquirer*, August 20, 2001.

101. "Poverty in Eastern Europe: The Land That Time Forgot," *The Economist*, September 23, 2000.

102. Richard Rose, "A Diverging Europe," in Diamond and Plattner (eds.), *Democracy after Communism*, 157.

103. On Nice and related issues, see Calleo, *Rethinking Europe's Future*, 250–98.

104. See the preface to the draft constitution of June 2003: http://europa.eu.int/futurm/constitution/index_en.htm.

105. Rumania and Bulgaria could not close all chapters. Their admission will probably be delayed until at least 2007.

106. The draft constitution is cited in Note 104.

107. The EU membership of twenty-five includes six states that do not belong to NATO: Ireland, Austria, Sweden, Finland, Malta, and Cyprus. NATO's non-American membership of twenty-four includes four European states that do not belong to the EU: Iceland, Norway, Rumania, and Bulgaria. They are all joined by democratic, fellow-traveling Switzerland, which has recently inched away from neutrality by joining the UN—altogether thirty-one states, for NATO also includes non-EU member Turkey, the only Muslim democracy in the Middle East prior to the democratic experiment in Iraq.

108. Serbia (with Montenegro and Kosovo), Croatia, Bosnia-Herzegovina, Macedonia, and Albania.

109. Russia, Ukraine, Moldova, Georgia, and Armenia.

INDEX